# New Institutional Economics

T0311566

Institutions frame behaviors and exchanges in markets, business networks, communities, and organizations throughout the world. Thanks to the pioneering work of Ronald Coase, Douglass North, and Oliver Williamson, institutions are now recognized as being a key factor in explaining differences in performance between industries, nations, and regions. The fast-growing field of "new institutional economics" (NIE) analyzes the economics of institutions and organizations using methodologies, concepts, and analytical tools from a wide range of disciplines (including political science, anthropology, sociology, management, law, and economics). With contributions from an international team of researchers, this book offers theoreticians, practitioners, and advanced students in economics and social sciences a guide to the recent developments in the field. It explains the underlying methodologies, identifies issues and questions for future research, and shows how results apply to decision-making law, economic policy, managements, regulations, and institutional design.

ÉRIC BROUSSEAU is Professor of Economics at the University of Paris X and Director of EconomiX, a research center jointly operated by University of Paris X and the CNRS (French National Science Foundation).

JEAN-MICHEL GLACHANT is Professor of Economics and Head of the Electricity Reforms Group in the ADIS Research Center, University of Paris-Sud XI.

# New Institutional Economics

*A Guidebook*

*Edited by*

Éric Brousseau and Jean-Michel Glachant

CAMBRIDGE
UNIVERSITY PRESS

# CAMBRIDGE
## UNIVERSITY PRESS

University Printing House, Cambridge CB2 8BS, United Kingdom

One Liberty Plaza, 20th Floor, New York, NY 10006, USA

477 Williamstown Road, Port Melbourne, VIC 3207, Australia

314-321, 3rd Floor, Plot 3, Splendor Forum, Jasola District Centre, New Delhi - 110025, India

103 Penang Road, #05-06/07, Visioncrest Commercial, Singapore 238467

Cambridge University Press is part of the University of Cambridge.

It furthers the University's mission by disseminating knowledge in the pursuit of
education, learning and research at the highest international levels of excellence.

www.cambridge.org
Information on this title: www.cambridge.org/9780521700160

© Cambridge University Press 2008

First published 2008

*A catalogue record for this publication is available from the British Library*

*Library of Congress Cataloging in Publication data*
New institutional economics : a guidebook / edited by Eric Brousseau
and Jean-Michel Glachant.
  p.  cm.
Includes bibliographical references and index.
ISBN 978-0-521-87660-5 (hardback) – 978-0-521-70016-0 (pbk.)
1. Institutional economics.  I. Brousseau, Eric.  II. Glachant,
Jean-Michel.  III. Title.
HB99.5.N4913 2008
330.15′52–dc22

                                              2008021977

ISBN  978-0-521-87660-5  Hardback
ISBN  978-0-521-70016-0  Paperback

To the more than six hundred fellows who have been teaching, thinking, learning, discussing, sharing meals, and even dancing at the European School for New Institutional Economics (ESNIE) every spring in Corsica since 2002

# Contents

# Tables

# Figures

# Contributors

LEE J. ALSTON is Professor of Economics and Director of the Program on Environment and Society in the Institute of Behavioral Sciences at the University of Colorado. He is a research associate at the National Bureau for Economic Research and is a past president of the International Society for New Institutional Economics (ISNIE). His current research focuses on the political economy of the historical USA and present-day Latin America, and on issues of land use and agricultural contracting in North and South America.

BENITO ARRUÑADA, Professor of Business at Pompeu Fabra University, Barcelona, has published widely on organizations and institutions in, among others, the *Journal of Law & Economics*; *Industrial and Corporate Change*; *Harvard Business Review*; the *Journal of Law, Economics & Organization*; the *Journal of Economic Behavior & Organization*; and the *International Review of Law and Economics*. The interaction between the law and private enforcement is a recurrent theme of many of his works. His latest projects deal with the institutions that make impersonal transactions possible in a market economy, focusing on cognitive property rights, and formalization issues.

LYDA BIGELOW is an assistant professor of strategy at the University of Utah's Dave Eccles School of Business. Prior to this she held the position of assistant professor at Washington University's Olin School of Business. Her research lies at the intersection of population ecology and transaction economics by studying how organizational and technology choices affect firm performance.

ÉRIC BROUSSEAU is Professor of Economics at the University of Paris X and a member of the Institut Universitaire de France. He is the director of EconomiX, a joint research center between the CNRS and the University of Paris X. He is also the director of the European School for New Institutional Economics (ESNIE). His research agenda focuses on the economics of institutions and on the economics of contracts, with two main applied fields: the economics of intellectual property rights and the economics of the internet and digital activities.

MICHAEL L. COOK is the Robert D. Partridge Professor in Organization Economics in the Division of Applied Social Sciences at the University of Missouri. His research activities include field studies in more than fifty countries and one hundred published works. Dr. Cook is a member of the core faculty of the Agribusiness Research Institute (ARI), and is a senior fellow with the Contracting and Organizations Research Institute (CORI) at the University of Missouri.

NICOLAI J. FOSS is a professor at Copenhagen Business School, and the director of the CBS Center for Strategic Management and Globalization. He is also a professor at the Norwegian School of Economics and Business Administration. His work has been published in leading journals in business administration, and he is the editor and author of several books on the theory of the firm and strategic management.

PIERRE GARROUSTE is Professor of Economics at the University of Lyon 2. He is also the Deputy Director of the ATOM Center at the University of Paris I. His research interests include Austrian economics, learning, and organization theories. (Website: http://atom.univ-paris1.fr)

JEAN-MICHEL GLACHANT is Professor of Economics at University Paris-Sud, and has been advisor to the French Energy Regulatory Commission and European Commission (DG Competition, DG Energy, DG Research). Formerly an elected member of the board of the International Society for New Institutional Economics (ISNIE), Dr. Glachant is a founding member of the European Energy Institute (EEI) and a partner of the Electricity Policy Research Group (EPRG) at the University of Cambridge. He edited *Competition in European Electricity Markets: A Cross-country Comparison* with D. Finon (2003) and *The Economics of Contracts: Theories, and Applications* with É. Brousseau (Cambridge University Press, 2002). (Website: www.grjm.net)

MANUEL GONZÁLEZ–DÍAZ is Associate Professor of Business Economics at the University of Oviedo. His papers have been published in journals such as *Industrial and Corporate Change*; the *International Review of Law and Economics*; and the *Journal of Economic Behavior and Organization*. His research focuses on make-or-buy decisions and hybrid organizations in different sectors.

CONSTANTINE ILIOPOULOS received his PhD in agribusiness economics from the University of Missouri–Columbia, USA. Currently,
he is a researcher at the Agricultural Economics and Policy Research
Institute, Athens, Greece. His research focuses on the organizational
aspects of producer-owned firms, with applications to financial and
collective governance constraints, entrepreneurship, and strategy. He
serves as a member of the International Editorial and Advisory Board
of the *Journal on Chain and Network Science*, and the European
Research Network on Agricultural Cooperatives.

PAUL L. JOSKOW is President of the Alfred P. Sloan Foundation and
Elizabeth and James Killian Professor of Economics and Management
at Massachusetts Institute of Technology. He has carried out research
in the areas of industrial organization, energy and environmental
economics, competition policy, and government regulation of industry. He is a Fellow of the Econometric Society, a Fellow of the
American Academy of Arts and Sciences, a Distinguished Fellow of
the Industrial Organization Society and a past President of the
International Society for New Institutional Economics.

PETER G. KLEIN is Associate Professor in the Division of Applied Social
Sciences at the University of Missouri and Director of the Contracting
and Organizations Research Institute. His research focuses on the
economics of organizations with applications to entrepreneurship,
innovation, financial economics, and corporate governance. He taught
previously at the University of Georgia and the Copenhagen Business
School, and was a senior economist on the Council of Economic
Advisors.

SANNY X. LIAO is a PhD student in the Business and Public Policy Group
at the Haas School of Business, University of California, Berkeley, USA.
Her research includes the study of incentives among public-sector
employees, political strategies used by firms.

GARY D. LIBECAP is Donald Bren Professor of Corporate Environmental Policy at the Bren School of Environmental Science and
Management, and Professor of Economics at the University of California, Santa Barbara, USA. Before this he was Anheuser Busch
Professor of Economics and Law at the University of Arizona. He is
also a research associate at the National Bureau of Economic Research
and a research fellow at the Hoover Institution.

ANTONIO NICITA is Associate Professor of Economics and Director of
the Center for Law, Economics and Institutions (CLEIS) at the

University of Siena, Italy. His area of interest is law and economics with specific focus on the economics of contracts and organizations, competition policy and antitrust, public law enforcement, property rights, and intellectual property rights.

JACKSON NICKERSON is Frahm Family Professor of Organization and Strategy at Washington University's Olin School of Business. His research focuses on organizational choice and various measures of performance, including innovation, and lies at the intersection of economics, sociology, and psychology. Outlets for his research include *Administrative Science Quarterly*; the *Journal of Political Economy*; *Organization Science*; and the *Strategic Management Journal*.

JOHN V.C. NYE is Professor of Economics at George Mason University and holds the Frederic Bastiat Chair in Political Economy at the Mercatus Center. Prior to this he was on the faculty of Washington University. He is a specialist in European economic history and the political economy of reform. He has been a National Fellow at the Hoover Institution and is a regular visiting professor at the Institut d'Etudes Politiques de Paris. With John Drobak, he was co-editor of *Frontiers in the New Institutional Economics* (1997). His most recent book *War, Wine, and Taxes: The Political Economy of Anglo-French Trade 1689–1900* appeared in 2007.

SONJA OPPER is Gad Rausing professor of international business at the School of Economics and Management at Lund University, Sweden. Her research agenda focusses on the application of new institutional economics on transition and developing countries. She is particularly interested in the explanation of patterns of institutional change and the interplay between institutional environment and institutional arrangements. In her empirical work, she has a strong focus on China's reform economy.

JOANNE E. OXLEY is Associate Professor of Strategic Management at the Rotman School of Management, University of Toronto, Canada, where she teaches international management and strategy. Her research focusses on international collaborative strategies for technology development and commercialization. She has published widely and currently serves on the editorial boards of the *Strategic Management Journal*; *Organization Science*; the *Journal of International Business Studies*; and *Strategic Organization (SO!)*.

UGO PAGANO is Director of the Doctoral School in Economics and President of the Graduate School S. Chiara at the University of Siena,

Italy. He is Visiting Professor at CEU (Budapest), where he also served as head of the Department of Economics. He obtained his PhD at the University of Cambridge, where he was also a lecturer and a fellow of Pembroke College. He is an editor of the *Journal of Institutional Economics*.

THIERRY PÉNARD is Professor of Economics at the University of Rennes 1 and Affiliate Professor at ESC Rennes Business School. He is also member of the Centre for Research in Economics and Management (CREM). His main fields of interest are the economics of networks (internet, telecommunication), the economics of contract (franchising), game theory, and antitrust policy.

YANNICK PEREZ is Associate Professor at University Paris-Sud 11. He is a member of the Networks Group Jean-Monnet and Laboratoire d'Analyse Économique des Réseaux et des Systèmes Énergétiques (LARSEN). His research focusses on the EU electricity reforms.

JEAN-PHILIPPE PLATTEAU is Professor of Economics and Director of the Centre de Recherche en Économie du Développement (CRED) at the University of Namur, Belgium. His main field is development economics and most of his work has been concerned with understanding the role of institutions and collective action in economic development, and the processes of institutional change. The influence of non-economic factors and various frontier issues at the interface between economics and sociology are a central focus of his research projects.

EMMANUEL RAYNAUD is Research Fellow at INRA SAD (National Institute of Agronomical Research) and a member of the ATOM Center at the University of Paris I. His field of interest covers the theory of the firm and organizations, and the economics of contracts and institutions. His current research focusses on vertical coordination and product quality in agrifood chains, franchising, and the economics of private institutions.

STÉPHANE ROBIN is Associate in Economics at the National Centre for Scientific Research (CNRS), affiliated with the GATE Research Institute, at the University Lumière Lyon 2. His research interests are in experimental economics, behavioral economics, industrial organization, and market design.

STÉPHANE SAUSSIER is Professor of Economics at the University of Paris I-Sorbonne. He is affiliated to the Gregor Research Center. His research interests include contracting practices, institutional economics and its relation to economic organization, and organization theories. (Website: http://iae.univ-paris1.fr)

BRIAN S. SILVERMAN is the J.R.S. Prichard and Ann Wilson Chair in Management at the Rotman School of Management, University of Toronto, Canada, where he teaches courses on competitive strategy, collaborative strategy, and managing innovation. His research focusses on how firms' competitive strategies and organization structures interact to affect their performance. He currently serves on the editorial boards of *Administrative Science Quarterly, Organization Science, Research Policy,* and *Strategic Organization (SO!)*. He was named a noted alliance expert by the Corporate Strategy Board in 2001.

PABLO T. SPILLER is the Jeffrey A. Jacobs Distinguished Professor of Business and Technology at the Haas School of Business, University of California, Berkeley, USA, and research associate, NBER. He has held academic positions at the University of Pennsylvania, Stanford University, and the University of Illinois at Urbana–Champaign. His most recent book (with Mariano Tommasi), *The Institutional Foundations of Public Policy in Argentina,* appeared in 2007. He is co-editor of the *Journal of Law, Economics and Organization* and associate editor of the *Journal of Applied Economics, the Journal of Comparative Economics, The Regulation Magazine,* and of *The Utilities Project.* He has been a special advisor to the Federal Trade Commission's Bureau of Economics, and is an elected member of the board of directors of the American Law & Economics Association and is the President Elect (2008) of the International Society for New Institutional Economics.

CARINE STAROPOLI is Associate Professor at the University of Paris I. She is a member of the Centre d'Économie de la Sorbonne (CES). Her research focuses on market, contract, and institutional design – mostly in the context of regulatory reforms. She has been involved in various projects using laboratory experiments as an empirical methodology to test new market design in the electricity industry.

MICHAEL E. SYKUTA is an associate professor in the Division of Applied Social Sciences at the University of Missouri–Columbia, USA. He is also Director of the Contracting and Organizations Research Institute (CORI), a multidisciplinary research center for empirical research on organizational structures, contracting, institutions, and their implications for the operation of the economic system. His research focuses on issues of organizational governance, contract structure, and political economy of market institutions and regulation.

LUIS VÁZQUEZ is assistant professor of Organization and Strategic management at the University of Salamanca, Spain. He received his PhD from the University of Oviedo. His research focusses on franchising, firm governance, and the determinants of superior organizational performance.

STEFAN VOIGT holds the Chair for Institutional and International Economics at Philipps University Marburg. His research focuses on the economic effects of constitutions and thus belongs to the research area of the new institutional economics. More specifically, his current research concentrates on the economic effects of the judiciary. In 2002, he published a textbook on the new institutional economics; in the fall of 2003 a two-volume set on critical writings in constitutional political economy appeared. He is a member of a number of editorial boards, including those of *Public Choice* and *Constitutional Political Economy*.

OLIVER E. WILLIAMSON is Professor of the Graduate School at the University of California, Berkeley, USA. He is one of the most quoted authors in the field. His major contribution is theoretical and empirical work on the transaction costs theory. He is the author of ten books and more than one hundred articles published in the most prestigious reviews, such as the *American Economic Review*, the *Administrative Science Quarterly*, and the *Journal of Law, Economics and Organization*.

# Acknowledgements

Every year in the spring, about one hundred scholars of more than forty different nationalities gather at the European School on New Institutional Economics (ESNIE), which is organized at the Scientific Institute of Cargèse, in Corsica (France). New institutional economics (NIE) is being taken in the broad perspective of understanding institutions, organizations, and contracts, through the lenses of economics (and vice versa). The aim of this annual event is to bring together distinguished scholars and PhD students, post-doctoral students, and researchers who are interested in developing the field to provide the latter with intensive training and to develop networking within the NIE community

ESNIE is characterized by multidisciplinary approaches, and by a variety of techniques and tools, and brings to the same place and for a short period of time a number of high-level experts from many different fields and traditions. The event is a unique opportunity to advance the state of the art of this field and, more crucially, to teach and transfer the methods, theories, and research practices of NIE. In return, the young scholars, on the basis of their innovation capabilities and dynamism, actively contribute to the development of the field.

ESNIE is progressively becoming a platform around which many cooperations are organized. Meetings, workshops, publications, research projects, and networks have been launched under the patronage of ESNIE, which is no longer seen as just a spring school nor just an organization, but, rather, as something of more value: a lively and permanently renewed community.

This book is one of the results of this community. It draws from lectures which were initially given at ESNIE and seeks to contribute to the diffusion of the knowledge which was developed and accumulated thanks to this open platform of exchange, discussion, and training.

We are indebted to all the first-class scholars who contributed to ESNIE, and to the development of its reputation, and to the many organizations which sponsored its performance. We are also grateful to those who actively contributed to the organization of the various ESNIE sessions and related events. These people and organizations are too numerous to be mentioned individually. All their names, and even more importantly, their contributions, are available online at www.esnie.org.

None of this would have been made possible without the dynamic initiated in 1997 by the founders of the International Society for New Institutional Economics (ISNIE). ISNIE and ESNIE are sister organizations and many of the contributors to one are also involved in the other. We wish to extend our thanks to those who funded ISNIE and developed its activities.

# Foreword

## The New Institutional Economics Guidebook

*Oliver E. Williamson*

New institutional economics (NIE) has been in existence for thirty years and counting. Periodic reassessments of accomplishments, limitations, and unmet needs are useful for a young field such as this. *The New Institutional Economics: A Guidebook* is such an undertaking.

Having previously written overviews on NIE, I refer interested readers to them.[1] But for a short introductory summary of key ideas and accomplishments of the NIE and some concluding remarks, I have organized the Foreword to this book around provocative passages from each of the chapters. On my reading, the chapters in this book provide corroboration for the proposition that "the new institutional economics is a boiling cauldron of ideas. Not only are there many institutional research programs in progress, but there are competing ideas within many of them" (Williamson 2000, p. 610). That is both the spirit of this guidebook and of my remarks on individual chapters.

The appearance and development of a *new* institutional economics presupposes a predecessor – to which NIE presumably both relates and differs. The common ground is this: unlike the neoclassical resource allocation paradigm (which focussed on prices and output, supply and demand, and was dismissive of institutions [Reder 1999]), both older- and newer-style institutional economics insisted that *institutions matter.* The older institutional economics fell on hard times, however, because it lacked a positive research agenda (Stigler 1983, p. 170) and eventually ran itself into the sand. What NIE does that is different is breathe operational content into the study of institutions. Accordingly, going beyond the proposition that institutions matter, NIE also demonstrates wherein *institutions are susceptible to analysis* (Matthews 1986).

Notwithstanding the many successes of institution-free economics in the thirty years after World War II, there is also a downside. As perceived by Ronald Coase (1937, 1960), and others who took a hard look, orthodoxy was beset with conceptual lapses – many of which were traceable, directly or indirectly, to the unacknowledged assumption that transaction costs were zero. Pushing the logic of zero transaction costs to completion often revealed that the emperor had no clothes. Slowly but surely the need to make provision for positive transaction costs and to ascertain how and why these differed among institutions began to register – with the result that gaps were filled, a deeper understanding of complex economic organization was realized, and public policy was reshaped. With the benefit of hindsight, key features of NIE projects include: (1) eschewing hypothetical ideals by focussing, always and everywhere, on feasible alternatives, all of which are flawed; (2) describing human actors in (more) veridical terms; (3) opening the black box of economic organization and uncovering the purposes served by the mechanisms inside; (4) adopting a main case orientation (of which transaction cost economizing is an obvious candidate); (5) operationalizing the project with reference to the microanalytics of transactions, governance structures, and the rules of the game; thereupon (6) deriving refutable implications and submitting these to empirical testing; and (7) working up the public policy ramifications.

NIE insights and reasoning have since displayed broad reach. Research in economics, the contiguous social sciences (especially political science, sociology, and the law), and applied fields of business (especially strategy, organizational behavior, and marketing) have all been invigorated. Understandably, a new field which displays such vitality has attracted the interest of young scholars – as witnessed by the names of the editors and contributors to this book.

This book, *New Institutional Economics: A Guidebook*, begins with Paul Joskow's introduction, "New Institutional Economics: A Report Card." The quotation that I have chosen from Joskow is this: "One of my colleagues recently suggested that institutional economists had 'won the war' in the sense that it is now widely recognized that understanding how institutions affect economic performance and why different institutional arrangements emerge in different social, cultural, and economic settings is now widely accepted" (pp. 17–18). With one small change, I completely agree. The change is this: rather than "won the war," I would say that we have "won many battles." That small change is consequential for two reasons. First, I am persuaded by Jon Elster's dictum that "explanations in the social sciences should be organized around (partial) *mechanisms* rather than (general) *theories*" (Elster 1994, p. 75; emphasis in original). On my interpretation, the focus on mechanisms directs our attention to the microanalytics of specific phenomena. That is where much of the action resides and where we have won enough skirmishes to persuade others that institutions truly matter and are susceptible to *analysis* (Arrow 1987, p. 734). Second, we are not really at war with anybody. Most students of NIE are pluralists and believe that it is useful to examine complex phenomena through several perspectives – of which the (more microanalytic) lens of contract is one and the orthodox lens of choice is another. Paul Joskow's own research illustrates the productive use of both of these.

Chapter 1, by Pierre Garrouste and Stéphane Saussier, deals with "The Theories of the Firm." The quotation that I have chosen for this chapter is this: "We believe that Coase's (1937) article is a natural and obliged-to-read paper as it contains all the ingredients for a theory of the firm . . . [Upon] looking at recent developments of the theories of the firm, [however,] it is clear that . . . a unified and unique theory of the firm is a challenge – such a theory [does] not exist yet. That has to be resolved in the next coming years," (Coase 1937 p. 39). My responses are "Yes" and "No." Yes, Ronald Coase (1937) wrote a foundational article that both deserves and occupies a place of great honor in the pantheon of economics. And, yes, the development of a unified and unique theory of the firm is a huge challenge.

But while everyone should read Ronald Coase in the original, I do not know what to make of the claim that the classic article "contains *all* of the ingredients" (emphasis added). Notwithstanding the extraordinary insights of Coase (1937), I would describe this paper as the first stage in a natural progression – from informal to preformal, semiformal, and fully formal stages of analysis. It is, furthermore, noteworthy that the 1937 paper was not self-actualizing – as witnessed by Coase's remark, thirty-five years later, that his 1937 paper was "widely cited and little used" (Coase 1972, p. 63). Progressive operationalization has nevertheless been accomplished in the years since. This has entailed naming a robust "main case" (of which searching for prices is not one), uncovering the relevant mechanisms that distinguish firm and market organization in main case respects (to which law, economics, and organization theory are all pertinent), working up the logic, deriving refutable implications, and submitting these to the data.

Also, it is not at all obvious to me that a "unified and unique theory of the firm" is something that "has to be resolved" soon – although such a theory, if it were not vacuous, would be an auspicious accomplishment. Whatever, those who have general theory ambitions must be urged to develop a general theory which has some teeth. In the meantime many of us will continue to work in the style of Elster (by focussing on specific mechanisms rather than general theories).

Chapter 2, by Éric Brousseau, is titled "Contracts: From Bilateral Sets of Incentives to the Multi-Level Governance of Relations." This is an ambitious survey of the vast economics literature on contracting which has been under development over the past twenty years. Éric

Brousseau's survey reveals that a variety of contractual approaches to economic organization has been developed and is being employed by an ever-growing number of economists.

What are we to make of and what are we to do with this bounty of riches? First of all, multiplicity is a good thing in a new field such as this, which is seeking to understand complex phenomena. In circumstances where "any direction you proceed in has a very high a priori probability of being wrong . . . it is good if other people are exploring in other directions" (Simon 1992, p. 21). Moreover, more than one theory may be instructive, in that different theories could inform different aspects of the complex phenomena in question.

Furthermore, promising theories that "fail" are nonetheless instructive: "science . . . advances primarily by unsuccessful experiments that clear the ground" (Friedman 1997, p. 196). Such ground clearing will be accomplished by examining each theory with respect to the four precepts of pragmatic methodology: keep it simple; get it right; make it plausible; and derive refutable implications to which the data are applied (Georgescu-Roegen 1971; Solow 2001). Sooner or later, all would-be theories need to stand up and be counted.

Chapter 3, by John Nye, examines "Institutions and the Institutional Environment," broadly in the spirit of Douglass North. The passage that I have chosen is this: "While . . . NIE work has begun to revitalize economics . . . the implications for policy are less encouraging. If the relationship between formal and informal institutions is critical to economic performance, if that relationship is poorly understood, and, worst of all, if our basic ability to alter slow-moving institutions is limited, we may not be capable of providing the policy advice that statesmen and bureaucrats regularly seek" (pp 79–80). I agree that NIE has had revitalizing effects and I also agree that giving policy advice is made difficult by our failure to better understand the relationships to which Nye refers. Nye presents us with a research challenge to do better. My advice is that we hold our course and "grow the knowledge" as we have in the past, in a modest, slow, molecular, definitive way. It is not in the least discreditable, moreover, if, often, we are unable to give precise policy advice to statesmen and bureaucrats. Everyone, including statesmen and bureaucrats, needs to come to terms with the limits of our collective knowledge as economists. Too many policy disasters are attributable to "one-handed economists" whose confident pronouncements are in error.

Chapter 4, by Benito Arruñada, deals with "Human Nature and Institutional Analysis," which plainly has a bearing on the provision of policy advice. Rather than deal with this issue, however, I consider instead what he refers to as "two prominent examples of emotional maladaptation with vast economic consequences: risk aversion and weakness of will" (p. 87). Most treatments of these and related matters operate at the level of the individual, and most of Arruñada's discussion is of this kind. I submit, however, that *organization* is important in both respects.

Not only does organization relieve individual risk aversion – by pooling risks and by hiring specialists to help us deal with risks that "we are programmed to (wrongly) perceive as affecting our survival and reproduction" (p. 87) – but, even more consequentially, organization often permits us to relieve weaknesses of will. Not only can we substitute "rational" economic routines for defective "mental modules" but we can also craft private ordering governance supports that better assure order, the effects of which are to mitigate the conflict that is posed by "maladaptive discounting." To be sure, organizations also pose dysfunctional consequences of their own, so allowance is properly made for these as well. My point is that the current focus of behavioral economics – which is a healthy development of which NIE is a beneficiary – on individual behavior and individual decision making may usefully be extended to make more prominent provision for organization to include both laboratory and field studies. (Some of these issues are raised in the last few pages of Arruñada's essay.)

Chapter 5, by Lee Alston, discusses "The 'Case' for Case Studies in New Institutional Economics." I am persuaded that case studies are both important to and are underutilized by NIE. I organize my remarks around Alston's statement that the benefits of "case studies include: the ability to first understand an issue prior to modeling it; the ability to test theoretical hypotheses; and the ability to shed credible light on the workings of the institutional and economic workings of society" (p. 121).

I concur, but emphasize the need for a *focussed lens* when doing case studies. That is because the phenomena are usually too complex to speak for themselves. Indeed, it has been my experience that a wrong-headed focussed lens is better than no lens at all, since we will then be confronted with contradictions in the data. Such contradictions invite us to rethink the issues by trying to ascertain what factors are responsible for the disparities and, if we are lucky, provide hints as to what *really is going on out there*.

My second remark on Alston is that I regard a case study less as a test of a theory than as a reality check.[2] And, I agree with Alston's third point: that case studies can and do shed light on the inner workings of complex institutions and economic organization. These microanalytics are where much of the action resides.

Chapter 6, by Michael Sykuta, examines the "New Institutional Econometrics: The Case of Research on Contracting and Organization."

Sykuta takes exception with the discriminating alignment hypothesis out of which transaction cost economics works, by observing that "Transactions at one level of the value chain are likely interdependent on the structure and governance at other levels of the supply chain . . . without an eye on the larger system researchers are likely to overlook ways in which organizational structure is influenced by its value chain context" (p. 140). I do not disagree, but would call attention to the first precept of pragmatic methodology: "keep it simple" (Solow 2001, p. 111).

Given the complexity of economic organization, we need to strip things down and identify the main case – which is not to say the only case. However, until such a main case is in place, an emphasis on second-order effects is apt to delay rather than promote the theory development exercise.

The advantages of a main case are these: it is transparent (simple); it is tractable; it invites others to advance rival main-case candidates; and it does not preclude subsequent refinement by making provision for second-order effects – which is good news! NIE is a work in progress for which new challenges are posed and new talents are needed.

Chapter 7, by Stéphane Robin and Carine Staropoli, discusses "Experimental Methodology to Inform New Institutional Economics Issues." Their concluding comment, which I agree with, is this: "We claim that EE [Experimental Economics] and NIE have already research points in common and . . . could mutually gain from common research projects" (p. 157). Earlier, they discuss how EE contributes to a "deeper characterization of the main behavioral hypothesis of NIE (bounded rationality and opportunism)" (p. 156). I offer a reciprocal example of how provision for organization can help to deepen our understanding of "bad games," of which the prisoners' dilemma is the canonical case.

The myopic version of the prisoners' dilemma is that two suspected criminals are apprehended and questioned about a crime. In the hope of extracting a confession, each is presented with payoffs that invite them to confess. Although both would be better off denying guilt, the calculus leads to what (for them) is a bad outcome: defecting is a dominant strategy.

Ways of overcoming this outcome have mainly emphasized spontaneous mechanisms. Camerer and Knez (1996, p. 94) summarize as follows: "[U]nder three conditions, games which are often classified as social dilemmas are [transformed into] games of cooperation. The first condition is that players get utility from [being nice and] cooperating with others who cooperate . . . The second condition is that [if] . . . players can be excluded from benefiting when others cooperate . . . then players [can be induced to] cooperate. The third condition is . . . [to repeat the game] with sufficiently high probability."

The first condition corresponds to conditional reciprocity, with a predilection to begin with a nice move. The second two conditions entail foresight but leave the basic game intact. None of the three conditions, however, contemplate what I would say is the obvious move: take deliberate action *to alter the payoff matrix by engaging in private ordering* (which also entails foresight).

The implicit assumptions in the classic game are that the police are clever and that thieves are myopic and suffer from "frailty of motive." Suppose, however, that some thieves (or their managers, perhaps the mafia?) have the capacity to look ahead while the robbery is in the planning stage. Suppose that they not only recognize that they might be suspected of committing the robbery, but they also perceive the possibility of being presented by the police with the payoff matrix of the prisoners' dilemma. In anticipation of this dilemma, and so as to better assure that neither defects, they take advance actions that penalize the defection option and make cooperation the dominant strategy. The farsighted or augmented game thus "defeats," as it were, the myopic game that they would otherwise be confronted with.

Predisposed to work out of spontaneous mechanisms, many economists eschew purposeful efforts to craft credible commitments. If, however, individuals have the capacities to recognize and reconfigure bad games, neglect of intentionality will miss some of the action. A researchable question, to which laboratory experiments could be applied, is "*What are the limits of intentionality*, if players are afforded this reconfiguration option, *in the repeated play of bad games?*" Such work has been taking shape (McCabe, Smith and LePore 2000).

Chapter 8, by Thierry Pénard, examines "Game Theory and Institutions" and advances the argument that ". . . game theory is highly useful in examining the rationale of institutions. Game theory is a rigorous framework for questioning the nature of interpersonal relationships." (p. 179). I agree, but would repeat that the pervasive importance of private ordering is often overlooked in game-theoretic treatments of economic organization. For example, Thierry Pénard tells us that cooperation, or agreement by parties to a contract, is "enforced by reputation and trust rather than by courts" (p. 172). True enough, but if the efficacy of reputation and trust vary with the circumstances then we need to ascertain when they work well and when poorly. Also, if access to the courts for purposes of ultimate appeal serves to delimit threat positions, that should not go unnoticed. More generally, the aforementioned neglect of intentionality, as in designing credible commitment mechanisms which have the purpose and effect of deterring inefficient breach of contract, bears repeating.

David Kreps's (1999, p. 122) views on transaction-cost economics (TCE) are pertinent: "speaking as a tool-fashioner interested in developing tools that better deal with the *world-as-it-is*, I believe that game theory (the tool) has more to learn from transaction-cost economics than it will have to give back, at least initially" (emphasis added).

Chapter 9, by Jackson Nickerson and Lyda Bigelow, on "New Institutional Economics, Organization, and Strategy" both surveys the empirical literature on TCE and describes awaiting research opportunities, with special emphasis on the latter. The workhorse that they rely on throughout is that of discriminating alignment; transactions (which vary in their attributes) are aligned with governance structures (which vary in their costs and competence) so as to elicit a transaction cost-economizing result. This is truly the big locomotive on which TCE relies.[3]

Note in this connection that TCE, always and everywhere, is an exercise in comparative economic organization. In as much as there is always more than one way to organize economic activity, this requires the student of TCE to come to terms with the defining attributes of each generic mode of governance.

As Jackson Nickerson and Lyda Bigelow show, this strategy for studying economic organization has had broad application, of which more is in prospect as numerous extensions and refinements upon the simple model are worked out.

Chapter 10, by Joanne Oxley and Brian Silverman, examines "Inter-Firm Alliances: A New Institutional Economics Approach." The authors extend the basic TCE logic and include parts of resource-based reasoning to examine how and why alliances vary depending on the attributes of the transaction and the history of the contractual relation between the parties. What appears at the outset to be a wide variety of contractual provisions reduces to three distinct classes: "alliances tend to cluster in discrete forms, within which there is significant variation but between which we can nonetheless identify step function differences in governance attributes" (p. 219). Specifically, technology-related alliances classify as unilateral-, bilateral-, and equity-based, where safeguards progressively build up among them and equity-based alliances have the most hierarchical features. The authors furthermore project that "insights from the existing body of research on vertical relationships may usefully be integrated into future research on alliances" (p. 220). Altogether, their extensions of TCE reasoning into the study of alliances reveals that many of the puzzles of alliances may be interpreted as variations upon a few key themes.

Chapter 11, by Emmanuel Raynaud, examines "Governance Structure and Contractual Design in Retail Chains." He mainly examines franchising as a mode of governance where, often, the franchisor both makes *and* buys the good or service in question, with benefits to both buy and make options. This is an instructive perspective and has ramifications for both TCE and marketing. Late in the chapter Raynaud examines the ramifications for antitrust, where monopoly (price theoretic) and efficiency (transaction cost) interpretations are contrasted. He observes in this connection that the "antitrust attitude toward the motivations behind vertical restrictions in distribution contracts has evolved considerably over years" and that the inhospitality tradition of ascribing monopoly purpose has been augmented to include a broader understanding of "the benefits of vertical restraints in promoting [efficiency]" (p. 247). I concur and take this to be one of the policy accomplishments of TCE.

Chapter 12, by Manuel González-Díaz and Luis Vázquez, examines "Make-or-Buy Decisions: A New Institutional Economics Approach." The authors mainly work out of a transaction cost setup in which asset specificity gives rise to hazards of bilateral dependency, and in which hazards are relieved by crafting credible commitments (hybrid contracts) or by unified ownership (vertical integration). They observe, however, that "solving the hold-up problem does not guarantee that other problems can be solved so easily, as, for example, monitoring" (p. 257), and subsequently discuss measurement costs as these bear on vertical integration.

I agree that measurement costs (which have their origins in information asymmetry conditions that are costly to rectify) have many ramifications for economic organization. I contend, however, that transactions between the firm and its customers, workers, and investors have more severe measurement problems than are experienced by firms engaged in intermediate product market exchanges.

The reasons are two, both relating to the proposition that organization matters. The first organizational difference is that it is much more economical for firms to acquire the requisite technical, legal, and managerial expertise to evaluate quality before taking delivery than it is for individual customers, workers, and investors. Second, (and related), intermediate product market transactions are presumed to take place between successive stages of production; each of which possesses the requisite scale and has perfected its internal governance mechanisms, thereby to qualify as a viable economic entity *unless* contractual complications arise at the trading interface.

To be sure, the foregoing applies more to trade between successive stages of production (both laterally and vertically) than it does to trade between a supplier and its distributor, which is often multiple, and hence takes the form of a *network*. As Klein (1980) describes, quality assurance (i.e., measurement) problems can arise between a franchisor and its network of franchisees for which credible contracting supports (in the limit, vertical integration) are needed. When it comes, however, to trade between successive stages of *production*, the trading relation is normally of a bilateral rather than network kind – in which event the main contractual concern is that of bilateral dependency (asset specificity).

Note, moreover, that the quality assurance problems that sometimes arise between the firm and its workers over due care and maintenance of equipment are normally of an *intra*stage rather than an *inter*stage issue. Thus, if it is very costly to monitor tool misuse and maintenance, then it may be better to concentrate the ownership of tools on the workers rather than the employer. Since that problem is posed whether successive viable stages are integrated or not, it should not be regarded as a separate "explanation" for vertical integration.

Chapter 13, by Gary Libecap, deals with "Transaction Costs, Property Rights, and the Tools of the New Institutional Economics: Water Rights and Water Markets." As many of us are vaguely aware, and as Libecap makes it abundantly clear, markets for water pose unusually severe problems, many with path-dependent origins. Once rights have been established, reallocations to elicit a shift from past and current uses to what have become higher-valued uses are deterred by many obstacles. One is that property rights for water in the American West are "incomplete [and] vaguely defined" (p. 271). Also, and less widely appreciated, current users with "established ties to politicians . . . are well placed politically to block reallocation" (p. 270). The early property rights literature (Demsetz 1967) easily relates to the first of these. The second poses political obstacles: with "many constituencies having a stake in existing allocations and a potential veto in any reallocation, a paralysis in present uses emerges" (p. 270).

I have elsewhere discussed the limitations of neoclassical resource allocation reasoning with reference to the "remediableness criterion" (Williamson 1996) – where the latter insists that reform proposals need to come to terms with both feasibility and implementation obstacles. Although no easy solutions emerge, the remediableness criterion has the merit of avoiding the hand wringing that attends "failures" to achieve hypothetical ideals of a zero-transaction cost kind. Although Gary Libecap has never been a hand wringer, I suggest that the short section of his chapter, "Policy Responses," could usefully be elaborated by the systematic application of remediableness reasoning.

Chapter 14, by Michael Cook, Peter Klein, and Constantine Iliopoulos, discusses "Contracting and Organization in Food and Agriculture." These authors conclude that despite its "unique institutional environment, the food sector faces the basic problems of economic organization: the need to reduce transactions costs, the need to protect relationship-specific investments, the need to design structures that adapt to change. For this reason, many NIE theories translate easily and naturally to an agricultural setting." I agree, and especially want to emphasize the impor-tance of the uniqueness of agriculture to which the authors refer.

What distinguishes the NIE is the combination of a focussed lens that operates at a microanalytic level with deep knowledge of the phenomena. Thus, the lens of contract calls attention to and interprets contractual regularities which hitherto had been slighted. In as much as the specifics vary, however, deep knowledge of the particulars leads to qualifications and refinements. The combination of deep knowledge of agriculture with the concepts and apparatus of the NIE is what Michael Cook, Peter Klein and Constantine Iliopoulos bring to bear.

Chapter 15, by Pablo Spiller and Sammy Liao, examines "Buy, Lobby, or Sue: Interest Groups' Participation in Policy-making: A Selective Survey." Although most of the chapters in this volume work from a TCE setup, Spiller and Liao work out of the "positive political theory" (PPT) branch of the NIE, which focusses on the rules of the game. As they point out, however, "The distinguishing feature of NIE . . . is its emphasis in opening up the black box of decision making [whether] understanding the rules . . . of the game [PPT, or the] play of the game [TCE]" (p. 303). Specifically, their objective is to "explicate the *micro-analytic* features of the way interest groups [*actually*] interact with policy makers" (p. 303).

This is very much in the spirit of Kenneth Arrow's (1987) remark that the "New Institutional Economics movement does not consist primarily of giving new answers to the traditional questions of economics – resource allocation and the degree of utilization. Rather, it consists of answering new questions, why economic institutions emerged as they did and not otherwise; it merges into economic history, but brings sharper nano-economic . . . reasoning to bear" (Arrow 1987, p. 734). Pablo Spiller and Sammy Liao not only take institutions seriously (by answering new questions) but examine the microanalytic mechanisms of buying, lobbying, and suing with reference to the institutional environment (polities, judiciaries) within which they are embedded and furthermore review empirical evidence that relates thereto. As compared to TCE (which combines economics with law and organization theory), PPT principally combines economics and political theory. NIE is greatly enriched in the process.

Chapter 16, by Jean-Michel Glachant and Yannick Perez, addresses "Regulation and Deregulation in Network Industry." The quotation that I have selected for this is: "The efficiency of [each ... type] of arrangement for network industries should thus not be seen [in absolute terms], but rather ... depends on [the comparative analysis of each feasible alternative]," to which they add that "there is no single 'best solution' applicable to all [network] ... industries" (p. 325). The move from examining actual modes in relation to hypothetical ideals by insistence upon examining feasible alternatives, all of which are flawed, is the first of the seven key features that I ascribed to NIE in my introductory remarks. Glachant and Perez's discussion of why regulation and deregulation need to be examined comparatively, and of the compli-cations posed by differences in the institutional environment across nation states, (with special reference to Germany and Great Britain), illustrates why there are no all-purpose solutions to network industries. Rather, the logic of comparative economic organization needs to be worked out with respect to the attributes of different network industry transactions in relation to the applicable nation-state rules of the game. This may be tedious, but global prescriptions are naïve and invite public policy error.

Chapter 17, by Stefan Voigt, examines "Constitutional Political Economy: Analyzing Formal Institutions at the Most Elementary Level." Stefan Voigt distinguishes between normative and positive branches of the economic analysis of constitutions, and associates the normative branch with James Buchanan, whereas Voigt's chapter deals mainly with positive constitutional economics.

Stefan Voigt makes note of many similarities between constitutional political economy (CPE) and NIE, and he avers that "CPE could greatly profit from positioning itself within the broader NIE" by making express allowance for the complications posed by pre-existing informal institutions when designing new constitutional rules and giving more prominence to problems of credible commitment (p. 366). More generally, the lens of contract approach (which Buchanan contrasts with the more conventional lens of choice) is instructive for studying both political and economic institutions, hence to both the CPE and NIE research agendas. These two have much in common and may be expected to "flourish together."

Chapter 18, by Sonja Opper, discusses "New Institutional Economics and Its Application on Transition and Developing Economies." This chapter contains a plethora of quotable insights and observations. One of these has to do with over-reliance on property rights reasoning by transition economists, where the propensity to focus on the "simple establishment of *de jure* property rights ... underestimated the complexity of the transition task" (p. 388). An obvious problem is that *de jure* property rights are sometimes compromised, with the result that de facto and *de jure* property rights differ. A less obvious point is that provision should also be made for governance efforts by which "individuals try to secure their interests by ... private ordering" (p. 389).

The NIE distinction between the rules of the game (of which property rights is one) and the play of the game (the governance of contractual relations) is pertinent. Among other things, the use of private ordering (governance) may relieve the limitations or defects, or both, in the rules of the game, property rights included. Although this has been recognized by some students of transition economics (Sonja Opper refers to the work of John McMillan and Christopher Woodruff (2000, 2002) in this connection), transition economics will benefit by making express provision for governance.

A second quotation from Opper concerns the concept of embeddedness. Albeit potentially important to an understanding of economic organization, we know very little about the mechanics of informal norms – possibly because "[Mark] Granovetter's (1985) concept of embeddedness, [which] has been the most influential approach so far, ... still awaits greater theoretical specification" (p. 397). The challenge here is to uncover and examine the obstacles to the operationalization of embeddedness. Unless operational life can be breathed into this vague concept, it will suffer the fate of other promising ideas by "running itself into the sand."

Chapter 19, by Antonio Nicita and Ugo Pagano, examines "Law and Economics in Retrospect." The quotation that I have selected from their paper is this: "[Ronald Coase and Oliver Williamson] ... share [with Richard Posner an] over-optimistic view of the legal process: when property rights do exist, in Coase and Williamson's studies, they are always well-defined, complete, clear, and fully enforced at zero [transaction] cost" (p. 411). I respectfully submit that Antonio Nicita and Ugo Pagano have it wrong, whereas Opper has it right. Specifically, my position on property rights reasoning is that it is important, but has overplayed its hand: "The claim, for example, that the legal system will eliminate chaos upon defining and enforcing property rights assumes that the definition and enforcement of such rights is easy (costless). Plainly, many transactions do not qualify," (Williamson 2000, p. 599).

Chapter 20, by Nicolai Foss and Peter Klein, examines "The Theory of the Firm and Its Critics: A Stocktaking and Assessment." Foss and Klein identify "four seminal . . . streams of research in the theory of the firm [which appeared in the 1970s], namely TCE . . . the property rights or nexus-of-contracts approach . . . agency theory . . . and team theory" (p. 420). Of these, they focus on TCE and property rights theory, which they then conflate with the observation that "we generally suppress the differences between Williamson's and Hart's versions of the incomplete contracting story" (p. 421, note 1). They then discuss several "underlying assumptions of the modern theory of the firm," three of which are these: "there is no . . . room for the emergence of new contractual or organizational forms"; "Low-powered incentives play a role only in multi-task agency problems;" and "the modern theory of the firm generally disregards coordination problems" (pp 422–423).

As I have observed elsewhere (Williamson 2000, 2002b, 2005), the transaction-cost theory of the firm as governance structure is not correctly described in any of those three respects. Specifically, the theory of the firm as governance structure expressly (1) makes provision for new contractual forms (such as the hybrid) and new forms of organization (such as the T-form), (2) ascribes low-powered incentives to firms as compared with markets, and (3) holds that adaptation is the central problem of economic organization (of which spontaneous and purposeful kinds are distinguished). The property rights theory of the firm makes provision for none of the above, on which account transaction-cost and property-rights theories of the firm *cannot be conflated*.

Much of the remainder of this chapter is illuminating and invites follow-on work. I therefore urge readers to focus on the remainder of the chapter, which examines a vast literature (some one hundred references), much of it in a nuanced way.

Chapter 21, by Jean-Philippe Platteau, discusses "The Causes of Institutional Inefficiency: A Development Perspective." Platteau successively examines transaction cost, principal agent, equilibrium of the game, and evolutionary approaches to inefficient institutions, where the latter two "lead to the conclusion that institutions may very well be inefficient over long periods of time," and the two former emphasize "(second-best) optimal institutional arrangements," in which inefficiency is judged with respect to a hypothetical ideal (p. 455). Although it is easy to display inefficiencies in relation to a hypothetical ideal (Dixit 1996), remediable inefficiency is judged in relation to *feasible* and *implementable* alternatives. The latter is what I recommend if specific applications are to be attempted.

## Conclusion

Overall, the chapters in this book reveal that NIE is very much a work in progress. The accomplishments of the past thirty years notwithstanding, challenges, controversies, and unmet needs beset the field – sometimes as posed by active participants, sometimes by skeptical outsiders. My recommendation is that these should be addressed in the manner of the best work in NIE – namely, in a modest, slow, molecular, definitive way.

A lasting accomplishment of NIE is that the importance and analysis of institutions has been securely placed on the research agenda. I project continuing progress for the foreseeable future as a new generation of NIE scholars takes the reins.

# A Road Map for the Guidebook

*Éric Brousseau and Jean-Michel Glachant*

New institutional economics (NIE) is the outcome of an evolutionary process, not a planned refoundation. Consequently, unlike neo-classical economics, it is not an integrated theory based on a set of common hypotheses, but, rather, a combination of bricks coming from different traditions. NIE scholars quote great minds as contrasted as Kenneth Arrow and Herbert Simon, Friedrich von Hayek, and Armen Alchian, or Mancur Olson and Sidney Winter. They borrow concepts from, and contribute to, many literatures and traditions, among which law and economics, organization theory, industrial organization, economic history, development economics, and public economics are not least. NIE is, nevertheless, built around a backbone of some fundamental and original contributions proposed, in particular, by Ronald Coase (1937, 1960, 1988), Douglass North (1990, 2005), and Oliver Williamson (1975, 1985, 1996). Together these contributions are not fully consistent, and many debates opposed the three scholars quoted above. They are, however, complementary in the sense that they fit together to compose not a general theory, but, rather, a frame proposing a new way of analyzing economic phenomena.

To NIE scholars, (economic) agents use resources and play games on the basis of rights of decision. Those rights are defined, allocated, and reallocated by various types of devices, in particular contracts, organizations, and institutions. Analyzing these devices highlights a new level of interactions among agents seeking to influence the way the rules of the games are built and evolve. These games are played either on a very local level (in bilateral interactions), or on a global level (in interactions encompassing all human beings), and on many intermediary levels between the two: communities, industries, countries, regions, and so on. The strength of NIE lies in its proposal to analyze governance and coordination in all sets of social arrangements: a vision in terms of design and enforcement of systems of rights (of decision, of use, of access) which results in the implementation of orders allowing agents to coordinate when using or producing resources.

Another powerful characteristic of NIE is its evolutionary perspective. This is a consequence of human nature and of the complexity of social systems composed of numerous interacting agents whose behavior cannot be fully anticipated (partly because their rationality is bounded, partly because they are innovators). Thus, the games mentioned above are not played by agents benefiting from perfect information and infinite computation capabilities enabling them to optimize and establish, in one shot, the optimal system of rights. The design of institutional systems is not based on optimization computation but on trial and error, on the implementation of solutions that should be recognized as imperfect and temporary (hence the concept of "remediability"). In such a context it is essential to take into account the management of changes, together with the processes of evolution.

This vision has two important methodological consequences. First, NIE is built from an applied perspective. Because scholars believe they should learn from facts and because of the complexity of the problems they are dealing with NIE leads scholars to focus on issues, and their research is strongly oriented toward decision making. Second, it makes NIE "open-minded." NIE is open to the "importation" of any contribution which may be relevant to dealing with the above-mentioned issues. For example, scholars as different as Georges Akerlof, Jean-Jacques Laffont, Jean Tirole, Reinhard Selten, Vernon Smith, and Ariel Rubinstein were involved in conferences held by the International Society for New Institutional Economics (ISNIE). More fundamentally, scholars who trained in different traditions and are recognized as key contributors to other domains have made distinguished contributions to the field. This is the case, for example, for Masahiko Aoki (2001) or Avihash Dixit (2005).[1] Also, NIE relies strongly on multidisciplinarity to benefit from fertilization from political sciences, anthropology, sociology, management sciences, and law in particular.

This openness of NIE results in a certain degree of heterogeneity. The literature pools a wide set of very different contributions which include in-depth case studies (with important benchmarks by Coase and Williamson), historical analysis (North, Greif, Weingast), econometric tests (Joskow, Masten), experiments (Smith, Fehr), and modeling (Kreps, Milgrom, Hart), and so forth. As a result, although rich at first sight, the contributions in NIE taken as a whole may appear inconsistent and lacking in identity (Ménard 2004). This heterogeneity is further strengthened because a growing body of research continues to explore how institutions evolve, how they could be enhanced through better design, and how they affect human behavior and economic performances. However, this eclectism is serving a clearly established scientific program aimed at identifying stylized facts, highlighting general causal regularities, building theoretical logic, and verifying and confronting theoretical propositions.

This complex nature of NIE explains why we felt a "guidebook" could be useful. It aims to clarify the unity and diversity of the field, to highlight established knowledge and point out future developments. The book seeks to provide the reader with a guide to link up the many developments carried out in the field. And this introductory "road map" aims to highlight the relationship between the chapters.

In his introduction to the book, Paul Joskow provides an historical overview of how NIE emerged in response to the shortcomings of traditional micro- and macro-economic analyses. He insists that NIE brought essential issues, which were neglected or not sufficiently taken into account owing to a lack of analytical tools, to the attention of the economic profession and decision makers. This resulted in some original and major achievements. However, the main success of NIE has occurred because issues originally highlighted by NIE scholars (such as coordination costs, design, and allocation of rights of decision, credibility of rules and commitments, complex multi-layer games among stakeholders, and many more) now lie at the heart of most developments of economics.

This book is divided into six parts. It starts in Part I by analyzing the origins of NIE, based on contributions focussing on coordination means – organizations, contracts, and institutions – and neglected by mainstream economics until the 1980s, which originally only focussed on market mechanisms. Part II focusses on the methodology of institutional analysis. The peculiarities of the performance of case studies, econometric tests, experiments, and modeling are discussed. Parts III–V consider the development of NIE in various fields of applications. Part III deals with issues related to management, in particular strategic reasoning and organizational design. Part IV deals with the organization of industries. Part V studies the complex issue of the design of institutional systems, which is a major policy tool, whether a matter of regulating business activities or promoting development and growth, or dealing with many other policies (education, crime, and so on). Taking stock of progress – whilst recognizing the shortcomings – of current developments in the economics of institutions, Part VI comprises three chapters which highlight some of the research directions to be explored in the future.

## Part I: Foundations

NIE started with studies of three categories of coordination devices: organizations; contracts; and institutions. In each case, the main challenge was to understand the very nature of these phenomena by explaining how they affect the performance of economic activities and how they are designed. In many respects these devices are different – organizations are collective and consciously designed, contracts are bilateral and consciously designed, and institutions are collective and self-organized – which leads to different analyses, refers to different traditions, and relates to different issues. However, they all frame the behavior of economic agents and influence the results of their inter-actions. Economists have been progressively paying attention to these devices to gain better theoretical foundations for analyzing economic issues and also to benefit from a more consistent theory of coordination in a decentralized economy. They progressively understood that the characteristics and limits of human beings explain why we need insti-tutions and organizations. Organizations permit coordination and cooperation, which allow human beings to exceed the limit of their individual capabilities, in particular their limited cognitive capabilities.

Historically, however, NIE did not start with concerted scientific initiatives. Several waves of applied and analytical developments, driven by specific issues, led to the development of three main bodies of lit-erature, initially relatively separated from each other. One is the eco-nomics of the firm and organizations. This started in the 1930s (with major development in the 1950s) owing to the development of large firms and their strong influence on the economics of markets and industries. Another is the economics of contracts initiated in the 1970s (with major development in the 1980s and 1990s). Both lines of thought led to a more consistent framework for studying coordination in a decentralized economy and addressing essential policy issues (Brousseau and Glachant 2002). The final literature is the economics of institutions initiated in the 1990s and inspired by the need to manage development and transition processes.[2] Following this sequence, our book starts by pointing out the contribution of NIE to the economics of firms, con-tracts, and institutions. Rather than following the path of the history of economic thinking, the four chapters in this section highlight the spe-cificities of the NIE approach when it deals with its core subjects.

Chapter 1 on the theories of the firm, by Pierre Garrouste and Stéphane Saussier, starts by pointing out that most of the fundamental questions (but not all the answers) structuring the economics of the firm were already raised in the contribution by Ronald Coase in 1937. This outstanding scholar delivered perfect insights into the nature of the firm. At the same time, these insights explain why building a theory of the firm is inherently difficult. Everything depends on the fact that organizations and markets are, at the same time, both substitutes and complements. First, the firm is sometimes an alternative mode of coordination which enables the same activity as markets – that is, enabling transactions among individual agents providing or benefiting from services – as proved by the divestiture of large firms and permanent movement of mergers and acquisition. However, it is sometimes an inherently different mode of coordination, as proved by the need to separate certain collections of resources (physical assets, financial means, and knowledge), from markets in order to generate new activities and build new capabilities, (e.g. the internalization of start-ups, the movement of alliances, and these large innovations are often linked to the emergence of large firms). Second, hierarchical coordination is a way to avoid the drawbacks of independent decision makers driven by their individual interests. This separation from the logic of market and competition creates principal agent-type incentive issues. The employer (she), as residual claimant, needs to extract information from the employee (her agent) and to incite him to act according to her will. Incentive mechanisms are thus created by reintroducing market-like mechanisms within the firms either by transmitting market pressures (e.g. bonuses indexed on sales) or by organizing competition (e.g. rank order tournaments). This double face of the firm highlights a key task for new institutional analysis: to identify interdependencies between alternative modes of coordination as complementary components of economic and social systems.

The NIE approach to contracting highlights such interdependencies (in Chapter 2, by Éric Brousseau). Since early developments in the economics of contracting centered on a fully decentralized economy, scholars focussed on understanding pure bilateral tools for coordination. This resulted in the theory of incentives which analyze self-enforcing coordination mechanisms. It also defines highly sophisticated mechanisms that would be too costly to implement in the real world where decision making is onerous. NIE, and also law and economics, propose an alternative vision based on a more applied approach. Individuals have a bounded rationality and are already embedded in an institutional framework. The latter empowers them to interact with the others whilst limiting their ability to do so. Institutions indeed grant them property rights and collective rules framing the exercise of these rights, and with coordination means (starting from marketplaces facilitating meetings between traders or dispute-resolution devices ensuring enforcement of commitments). Contracting allows agents to redesign and transfer their rights between one another. Those contracts are embedded in the institutional framework – social customs, laws, judiciary, and so forth – simply because the agents' ability to contract and the cost of contracting depends on it. The institutional environment is therefore the primary factor for agents' contractual choices. The latter are based on trade-offs between the costs and benefits of relying on alternative coordination mechanisms either designed by agents (contracts) or provided by society (institutions). These trade-offs lead to combine mechanisms which complete with each other, leading to the idea that coordination is ensured by multi-level governance – and the consequent need to analyze institutional and contractual coordination together.

However, building an economics of institutions forces a change of vision from that of institutions as the result of rational design. Although the purpose of NIE is to apply rational choice to the understanding of coordination devices, John Nye and Benito Arruñada explain in their stimulating contributions (in chapters 3 and 4, respectively) why it is misleading to consider institutional systems as the result either of efficient coordination decisions aimed at optimizing the collective economic outcome, or as the result of a process of selection allowing more economically efficient social arrangements to surpass alternatives.

Because social systems are made up of heterogeneous individuals interacting through a wide diversity of coordination mechanisms, which change and whose combination evolves with the passing of time, in Chapter 3 John Nye recommends analyzing them as biological systems rather than mechanical devices. This puts the focus on the diversity of the processes of evolution, since efficiency is not synonymous with the ability to survive. As pointed out in biology, but also in history, what is "efficient" at a given point of time may evolve the wrong way, and inefficient but evolving or invading arrangements may surpass "efficient" ones. However, biological analogies have their own limits when it comes to understanding the dynamics of institutions since the interacting units in a social system are capable of reflexive analysis, which leads to innovation. Thus, on the one hand, to economize on cognition capabilities – and on coordination costs – agents may rely on routines and beliefs to coordinate. This is one of the major factors of institutional stability and the slow pace of change. On the other hand, since they are able to analyze the shortcomings of a given equilibrium, and if some specific conditions arise, they are sometimes able to switch to a new equilibrium. This is why endogenous radical and rapid changes may occur in social systems. Consequently, the complex interplay between trends to stability and trends to change calls for in-depth analysis at the frontier of several social sciences: anthropology, sociology, politics, history, and so on.

This is the kind of exercise proposed by Benito Arruñada in Chapter 4. He explores the features of institutions on the basis of very long-term historical analysis, cognitive sciences, and anthropology.

Institutions have to be understood as tools built by humanity to coordinate, despite the inability of human beings to be perfectly rational. They succeeded in domesticating nature thanks to technology. In doing so they dramatically changed the material and social conditions of their lives, and they did it at a pace that totally surpassed the biological pace of evolution, in particular the capability of the brain to evolve. Institutions must therefore be understood as tools built to overcome the cognitive limits of human beings. They constrain behavior to allow individuals to behave – individually and collectively – more rationally than they could do otherwise. They are able to do this because institutions are the products of a long process of trial and error. However, since this process is not perfect, since formal institutions are designed and run by individuals with bounded rationality, and since technological and social changes are constantly accelerating, institutions are never neither fully adapted to coordination needs, nor are they fully efficient.

### Part II: Methodology

The economics of institutions deals with complex issues owing to the complexity of social systems. Whilst rooted in economics, it calls for analytical innovations to better grasp the specificities of dynamic social interactions, the games played by agents around rules they might decide to comply with or not, complementarities among different types of coordination devices, and so on. This is why NIE relies on a combination of several methodologies, whose usefulness and specificity are discussed in the second part of the guide.

Being a scientific movement NIE aims to identify and control causal relationships. Because the devices and issues dealt with are numerous, and because there are many differentiating factors among them, one size does not fit all and several methodologies have to be combined.

Of course mathematical modeling is a key tool. It is a way of making progress since modeling allows for the systematic checking of logical consistency and tracking of chains of cause and consequence. However, in its current state of development, the economics of institutions still has to identify the regularities and the causal relationships to be examined to check whether the burgeoning theories fit the facts. Indeed, rational choice analysis led to the development of a wide corpus of recommendations on supposedly "efficient" rules and coordination devices. However, most of these propositions are based on oversimplified assumptions, on biased equilibrium analysis, and on overstatic reasoning. It is thus important to assess whether these unavoidable assumptions are satisfactory heuristics or not, and, if not, how they should be reshaped. To make progress various methodologies must be combined.

An initial stage is identifying the most relevant regularities to be explained – the "stylized facts" – and carrying out a preliminary test of the complex interrelation of causal relationships. This calls for the collection of wide sets of qualitative and quantitative data. This may be done through the systematic performance of case studies – which are of value in themselves, and which also gain value as they are accumulated by the scientific community. In Chapter 5, Lee Alston illustrates how, and in what conditions, narratives may become insightful from an analytical point of view. It is indeed often forgotten that the revolutionary and fundamental contributions by one of the founding fathers of the discipline, Ronald Coase, are all based on the accumulation of careful observations of how real-world problems actually arise and are dealt with.

A second stage comes when stylized facts are identified. Then, economic modeling, and especially that carried out by game theory, is a good way of exploring their rationalization. Thierry Pénard explains, in Chapter 8, why this type of analysis fits well with the analysis of institutional systems because we are dealing with interacting agents playing rules. Moreover, the flexibility of game theory makes it a useful tool for analyzing issues that are fundamental when dealing with institutions such as credibility or the convergence of equilibria. Path-breaking contributions, such as those by Aoki or Dixit, demonstrate how game theory is a fundamental fuel for developing institutional economics.

Third, to control possible explanations, econometrics is a vital tool since it allows for the control of various alternative explanations and for the impact of multiple factors that interrelate (interdependence tests). Michael Sykuta details, in Chapter 6, the specificities of the constraints of econometrics with regards institutions. First, we process qualitative rather than quantitative data. Second, since the issues raised by institutional scholars are relatively new, most statistical systems are not capable of providing scholars with relevant data. Efforts are therefore oriented not only toward processing existing data, but also towards the development of new data sources. Although widescale systematic data collections would be needed, most current knowledge relies on ad hoc, incomplete, and partial databases, raising concerns of replicability and insufficient controllability of results. Despite these boundaries, great progress has been made and further progress is expected because of the increase in attention paid by decision makers to institutional drivers of economics performances. Indeed, increasing means and efforts are being dedicated to measuring institutions, their outcomes, and to improving methodologies (*see also* the contribution by Stefan Voigt; Chapter 17 in

Part V). However, although plenty of work remains to be done, past research has already provided valuable knowledge.

Fourth, since we are dealing with human behavior, the complexity of which is still poorly taken into account in the core of economic theories, experimental economics is one way of improving our knowledge. It reveals how "agents" behave in socio-economic interaction interactions, with the scientist in a position to control the parameters of the rules of the game to check the effects of some of them. Moreover, laboratories allow the actual decision made by agents, and sometimes their motivations, to be observed. In Chapter 7, Stéphane Robin and Carine Staropoli provide the reader with insights into the possibilities offered.

So, Part II of the book explains how developments in the economics of institutions should be expected after the presentation of new theories. The latter will be drawn from the accumulation of narratives aimed at identifying stylized facts combined with studies inspired by game theory reasoning. They should result in testable propositions that would have to be more systematically tested through econometric efforts – conditioned by the development of relevant databases – and the design of ad hoc experiments.

### Part III: Strategy and Management

In Part III of the book the unit of analysis is the firm, where many of the "strategic" decisions are organizational in nature. Firms choose how they organize their internalized activities and how they coordinate with others within alliances, partnerships, and networks.

It is generally assumed that NIE, and especially transaction cost economics (TCE), offer a simplistic analysis whereby simple optimal static solutions meet transaction situations. Transaction attributes would call for a single optimal governance mode. On the contrary, the accumulation of results and recent developments show that this approach first takes stock of the need for dynamic adaptations and therefore focusses on managing change; second, it reveals how governance relies on the complex combination of various means which cannot always be "aligned" and managed efficiently; third, that organizational performances are strongly dependent upon the institutional context in which alternative organizational tools are implemented.

TCE cannot be static. The problem is not to minimize transaction costs in a static perspective because (i) the strategic environment of a firm is mobile and (ii) costs are generated by organizational changes, while (iii) lack of adaptability associated to routinization generates costs (attributable to [i]). This gives rise to three insights developed in Chapter 9, by Jackson Nickerson and Lyda Bigelow, on the state of the art in organization and strategy. First, organizational design refers to the ability to minimize dynamic misalignments (because of [i]; see Williamson, 1991a, 1991b). Second, one of the advantages of hierarchy as compared to market is its inertia in an unstable context (because of [ii]). Third, organizational vacillation (among alternative designs) may be optimal in a stable environment (because of [iii]).

TCE develops the idea that governance is a complex matter since it results from the combination of various mechanisms. This can be interpreted in two ways.

First, analysis of the discrete governance mechanism reveals that problems as "simple" as incentive issues call for a combination of mechanisms to deal with vertical and horizontal interdependencies (as pointed out by Emmanuel Raynaud in Chapter 11 on the case of governance of distribution channels). The incentives approach is reinforced by the knowledge perspective, which points out the perils and virtues of authority in managing knowledge. Market supplants hierarchies to solve cognitive problems in some cases, but the reverse is true in alternative contexts (Jackson Nickerson and Lyda Bigelow; Chapter 9). As a result, there is no one best way to organize firms, either from a transaction or from a problem-solving perspective. This is why firms have to rely on hybrid modes of governance and on a combination of hierarchy, market, and networked long-term cooperative relationships to manage complex problems raised by innovation, fragmented markets, and transaction chains. Hierarchies and hybrids may be considered complementary tools, either because they enable the management of different types of transactions (as developed in Chapter 10 by Joanne Oxley and Brian Silverman, on inter-firm alliances and management of innovation) or because hybrid governance allows reliance on complementarities between modes of governance in managing a given type of transaction (Emmanuel Raynaud; Chapter 11).

Second, within a firm various levels and problems of coordination have to be managed, from shop floor to shareholder and manager relationships, and including research and development (R&D) management and coordination with suppliers. Interdependencies of governance exist among these levels, together with coordination problems, which might explain why governance solutions fail to meet governance needs at the transaction level perfectly.

Finally, TCE points out that any reasoning on the choice of a governance mode should be contextualized institutionally. First, the institutional environment influences the relative efficiency of alternative organizational arrangements. Indeed, the quality of property rights, the design of laws, mutual trust among agents, and so on, are the foundations on which arrangements are established. Agents rely simultaneously on both levels of governance which interplay; and sometimes they build hierarchies and hybrids to compensate for the insufficiencies of the institutional environment. Transactions with the same attributes may optimally be governed by alternative organizational arrangements in contrasted institutional contexts (known as Williamson's shift parameter). Second, the institutional environment establishes the selection mechanisms that make alternative governance arrangements viable or not. Indeed, contractual and organizational viability does not depend on a "natural" (or "physical") law that eliminates less efficient solutions. It depends on human-built institutional rules and the convergence of anticipations to set the boundaries of socially acceptable behaviour and arrangements (Jackson Nickerson and Lyda Bigelow, Chapter 9; Brousseau 2000a).

From a methodological point of view, the NIE approach to organizational issues imports insights drawn from an evolutionary perspective. In particular, to understand firms and inter-firm networks the "resources-based view" (RBV) is essential since it points out the specificity of knowledge as a common asset built by non-market forms of organizations; because rights of access and use over such intangibles are difficult to secure and manage. Also, a lot has to be learned from the evolutionary analysis of selection processes.

## Part IV: Industrial Organization

Applying NIE to management issues highlights how the institutional environment is an essential variable of organizational strategies. The contribution of NIE to industrial organization is to further explore the nature of the constraints faced by firms when building organizational arrangements. Firms are constrained, first, by the nature of their coordination needs. The latter – which relate to the notion of transaction attributes – are both the consequences of some "natural" constraints and the unintended results of past technological and relational choices. These choices determine how tasks are presently divided among firms. Past choices influence, in particular, the fragmentation of the production process into separated tasks, the interdependences among them, and the degree of standardization of interfaces along transactions chains (which relates directly to the notion of asset specificity). The second constraint is the shape of the institutional environment which sets the existing nature and distribution of (property) rights among economics agents, which opens or closes opportunities in terms of organizational design. The resulting complex interplay between individual choices and collective constraints explains the organization of industries, and is a subject studied by NIE scholars.

Manuel González-Díaz and Luis Vázquez clearly illustrate this in Chapter 12, on "make-or-buy" decisions. TCE claims that the governance of transactions, and of transaction chains, is, at first sight, the result of the will of agents who simultaneously choose transaction attributes and modes of governance. More recent developments insist on the fact that relevant transactional features (interconnectedness, risk, measurability, and so forth) are the results of systemic constraints attributed to choices made earlier by other agents in the industry.

Cases of industries dealing with natural resources also reveal systemic constraints framing organizational choices. They also highlight that these constraints are less "natural" than "institutional." Indeed, the characteristics of transactions (measurability, risk, and so on) calling for the implementation of alternative governance solutions fully depend on the division of labor mentioned earlier, and on the development of institutional solutions aimed at alleviating these problems by providing economic agents with credible measurement means, solutions to socialize risks, and so forth. This is particularly well developed in the contribution by Gary Libecap (Chapter 13) on the management of a resource – water – generally considered a "public good." He shows that the notions of rivalry or non-rivalry, and excludability or non-excludability, are not natural but result from the institutional framework which first establishes, or not, rights – property rights, but also right of access and use – and, second, permits, or not, their redistribution.

NIE goes further by comparing alternative institutional arrangements. When rights are poorly established a decentralized system of negotiation among users of a resource cannot operate properly, and the resource is de facto managed through a political and bureaucratic process. This induces biases in decision making since decision rights may be totally unrelated to (individual and collective) economic interests. Moreover, these processes tend to lack flexibility since those benefiting from established advantages have a de facto power of veto against any attempt to change the principles according to which the resource is managed. On the other hand, establishing a decentralized and flexible process of collective management necessitates the establishment of an adequate institutional framework consisting of (costly) mechanisms to establish property rights, and of (costly) devices aimed at fluidifying and overseeing the performance of the market through which they are redesigned and redistributed. The choice between two institutional alternatives should balance the cost of the underperformance of political and bureaucratic management processes with the costs of implementing and running a market. This last point illustrates one of the main lessons drawn from NIE: institutional frameworks should be considered as processes for producing coordination capabilities among economic agents. Alternative "technologies" deserve to be compared in terms of overall costs and benefits.

While institutions matter, "natural" constraints exist nevertheless. As pointed out in Chapter 14, by Michael Cook, Peter Klein and Constantine Iliopoulos, agriculture, not because it deals with "the" nature, but with hazards and team production, tends to maintain small entrepreneurship firms such as family-owned farms. Indeed, the activity is characterized by multiple, interrelated, seasonalized, localized, and difficult-to-observe tasks, which are poorly adapted to tailoring of the production process, and which raise complex issues in terms of coordination and incentives. Family-based teams seem to be a good second-best solution because solidarity among members can align the interests of the team members, and the "natural" structure of authority allows decision making. However, family businesses remain inherently small. To face natural and coordination hazards collectively and to benefit from economies of scale, both up- and down-stream, operations are managed by cooperatives (of farms). Cooperatives are nevertheless inherently inefficient – especially in accumulating capital and reacting quickly to shocks – because of the difficulties in making decisions and managing incentives in a group of "peer residual claimants" with diverging interests. So, Chapter 14 clearly illustrates the combination of constraints and the systemic effects framing the design of industries.

Reciprocal interdependencies are one of the reasons why organizational and institutional arrangements may persist over time. In response to the lack of an existing coordination framework, agents can develop ad hoc complementary coordination devices. The latter hinder incentives to reshape the inefficient framework, and may even raise barriers to change, since both the weak framework and its organizational cure must be transformed. Such institutional complementarities explain stability and resistance to change, but they may also be considered drivers of change when certain conditions are met.

## Part V: Institutional Design

At first sight, the idea of institutional design does not fit with the "evolutionary" nature of institutional frameworks, characterized by reciprocal interdependencies and a chain of strategic reactions to existing rules or changes. At the same time, since policy-making aims, to a large extent, reshape a given institutional system to improve its capability, it is crucial to better understand how institutional changes may be influenced, taking into account the fact that existing institutional frameworks are the unintended collective outcomes of deliberate attempts to improve efficiency locally.

The existing institutional framework is, to a large extent, mandatory and not optional or voluntary. We may analyze its properties, but it is difficult to make changes because this induces redistribution of decision rights (then power) and of use and access rights (then wealth). Any "social planner" faces the unavoidable constraint of being both a long- and short-termist. He has to develop a long-term and general vision to propose solutions to deal better with collective problems – both social coordination and collective action – and a pragmatic approach. Pragmatism is a response to the ability of agents to behave strategically and bypass collective constraints to protect their interests and enhance their individual wealth. Here, NIE first provides a better understanding of how institutional frameworks produce economic outcomes by analyzing how individuals and groups play with and bypass them. Second, NIE analyzes the processes by which changes occur, often by accumulation and propagation of micro-institutional reforms for fixing local problems.

In Chapter 15 Pablo Spiller and Sanny Liao point out that business regulations and competitive policies are influenced by the way interactions among groups of interest take place. Those in charge of designing the rules which frame business activities need to access relevant information and knowledge. Various interest groups are motivated to provide this information, of course, biased according to their particular interests. "Rulers" and "Arbitrators" are therefore motivated to gather information from different groups. The way interactions between rulers and arbitrators, and those groups, occur depends on the structure of the political institutional environment. The respective organization and the interactions between legislators, courts, and bureaucracy explain how the various stakeholders select the most relevant communication strategies and targets to promote their interests. These games of influence occur in any institutional settings, not only in "corrupted" countries. Only the modalities differ across socioeconomic systems. They result in complex combinations of strategies among the different players – holders of interest, but also the general public, politicians, and bureaucrats – inducing processes of evolution that are highly unlikely to be driven by the desire for efficiency and to converge toward similar (and even compatible) equilibria across countries.[3] Although perfection is out of reach, more transparent political institutions and checks and balances should lead to more efficient changes because the ability to identify weaknesses is enhanced and greater incentives to cure them exist.

In a complementary approach, based on a survey of the process of regulatory reforms in network industries, Jean-Michel Glachant and Yannick Perez highlight (in Chapter 16) other reasons for the path dependency characterizing the processes of institutional redesign. Managing reforms does not involve designing, from scratch, optimal market and ideal industry structures which would depend on "natural" conditions, nor on the "technology", for two reasons. First, technology is endogenous, as pointed out by the fact that past reforms in those industries has led to many technological changes – standardization, measurement techniques, structuring of networks in "hub and spokes", and so on – to comply with competitive logic. Second, reforms are, most of the time, hardly politically sustainable since they result in the redistribution of power and wealth. There are few chances of benefiting from a perfect alignment of stakeholders' interests with adequate incentives for political or judicial authorities to allow for consensual reforms. Rather, the institutional protection of existing rights always allows some parties to exercise their veto (also because some bureaucrats and politicians may have an interest in maintaining the status quo or in protecting groups harmed by the reform). Reforms are inherently progressive, and generate political games at each stage, with outcomes that are difficult to predict because the various institutional decision makers are loosely coordinated (both for good reasons – separation of powers – and bad ones – divergence of interests). Such conditions hardly guarantee efficiency and may even lead to inconsistent new regulation regimes submitted to potential major failures (such as electricity black-outs or financial crises). Step-by-step implementation of "institutional patches" aimed at fixing the worst effects of institutional regimes do not guarantee success, but limit the danger of major failures because adjustments to the reforms may be made (leading to the concept of remediability).

The complexity of managing institutional changes also lies at the core of developmental policies. In Chapter 18, Sonja Opper points out that besides the management of diverging interest, the necessary consistency among institutional components – that is, the institutional complementarities – makes change difficult to manage. First, institutional components do not have the same degree of manipulability. Whilst it might be possible in certain circumstances to transform certain formal institutional components, it is vital they remain consistent with other institutional components – especially informal ones – which cannot evolve or which change at different paces. Second, complementarities among institutional components are complex to manage because the properties of alternatives are context dependent. For instance, a private body may do what a public one cannot in a specific environment. The same occurs for formal versus informal institutions, and so on. As a consequence, any institutional framework is highly specific, and the combination of mechanisms performing well in one context may prove powerless in another. This means that those who are in charge of managing the processes of institutions face difficulties when trying to learn from other experiences and while they are managing complex systems in which the consequences of changes are difficult to predict. Thus, the inherent difficulties of managing institutional change and implementing institutional frameworks to promote economic efficiency are partly caused by a lack of knowledge about the complex interplay between institutional components. The same applies to knowledge of the way institutional constraints create socio-economic outcomes by taking into account the actual strategic reactions of agents to institutional constraints. In his essay on the state of the art of constitutional political economy (Chapter 17), Stefan Voigt highlights how it is possible and worthwhile carrying out systematic positive analysis, based on patient efforts to measure institutions and their impacts, and to unbundle the many components of the complex phenomena. Normative constitutional analysis, based on a contractual approach to constitutions (as developed by Buchanan), provides normative tools for judging the efficiency of alternative constitutional regimes. However, the very nature of institutional frameworks – more in line with the spontaneous order à la Hayek than with a consciously designed order – means that these criteria are irrelevant when it comes to studying existing institutional frameworks. To overcome these shortcomings, and thanks to new econometric methods and databases, several scholars have launched initiatives to measure how institutions affect performance. However, we lack knowledge of complex transmission mechanisms to explain the relationship between an observed outcome and observed formal institutions, and this makes it hard to learn any relevant "lessons" for directly building policies from results obtained during the last decade. Nevertheless, ongoing efforts to measure teach us more about what needs to be investigated further via various methodologies (from econometric to anthropologic observations, and including experimentation), and opens up avenues for further research which should deliver useful knowledge for managing institutional changes.

## Part VI: Challenges to Institutional Analysis

One of the key views of NIE today is that the processes of institution-building and institutional evolution do not guarantee that the most efficient forms of governance are selected. Institutions may be durably inefficient. Even the notion of institutional efficiency is questioned. This is not only because selection failures occur, but also because institutions are made up of various coordinated equilibria among individual strategies in games played in a wide number of institutional arenas – the components of the institutional framework – which do not spontaneously match and lead to efficiency. This links up the viewpoint developed by Aoki – who sees alternative institutional arrangements as various combinations of equilibria in different institutional spheres – with the approach proposed by North – of a constant challenge to align various kinds of institutional components which do not evolve at the same pace (such as formal and informal institutions).

In such a context, it is useful to examine institutions, organizations, and contracts through lenses that are different from those traditionally used. As illustrated by the evolution of the TCE approach to governance (Part III), it is useful to remember that the primary purpose of coordination mechanisms is not to reduce – or even annihilate – transaction costs, but to empower human beings. Such an approach does not contradict the one that was dominant in the past, but enlarges the perspective and allows it to better take into account four dimensions.

Institutional issues are inherently dynamic, and the processes of evolution are characterized by path-dependency and tensions because of contrasting paces of change.

- Institutional systems are complex by nature and made up of interacting components which are both complements and substitutes, and whose regimes must be compatible. Although they result from human action, some of these components – in particular, informal institutions such as beliefs, patterns of behavior, and so on – are difficult to change voluntarily.
- Any given design for an institutional framework establishes distribution of wealth and power. Vested interests render the management of institutional change inherently difficult, particularly because the high number of stakeholders makes it difficult to organize negotiation and compensation.
- This is reinforced by the myopia of players – whoever they are: stakeholders, rulers, or arbitrators – because bounded rationality and information costs prevent them from having a complete, and therefore common, vision of the whole game.

Part VI of the book pools chapters on how to draw up the research agenda to be explored to develop the analytical tools linked to this enlarged vision.

According to Antonio Nicita and Ugo Pagano (Chapter 19), it should be recognized that the legal order is inherently imperfect. There are always incomplete property rights, biased legal rules, and flawed enforcement mechanisms because the process by which a legal order is built guarantees legitimacy, but not consistency and efficiency – members of the society decline to refer to it and use it. Boundedly rational agents who have vested interests accept and contribute to implementing changes in the pre-existing order, but do it sub-domain by sub-domain both because of the complexity of a general reshaping and because of difficulties in reaching agreements. Any process of legal evolution should recognize this.

The many chapters insisting on path dependency and the uncontrollability of institutional evolution could lead to the conclusion that processes of evolution are caused by the combination of random changes – "small events" – and the dynamics of network externalities – path dependency – in a purely biological logic if we lose sight of the figure of the "entrepreneur." In Chapter 20, Nicolai Foss and Peter Klein opportunely remind us of the fundamental role this figure should play in the economics of the firm. And we think this role should be highlighted more generally in the economics of institutions to help understand the process of economic change. Entrepreneurship refers to the specific skill of identifying new opportunities and new combinations, to realize them, especially when uncertainty prevents the ability to predict the precise results of decisions. Entrepreneurs build on the pre-existing coordination structure because the latter are the result of the accumulation of previous solutions to problems solved by human beings. And it would be inefficient to re-invent everything from scratch. Entrepreneurs are empowered by the knowledge embodied in social rules, which are the concrete forms of the collective capabilities put forward by the RBV. They are also empowered by the assets acquired thanks to pre-existing institutional structures (human capital, infrastructure, trust, and so on). Entrepreneurs are, nevertheless, necessary tools for change because social selection processes do not work spontaneously and eliminate inefficient solutions. Therefore, understanding the process of institutional and organizational evolution requires in-depth analysis of the ways entrepreneurs invent, of their incentives to push for adoption of their inventions, and of their strategies for coping with the competition.

Beside drivers for change, analyses of the many factors hindering change and evolution should also be developed, as we are reminded in Chapter 21, by Jean-Philippe Platteau, who surveys the state of the art on the matter. First, information and decision costs may conceal the fact that a given institutional framework is inefficient and that an alternative is feasible. In a large community transaction costs for renegotiating a better "social contract" – to draft it and have it adopted by each member of the community – might be prohibitive. Second, a collective action problem occurs. Even if each member of the society is convinced that a better equilibrium exists, and even if they all agree on its characteristics, it might be too risky for each member to switch unilaterally to the new equilibrium. The old Nash equilibrium is inherently stable.

This dialectic between elements of change and stability explains why the economics of institutions is unable to propose clear political recipes for "rationally" building or rebuilding institutional settings, and for "driving" institutional reforms. Although institutional policies are increasingly recognized as main policy tools, compared to direct governmental intervention, or tax and subsidies, economists are only able to propose "insights" into running reforms.

Whilst it is impossible to design "turnkey" policies based on present knowledge, it is nevertheless becoming increasingly obvious that, because of the interplay between informal institutions (in particular, beliefs and customs), formal institutions (laws), and strategic reactions of economic agents, two approaches to managing changes must be combined.

Changing or manipulating beliefs is essential since changes to formal rules are insufficient to affect actual business and social practices. While "standard" theory – North (1990), for example – states that beliefs evolve very slowly, empirical evidence shows that they sometimes can change quite quickly (such as transition in eastern Europe, deregulation of network industries).

Implementing "institutional patches" (such as ad hoc licenses, decrees, administrative procedures, and so on) may be efficient because attempting to directly overwhelm the distribution of property rights leads to clashes among group of interests, with incumbents able to protect their established right thanks to powers of veto (either exercised thanks to political lobbying or judicial suits). Light and local reforms to procedures might result in "viral" effects, generating major changes in the end.

Although this theory is missing, this book shows that the logical foundations are almost in place.

As institutional economists, we are witnessing a kind of Hayekian revival today. NIE highlights the fact that instead of being constructed though a process of rational choice and efficiency-driven selection, society has built its own rationality by building a social order on the basis of the definition and reorganization of rights and rules. The latter permits collective action and empower individuals, but there is neither any specific end nor stable final state to be reached. Like biological systems, institutional systems are out of equilibrium.

# Introduction to New Institutional Economics: A Report Card

*Paul L. Joskow*

## Introduction

During the first three decades after World War II, mainstream academic economists focussed their attention on developing and expanding the theoretical foundations for what is commonly called neoclassical economics, and on the development and application of econometric techniques to measure empirically the parameters of these theoretical models, and to test hypotheses about their properties. In microeconomics we saw the development of rigorous theoretical models of consumer demand, firm production, and cost functions; the foundations of competitive market equilibrium, with and without uncertainty; and the implications of a wide range of market imperfections (e.g. externalities, oligopoly, asymmetric information) on firm behavior and market performance. Econometric techniques to estimate the parameters of demand and cost functions, and to measure the effects of market imperfections on prices, costs, and other market attributes, were also developed and applied.

In macro-economics we saw the development of theoretical models to explain key determinants of aggregate economic activity – income, consumption, investment, inflation, unemployment, and economic growth. This work focussed initially on the rigorous theoretical articulation of the foundations of Keynesian economics, and then on alternative non-Keynesian and post-Keynesian models linked more closely with neoclassical micro-economic foundations of firm and consumer decision making, price and wage formation in markets, and investments in human capital. This theoretical work was accompanied by new econometric techniques to use macro-economic data to estimate the parameters of key aggregate economic relationships. These empirical relationships were used, in turn, to create large macro-economic models to assist in making predictions of the components of aggregate economic activity and the effects of government tax, expenditure, and monetary policies on these variables.

In parallel with these developments in "positive" micro-economics and macro-economics substantial efforts were made to develop rigorous theoretical foundations and supporting econometric techniques for evaluating the societal implications of individual and market behavior and performance, and the effects of various public policies on social welfare – modern welfare economics. Going beyond simple utilitarian models of social welfare, this work confronted the challenge of dealing with diverse consumer preferences and interpersonal comparisons, aggregation of consumer preferences, and the ethical implications of wide distributions of income and wealth in the population.

There can be no doubt that the developments in economics during the three decades following World War II were extremely important from both an intellectual and a practical perspective, and they have helped to expand dramatically our understanding of many aspects of market structure, economic behaviour, and economic performance, especially in developed economies. The tools that were developed are widely used in government policy making and business decision making. And progress continues in theory and empirical applications within the neoclassical tradition. Nothing in this essay is meant to diminish the many important advances in economics that have been achieved during the last fifty years.

It appears to me, however, that the incremental knowledge resulting from the ongoing work in this neoclassical tradition, especially in micro-economics, began to yield significantly diminishing returns by the late 1970s. The low-lying fruit had been picked and the remaining fruit in the tree began to become much more difficult to find and harvest. Moreover, in many ways these developments were less than fully satisfactory, or at the very least, provide an incomplete framework for understanding many important economic phenomena.

This work had a number of deficiencies. It adopted either an *a*-institutional or a *non*-institutional approach to economic analysis. The basic underlying legal institutions that are widely assumed to be necessary to support the behavioral assumptions and market structures being analyzed – such as credible property rights, enforceable contracts, private ownership, well-functioning capital markets, and corporate governance systems – were either implicitly assumed to exist and to operate costlessly and perfectly (or not at all in the case of externalities), or were effectively ignored completely or swept under the rug. Firms were black boxes characterized by productions functions and their horizontal expanse governed by economies of scale driven by the underlying technological attributes of these production functions. The inability to measure significant economies of scale at the plant level econometrically led many industrial organization economists to the conclusion that firms were too large and that deconcentration policies would have potential competitive benefits with little potential economic costs. Vertical integration and associated vertical contractual arrangements were difficult to explain with the prevailing tools, except trivially by appeals to unspecified "economies of vertical integration" or as strategic responses of firms to increase market power at one or both levels of the production chain (Joskow 2004). Technological changes which led to the introduction of new products and new production processes were understood to represent important components of economic growth and consumer welfare, but the theoretical and empirical foundations for understanding the rate and direction of innovation and how they are influenced by micro-economic, macro-economic, institutional, and policy considerations was poorly understood. Economic growth was driven by changes in capital and labor inputs, exogenous technological change, and poorly understood differences between countries over time and space.

Benevolent governments with public interest goals and perfect information were available to make policies "in the public interest." Whilst it was recognized that governments could do things which could either improve or undermine economic performance, the economic and political considerations that led to alternative government policy initiatives, and affected the structure and behavior of government institutions which influenced economic growth, from legislatures to courts, were largely ignored. Micro-economic theory focussed on private profit-maximizing firms while large portions of economic activity were governed by state-owned firms, state agencies, and non-profit organizations. The nature of the choices between different governance arrangements and their consequences were largely ignored. Finally, although the theory and associated empirical analysis developed during this post-World War II period was "generic", in the sense that it was thought to be applicable to any economy, in practice it was difficult to apply generically. This was particularly problematic in application to developing countries without somehow taking account of the "idiosyncratic" and unmeasured attributes of social, political, and economic attributes of "institutions" in different countries. There was little progress in understanding these "idiosyncratic" attributes which characterized institutions in different countries, how and why they mattered, their linkages to historical and cultural attributes, and how they could or would change over time in response to changes in the economy, economic growth, changes in government and legal institutions, and to policy initiatives mediated through these institutions.

These limitations of neoclassical economics are now widely recognized, and "mainstream" economics has now moved forward to address them. A growing number of scholars are engaged in research to respond to these limitations in a number of different ways. We see this evolution in several apparently different but fundamentally interrelated "new" fields of economics: law and economics, political economy, behavioral economics, organizational economics, evolutionary economics, the economics of contracts, and new institutional economics (NIE). In some ways these fields are not "new" at all since their origins may be traced back to pioneering research, sometimes largely ignored at the time, which was produced decades ago. However, in other important ways these fields are indeed new. First, they do not reject the basic progress which has been made in the neoclassical tradition over the last fifty years, but recognize both its strengths and its limitations. Second, they do not reject the basic analytical tools that have been developed over the last fifty years – mathematical modeling and econometric analysis – but use these tools to address a broader set of issues. Third, they supplement these methods of modern economic analysis with additional analytical and empirical methods and analyses which include, for example, case studies and experimental methods which are appropriate for addressing the relevant issues more completely. Fourth, they draw on scholarship from a broad range of social and behavioral sciences: history, law, political science, anthropology, psychology, sociology, and other disciplines to address issues that neoclassical economics addresses poorly or not at all. Fifth, they recognize that economic theory and empirical regularities are often not "generic," and are more or less relevant, or relevant in different ways, depending on economic, social, political, and legal attributes of different countries. One size does not fit all and, in particular, differences between developed and developing countries can lead "reasoning by analogy" to result in serious errors. Finally, rather than taking a position outside of economics and looking in at it, often critically, these efforts seek to be fully integrated into advances in economic theory, empirical methods, and applications. This transformation of economic analysis was, and continues to be, heavily influenced by the perspectives and pioneering research undertaken under the banner of "New Institutional Economics."

## What is new institutional economics?

The effort to move economics beyond the limitations of neoclassical methods and models, and the progress that is being achieved, is truly exciting. It is not my intention, however, to discuss all of these developments. Rather, I want to focus on developments in institutional economics or, more precisely, NIE, which motivated the founders of the International Society for New Institutional Economics (ISNIE) in 1997. I recognize that "mainstream" economic research has now turned its attention to many of these issues. However, this transformation both preceded and was heavily influenced by the work of scholars who we associate with NIE.

The founders of ISNIE had (and have) a broad range of interest in and approaches to economic analysis. Nevertheless, they shared a common set of basic beliefs which defined the research topics they would focus upon and the research methods that they would use and sought to foster:

- Legal, political, social, and economic institutions ("institutions") have important effects on economic performance. The effects of alternative public policies aimed at improving economic performance in various dimensions will vary along with the institutions that are available to respond to them.
- Institutions may be analyzed using the same types of rigorous theoretical and empirical methods which have been developed in the neoclassical tradition whilst recognizing that additional tools may be useful to better understand the development and role of institutions in affecting economic performance.
- Theoretical and empirical analysis should be interactive and evolve together over time. Theory identifies relationships that may be examined empirically, whereas empirical regularities and "anomalies" raise questions about the relevance of received theory and suggest new targets of opportunity for theoretical advances.
- Interdisciplinary research may make important contributions to understanding the role of institutions and how they affect economic behavior and performance. Contributions from history, law, psychology, anthropology, sociology, religion, and related disciplines may play an important role in advancing our understanding of institutions and their effects on the economy and the consequences of economic policies.
- Longer-term dynamic considerations associated with technological change, the diffusion of innovations, and the impacts of institutions on both should play a more central role in economic analysis.
- Our understanding of institutions should be rich enough to allow us to apply economic theory and empirical knowledge to a wide range of economic, cultural, and political settings: developed and developing countries; countries with a range of political systems, including

variations of the implementations of "democracy"; countries with a range of cultural, religious, ethnic, tribal, and family traditions.

- Institutional analysis seeks to understand the role of government and political institutions in policy formation, implementation, and economic performance, but it does not itself have a political agenda.

When we adopt a phrase like "new institutional economics" to define a framework for social science research it is fair to ask how this work differs from "old" institutional economics. It is quite clear that "institutional economics" had achieved a bad reputation among post-World War II academic economists in the USA and some other countries. Indeed, the economic research which flourished during this period was, at least in part, a reaction to the "old" institutional economics which was the focus of economic research in the previous decades. The criticisms of "old" institutional economics, while perhaps not entirely fair, are important to understand. Much of what passed as institutional economics lacked rigorous and systematic theoretical foundations. It lacked comprehensive supporting empirical analysis. It was often country specific or even case specific and little effort (or non-credible effort) to generalize was made. It tended to become politicized and driven by political agendas. The identification of institutional economics with Marxist economic theories and political agendas was especially damaging, though many institutional economists (e.g. John R. Commons [1932–33]) were hardly Marxists. Moreover, as neoclassical economics became the central focus of modern economic analysis institutional economics became the home of the disgruntled and disaffected critics of the new methods being used in economics, and of modern market economies more broadly. We see this no more clearly than in France where a schism emerged between "institutional economists" in university positions, and neoclassical economists, often trained as engineers, using mathematical methods and empirical analysis in engineering schools, public enterprises, and some research institutes. Clearly, NIE is very different from old institutional economics.

We should recognize as well that the reaction to old institutional economics also reflected its perceived failure to explain the economic issues and problems which were revealed by the Great Depression and the associated failure of micro-economic and macro-economic policies to bring the world quickly out of the Depression. The consequences of the Great Depression, and the difficulties economists and policy makers had in explaining or responding to it, brought a new generation of brilliant individuals into economics seeking to better understand economic phenomena so that economics and economic policy could better serve the interests of the people. From this perspective, NIE may be somewhat more in the position held by neoclassical economics at the end of World War II: it is a reaction to perceived deficiencies in the state of economic science. But, whilst there were many outstanding post-World War II economists who remained interested in important foundations and aspects of economic institutions (e.g. Ronald Coase, Herbert Simon, Richard Cyert, Jacob Marshak, Roy Radner, Kenneth Arrow, and others), much of this work was largely ignored by mainstream economists until relatively recently. In this sense, mainstream neoclassical economics may have thrown some babies out with the bath water, though the bath water was not lost for ever.

### A framework for new institutional economics

When we seek to examine the role of "social, cultural, political, and economic institutions" on "economic behavior and performance" we have cut a very large slice of cake to chew on. As I will discuss presently, NIE has not tried to focus on all institutions that might fit under this umbrella. Nor has it focussed on all aspects of economic performance. Whilst the field has been reasonably inclusive, it has also been reasonably well-focussed. To better understand the (perhaps soft) boundaries of NIE it is useful to work from a more expansive description of the full range of relevant institutions, and the relationships between them, and then to identify the subset of institutions upon which research in NIE has focussed.

The most useful framework to work from is the one proposed by Oliver Williamson (2000) a few years ago. I will make use of Williamson's analytical framework here, including a number of adaptations of my own to it. Williamson's framework identifies four interrelated levels of social or institutional analysis.

*Level 1: Embeddedness, or Social or Cultural Foundations.* The highest level of the institutional hierarchy encompasses informal institutions, customs, traditions, ethics and social norms, religion, and some aspects of language and cognition. This level provides the basic foundations for a society's institutions. These basic social and cultural institutional foundations change very slowly over time, with adaptation periods of as long as a thousand years and no shorter than a hundred years.

*Level 2: Basic Institutional Environment.* This second level of the institutional hierarchy encompasses the basic institutional environment or what Williamson calls "the formal rules of the game." At this level are defined constitutions, political systems, and basic human rights; property rights and their allocation; laws, courts, and related institutions to enforce political, human rights and property rights, money, basic financial institutions, and the government's power to tax; laws and institutions governing migration, trade, and foreign investment rules; and the political, legal, and economic mechanisms which facilitate changes in the basic institutional environment. The nature of the basic institutional environment at any point in time reflects, among other things, the attributes of a society's basic social and cultural foundations. In a society in a dynamic equilibrium, a given set of basic institutions at this level will be compatible with the society's social foundations at any particular point in time. Changes in the basic institutional environment occur more quickly than changes in the cultural or social foundations (Level 1), but change is still relatively slow and partially constrained by the slow rate of adaptation of the underlying social and cultural foundations, with response times as short as ten years but as long as a hundred years.

*Level 3: Institutions of Governance.* This third level of the institutional hierarchy encompasses what Williamson calls "the play of the game." Given the basic institutional environment, choices are made about the institutional (governance) arrangements through which economic relationships will be governed given the attributes of the basic institutional environment. The basic structural features of the institutions (e.g. competitive markets), through which individuals trade goods, services, and labor are defined; the structure of contractual or transactional relations, the vertical and horizontal structure of business firms, and the boundaries between transactions mediated internally and those mediated through markets; corporate governance, and financial institutions that support private investment and credit, are defined at this level. The choice of governance arrangements is heavily influenced by the basic institutional environment as well as by a country's basic economic conditions (e.g. natural resource endowments) at any point in time. Changes in governance arrangements also take place more quickly than do changes in the basic institutional environment. Williamson suggests a change time frame of one to ten years.

*Level 4: Short-term Resource Allocation (Neoclassical Market Economics).* This level refers to the day-to-day operation of the economy given the institutions defined at the other three levels. Prices, wages, costs, and quantities bought and sold are determined here as are the consequences of monopoly, oligopoly, and other neoclassical market imperfections. Williamson would include agency theory and incentive alignment within and between organizations here. I would, instead, consider these arrangements to be more appropriately included under the Level 3 institutions of governance. Indeed, these developments reflect the shift of "mainstream" economic research to the consideration of governance arrangements and institutions more generally.

The division of social, political, legal, and economic institutions into four levels is necessarily somewhat arbitrary. However, I think that this qualitative characterization is quite useful. A society's social and cultural foundations place constraints on the attributes of the basic institutional environment that will be feasible at a particular point in time. For example, societies that have no tradition of private property, and have relied instead on communal exploitation of resources and collective allocation decisions, cannot be expected overnight to successfully adopt the basic institutions of capitalism that characterize the USA or Western Europe. Nor will societies with hierarchical non-democratic political systems, easily shift instantly to modern democratic political or human rights institutions (these are positive not normative observations). Similarly, when certain basic institutions, such as private property rights, centralized monetary institutions, and decentralized credit institutions, first begin to be introduced we cannot simply assume that they will instantly have the same attributes as they do in societies with many years of experience with them. Moreover, the institutions of governance that have attractive allocational and adaptive properties with one set of basic institutions may have different and less-attractive attributes with another set of basic institutions. Finally, familiar capitalist market institutions may not work very well if the supporting institutional infrastructure composed of basic institutions and compatible governance arrangements is not in place. Alternative allocation mechanisms may be better adapted to the supporting institutions that are in place at any particular point in time.

Williamson's framework also makes important observations about the speed with which adaptation may be expected to take place. Changes in basic social and cultural foundations take place most slowly, and are most "embedded" in the institutions of a society. To the extent that changes to the basic social and cultural environment also constrain the choice of basic institutional arrangements, adaptation at this second level may be slowed as well. Within the boundaries established by the basic social and cultural environment, the basic institutional environment may also be expected to change fairly slowly. This not only places limits on the speed with which the basic "modern" institutions of capitalism will be adopted and work well, but may also influence the most effective intermediary governance arrangements compatible with the state of the basic institutional environment. Periods of relatively rapid change in social and cultural norms, and the basic institutional environment, may be expected to lead both to rapid change and potentially significant instability in governance arrangements as well. Adapting to rapid changes at these levels may lead to major dislocations and adaptation costs as a society moves forward (or perhaps two steps forward and one step backward) with fundamental changes at all levels.

Williamson's framework also makes it clear that the speed and direction of changes at these levels is not exogenous or necessarily monotonic. Change is stimulated through two basic paths. First, the performance of the society, broadly defined to include aggregate income and wealth (the size of the pie), distributions of income and wealth (how the pie is shared), quality of life and its direction of change, the incidence of poverty and starvation, personal and family security, responses to changes in the availability of natural and human resources (driven by natural, human, and political variables), and opportunities for individuals to fulfill their ambitions for themselves and their families will influence the rate and direction of change. Good performance supports the status quo. Poor performance stimulates change, but not always in a direction that makes thing better overall.

Second, changes in lower-level institutions in the hierarchy may stimulate supporting changes in higher-level institutions. For example, increased reliance on long-term contracts between "strangers" rather than relying on transactions between members of the same family or ethnic group (Greif 1993) may lead to pressures to better define the basic institutions governing enforcement of private property rights and contractual performance. Or the effects may be more indirect: industrialization may lead to more air pollution and, in the absence of clearly defined property rights and enforcement institutions, or more informal institutions to mediate between those who benefit and those who are harmed by pollution, may create pressures for governments to enact laws to control pollution, effectively deciding who has the property rights to clean air and water.

Whatever the pathways of change, both the speed and nature of any changes will necessarily be affected by the time that it takes to make significant adjustments in the attributes at the different levels of this institutional hierarchy. Adjustment and adaptation lags, and costs, become important considerations in implementing public policies to improve economic performance.

NIE has focussed primarily on analyses of aspects of institutional arrangements that fall in Level 2 and Level 3 of this hierarchy (or both). At the ISNIE annual conference in 2003 about 85% of the papers presented fell within these categories and were divided roughly equally between them. Only 5% of the papers were on topics that would be categorized as Level 4 (and some of these featured applications of experimental economics), whilst about 10% involved issues on Level 1 of the hierarchy focussed heavily on the role of religion, ethics, and social norms. Although a large number of topics may fit easily into levels 2 or 3, the bulk of the research presented at the conference fell into a fairly well defined subset of topics that lie at these levels. Among those papers which fell into levels 3 and 4, the vast majority focussed on issues associated with the definition, allocation, and enforcement of property rights and their effects on economic performance, contracts, vertical integration and various hybrid organizational forms, privatization, positive political economy, regulation, deregulation and industry restructuring, and competition policies. Most of these papers involved empirical analysis (including case studies) and many focussed on developing countries. It is also my impression that there has been growing interest over time in issues that naturally fall into Level 1 and their implications for the attributes of the basic institutional environment of Level 2.

### Substantial progress has been made

Looking back over research in the general area of institutional economics over the last ten or fifteen years, it is clear to me that very substantial progress has been made. There also remains much to do to advance our understanding of institutions, how they affect economic performance, and how they change. Perhaps most importantly, the central role of institutions in understanding economic performance, growth and development, and the strengths and weaknesses of alternative public policies aimed at promoting improvements in individual welfare is now widely accepted by the economics profession and has become an important part of "mainstream" research in many fields. While there remain (healthy) differences in views about which institutions are most important, how they should be analyzed, and the relative importance of formal theory, less formal theories, and empirical analysis, research devoted to institutional economics has increased dramatically and has become a fairly mainstream topic. This is a very dramatic change over a period of less than two decades.

Identifying the specific issues upon which the most progress has been made is necessarily a matter of taste. Let me identify my own "top three" areas where I believe substantial progress has been made in the last two decades. In my view, very substantial progress has been made in understanding the definition, allocation, and enforcement of property rights in different Level 1 and Level 2 institutional settings, how property rights affect key attributes of economic performance, and, in turn, how the role of property rights is affected by economic performance and other attributes of the social, cultural, and basic institutional environment (Acemoglu 2003; Alston, Libecap and Schneider 1996; Davis and North 1971; Libecap and Smith 2000; North 1991, 1994). The research here has gone well beyond fairly banal observations such as "well-functioning markets require credible property rights" to explore more fundamental issues of how property rights emerge, what they mean, how they are enforced, how these rights are limited and adjusted in very different institutional settings. Historical, cross-country, cross-cultural, and developing country studies have been especially powerful in developing a much more complete understanding of property rights and their effects.

Another area in which I believe very substantial progress has been made is in understanding vertical integration, or the "make-or-buy" decision, and associated issues of comparative governance arrangements for commercial transactions (Joskow 2004). Indeed, from both a theoretical and empirical perspective there is perhaps no other Level 3 arena that has been worked on so extensively (Williamson 1985, 2000). I will discuss the work on vertical integration in more detail presently. Related research on relational contracting, contract enforcement mechanisms, and hybrid forms has also progressed very nicely from both a theoretical and an empirical perspective.

The third area where I think very significant progress has been made is that of positive political economy. Important research work here involves both Level 2 and Level 3 lines of inquiry (Acemoglu, Johnson and Robinson 2001; Dixit 1996; Weingast and Marshall 1988). From a Level 2 perspective we have gained a much better appreciation of how the institutions of government, broadly defined to include election rules, legislative, executive, and legal institutions, may affect economic behavior and performance and, in turn, how economic behavior and performance may affect the basic institutions of government. From a Level 3 perspective we have learned a lot about how the structure of government and supporting institutions have evolved to respond to instabilities and various transactions costs associated with pure democracy and, as well, the key role of interests groups in determining the behavior of government and political institutions. Related work on the structure, behaviour, and importance of regulatory agencies and supporting institutions has also progressed significantly (Levy and Spiller 1994).

### Vertical integration and the comparative governance paradigm

It is not my intention to review all of the research accomplishments which may (loosely) be placed under the umbrella of NIE. Instead, by way of example, I will explore (relatively briefly) the progress that has been made in understanding why firms become vertically integrated (or de-integrated) backward into input production, or forward into distribution and retailing (the "make-or-buy" decision).* Understanding the factors that determine which types of transactions are mediated through markets and which within hierarchical organizations called firms has been an important subject of theoretical and empirical work in microeconomics generally and is central to work in NIE in particular for at least the last 25 years. Much of this research falls squarely into Level 3 consideration of governance arrangements, focusses on the role of transactions costs (broadly defined) arising from incomplete contracts and relationship specific investments, and adopts the powerful comparative institutional analytical framework. I will refer to this line of research as transaction cost economics (TCE), which is a component of NIE. Pioneering theoretical research in this general area may be attributed to Ronald Coase (1937), Oliver Williamson (1975), and Oliver Hart (1995). Perhaps more importantly, a vast empirical literature now exists, which provides very strong support for, in particular, the transactions cost or comparative governance approach to understanding the choice of organization structure to govern commercial transactions most effectively.

Virtually all theories of vertical integration turn in one way or another on the presence of market imperfections of some type. Traditional approaches to vertical integration have tended to focus on vertical integration as a response to pre-existing market power problems (e.g. double marginalization) or as a strategic move to create or enhance market power in upstream or downstream markets (e.g. foreclosure strategies). Whilst not excluding these rationales for vertical integration, the NIE approach to the analysis of alternative market and internal organizational governance arrangements is much broader. It focusses on a well-defined array of attributes of individual transactions between buyers and sellers of goods or services and how they affect the performance (total cost) of alternative governance arrangements. It recognizes that there is a wide array of governance structures through which transactions can be mediated – from anonymous spot markets to internal administrative procedures within hierarchical organizations. It recognizes further that the task of consummating transactions must confront a variety of potential transaction costs, contractual, and organizational hazards, which are related to the attributes of the transactions at issue and their interplay with the attributes of alternative governance arrangements. These transaction costs involve the direct costs of writing, monitoring, and enforcing contingent contracts as well as the costs associated with the *ex ante* investment and *ex post* performance inefficiencies which arise as a consequence of contractual hazards of various types and various bureaucratic costs associated with internal organization.

The transactions costs of particular interest are those that arise as a consequence of *ex post* bargaining, haggling, pricing, and production decisions, especially those that arise as the relationship must adapt to changes in supply and demand conditions over time, though inefficiencies in *ex ante* investments are also relevant (Williamson 1975, 2000). The governance structures that are chosen, whether market or hierarchical, are those that are best adapted to the attributes of the transactions of interest in the sense that they economize on the total costs (including transaction costs) of the trading relationship.

Contractual incompleteness, and its interaction with the attributes of different types of transactional attributes, including asset specificity, complexity, and uncertainty, plays a central role in the evaluation of the relative costs of governance through market-based bilateral contracts versus governance through internal organization. Contracts may be incomplete because of the direct costs of specifying and writing contracts that anticipate all contingencies, because of "bounded rationality," which makes it unlikely that the transacting parties can foresee all possible contingencies, and/or because of high monitoring, verification, and enforcement costs. When transactions are mediated through market-based contracts circumstances may arise where the buyer and seller have conflicting interests. The potential advantage of internal organization in this case is that internal organizations are likely to better harmonize these conflicting interests and provide for a smoother and less costly adaptation process under these circumstances, facilitating more efficient *ex ante* investment in the relationship *and* more efficient adaptation to changing supply and demand conditions over time.

If hierarchical organizations have these attractive properties why don't we see more economic activity taking place within very large organizations rather than through markets? The answer is that internal organization is good at some things, but not at others. Williamson (1996; *see also* Chapter 4) observes that when we look at the bigger dynamic picture, internal organization is a last resort that we turn to only in the presence of significant contracting hazards and associated transactions costs. This is because, opportunistic behavior associated with specific investments aside, decentralized market arrangements have superior adaptive properties to internal organization in many *other* important dimensions. For example, employees may be less willing to reveal information that adversely affects their promotion possibilities or continuing employment. The kinds of low-powered incentives which characterize internal compensation arrangements may also mute incentives to exert the optimal amount of worker effort (Holmström and Milgrom 1994; Williamson 1985; *see also* Chapter 6). In addition, although internal organization is likely to be better at removing certain kinds of internal information asymmetries in the short term, it may be an inferior structure for obtaining, processing, and using external information about prices, costs, quality, and technological change in the long term compared to repeated market transactions. For example, when a firm vertically integrates (or enters into a very long-term full requirements contract) it is likely to lose some of the benefits associated with continually examining and accessing outside opportunities through repeated contracting. These opportunities include information about the "least-cost" prices of the goods and services which the firm is producing internally and the availability of new technologies and production methods.

For these reasons, even in the face of significant contractual hazards resulting from specific investments and incomplete contracts, firms may still find it advantageous to continue to rely on arm's-length market transactions for all or a fraction of their input or distribution requirements (dual sourcing) involving specific investments rather than turning to complete vertical integration.

*The bottom line is that there are benefits and costs of internal organization.* Market transactions incur transactions costs associated with writing and enforcing contingent contracts and the inefficiencies *ex ante* and *ex post* resulting from opportunistic behavior which exploits specific investments. Internal bureaucratic allocation mechanisms may help to mitigate these types of transactions costs but incur other types of transactions or organization costs. The costs of internal organization are associated with the relatively inferior adaptive properties of bureaucratic hierarchies to rapidly changing outside opportunities over the longer term and the difficulty of designing compensation mechanisms to give managers and employees appropriate incentives to control costs and product quality. No governance structure is free from at least some transactions costs. The decision whether or not to vertically integrate then becomes a trade-off between the costs of alternative governance arrangements. Vertical integration is favored when the benefits of mitigating opportunism problems by moving the transactions inside the firm, by reducing *ex ante* investment and *ex post* performance inefficiencies, are greater than other sources of static and dynamic inefficiency associated with resource allocation within bureaucratic organizations.

The choice of governance structure, and how this choice is affected by transaction cost considerations, has attracted considerable empirical study. There have been at least five hundred papers published that have examined various aspects of comparative institutional choice from a TCE perspective. A significant fraction of these studies have examined the vertical integration or "make-or-buy" decision. There have also been several survey articles that have reviewed the empirical literature stimulated by TCE theories, including many related to vertical integration and non-standard vertical contracting arrangements (Coeurderoy and Quélin 1997; Crocker and Masten 1996; Joskow 1988a; Shelanski and Klein 1995; Vannoni 2002) .

These empirical studies of vertical integration and how the choice of this governance structure is influenced by the importance of specific investment and other variables that could lead to *ex ante* and *ex post* contractual inefficiencies overwhelmingly show that the importance of specific investments is both a statistically and economically important causal factor influencing the decision to vertically integrate. Indeed, it is hard to find many other areas in industrial organization where there is such an abundance of empirical work supporting a theory of firm or market structure. And it is the combination of compelling theoretical analysis combined with a large body of supporting evidence that makes the TCE approach to understanding vertical integration and alternative vertical governance arrangements so important.

Does the extensive theoretical and empirical analyses of vertical integration lead us to conclude that the topic has been so well worked over that there is little more to do on it? I believe that the answer is "No." As Scott Masten, James Meehan, and Edward Snyder (1991) show (*see also* Joskow 2004), the empirical tests which have characterized much of the econometric literature on vertical integration are not nearly as powerful as first meets the eye. The primary problem is that the literature has focussed primary attention on the causal variables which are thought to affect the costs of *market contracting*. However, relatively little attention has been paid to the state and dynamic costs of *internal organization* and the variables that affect these costs. As previously noted, the comparative governance approach teaches us to compare the costs of alternative governance arrangements. By focussing on the factors which affect the costs of market contracting only, we are implicitly assuming that the associated variables do not also affect the costs of internal organization. This may not be a good assumption in all situations. Moreover, most of the empirical research does not measure the costs of alternative governance arrangements directly, but, rather, measures the variables (often ordinally) that are thought to influence their relative costs, relying on the revealed preferences of economic agents, revealed through their choice of governance arrangements, to identify the importance of various causal variables.

It seems to me that the empirical analysis of TCE theories of vertical integration may be improved in a number of ways. More attention should be paid to both the attributes and costs of internal organization. Direct measurement of the costs of alternative governance arrangements would also increase the power of the empirical tests. Finally, research that examines dynamic shocks to demand or cost attributes, and the associated responses of governance arrangements would also add power to the empirical analyses of TCE theories of vertical integration.

There are also significant theoretical disputes about the factors which influence the make-or-buy decision (Gibbons 2005). Property rights theories of vertical integration (Hart 1995) have attracted a lot of attention, in part because they are more formal than TCE theories. Some view the property rights theories as formalizations of TCE theories. This view is incorrect. Property rights theories focus primarily on the effects of incomplete contracts and specific investments on *ex ante* investment incentives with or without vertical integration. TCE theories focus on *ex post* adaptation problems while recognizing that *ex ante* investment incentives cannot be ignored. The property rights literature assumes that *ex post* bargaining is efficient. Moreover, the property rights theories' characterizations of what constitutes a firm and the nature of internal governance arrangements is quite different from the nature of firms laid out in TCE and many other theories of organizations. In my view, the property rights approach strips the firm of most of its organizational features and focusses on how ownership and the associated residual rights of control affect the bargaining power of otherwise self-interested economic agents engaged in bilateral trade. This approach does not allow for any other changes in incentives and behavior of the transacting parties when the relationship is brought from the market inside of the firm (vertical integration). Thus, it largely ignores important differences between market transactions and internal organization other than simply a change in relative bargaining power between self-interested managers (Williamson 1996; *see also* Chapter 4), despite the fact that the objective functions possessed by managers, and the incentive and payoff structure that they face, are different for managers within a firm as compared to managers in separate firms. Nevertheless, gaining a better understanding of the similarities and differences theoretically between property rights and TCE theories of vertical integration would be very useful.

## Conclusions

One of my colleagues recently suggested that institutional economists had "won the war" in the sense that it is now widely recognized that understanding how institutions affect economic performance and why different institutional arrangements emerge in different social, cultural, and economic settings is now widely accepted by economists and increasingly reflected in mainstream economic research in many fields. It may be that in this sense the war has been won. However, there is still much work to do. As the discussion of vertical integration in the previous section should indicate, even in this relatively well worked-over area, there are still unresolved theoretical questions and opportunities to improve the quality of empirical analysis. As we consider the state of knowledge in other less well-developed areas it is clear that whatever war has been won there are still many important issues that are targets of opportunity for theoretical, empirical, and policy-oriented research on institutions and their effects on economic performance.

The broad acceptance that "institutions matter" has meant that there are many scholars working on institutional issues from a variety of different perspectives. In my view NIE has not done enough to reach out to the research relevant to institutional economics that has emerged from other fields of economics which have begun to address related issues in the last couple of decades. Perhaps the field has become too insular and runs the danger of being isolated as scholars working in other fields turn their attention to institutional issues. For example, I believe that NIE has devoted too little attention to the details of individual decision making, relying on broad characterizations of bounded rationality and self-interest seeking behavior. Expanding analyses of, and integrating research on, individual decision making and cognition (psychology) in the presence of uncertainty, imperfect information, and various social and cultural norms – the focus of the rapidly growing field of "behavioral economics" – into research on institutions could be very productive (Kahneman and Tversky 1979; Rabin and Thaler 2001; Thaler 1992). Concepts of altruism, trust, and human responses to uncertainty, information, search, and cognition costs clearly have implications for institutional choice and impacts. Behavioral economics can play an important role in accounting for these dimensions of human behavior more directly. The increased use of experimental methods widely used in behavioral economics may help to expand the data available to test hypotheses about the formation of and impacts of different types of institutions.

Much of the work in the comparative governance arena (Level 3) traces its origins to work done by researchers identified with the "Carnegie School" in the 1950s and early 1960s (Cyert and March 1963). Concepts of "bounded rationality" articulated by Herbert Simon (1957) are central to the analysis of incomplete contracts as well as to recent research in behavioral economics. Efforts to integrate behavioral economics into institutional economics thus will, in a sense, bring institutional economics back to its roots. So, too, would more research devoted to the structure, behaviour, and performance of organizations (private, public, for-profit, not-for-profit), their internal structures, their behavior and performance. These were topics of particular interest to the Carnegie School, which has somehow attracted much less attention than it deserves in the comparative governance literature, as I noted in the previous section.

It is also my view that NIE has had too limited an impact in the public policy arena. Some of the problems that have emerged in the privatization, restructuring, and deregulation of electric power networks during the 1990s may be traced to a failure to incorporate learning from NIE into the restructuring and market design process (Joskow 1996). This reflects, in part, the heavy reliance on "economists" trained in engineering and operations research, and who have no appreciation for the subtleties underlying simple economic principles and the importance of institutional economics considerations. In the area of economic development policy it has become routine for policy makers to trumpet their recognition that institutions matter and that development policies must be tailored to the institutional attributes of the particular countries to which they are applied. In practice, however, these institutional considerations are often ignored and policy prescriptions often continue to reflect the application of developed country concepts to countries with very different Level 1 and Level 2 institutional environments which also imply effective Level 3 governance arrangements that may be quite different from those that characterize developed countries. There is very exciting academic research going on in the field of development economics (Banerjee and Duflo 2000; Banerjee and Iyer 2004; Banerjee and Munshi 2004) which may, and should be, integrated into the work on NIE as it applies to developing countries, helping to move policy makers away from banal prescriptions for developing countries that ignore relevant developing country institutions.

NIE gets a very good report card in most dimensions, but there are still important intellectual challenges and a lot of interesting work to be done.

*Part I*

# Foundations

# 1     The Theories of the Firm

*Pierre Garrouste and Stéphane Saussier*

## 1.1     Introduction

What is a firm? Since the seminal article on the nature of the firm by Coase (1937), this question has been put under the attention of a growing number of economists looking for a theory of the firm, and, since the beginning of the 1970s, significant progress has been made. Yet, despite the important literature on the subject, this question is still an empirical as well as a theoretical challenge (Garrouste and Saussier 2005; Gibbons 2005).

The empirical challenge comes from the difficulty to form a complete picture of the phenomenon since firms have a large spectrum of more or less formal governance structures, which range from hierarchy to outsourcing and from outsourcing to internalization (Ménard 2004b). The theoretical challenge comes from the multifaceted nature of the phenomenon, which can hardly be grasped by a unique theory, thus leading to the multiplication of theoretical approaches which may be considered as complements or substitutes, depending on the question they try to answer. In fact, a theory of the firm has the difficult task of being able to answer many questions. First: the question of the nature and boundaries of the firm. Why are some transactions internalized, others externalized, and others both internalized and externalized at the same time? Second: the question of the internal structure of the firm. How is the firm organized? How is production organized? What incentives, controls, internal hierarchies exist? Third: the question of the relations between firms and the market. Are firms a substitute for the market? What are the limits of the firms?

In this chapter, we will focus on the question of the nature of a firm. The issue of how a firm should be organized internally falls outside the scope of this chapter and is treated elsewhere (Garrouste and Saussier 2005). We first go back over Coase's (1937) article on the nature of the firm. We show that this seminal article contains an "incomplete" theory of the firm, which is nevertheless a good benchmark in order to

23

introduce more recent ones. We argue that Coase's (1937) theory of the firm is not given sufficient credit. Indeed, Coase did not only raise the question of why firms may exist but he also provided many (if not all needed) "ingredients" for a theory of the firm. We then examine recent competing theories of the firm, showing how their assumptions depart from Coase's theory and how their propositions differ. We show that the firm may be viewed as a way to solve coordination problems or as a collection of assets, the distribution of which has an impact on incentives to invest. Those two views are clearly different and, respectively, correspond to the transaction cost theory and the incomplete contract theory of the firm. We also show that the firm may be viewed as a collection of assets as well as an internal incentive system which play complementary roles, but also as a place where learning is easier than it is on the market. Those two last parts of the paper correspond to the incentive and resource-based views of the firm. We conclude this chapter by identifying the important challenges to be faced in the near future in order to construct a theory of the firm that does not exist yet.

## 1.2    The nature of the firm: seventy years after

Many (if not all) of the existing theoretical frameworks available to analyze firms make use of Coase's (1937) seminal article as background. This article, written more than seventy years ago in 1935, points out the need to incorporate transaction costs in the analysis of contractual decisions. Coase reaffirms this later, in his 1960 paper, and the so-called Coase's theorem points out that without any transaction costs institutional choices are not an issue.

Coase's (1988) article on the nature of the firm has long been viewed as giving tautological propositions with regard to the driving forces underlying the choice of a particular organizational arrangement. As Williamson (1975, p. 3) wrote concerning Coase's (1937) paper: "Transaction costs are appropriately made the centerpiece of the analysis but these are not operationalized in a fashion which permits one to assess the efficacy of completing transactions as between firms and markets in a systematic way."

Nevertheless, it is only fair to recognize that if the analysis of Ronald Coase was not based on clear assumptions, giving rise to a precise definition of what is a firm and clear propositions about when to substitute coordination on the market by coordination in the firm, many of the premises of a theory of the firm were already present in his work.

### 1.2.1    Bounded rationality

Coase's (1937) article stressed the importance of taking bounded rationality into account when constructing a theory of the firm. The bounded rationality of entrepreneurs is discussed in this article, and mobilized in order to explain the limits of the firm. As noted by Coase: "It may be that as the transactions which are organized increase, the entrepreneur fails to place the factors of production in the uses where their value is greatest, that is, fails to make the best use of the factors of production" (pp 394–5). To put it differently, "A firm will tend to be larger the less likely the entrepreneur is to make mistakes" (p. 396). Furthermore, Coase pointed out that the "dissimilarity of the transactions" (p. 397) would increase the cost of organizing a transaction within a firm.

As we will see below, this gives rise to the idea of focussing on core transactions. Indeed, firms should focus on the transactions they know how to handle best because the attention of firm managers is limited. This assumption therefore allows Coase's theory to explain what should be organized in the firm, and what its limits are. An important reason why the firm has boundaries is that managers have a bounded rationality that does not allow them to organize as many transactions as they would like to. If it is possible to outsource part of the product to other firms (without monopoly power) the manager should then do it.

### 1.2.2    Uncertainty

Furthermore, the role of uncertainty is referred to in order to explain why, depending on sectoral considerations, firms may be more or less present (p. 392). This led Coase to put forward propositions almost similar to those advanced many years later by transaction cost economics (TCE). For example, considering the use of long-term contracts, Coase stated that "owing to the difficulty of forecasting, the longer the period of the contract is for the supply of the commodity or service, the less possible, and indeed, the less desirable it is for the person purchasing to specify what the other contracting party is expected to do" (p. 391). This statement is close to what is to be found in recent analyses made by transaction cost economists (Crocker and Masten 1991; Crocker and Reynolds 1993; Saussier 2000).

### 1.2.3    Institutional environment

Finally, Coase considered how change in the institutional environment may affect the decision to create firms stating that "if we consider the operation of sale tax, it is clear that it is a tax on market transactions and not on the same transactions organized within the firm. Now since these are alternative methods of 'organization' – by the price mechanism or by the entrepreneur – such a regulation would bring into existence firms which otherwise would have no *raison d'être*" (p. 393).

### 1.2.4    An "incomplete" theory of the firm based on the comparison between markets' and firms' characteristics

The elements listed above clearly show how advanced Coase's analysis was. Indeed, his reasoning was already based on a comparative analysis of markets' and firms' characteristics: "Outside the firm, price movements direct production, which is coordinated through a series of exchange transactions on the market. Within a firm, these market transactions are eliminated and in place of the complicated market structure with exchange transactions is substituted the entrepreneur-coordinator, who directs production. It is clear that these are alternative methods of coordinating production," (p. 388). Markets and firms are thus primarily analyzed as substitutes rather than complements. More precisely, firms need markets only because they allow some transactions not internalized by firms to be realized between them.

Nevertheless, if we agree with Coase's answer to the question of why firms exist other issues are still open to discussion at the end of his 1937 work. The definition of the firm viewed as the place where the coordination through prices is replaced by coordination through authority is vague. Many aspects of such authority relationships may be found on the market as well. Coase does not analyze the internal organization of the firm in as much as he reduces it to authority and command. But the firm's internal organization is actually something more complex, as Holmström (1999) and Holmström and Milgrom (1994) stress it. Besides, the relationships between markets and firms are also weakly analyzed. Finally, the refutability of Coase's approach has been questioned on the basis of an impossibility to assess transaction costs for alternative contractual choices, letting the door open for *ex post* rationalization. Those issues are still at the top of the agenda even if recent theoretical developments are trying to remedy such weaknesses.

Let us now turn to recent theories of the firm and their connections to Coase's foundations. The "natural" follower and improver of the Coasian approach is, without any doubt, Williamson with his transaction cost theory of the firm. The new property rights theory of the firm as well as the incentive theory are answering the Coasian question differently, and are proposing much more formalized conceptions of the firm's scope. All those approaches concerning the question of the boundaries of the firm are clearly more substitutes than complements. Finally, the resource-based view of the firm, even if founded on different assumptions, also refers to Coase's article. The importance attributed to knowledge and competences by the resource-based view is clearly absent from Coase's theory.

## 1.3    The firm defined as a low-incentive arrangement to solve coordination problems

Because of the coordination problems that may arise on the market, the firm may be viewed as a way to have access to coordination mechanisms that are superior, in some particular situations, to those available on the market. That is the view taken by the transaction cost theory (TCT) (Williamson 1975, 1985, 1996).

### 1.3.1    Assumptions and sketch of the argument

TCT endeavors to analyze "man as he is" and posits that the firm is the chosen organizational form as soon as contracting on the market is not feasible because of prohibitive transaction costs. The chosen behavioral assumptions insist on the fact that economic actors have a bounded rationality but also a far-sighted behavior, and they might, therefore, behave opportunistically.

The fact that economic actors have a bounded rationality is not a problem as long as the environment characterizing the world they live in is not uncertain. Under such circumstances, bounded rationality does not prevent economic agents from coordinating their activities. However, when the levels of uncertainty are high the main consequence is that agents can only sign incomplete contracts.

Signing incomplete contracts is not usually a problem, even if we face opportunistic behaviors, as long as we may resort to market sanctions. That is the case when contracting parties are not dependent. But when they are in a "small number" relationship (Williamson 1975), the problem is more crucial since they cannot shift from one partner to another. That is typically the case when one or both parties develop specific investments in order to realize a transaction. Specific investments, which may be defined as specialized investments that cannot be redeployed for alternative use or by alternative users except at a loss of value, generate a bilateral dependency. Such dependency generates contractual hazards in the face of incomplete contracting and opportunism. The main consequence is that contracts cannot rely on promises, but must be supported by credible commitments when possible. But when this is impossible (uncertainty and asset specificity are too high) the firm is chosen to replace market relationships.

### 1.3.2    Departures from Coase's theory and definition of a firm

Even if TCT may be viewed as a natural extension of Coase's (1937) article, it departs from the latter in retaining the assumption of opportunism and focussing on asset specificity as a crucial element in explaining the existence of the firm. Coase pointed out that such a concept of economic relationships differs from his. More precisely, Coase (1988) defends the idea that reputation effects may in very frequent cases annihilate the risk of opportunism. Such a difference leads TCT to give a definition of the firm that substantially differs from that of Coase.

In the transaction cost economics (TCE) framework, the firm is viewed as very distinct from the market since markets and hierarchies have different access to fiat (Alchian and Demsetz 1972; Williamson 1996) and there is a differential with respect to bureaucratic costs. More precisely, the firm is described mainly as a coordination mechanism in which low-powered incentives and extensive administrative controls are to be found, and which has its own dispute settlement machinery; (courts will often refuse to hear intra-firm disputes, thus making the firm its own court of ultimate appeal). More recently, considerations of differential probity have been examined (Williamson 1999a) in the context of transactions where failures of loyalty and real-time responsiveness could undermine integrity.

The main idea developed by TCE is that the firm, with its distinctive capabilities, is able to govern transactions of a particular kind, for which markets are not suitable, by reducing or controlling more strongly opportunistic behaviors and transaction costs which may arise as soon as economic actors are in a relationship of dependency (Joskow 2004). However, such control implies high transaction costs (e.g. higher transaction costs than on the market, with transactions characterized by a lower level of asset specificity) owing to a loss of incentive intensity (e.g. bureaucratic costs).

As far as the boundaries of the firm are concerned Williamson improved the Coasian analysis by defining precisely the nature and sources of transaction costs. The difference he made between the different environmental factors (uncertainty, frequency of transactions, and asset specificity) as well as between behavioral factors (bounded rationality and opportunism) allowed the introduction of some analytical ways of distinguishing the reason why the market, hierarchy, and sometimes hybrid forms are selected.

The firm is "needed" (by means of a selection process) when there is a possibility to avoid the *ex post* negative impact (for one of the parties) of opportunism on the execution of the contract, in a context of asset-specificity. The definition of the scope of the firm is then based on a much more precise analytical background than it is in a strictly Coasian perspective. What is very interesting is that even if the TCE approach is not linked with formal models it still offers "empirical success stories" in as much as many empirical tests flourished and corroborated propositions on make-or-buy issues (Boerner and Macher 2001; Masten 1999; Masten and Saussier 2002).

Nevertheless, the theory is calling for an "underdeveloped" theory of intra-firm organization to explain what changes as soon as a transaction is internalized (Grossman and Hart 1986; Holmström 1999). The need for bureaucratic costs, the impossibility of selective intervention, as well as the assumption that transaction costs inside the firm are generated by the same sources on the market[1] reveal the weakness of this theoretical framework.

As far as formalization is concerned, property rights theory and incentive theory seem to be more satisfactory, even if the way in which they analyze the scope of the firm is apparently very poor. Furthermore, both theories challenge the definition of the firm given by TCT.

## 1.4    The firm defined as a collection of assets

Instead of considering both a theory of the limits of the markets and a theory of the limits of the firm we may look for a definition of the firm which permits the assessment of firm boundaries within an integrated framework. That is the view taken by the incomplete contract theory (or the new property right theory) (Garrouste 2004; Grossman and Hart 1986; Hart 1995).

### 1.4.1    *Assumptions and sketch of the argument*

Incomplete contract theory proposes a unified framework to explain both the limits of the market and those of the firm. This theory challenges the assumption that we need to use, on the one hand, the hold-up problem in order to explain the limits of the market and, on the other, the existence of bureaucratic costs to explain the limits of the firm.

Defining the firm as the collection of the assets it owns (Grossman and Hart 1986, p. 692), the theory focusses on ownership as the purchase of the residual rights of control that exist as soon as we consider incomplete contracting. The idea is that firm boundaries define allocation of residual rights. Those rights, when an incomplete contract is signed *ex ante* and may be completed *ex post*, modify the *ex post* bargaining position of an asset owner, and thereby increase his incentives to make specific relationship investments.

Models developed in this theoretical framework generally assume information symmetry between contracting parties. Furthermore, the theory challenges the idea that bounded rationality is needed in order to analyze organizational choices (Hart 1990), at least as far as contracting parties are concerned. Contractual incompleteness is only attributable to external constraints (Kreps 1996), namely the bounded rationality or asymmetric information situations of the third parties in charge of the enforcement of contracts. In such incomplete contracts no previously unexpected contingency can arise to disrupt the contract's fulfillment – for example there is no uncertainty. Incompleteness is postulated rather than actually explained by models. The incomplete contract theory sheds light on the impact of contractual incompleteness, but is of no help in understanding differences in contractual completeness levels – nor does it measure the extent to which those levels result from the parties' goodwill. Contractual incompleteness is exogenous and does not result from a trade-off made by economic actors (Saussier 2000). As pointed out by Hart and Moore (1999, p. 134), a contract is incomplete when "the parties would like to add contingent clauses, but are prevented from doing so by the fact that the state of nature cannot be verified (or because states are too expensive to describe *ex ante*)." Generally, this theoretical framework predicts an all-or-nothing solution: the contract is either complete or totally incomplete (i.e. no contract is signed).[2]

Nevertheless, such a theoretical approach sheds some light on firm boundaries. Incomplete contract theory (perhaps because it is more formalized) offers a richer set of predictions than TCT does concerning the make-or-buy decision. Whilst TCT is concerned mainly with the size of the quasi-rent generated by specific investments, incomplete contract theory focusses on marginal returns to non-contractible investments, which gives rise to a richer set of predictions. That is why the verifiability status of investments, their nature (self-investments versus cross-investments; Che and Haush 1999) and the verifiability or observability status of asset specificity levels appear crucial.

What is central in TCT is not so much the amount or the level of asset specificity as the size of the appropriable quasi-rent that is generated by the specificity and amount of assets. Incomplete contract theory (ICT) points out that as long as such investments are observable and verifiable the quasi-rent they generate might not be appropriable (if uncertainty is low) and might generate different effects from those predicted by the TCE framework. Furthermore, ICT does not suppose a monotone relationship between the size of the surplus and the probability of integration (Hart 1988). It is important to know who owns the assets and their marginal returns, but also what direction integration is taking, which is not the case in the TCE framework.

### 1.4.2   Departures from Coase's theory and definition of the firm

Contrary to what is often believed, the ICT of the firm is not a formalization of TCT (Fares and Saussier 2002; Gibbons 2005; Whinston 2003). By making the assumption that agents are rational and the environment not uncertain this theoretical framework clearly departs from TCT and from Coase's assumptions, thus giving rise to a different definition of the firm.

In ICT, the firm is viewed as providing a way to define who owns the assets and, therefore, who has the residual rights of control over those assets. Those rights are important because they have some impact on the way contracts are renegotiated, regardless of what the manager decides to do (whether or not to externalize the product). Renegotiation may indeed take place with an employee as well as with an independent contracting party.

Although this theoretical framework gives rise to a richer set of predictions than does TCT testing incomplete contract theory is bound to be an extremely demanding task as far as data collection is concerned (Baker and Hubbard 2001). Propositions are "nearly untestable" (Whinston 2003). However, some attempts to test ICT have been made in more recent work. Baker and Hubbard (2004, p. 1478) answer the question of "what determines who owns the assets" by looking at the US trucking industry. They find evidence that contractibility influences ownership. More precisely, the introduction of onboard computers improves the possibility of contracting and also leads to more integrated asset ownership; that is to say, more integration. Elfenbein and Lerner (2003) evaluate the effects of the control rights on ownership in internet alliances. Analyzing one hundred contracts, they show that there is strong evidence in favour of Grossman and Hart's (1986) ideas. However, control rights appear to be also related to the bargaining power of the parties. This result is not in line with the "traditional" ICT models and is interesting in as much as it stresses the notion that ownership and control are not necessarily the same thing.

Furthermore, the criticism already addressed to TCE, namely the absence of a theory of intra-firm organization, may be re-addressed to ICT (Holmström 1999). Indeed, this theory makes little room for issues of organizational structure, delegation of authority, or hierarchy.

Finally, ICT clearly is a theory of the firm without managers (Gibbons 2005; Holmström 1999). As acknowledged by Hart and Holmström (2002), it describes owner-manager firms better than large companies. In ICT, decision makers also own the firm's assets and, in this respect, Hart and Holmström (2002) are in fact attempting to disconnect decision making from ownership. Nevertheless, many incentive mechanisms, which are internal to the firm, are not studied here and may complement or substitute incentives created by the repartition of the firm's assets (Holmström 1999). This issue is considered in much more detail by the incentive theory of the firm.

## 1.5    The firm defined as a collection of assets and internal incentive mechanisms

One way to take a further step toward a unified theory of the firm would be to combine incentives coming from the distribution of property rights with incentives coming from internal organization strategies.

This conception of the firm has been chosen by Holmström (1999) who argues that the way in which incentives are designed within the firm is connected to the repartition of ownership and other elements. More precisely, internal incentive design may benefit greatly from the control of a wider range of instruments often available through the ownership of assets. That is why internal incentive strategies and ownership of assets are connected.

### 1.5.1    Assumptions and sketch of the argument

The assumptions advanced in such a theoretical framework are those of the incentive theory. Economic actors are supposed to be rational and live in a world free from radical uncertainty. Nevertheless, they may be in possession of some private information likely to impede the signing of complete contingent contracts.

The basic idea developed by such an approach is that there are complementarities between several elements explaining why firms are chosen and how they are internally structured: "We cannot claim to fully understand either the internal organization of firms or the operation of markets by studying the two in isolation. We need to analyze how they interact as organizations; how they compete as well as complement each other in matching individuals with tasks and in providing proper individual incentives for carrying out those tasks" (Holmström 1999, p. 100).

In fact, as Holmström (1999) recognized, "The strength of the property rights view is that it articulates so clearly the role of market incentives and how they can be altered by shifts in asset ownership. But it says nothing about the incentives that can be created within firms. The real challenge is to understand how the two forms of organization complement each other as well as compete with each others' mechanisms for influencing individual incentives" (Holmström 1999, pp 76–7). "Indeed the very fact that workers can exit a firm at will and go to other firms, and that consumers and input suppliers and other trading partners can do likewise, limits the firm's ability to exploit these constituents" (Holmström 1999, p. 90). This leads us to consider markets and firms not as mere substitutes but rather as complements. The role of the market with regard to the firm appears through its influence on the level of outside options available for agents. In this view, the firm is not any longer considered as emerging where the market failed without the market being attributed some role in explaining organizational choices.

Holmström and Milgrom (1994) give a complete analysis of the relationships between incentives and firm boundaries when they show that it is possible to put the existence of complementarities between different kinds of incentives to the fore.

### 1.5.2    Departures from Coase's theory and definition of the firm

This theoretical framework is clearly based on a set of assumptions which differ from those expressed in Coase's (1937) paper. It is also a more ambitious framework as its goal is to analyze, within a unified framework, the existence of both the firms and their internal organization (incentives, multi-tasking, authority delegation ... ). Nevertheless, it remains a programmatic project without clear propositions that may be tested. Furthermore, the basic assumption that founds the incentive theory of the firm has been recently challenged. The idea that, in a principal or agent relationship, incentives are always efficient in terms of the agent's effort has been discussed by analytical models (Benabou and Tirole 2003; Harvey 2005), experimental economics (Fehr and Gächter 2002; Frey and Oberholzer-Gee 1997; Gneezy and Rustichini 2000) and cognitive psychology (Gagné and Deci 2005).[3] Moreover, dynamic issues are not incorporated in the framework of the incentive theory of the firm. Such issues are emphasized by the resource-based view of the firm.

## 1.6    The firm defined as a collection of historically constructed capabilities

Looking for a coherence of the firm, linking its internal and external strategies, requires that the capabilities and knowledge it acquired through past choices and accumulated experience be somewhat taken into account. Capabilities are usually defined as a set of "know" and "know-how" more or less embedded in equipment. What makes this approach interesting is that, unlike the previously analyzed theories which underestimate the learning processes taking place at both individual and organizational levels, theories based on the notions of capabilities and knowledge emphasize their importance.

Despite their differences, the evolutionary theory and resource-based view of the firm are both knowledge-based explanations of the firm.[4] They share (a) behavioral assumptions (learning- and rule-guided behaviors) and (b) a belief that knowledge and capabilities represent the firm's critical and distinctive resources. The competence perspective advocates that firms have to build up some kind of specific knowledge in order to be able to follow the complicated procedures needed to carry out difficult tasks such as producing aircraft, shoes, transportation services, and so on. This raises the question of the difference between the market and the firm when it comes to the acquisition of knowledge.

### 1.6.1    Assumptions and sketch of the argument

The assumptions advocated by such approaches are quite similar to those advanced in TCT of the firm, except that these new theories push problems linked with opportunism[5] into the background and put forward issues related to knowledge and learning.

The actions taken by firms are based on routines and capabilities that indicate where a firm's distinguishing competences lie. There are three reasons why the firm is best suited to the development of knowledge. First, knowledge is the result of learning and experience. Second, since knowledge is the result of learning, it is context- (local) and path-dependent (historical). Finally, knowledge is partly tacit and the organization remains partially unaware of its existence since it is embedded in organizational routines and individual skills (Cohen *et al.*, 1996; Nelson and Winter 1982). Therefore, knowledge may only be transferred to a third party who has some absorbing capacity: a party that has already accumulated the knowledge required to understand and integrate the knowledge developed. Should the third party lack this absorbing capacity the transfer would be too costly to be implemented.

Then, why should a firm buy knowledge on a market when it has the capacity to build it internally? What is the definition of the firm?

### 1.6.2    Departures from Coase's theory and definition of the firm

Why should a firm buy knowledge on a market when it could build it internally? The answer to this question is: "there is no reason for it." Knowledge is not developed in a vacuum, it is built as coordination and communication mechanisms emerge and become embedded in some shared identity (Kogut and Zander 1996). Consequently, this common identity lowers the cost of communication for future research and learning: "As an activity becomes more specific to the firm, it increasingly accesses and develops a common organizational communication code which both codifies knowledge and facilitates its efficient dissemination and protection" (Poppo and Zenger 1998, p. 857). Firms are therefore viewed as governance structures which have the advantage of generating firm-specific languages and routines that, in turn, produce valuable capabilities. When knowledge is tacit and difficult to transfer, the use of independent contractor relationships to develop new knowledge may become very costly in terms of transactions and even impossible without facing opportunistic behaviors: "The key is that some of each person's knowledge necessarily remains private, as established by the bounded-rationality corollary. Honest persons ... may disagree about the best course of joint (or even individual) action, or the division of gains. ... The person's 'discovery' may produce lengthy and costly negotiation, which includes efforts to convey to the others both the originator's analysis and the knowledge on which it is based. Because of irreducible individuals, adoption of the innovation may not be automatic." (Conner and Prahalad 1996, p. 483). Only under the cover of hierarchy can communication be easier and disagreement easily settled through authority. TCT confines the role of organizations to one of restricting the scope for opportunism given by the market. This is not the view defended by the competence perspective (Moran and Goshal 1996).

To summarize: hierarchy, through the formation of routines, can induce more efficiency than the market does. This is especially true when we consider activities that are specific to the firm. Therefore, activities that need specific human investments are supposed to be internalized (owing to the enhanced governance efficiency when specific asset are needed, especially because firms have advantages and more capabilities than the market to develop these specific human assets). In other words, transaction costs inside the firm are not increasing but decreasing with human asset specificity. This statement is incompatible with the TCE view and generates a proposition that is clearly in competition with the transaction cost view of the firm (Plunket and Saussier 2004).

If those approaches try to take capabilities, knowledge, and learning processes into account when giving an explanation of firms' existence, we must note the poverty of such analyses when it comes to the question of incentives. Individuals seem to have a natural tendency for cooperation. For example, Kogut and Zander (1996, p. 506) assume that "firms provide the normative territory to which members identify." The firm identity improves the way in which coordination, communication, and learning are taking place. The set of incentives is not explicitly analyzed. It is supposed to be the natural outcome of the fact that the members of the firm are integrating the firm's identity. The fact that incentives are not taken into account is a weakness shared by all evolutionary theories of the firm. The reason for this is simple. In this perspective a firm is defined by its routine (Nelson and Winter 1982), which becomes the unit of selection of the evolutionary process. Since a unit of selection is defined as an entity characterized by the fact that all its elements cooperate, it is implicitly assumed that all the members of a firm have to cooperate.

## 1.7    Conclusion

Let us conclude by reaffirming once more what we said in the Introduction and believe is essential for young fellows who would like to study or do research in the field of the theories of the firm. First, we believe that Coase's (1937) article is natural and essential reading as it contains all the necessary ingredients for a theory of the firm. Second, looking at recent theoretical developments makes it clear that finding a unified and unique theory of the firm is a challenge – such a theory does not exist yet! That has to be resolved in the near future. This is a very important issue since developing a theory of the firm implies solving important questions, namely: Why firms exist? What are their boundaries? How are firms structured internally, and how should they evolve through time? These many questions are of primary interest for economists, management, and business scholars, but also for policy makers since such issues necessarily have some implications for competition policies and more broadly for industrial policies.

# 2 Contracts: From Bilateral Sets of Incentives to the Multi-Level Governance of Relations

*Éric Brousseau*

## 2.1 Introduction: contracts ... and institutions

### 2.1.1 *Contracts as analytical tools, contracts as objects of analysis*

Although many textbooks point out that new institutional economics (NIE) brought firms, institutions, and property rights to the forefront of the research agenda of economists it should be highlighted that it strongly contributed to turn contracts into essential analytical tools in economics and as a central object of investigation. Contracts are fundamental in NIE: Ronald Coase (1937) developed a contractual approach to the firm; Oliver Williamson (1975, 1985) developed a contractual approach to the governance of transactions. Their efforts – together with those of other scholars closer to the neoclassical approach who were seeking to renew the theory of prices – led to renew economics.

There are two ways of considering contracts in economics. Contracts may be considered, first, as analytical tools. The contractual approach applies, then, to almost any relationship: from transactions between firms to any relationship among entities. This way of relying on a very abstract notion of contract – which may be social, implicit, and so on – does not take into consideration, however, the conditions in which agreements are settled and enforced. Alternatively, contracts may be considered as actual means of coordination, organizing coordination among agents, thanks to a set of mutually agreed promises.[1]

In this chapter we will concentrate on this last vision since we would like to highlight the contribution of NIE and sister approaches – especially applied law and economics – to the understanding of contractual problems. NIE points out that contracts are costly to design and manage. These costs lead to "imperfections" if we compare them to ideal contracts. In particular, contracts do not solve *ex ante* all dimensions of coordination problems calling for *ex post* adjustment. Contracts implement, therefore, governance mechanisms to ensure coordination *ex post.* In addition, contracts are never perfectly enforced, both because they are imperfect and because enforcement is costly. This has two consequences. First, enforcement constraints affect the design of contracts. Second, a way to influence contractual performances is to modify the institutions framing enforcement. Contracts are therefore embedded in institutional framework.

### 2.1.2    *Contracts as tools to control transactional hazards*

The main problem dealt with by the economics of contracts is the control of hazards induced by the performance of transactions which are caused because the parties exchange promises to give (and receive in exchange) which, most of the time, are not fulfilled simultaneously but at moments when the parties agreed it would be mutually beneficial deal. The gap between the moment at which a promise is made and the time it has to be honored generates risks because the reason that made the parties likely to give what they promised may have changed. First, one of the parties (she) in question may have received what the other (he) was ready to give. She is therefore better off if she does not deliver, or if she delivers less than expected. Second, the situation may simply have changed and she may have better trading opportunities with other partners in the economy.

To overcome these hazards agents have to make their promises credible. Commitments may become credible if, in last resort, the cost of not fulfilling her obligation is higher than the cost of fulfilling (i.e. of giving what was promised.) The first way to do so is to provide the other party (or a third party) with a means to retaliate in case of unfulfilment of her obligations. This is the logic of hostages. If she does not comply he becomes the owner of the hostage whose value she therefore loses. The second way is to grant a third party with the responsibility of enforcing the agreement. This third party should benefit from the capability to punish the parties when they do not honor their promises; for instance, because it can ultimately rely on violence. In the latter case, the credibility of a promise is dependent upon the probability of having this third party detect infringements, and of the cost of the sanctions it can impose in comparison to the potential benefits of the infringers.

### 2.1.3    *From contracts to their institutional framing*

In practice, the third party in question may be an individual or an organization which provides the exchanging parties with an enforcement service. This is, for instance, one of the purposes of mafias in societies characterized by disorganized public authorities. The main problem is that the "enforcer" may always use his strength to capture the wealth of the parties. A component of the institutional environment may also provide this enforcement service. Advantages are twofold, at least in the case of institutional systems built on the "rule of law." First, citizens' fundamental rights are recognized, which restrains the capability of capture of the last-resort enforcer. Second, the costs of the enforcement mechanism can be shared among the citizens.

When we consider the provision of an enforcement capability the nature of the mutual obligations which can be contracted depends strongly upon the capabilities of the mechanisms that ensure enforcement. These capabilities can be described in terms of costs: costs for observing compliance to commitments; costs for making decisions; costs for exercising constraints. These costs affect the probability and the level of sanctions which can be actually exercised on contracting parties, and therefore on their likelihood to comply with their commitments. The "quality" of the institutional environment, which results in a degree of credibility of the mutual commitment between parties, influences the security of exchanges and thus transaction costs.

There is, however, a second way by which the institutional environment influences the nature of contracts and transaction costs. According to North (1990), the institutional environment is the set of rules that frame agents' behavior (and which ultimately results in rights to decide and to do). It therefore binds agents' capability to act. When it comes to contract the institutional environment therefore affects the nature and level of hazards agents have to deal with.

Lastly, contracts are embedded because the institutional framework set the endowment of agents in terms of right of decisions. Not only does it fix the set of assets, of which use may be decided by agents, but it also delimitates these rights of decisions (and therefore of contracting).[2]

All of the above call for a joint analysis of contracts and institutions. Governance is, indeed, multi-level in the sense that it depends upon operations which are carried out at a collective level by institutions and at an inter-individual level by contractual arrangements.

In this chapter we will first come back to the analysis of contracts as governance mechanisms, and show why most scholars have been led to accept the idea that most contracts are aimed at implementing governance mechanisms rather than consisting only of incentive mechanisms solving *ex ante* all coordination problems (*see* 2.2). Then we will consider the embeddedness of contracts in institutional frameworks.

We will start by considering the trade-off between relying on institutional rules to coordinate and relying on bilateral contracting (*see* 2.3). We will then consider various aspects of enforcement by pointing out that there are two sets of questions. First, the optimal principle of action of the enforcement mechanism results in a dilemma of "protection versus flexibility," which is to be arbitrated differently when different circumstances and, before all, "contrasted" logics of contracting are considered (*see* 2.4). Second, the principle on which institutional enforcement is organized has a cost and frames the contracting capabilities of agents. Its performances are dependent on the available institutional alternatives (*see* 2.5).

## 2.2     From incentives to governance

Oliver Williamson is, for sure, the father of the idea that contracts not only implement self-enforcing rules, but that they organize the distribution of rights – to make decisions and to access information – to the various parties involved in a transaction (in particular in Williamson 1985, 1991a). These ideas draw from MacNeil's (1974) analysis of the differences between transactional and relational contracting, which contrasts contracts aimed at organizing the simple transfer of a good and contracts framing long-term cooperative relationships.

Throughout the 1980s and 1990s a debate developed among economists to assess whether the two conceptions of contracts were lying in the question of the completeness or incompleteness of contracts (Brousseau and Fares 2000). The so-called "incomplete contract theory" (ICT) arose claiming that it was a model of "Williamson's insights," and controversies developed about the consistency of this theory and its ability to grasp Williamson's essential ideas. Today it is clearer that the essential contrast between approaches to contracts does not lie in the degree of completeness, but lies in the hypothesis about the ability of parties to implement *ex ante* a coordination mechanism that guarantees efficient coordination *ex post*. We will show that the theory of incentives – which encompasses both the theory of complete contracting and ICT – relies on the assumption that agents can design *ex ante* a mechanism that will solve any crucial problem in the future (*see* 2.2.1); whereas NIE supposes that this is reached only in very specific contexts, leading contractual arrangements to organize a framework that will help agents to coordinate *ex post* (*see* 2.2.2). Detailed presentation of the three theories and basic models is available in Brousseau and Glachant (2002).

### 2.2.1 Contractual completeness and incompleteness in the theory of incentives

*2.2.1.1 Complete incentive contracts* In the early 1970s, whilst Williamson was developing his analysis of actual contracting, several theoreticians initiated the incentive theory. Initially, the issue was to understand how markets were performing, not to grasp contract design. Contracts were tools to represent a really decentralized economy in which agents deal bilaterally (Akerlof 1970; Arrow 1971; Stiglitz 1974, 1977). The goal was to understand the performance of markets, in particular the labor market, and the forming of macro-economic equilibria. These early developments were the seeds of a major evolution in the understanding of coordination mechanisms at the micro-level. By the end of the 1970s, and in the 1980s, the mechanism design approach developed. It attempted to characterize optimal contracts, controlling *ex ante* for the complex strategic games among parties (Laffont and Maskin 1982; Laffont and Tirole 1993; Maskin 1985). Interestingly, the approach was not primarily applied to the actual contracting process. Many developments addressed the issue of the production of public good (understood as a problem of preferences revelation), of regulation (understood as a contract between the regulator and the firms), and of corporate governance (considered as a problem of agency between the shareholders and the managers). Later, however, the approach was applied to some specific contracting practices especially sharecropping, franchising (in the distribution chains), and public procurement.

For a long period, therefore, the incentive approach did not rely on any analysis of contractual practices, resulting in two consequences. The approach was mainly theoretical and based on few pieces of empirical evidence (Masten and Saussier 2002). The approach considered any system of incentives rather than contracts *per se*; that is, a system of negotiated, mutually agreed, and explicit reciprocal obligations. These theoretical developments taught us a lot on the potentialities and limits of incentives mechanisms aimed at channeling *ex ante* the *ex post* behaviors of agents. The theory pointed out the complexity of optimal contracts – which have to anticipate and control for all possible *ex post* strategic behaviors – and their sensitivity to the context – that is, to the nature of information asymmetries, to the number of players, to the observation capabilities of the enforcement device, to the degree of competition among potential contractors, and so on. It resulted in a limited number of contracting principles that were applicable to a wide set of situations. It also allowed economists to point out the impossibility of implementing "first best" solutions in many complex coordination situations: (the impossibility of reaching complex objectives in case of muti-tasking; collusion in "more than two players" situations; non-separable equilibria in case of competition; and so forth). The theory nevertheless provided insights about the design of incentives and revelation mechanisms, and led us to identify the inefficiencies of many actual practices. It helped to identify the capture or revelation dilemma and therefore the strong contrast between one-shot and repeated games. It also revealed the power of incentives schemes which, when implementable, provide far more flexible solutions than do mandatory rules. Incentives schemes provide benefits from the information or knowledge of the "agent," and limit the need to exchange information between the "principal" and the "agent."

*2.2.1.2 Are incomplete contracts consistent in a world of perfectly rational agents?* All these developments, however, set aside any endogenous explanation of the existence of non-market coordination. Indeed, the contracts in question are never hierarchic. The principal has no authority upon the agent. He is the client of a service provider. This deprived the theory of any ability to explain the existence of firms. This is why ICT developed. It began with the contributions of Grossman and Hart (1986), and Hart and Moore (1988); both written with the explicit will to found contractual incompleteness within the perfect rationality approach (i.e. the rationality axiomatized by Savage in 1954). Two lines of analysis developed. The first sought the foundation of contractual incompleteness in a world characterized by the absence of cost of decision and of any limit to the computation capabilities of agents. The second simply investigated the consequences of the impossibility of designing complete contracts, both in terms of best contractual design and efficiency of outcome.

There are two possible sources of contractual incompleteness. The *ex ante* cost of "writing" a contract – which is not the cost of paper and ink, but the cost of the efforts of settling an agreement and designing coordination rules – may prevent the parties from establishing a complete contract. The *ex post* costs of having the parties comply may lead us to exclude from the contract requirements which would be more costly to enforce than the benefit they would bring to the parties. As pointed out by Tirole (1999), and agreed upon by Hart, assuming positive "writing" costs is assuming that decision is costly for the agent, which is inconsistent with the assumptions of Savage on rationality. This inconsistency led those who worked on the foundation of contractual incompleteness to focus on the explanation based on enforcement costs.[3] These costs are linked to assumptions about the ability of the device responsible for enforcement in the last resort – the "judge" – to perfectly, or not, guarantee that the parties will actually and fully comply with their commitments. In the theory, two possible sources of imperfection are discussed. They are both linked to bounded observation ability. First, the judge may be unable to observe (verify) a relevant variable that is observable by the parties. Second, the judge may be unable to prevent renegotiations among the parties. This is so if the parties can fake their exchange to the judge. In both cases, this leads to the idea that the contracts are incomplete because the parties anticipate that certain relevant contractual provisions will not be enforced. These foundations for the incompleteness of contracts are, however, logically inconsistent with perfect rationality assumptions. Unless he has bounded rationality, the judge should be able to implement a revelation mechanism that would lead the parties to reveal the relevant information to allow him to oversee the performance of the contract (Tirole 1999).

*2.2.1.3 The consequences of contractual incompleteness* Beyond these controversies, the consequences of the impossibility of signing complete contracts have been investigated, mainly by Oliver Hart and his co-authors (with also a very important contribution by Aghion, Dewatripont, and Rey in 1994). For the reasons just mentioned above, many of these contributions were criticized on the basis of the ad hoc nature of their assumptions. They provided, however, stimulating insights on the nature and properties of incomplete contracts. All the models deal with the same structural problem. A pair of transacting parties cannot commit on variables – qualified as "investments" in the model, but they could be efforts or quality of inputs – that are essential in the exchange. The only verifiable variable is the volume of trade. They are then facing a security versus flexibility dilemma. If they commit too strongly on the level of trade they will not be able to adapt to *ex post* contingencies (including the actual contributions of both parties). If they commit too loosely, the parties will not be incited to invest optimally. The idea of non-contractible investments is a very powerful one. It translates the idea that a third party, responsible for the enforcement of the mutual promises, cannot check the quality of the investment or efforts made by the parties, and that the parties cannot therefore contract on such an issue. The alternative models developed by the theory point out that the ability to deal with security (of investment) versus flexibility dilemma depends upon the ability of the parties to implement a more sophisticated system of rights to set *ex post* the terms of exchange – which is itself dependent on the enforcement context.

When these rights cannot be disentangled and clarified between parties the outcome is less efficient than when many different rights or duties may be distinguished and distributed on a very specific basis to provide each party with incentives to behave optimally.

Initially, the approach did not explicitly focus on contracts, but on property rights. In Grossman and Hart (1986), since the parties cannot contract, they play on property rights understood as the right to capture the surplus resulting from the joint operation of assets. These rights provide therefore incentives to invest in non-contractible assets (or efforts). Since these rights lead to discrete choices – they belong to one of the parties or are shared; only a second-best solution may be implemented because it is impossible to fine-tune the allocation of these rights to the optimal level of investment required of each of the parties. The strength, and the limit, of this approach is that because it considers situations in which *ex post* decisions are not contractible it investigates the consequences of the transfer of rights to capture residual surplus. It has, however, been intensively applied to the analysis of vertical integration and to public–private partnerships.

*2.2.1.4 Three "incomplete contract" theories*    The criticisms of the earlier "property-rights" models led to the development of more "contractual" ones, which may be qualified as such since subtle ways of distributing rights to capture the surplus can be managed thanks to the design of "renegotiation frameworks" which organize *ex post* decisions about the actual conditions of exchanges. Three types of models have been developed.

First, in the line of Hart and Moore (1988) and of Aghion, Dewatripont, and Rey (1994), the incomplete contracts are made of a default provision setting minimal conditions of exchange, and of a renegotiation mechanism by which all the bargaining power to set new conditions of exchange is provided to one of the parties. The spirit of these models is that each of the parties is "protected" by one of the two mechanisms. In such a framework, an "incomplete contract" is nothing but a "renegotiation" mechanism through which implemented constraints lead one party to decide the conditions of exchanges, which is a collective second-best given what happened among the parties and in their environment. This family of models is a refinement of the property-rights models and is therefore submitted to similar criticisms. Only rights to capture the surplus are transferable through the contract and the contract does not really establish authority since the rights to decide *ex post* are severely bounded: the deciding party decides only among a set of options that might be described *ex ante*.

In a sense, the same criticism applies to the second type of models developed in the line of Hart and Moore (2004), which is also close to the spirit of the model developed by Simon (1951). In these models contracts are a list of trading options. *Ex post*, the parties bargain freely over the option that is implemented. Hart and Moore (2004) contrast "loose" contracts – which consist of a long list of options that maximize flexibility but reduce *ex ante* incentives to invest – and "tight" contracts – which implement only a short list of options and therefore protect more efficiently the investments made by the parties at the cost of *ex post* inefficiencies.

More recently, Baker, Gibbons, and Murphy (2004) proposed a third family model. They try to overcome the criticisms addressed to the two first categories. In this framework, contracts are a combination of rights to decide and of rights to capture which may be distributed in complex ways among the contracting parties (and a third party). This enables the authors to generate a wide set of contrasted contracts which permit adaptation to contrasted transactional situations.

*2.2.1.5 Incomplete contract theory and transaction cost reasoning*
ICT may, to some extent, be interpreted in terms of hybridization between incentive theory (IT) and transaction cost economics (TCE). However, it is clearly closer to the first than to the second. ICT shares with TCE the idea that bounded rationality – that is, decision costs (cf. Simon 1976) – forbids implementation of too-subtle incentives systems and leads therefore to discrete alternatives which lead to second-rank solutions (because a perfect alignment to rules of behavior with coordination situations is out of reach). However, only the enforcer or judge's rationality is bounded in ICT. This brings it quite close to IT. In both theories contractors may make accurate anticipations about the future problems to be solved. They are able to align *ex ante* (before coordination) incentives of the parties so as to yield the best possible response to all future contingencies. Because all *ex post* cheating possibilities have been anticipated they are addressed by the incentive scheme, which makes the contract self-enforcing. Breach is never appealing.

The only difference between the IT and ICT approaches is that the enforcement environment is imperfect in the latter, reducing the ability of agents to implement the first best response to all future contingences. ICT teaches us a lot about the effects of alternative enforcement contexts. It allows recognition and analysis of one of the roots of institutional embeddednes of contracts. However, unlike TCE, the contracts are not really understood as a governance mechanism aimed at reorganizing coordination among the parties during their own performance.

In TCE agents have to economize on costs of decision and to avoid errors found in designing solutions that will be *ex post* maladapted to problems they were unable to anticipate perfectly. They build mechanisms to permit them to decide how to behave *ex post* while saving decisions. In particular, they rely on pre-existing collective rules to save on effort in designing bilateral rules and bound errors (since institutional rules have been tested). Bounded rationality of agents – not only of enforcers – is another reason for the institutional embeddedness of contracts.

### 2.2.2    The governance approach to contracts

Two essential ideas are at the origin of the new institutional approach to contracts. First, Oliver Williamson highlighted the consequences of the adoption of realistic assumptions: contracting is costly and contracts are therefore quite imperfect. These are the consequences both of the agent's bounded rationality and of the imperfection of the institutional framework on which contracts stand. The imperfections of the institutional frameworks are themselves attributed to the bounded rationality of the agents who design or run them and to their opportunism (since rent seeking plays a role in institutional design and in the performance of institutional frameworks; *see* Arruñada 2001; North 1990).[4] Second, Ian MacNeil (1974) pointed out that many contracts are relational. They implement loose commitments which "frame" the mutual behavior of parties[5] rather than precisely designing a formal renegotiation framework. A relational contract aims therefore at making explicit the "object" and the "spirit" of a cooperative process rather than stating a clear delineation of rights of decision and of rights to capture the surplus (as in Baker, Gibbons, and Murphy 2004). According to MacNeil (1974), relational contracts initiate renegotiations between the parties that permanently redefine the purpose and the modalities of their cooperation. To allow themselves, nevertheless, to save on negotiations and enforcement the parties rely on formal and informal institutional frameworks (in particular social networks) since these provide them with rules and resources to coordinate. This is why relational contracts are embedded in institutions.

In the NIE framework contracts are therefore imperfect and incomplete. They implement governance regimes that allow coordination because, on one hand, they protect the parties, and, on the other, they allow them to adapt and learn. Contracts organize the frame of future coordination. They are necessary for coordination, but not sufficient in guaranteeing its efficiency. A lot depends upon the mutual behavior of the agents, upon the dynamics of their relationship, and upon the quality of the institutional environment.

A second consequence of the NIE understanding of contracts is the complementarities between formal contracting and informal coordination rules. Formal contracts and relational governance are complements. Rather than hindering or replacing relational governance contracts may promote the formation of long-term, trusting exchange relations (e.g. Poppo and Zenger 2002). Contracting and the logic of credible commitment (and retaliations) are tools to substitute for trust and allow the parties to coordinate when the fear of opportunistic behavior would otherwise prevent them to do so (Williamson 1993), but is also a tool to generate trust and allow cooperation (*see* 2.4.2.)

In that spirit a contract establishes the logic of the relationship among the parties and involves them in contrasted patterns of relationship (corresponding to the categorization of "market," "hybrid," and "hierarchy".) Engaging the parties on various paths of relations is dependent on the implemented contract that sets:

- a regime of decision: by allocating decision rights to one of the parties, to a third party, or by setting a negotiation procedure;
- a regime of risk-sharing: the rules according to which the surplus will be shared establish either a regime in which risks are borne by the parties or only by one of them;
- a way to recourse to external resources, and, in particular, to institutions to guarantee the mutual promises or to resolve disputes they might generate.

Since boundedly rational agents design contracts in an imperfect institutional environment, contracts are not only incomplete, they are also imperfect. This leads to two important ideas. First, contracts should be remediable. They should always be somehow revisable either to implement changes caused by poor conception of the coordination rules (since their actual consequences where wrongly anticipated *ex ante*) or because experience and learning allow discovering more efficient solutions. There is therefore no rigid trade-off between flexibility of mutual commitments and credibility. Adaptation allows higher performance and therefore ensures credibility (in the logic highlighted by Crocker and Masten 1991). However, at the same time the revisibility of contracts opens the door to opportunism and induces *ex post* costs. Second, contracts cannot be analyzed in abstract outside their institutional contexts. Since they are imperfect and costly to manage contracts should be considered as tools complementary to mechanisms that are relied on to reduce the costs of contracting – for example enforcement may rely on the enforcement mechanisms provided by the state (i.e. the judiciary) because it is less costly and more powerful than a mutually agreed upon and mutually run enforcement mechanism – and to control for the worst deviation of the contracts – for example the judiciary may be relied on to void mutual obligations that are considered as unfair, unjustifiable, or contrary to the general interest.

## 2.3    Contracts within their institutional framework

Thus, in the governance approach to contracting the analysis of contracts is indissociable from analysis of the institutional framework and vice versa. The incentives approach – through ICT – also provides many insights about the relationships among contracts and the institutional framework. Several applied analyses, relying on ad hoc but fruitful assumptions, also highlight how institutional constraints frame the design of contracts. Many of them have been developed in the framework of law and economics. Since the demand for analyses of contract law or contract regulation has been strong for the past thirty years, a literature has been developing to analyze the principles which should frame the freedom of contracting and the justifications for any regulation of contracting practices (*see* 2.3.1). Most of the literature, however, has been dedicated to analysis of the effect of the enforcement context on contractual practices and their performance (*see* 2.3.2). As will be developed in the remaining sections of this chapter, the issue is either to provide the last-resort enforcer – often the judge – with optimal decision rules (*see* 2.4), or to think of the optimal enforcement environment (*see* 2.5).

### 2.3.1    *Contractual regulations, mandatory, and default rules*

*2.3.1.1 Law as complementary to contracts*    In a world of zero transaction costs coordination would be purely contractual and bilateral. In a world of positive transaction costs there is a trade-off between relying on general rules, which induce malalignment to transactional characteristics and to individual preferences of the parties generating maladaptation costs, and bilateral agreements which lead parties to bear transaction costs (Brousseau and Raynaud 2007). If transaction costs are positive governance is multi-level because efficiency gains may result from the combination of contractual and institutional coordination.

A more conventional way to express this idea is in use in law and economics. General or legal rules may be set up to decrease social transaction costs for two main reasons. First, because of the bounded rationality of the parties, contract law may propose contractual "turnkey" terms to economize on transaction costs. Second, because of cognitive asymmetries among parties, some could impose unfair contracting conditions on others, which might be avoided by a regulation guaranteeing fairer and therefore more efficient conditions of exchange.

Contract law may thus be considered a crutch for contracting parties. It can impose contract terms in order to reduce waste. However, this may require a perfectly rational (and purely benevolent) regulator, which is highly unlikely to exist. There are nevertheless two ways of justifying the enlightenment of contracting parties by law.

First, market selection[6] and collective learning (though precedent) allow for the discovery of efficient contracting practices (Arruñada 2001; Chakravarty and MacLeod, 2004). This helps to identify the best learning institutional framework. Until now this important issue received only limited attention. There is obviously the theory – developed, in particular, by LaPorta *et al.* (1999) and Posner (2003) – that common law principles are superior to those of the civil code because they allow a wide and systematic assessment of rules and an accumulation of the knowledge related to them. It is, however, clear that more in-depth studies are needed to ground these opinions. Arruñada and Andonova (2005) or Lamoreaux and Rosenthal (2004), for instance, pointed out the historical specificities of the rationale behind the logic of the civil code (which was a way for an enlightened elite to boost the implementation of more efficient legal standards in a context in which these standards were not spontaneously adopted by the majority). Deffains and Kirat (2001) or Hatzis (2000, 2006) also developed convincing arguments about the ability of civil code institutions to provide users of the law with efficient norms because the process of law making combines both in-depth philosophical reasoning and studies of current practices and their outcome.

Second, as pointed out by Arruñada (2001), a way to avoid implementing inefficient legal principles when not needed is to make their use optional. This calls for the implementation of default rather than mandatory rules.

*2.3.1.2 Complementarity depends on bilateral context and on the design of institutions*   In any case, different situations should be contrasted. In relationships between firms it is often not relevant to consider that the two parties have a bounded rationality when regulating contracts. Indeed, firms may dedicate cognitive means to contract efficiently. If a regulation protects parties because they did not foresee future coordination difficulties it may incite firms to under-invest in their coordination arrangements. On the other hand, when two individuals contract – as is the case in the relationship between members of a family – it may be efficient to protect parties from their lack of awareness of their own weaknesses simply because more incentives to be far-sighted could simply be useless.

This is also true when there are structural asymmetries between parties, as is often the case between firms and individuals citizens (e.g. business-to-consumer or business-to-labor relationships). In these asymmetric situations the weak party is often a contract-taker. It accepts or refuses the contract designed by the other party. The boundedly rational non-drafting party will usually not be able to review all the details of the contracts, and if he does, he is unable to renegotiate the terms. The drafting party has, therefore, incentives to include terms in its standard contracts which work in his favor, despite whether such terms are efficient. In such a case, more intensive recourse to mandatory contract terms would be an efficient policy. This is widely recognized in civil code countries for relationships between individuals and firms (*see* Korobkin 2003; Rasmunsen 2001). However, as in the previous case, it supposes the design of mandatory terms is based on efficiency, whereas the lack of capabilities of the social planner and the ability of private interests to influence its decision may lead to less than optimal results (*see* Arruñada 2001). This leads us back to the issue of the logic of the legal rule-making process.

Beyond contract law *per se*, a great deal of the legal or institutional environment plays an important role, too. This is pointed out in the excellent study by Hadfield (2005). First, the regulation settling how contracts should be legally established (procedural law) affects their quality – for instance, the mandatory intervention of a lawyer favors a systematic quality check – their credibility, which is reinforced when notaries and other independent third parties oversee the settling and enforcement of promises, and the control of domination effects, which are more difficult to exercise when contracts have to be made public or when an explicit "manifestation of the will" by each party is made mandatory (as in French code). Second, and more generally, the legal context affects the ability to implement specific contractual terms and to guarantee their enforcement. This is the case, for instance, for liability principles, for debt obligations and bankruptcy laws, for shareholders rights, and so on. Third, the organization of the legal profession (which drafts contracts and is involved in their litigation) also affects contractual practice. It is both a matter of equilibrium (among the strategies of the various parties in the system) and a matter of organization of, or oversight by, the profession, which may be self-regulated, regulated by law, or regulated by judges and courts.

However, plenty of research needs to be done, since the trade-offs between rules set at collective levels and rules that are decentrally contracted by agents must be explored more carefully than has been done in the past. In particular, these trade-offs are affected by the nature of the issue addressed. Moreover, there are different collective levels (from local or trade community to global, plus national and regional). In addition, these trade-offs are affected by the ability of agents to rely simultaneously on rules defined at different levels. These questions and the related research agenda are explored by Brousseau and Raynaud (2007).

### 2.3.2 Enforcement

The question of enforcement has been receiving more attention over the past twenty years. This is because of the need to provide judges with decision rules. Although much remains to be done to produce a comprehensive theory, a lot has already been achieved. The principal weakness of the theory today is that it is made up of a wide number of ad hoc models, and up to now, specific studies did not produce a consistent analysis. In addition, there is clearly a lack of systematic empirical evidence.

The problem is the following: contracts are *ex ante* commitments to behave in a certain way *ex post*. However, most contracts are settled in the shadow of doubt so that *ex post* unanticipated circumstances make *ex ante* promises no longer the preferred choice (and sometime a possible choice) of at least one of the parties. This raises the question of the optimal decision to be taken by the last-resort enforcer of the contract (most often a judge).[7] Upstream, the design of the institutional system (here the judiciary) can be discussed. Indeed, the quality of decisions by last-resort enforcers might well depend upon their skills and incentives, which are influenced by their identity, the way they are appointed, the mechanisms overseeing their decisions, and so on. Downstream, optimal rules of decision may be designed to allow the judge to settle conflicts in ways that result in gains in collective efficiency in the long run. Thus, two issues have been studied – rules governing breach remedies and the structure of enforcement institutions – and they are addressed from two perspectives. The first is the incentive approach to contracts; the second is the governance perspective. Table 2.1 summarizes both. Each of the boxes will be further explored in the next four sections.

It is worth noting that, in the first column, the normative conclusions drawn from the theory should be carefully analyzed in the light of the ad hoc assumptions that are generally made in the literature. On one hand,

Table 2.1 *Contract enforcement: two visions and two issues*

|  | Incentive contracting (coordination problems optimally solved *ex ante*) | Governance contracting (combination of *ex ante* and *ex post* solution to allow coordination) |
|---|---|---|
| Breach remedy: optimal decision rules (to be followed by the enforcers in last resort) | Breach remedies Interpretation rules *Section 2.4.1* | Contract and incentives to cooperate *Section 2.4.2* |
| Institutional design (Public versus Private // Specialized versus Generic //) | Specialization and the matching between Human K and Judicial decision rules Optimal institutional design to allow for impersonal exchange *Section 2.5.1* | Advantages and limits of interpersonal links Public verus Private (self) (or formal versus informal) Logic of observability and exclusion *Section 2.5.2* |

the theory refers to a world of perfect rationality. When they design contract agents may anticipate the decisions of the last-resort enforcer if disputes arise. The contract is designed accordingly and corrects any potential bias or weaknesses in the enforcement mechanism. On the other hand, legal and economic reasoning rely on the "realistic" assumption that parties bear decision costs. Many models applied to studies of conflict settlement often rely on specific combinations of partly conflicting assumptions which are made to "rationally" explore the consequences of imperfect contracts or regulations, or both. Thus, normative conclusions should be analyzed carefully. For instance, several scholars call for no interpretation by courts of contractual terms in the case of litigation so as to incite parties to write complete (customized) contracts. This is optimal if, and only if, there are no decision costs. When decisions are costly it is justifiable to leave some incompleteness in the contracts, and might therefore be efficient to interpret the contractual terms *ex post* (even if parties are encouraged to write as complete as possible contracts).

## 2.4    Enforcement rules

### 2.4.1    Breach remedy and interpretation rules

As pointed out by Craswell (2001), the economic analysis of contract enforcement does not equate efficiency with the ability to carry out promised actions. It recognizes that legal enforceability triggers a much more complex set of effects. For example, enforceability influences not only whether the promise is carried out, but also whether the promise gets made at all, or how carefully the promisor thinks about the promise before making it, or how much the promisor spends on precautions guarding against accidents that might leave him unable to perform in the future and so forth.

*2.4.1.1 Optimal damages*  The theory of breach remedy, as developed over the past decades, depends on the principle of efficient breach. Although obvious to an economist, this principle is not so obvious to many legal traditions, which insist, in particular, on security being provided by law, or on the inalienability of the given word. The doctrine of efficient breach states that if an action taken *ex post* results in a higher collective surplus than the one resulting from the action committed to *ex ante* it is efficient to breach the arrangement. There are two cases. If negotiation is possible, and non-costly, then the party who wants to breach, because it will get a benefit higher than if he would not breach, will be able to compensate the other party for its potential losses. Letting the parties freely renegotiate their mutual commitment is optimal since breach will occur only if the surplus brought by the breach is higher than the losses incurred by all parties. Flexibility will then allow adaptation to unforeseen circumstances.

When renegotiations are costly it may be more efficient to allow unilateral breach and to apply a general principle to compensate the victim. Literature on breach remedies discusses alternative principles of compensation. As this is certainly the topic that is addressed by the larger number of contributions quoted in this chapter, it is impossible to survey all the refinements (*see* Cooter and Rubinfeld 1989). Here we will point out the main principles and achievements, and then discuss them in relation to the governance approach to contracting. There are three main regimes for breach remedies: expectation damages; reliance damages; and specific performance. In the next two paragraphs we will compare the first with the last two, and use examples adapted from Edlin (1998) to clarify.

When *expectation* damages are applied the victim is compensated according to the benefits he would have if the deal had been completed. With *reliance* damages the victim is compensated in order to return to the initial situation when the contract did not exist. The first rule leads the party who breached the contract to internalize the costs of the other, and therefore to breach only when efficient. This is not the case for the second rule. To illustrate, let us take an example: a client who would like to get an old-style desk orders a copy from a craftsman for €1,000. At time (T1), the craftsman has already spent €350 in supplies and efforts to build the ordered desk, while the client discovers, at an antique dealer's, the original desk he wanted. He therefore decides to breach the contract with the craftsman. The latter was expecting a profit of €400, because costs were anticipated to be €600. If a rule of expected damages could be applied compensation to the craftsman should be €350 + €400 = €750. In the case of reliance damages the compensation would be only €350. Thus, in case of expectation damages the buyer breaches if, and only if, the surplus of value (v) of the copy compared to the antique desk, is less than €250. In the case of reliance damages the buyer breaches inefficiently if €250 < v < €650, and, of course, efficiently if v < €250. Thus, the difference between the two regimes is that reliance damages can lead to a socially inefficient outcome. Expected damages are, however, more complex to manage (see below). It is worth noting, however, that the two regimes may be equivalent in certain circumstances. First, the efficient versus inefficient character of the breach depends on the buyer preferences. In certain cases, the two regimes lead to an efficient breach. Second, the degree of competition matters. If competition on the handmade desk market was higher prices would tend to marginalize costs and the price of the desk would reach around €600, which would reduce the level of expected damages.

Specific performance involves forcing parties to comply with their prior commitments, whatever the cost. The example here is a tenant who rents an apartment for twelve months. He discovers a new flat after four months and decides to move. In the case of specific performance he will have to pay the lease for the eight remaining months. In case of expected damages he will pay the lease for the period during which the apartment is unoccupied. He is therefore strongly encouraged to take the new opportunity and find a new tenant for the apartment. Again, expectation damages lead to a more efficient outcome. It protects parties like specific performance does, but allows them to benefit from flexibility, if needed.

So, expectation damages seem to be at first sight an optimal solution for contractual breaches. Its implementation is, however, complex in practice and may result in inefficient incentives. Let us point out three issues. First, it provides low incentives to protected parties to reduce costs and so to favor efficient breach. In the example of the desk, the craftsman is sure to be compensated up to €600 of expected costs, and has no incentives to reduce them. If he was unsure of being compensated for the costs he anticipated he would have incentives to reduce them. This is the same for incentives to find a new partner. In the case of breaching the craftsman is not encouraged to search for a new client, although this would enhance collective efficiency if he would find one (as in the case of the rented apartment). Second, as pointed out when we compared expectation with reliance damages, the actual efficiency or inefficiency of the alternative rules pretty much depends on the context. Given the relative costs of negotiation, renegotiation, and conflict settlement, the distribution of preferences, the information asymmetries, and given the level of competition on the market in question, negotiation of ad hoc damages could lead to a more efficient outcome. The expectation damages rule is not always optimal, even if it is most often the most efficient breach remedy. Third, the main weakness of the expected damage rule lies in its implementation limitations. It supposes that parties assess "expectations" *ex ante*, and that this information can be verified by the courts. It is easy to understand in the desk case that the craftsman has no incentives to reveal costs. If, in the negotiation phase, the buyer discovers the expected profit is two-thirds of the costs he will negotiate a much lower price. If the craftsman does not reveal his costs *ex ante* then efficient breach will never be guaranteed because damages will be computed *ex post* by an investigation by the courts, meaning that the client would have to choose to breach, or not, without knowing the damages he would pay. In addition, if the court bears the information and decision costs it might well make mistakes in calculating damages, which will result in inefficient compensation.

*2.4.1.2 Interpretation rules*  Another important part of the literature discusses the principles by which contracts should be interpreted. Cheating on a complete contract (to the extent that they exist in the real world) is useless since, by definition, the payoffs for every relevant action and the corresponding sanctions for non-performance are prescribed in the contract. Parties may, however, have incentives to cheat by exploiting gaps in incomplete contracts. Making the verifiable terms of the contract legally enforceable and regulating incompleteness is a consistent strategy for reducing, but does not annihilate, these incentives to cheat. There are three basic interpretation rules that could be used by a court.[8] The majoritarian rule corresponds to the understanding most frequently used in similar contracts. The penalty default rule involves choosing the interpretation that is most unfavorable for the victim. A literal interpretation considers only what is written down. Borrowing from Posner (2003) let us take an example to study the consequences of these three rules. A contract states that a poultry farmer should deliver a certain quantity of broilers to a restaurant owner, while the quality of the broiler is not specified in the contract. There are three possible levels of quality: premium, standard, and first-price. The restaurant owner is expecting premium, since it is obvious for him that he needs this level of quality for his customers. He is dissatisfied with the delivered quality, first-price, and so sues the farmer. If the court uses the majoritarian rule it considers the farmer cheated according to usual practices and requests he compensate the restaurant owner, but only for the difference of value between the first-price and standard quality. If the court applies the penalty default it considers the farmer did not cheat and does not request compensation. This is the same if the court applies a literalistic interpretation because the broilers have been delivered. If the farmer does not deliver then he will have to pay compensation related to the value of standard quality if the majoritarian rule applies, to the premium quality if the penalty default applies, and to the first-price if the contract is interpreted literally. It is clear these rules provide asymmetric incentives to cheat and breach. Studies of the respective advantages of the majoritarian versus default rule point out that their respective efficiency depends on the costs of negotiation, renegotiation, and conflicts; the distribution of preferences within the population; the balance of market power; the ability of the seller to influence quality; and so on. There is no optimal solution. When it comes to comparing the majoritarian and the literalistic interpretation rules analysis is clearer. Literalistic interpretation provides parties with incentives to write more complete contracts, which are more efficient because they generate fewer conflicts *ex post*. In other words, parties internalize and therefore minimize the costs of conflicts. However, this increases the cost of writing contracts.

The literature which attempts to provide optimal decision rules for entities responsible for enforcing contracts reveals that the rules more efficient in many situations are not optimal in all conditions. Optimality depends on a wide set of conditions that are specific to each transaction. This calls either for specific judgment of each case or for contingent rules. The problem with both solutions is that they do not provide agents with capability to foresee what will actually happen, and consequently, no security or clear incentives. If remedies to be applied *ex post* depend on the judge's discretionary powers (or interpretation of the situation) conflicts are likely to occur frequently because parties will have an incentive to cheat, breach, and sue (since uncertainty leads to expected benefits). Contracts will thus fail to provide the right incentives. Underperformance may be expected. This is why, in the world of "transactional" contracts between professionals strong incentives should be given to parties to write fully detailed contracts stipulating, in particular, adequate solutions for cheating and breaching. This is the argument proposed by Schwartz and Scott (2003) and many others keen to keep contract law as minimal as possible in order to stimulate efficient and ad hoc contracting. However, there is a non-reducibility to contract law if agents face decision costs, since, as argued above, default rule and principles of interpretation allow agents to save on writing costs (Shavell 2006).[9]

### 2.4.2 Contracts and incentives to cooperate

To establish clear rules of behavior for the last-resort enforcer of a relational contract is even more difficult. It may be illustrated by the case of contracts sustaining cooperation. Indeed, such contracts do not "drive" cooperation, but create a climate favorable to it. Cooperation, especially when closely linked to innovation, requires initiatives to test new solutions and seize opportunities, while success is not always guaranteed. Permanent renegotiation could be slow and costly. This is why these processes rely on freedom to experiment, mutual adjustments, and *ex post* negotiations to adapt the formal arrangements to the new resulting situation, in a context where initiatives could also be interpreted as strategic and hostile moves.

On one hand, what often matters is the dynamics of interactions, since it results in mutually built assets of value to both parties, and creates *ex post* solidarities which contribute to solving potential tensions caused by selfishness. This is why the evolutionary approach and the resource-based view (Dosi 2000; Dosi and Marengo 1994; Teece *et al.*, 1994; *see also* chapters 1 and 20 in this volume) state that the first coordination difficulty to be considered is the complexity of associating and accumulating knowledge in a world where agents are cooperative. On the other, as highlighted by mainstream economists and also by NIE scholars, any cooperative process is threatened by a "tragedy of the commons" type of problem. Incentive schemes and governance frameworks therefore matter, and are enabling conditions for the emergence of cooperation. Literature on cooperation among firms (*see* Chapter 10) points out that contracting does matter. However, the contract does not seek to protect against any kind of opportunism. It allows for the creation of mutual trust. Of course, trust can result from sources other than contracts; in particular, from social networks. However, if social networks do play a role in the shaping of relationships between firms it is limited. Firms are collective entities somehow detached from their members. Social networks in which the latter are embedded are not enough to guarantee efficient interactions.

As we are reminded by Oxley and Silverman in Chapter 10, empirical evidence suggests that firms involved in a cooperation process, typically in technological partnerships, do sign contracts that become less and less incomplete during the development of their relation (Ryall and Sampson 2003). They also carefully implement last-resort retaliation mechanisms and termination provisions (Parkhe 1993). So contracts are signed and seem to matter. Based on the same stylized facts, Brousseau (2000a) proposes an interpretation of the role of the contracts in cooperative processes. Since these processes are characterized by innovation (often in an uncertain context because competitors are also innovating, and because the behavior of the demand is difficult to foresee) it is impossible to sign contracts that will *ex ante* establish a set of actions or even development plans. Contracts are nevertheless signed to publicly highlight the will to cooperate. Usually, alliances are advertised in the press. At this stage, however, the contract is generally nothing more than a few pages by which the parties state their will to cooperate. Projects are often still fuzzy, but the initial commitment guaranteed by their reputation is needed to allow further discussions, during which parties progressively explore what they can actually do together, which supposes the mutual revelation of trade and technical secrets. Of course, this commitment to cooperate is too loose to guarantee the continuation and development of the project. The latter relies on the development of mutual trust between parties. In parallel to exchanges aimed as defining their common project and respective contributions, parties have an interest in progressively "tying up" more and more closely "their hands" by proposing to subscribe additional binding commitments. Providing the other part with credible hostages is a good way to prove our spirit is cooperative and that we do not fear retaliation.

Contracts are thus one of the tools used in the multi-channel and continuous mutual screening of the willingness to cooperate – which allows establishing trust; (*see* Dixit 2004) – that is, enabling conditions of processes of cooperation aiming at managing hazards and adaptation. This is why partnerships often rely on the permanent renegotiation and "upgrading" of contractual commitments, and on the implementation of formal mechanisms to signal the end of a cooperative behavior, should it occur. The goal is to avoid distrust in the case of behavior that could be interpreted as apparent opportunism (like an experience that fails and harms the other party).

The many applied studies highlighting the fact that contracts are not relied on in day-to-day business (Macaulay 1963; Deakin and Michie 1997a, 1997b; Contractor and Lorange 1988; Gambetta 1988; Ring and Van de Ven 1992) are right. The contract has to be "locked into a safe box," since its purpose is not to manage the cooperation process that relies on mutual and informal adjustments (to optimize flexibility and minimize costs). Parties shall avoid enforcing the contract as it stands.

They must comply with its spirit only. For instance, in the case of delayed delivery or wrong quality parties should rather meet, try to understand the cause of the problems, and fix it cooperatively, rather than applying penalties and litigating. However, the cooperative process is performed in the shadow of this contract aimed at credibly guaranteeing the cooperative minds of both parties.

So in relational contracting contracts must be seen as crash barriers framing the process of cooperation rather than tracks organizing it. They establish and maintain mutual trust, which is a necessary condition for sustaining cooperation (*see also* Kale, Singh, and Perlmutter 2000; Poppo and Zenger 2002). In this context, how should the last-resort enforcer behave? On one hand, the contract implements mechanisms allowing punishing deviation from the formal contract; on the other, even when no conflict occurs, parties are always deviating from formal contracts, taking them seriously in spirit but not in words. In such a case, a judge should behave as a marriage guidance counselor rather than a police officer, noting and punishing infringements. In case of conflict he should assess if cooperation remains mutually beneficial. If yes he should try to restore trust by analyzing the causes for not complying with the spirit of the agreement, and by discovering possible compensation. If no he should manage efficient breach by avoiding, in particular, the vicious loop of retaliation. However, fundamentally, such cooperative agreements should be self-enforced. When a conflict requires a third party to be solved it tends to be hopeless.

By comparing the approach of the last-resort enforcer in relational contracting (*see* 2.4.1) with the same in transactional (*see* 2.4.2), it is clear that the more "relational" the contract, the more the judge should be a mediator (or go-between) rather than a judge *per se*.

## 2.5    Enforcement institutions and their structure

### 2.5.1    Specialization and organization of the judiciary

When scholars discuss optimal rules (contractual breach, interpretation, default, and so forth) they assume that the enforcer – implicitly the judiciary – benefits from a perfect (at least a higher) rationality that allows him to compensate for the imperfect rationality of the contracting parties.[10] Such an assumption was strongly criticized by Williamson from the very beginning of TCE. It also goes against the common knowledge of any practitioner (e.g. Posner 2005). It is therefore vital to take into account that enforcement devices are imperfect, since this influences the decision rule to be implemented. Posner, for instance, insists that laymen in juries interpret differently than professional judges because they lack experience. In addition, they may be biased. For instance, they could feel empathy for one of the parties. Of course judges may also be biased, but their statute can be designed to protect them from pressures and prevent them yielding to entreaties by involved parties. Consequently, when laymen play a key role in the decision-making process default rules are preferable to interpretation. This is the reasoning behind talks about the strength and weaknesses of juries, and the need to frame their decision-making process. Arruñada and Andonova (2005) develop similar ideas about the optimal logic of legal enforcement when comparing the different degrees of judicial discretion adopted by English Common Law and in the Continental Civil Code legal traditions of the nineteenth century. They claim that the market-friendly climate in Great Britain allowed for reliance on the discretionary power of judges to progressively adapt common law to the requirements needed by the industrial revolution and for developing markets. On the other hand, judges and public opinion were much less oriented toward free-markets on the continent. Constraining judicial discretion was essential for strengthening the freedom of contracts and establishing a market economy.

These highlight two facts. First, (optimal) contract design and (optimal) contract regulation are a matter of institutional capabilities. Second, designing the enforcement framework is an essential policy tool even if it is difficult to foresee the precise impact of an institutional reform because of the complex games among the contracting parties and the enforcer. Let us briefly review these two lines of thought.

*2.5.1.1 Specialization of rules and specialization of enforcement mechanisms: costs and benefits*    One essential insight, provided by Williamson as early as 1975, was the idea that litigation by courts takes time, results in errors, or in the absence of choice (dismissing the case for lack of evidence); and this justifies opting-out of legal enforcement in certain circumstances (in TCE when asset specificity is high). In 1975, this statement was the main reason for the emergence of hierarchies. In 1985, it became a more general reason for the oversight of contracting parties by private and specialized third parties.

A direct consequence of Williamson's analysis is to analyze the overall impact of poor performances of courts on contractual performances. Indeed, if private ordering is the best response to some institutional inefficiency it does not mean that higher overall efficiency would not result from a better institutional design.

When courts become more efficient, contracting parties can rely more on collective regulations and enforcement. This brings advantages. First, agents do not have individually to bear the direct costs of implementing solutions aimed at guaranteeing enforcement. Second, they can benefit from efficiency gained by socializing the design and the enforcement of their rules. This is the reasoning behind Williamson's idea that coordination via the market is less demanding for agents in terms of governance than coordination via the hierarchy, since markets rely on sophisticated institutional infrastructures.

The general economy of the contract or institutional framework system needs to be developed in reference to the degree of specialization of institutional components. It is essential to better understand the benefits and costs of relying on more standardized rules and related enforcement mechanisms versus the use of more specific contracts; given the cost of building skilled and reliable enforcement organizations, and given the efficiency or cost of these organizations in enforcing specific contracts rather than generic rules.

It is not, however, only a question of standardization versus customization of coordination principles. Some literature explores other dimensions of the trade-offs at play when contractual imperfections have to be balanced with institutional imperfections. Schwartz and Watson (2004), for instance, take into account the costs of drafting complex and specific contracts, and the costs of *ex post* renegotiations of these contracts, and balance them with the risk of *ex post* capture of surplus given the enforcement costs and the law's interpretive rules. Other approaches, by Bull and Watson (2001) or Triantis (2002), suggest that the chosen reporting technology to bring evidence to the enforcer influences the contract terms which may be implemented and vice versa. In this type of study the verifiability constraint is no longer exogenous and dichotomic. Agents simultaneously choose the design of the contract and of the enforcement system, and take into consideration the benefits and costs of both.

*2.5.1.2 Designing more efficient institutions* The other consequence is to consider the changes needed to benefit from a better enforcement context. This leads us to analyze the impact of the organization of the judiciary on its ability to enforce contractual arrangements.[11] The key issue is to assess the incentives of those involved in the litigation process to perform efficiently, or at least to understand the drivers of decision making in alternative types of enforcement institutions. A systematic approach is needed since many issues must be dealt with. They concern, in particular:

- the benefit instead of: cost ratio of enhancing the quality of the human capital involved in dispute settlement (involving studies of the impact of skills on the quality of decisions), and how to obtain a higher quality decision (which should depend on many variables since remuneration schemes and career management could greatly impact on incentives to learn, to specialize, and so on);

- the impact of the organization of the decision process – that is, the way cases are documented, judgments are formed, sentencing is decided. For instance, accusatory and inquisitory procedures have differing properties in practice. While accusatory procedures imply redundancy of efforts, and might result in manipulation, competition between parties leads to greater revelation. We have also already mentioned the idea that sentencing by juries and judges leads to different biases.

These questions need to be investigated more systematically, and there is plenty of research ahead of us. Indeed, today there is much evidence provided via case studies, but these observations do not deliver systematic assessment and comparisons that allow for controllable tests. We therefore lack systematic studies on the effects of the design of enforcement institutions on the design and performance of contracts. We also lack of systematic assessment of alternative contractual practices within alternative institutional frameworks that would allow for comparisons of the joint efficiency of contracts and institutions. There are only few systematic studies on contractual enforcement. There are many such studies focussing on the enforcement of property rights (*see* 2.4; *see also* Chapter 17; and, obviously, the papers by La Porta *et al.* [1999] and Djankov *et al.* [2003]). Some studies on the alternative organization of property right systems (e.g. Arruñada and Garoupa 2005; Brousseau and Bessy 2006) could be extended to contractual enforcement, but this has yet to be done.

### 2.5.2    *Public versus private or self-enforcement*

Although, to date, designing formal institutional frameworks to optimize the enforcement of contracts has not received sufficient attention, at least sufficiently systematic attention, one of the questions explored most by NIE scholars with regard to institutional design is the performance of self-enforcement (or at least of non-judicial enforcement) and its interplay with public enforcement. It arose from two questions. How does trade occur and how are contracts enforced in a "weak" institutional environment (Dixit 2004; Fafchamps 1996; Greif 1993, 2006; Greif, Milgrom, and Weingast 1994; Milgrom *et al.* 1990; Weingast 2007)? Why do some traders opt out of the legal system in a sophisticated institutional environment (Bernstein 1992, 2001)?

This resulted in the development of what is called the economics of non-judicial enforcement, which highlights both the strengths and the weaknesses of extra-legal mechanisms (and therefore reveals plenty on legal ones). Traders and peers benefit from two advantages which reduce enforcement costs (or enhance the quality of enforcement). First, peers have a greater ability to verify what is going on in the frame of a partnership since they have close access to information, and because they have the skill to interpret it. In addition, in a community each trader is supervised by "many pairs of eyes" belonging to potential counterparts in exchanges, who therefore have incentives to detect and retaliate against infringers. Second, partners in the exchange benefit from a "natural" and "cheap" means of retaliation: to stop trading. At a community level, this results in ostracism that is not costly to exercise, but costly when subjected to (because an ostracized individual does not benefit from many counterparts in the exchange, and is in a weak bargaining position with the few who trade with him). The capability of partners and communities of peers to oversee contractual behavior and punish infringers by being able to replicate and leverage the advantages of the threat to stop trade (Corts and Singh 2004; Kreps *et al.* 1982; Milgrom, North, and Weingast 1990) is, however, bounded. It is first limited by the spread of information across networks because information asymmetries and information costs prevent perfect transmission of information among peers (*see* Cooter and Landa 1984). It is also limited by the relative low cost of ostracism as a unique sanction in several cases. For instance, Bakos and Dellarocas (2003) illustrate the limits to reputation effects in communities of online traders. Milgrom, North, and Weingast (1990) point out how profitable "hit and run" strategies are not discouraged when the profit of infringements are much higher than the cost of being definitely expelled from a community (which is partly linked to the size of the community).

With some infringements being hardly visible to members of a community and some infringers being out of the reach of the natural sanction mechanism the ability of community mechanisms to guarantee the fulfillment of promises is limited. This is the reason for the existence of specialized third parties (and organizations) to optimize the extraction of information and the exercise retaliation. This is well highlighted by Milgrom, North and Weingast. There is an unavoidable trade-off between the proximity to transaction (and low-cost observation and retaliation) and a generic enforcement by a specialized third party (which raises issues of additional information asymmetries, costs of sanctions, potential inefficiency of the third party that has to be incited and that could divert its sanction capability to capture wealth, and so forth). However, studies point out the advantages of market intermediaries and private judges (compared to the judiciary). This literature insists, in particular, on the expertise, speed, and privacy provided by private institutions (Bernstein 2001; Hadfield 2000), which are of value to the contracting parties in many circumstances; whilst, as pointed out by Richman (2002), these private institutions are unable to oversee the performance of highly complex behavior and situations. They might also be too weak to exercise retaliations that have a deterrant effect.

Since non-judicial enforcement displays "imperfect" performances, it is an add-on to judicial enforcement (Brousseau and Raynaud 2006). This is at the origin of two perspectives. On one hand, institutional frameworks may be seen as alternatives. This leads to the idea of alternative regimes. When the formal institutional framework can provide third-party neutral enforcement at a low cost then the market can emerge. Exchange is based on public order. When this is not the case social networks providing self-enforcement permit the development of relational contracts (*see* Brown, Falk, and Fehr 2003; Bueno de Mesquita and Stephenson 2006). On the other hand, enforcement frameworks may be see as complements. Lazzarini, Miller, and Todd (2004), for instance, find that contracts facilitate the self-enforcement of non-contractible dimensions of the exchange.

Besides this static understanding of complementarities, Johnson and McMillan (2002) propose a dynamic analysis, which falls in line with our study above of the emergence and dynamics of trust (*see* 2.4.2). They point out that established interactions are driven within the framework of "relationships" that are self-sustainable. However, "courts" and formal institutions are needed to generate new relationships by providing guarantees to initial interactions.

## 2.6    A research agenda

Despite the focus on contracts over the past thirty years, much remains to be done to better understand them and their interactions with the institutional frameworks. In line with this chapter, and in complement to the research directions that have already been highlighted, at least three essential dimensions have to be deepened.

First, much more needs to be known of the way contracts are designed by agents. Today there is little theory and evidence on the way agents actually choose contracts – and this is of great importance both for theoretical and applied reasons. For instance, do agents select polar forms of coordination (market, hierarchy of hybrid) and then refine the contract design within each of these alternative forms (as suggested by Oliver Williamson)? Or do they select a set of provisions after identifying the coordination problems they face, and try to address potential discrepancies among them? In the first case we should observe clusters of contract types in an economy, whereas in the second, more homogeneous distribution should occur. This is important, both for understanding the property of an economy and for implementing institutional reform aimed at favoring the adoption of more efficient forms of contracting. Another important issue to implement reforms in an economy is to analyze whether agents write new contracts from scratch by analyzing coordination problems and by designing the best responses, or if they do so by imitation and progressive amendments of pre-existing contracts. If the latter is true, the pace at which institutional reforms generate changes may only be progressive and strong-path dependency effects should occur. In addition, in this latter case, the institutional framework plays a key role both because it is the matrix in which contracts are embedded, and because it organizes the competitive selection of "efficient" contractual forms. Institutional mechanisms – for example contract law, antitrust regulations, specific "professional" regulations, financial regulations, the openness of the economy, and so on – all determine to what extent contractual practices are sustainable. They provide (or not) incentives for organizational change at a micro-level.

Second, better understanding of the economics of multi-level governance is needed. Contracts interact with other governance mechanisms aggregated at different "levels": local and professional communities, nations, coalitions of states organizing some integration between their institutional frameworks (regional unions, political alliances, and so forth), and even the global arena. It is important to better understand what kind of problems are solved better bilaterally than collectively, and, for the latter category, what is the relevant level? Moreover, interdependencies between these levels or modes of governance must be studied to design better contracts and institutions (*see* Brousseau and Raynaud 2007).

Lastly, another very important research target is to better understand the relationship between contracting arrangements and patterns of behavior. There are complex relationships between the features of contracts and rationality of agents. Contracts are responses to decision costs and means to surpass the boundaries of individual rationality. The ability to design efficient contracts strongly depends on the rationality of contract drafters and the third party involved in contract oversight. In a situation where agents are empowered by the development of Information Technologies, and benefit from evolving means of coordination (thanks to the development of the legal profession and to the standardization of practices worldwide), it is a challenge to disentangle the phenomena that affect the evolution of our economies (Baker and Hubbard 2004; Brousseau 2004). Another challenge involves digging deeper into studies on economic action from a motivation perspective. We have already mentioned the complex relationship between seeking to cooperate and the pursuit of selfish interest. For more than two decades it has been a major axis of differentiation between the evolutionary approach, on one hand, and the standard and NIE approaches, on the other. No convincing conclusions about the factor that should rank first in the analysis and the way to merge the two approaches have been reached. There have been several attempts to do so, highlighted in Chapter 9 and in Chapter 20, within the framework of theory on the firm. The other approach is to further explore the complex relationship between intrinsic and extrinsic motivation, and the lessons to be drawn for designing contracts, as explored by Fehr and Gächter (2002, 2006) and Benabou and Tirole (2003). Indeed, as pointed out by Scott (2003), reciprocal fairness could explain endogenous contractual incompleteness and would change, to a large extent, our current understanding of contracts.

All these evolutions call for theoretical development and, before all, systematic application of contractual analysis to all kind of applied issues.

# 3    Institutions and the Institutional Environment

*John Nye*

## 3.1    Introduction

How may we explain the varied performance of the world's many economies? The founders of modern economics – especially Adam Smith – would have had no trouble pointing to the institutions of each nation including issues such as the security of property rights, the presence of stable rules, and the reliability or avarice of the nation's rulers as playing a large role in the explaining these differences. After several decades of paying a great deal of attention – probably overmuch so – to issues like the availability of capital, the presence or absence of natural resources, or access to the latest technology, the economics profession is once again coming round to the classical view of the central importance of institutions in economic performance. But this time around the study of institutions is taking place with the benefit of the tools and insights of modern theory developed in the last century.

It is important to begin with a definitional clarification. Throughout this work we use the word institutions in the way first advocated by Douglas North. Using this definition, institutions are the rules and laws, both formal and informal, and the enforcement mechanisms that make up a given institutional matrix or environment.[1] The word "institution" is often used in everyday parlance to refer to groups like the World Bank or the US Treasury. However, following the usage advocated by North, these are not institutions but rather, organizations. Hence, the World Bank or the Customs Office contribute to the maintenance and functioning of any number of institutions but are not themselves institutions.

In this chapter, the next section will tell the story of how institutions regained prominence in economic writings. Next, one of the major issues concerning new institutional economics (NIE), the role of the government, will be discussed. This will be followed by sections on institutional change, complexity issues arising in understanding institutions, and problems inherent in implementing institutional change. Lastly, a conclusion for this chapter will be offered.

## 3.2    The revival of institutional economics

The role of institutions in economics has a long and distinguished pedigree going back to writings that even preceded the work of the first modern economist, Adam Smith. Despite this early interest, almost all economic work focussed on the role of capital, labor, and technology in explaining economic growth. The revival of attention to institutions in late-twentieth century economics and development literature derives from the failure of the technologically centered aid programs which were the norm in the decades after World War II, and to the renewed interest in property rights, law and economics, and the historical, institutional foundations of the modern market economy.[2]

The new institutional approach to economic history and development owes much to the advocacy and research of Douglas North. At the very end of the 1960s, when North first began working on this topic, it was commonplace in discussions of economic development and growth to downplay the role of institutions and to focus on the twin problems of capital accumulation and technology transfer. Although the pioneering scholars in the theory of economic growth, including Simon Kuznets and Robert Solow, were quite aware of the significance of institutions in differentiating country performance the models that were then in vogue and the particular conceptions of development commonplace in the 1960s tended to discount their role in policy matters. This was partly because the formal models of economic growth that had been developed had no place for institutions and only the most rudimentary accommodation for technology.[3] Also, the shared ideology among many thinkers, politicians, and the general public was that what primarily separated the richest from the poorest nations was indeed access to capital and good technology.

Furthermore, belief in some form of planning – whether the rigid planning of overt communist and socialist governments, or the milder form of planning typical of mixed economies taking advantage of the macro-economics of a Keynesian–neoclassical synthesis – led to policy makers and academics seeing the economy as a machine rather than as a living, organic entity. To a first-order approximation, most of the vast sums of money sent in aid from the developed to the underdeveloped nations during this time, and indeed well into the end of the century, focussed on transferring capital, technical training, or promoting enhanced education.

At the same time, economic history was – thanks to the work of scholars such as W. W. Rostow and Alexander Gerschenkron – preoccupied with trying to understand the Industrial Revolution in eighteenth-century

Great Britain and its eventual transfer to the European continent. As with the development literature the emphasis here conformed to the theorists' focus on capital and technology. Unsurprisingly, writing about industrialization tended to reflect this preoccupation with the arrival of a "wave of gadgets" (as T. S. Ashton once jokingly referred to it).

But, by the end of the 1960s, doubts had begun to creep into this picture. Work in the emerging new economic history suggested that the simplified accounts of a take-off (Rostow) or "great spurt" (Gerschenkron) were not good templates for understanding the rise of the West. The narrow focus on technology and capital left much still to be explained.

North basically took the new economic history approach to its logical end with a wholesale abandonment of the logic of capital and technology transfer. He argued that technology could not be seen as the cause of growth or the Industrial Revolution. Rather, accelerated technical change was itself merely a symptom of an underlying, fundamental transformation of society that produced both economic growth and technological innovation. It was the institutions of capitalism, or more generally growth-enhancing aspects of Western institutions, that accounted, in the long term, for economic success; however much technical transfer or problems of capital accumulation may have been relevant for short-term variations in economic performance or for the relative advancement or retardation of any individual nations (North and Thomas 1973).

This point of view was extremely controversial at first. Yet over time, this idea, which accompanied a parallel decline in the belief in favor of naïve Keynesianism and all forms of socialist planning, seemed well-attuned to the late-twentieth century's revival of interest in the virtues of the market.

The market, it turns out, was a complex phenomenon, poorly understood and difficult to develop in societies – such as the new Russia after 1991 – which sought to adapt it. As was increasingly clear, the great differences in prosperity between the rich and poor came from neither natural resources nor access to capital. Rather, the ability to harness political and social institutions to a flexible system that was supportive of growth seemed key to closing the gaps between the richest and poorest nations. The differences in market openness between the USA and Sweden or Japan, for example, were nothing compared to the economic gaps that had emerged between all these countries and the failed states of sub-Saharan Africa or inflation-ridden South America.

It is important to recognize that these transformations in our views of economic growth were paralleled by a similar evolution of views in the literature on economic development. As discussed in Easterly's *The Elusive Quest for Growth* (2001), development economists started out with institution-free explanations that focussed on problems of: (1) poor geography and lack of resources; (2) insufficient capital; (3) lack of technology; (4) insufficient education; or (5) bad macro-economic policies. Yet, one by one, each of these explanations was found to be severely lacking. In many cases, these explanations even seemed almost irrelevant to the presence or absence of successful economic growth. As with economic historians, the record of growth performance around the world, and the verdict of well-specified empirical studies, was that none of the standard arguments could explain why South Korea or Taiwan had grown rich and prosperous while India and Argentina had stagnated. Nor could most explanations of poor Chinese performance under Mao come to grips with the startling Chinese success under Deng Xiao Ping and his successors. At the end we were back to the role of politics, law, and history.

### 3.3    The role of government in new institutional economics

Despite the realization of the importance of institutions, in focussing on the political and institutional prerequisites of economic progress, the profession was faced by a harder task: the explanation of the origins of good or bad institutions. This is difficult for the economist; partly because it ultimately demands an interdisciplinary perspective drawing on political science, law, demography, anthropology, history, even cognitive science. Further, economics itself, especially of the dominant neoclassical variety (especially macro-), also was further limited by its usual taking of the market or the institutional environment as a given. It seems that economists were rediscovering Hobbes at the same time as they were returning to the core wisdom of Adam Smith.[4]

In looking at this problem, North, in cooperation with Barry Weingast, identified the central dilemma confronting us in our study of the institutions of development. Specifically, economics functions in the realm of voluntary transactions, but those transactions generally need to take place in a market in which (following Ronald Coase 1960) property rights are clear and well-defined, and contracts may be enforced. Usually, the existence of this market requires a third party or outside force with the power to enforce the law. This leads naturally to a contradiction. Any group or organization or individual with the power to make laws and guarantee the functioning of market institutions is also powerful enough to abuse those who need such protection. Hence, the great temptation for all rulers and governments throughout history has been, "Do I (We) do better by encouraging enhanced economic performance or by simply preying on those who produce, and redistributing the surplus to ourselves and our friends?" In short, this is the problem of "Take or Make". As is clear from the economic history of the world, taking has been at least as common as making, even when it was clear that encouraging further economic growth would leave more for everybody.

In their seminal article, North and Weingast (1989) sought to explain the success of England in the late-seventeenth and early-eighteenth century in terms of the creation of institutions which limited the King's prerogatives by establishing a state in which the powers of the King and Parliament were held in check by each other. Thus, property rights could more credibly be guaranteed, and, as a result, investment could be encouraged. More specifically, North and Weingast (1989) argue that institutional checks on the King's power to tax and to arbitrarily renege on the debts that he incurred actually made it easier for the Crown to borrow. By increasing the number of interested parties deciding on whether or not to renege on loans made by members of Parliament the capacity of the King to default was checked considerably, since now he had to first convince Parliament that this was the best plan of action.

As a result of this new-found ability to raise revenue through taxation and borrowing England rose to dominant status in Europe. England was able to acquire revenue, for use in war, at rates that were lower than those of its main rival, France. It then was able to launch successful wars against France, furthering England's rise in military and naval importance. In so doing, the British also provided the prerequisites for the Industrial Revolution that was to come, all the while playing a role in creating liberal institutions by enhancing the role of voice and representation in the conduct of government.

Alternative explanations of British success during the Industrial Revolution tend to merely identify the most proximate causes of growth – for example, the rise of a new technology in a specific industry – or, in the worst cases, point to explanations that are virtual tautologies (see Mokyr 1977 for the problems with many standard explanations). Though institutional explanations lead to even more secondary questions there does not seem to be a recourse to talking about the rise of Western Europe from the eighteenth century without considering how institutions operated in differentiating the growth paths of even fairly similar nations such as France and Britain which, nonetheless, did not share equivalent paths to material success.

North's contribution to understanding the checks on governments did not cease here though. His most recent work, *Understanding the*

*Process of Institutional Change* (North 2005), provides a more dynamic system of checks on a government. In particular, North argues that three underlying sources of bargaining strengths determine whether or not a government will choose confiscation. First, the potential gains to confiscation by the government must be considered. For, specifically, the lower these potential gains, the less likely a government will confiscate property. Second, the greater ability of other potential governments to gain power increases the potential loss to a government by confiscation. To explain, if groups within the country possess enough power to pose a threat to the current government confiscation may cause popular support to these potential revolutionaries and, ultimately, cause the government to lose control altogether. Third, the economic structure that determines the yield of taxes also acts as a potential determinant of governmental behavior. If the system of taxation requires good faith on the part of taxpayers and yields high levels of revenue a government will be less willing to confiscate owing to the loss of trust by taxpayers.

Applied to the case of seventeenth-century England, this new approach to identifying constraints strengthens the argument first presented by North and Weingast in 1989. In particular, at the time of the Glorious Revolution an improved economic structure for taxation and borrowing was implemented by Parliament in order to guarantee to the King enough finances to successfully wage war against the French. The institutional developments of most importance were the creation of special taxes by Parliament used specifically to fund specific wars, and the creation of the Bank of England, the organization to collect funds voluntarily for loans made to the King. Since these institutions were controlled by the Parliament any form of confiscation or reneging by the King may have led to the removal of the King's privilege to or, at least, a diminished ability to draw upon these for funding. As a result the King would be less willing to confiscate owing to the fear of significantly reducing future wartime funding.

## 3.4    The dynamics of institutions

One of the most serious difficulties in dealing with institutions is the problem of endogeneity or exogeneity. The inescapable fact is that institutions affect the economy and are themselves shaped by the behavior of the actors in the economy. The usual attitude of scholars in NIE is to treat institutions as exogenous to most people's behavior in the short term, while being almost completely endogenous in the long term. In between, the trade-offs between institutions as constraints and framing rules versus treating institutions as equilibria of games depends to a great extent on the specifics of any given situation, in particular the costs of creating new institutions or changing existing ones and the relevant capacities of the actors to instigate such changes. Thus, equally effective institutions in the short term will, once established, have longer-term implications for the working of the economy. Hence, a great deal of attention is beginning to be paid to the question of which institutions prove more adaptable in the long term.

Avner Greif (1989) has brought this idea to the forefront in his work on eleventh-century Maghribi trade and on twelfth-century Genoese commerce. Greif points out that the Maghribi system of collective constraints on behavior worked well to permit an efficient, large-scale trading network through a combination of overall reputation and collective responses to cheating and opportunism. Further, because the small community of Maghribi traders had a system of only working with traders for whom a personal relationship existed reputation mechanisms were quite capable of providing checks on the desire of each party to renege on an agreed deal.

In contrast, the more individualistic Italians had to rely on third parties to settle disputes, and they made extensive use of costly instruments such as written contracts. Genoese trade, in contrast to Maghribi trade, occurred between merchants belonging to separate towns, religions, cultures, and, especially, local laws. As a result, formal rules and methods for enforcing contracts had to be used in order for all parties involved in the trade to respect and recognize the property rights of the other members involved. Despite these complex necessities for trade, the instruments had the advantage, once discovered, of permitting the Genoese to expand the number and types of people engaged in trade and contracting.

The more personalized and collective network of the Maghreb made for a high degree of security and reliability, but it was not well-suited to adaptation to dynamic changes in the world economy brought on by technology, demographic expansion, and expanding trade. Relying on personal relationships proved unsustainable given the growth in trade, causing the Maghribi system to become less and less effective. On the other hand, impersonal arrangements, as practiced by the Italians, have the virtue of being more easily extended to people who do not have the same beliefs and attitudes of the original traders. In all, despite the early advantages of the Maghribi system, the Genoese system proved to be more efficient, and, ultimately, more successful over time owing to its ability to cope with changes in demographics, technology, and trade.

## 3.5    The complexity of institutions

Greif's work leads into another dilemma faced by NIE, namely the intertwining of informal and formal rules. To explain, this work does not mean that trust and reputation are unimportant; rather, they are complemented by these anonymous institutions of exchange. It has been common to speak of anonymous exchange replacing personalized exchange in the course of economic development. Phrased differently, it is viewed that primitive exchange ostensibly relies on trade between parties that are tied together by social, ethnic, and familial ties, whereas modern commerce is an activity between complete strangers. But, in our view, this is a misunderstanding. Personalized exchange remains and always will be important. Rather, the existence of improved institutions such as courts, written law and contracts, and the development of improved mediating organizations permit us to economize on our personal exchange and to save our personal attention for those matters of higher significance such as friendship, marriage, or even high-level business transactions. We have only a finite amount of time and attention to devote to personalized transactions, so the modern marketplace makes it possible to economize on such exchanges.

Put another way, without a well-developed economy and having no external institutions to aid him primitive man had to devote an enormous amount of effort to verify the reliability of the most basic transactions. Obtaining food, shelter, and clothing, and keeping his possessions safe from predation were daily preoccupations. Without more complex social and economic arrangements man must rely on ties of family or friendship to assure the reliability of the most basic exchanges. In contrast, the consumer in a modern economy may engage in buying and selling extremely complicated items from perfect strangers. Food and medicines, clothing and transportation can all be more easily obtained because the network of trust and reputation built into the mix of high-reputation market brands and legal enforcement we use today allow us to minimize our personal involvement in an enormous range of transactions. Yet, it is likely that we engage in almost as many personalized exchanges as our ancestors, only we are more selective now. Even so there is still a great deal of room for equally effective variation in terms of choosing what mix of formal and informal institutions will support economic growth.

The question of what activities will be ruled by anonymous exchanges and the formal laws of contract versus those which will be shaped by social rules and informal norms is an important factor in shaping which institutions are needed and which are liable to play a large role in the economy. It is likely that countries with highly homogeneous populations with limited racial, ethnic, and social variation, can economize on many of the transactions costs of formal contract and enforcement because of their shared heritage, the greater presence of common knowledge, and the ability to rely on social enforcement in lieu of formal constraints on opportunistic behavior. Such countries can have very well-developed anonymous institutions of exchange, but it is likely that, at the margin, the importance of formal intermediaries such as lawyers will be less noticeable than for countries with more heterogeneous populations.

On the other hand, following the logic of the Maghribi versus Genoese case, homogenous societies will have to struggle to adapt to newer groups and may be less capable of dealing with rapid social change or a fast-changing market environment. The more heterogeneous society will be able to specialize more easily in a variety of activities while carrying a greater burden of laws and regulations and having to adjudicate minor conflicts between different groups, while always running the risk of more severe group conflict which could lead to outright warfare or to the "Balkanization" of the nation.

Just as important, the solutions to both sets of difficulties in homogeneous and heterogeneous societies may also run the risk of establishing serious rent-seeking opportunities, and the resulting political compromises which emerge could lead to serious impediments to innovative and productive activity. After all, no country has ever been completely devoid of any type of corruption; it has occurred in grand scales in seemingly the most homogenous countries, such as England, and the most heterogeneous, such as India. This concern, though, is just one of the problems confronted by those attempting to implement improvements to existing institutions.

## 3.6    Implementing institutional reform

Even in the cases where we clearly believe that an existing set of institutions is inefficient, and where policy makers have identified a clear set of market institutions they would like to implement, the actual policy problem is bedeviled by the need to find a good method of transition from one regime to the other. The social sciences have, at best, only the most rudimentary understanding of the dynamics of institutional change and, given the limits of a human science, are unlikely to ever produce a truly detailed understanding of the dynamic processes which underlie human activity, even restricting ourselves to the economy. For example, in light of the last section, there is often a great divergence between the formal, legal rules which govern a nation's institutional environment and the de facto mix of formal enforcement and informal norms which often determine how any given set of laws will function in practice.

Some insight may be had by seeing what neoclassical theory has to say about the direct incentive effects of the laws as they are formulated and the actual incentives in place for the administration, bureaucrats, and the citizenry to comply with said rules. Here, NIE focusses on the transactions cost surrounding exchange, for which the extent to which participants in the economy share a common understanding of exactly what goods and services are being offered, and how ignorance or mis-understanding is managed, are especially critical. Work combining the insights from game theory and modern political economy takes its cue from the ideas of Mancur Olson, whose book, *The Logic of Collective Action* (1965), clarified one of the most important reasons for good institutional environments.

Although most people benefit from enhanced cooperation with each other, many situations are routinely encountered where the incentives facing a narrowly self-interested individual are at odds with the well-being of a group. For example, although cooperation on a joint com-munity project, such as digging a ditch, may jointly benefit everyone, the awareness that the shirking on the part of a single individual will have little effect on the final success of the project may cause so many to hold back that the project may be more difficult to complete or, in an extreme case, may not even get off the ground. Primitive societies and people living in small, fairly homogeneous communities can often deal with these problems through moral persuasion and community vigilance. But as the group grows larger, the need for formal rules to encourage cooperation and discourage opportunistic behavior leads to structures that grant enforcement authority to some persons or groups. As we have already discussed in an earlier section on credible commitment such enforcement power leads to the potential for abuse or rent-seeking, or both.

A more significant problem for the study of institutional change is to take into account the degree to which people are poorly informed about the overall institutions themselves and what beliefs they hold about the rules and the effects of any proposed changes. Given the extremely weak feedback between any given change in the rules and its eventual effects on the whole community, uninformed and even irrational beliefs may interfere significantly with the process of reforming an economy. Whereas it is quite clear that jumping in the river is likely to get us wet, it is not so clear that a given change in taxes or in regulation will result in outcomes that are predictable or desirable. If it is also difficult to assign responsibility for any specific effects of an institutional change, it is difficult to hold public officials accountable for their mistakes. Consequently, bad institutional environments might persist or even flourish in the short run, while good ones may not survive for long enough to have observable effects.

The remedy to these problems of implementation must then, have to encompass work which cannot be done exclusively within the realm of economics. However, entering the study of beliefs and ideology requires an even more eclectic mix of ideas and research derived from work in cognitive science, psychology, sociology, and anthropology, as well economics, political science, and law. Though there is much hope that such work will come to inform future discussions of institutional change, it is still an open question whether the larger scholarly agenda that encompasses virtually the whole of the social sciences will eventually provide us with concrete guidelines that will improve our policy recommendations. It is even more difficult to see whether policy makers will be able to assimilate such work and willingly choose to reform economies whose defects many bureaucrats currently benefit from.

### 3.7    Further work in new institutional economics

Because of the inherent complications in both studying and defining the limits of institutional analysis, Greif (2004), in his manuscript "Institutions: Theory and History," proposes a different definition of institutions than simply rules and enforcement mechanisms. For him, enforcement mechanisms are not primitives. He proposes a broader, alternative definition encompassing North's definition as well as those commonly in use in sociology and political science. Central to his definition is the concept of institutional elements, which are man-made non-physical factors exogenous to each individual whose behavior they influence. These include shared beliefs, internalized norms, shared cognitive systems, and socially articulated and distributed rules. An institution is then defined as a system of institutional elements which conjointly generate a regularity of behavior by enabling, guiding, and motivating it.

This approach leads to a context-specific analysis of institutions. Every institution must be seen as having developed within a framework of beliefs, norms, and shared mental models that may be unique for that given institution. This is essential because multiple equilibria are possible when institutions are formed in a given set of circumstances. Examining the contextual detail helps to clarify why particular institutions emerged in a specific setting and how they may be sustained. For example, attempting to understand the reasons why ancient Athens had democratically elected positions in all areas except military and sanitation requires, at least, an understanding of the culture, foreign relations, and political motivations within ancient Greece.

Three aspects of this approach enable studying institutional dynamics as a historical process. First is the explicit elaboration of how institutions generate the behavior that reproduces them (using primarily game theory) to reveal the sources of institutional path-dependence. Second, recognizing that institutions have unexpected, partially observed, and poorly understood implications reveals the sources of their endogenous change. Finally, recognizing that institutions are systems of institutional elements exposes why and how history plays a crucial role in the evolution of institutions. Unfortunately, all this suggests how far we are from a definitive understanding of the role of the institutional environment in an economy's performance, and how much farther we are from a simple "cookbook" approach to policy questions.

Those seeking coherence in the new approaches to institutional questions that are often grouped under the heading of NIE are quick to note the contradictions between the North–Weingast-style views of institutions and the more equilibrium-oriented ideas of Greif or, similarly, Masahiko Aoki. Some have tried to deal with this through various classification schemes.

Oliver Williamson – perhaps the earliest proponent of the term "new institutional economics" – initially referred to institutionalism more narrowly applying to issues of hierarchy in organization, more specifically the business firm. The rise of an industrial organization literature on transactions costs and their analysis in the firm would seem to be quite different from the broader, more societal-level analysis promoted by North, and those working in related areas of political economy such as Mancur Olson or Elinor Ostrom. Williamson has sought to deal with the expanded view of institutionalism which has become commonplace by treating the various strands of the literature as dealing with different time frames. In his schema, institutions are ranked in terms of a hierarchy from those that are endogenous in the short term, such as firm organization, to medium-term variables, such as the institutions of law and other formal rules and regulations, and to those characteristics of culture, belief, or ideology which require a much longer time frame to adjust and which are themselves often subject to grand forces such as long-term demographic trends or shifts in the global technological frontier (Williamson 2000).

More recently, a related schematization has been suggested by Gérard Roland (2004) which focusses more precisely on different scales of social change. In this analysis, the critical element is the speed of institutional change. For Roland, beliefs, norms, and culture are all characterized as "slow-moving" institutions, since the relevant measure of time for change is centuries. Likewise, political and legal institutions are considered "fast-moving," since much less time is needed for these institutions to change.

Roland uses this distinction to explain North's views on why institutional changes work so poorly in many countries because the formal changes are so poorly matched to the underlying informal habits, beliefs, and norms of the people. Emplacing new formal rules occurs quickly, but in order for informal rules to change to match the incentive systems created by these emplaced formal rules a considerably longer period of time must pass. Typically, this amount of time is not allowed to pass, since the poor immediate performance of the formal rule change ushers in a new regimen and a new set of emplaced formal rules. This conforms to the many observations we have of the difficulty of social and economic reform, most recently seen in the varying degrees of success enjoyed by the nations that made up the former Soviet or East European bloc.

However attractive this approach seems, there is a counter view that stems from doubts about the extent to which beliefs and culture always remain exogenous to political and rule changes, and, hence, doubts as to which institutions are in fact the "slow-moving" ones. For example, we have often seen situations in which groups of people and even nations have changed their religious beliefs – and not just superficially – for the benefit of improved trade and the formal institutions that are attached to membership in a religious group. In some situations, it may be that the classifications formulated by Roland may not apply or, at worst, are even reversed.

Jean Ensminger, in her book *Making a Market* (1992), argues that this, indeed, may be the case. Specifically, Ensminger has noted how pastoralists in West Africa converted to Islam in earlier centuries partly as a means of benefiting from the commercial and legal institutions of the Islamic cultures. More exactly, for the case of commercial activity, Muslim law dictates that Muslims can only trade with Muslims, a rule that was typically applied in this period. Coastal West Africans then, had to convert in order to trade with these Muslim merchants from the Arabian Peninsula. Conversely, legal and property rights reforms in the twentieth century have been especially difficult and contentious. In these cases, beliefs – even those as seemingly fundamental to the individual as religion – seem to have been more malleable than political institutions.

## 3.8   Conclusion

Whilst all this work has begun to revitalize economics and indeed, much of the social sciences the implications for policy are less encouraging. If the relationship between formal and informal institutions is critical to economic performance, if that relationship is poorly understood, and, worst of all, if our basic ability to alter slow-moving institutions is limited, we may not be capable of providing the policy advice that statesmen and bureaucrats regularly seek. This suggests a pessimistic view of development that provides less hope than the promises of earthly nirvana from the most extreme proponents of early socialism, or less ambitiously, even the smoothly shifting macro-economic machine held out by naïve proponents of Keynesian fine-tuning in the 1960s. However, abandoning these extreme scenarios does not leave us with nothing to do. We can strive to eliminate the most blatantly harmful and counterproductive prescriptions from our policy repertoire. Moreover, proponents of the newer approaches hold out hope that better research may help to rank reasonable alternatives in a sensible hierarchy of priorities. In particular, political economy can help us to identify which sorts of reforms are liable to encounter the highest degrees of resistance and which provide insufficient incentives for the maintenance and extension of reform in the longer term.

If it is difficult to prescribe social and economic cures as easily as a physician prescribes pills for a headache or flu, we can at least emulate those doctors who live by the dictum "First, do no harm."

# 4    Human Nature and Institutional Analysis

*Benito Arruñada*

## 4.1    Introduction

The human mind was mainly designed in a competitive process of natural genetic selection, which is characterized by random genetic mutation – producing new traits, and cumulative selection of those traits that allow individuals who carry them to survive and reproduce more. Natural selection thus acts as a chief design engineer even if other forces, such as sexual selection, path dependency, and simple noise, are also present. We see well now only because a long series of mutations triggered redesigns which permitted our ancestors' sight to improve. The same happens with our mental processes, even those considered more rational, involved in making decisions and interacting socially.

Modern cognition sciences perform a sort of "reverse engineering" of these mental processes. Their findings may trigger a scientific revolution of Copernican proportions in the social sciences and, in any case, require a full reconsideration of standard assumptions about human behavior, related to both rationality and cooperation.

This chapter reviews some of these findings and examines some of their consequences for the analysis of institutions and organizations. We start by exploring the consequences of our specialization in producing knowledge, which are twofold: it has ensured our success in dominating the environment but has also changed the environment very fast and radically. This change occurred so fast that it did not allow time for natural selection to adapt our biology, causing us to be maladapted in important dimensions. To adapt we therefore need the artifacts we call institutions. A new view of institutions thus emerges which sees their function as that of filling the gap between our biology, which is still adapted to our ancestral environment as hunter-gatherers, and the demands of our relatively new environment.

The development of institutions therefore facilitates cooperative transactions which seem to rely less on our instinctual psychology and more on artificially designed structures of enforcement. These artificial systems rely on instincts, however, as they recruit them for performing new functions within the institutional arrangement.

Consequently, cooperation is not only grounded on a calculation of costs and benefits, as it is sometimes assumed in utility-maximizing models of human behavior. Automatic mechanisms, evolved in ancestral environments, play essential roles, and their functioning has to be understood for wisely structuring our artificial enforcement systems (including those of firms), as well as for using our calculative rationality successfully when we interact with other individuals.

This emphasis on instincts ties in with classic and institutional economics. For instance, Adam Smith saw humans as essentially instinctive (Coase 1976) and he correctly understood that instincts (i.e. his "sentiments") are adaptive and, under normal circumstances, make no mistake. This is why affairs of survival importance, such as self-preservation and reproduction, are not "entrusted to the slow and uncertain determinations of our reason" but to "original and immediate instincts" (Smith 1759, II, iii). Instinctive Darwinian psychology was also important for institutional analysts such as Veblen (Hodgson 2004a, 2004b), because they saw habits as the basis of human behavior, and habits are close to current views of the mind, based on modules and heuristics.

This chapter will proceed in four stages. First, it will examine how the specialization of human beings in cognition leads to a modular design of the human mind and how it grants both biologic success and maladaptation. Next, it will explore the consequences of this view, in terms of modular instincts and environmental maladaptation, for the two key behavioral assumptions, those of rationality and cooperation. Then it will explain how institutions allow us to fill the gap in our innate maladaptation, a job for which institutions often recruit instincts originally designed for other purposes. A final section concludes.

## 4.2    Consequences of our cognitive specialization

### 4.2.1    *Human beings are specialists in the cognitive niche*

We are not very good at flying but we do build planes that fly faster than any animal. Already in ancestral times we were the best predators; thanks to our hunting technologies, both physical and social, we were able to hunt animals that were too big to be hunted by any other predator. We achieved it all by becoming knowledge specialists, by entering the "cognitive niche" (Tooby and De Vore 1987), and developing increasingly sophisticated tools, with which we have radically changed our environment.

This specialization in cognition and technology constrains our design but also explains our dominant position in mature performance. Our design is constrained to have certain physiological and social constraints that make brain development possible, and, most importantly, to have a modular mind instead of a general processing mind. Cognitive specialization also brought about a substantial comparative advantage over our animal prey and competitor animals, with the side consequence that we also became maladapted to the rapid changes we cause in our own environment.

### 4.2.2   Modular design

First, an intelligent mind has to be produced and has to function economically, because brains are very costly to operate: our brain weighs only 2% of our total body weight but it spends around 20% of our energy. To be efficient cognitive specialization requires a certain degree of modularity in the internal workings of our mind, as any other complex system (Simon, 1962). Otherwise, a general-purpose mind would have to use the same methods and tools for different problems which present different information structures. In contrast, specialized modules make it possible to optimize the use of the information available in the environment. With this specialization, the mind contains mechanisms that are, in a sense, "better than rational" because they minimize the use of information, speed up decisions, and produce sophisticated solutions (Cosmides and Tooby 1994). We will see below that instincts provide speedy optimal solutions without conscious rational thinking and emotions even achieve optimal strategic self-commitment by suspending rationality.

### 4.2.3   Success – and maladaptation

Second, intelligence confers on human beings a huge comparative advantage over most other animals because we are able to develop new technologies, including weapons and hunting techniques, faster than our prey and competitors can evolve defenses against them, given that they develop them only by natural selection. We therefore become dominant and much of our prey tends to go extinct, as shown by the now abundant record that we exterminated big animals each time we first arrived on a continent.

However, our cognitive specialization has the paradoxical consequence that we outrun not only our prey but also ourselves. In the last ten thousand years (an instant for natural selection) we have also changed our own environment far faster than our own genetics could adapt. Natural selection is powerful but slow, requiring thousands of generations. The human brain thus evolved under the selective pressures faced by our ancestors in the ancestral "environment of evolutionary adaptedness" of the Pleistocene period (1.8 million to ten thousand years ago), the only interval long enough to allow significant genetic adaptation.

Our mind is therefore designed to cope with the problems relevant for survival and reproduction at that remote time – those of habitat selection, foraging, social exchange, competition from others, contagion avoidance, and sexual rivalry. Our mental hardware is fine-tuned to live in small nomadic tribes, hunting and gathering fruits, in a world with few technologies – just fire as well as stone and wood tools, and little interaction and trade outside the group.

In a manner consistent with our cognitive specialization, the solution for this maladaptation has also been technological: we use institutional "technologies" to improve our fitness. The function of institutions is therefore to enhance our capacity to reason and interact, allowing us to overcome our own evolutionary constraints, mainly through self- and social control.

## 4.3    Rationality

When engineers started to design mechanical robots they soon realized that seemingly simple tasks, such as recognizing objects, are instead tremendously complex and achievements in such tasks have been slow. Computers are now very good at using mathematical and logical rules, and one of them even beats the world chess champion. At the same time, experimental psychologists have shown that human beings err systematically in simple logical problems and poorly assess the probability of individual events. Why is our mind so powerful and, at the same time, so limited? Why do bumblebees perform better than most humans at probabilistic induction? The answer is simple. Our mind is *powerful but economical* in the use of resources. It spends resources in solving problems which were relevant for survival in our evolutionary past, but it does not care about those that were irrelevant.

Make no mistake. The human mind is very *powerful* indeed. It routinely, even effortlessly, manages to solve the most difficult problems: those without solution, such as identifying the factors in a product – so-called "ill-posed" problems. It is so powerful that we are *better than rational* on evolutionary recurrent tasks, such as recognizing objects, acquiring grammar, or comprehending speech. Robot designers soon realized how difficult it was to endow their creatures with the crudest rudiments of sight or walking. After several decades of research even purpose-designed robots are only able to walk clumsily, or to identify only the set of forms that they have been programmed to "see."

But our mind is also *economical*, meaning that it uses only those resources required to succeed in a given environment. Our mind does not produce "scientific" solutions, with general validity, but solutions which are good enough to master the local environment. Our rationality is bounded not only because it is subject to constraints, but because it is developed and adapted to certain environments: it is *ecological*, meaning that it is adapted, first, to our common ancestral environment of evolutionary adaptation, and, second, to our learning environment, probably with much more malleable consequences.[1]

Many observed decisional "failures" in the artificial environments of experimental psychology, and economics may therefore be a consequence of its artificiality, its absence in the natural environment. For example, humans "fail" when applying probability theory. For instance, we fall prey to the "gambler's fallacy," feeling that, for example, lottery numbers with all their digits repeated (e.g. 33333) have a lower probability of winning than numbers with variable digits (53487). But it might well be the case that our mind is adapted to environments in which very few events are independent and most variables are correlated. In nature, very few successes are independent, and it is unclear how many there are in the current world, perhaps with the exception of some casinos and stockmarkets. Independence is often open to question. After an aircraft crash most people are more afraid to fly. That would not make sense if aircraft crashes were independent events, but are they really independent?

Similarly, our mind seems to have developed an ability to process probabilities in terms of relative frequencies in the long term, not as numbers expressing confidence in a single event. This explains that, when probabilities are presented as frequencies ("one out of one hundred is sick") instead of single events ("probability that John is sick"), people are much more accurate. This "frequentionist" view of the mind somehow dilutes the claims about several alleged biases and fallacies, such as overconfidence bias, conjunction fallacy, and base-rate neglect.[2]

### 4.3.1 Instinctive rationality

During the last few centuries we have become accustomed to separate reason and emotions, also considering emotions as inferior to reason. This

Cartesian separation of emotions and reason is seriously flawed, however. Our mind relies on instinctive mechanisms, including emotions, to solve the most relevant problems, those on whose correct solution hinged our survival and reproduction. Furthermore, emotions are a necessary ingredient of rationality: ill people who have lost part of their frontal lobe are "perfectly rational" but their loss of emotions seems to damage their decision-making capacities. They are often incapable of deciding and, instead, keep evaluating advantages and disadvantages without ever reaching a conclusion (Damasio 1994).

The adaptive consequences of emotions are obvious in simple ones, such as hunger, which moves us to search for food, and the pleasure of eating, which leads us to accumulate reserves in our bodies. Furthermore, emotions are often adaptive even when they seem to harm the individual, and tend, therefore, to be considered "irrational." For example, having a hot temper that leads us to react violently to even minor offenses may have a deterrent effect which helps such person in a lawless context.

More complex emotions also have adaptive value. For instance, happiness mobilizes resources to fit in our environment and to reproduce. The paradoxes of happiness may be explained from this perspective. First, we feel happy when we observe that our *relative* position is good. This seems silly but it is not because relative positions inform us about which level of achievement we should be aiming for. Second, in determining the degree of happiness we give greater importance to changes than to levels of achievement. This emphasis on changes renews our motivation to strive in the search for happiness and, therefore, environmental fitness – both people who win a lottery or whom suffer misfortune adapt fast to their new situation. Third, we feel more negative than positive emotions and we tend to grant greater weight to losses than to gains. This asymmetric feeling may also be adaptive because the consequences of losses and gains are intrinsically asymmetric, given that losses threaten survival while gains do not increase reproductive success in an equivalent proportion. There are, in a sense, diminishing returns to wealth in generating fitness.

### 4.3.2    Ecological rationality: the maladaptation of our instincts

There are many examples of emotions that no longer seem well-adapted, however. For instance, our feeding emotions were probably useful in our ancestral set-up, characterized by unreliable food supply, but are badly adapted for wealthy societies. Consequently, we now need to spend resources and develop self-controlling mechanisms to avoid dying earlier from overeating. Without self-control, we tend to eat too much, especially sugar, fat, and salt. A taste for sweetness motivated our ancestors to eat fruits, but it became maladapted when we recently developed sugar and candy, transforming the taste for sweetness into a damaging sweet tooth.

Let us examine two prominent examples of emotional maladaptation with vast economic consequences: risk aversion and weakness of will.

### 4.3.3   Risk aversion

As any other essential trait of human beings, risk aversion probably has an innate component as shown by a certain asymmetry of gains and losses and perhaps even excessive risk aversion.

Evolutionary optimal preferences about risk should be adapted to the ancestral environment in which people were living on the edge of subsistence. Under such dire straits it makes sense to evolve risk-aversion preferences, especially toward losses, and this may be behind some forms of asymmetry which have been observed in experiments. Our current environment is less uncertain and its optimal rate of risk aversion may well be lower. However, natural selection is too slow to catch up with fast environmental change. Therefore, instinctive risk aversion may be leading modern humans to excessive prudence. We are risk-averse to avoid risks that we are programmed to (wrongly) perceive as affecting our survival and reproduction.

### 4.3.4   Weakness of will

Most human beings suffer difficulties identifying what they want and being consistent about it. This may be a natural consequence of at least two factors: conflict between mental modules and maladapted discounting.

The modularity internal to the human mind causes a typical trade-off between specialization gains and transaction costs. Developing specialized mental mechanisms to solve different problems might incur substantial transaction costs that will take the form of discrepancies and conflicts between these specialized modules, as each one optimizes the allocation of scarce resources toward a different goal. In addition, it would be too costly to eliminate these transaction costs, achieving a perfect fit between the aggregation of locally optimal partial solutions reached by different modules and the optimum for the whole. Current knowledge on consciousness is too weak to reach a definite conclusion,[3] but the existence of internal mental conflict is supported by biological evidence on apparently awkward conflicts, as those between cells and organs within a body as well as those between a pregnant mother and the fetus in her womb.

Daily life is also full of instances in which we make inconsistent decisions over time, from the difficulties of following a diet or quitting smoking to the tricks we use to get out of bed in the morning or to study regularly. These weaknesses of will may emerge because of maladaptation to our current environment, which is substantially less risky than our ancestral environment and therefore makes it optimal to postpone gratification whilst we have evolved to emphasize present consumption. Let us see why.

Human beings constantly allocate scarce recourses over time through saving and investment decisions which confront present against future consumption, decisions which are driven by both reason and emotions. Evolution has also developed automatic mechanisms to cope with this allocation problem and to maximize the chances of reproduction. It is also likely that innate traits have evolved for decision-making, a sort of "subjective discount rate" finely tuned to our expected longevity and the level of risk in our environment, and both affecting and embedded in our emotions.[4]

It is likely that such innate discount rate is too high for our current stable environment and long life. Risks were much greater in the ancestral past, because of lesser control on nature and the prevalence of warfare. Therefore, life expectancy was very short and, in accordance with such circumstances, we probably evolved a high subjective discount rate which ceased to be optimal when, quite recently, we achieved a safer environment.

This may explain that we now need artificial technologies of self-control to be able to postpone gratification and better adapt to our environment. For instance, it is clear that much of our educational effort is directed to change children's preferences in order to postpone gratification, inculcating them with a lower discount rate. This cultural lowering of the subjective discount rate is most noticeable when lacking: many children who are raised in broken families and ghettos easily fall prey to drug addiction and all kinds of short-sighted behavior.

## 4.4    Cooperation

Specialization increases productivity but requires cooperation, and is often costly to achieve. Only in the less-interesting cases do cooperation benefits come at no cost to cooperators. Symbiotic interaction is the paradigm of this sort of costless and non-conflictive cooperation. It explains, for example, why some animals live together in amorphous shoals or herds in order to be better protected from predators. When we trade simple commodities in the spot market we are also close to such ideal of mutuality.

The most interesting cases of cooperation, however, are those in which cooperation benefits involve substantial costs for cooperating parties. Their interaction is therefore prone to conflicts of interests, as each cooperator tries to reap the benefits of cooperation without paying the corresponding share of the costs. In such cases cooperation requires enforcement mechanisms to make sure that parties comply.

This enforcement is produced by different means, which rely more or less heavily on innate instincts. The most simple of these instincts are linked to genetic relatedness, which grounds cooperation between relatives. The most complex are those instincts supporting cooperation between genetically unrelated individuals. They play a role even for achieving cooperation between total strangers.

Let us examine some elements of this arsenal of cooperative instincts, how they work, and to what extent they are maladapted.

### 4.4.1 Instinctive cooperation

*4.4.1.1 Genetic relatedness* By helping their children parents promote the survival of their own genes. More precisely, genes driving parents to help their children had a better chance of survival and became dominant. This explains why humans in all cultures are benevolent toward their own descendants and relatives, the more so the greater their genetic relatedness, leading to nepotism, which has been shown to be universal.[5]

The common practice of taking the family as a rhetorical model when we want to emphasize cooperation suggests that genetic relatedness is effective. Managers, for example, claim that "our firm is a family," and believers of many faiths treat co-believers as brothers and sisters, and priests as fathers. In addition, genetic relatedness does not require external enforcement, because parties are pre-programmed to cooperate. On the negative side, however, it motivates rent seeking in the form of cuckoldry and, correspondingly, spending resources to avoid it. Furthermore, nepotism often conflicts with "higher" forms of cooperation, which explains that, despite being universally present, the most developed cultures try to repress it. In addition, cooperation grounded on genetic relatedness is limited to a few individuals, and, as a consequence, it does not allow much specialization.

*4.4.1.2 Emotional commitment*   Genetic relatedness is only the tip of the iceberg of cooperative instincts. Even strangers playing standard non-repetitive cooperation games cooperate more than pure logic predicts, especially when they are allowed to talk with the other players (e.g. Valley *et al.* 2002). It seems that we are able to evaluate, detect, or link emotionally to our mates, and this allows us to overcome part of the cooperative dilemma we are facing.

The implementation of these detection and reciprocity strategies requires a sophisticated mind, which has to be capable of, at least, forming cooperative initial expectations, foreseeing future interactions, distinguishing cheating from cooperative behavior by partners, and keeping a record of past interactions. Human minds are equipped with tools designed for overcoming these problems because they were important in our evolutionary past.

The simplest evidence on the existence of these instincts comes from the physiological consequences of insincerity: blushing often follows lying, and most people cannot avoid showing their feelings. This explains why business travel continues being important in these times of the internet and teleconference, as people have difficulty in evaluating trustworthiness by telephone or e-mail.

These cooperative tools, from the relative simple, such as facial expressions, to the most sophisticated, such as love, are instinctive and not calculative because it would be inefficient to solve most of these cooperation problems by rational calculation, using a general-purpose mental process. Couples rely on love and attachment to safeguard their cooperation. In a similar way, criminals ground their cooperation on their urge to defend their reputation and territory, which leads them to costly and seemingly irrational fights and revenges. Emotions thus provide solutions that are "better than rational" when they commit individuals to a certain behavior which is optimal in the long-term.

Emotional responses often seem irrational and maladaptive, as when we die to save a loved one or to punish an enemy. However, these emotions are part of an efficient commitment strategy. If he is willing to die for her she will be much more willing to take him as a partner. If a criminal is offended he will retaliate against the offender to deter a further offense. The problem of both, lovers and criminals, is to make their disposition credible, as, after the fact, it would pay to change their minds and avoid his giving up life or inflicting a costly punishment. Being emotionally driven provides this credibility. He falls in love so much that when faced with the situation of risking his life he does not calculate costs and benefits. He simply cannot help but throwing himself to save her. The criminal's rage and urge for revenge may play a similar role. For both, their emotional responses will occasionally seem inefficient when they are activated, but this apparent inefficiency is hiding that such instances of activation make it possible achieving greater efficiency in many other cases. In a sense, *ex post* "irrational" emotions are introducing greater *ex ante* rationality.

*4.4.1.3 The tools of reciprocity*   The human brain is also well endowed to distinguish cooperators from cheaters among potential partners and to distinguish cooperative from cheating behavior. Think that, to be fruitful, emotional commitment requires that prospective parties are able to distinguish cooperative individuals from cheats beforehand. Similarly, reciprocity, which is probably the basis of most cooperation in modern societies,[6] also requires that participants be able to distinguish at least compliant from cheating behavior after the transaction. For instance, playing even the simplest reciprocity strategy, such as "tit-for-tat,"[7] requires us to distinguish cooperative from cheating behavior a posteriori.

Both abilities, detecting cheats *ex ante* and *ex post*, are related and have to cope with the possibility of error and mimicry: those who read a cooperative move as cheating when playing tit-for-tat are inviting retaliation on themselves; those who take a cheat for a cooperator will get the worst of their association. Understandably, human beings seem to have developed specialized innate abilities to detect cheating behavior, as well as to signal and distinguish cooperators, which make it possible for human populations to reach stable polymorphic equilibria with different types, for instance cooperators, reciprocators, and cheats.[8] Some biologists have even argued that our brains develop in the "arms race" of deception and detection. In sum, reciprocity is grounded on complex mental tools of detection and commitment. Two of these tools are our ability to detect cheats and our urge to retaliate when we feel that we have been cheated.

*4.4.1.4 Cheating detectors*   The presence of mental resources specialized in detecting cheats has been shown by an adaptation of the Wason psychological tests by Leda Cosmides (1985, 1989; Cosmides and Tooby 1992). The original test measures humans' logic ability by trying to find out how good we are at falsifying hypotheses. For example, a set of four cards with letters on one side and numbers on the other, such as

$$\boxed{D} \quad \boxed{F} \quad \boxed{3} \quad \boxed{7}$$

is shown to a sample of individuals who are then said to test the rule "If a card has a $D$ on one side, it must have a 3 on the other" by turning over as few cards as possible. It results that only between 5% and 15% of people get it right ($D$ and 7 in this example).[9]

However, as shown by Cosmides, the same task becomes much easier if it is expressed in terms of contractual exchange, when finding a false is equivalent to detecting a cheat. Imagine, for example, that you are enforcing the rule "If a person is drinking beer he must be 18 or older" by checking either their drink or their age.

$$\boxed{\text{Beer drinker}} \quad \boxed{\text{Coke drinker}} \quad \boxed{\text{25-year-old}} \quad \boxed{\text{16-year-old}}$$

In this case most people get it right (checking the beer drinker and the 16-year-old) despite the fact that the logical structure of the problem is exactly the same as before. Furthermore, the improvement in solving the puzzle is not caused by the concreteness of the story because most people also fail when it is told in a concrete set-up without a cheating element. For example, falsifying the rule "If a person eats hot chili peppers (HCP) then he must drink cold beer," where SCP represents sweet chili peppers, is not easier than the example with the abstract cards *DF37*.

$$\boxed{\text{Eats HCP}} \quad \boxed{\text{Eats SCP}} \quad \boxed{\text{Drinks beer}} \quad \boxed{\text{Drinks Coke}}$$

In conclusion, it seems that our ability to obtain the right solution is higher in a cheating situation thanks to our use of mental resources which work faster and better than when processing the abstract rules of logic.

*4.4.1.5 Strong reciprocity* Reciprocity seems well suited for repeated interaction, but experiments also show that humans often practice a *strong* form of reciprocity that is well suited to one-shot transactions: we are willing to incur costs to punish cheats even when there is no prospect of further interaction. Interestingly, this propensity to punish ends up achieving greater cooperation when parties anticipate the possibility of costly retaliation.

Both results have been proved in many experiments (Fehr and Gächter 2000). In those with an "ultimatum" game, an individual, $A$, divides €1000 between himself and $B$, but none of them gets a cent if $B$ rejects the offer. Usually, the distributor $A$ divides by half and, interestingly, $B$ rejects offers below 30%, even for stakes of as much as three months' earnings. Given that distributors are less generous when $B$ cannot reject and $A$ acts as a dictator, it seems that the expectation of $B$'s rejection helps in eliciting generous offers.

The psychology of retaliation is also revealed in experiments that test our reactions in "public good" games. In these a number of people contribute money to a common pool expecting to be compensated later with an equal share in a multiple of the pool. In one-stage games people often contribute half their wealth. In multiple stages, however, people start contributing more but their contributions decay with time and approach zero at the end. This fall is not driven by learning but likely by the fact that, in the experiment, the only punishment cooperators can inflict on free riders is by cheating themselves. Remarkably, when the game is redefined so that cooperators can punish free riding, even at a cost and without prospect of future interaction ("strong reciprocity"), they do punish them, and this increases cooperation. Therefore, depending on circumstances, either cheats lead cooperators who are incapable of retaliation to cheat, or cooperators who are willing to incur costly retaliation lead cheats to cooperate.

### 4.4.2    Ecological cooperation: the maladaptation of our instincts

Whatever the power of cooperative instincts their adaptation to the hunter-gatherer environment of our ancestors means that they may be maladapted to the cooperative demands of our current environment. We will now comment on the limits of cooperation grounded on cooperative instincts to examine, next, how these limits constrain the characteristic form of modern cooperation – that taking place through market exchange.

*4.4.2.1 The limits of instinctive cooperation*    Cooperative instincts are powerful but limited to certain forms of cooperation, mainly within small groups of known people. These limits are most prominent for genetic relatedness, which promotes cooperation only among relatives, but other mechanisms have also their particular, even if less strict, limits. Thus, most emotional commitment and cheating detectors require personal interaction. Direct reciprocity is also limited to relatively small groups because it requires us to know others and to keep track of their behavior.

We now live in large groups, with anonymous and more impersonal, indirect, and superficial interactions. In part, we rely on direct reciprocity. For example, brand managers are well aware that consumers have a personal and emotionally loaded relationship with the brands that they consume. We rely more, however, on mechanisms of indirect reciprocity. In the market, for example, we reward a merchant who rewards another merchant, and so on, until, after several more steps, a manufacturer is rewarded for producing a good product. But, not only in the market place. The legal order is grounded on indirect reciprocity by the use of third-party (mainly judicial) enforcement.

*4.4.2.2 The unnaturalness of market exchange*  Most of these mechanisms of indirect reciprocity are institutional. They are designed to promote a certain type of exchange for which we are poorly endowed by nature, for example trade between anonymous parties. The design and difficulties of such institutions are often connected to this intrinsic maladaptation.

This reasoning is especially applicable to markets. Market dealings may suffer all sorts of problems and therefore require substantial institutional support. Given that, in the evolutionary timescale, at least some forms of market exchange are very new they are prone to conflict with our instincts.[10] Several types of conflict appear when considering that these instincts, well adapted to the economic environment of our hunter-gathering ancestors, will tend to bias us against anonymous parties and at least certain forms of trade, insurance and capital, including wealth accumulation and credit.

Our hunter-gatherer grandparents lived in small bands of no more than a hundred or 150 individuals, which limited social interaction and economic specialization as most interactions were with identifiable people who you knew personally. A bias against unknown, anonymous people likely developed as a consequence.[11] In addition, the value added by those making indirect trade possible (intermediaries) and abstract forms of trade (e.g. in services, intangibles, or capital) may be more difficult to grasp. Furthermore, warfare among bands was prevalent, much more so than in modern societies (Keeley 1996), which throws doubt as to how much are we naturally endowed to gain through production and trade or, instead, to expropriate strangers through violence.

With respect to distribution, hunter-gatherers distributed their production following a mixed pattern of sharing and private appropriation. This agreed with economic logic, as they shared resources (big game) as insurance against exogenous risks and privately appropriated those resources (fruits) whose production would have suffered the most from the perverse incentives caused by sharing (Bailey 1992; Cashdan 1980; Kaplan and Hill 1985). This predisposition to compensate exogenous risks now likely poses systematic problems to insurance markets. Given that human societies are predisposed to compensate bad luck *ex post*, it does not make sense to buy insurance *ex ante*. The argument can be applied widely in all sorts of insurance, from farm production to earthquakes or, most importantly, healthcare; and also provides support for welfare states.

Lastly, the ancestral situation with respect to capital and technology also holds important consequences. First, the need of mobility meant that our ancestors only accumulated portable capital. This may have hindered our ability to understand the productivity of capital and the basis for paying interest. Second, technical change was extremely slow, causing a practical absence of economic growth (Kremer 1993). This may have predisposed humans against inequality and even wealth because, in the absence of growth, the economy becomes a zero-sum game and individual inequality and wealth are more likely to proceed from expropriation than from socially productive activities.

## 4.5    The role of institutions

Against this background, institutions act as rationalizing and cooperative mechanisms that enhance our fitness in new environments. They are, however, grounded on our human nature: in a sense they "recruit" and mold our instincts to build more effective mechanisms. We will briefly examine this recruitment process to focus on the role of institutions.

### 4.5.1    Instincts as building blocks of institutions

Natural selection has often recruited body organs to perform functions different from the ones that they were originally designed to do. For example, our limbs were developed starting from the swimming fins of our fish ancestors.

Similarly, institutions recruit instincts as building blocks of their machinery, often to create enforcement mechanisms. A simple case is that of disgust, an emotion that was originally useful to avoid poisoning; an important risk for omnivorous animals. For example, food taboos (e.g. against eating pork) seem to be exploiting the psychology of disgust during the period when children learn their food preferences, probably to make for them more difficult to interact with members of neighboring groups when they are grown up. These cultural taboos show enormous variety but all of them rely on the same instinctive mechanisms. In the case of disgust this mechanism is related to the idea of a polluting substance; what explains that the feeling of disgust is independent of the amount of contact or how much the substance is diluted.

Applications of the recruitment of instincts for higher ends abound. We have seen above how our drive for fairness triggers retaliation *ex post* and elicits cooperation *ex ante*. Many religions rely on fear of a punishing God and some on love of God to motivate good deeds, and feelings of shame and guilt are present in most correctional institutions. In general, different emotions seem to be active in different kinds of enforcement mechanisms.

### 4.5.2  *Institutions as complements of human nature*

Filling the adaptation gap between our ancestral and current environments requires us to manage our instincts on both the rationality and cooperation fronts. In terms of rationality, the paramount issue is one of self-control, postponing gratification, while, in terms of cooperation, it is fundamental to control antisocial behavior. Self-control means greater control of our emotions to improve our individual fitness; for example, instilling a lower subjective discount rate by education. Social control means controlling free riding. In a sense, it can be understood as a way of dealing only with cooperators.

### 4.5.3  *Institutions as enforcement*

Focusing on social control institutions act as enforcement mechanisms, which permit human groups to achieve greater cooperation within the group and makes them more competitive against other groups. Considering which of the exchange's parties is acting as enforcer, three kinds of enforcement may be distinguished, and institutions play an important role in all of them.

Under *first party enforcement* it is the obliged party who acts as enforcer, relying for punishment on emotions like guilt and shame. To function properly it requires previous indoctrination and selection of types before contracting. The role of institutions lies mainly in defining and indoctrinating a moral code, whose violation triggers innate guilt and shame emotions. On occasion, institutions are also involved in helping to enforce the moral code.[12] In addition, this code may have very different properties and, therefore, facilitate different kinds of cooperation. For instance, Protestantism seems to promote values that support anonymous exchange while Catholicism is more hospitable to smaller communities (Arruñada 2004).

*Second party enforcement* is grounded on reciprocity, as the receiving party is the one who sanctions the defaults. Emotions triggering seemingly inefficient *ex post* retaliation act as important enforcement mechanisms, deterring cheating in anticipation of retaliation. A key activity is the correct evaluation of performance to avoid unjustified retaliation. Understandably, evolution has dedicated specialized mental resources to provide us with innate cheating detectors. The role of modern institutions, however, is often to channel or impede private retaliation. For example, criminal law punishes retaliation and rules and courts restrain asymmetric relational contracting.

Within *third party enforcement* other persons act as enforcers. It can be informal and decentralized, as in the functioning of a commercial market or a social network, or highly formal and centralized, as in judicial procedures. Decentralized enforcement relies on different forms of reputational investments and gossip, including at present the activity of the mass media. Centralized enforcement relies on litigation and accumulation of sentences. It suffers the same problem as any other specialization: positive transaction costs, given that third-party enforcers, as any other specialist, may pursue their own interests to the detriment of the underlying transactions.

## 4.6    Where are we humans heading?

Analyses of human behavior that point out the presence of innate traits used to be wrongly read as genetic determinism, as prevalence of nature over nurture. This should not happen with modern cognition science because it surpasses this controversy on the relative importance of nature and nurture on behavior by emphasizing that both, nature and nurture, interact in a way that makes them not separable. They act as complements more than as substitutes. For example, children learn to speak different languages by growing up in different environments, but they learn by using a highly developed innate learning mechanism that includes most structural grammar, which explains why they learn to speak so fast and suddenly, almost exploding to speak between two and three years of age (Baker 2001; Pinker 1994).

The interaction also takes place at the institutional level. The previous analysis of the adaptive role of institutions should help us in avoiding the mistake of genetic determinism because institutions interact with our instinctive traits, both recruiting them and complementing them. Institutions mold the nurturing process and display a full array of enforcement mechanisms that greatly affect our self- and social-control abilities. And institutions are the product of intentional design, relying on instincts, as explained above, but intentionally designed. This might reduce the influence of genetic selection, sitting human beings at the wheel of their destiny.

We now interact technologically with our nature, as we have greater control over it: we achieve the pleasures that nature used to drive our behavior without incurring the costs of such behaviors: contraceptives allow us to have sex without producing children; saccharine satisfies our sweet teeth without obesity; and so on.

More importantly, institutions allow greater human interaction, enhancing specialization and multiplying our productivity. Institutional enforcement not only boosts within-group cooperation by punishing free riders but also enlarges the cooperative group. For instance, the rule of law makes trade with strangers much easier. It also channels between-group conflict to productive ends, by precluding violence, as it happens, for instance, in market competition between firms, ending up with multiple levels of cooperative groups.

Furthermore, the process of institutional change is different from natural selection. It is constrained by the genetic background, but is substantially influenced by learning, decision making, and imitation. Interbreeding is also possible, triggering processes similar to contagion and infection. To some extent, acquired behavioral features may also be transmitted from one generation to the next.[13]

Institutional change is also *intentional,* the consequence of individual decisions.[14] Intentional does not necessarily mean successful, however. We develop technologies only to be surprised by their unintended consequences, and our abilities at institutional design are probably even lower. Therefore, even if we are now at the wheel of our destiny, we are barely learning to drive it.

### Acknowledgements

The author thanks Jean E. Ensminger, Jean-Michel Glachant, Geoffrey M. Hodgson, Paul H. Rubin, Marta Serra, Robert L. Trivers, Xosé H. Vázquez, David Sloan Wilson, and participants at European School of New Institutional Economics (ESNIE), the Ronald Coase Institute, Universidad Pablo de Olavide, Université de Paris I, Université de Paris

X, Universidades de Castilla-León, and the Gruter Institute for Law and Behavioral Research, for their comments; also for financial support the MCYT, an agency of the Spanish government, through grant no. SEJ 2005-03871/ECON, and the European Commission through the Integrated Project C1T3-513420. Usual disclaimers apply.

*Part II*

# Methodology

# 5 The "Case" for Case Studies in New Institutional Economics

*Lee J. Alston*

## 5.1 Introduction[1]

In the economics profession at large the use of case studies is not the norm. Case studies may be frowned upon as simply individual narratives and thus do not fit one of the criteria for good scientific research: generalization – the more general the result the better the theory. This still holds for case studies so the scholar needs to take care when selecting the case study to be aware of the "big picture." Indeed, I advocate the use of case studies because it allows the analyst the ability to isolate the impact of a theoretical concept in a more detailed and potentially more compelling manner. Case studies are especially important for new institutional economics (NIE) because they enable us to analyze both the determinants and consequences of institutions and institutional change.

Case studies in NIE are also known as "analytical narratives."[2] The term "analytical" conveys the use of a theoretical framework or set of theoretical concepts and the term "narrative" conveys the use of historical qualitative evidence.[3] Though narratives use historical evidence, including at times accounts by individuals, the style also endorses quantitative evidence, including the use of econometric tests. One of the differences between the use of quantitative evidence in case studies as opposed to many broader analyses is that the scholar typically has a very thorough understanding of the data used in the analysis and, in some cases, may have collected the data, as is typically the case for anthropologists as well as some development economists. For historical data, some economic historians have created the data series from a variety of sources; for example this is the case for most statistics on national accounts. Scholars working in the field of case studies may also have relied on surveys and interviews as input for study. Interviews can be extremely helpful for the scholar to more thoroughly understand an issue before embarking on modeling and testing. Surveys can be crucial for testing some hypotheses because of a lack of data. Although surveys may have their biases, we have come a long way, largely due to work outside of standard economics, in our ability to conduct a survey and understand potential biases.[4] A deep understanding of data and their limitations is important because statistical work then becomes more believable if we have faith in the underlying data-set.

Narratives in NIE have taken two branches: micro and macro. "Micro" studies in NIE preceded "macro" studies, partially because they tended to hold constant the broader institutions of a society and focus on isolating a particular theoretical concept. Narratives have been especially useful in illustrating what might otherwise be anomalous in contracting. Much of the work of Ronald Coase falls into this category. Coase is a particularly apt example because his first published article was about the neglect of transaction costs in the theory of the firm and, in particular, the important role of transactions costs in vertical integration and disintegration. Numerous narratives then analyzed specific cases, perhaps the most famous being the integration of the Fisher Body Company into General Motors. Other early micro-narratives include cases of long-term contracting.[5] As a result of narratives, theorists have incorporated many insights into a much richer theory of contracting.[6]

Narratives are ideally suited to make comparisons across time, a period long enough to isolate the determinants or impacts of institutional change.[7] Through case studies scholars can study the dynamics of individual societies and begin to understand the lack of worldwide development. Particularly puzzling is why there exists so much "institutional lock-in" given the poor economic performance in many countries.[8] Recently macro-theorists have utilized narratives to help them build broader theories for explaining the lack of worldwide development.[9] Case studies have also been used to make comparisons across space; for example, by holding constant a sector the analyst can make better inferences of the role of political institutions on economic outcomes.[10]

As all of those who work in NIE understand, there is no grand all-encompassing theory of institutional development and change. For this reason alone case studies are important for the profession because they form the building blocks for a framework for understanding the role of institutions in societies. It is for this reason that is critical for scholars who develop case studies to do so with an understanding of how their work fits into either a broad framework of the either the determinants of institutional change or the impacts of institutions on political and economic outcomes. This is true for both "micro" and "macro" studies. For micro-studies the economic outcomes typically entail a particular type of contracting.[11] For macro case studies economic outcomes include indicators such as gross domestic product (GDP) per capita, income distribution, or economic opportunity. By political outcomes I mean indicators such as the degree of political competitiveness. One of the more difficult tasks of scholars in NIE who utilize case studies is to prevent the research from becoming simply a "good story." To increase the analytical component it is critical to isolate what is exogenous and what is endogenous to the actors in the system that we are trying to understand. In this way we can make headway toward a more general understanding of the dynamics. In this chapter I illustrate the use of case studies by describing some research in three broad areas in which I performed research: the role of property rights to land and the causes of insecure property rights for land; the importance of beliefs in the rule of law; and the roles of economic incentives and political abilities in shaping policy outcomes.

## 5.2    Titles, conflict, and land use in the Brazilian Amazon

It is now received wisdom that secure property rights promote economic growth yet, surprisingly, there has been little empirical work on the precise mechanisms by which secure property rights promote growth or on the quantitative impact of property rights on growth.[12] Case studies can fill this void. In this section I summarize the methodology that we used and some of the empirical results from our research on titles and land use in the Brazilian Amazon.[13] By property rights I mean both the specified and enforced rights that individuals have to resources. Specified (i.e. legal) property rights to land may include: the ability to use the land, including keeping it idle; the right to sell the land; the right to bequeath the land; and the ability to use the land as collateral. Enforcement of property rights include: social norms (when scarcity values are low): private enforcement, such as fences that deter encroachment; and government enforcement, such as forced evictions by police.

Secure property rights may influence economic growth through several mechanisms: (1) secure property rights provide the incentive to maintain the value of an asset; (2) secure property rights provide an incentive to enhance the value of an asset through investment; (3) secure property rights provide the ability to invest by enabling the property right-holder to use the asset as collateral for a loan; and (4) secure property rights increase the extent of the market and thereby may increase the exchange value of an asset by enabling outside investors to compete for the ownership of the asset.

It is the enhanced value of assets from secure property rights that causes individuals to "demand" property rights. Underlying the analysis is the notion that the potential rent generation from more secure property rights increases as the resource becomes scarcer. The difference

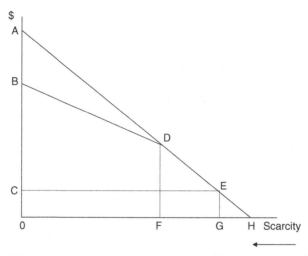

**Figure 5.1** The demand for, and evolution of, property rights.

between the rental streams from an asset with more as compared to less secure property rights generates a "demand" for secure property rights. In Figure 5.1 the horizontal axis measures the relative scarcity of a given resource (from right to left) and the vertical axis measures the net present value that accrues to the owner of that resource.[14] Line A–H shows that the net present value of the resource increases as it becomes scarcer. In the case of land the measure of scarcity could be the distance of a plot of land to a market center, as transportation costs are often the main determinant of land value.

At point H land is so far from the market center that the economic return given the transportation costs to market is zero. The segment B–D–E–H represents the net present value of land under a commons arrangement.[15] Zero–C represents the opportunity cost of the marginal laborer. Thus, point G represents the economic frontier where, provided costs of migration are low, it becomes worthwhile for labor to migrate to the frontier. In our model distance represents the frontier but it could be technological, for example broadcasting on previously unused frequencies at the spectrum frontier.

At points between G and F property rights are not formally defined or enforced, but this does not affect the return to the resource given that it is still abundant relative to the competition for it. As the net present value increases new users arrive yet they are able to get access to the resource without detracting much from the use of those who were already there. At this stage resource users will tend to be relatively homogenous and informal property rights arise that are sufficient to arbitrate the existing competition. Any potential disputes are easily defused as accommodation yields higher expected returns than confrontation. Squatting prevails yet absence of government-enforced private property rights does not pose significant costs.[16] Note that the emergence of informal property rights at this point is already a case of institutional change.

At points to the left of F the returns to the resource have risen and start attracting an ever-growing number of individuals. This new migration typically brings heterogeneous individuals with differing amounts of wealth or human capital, nationalities, cultures, or objectives. The informal institutions that developed can no longer cope with the increased competition for the resource. It becomes necessary to expend effort, time, and money to assure continued possession of the resource and the income derived from it. This may involve incurring costs to exclude others or the cost from sub-optimal uses. It may also include the costs to lobbying for changes from informal to formal property rights. At some point it becomes beneficial in the aggregate to have officially defined and enforced property rights. The pie-shaped area A–B–D represents the increased value of land with secure formal property rights versus the next-best commons arrangement for property rights. A–B–D is the potential rent that forms the basis for the demand for property rights.[17]

In our exposition we used distance as the proxy for scarcity but we could also use fertility of the soil or population density as alternative measures of scarcity.[18] The framework is flexible to allow for changes in technology, preferences, or new market opportunities. For example, if the demand for the output of the land increases the divergence between the rental streams may emerge at E, corresponding to the distance 0–G from the market center.

To put meat on the analytical bones detailed above, we (Alston, Libecap, and Schneider 1996) conducted 249 surveys in 1992 of smallholders in the Brazilian Amazonian state of Pará. We choose the state of Pará because it was the most populous Amazonian state and the area where land conflict was the most prevalent. This was still true as of 2004. Four different areas were selected for the surveys in order to control and test for the importance of various attributes. The mix of sites allowed us to analyze the effects of different agency jurisdictions and settlement processes: Altamira, on the TransAmazon highway was one of the original planned colonization sites by the Federal land agency; Tucumã was initially a private settlement area that reverted to the

Federal land agency after difficulties in preventing land invasions; and São Felix and Tailândia were settlement sites, one old and one new that were under the state land reform agency.

Designing the survey ourselves enabled to us to collect data on the factors important for a study on the role of property rights.[19] We asked whether the land operator had a permanent title or informal rights. In our survey 56% had a formal title; 12% stated that they had a sales receipt indicating the occupant paid cash to another squatter; and 32% had no documentation. We also documented the degree of investment by asking the percentage of area in pasture, requiring site-specific investments in fencing, and the percentage of area in permanent tree crops. We also asked a variety of questions relevant to better understanding the settlement of a modern frontier: age of the head of household (mean forty-three years); years of education (mean of two years); years on the plot (mean of eight years); and number of migrations (mean of three).

Undertaking a case study enables the analyst to better understand exactly what the proxy for property rights conveys. In the present case formal titles were used as the proxy for secure property rights. We maintained that titles conveyed a lot of information about security to the land. Title is a formal document, issued by the Brazilian federal government or the state government, depending on jurisdiction, that signifies government recognition of an individual's property rights to land. Having a title not only gives legal standing to the land owner, but the recording of the title in the local land registry (*cartório*) includes survey descriptions (*memorial descritivo*), the location of boundary markers, and the date of recording to establish precedent for the land claim. Land exchanges are recorded by the *cartório* in a document which includes a *cadeia dominal*, a list of previous owners. This record can be valuable if there are disputes over land transfers. With title, the police power of the state is used to enforce private property rights to land, according to surveyed and recorded individual property boundaries. The courts issue eviction notices or arbitrate boundary disputes, and law-enforcement officials implement court orders.

As the most visible form of ownership recognition by the government, having title reduces private enforcement costs, provides security and collateral for long-term investment in land improvements, and promotes the development of land markets. All of these activities are wealth-enhancing. The role of title in Brazilian law is recognized throughout Brazil, and, for the most part, title functions well and is respected.

Although frontiers are remote by definition, there are strong reasons to believe that title on the frontier plays at least some of the roles described above. First, consider the collateral argument. Even though credit may be quite limited on a frontier that is not the case for the rest of Brazil, where agricultural credit has been commonplace and requires title. Migrants to the frontier, mostly from rural areas, likely carry this understanding with them.[20] Settlers are aware that as financial markets extend to the frontier credit will become more available and having title will assist them in obtaining funds. Moreover, practically every small urban center in Brazil has a branch of *Banco do Brasil*, which historically has provided credit to agriculture. Further, living under inflationary conditions of up to 50% a month resulted in a population that was accustomed to dealing with banks and other financial institutions in efforts to respond to inflation.

The arguments also apply to the role of title in promoting land exchanges. Throughout Brazil title is a recognized institutional device for designating private property rights and facilitating land transfer agreements. Formal titles are exchanged with land to document the transfer of ownership of land. Land exchange contracts and titles are recognized throughout the country and defendable in court. Hence, they provide security for those more-remote, potential purchasers (say, from more settled areas), who might be interested in purchasing frontier land. In the absence of titles individual holdings are based on squatter claims and subject to local agreements and practices. Potential purchasers, who are not part of such arrangements, may have little understanding of local conditions or confidence in the property rights they provide. Although there is a market for land without title, having title is perceived as an advantage by settlers for broadening the range of potential purchasers.[21]

Finally, consider the ability of title to reduce private enforcement costs. With state-recognized title land owners can appeal to the police to patrol property boundaries and to evict trespassers. Further, the judicial system may be used to issue injunctions against squatters who invade private property. A review of land-conflict records held by the state land agency, the Pastoral Land Commission, and other federal and state government agencies shows that having title facilitates the introduction of the rule of law in resolving land disputes.

With a firm understanding of what rights title conveyed we then could proceed to estimating the impact of land titles on land investment and land values.[22] Controlling for a host of individual characteristics we estimated the percentage of total farmland representing investments for those with and without a title. The results across our sites are shown in Table 5.1.

The amount of land devoted to pasture or permanent crops represent large investments in materials, effort, and patience (in the case of tree

Table 5.1 *Percentage of hectares devoted to pasture or permanent crops*

|  | Without title | With title |
|---|---|---|
| Altamira | 26 | 55 |
| São Felix | 7 | 28 |
| Tailândia | 12 | 33 |
| Tucumã | 32 | 80 |

crops). Of those who had pasture the mean level of fencing was 1,181 meters, which represents an investment of approximately US $550. The effects are large and, importantly, believable because of the care that went into understanding the local context and therefore the survey design.

We also estimated the impact title on land values, over and above its impact on investment. Land values should increase above investment because settlers have to expend less time enforcing their own claims and it increases the extent of the market for their land. For example, most investors in São Paulo or Rio de Janeiro would only buy titled land. The increased value of a title is greater for land that is closer to a market center. For land at the market center our estimates indicate that a title would increase land values by 189%. For land that is forty kilometers from the market, land would increase by 72% with a title; and for land 140 kilometers from a market land values would increase by 45%. These estimates make sense because titled land closer to a market should have a greater value owing to increased competition for the land. By controlling for distance we show that title matters more; not surprisingly, the greater the competition for land which we proxied by distance to the market. It is the potential impact of property rights to land that will drive the "demand" for property rights – *see* Figure 5.1. But property rights are not supplied without cost nor are the incentives identical across titling agencies in Brazil. In our work on the Amazon we used proxy variables for both demand and supply side variables and estimated the determinants of property rights. Not surprisingly, as the potential impact of secure property rights increased so, too, did the probability of having a title. Perhaps more innovatively we were able to test for the impact of different suppliers of title on the likelihood of an individual having a title. It turns out that state land agencies title more, holding all else constant than federal land agencies. This makes sense given that there is a greater electoral connection between landholders and local politicians who tend to title prior to elections as a quid pro quo for a vote.

Though many landholders in the Amazon and elsewhere in rural Brazil have a legal formal title, property rights for many large land-holders remain insecure. Several factors account for the insecurity. Brazil has the highest level of land inequality in Latin America and this produces a consensus view in Brazil for land reform. Yet, there is also a consensus that property rights and land titles should be upheld. In the 1988 Constitution, as well as earlier constitutions, there is a provision allowing squatting on private land if the land is not "beneficially used." If land is not used productively the state has the right to expropriate it (with compensation). As a result of these constitutional measures, the Landless Peasants Movement has organized land invasions in the hope of prompting the government to expropriate and redistribute to the invading group. This leads some farmers in the Amazon to cut trees prematurely in order to show "beneficial use." In all regions the invasions and reactions of land-holders has led to violent conflict. We may view the conflict, at a higher level, as that between the federal government responding to the general interests of the public for land reform and the courts who adjudicate according to Civil Law which guarantees the rights of private property holders. In an even broader sense there is a political conflict present in all societies to a greater or lesser degree of promoting efficiency through secure property rights and promoting equity through redistribution.

The goal of describing the work on property rights in the Amazon was to provide sufficient description to illustrate some of the benefits of the case study method as discussed earlier in this chapter. By providing sufficient detail, in this instance the role of land titles in the Brazilian Amazon, we can first understand the issue and thereby better isolate the theoretical concept and, as a result, the argument becomes more compelling. I also tried to emphasize the importance of being analytically clear on the determinants of institutional change, here the demand for and supply of property rights, and the impact of a given institutional change, in this case the impact of having a land title on investments in land and land values. The results of a case study should also shed light on a bigger issue. In this case it is the role of property rights in fostering economic development. I trust that it is obvious that to the extent that titles affect behavior in the Brazilian Amazon they most likely would function in a similar fashion in most other countries in Latin America.[23] The case study of property rights in the Amazon dramatically raises the question: If secure property rights are so wonderful for promoting economic growth why are they not always provided? The next case study demonstrates the importance of beliefs in shaping policies. The case study analyzes why Argentina moved from protecting secure property rights to agricultural land from the mid-nineteenth century until the 1940s when it began to infringe on the property rights of agricultural landowners.

## 5.3    The erosion of checks and balances in Argentina, and the rise of populism

At the dawn of the twentieth century Argentina was in the top ten in GDP or per capita in the world.[24] At the dawn of the twenty-first century, Argentina is a middle-income country. Why did the fall occur? Cross-country econometric evidence would probably do little to help us answer this question because regression analysis tells us about behavior at the mean. On the other hand, a detailed case study may give us a better understanding of off-path behavior, which in turn may help us produce more enlightened policies for economic development. This case study also illustrates the role of beliefs in shaping economic policies, especially in the long term, when economic performance is poor. We might expect that policy makers would change institutions in the presence of poor economic performance. The role of beliefs is important for theorists to understand in their quest as to why there has not been convergence in GDP across countries.

From the late-nineteenth century until 1914 Argentina was run by the conservative autocratic elite. In 1912 Argentina established the secret ballot and embarked on its way towards becoming a country ruled by a legitimate democracy. As a result of the secret ballot, the Radical Party secured majority representation in the Chamber of Deputies and the Presidency from 1914 to 1930. The Conservative Party maintained its majority in the Senate. During this period Argentine citizens began to develop a belief in the rule of law, with the Supreme Court acting as independent check on the executive and legislative branches.[25] During this period Argentina continued in its mode of sustained economic growth. The virtuous feedback from divided government and economic growth on belief in the rule of law came to an end with the first successful military coup in Argentine history in 1930. The Conservative Party openly supported the coup, as did the Supreme Court and some people within the Radical Party.

The Conservatives planned on moving back to open democracy and held a fair election in the province of Buenos Aires in 1932. The Radical Party won the election and the Conservatives, fearing defeat at the National Election, annulled the vote. The Conservatives in particular were afraid of turning over economic policy to the Radicals during the Great Depression. Though conducting economic policy well during the Great Depression, the Conservatives continued to engage in fraud in several leading Provinces, in particular Buenos Aires, in order to stay in power.[26] As a result the Conservatives eroded the belief in the rule of law and set the stage for the next military coup in 1943 and the support for populism.

Following the coup, Juan Peron won the Presidential election fairly in 1945.[27] His platform consisted of a series of populist policies, part of which entailed abridging the property rights of landowners in the Pampas. This would not have been possible had it not been for the impeachment of all but one of the Supreme Court Justices. In the hearings for the impeachments it was clear that the rationale was the countenance of fraud during the 1930s. In the accusations made in the Chamber of Deputies over the impeachment of the Supreme Justices, we may extract the prevailing sentiment:

Since a military government interrupted the normal cycle of constitutional government [1930], and after the Court granted this victorious movement both a title and its overt recognition, the country saw the disconcerting show of arbitrariness. This episode lasted almost seventeen years. Those were seventeen long years in which the basic principles of our constitutional system have expired right in front of those in charge of keeping them with all the integrity with which they were created. This fact has been stated by respected sectors of public opinion and the general media. After this military government legitimized by the Court recognition, there was a succession of arbitrary governments of fraud, treason, and lies. Governments openly called constitutional, which in fact were merely – or, better said, continued to be – de facto. They applied the theory wrongly used by the Court when it legalized an unconstitutional government violating the Constitution. The initial mistake of the Court and its lack of courage to impose the return to the true constitutional path cost the country a new military movement [1943]. Luckily, it would have the glorious deed of honor after a hard path filled with ups and downs, surrounded by difficulties – which the Court also experienced – to restore the entire rule of the Constitution. These difficulties were overcome by a magnificent movement of social justice led by the creator of the Secretary of Labor and Prevision, Colonel Peron. The recognition of two outlaw governments and its guilty passivity during the years of the reign of arbitrariness and unruliness have given the highest justice tribunal of the Nation a loss of reputation. The role of the Court played in the latest years until recently has reinforced it." [28]

The Deputies went to great lengths to tie the impeachment of the court not only to their denial of reform but to their duplicity in passively accepting the fraud perpetuated by the Conservatives in the 1930s. Following the impeachment, the Peronists began to craft a new Constitution, which they submitted for approval in 1949. Without a backstop of an independent judiciary, and a new constitution in hand the Peronists were able to have their way until the next military coup in 1955.[29]

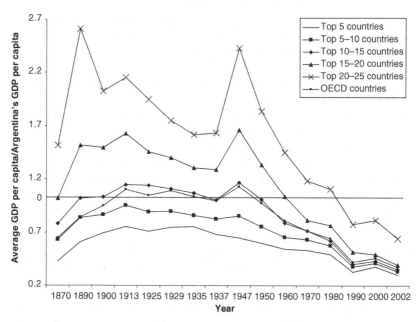

**Figure 5.2** Comparison: Argentina (GDP per capita) and other top countries.
*Source*: own elaboration based on Madisson (1995) and WPT 6.0.

After the impeachment process and new constitution, Argentina has never been able to return to its former institutional path of upholding property rights through the rule of law. The aftermath of Peron witnessed a departure from its historical growth trajectory compared to other high-income countries (Figure 5.2).[30] In 1947 Argentina was ranked tenth in the world in per capita income. Relative to various cohorts with whom Argentina might be compared, relative income per capita fell precipitously.

Successive military and populist governments appointed their own Supreme Court Justices in order to accomplish their political goals. But, without the court as a backstop, institutional volatility ensued.[31] Until Peron no Justices had been impeached or "forced" to resign. After Peron only five of the fifty-eight changes in Justices have been attributed to death or retirement. Before Peron governments appointed a new Justice approximately every two years. After Peron governments appointed a new Justice every eleven months. An alternative measure of instability is tenure: pre-Peron tenure of Justices was nearly ten years, whilst in the post-Peron years tenure has fallen to approximately six years. Oscillations between military and democratic governments matched the instability of the court.

The only time when Executive, Legislative, and Judicial branches were close to the ideal of the Constitution was the Camelot period of 1912–1930. After the military coup of 1930, instead of returning to open democracy the conservative elite resorted to fraud in order to stay in office and dictate economic policy. The Conservatives may be given high marks for economic policy but their short-sightedness gave rise to oscillations between democratic or populist and conservative or military governments. With this background we cannot be sanguine about the future institutional path of Argentina.[32] Until Argentina moves to back to a respect for rule of law, with an independent court and constitutional review, it seems highly unlikely that short-term economic policies can re-ignite economic growth. In this case study we demonstrated how the beliefs of those in power shape policy outcomes. In the next case study we analyze how the economic incentives of those with political power can sustain policy outcomes even when the outcomes may not be those favored by the majority of the population nor be those that lead to the highest rate of economic growth.

## 5.4   Southern paternalism and the American welfare state: the dynamics of institutions

Temporal analysis of the determinants and impact of institutions is necessary in order to better understand the dynamics of institutional change.[33] Case studies are ideal for this task because they enable the analyst to construct an analytical narrative. Narratives allow the combination of a deep understanding of the historical and institutional context with a theoretical framework. Temporal narratives also allow the scholar the ability to address the "big picture," that is, both the consequences of institutions on economic performance and the feedback of economic performance on institutional change.

Generally, it is an easier task to analyze the impact of institutions on contracting and, in turn, economic performance. I use "contracting" in the very general sense, that is, how participants interact to best exploit potential gains from trade. The beauty of a case study is that it allows us to keep these abstractions in mind while engaging in the specifics of time and place, which Hayek and Coase viewed as essential for theoretical (Hayek) and empirical (Coase) work.

Here I will detail the rise and fall of paternalism (a part of contracting) in Southern agriculture and then the impact of paternalism on the shape of the American welfare state (a set of institutions). Before analyzing paternalism it is important to set the stage or establish the background conditions. From its initial settlement by Europeans in the early seventeenth century to the mid-twentieth century, the US South was dominated by agriculture both economically, in terms of employment, and politically, in terms of representation. My analysis focuses on the post-Civil War (1865) period until c. 1970. Throughout this period the South may be characterized as a "low-wage" and "low-education" region, and one where, from the late-nineteenth century, there was effectively only one political party: the Democratic Party.

Because of the legacy of slavery and massive immigration to the US North in the late nineteenth and early twentieth centuries, the South was home to the vast majority of the black population in the USA until after World War II. Furthermore, most of the black population resided in rural areas and worked in agriculture, many on plantations where their predecessors toiled. On large plantations paternalistic relations predominated. By paternalism I mean an implicit contract in Southern agriculture that emerged after the Civil War. Under a paternalistic contract agricultural workers (more often black than white) exchanged "good and faithful" labor for a variety of in-kind goods and services, most notably protection from civil rights abuses.

Workers had a "demand" for paternalism because of the presence of discriminatory laws and practices in the South and the absence of any federal or state welfare programs. For example, by the 1890s, the Democratic agricultural elite managed to disfranchise most blacks (and many poor whites) through the establishment of literacy tests and poll taxes. Lynchings – public murder – peaked in the 1890s. In this atmosphere, labeled "an armed camp for intimidating black folk" by W. E. B. DuBoise in the early twentieth century, it made sense for black workers to attach themselves to a white protector who could protect them from the most vicious abuses and also provide them with the modicum of social insurance, for example a house, medical care, garden plots, and, for the most loyal workers, old age assistance.

Landlords had an incentive to "supply" paternalism because of the high monitoring costs in pre-mechanized labor-intensive agriculture. By offering a paternalistic contract planters could induce greater work effort and reduce turnover by supplying goods and services (protection from civil rights abuses) that were difficult if not impossible to procure in the market. In the language of labor economists, paternalism functioned as an efficiency wage; for workers the landlords offered a total compensation package that had a greater value than an alternative compensation package, which was the casual labor market. The simple "demand" and "supply" framework for paternalism that I sketched out examined contracting and took institutions as exogenous. I now turn to an examination of political institutions.

Paternalism rested on the political ability of Southern Congressmen to maintain social control in the South and prevent northern interference in race and labor relations. The disproportionate ability of Southern Congressmen to ward off northern attempts to reform the South rested on two main institutional factors which I also take as exogenous to this analysis. The first important institution in the South was the creation and maintenance of the one-party system in the South. Having one party gave disproportionate seniority to Southern Congressmen, which, in turn, allowed Southern politicians to occupy nodes of power in the US Congress; in particular, chairs of committees. Chairs of committees have considerable agenda-setting power which gave Southerners power of veto over legislation that, as a whole, they did not want, and the ability to shape bills to their preferences.

Further bolstering Southern political power was their ideological position within Congress. Overall, they occupied a pivotal position. On labor and race relations they aligned themselves with Republicans, but on other issues they sided more with the populist side of the Democratic Party. Ideology and agenda control enabled the South to shape the welfare state in the USA for more than fifty years. I stress that here the analysis takes welfare policy as endogenous to the political actors in the South because of exogenous institutions giving them disproportionate political power. Evidence that Southerners were able to prevent any interference in agricultural labor relations includes: (1) Agricultural workers were excluded from the first two major welfare and labor relations programs passed during the 1930s – the Social Security Act and Fair Labor Standards Act; (2) Southerners were decisive in cutting appropriations to the Farm Security Administration (FSA) in the late 1930s when the FSA turned its agenda from recovery to reform; (3) Southerners were instrumental in establishing deferments from the military draft for agricultural workers during World War II; and (4) Southerners initiated and maintained the "guest worker" program for Mexicans to work in US agriculture, mostly outside of the South, as a means of discouraging outmigration of its own agricultural labor force.

So far I have described how paternalistic relationships in Southern agriculture emerged and were sustained because of the economic incentive and political ability of Southerners to keep labor cheap and dependent. In this part of the analysis we took paternalistic relations as the "dependent" variable given a set of institutions. In another part of the analysis we showed how another set of exogenous institutions, for

Table 5.2 *Seniority of Southern Democratic Congressmen: 1947–1970*

| House committees | Years chaired by Southern Democrat | | | Ave no. of five most-senior seats | | |
|---|---|---|---|---|---|---|
| Committee | 47–60 | 61–64 | 65–70 | 47–60 | 61–64 | 65–70 |
| Rules | 6 | 4 | 6 | 3.0 | 3.0 | 3.0 |
| Appropriations | 0 | 0 | 6 | 2.3 | 2.0 | 3.3 |
| Ways and means | 10 | 4 | 6 | 3.4 | 2.0 | 2.7 |
| Agriculture | 10 | 4 | 6 | 4.7 | 5.0 | 5.0 |
| Education/Labor | 8 | 0 | 4 | 2.0 | 2.0 | 1.0 |
| Judiciary | 0 | 0 | 0 | 1.3 | 1.5 | 1.0 |

example the one-party system coupled with strong committee power, enabled the South to shape the welfare state which, in turn, fed back on paternalistic relations.

The dynamic maintaining paternalism began to change in the late 1950s and early 1960s, and, by c. 1970, we see little paternalism in Southern agriculture. Given that paternalism rested on the economic incentive in Southern agriculture, and the political ability of Southerners to shape labor relations, one or both had to change. We argue that the economic incentive to continue paternalistic contracting changed with the mechanization of cotton and complementary technology which came to fruition around 1960.[34] Recall that the "supply" of paternalism rested on the ability to reduce monitoring costs. Mechanization of Southern agriculture reduced monitoring costs in two ways: (1) by displacing thousands of workers unemployment and underemployment increased labor effort without close monitoring in an effort to retain employment; (2) mechanical harvesting reduced the variation in the marginal productivity of labor thereby making it easier to assign effort to outcomes. Evidence consistent with the decline of paternalism in Southern agriculture was the virtual disappearance of sharecroppers by 1970. All qualitative evidence links paternalism and sharecropping.

A competing though not necessarily contradictory explanation for the decline of paternalism is that the political ability of Southerners to resist the expansion of the welfare state declined. We find the evidence inconsistent with Southerners losing political power. The evidence in Table 5.2 and Table 5.3 indicates that Southerners did not lose their dominance of the committee hierarchy in the 1960s. The committees selected are either those dealing with labor relations directly (e.g. agriculture and labor) or indirectly (e.g. appropriations). I also stress that it was not necessary for

Table 5.3 *Seniority of Southern Democratic Congressmen: 1947–1970*

| Senate committees | Years chaired by Southern Democrat | | | Ave no. of five most-senior seats | | |
|---|---|---|---|---|---|---|
| Committee | 47–60 | 61–64 | 65–70 | 47–60 | 61–64 | 65–70 |
| Rules | 0 | 2 | 6 | 1.0 | 1.0 | 1.3 |
| Appropriations | 4 | 0 | 2 | 2.7 | 3.5 | 4.0 |
| Finance | 10 | 4 | 6 | 3.5 | 3.5 | 3.3 |
| Agriculture | 10 | 4 | 6 | 4.0 | 5.0 | 5.0 |
| Labor | 6 | 4 | 6 | 1.4 | 2.0 | 1.7 |
| Judiciary | 4 | 4 | 6 | 2.5 | 4.7 | 3.2 |

Southerners to dominate a particular committee in both houses of Congress; seniority in one chamber is sufficient to act as a veto.

With the economic incentive to supply paternalism obsolete and with it the fierce opposition to the rise of the federal welfare state, we argue that Southern Congressmen allowed and shaped the expansion of the modern American welfare state. Evidence consistent with this view includes: (1) the passage of the Economic Opportunity Act in 1964, which was the first significant federal legislation dealing with welfare policy and the first legislation to encourage migration out of the South by allowing state control of welfare benefits, even though the benefits were partially funded by the federal government; (2) the termination of the guest worker program for Mexicans in 1963;[35] (3) the passage and expansion of the Food Stamp program;[36] (4) the South began to actively solicit outside capital;[37] and (5) expenditure on Southern primary and secondary education increased dramatically.[38]

The rationale for the detail in this case was to show how to use case studies to illustrate and test the dynamics and feedback loops among institutions, economic contracting, economic performance, technological change, and institutional change. Like all of economics it is crucial for the analysis to be explicit about what is exogenous and what is endogenous. Unless we do so the narrative strays from being analytical with general lessons to being a unique story.

## 5.5    The lessons from case studies

In this chapter, I have tried to demonstrate the value of case studies by detailing three specific examples. The tools used in case studies are similar to those used elsewhere in NIE: a theoretical framework emphasizing the interaction of institutions and economic performance, and empirical testing using both qualitative and quantitative evidence, including econometrics. Case studies have value, in part because they enable the scholar to be very detailed and specific about both causation and testing whilst illustrating a general proposition. Indeed, the ability to move from the specific to the general case may be the most difficult methodological hurdle faced by analysts working with case studies. In our analysis of Brazil we provided a clear description of the possible benefits of having a title and how land values vary with the distance from a market. This enabled us to perform very clear tests which generated believable results about both the determinants and impact of land titles. The importance of the study is both in the issue itself, the Amazon being one of largest remaining frontiers in the world, but also because it clearly illustrates and quantifies the role of secure property rights.

Case studies may also enable the analyst to examine off-path behavior and the role of beliefs in shaping economic policies, which, in turn, shape economic performance. The most general characteristic of societies is stasis but there are critical turning points. Detailed case studies may be the best way to examine moments in the history of a country which have long-term effects. We argued that the electoral fraud in Argentina in the 1930s promoted a belief in populism, which led to erosion in the rule of law which, in turn, led to a declining relative economic performance. Argentina fell from one of the top GDP per capita countries in the world to a middle-income country. Like the case study of the Amazon, the analysis of Argentina goes beyond an understanding of Argentina toward a general lesson on the role of beliefs in shaping policy outcomes.

One of the hallmarks of NIE is its ability to examine the dynamics of institutional change and economic performance. To do so requires the analyst to be careful about what is exogenous and what is endogenous to the actors in the system. In the case study of paternalism in the Southern US agricultural labor contracts we tied the prevalence of paternalism to the high supervision costs of monitoring labor prior to mechanization of Southern agriculture. But, for paternalism to reduce monitoring, workers needed to be dependent on their landlords. This dependence required the absence of welfare programs which, because of political institutions in the USA, the South was able to shape. Once mechanization became available the South again shaped welfare policies, only now in a way that encouraged migration out of the South. The general lesson from this case study is that economic incentives at the micro-level matter at the macro-policy level in order to provide a deep understanding of the "supply" side of government, that is, the political institutions of a country.

The goals of case studies include: the ability to first understand an issue prior to modeling it; the ability to test theoretical hypotheses; and the ability to shed credible light on the workings of the institutional and economic workings of society. At the current stage of development of NIE, case studies form the building blocks upon which we can erect a more solid theoretical and empirical foundation for a theory of the dynamics of institutional change.

# 6 New Institutional Econometrics: The Case of Research on Contracting and Organization

*Michael E. Sykuta*

## 6.1 Introduction

From its inception, new institutional economics (NIE) has been characterized by its emphasis on empirical research. This is not to say that NIE is hostile or even ambivalent toward formal theory; quite the contrary. Rather, it is to say that NIE places a premium on realism that is absent in much of traditional neoclassical economic theory. Indeed, NIE is frequently defined in terms of its relaxation of certain restrictive assumptions in neoclassical theory, most notably the existence of positive transaction costs, the role and influence of the institutional environment, and the limited rational abilities of economic actors. Consequently, empirical observation and analysis play a central role in the development of NIE.

The real-world orientation and focus of NIE on empirical research have expanded the scope of economics research by broadening the focus from price and quantity analysis to the existence and structure of economic systems.[1] Nowhere is this broader scope more evident than in micro-economic theories of firms and markets. NIE has led researchers not only to crack open the black box of production known as the firm, but also the market itself, examining the structures of individual transactions and their implications for firm and market performance. The result is a burgeoning field of research on the causes and consequences of different modes for governing the allocation and coordination of resources in an economy. Oliver Williamson (2000, p. 610) characterizes new institutional economics as "a boiling cauldron of ideas." He goes on to state that: "Not only are there many institutional research programs in progress, but there are competing ideas within most of them." This bubbling mix of competing ideas manifests itself as a wide range of questions and perspectives on economic organization. Several reviews of these competing theories as well as of the empirical literatures they have spawned are available elsewhere.[2] The purpose of this chapter is to provide an overview of econometric techniques appropriate to NIE research and some of the empirical and theoretical challenges facing scholars in this field.

The chapter proceeds with a discussion of common research questions and their corresponding econometric approaches. Section 6.3 presents some empirical challenges resulting from the nature of the decisions modeled and the availability of data; Section 6.4 considers some conceptual and theoretical issues that hamper empirical research; and Section 6.5 provides concluding thoughts.

## 6.2    Matching a model to the question

The empirical tools used by students of organizations and contracts are as wide in range as the questions being addressed. An exhaustive review of the many econometric models, their applications, and their estimation issues (in particular issues about poorly behaved data and error structures) would require a book unto itself. Most economics researchers are well acquainted with ordinary least squares (OLS) estimation techniques, but may be less familiar with estimation tools specifically designed for discrete-type dependent variables. Since much of the research in NIE is driven by questions of a discrete choice nature, I focus primarily on these less familiar models as they relate to the types of questions frequently investigated by NIE scholars. The discussion also refers to a limited number of research papers employing each econometric method. Again, these are intended to be illustrative rather than representative.

### 6.2.1    To be or not to be, the simple question

The most basic question in NIE research dates back to Ronald Coase's original (1937) inquiry: Why use a firm (managerial control) instead of the market (price mechanism) to coordinate the allocation of resources? Coase addresses this general question in two steps. First, he considers the question of "why a firm emerges at all in a specialized exchange economy" (p. 390). His proposed answer, as is now familiar to many economists, is that there are costs to using the price mechanism that may make internal organization more efficient. However, this raises the second point Coase considers, namely "why is not all production carried on by one big firm" (p. 394). Employing the principles of marginal analysis, Coase argues that the costs of managerial coordination increase as firm scale and heterogeneity of transactions increase to the point that the marginal cost of internalizing another resource allocation decision (transaction) exceeds the cost of using the price mechanism.[3] Hence, the basic empirical question resulting from Coase's insights may be summarized as "what factors affect the relative costs of internal coordination and market transactions that determine whether a firm will internalize resource allocations or use the price mechanism?"; that is, the make-or-buy decision.

Empirically, the make-or-buy decision would seem to present a straightforward econometric problem. Given the dichotomous nature of the decision, a simple dummy variable is sufficient to capture the distinction; either the activity is internalized ($y = 1$) or it is not ($y = 0$).[4] The econometric problem, then, is to estimate the probability that the activity will be internalized, based on a set of explanatory variables hypothesized to affect the relative costs of managerial and market coordination. The issue is how best to estimate the relationship between the discrete choice of internalization and the set of explanatory variables.

Simple linear regression models fail to generate probabilistic estimates constrained by 0 and 1, thus a *probit* or *logit* model is typically used for estimating such relationships. The difference between the two is the nature of the underlying probability distributions; probit models assume a normal distribution whereas logit models assume a logistic distribution. Specifically, a probit model is given by:

$$\Pr(y = 1 | \mathbf{x}) = \int_{-\infty}^{\mathbf{x}'\beta} \phi(t)dt = \Phi(\mathbf{x}'\beta) \qquad (1)$$

where $\mathbf{x}$ is a vector of explanatory variables, $\beta$ is a vector of coefficient parameters, and $\Phi(.)$ represents the standard normal distribution function. Similarly, the logit model is given by:

$$\Pr(y = 1 | \mathbf{x}) = \frac{e^{\mathbf{x}'\beta}}{1 + e^{\mathbf{x}'\beta}} = \Lambda(\mathbf{x}'\beta) \qquad (2)$$

where $\mathbf{x}$ and $\beta$ are the same as above and $\Lambda(.)$ represents the logistic cumulative distribution function.

William Greene (2003) asserts that "in most applications, the choice between these two seems not to make much difference" (p. 667).[5] However, the two models are likely to generate different results if: (1) there are relatively few internal or market transactions in the data (i.e. few 1s or few 0s); (2) there is an independent variable with a very wide variation; or (3) the data include relatively few observations. From a pragmatic perspective, the advantage of the logit model is computational ease, which is less of a constraint given the computational abilities of most computers and statistical software packages on the market. In fact, we may easily run both specifications to check for robustness in the results.[6]

The nonlinear nature of the probit and logit models makes interpretation of the estimated coefficients less straightforward than linear or log-linear regression models. While the statistical significance of the parameter estimates can be judged directly from the coefficient test statistics, the economic significance (or marginal effect) of a particular independent variable on the decision variable is more complicated. Given the specification in equations 1 and 2, calculating the marginal effect of $\mathbf{x}$ on the expected probability ($y$) results in the following for the probit and logit models, respectively:

$$\frac{\partial E[y|\mathbf{x}]}{\partial \mathbf{x}} = \phi(\mathbf{x}'\beta)\beta \tag{3}$$

$$\frac{\partial E[y|\mathbf{x}]}{\partial \mathbf{x}} = \Lambda(\mathbf{x}'\beta)[1 - \Lambda(\mathbf{x}'\beta)]\beta \tag{4}$$

where $\phi(.)$ is the standard normal density function. Since the marginal effect is obviously dependent upon the value of $\mathbf{x}$, it is common to report the value of the marginal effect at the means of the independent variables. However, special care must be given when calculating the marginal effect of dummy variables (perhaps representing an exogenous institutional shock or dichotomous transaction characteristic). In those cases, the marginal effect is simply the change in the expected probability, evaluated at the mean values of remaining independent variables, when the dummy variable changes from 0 to 1.

These binomial choice models are appropriate not only for examining determinants of make-or-buy decisions, but for any problem with a dichotomous decision variable. For instance, Glenn Hubbard and Robert Weiner (1991) use a probit model to estimate the use of most-favored-nations clauses in natural gas contracts.[7] Douglas Allen and Dean Lueck (1992, 1998) use logit models to examine choices of agricultural contract structures (cash rent versus cropshare) and farm organizational form (family versus corporate farms), while Harvey James and Michael Sykuta (2006) use a probit model to model farmers' choice to market their commodities to producer-owned versus investor-owned firms. Eric Helland and Michael Sykuta (2004) use a probit model to examine the effect of a change in regulatory regimens on the likelihood regulated firms appoint former regulators to their corporate boards. Richard Geddes (1997) uses logit models to explain managerial turnover in electric utility firms.

### 6.2.2   One form, two forms, three forms, more?

The make-or-buy decision is caricatured as the choice between two extremes: (spot) market transactions and internalization. However, between spot markets and hierarchy there is a wide range of contractual relations that exemplify characteristics of both spot (autonomous) transactions and managerial coordination to varying degrees. This is the grey range of organizational structure called "hybrids" (Williamson 1991a; Ménard 2004b). The addition of hybrids to the analysis simply adds one more choice in organizational structure: market, hybrid, or hierarchy. Of course, hybrids themselves may range from long-term contracts between two otherwise autonomous parties to joint ventures and strategic alliances that involve more mutual investment and governance to franchise agreements with a quasi-managerial contractual control.

The first question to address with more than two discrete choices or outcomes is whether the choices are inherently ordinal or simply represent multiple alternatives. For example, consider how the degree of asset specificity affects governance structures. Williamson (1991a) suggests that as the degree of asset-specificity increases, the optimal organizational structure moves from market to hybrid to hierarchy. If we consider market, hybrid, and hierarchy as degrees of hierarchical control, then a discrete choice variable taking on values of 0, 1, and 2, respectively, makes ordinal sense. Hierarchy (2) is more control than hybrid (1), which is more control than market (0). As with the make-or-buy decision discussed above, the richness of these differences are difficult to capture in discrete choice models, although in principle increasingly fine categorizations of "hybrid" could be addressed by simply allowing more discrete values for the dependent variable.

When discrete choices have ordinal relevance, an *ordered probit* or *ordered logit* model may be the most appropriate specification. The underlying structures for these models are similar to their binomial counterparts discussed above. Given the similarity of the two models' relative performance, this section discusses only the ordered probit for brevity's sake. For the above example of choice among market, hybrid, and hierarchy, the ordered probit probabilities for each of the three is given by:

$$\Pr(y = 0|\mathbf{x}) = 1 - \Phi(\mathbf{x}'\beta) \tag{5a}$$

$$\Pr(y = 1|\mathbf{x}) = \Phi(\mu - \mathbf{x}'\beta) - \Phi(-\mathbf{x}'\beta) \tag{5b}$$

$$\Pr(y = 2|\mathbf{x}) = 1 - \Phi(\mu - \mathbf{x}'\beta) \tag{5c}$$

where $\mu$ is a threshold parameter that is estimated with $\beta$.[8]

Interpreting the coefficients of the ordered probit model is more complicated than for the binomial probit, and caution should be exercised in discussions of marginal effects. Mathematically, the marginal effects of the ordered probit are given by:

$$\frac{\partial \Pr(y = 0|\mathbf{x})}{\partial \mathbf{x}} = -\phi(\mathbf{x}'\beta)\beta \tag{6a}$$

$$\frac{\partial \Pr(y = 1|\mathbf{x})}{\partial \mathbf{x}} = [\phi(\mathbf{x}'\beta) - \phi(\mu - \mathbf{x}'\beta)]\beta \tag{6b}$$

$$\frac{\partial \Pr(y = 2|\mathbf{x})}{\partial \mathbf{x}} = \phi(\mu - \mathbf{x}'\beta)\beta \tag{6c}$$

Assuming $\beta$ is positive, increasing one of the $x$'s while holding the parameters constant effectively shifts the probability distribution to the right. In this case, the $\Pr(y = 0|\mathbf{x})$ must decline and the $\Pr(y = 2|\mathbf{x})$ must increase as the probability distribution shifts to the right. Thus a positive value for $\beta$ may be correctly interpreted as implying a positive relation between the variable of interest the probability of $y = 2$ (in this case, hierarchy). However, because the relative mass of the distribution moving from $y = 0$ to $y = 1$ may be more or less than the mass of the distribution moving from $y = 1$ to $y = 2$ the net effect on the $\Pr(y = 1|\mathbf{x})$ is ambiguous and requires more detailed examination.[9] Thus, a statistically significant positive value for $\beta$ is not sufficient to conclude that the probability of all higher outcomes increases. Researchers should be careful in interpreting their results to ensure their conclusions are accurate.

Thomas Hubbard (2001) uses an ordered logit to estimate the choice of common carriers, contract carriers, or private fleets in the US trucking industry. James and Sykuta (2005) use an ordered logit to examine the relation of property rights among cooperative firm members and trust within the organization, while James and Sykuta (2004) use an ordered probit to examine the level of trust agricultural producers have in agricultural organizations.

For multiple discrete outcomes that do not have an inherently ordinal relation, a multinomial logit model provides an appropriate mechanism. The multinomial logit generates a different set of probability parameters for each of the possible outcomes. However, the model is inherently under-identified, meaning parameters cannot be estimated for every choice. The solution is a normalization procedure that effectively constrains the parameters of a "default" choice to be zero, resulting in probability estimates for each of the N-1 remaining choice outcomes.

Given this normalization, the estimated coefficients for each choice effectively capture the relative probability of the estimated choices with the respect to the probability of the default choice. This is a particularly convenient implication if the default outcome is a "status quo" choice, since the estimated parameters provide the probability of a change from the default choice to any of the alternate choices. Unfortunately, without such a rationale for selecting the default choice it is difficult to make meaningful economic inferences from the coefficient estimates since the results are dependent on the arbitrary choice of default outcome. On the other hand, unlike the ordered probit, multinomial logit models are not subject to ambiguity about the direction of influence of the independent variables on any of the estimated choices relative to the default choice.

For example, the multinomial logit is useful for studying the selection among more than two organizational alternatives. Keith Crocker and Masten (1991) employ a multinomial logit to examine the choice of price adjustment mechanisms in long-term natural gas contracts. Ménard and Saussier (2000) examine the choice by local governments to outsource their water supply services and the type of contract under which outsourcing was conducted.

### 6.2.3    Counting questions: how many to be?

The preceding models are well-suited to studies of choices between two or more discrete choices such as choices among organizational forms, whether to include or exclude a particular characteristic or contract term, or choices reflecting varying degrees of an attribute. A different set of research questions focusses on cardinal measures of organizational and contractual characteristics such as the number of terms included in contracts, the number of business divisions or production lines in a firm, or the number of members of corporate boards. Questions such as these suggest use of a counting model such as a Poisson regression model. The Poisson model is given by:

$$\Pr(Y_i = y_i | \mathbf{x}_i) = \frac{e^{-\lambda_i} \lambda_i^{y_i}}{y_i!}, \ y_i = 0, 1, 2... \tag{7}$$

where each $y_i$ is drawn from a Poisson distribution with parameter $\lambda_i$. Greene (2003) asserts the most common formulation for $\lambda_i$ is the log-linear model:

$$\ln\lambda_i = x_i'\beta \tag{8}$$

Paul Gompers and Josh Lerner (1996) use a Poisson model to estimate the number of covenant clauses in venture capital partnership agreements. Helland and Sykuta (2004) estimate the number of different types of board directors for firms in changing regulatory environments.

### 6.2.4   Constrained to be

In addition to discrete dependent variables, NIE research on contracting and organizations often encounters data that are in some way constrained or censored. A dependent variable is said to be censored when values in a certain range are transformed to or reported as a single number. For instance, reported price data may be subject to regulatory constraints, trade volumes may be subject to quota limitations, or survey data may assign limit values to extreme observations (e.g. max sales volumes, and so on). For such cases, a Tobit model may be used. The general formulation of the Tobit is given by:

$$y_i^* = x_i'\beta + \varepsilon_i$$

$$y_i = 0 \quad \text{if} \quad y_i^* \leq 0$$
$$y_i = y_i^* \quad \text{if} \quad y_i^* > 0$$

$$[y_i = \bar{y} \quad \text{if} \quad y_i^* \geq \bar{y}; \text{ in the case of an upper limit}]$$

Joseph Fan (2000) uses a Tobit when estimating an index variable (a firm self-sufficiency ratio) which is non-negative by constructions.

Crocker and Masten (1988) use a Tobit formulation to estimate a shadow price for natural gas using price data subject to a regulatory ceiling.

Another form of censoring may occur when the data reflect a survivorship bias. Paul Joskow (1987) and Crocker and Masten (1988) encounter this problem in their analyses of contract duration in coal and natural gas, respectively. Given samples of contracts at a point in time, the prevalence of long-term contracts may be biased by the absence of shorter-term contracts that may have been signed at the same time or later than the observed contracts, but expired prior to the sample period. Similar problems are faced when studying the age of firms or tenures of managers at a point in time, since other firms or managers may be omitted from the sample due to their shorter tenures. Such truncation of the dependent variable may cause biases in ordinary least-squares regressions (Maddala 1983, pp 166–167). Both Joskow and Crocker and Masten use maximum likelihood estimation techniques to account for these potential biases.

### 6.2.5    "Not-so-ordinary" least-squares?

From the above discussion we might presume that most empirical research on organizational and contract structure involves discrete measures of governance types or characteristics, and that ordinary least-squares (OLS) estimation techniques are not-so-ordinary in NIE research. While it is true that many of the decision variables of interest in NIE research are of a discrete nature, OLS remains a useful tool for many types of organizational economics research. In instances where the assumptions of OLS systems are challenged by the data (as in Joskow [1987] and Crocker and Masten [1988], discussed above), researchers occasionally employ both OLS and maximum-likelihood estimation (MLE) models to demonstrate robustness of their results.

### 6.3    Econometric challenges and data pitfalls

The very nature of the questions raised in NIE theories of the firm and contracting pose fundamental problems for statistical modeling. For instance, observed organizational forms often fail to conform to our empirical classifications and result from endogenous decision making. The equilibrium approach typically underlying empirical research also poses problems for making accurate inferences. Data problems create statistical quandaries for researchers in a discipline most comfortable with large sample regression analysis. This section briefly discusses these issues and offers some examples of research that attempt to constructively deal with the challenges.

### 6.3.1   The fallacy of dichotomous choice

The above discussion of the make-or-buy decision suggests such a simple choice would *seem* simple to model econometrically. This would be true if firms only chose one of the two forms of coordinating resources. In reality, however, firms often choose to both make *and* buy. This poses two sets of problems for those interested in explaining the decision to internalize resource allocations: how to determine for modeling purposes whether the activity is ($y = 1$) or is not ($y = 0$) internalized, and whether the theoretical underpinnings are consistent with the coding decision.

Kirk Monteverde and David Teece (1982) encounter this problem in their study of parts supplies in the US automotive industry. They construct a dichotomous dependent variable to reflect whether each of the sample component parts is "predominantly manufactured either in-house or by an external supplier" (p. 207). In this case, predominantly is defined as 80% or more manufactured in-house. Recognizing the arbitrary nature of their classification the authors then recalculate the dependent variable with thresholds of 70% and 90% and re-estimate the probit estimation to verify the robustness of their results. They find that parts are more likely to be manufactured in-house when the application of engineering effort in the development of the part is high and when the part is specific to a particular manufacturer's automobile, regardless of the threshold used.

Fan (2000) adopts an alternate approach to the mixed method problem by developing a measure for the degree of internalization. Rather than use a dichotomous dependent variable based on some threshold of in-house production Fan calculates the firm's input self-sufficiency rate, the proportion of in-house input production to the firm's total input requirement. Input requirements are based on input–output tables and the firm's production capacity. He then estimates Tobit regressions to test the relation between self-sufficiency and transaction cost variables such as proxies for asset-specificity and price uncertainty.

Make-*and*-buy arrangements raise other issues as well, such as the factors determining the share of in-house production whenever and the economic consequence of different in-house production shares. For example, the theoretical argument for Monteverde and Teece's empirical test is that transaction-specific know-how and skills will increase the cost of switching suppliers and therefore make the assembler subject to potential opportunistic recontracting or loss of transaction-specific know-how, leading the assembler to manufacture in-house. But what level of in-house production is sufficient to ensure the assembler retains access to transaction-specific know-how? If in-house manufacturing at any level of production is sufficient would Monteverde and Teece's results hold for much lower thresholds than the super-majority percentages employed, and how would that affect interpretations regarding potential opportunistic recontracting?

Similar questions arise in research on franchising, where franchise systems typically include both company-owned stores as well as franchised stores. Francine Lafontaine and Kathryn Shaw (2005) review a substantial theoretical and empirical literature on the choice of company ownership, then examine the level (or proportion) of company ownership in franchises over time. Contrary to much of the earlier literature, Lafontaine and Shaw find franchise organizations appear to target fixed proportions of company-owned versus franchised outlets over time, although the specific level of ownership differs across firms. In particular, they find a strong relation between brand name value and company ownership.

Rarely is empirical research as clean-cut as our theoretical models. The boundary of the firm – where the last transaction is internalized at the margin – has been a principle focus of NIE research for decades. Nonetheless, our theoretical tools frequently cut too broad a swath to capture the variety of organizational structures we have to study. Care must be exercised to consider the implications – econometric as well as theoretical – when fitting the data to our models.

### 6.3.2    Endogenous decision making and self-selection

Most of the empirical research on contracting and organization attempts to explain some attributes of governance mechanisms based on, or given, the characteristics of the transaction being studied. However, it is clearly the case that in many instances transaction characteristics as well as governance attributes are endogenously determined. For instance, the level of specific investment and the nature of protections against post-contractual hazards related to those investments may be simultaneously determined. Indeed, the incomplete contracts theory of the firm (Grossman and Hart 1986; Hart and Moore 1990) implicitly recognizes this, as the *ex ante* ownership arrangement is chosen based on its expected effect on the level of specific investment. More generally, decision makers choose (self-select) a governance mechanism with the objective of maximizing their payoff.

Linear estimation techniques have typically used instrumental variables and seemingly unrelated regression (SURE) models as means of controlling for endogeniety. Barton Hamilton and Jackson Nickerson (2003) develop a reduced-form switching regression approach specifically to relate choice of governance structure and performance. Kyle Mayer and Nickerson (2005) use the model to estimate the effect of governance structure on performance in the information technology industry. Daniel Ackerberg and Maristella Botticini (2002) use a full information maximum likelihood approach to account for self-selection between landowners and tenant farmers and compare their results to both simple (non-adjusted) linear models as well as linear models using instrumental variables to control for the endogenous choice. They demonstrate the effect of modeling approaches on the relative significance of important theoretical findings.

A related issue is the endogeneity of terms within a contract and the relationship between various contract terms. Michael Sykuta and Joe Parcell (2003) argue that transactions have three fundamental characteristics: the allocation of value; the allocation of exposure to uncertainty; and the allocation of decision rights. Terms affecting any one of these three allocations are likely to have implications for allocations elsewhere in the contract. Thus, it is important to consider the complete set of contract terms rather than focusing on individual terms in isolation. Both Joskow (1987) and Crocker and Masten (1991) examine the interaction between contract terms using standard simultaneous equation techniques. In discussing this challenge, Masten and Saussier (2002, p. 291) claim "[t]he binding constraint is not technique, but data availability. As the number of provisions analyzed increases, the number of explanatory variables and the size of the data set needed for statistical identification multiplies. Often, sufficient numbers of observations to analyze more than two or three provisions at a time will simply not exist."

### 6.3.3  Constraints of the equilibrium approach

Most empirical research on comparative governance mechanisms implicitly assumes equilibrium conditions. As Williamson (1985, p. 22) states "the question is whether organizational relations (contracting practices; governance structures) line up with the attributes of transactions as predicted by transaction cost reasoning or not." The hypothesis test, then, is based on the assumption that if we do not observe the expected relation between transaction cost factors and (presumably efficient) organizational design, the theory is not substantiated. The possibility of misalignment and dynamic adjustment has not been well addressed. In short, little work has been done directly examining the performance (or transaction cost) implications of governance design and the dynamics of governance structures.

Although there have been attempts to measure the relation between organizational design and performance (Armour and Teece 1978; Silverman, Nickerson, and Freeman 1997; Poppo and Zenger 1998), there is little conclusive evidence. Masten (2002) explains the methodological and empirical challenges for establishing a causal relationship between organizational form and performance. A major impediment is the ability to measure performance at the unit of analysis: the resource allocation decision or transaction. An important exception is Mayer and Nickerson (2005) who actually examine transaction-level financial returns as a function of organizational form. Using data on individual information technology service agreements, the authors find that service agreements structured in ways consistent with transaction cost-based predictions have higher financial returns, suggesting governance structure matters for performance.

Although not direct tests of the link between organization and performance, recent studies do offer indirect evidence. Nickerson and Silverman (2003) examine the dynamic implications of organizational misalignment in the US for-hire interstate trucking industry and find that firms with structures inconsistent with transaction cost economics (TCE) predictions "realize lower profits than their better-aligned counterparts, and that these firms will attempt to adapt so as to better align their transactions" (p. 433). Nicholas Argyres and Lyde Bigelow (2005) incorporate transaction cost economizing in a life cycle model for the early US automotive industry and find firms that were not organized in transaction cost economizing ways were more likely to fail during the industry's shake out period in the 1920s.

The dynamics of contract structure – that is, how contracts evolve and whether contracting parties learn from their experiences – have also received little attention. This is a different question than the effect of repeat dealing or reputation on contract design (Crocker and Reynolds 1993). Claire Hill (2001) provides a legal production function explanation for the persistence of poorly written contract documents, explaining how judicial institutions and the nature of legal work limit lawyers' incentives to innovate or improve upon previously sanctioned contract language. Argyres and Mayer (2004) conduct an in-depth study of a series of contracts between two parties to determine when and why contract terms change, and find many changes that cannot be readily explained by changes in the assets at risk. They also find a positive relation between inter-organizational trust and contract length, if not contractual completeness.

### 6.3.4  Data limitations on statistical techniques

As noted above in the quote from Masten and Saussier (2002), often the binding constraint on empirical research on contracting and organization is simply a lack of available data. Boerner and Macher (2001, p. 9) find that "[t]he most common means of primary data collection in empirical TCE research are mail surveys, interviews, and firm visits." Secondary data generally come from published data sources such as trade publications, government data, newspapers, and archival sources. In some cases, researchers examine actual contracts. Given the costs associated with these data collection efforts and the proprietary nature of contract documents, sample sizes in this field tend to be small – so small as to preclude effective use of most of the econometric techniques described. Researchers are left to conduct simple analysis of variance, categorical frequency statistics, and inductive reasoning to illustrate consistencies between patterns in the data and the theoretical expectations.

Commercial databases such as Thomsen Financial's SDC Platinum or Standard & Poor's ExecuComp provide large sets of data on key contract terms for a variety of financial, organizational, and executive compensation contracts. Although expensive, these data sets provide large, cross-sectional and inter-temporal samples. Their principal drawback is the lack of detail for the actual contracts available in the data set and the primarily descriptive nature of many contract terms (e.g. dummy variables for the presence of a particular term, without details on the exact nature of the term).

The Contracting and Organizations Research Institute (CORI) at the University of Missouri maintains a large collection of contract documents for a wide range of transaction types and industries.[10] Unlike the commercial databases above the entire text of the contract is available for inspection, allowing researchers to study the specific structure of individual contract terms and the inter-relation of terms with the contract. However, individual terms and firm characteristics are not already coded. This allows researchers to construct measures best suited to the specific contract terms of interest, but at the expense of the convenience associated with many commercial databases. While many of the contracts in the CORI collection come from similar sources as those of Thomsen Financial and Standard & Poor, the CORI collection includes material from a wider variety of sources, including regulatory agencies, government contracts, and proprietary contracts.

A final challenge for empirical research on contracting is the simple fact that the contract documents the researcher observes are a very limited picture of the actual economic relationships the documents represent. Contracts provide, at most, the details of the rules of the relationship as originally envisioned and negotiated by both parties. To view the relationship solely through the document is like looking through a glass dimly. To study the true relationship reflected in the contract requires more in-depth interaction with the parties themselves. Thus, some of the most insightful research to be conducted will not be achieved by the best econometric tools, but by case study research.

## 6.4    Theoretical and conceptual challenges in new institutional economics research

Empirical research on contracting and organizations has generally been successful, in particular the applications of Williamson's TCE theories. However, challenges still exist. Key terms and concepts in the underlying theories are both poorly defined and difficult to measure. This section briefly highlights these areas of potential concern not as a warning sign against proceeding, but simply as a caution or perhaps as a call for intentional focus to address these challenges. Measurement is a funda-mental difficulty in empirical NIE research. Although measurement problems are often the result of imperfect data, several key measurement problems result from theoretical concepts that are not well-defined. It is difficult to measure appropriately something that is not clearly defined. This section highlights particular terms and concepts that hamper effective research on contracting and organizational structure.

### 6.4.1    Vertical integration

From Coase's original work in 1937, the make-or-buy decision has been a focal point for empirical research. However, the concept of vertical integration is not well defined either in NIE or in the traditional industrial organization literature. The unanswered question about ver-tical integration is the economic relevance of the concept. Without that understanding we cannot begin to determine the appropriate measure of vertical integration.

Perhaps the most common understanding of vertical integration is ownership of productive assets at consecutive stages of production. Whilst measuring ownership of assets at two stages of production is rela-tively straightforward, such a measure ignores two important economic implications. First, such a measure does not address whether the volume of production at one stage corresponds with the volume at the other stage, what might be called the *degree* of vertical integration. A firm that vertically integrates 10% of its input requirements is not the same as a firm that integrates 100% of its needs. Fan (2000) and Fan and Lang (2000) develop a measure of relatedness using input–output production ratios to calculate the relative share of the vertically integrated resource. Such a measure provides a better perspective of the economic relevance of the integrated activity.

Second, defining vertical integration based on asset ownership at consecutive stages of production may miss the economic point. In Coase's (1937) paper, the economic question is not why assets are commonly owned, but why resources are allocated by managerial control rather than by the price mechanism. Common ownership of assets is neither a necessary nor sufficient condition for managerial (or non-price) coordination or control of resources. It is not uncommon for commonly owned divisions of a company to operate autonomously in the market place without direct managerial intervention. Similarly, ownership is not required to exert managerial control over assets. This is amply clear in US agriculture where production contracts in poultry and hogs, among other products, stipulate many managerial practices and asset allocations – to the point that such independent contracting arrangements are under scrutiny for appearing too much like employment contracts.

An alternate definition of vertical integration would be based on control of productive assets at adjoining stages of production. We might envision a measure similar to Fan's capturing the percentage of input needs (distribution access) controlled. However, since assets can be controlled by managerial discretion either through ownership or by contract, such a definition of integration would fail to discriminate between the types of governance mechanism used. Moreover, at least in the case of contractual control, contractual incompleteness may give rise to circumstances in which the residual rights of control do not correspond to the contractual control rights, raising the question of which party actually "owns" the asset (the basis of the Grossman–Hart–Moore (G–H–M) framework).

These are difficult questions that NIE scholars have yet to fully address. However, if the questions are ever to be answered theories of economic organization are more promising sources for those answers than is the traditional industrial organization literature. In the meantime, while a clean, theoretical definition of vertical integration may not be readily forthcoming, researchers need to be intentionally specific in how the term is used and operationalized in empirical research to ensure the phenomenon being investigated is the one with the most economic relevance.

## 6.4.2    Asset specificity

The concept of asset specificity plays a prominent role in NIE theories of the firm, in particular in Williamson's TCE, but to a degree in G–H–M incomplete contract theory as well. The argument is that asset specificity creates a quasi-rent in the transaction relationship that may induce one party or the other to engage in opportunistic behavior or costly negotiations, or both, in attempt to appropriate the value of the quasi-rent. These quasi-rents are typically considered the difference in the value of the specific asset in its current use versus its next best use, net of any conversion, re-tooling, and redeployment costs. Another way of thinking about the quasi-rent is as the difference between the price that is currently being paid for the asset and the price required to keep the asset employed in its current use (i.e. its shutdown or reservation price). The greater is the quasi-rent, the greater the incentive for at least one party to attempt to appropriate the value of the quasi-rents. Thus, the key for arguments of asset specificity rests in the size of the quasi-rent.

Empirical research examining the role of asset specificity rarely uses direct estimations of the size of the quasi-rent itself owing to the difficult nature of measuring opportunity costs.[11] Rather, most research asserts a positive correlation between certain characteristics and the size of the quasi-rent, and attributes any incentives resulting from asset specificity to the characteristics themselves. For instance, Fan (2000) uses geographic proximity among petroleum refiners to proxy for specificity. Joskow (1987) uses both the physical proximity of electric plants and coal mines and the type of coal available from the mines as measures of geographic and technical specificities. Scott Masten, James Meehan, and Edward Snyder (1991) use survey results from production managers rating the degree of specificity and complexity of component parts in ship building. Saussier (2000b) uses a dummy variable to indicate whether suppliers deliver to facilities requiring specially designed physical assets. While the link between such measures of specificity and the existence of a quasi-rent are intuitively reasonable, the size of the appropriable rent and hence the incentive for opportunistic behavior are imperfectly captured, at best.

A more appealing proxy for asset specificity may be the amount of investment required in non-redeployable assets, such as Saussier's (2000b) measure of site-specific investment. However, while quasi-rents may be attributable to such sunk investments, a measure of *re*-deployment costs rather than initial deployment costs would be more accurate. Obviously, quasi-rents are difficult to measure empirically and proxies such as those described may be the best alternative available to researchers.

Nonetheless, researchers should bear in mind the goal of measuring the size of the appropriable quasi-rent itself rather than immediately relying on characteristics of assets that *may* generate such rents.

A more fundamental question that researchers must address is "specific to what?" The general premise in NIE theories of the firm is that investments or assets that are *relationship*-specific give rise to potential quasi-rents and associated behavioral ills. What is less clear is whether, or when, assets that are firm-specific or industry-specific are necessarily relationship-specific. For instance, Craig Pirrong (1993) and Thomas Hubbard (2001) use "thinness" of the market to proxy for specificity of assets that, of themselves, are not necessarily specific to a particular transaction or trading partner. Thinness in the market creates a potential temporal hazard like unto that in Masten, Meehan, and Snyder (1991). However, in the former case, the temporal specificity derives from the sequential nature of a production process rather than market structure characteristics. We may ask to what extent the optimal governance response for such temporal specificities depends on the source of the specificity, or the circumstances under which the implications of the empirical results are more or less generalizable.

### 6.4.3  An economic system perspective

Williamson's (1985, p. 18) characterization of the nature of comparative organizational economics research has become known as the *discriminating alignment hypothesis*: "Transaction costs are minimized by assigning transactions (which differ in their attributes) to governance structures (the adaptive capabilities and associated costs of which differ) in a discriminating way." As noted above, this fundamental principle has been empirically supported by a wealth of empirical research.

An unfortunate consequence of this framework is that it tends to promote the perspective of governance structures and transaction attributes as commodities. Given two transactions with identical attributes the discriminating alignment hypothesis would suggest both transactions should have the same governance structure. What is missing from this analysis is an understanding of the motivations of and the relationship between the contracting parties, as well as the social and economic contexts within which the two parties are contracting. At the party level we might respond that such factors are simply additional dimensions of the transaction, hence otherwise identical transactions between parties that have a different relationship or different objective functions may have different governance mechanisms, and that would be a fair response. However, these particular characteristics have thus far not played a significant role in either the major theoretical or empirical works in the field.

An example of the importance of this issue at the contract party level may be seen in the agricultural sector. The agricultural sector is relatively unique in the widespread co-existence of cooperative or agricultural producer-owned firms (POFs) and investor-owned firms (IOFs), particularly in the first-stage handling of agricultural products. Michael Sykuta and Michael Cook (2001) argue the difference in objective functions between POFs and IOFs should be reflected in their contractual relationships with agricultural producers. Harvey James and Michael Sykuta (2006) find that producers of agricultural commodities not only perceive a difference when marketing to POFs versus IOFs, but also accept significantly different prices for their commodities based on the nature of their marketing counterpart holding other factors constant.

We might suggest that the above argument seems very close to the resource-based, or competence perspective of the firm discussed in some of the strategic management literature (Collis and Montgomery 1995; Conner and Prahalad 1996). Williamson (1999b) provides a useful discussion of governance versus competence theories of the firm and argues they are more complementary than rival. There are certainly dimension on which a competence perspective may enhance TCE. Williamson (1996b, p. 1106) concludes, "Both [governance and competence perspectives] are needed in our efforts to understand complex economic phenomena as we build towards a science of organization."

However, the system perspective envisioned above extends beyond simply recognizing the differences in capabilities and objectives of the specific contracting parties. Transactions at one level of the value chain are likely interdependent on the structure and governance of transactions at other levels of the supply chain. Contracts between retailers and product manufacturers create the context within which manufacturers choose their own governance and contractual structures with suppliers. The structure of supply relations affects a manufacturer's approach to contracting with its consumers. Without an eye on the larger system researchers are likely to overlook ways in which organizational structure is influenced by its value chain context.

## 6.5    Conclusion

From the original seeds sown by Coase's inquiry into why we observe firms in a specialized market economy, NIE research on the existence and structure of transaction governance mechanisms has been characterized by an interest in developing theories "where the assumptions may be both manageable and realistic" (Coase 1937, p. 386). This intention to develop models based in realism places a premium on quality empirical research both to test alternative theories and to identify empirical phenomena that might spur further innovations in our theoretical frameworks. The tremendous variation in governance structures and transaction attributes observed in the economy suggest numerous types of inquiries, each with different statistical characteristics. Therefore the econometric toolkit for researchers in new institutional economics must encompass a wide array of formulations and researchers must be flexible in their abilities to adapt to new techniques as are appropriate to their investigations.

Despite the large number of empirical studies to date, and the general consistency of empirical results with transaction cost-based theories of economic organization, there is much work to be done. Theoretical concepts must be refined to provide clearer insight into the nature of organizational structure. Competing theories suggest opportunities to take what is best from each to develop a more complete whole. New and better sources of data on contract and organizational structures will provide fuel for empirical research and facilitate more robust statistical analyses of the causes and consequences of alternate governance forms. Though challenges exist, our understanding of how the economic system works will be greatly enhanced as scholars continue their work.

# 7 Experimental Methodology to Inform New Institutional Economics Issues

*Stéphane Robin and Carine Staropoli*

## 7.1 Introduction

Traditionally, economics has been viewed as a non-experimental science that has to rely exclusively on field data. However, this was seen as an obstacle to the continued development of economics as a science, and as strongly restricting the possibility of testing economic theory. This view has been challenged by the growing development of experimental economics since the 1960s.[1]

Recent contributions by leading NIE scholars are viewing experimental economics as a promising method for future development of the NIE research program (Ménard 2001; Joskow 2003). These claims remain vague. The aim of this chapter is to suggest how NIE economists could benefit from carrying out experiments in addition to other empirical methodologies they are already using.

The paper is divided into three sections. Section 7.2 briefly presents the basic principles of experimental economics. It insists that, among the various uses to which laboratory experiments have been put in economics, the most useful for NIE lies in its capacity to generate laboratory data which may be used to test predictions and refine behavioral hypotheses. We then highlight two fields of research for which we think there are adequacies of research agenda between experimental economics (EE) and NIE: analysis of individual behaviour (Section 7.3) and assessment of institutional properties and performance as well as institutional design (Section 7.4). The main results obtained in these fields are then presented, focussing on their originality and how they might fit into the NIE research agenda.

## 7.2 Principles of experimental economics

The experimental laboratory aims to create a real economic situation where principles of economics apply, as they do outside the laboratory. The economic situation is characterized by rules that are explained to

142

real interacting people (they are called "subjects" in the laboratory) who may gain real and substantial payoffs, depending on their action in the laboratory. The experimenters observe how subjects behave in the laboratory through an *institution* in a controlled *environment*. In this sense, experimental economics is not a simulation.

The *environment* ingredients are the endowments and preferences of subjects. Control of motivation and the subject's preferences are determining factors in the experimental design. The incentive mechanism used for this control is based on a real reward medium (usually currency) that participating subjects may earn. The reward mechanism must meet three main conditions known as monotonicity, salience, and dominance (Smith 1976). "Monotonicity" refers to the fact that subjects must prefer more reward medium to less, and that they must not be satiated. "Saliency" refers to the fact that the reward received by a subject depends on his action (and those of the other agents he interacts with in the laboratory) as defined by the institution. Of course, the subject is aware of the rules for gaining a reward and the experimenter must make sure he understands them. "Dominance" refers to the fact that changes in subjects' utility during the experiment mainly result from the reward medium, and other influences are negligible.

*Institution* refers to the protocol the subjects must follow to interact in the laboratory. In a game experiment the institution is simply the rule of the game: the action profile of the player (buyer, seller . . . ), the order of moves, and the information set of the players at each stage of the game. In a market experiment the institution refers to the market exchange of information (bids, asks, acceptance procedures), the protocol for exchanging information (centralized or decentralized institution) and the rules whereby offers become real transactions.

Replication and control are the two primary motivations for carrying out the experiment instead of observing natural situations and using field data. As a condition for replication, environments and institutions used in an experiment must be clearly specified in the experiment protocol. Empirical researches are also facilitated in the laboratory since there is little or no measurement error. Control and replicability open the door to different research strategies. In accordance with the didactic classification by Alvin Roth (1995), there are three reasons for carrying out an experiment: "speaking to theorists"; "searching for facts"; and "whispering in the ears of the prince."

*"Speaking to theorist experiments"* are initially motivated by theory literature.[2] Experiments may be used to test theoretical predictions under precisely controlled or measured conditions, or both.[3] The idea is that general theories and models should apply to all special cases. Notably,

they should work in the special case of laboratory situations. As theory offers predictions embedded in a set of assumptions, experimental method produces data with an environment and institution that closely fits this set of assumptions. Then the question is to compare the experimental observations and theoretical predictions. If the observations target the predictions with a frequency higher than occuring by chance the strategy could then be to test the robustness of the theory by looking at how theoretical models react to disruption in environment or to the institution, or both. Otherwise, when the experimental observations fail to meet theoretical predictions a preliminary investigation checks to see whether this gap between theory and observation is not a laboratory artifact. Then it is possible to examine experimentally the causes of the failure of the theory by use of specific tests.

Most of the time, establishing a positive theory follows on from observations. "*Facts searching experiments*" are designed from this aim. Experimental methods document surprising regularities and stylized facts between observed and controlled economic variables. These empirical results could then serve as the basis for a new theory with a clearly identified link between the variables theorists must work on.

"*Whispering in the ears of princes experiments*" refers to the growing use of laboratory research. These experiments are designed to study new institutional designs or evaluate policy proposals in the laboratory before introducing them in the field, just as aircraft engineers study a small-scale model in a "test-bed" before trying to build and fly a new aircraft. Here again, with control and replicability, experiments may be designed to compare and evaluate different institutions, or to test new market institutions and evaluate their robustness to changes in the environment.

Each of these motives for carrying out experiments is interesting for NIE. NIE is presented as an "empirical success story" by its supporters, which does not mean everything has already been done. There have been hundreds of tests on transaction cost economics (TCE), yet many aspects of the research program still need to be tested. The main approach to testing NIE predictions so far involves statistical evidence and econometric test, often based on new sets of data from scratch. However, data may be unavailable in the field or irrelevant for testing NIE predictions. Indeed, field data are often difficult to collect ("because the attributes of transactions (and, for that matter, of governance structures) are rarely reported in published sources, empirical research in transaction cost economics often requires the collection of original data").[4] In the case of new institutions such as new electricity markets, created as part of the competitive reforms in many developed countries or the FCC spectrum auction in the USA, it is simply impossible to collect price data before the market has been implemented or the auction run. However, public authorities need some empirical material to have more visibility on the properties of the institution before its implementation. Typically, in the FCC auction design process, Milgrom reports that Plott experimental results (Plott 1997) convinced the FCC to adopt the Milgrom–Wilson auction design (Milgrom 2004).

More generally, Ménard (2001) argues that the concepts used by NIE are often too general making the collection of relevant data to test theoretical predictions more difficult. One solution might be to create its own environment in the laboratory, with parameters describing the environment which fit, as closely as possible, those used in the theoretical framework. Data obtained in the laboratory would thus be adequate for testing.

## 7.3    Behaviour in the laboratory: bounded rationality and social preferences

This section emphasizes the way EE deals with the two behavioral hypotheses central to the framework of TCE: bounded rationality and opportunism. It reveals how "learning experiments" help further understanding of the decision-making process in the context of bounded rationality, whereas the impact of social preferences is crucial for assessing the level of opportunism and better characterizing the determinants of such behaviour.

Interestingly, when new institutionalists refer to experimental work as a way of enriching studies on bounded rationality for their own purpose, they mostly refer to experimental psychology inspired by cognitive psychology (Williamson 2000). Although there are strong links between psychological assumptions and economic theory (notably through the recent development of "behavioral economics," which, according to Colin Camerer, reunifies the two disciplines), psychology and economics remain two different disciplines, notably in their experimental approaches (Camerer 2003). Here, the focus is on the sole experimental economics approach.

The first paragraph presents the main results of "learning experiments" – considered as those that have helped the most in specifying the concept of bounded rationality. We then present the main results of studies on opportunism, as defined by Williamson (1975), arguing that these concepts would benefit from analysing social preferences. According to Fehr and Fischbacher (2002), "a person exhibits social preferences if the person does not only care about the material resources allocated to her but also care about the material resources allocated to relevant reference agents." There are various types of social preferences, including "reciprocity" (both positive and negative), "inequity aversion," "pure altruism," and spiteful or envious preferences.[5] We focus on the Ultimatum Game, which is the known and used illustration of the impact of social preferences.

### 7.3.1 Clarifying the concept of bounded rationality: "learning experiments"

In traditional micro-economic theory, the *homo economicus* decision maker has a huge capability for solving simply structured problems. In reality, the decision maker is subject to rationality boundaries: he has limited perceptional, cognitive, and intellectual capabilities. Bounded rationality is central to NIE behavioral theory. However, its use is criticized for various reasons. Some economists criticize the lack of mathematical models for supporting reasoning on bounded rationality and evaluating its consequences. Although there is a growing body of work trying to find ways to model bounded rationality (Maskin and Tirole 1999) this is not yet the case. Further criticism comes from Herbert Simon himself who complains about the inappropriate and partial use of bounded rationality in the NIE framework (Simon 1997). In the NIE framework bounded rationality is not used as a "decision process response" at individual agent level for explaining administrative behaviour, as in Simon (1947), but, rather, for developing a theory on organizational choice (Williamson 1985). Bounded rationality is not invoked because it is itself central, nor is it modeled. Although considered a necessary assumption in the TCE framework, bounded rationality is still limited to what Foss (2002) calls "rhethorical use"[6] in the work of organizational economists. Its principal ramification for economic organization is that all complex contracts are unavoidably incomplete – a key feature for NIE.

As claimed by Joskow (2003), there is certainly much more work to be done to expand studies on bounded rationality and integrate work on individual decision making and cognition with imperfect information and uncertainty into new institutional analysis. This would re-legitimate or at least give more weight to Simon's contribution to NIE. We argue that what is done in the laboratory on individual decision making helps to further clarify studies on bounded rationality for NIE research. Indeed, in 1947, Herbert Simon himself argued that laboratory experiments and empirical studies on the behavior of consumers, or of business firms directly, should help further studies on organization.

The consequence of bounded rationality is that in order to reach a solvable decision problem, any individual who has to make a decision (decision maker) must first reduce its complexity by neglecting some aspects of the situation.[7] To do so, the individual has, notably, to learn from past decisions. Progress in the study of bounded rationality implies being able to determine these simplification rules (Tietz 1990). From a dynamic point of view, the decision maker must be able to detect errors he may have made, correct his preliminary decisions via feedback, and, more generally, learn about the impact of his decisions. In other words, he has to learn.

In an experiment, learning is related to incomplete information. This incompleteness is linked: sometimes to how the experiment is designed, and very often to the rationality or motivation of other participants. So there is a learning dimension to most experiments, no matter what the situation under consideration.

However, the most convenient way to benefit from experiments on learning is to take into account experimental tests of learning models. Indeed, learning is a field of research with fruitful exchange between experiments and theory. These experiments are mainly "Game experiments," where special attention is given to what subjects really know about the future and what they have experienced in the past. Their purpose is to validate or reject alternative models of learning, and to find out which one is the most appropriate given the circumstances. Using these models it is then easier to figure out the characteristics of learning processes from these experiments.

There are numerous kind of learning models based on different approaches to the learning process: evolutionary dynamics; reinforcement learning; belief learning; experience-weighted attraction; imitation; directional learning; or rule learning (Camerer and Ho 1999). In evolutionary dynamics models, learning is considered at a collective level.[8] For a given population some agents are endowed with a strategy and use it with the other players in the population. Then, the part of the population with unsuccessful strategies decreases, while the part which uses successful strategies increases. This collective approach to learning cannot explain the rapid learning of subjects in the laboratory.

Individual learning models better fit behavior observed during experiments. Reinforcement models – belief learning and imitation learning – are the two fundamental approaches to individual learning.[9] With the reinforcement approach the agent starts by using different strategies, and gradually selects those with a view to the payoffs they gave in the past. Belief learning models are more interactive. Here, the agent has beliefs about what the other players will do in the coming period, and he updates these beliefs depending on the effective behavior he observes. Given his beliefs, he chooses the strategy which should give him maximum expected payoff. Finally, in an imitation learning model the agent chooses the best strategy from among those used by others agents, and he uses it during the coming period. The imitation learning approach gives a good prediction for symmetric game. However, imitation learning cannot be generalized to a general type of learning environment.

Experiments for testing the reinforcement of learning models (Roth and Erev 1995) and belief learning models (Crawford and Broseta 1998) show that, in most situations studied, learning theories are more accurate than the equilibrium concept for predicting the development of effective behavior. For sure, equilibrium theories give no clues about how people really evolve toward equilibrium. So it is not surprising that learning models better fit learning processes with good predictions of the direction of learning. But more than that, the learning process could drive people away from the equilibrium predicted by theories. Is it possible to say whether one model of learning is better than others through comparative studies? Judging from the comparison between reinforcement and belief learning, the answer is "No." In fact, the logic of learning depends on the type of situation people face. For instance, reinforcement learning fits better than belief learning in games with only mixed-strategy equilibria (Mookherjee and Sopher 1997). But belief learning gives a better prediction than reinforcement in coordination and dominance-solvable games (Ho and Weigelt 1996).

So, it seems that learning depends on the type of economic interaction. Concerning individual behavior, results show that people use all the information they accumulate from experience (payoff, strategy, behavior of other players) and reveal that they are motivated to research information about foregone payoffs. These observations have resulted in further research on more general models capable of incorporating these features. Experience-weighted attraction models (Camerer and Ho 1999) and rule learning models (Stahl 1996) are designed with this aim in mind. These models predict better than simpler theories, but the models require more parameters. One of the next steps for this field of research is to integrate interactive learning: how people take the learning of others into account in their own strategies.

Overall, understanding how people learn in a given situation is an important step toward a better understanding of bounded rationality, which is central to the NIE analytical framework.

*7.3.2    Opportunism and social preferences in the laboratory*

Selfishness is one of the most common assumptions of standard economics. It means individuals are exclusively motivated by material self-interest. This hypothesis is a convenient simplification, notably for comparative static predictions of aggregate behaviour of self-interested models. But findings reveal that reality is more subtle. As seen earlier, for the self-interest-seeking-assumption, NIE adds "allowance for guile" (Williamson 1975). This slight difference is important since it includes new kinds of behavior even more diverse than those involved in the adverse selection and moral hazard ones in a principal-agent relationship. Also central to the opportunism concept, as opposed to the standard selfishness hypothesis, is the fact that there may be various degrees of opportunism. In other words an individal is, by definition, opportunist, but he may be more or less so. Furthermore, the degree of opportunism may be more or less consequential depending on the situation (notably, depending on the level of bounded rationality and, from a TCE perspective, features of the transaction). All this further complicates decision making compared to the standard self-interest hypothesis.

Since Adam Smith, influential economists such as Gary Becker, Kenneth Arrow, Douglass North, and Amartya Sen have pointed out that people often care for social preference motivations, others-regarding and process-regarding preferences (Fehr and Fischbacher 2002). Recent laboratory findings confirm such preferences, and refute the self-interest hypothesis. They reveal how concerns about reciprocity have a significant impact on bilateral negotiations, on the functioning of markets and incentives, on the structure of property rights and contracts, and on laws governing collective action and cooperation. These results suggest individuals are less willing to act opportunistically, or to a lesser extent, if influenced by fairness and reciprocity.

The first experiments on social preferences aimed to detect this kind of preference in a one-shot relation with anonymity and no reputation effect. In 1982, Werner Güth, Rolf Schmittberger, and Bernd Schwarz (1982) carried out the first Ultimatum Game experiment (henceforth referred to as UG). In this UG, two individuals must agree how to divide a sum of money (the pie). In the sequential form of the UG used by Güth *et al.* (1982), the first player (the sender) makes an offer about dividing the pie to the second player (the receiver). If the receiver accepts the offer he receives the offered amount, while the sender's payoff is the stake minus the offer. If the receiver rejects the offer both players obtain a zero payoff.

Assuming players are rational, risk-neutral, and only motivated by selfishness, the receiver will probably accept any offer made by the sender, even the smallest. Consequently, the sender's decision should be to offer the smallest subdivision allowed. Except for narrow-minded economists, most will predict unfair shares will be rejected and fair shares proposed. This is what Güth *et al.* (1982) observed in their experiment: the rate of rejection increases when the offer moves away from the fifty-fifty offer; offers that are inferior to the 20% of the stake are rejected with over 50% probability; and the average offer is between 30% and 40% of the stake. People in the laboratory, in an artificial, anonymous, and non-repeated relationship, are not only selfish but they also take care of the welfare of the other people they face.

Several explanations attempt to resolve the obvious differences between standard theory and empirical findings. Most focus on the social norms individuals bring to the game, which affect their behavior beyond what standard theory commonly assumes. According to these explanations, the utility players may derive from the game includes social factors such as the relative standing of each player after bargaining is concluded, and how the agreement is reached.

Since the experiment by Güth *et al.* (1982), UG has been the object of extensive experimental studies, the main goal being to test the validity and robustness of the results they obtained. The robustness of UG results was tested with regard to design variables (repetition, stake, understanding, anonymity between subjects, or anonymity vis-à-vis the experimenter), demographic variables, or culture. After these results were proved generally robust (Camerer and Thaler 1995; Camerer 2003), a second wave of experiments was designed to characterize the social preferences expressed in this category of interactions. This research resulted in new mapping of preferences modeled in utility function incorporating social preferences. There are two categories of model. On one hand, a large set of models focus on feelings of "envy" or "injustice" which extremely unequal bargaining outcomes trigger. The "degree of envy" or the "aversion to inequality" determines to what extent division of the stake will be accepted, even if different from the equal split (Bolton 1991; Fehr and Schmidt 1999). On the other hand, models of intentional or reciprocal behavior (Rabin 1993; Dufwenberg and Kirchsteiger 2004) assume a rational reason for taking action is to reciprocate what one's opponent is expected to do, or to respond to what he actually does. Models of intentional or reciprocal behavior also include notions of fairness or justice, not directly to defend the individual's utility function, but mediated by the individual's understanding of the norm in a given circumstance. Fairness is a rewarding response to fairness, just as unfairness is a retaliating response to selfishness; in the UG, receivers accept offers only when they consider them sufficiently fair; otherwise, they reject them.

Observing real behavior in the laboratory reveals how people are unselfish, but this does not mean they are altruistic. Opportunism drives behavior in the laboratory, as it does in real life, but this opportunism incorporates social preferences related to fairness and reciprocity. These results raise important issues about the norms of fairness and common knowledge about this norm. Even in a game with perfect information on its structure and player payoff, there remains incomplete information related to the norm of fairness of the player and the importance of their respective social motivation (Meidinger, Robin, and Ruffieux 1999).

## 7.4    "Institutions matter": playing with the rules

EE and NIE share the same credo: "institutions do matter." Even if the term "institution" refers to different types of reality for EE and NIE, both involve at least two tasks regarding institutions: first, the assessment of institutional properties and performances; and, second, how institutions are really created. Indeed, most institutions do not emerge spontaneously. They are, rather, designed and implemented by decision makers (public authorities, managers, market makers ...) in a specific institutional or industrial context (deregulation and privatization, creation of new market places, provision of public goods, developing internet ...) Economists have played an active role in this design stage, boosting the role of economics as an "engineering" discipline capable of providing guidance on matters of institutional design, in creating public policies, and selecting contractual forms, as well as providing advice on policy issues whose answers lie beyond the reliable scientific knowledge of the profession (Wilson 2002).

In the last two decades, governments and public authorities have had to design procurement contracts, new auctions, and markets in the context of the progressive liberalization of public utilities. In this design task economists face the challenging issues of assessing "good" or "efficient" market designs, given that significant consequences may arise if mistakes are made. Recent experiences – the best-known include UMTS auctions in Europe in the early 2000s and the electricity market crisis in California in the summer of 2000 – emphasize the negative consequences and costs of "bad institutional design," and how difficult and costly it is to correct initial errors. Famous experimentalists have focussed their research on these tasks while working as consultants for public authorities. In 2002, Vernon Smith was awarded the Nobel Prize for his contribution to EE, and notably for pioneering the use of controlled laboratory experiments as wind tunnel tests of new auction design before being used in practice. His work has been applied to the provision of public goods, the allocation of airport time slots using computer-assister markets, and, most recently, on alternative ways of organizing electricity markets. Other well-documented experiments on market design include, for instance, the gas transmission auction, FCC spectrum auction, the allocation of rights to use railways tracks or airport slots, medical clearing houses, or the auction of the irrigation system in Georgia.

Among the many institutions studied in the laboratory (bargaining procedures, contracts, and markets), we focussed on one specific type of institution: markets organized as auctions. We mentioned earlier the important experimental findings on bargaining procedures and coordination games, through the lens of the behaviors of transactors. Experiments focussing on contracts are also interesting for NIE but, from our point of view, to a lesser extent, since EE mostly considers contractual issues with reference to the principal-agent paradigm (Willinger and Keser 2000). However, recent experimental results contribute to the literature on incomplete contracts, which falls in line with the NIE research agenda but is still in its infancy in the laboratory (Fehr, Klein, and Schmidt 2001). On the contrary, market experiments contribute largely to EE, with significant results on the assessment of market properties and performances, as well as institutional design.

Since the early 1950s, EE has helped to open up the "black box" of the markets by producing many results on the characteristics of detailed mechanisms governing market exchanges, the so-called market rules. Early market experiments were based on theories of industrial organization.[10] These kinds of experiment were usually quite simple in design, with the standard underlying belief that market efficiency is mostly determined by market structure (the point of view of imperfect competition theory).

The aim was to test theoretical predictions on the behavioral characteristics of markets. Given an initial experimental design (one environment and one institution), a so-called "treatment," it is possible to elaborate other treatments which differ from the initial one by modifying (even marginally) one or more variables, keeping the others constant. The variable in question may be the nature of the object being transacted, the number, and the respective size of players to figure out market concentration, the information endowment of each subject, or the auction rule. By comparing results obtained in the two cases it is possible to assess the impact of this variable. This makes the assessment of institution properties and performances more powerful than analytical approaches, notably by allowing for a more complex environment and by allowing refinements in comparative analysis.

Overall, most market experiments confirm the crucial role of information and market structures in the performances of a market, as predicted by most standard theoretical approaches such as imperfect competition, information theory, and game theory.

However, even if most standard theoretical predictions on the accuracy of models to predict market behavior have been verified, they have also been shaken up by experimental evidence that emphasizes how market institutions may have a substantial influence on performance, even stronger than market concentration and relative firm size. For example, the monopoly experiments by Smith (1981) on two alternative institutions (oral double auctions and posted prices) show that when the market is organized as an oral double auction the standard monopoly model does not perform so well: prices have a tendency to erode away from the monopoly equilibrium price. Unlike the monopoly model it seems that the behavior of buyers may have some influence.

Even more striking are the experimental results that overtake theory, notably when there are no theoretical predictions, or when their explanation is limited.

A famous case is the Vernon Smith (1962) seminal experimental results on the efficiency of the oral double auction, which were far ahead of any analytical contributions at the time. Auction theory was just emerging, and the oral double auction not yet formalized. This meant Vernon Smith's results were particularly valuable, given the large use of double auction in markets in practice. He emphasized that the competitive model works best when markets are organized as an oral double auction, compared to other institutions (posted price in his experiments, or multilateral bargaining as used by Chamberlin [1948], even with very few traders. These primary results, and the many others that have since followed on the properties of the double oral auction, have emphasized how environmental and institutional conditions for market efficiency are not that constraining in the laboratory. Indeed, the robustness of this institution is high in the sense that if changes are implemented, such as a shift in demand or offer or the introduction of transaction costs, the prices converge to the new equilibrium after few periods.

The lack of theoretical predictions, or their limited explanatory power, may also be explained by the fact that many real situations are too complex to be dealt with analytically. So, theoretical models need to be passed over. For example, some goods induce the use of complex auction in practice (multi-unit objects, combinatorial goods, repeated games, sequential and interdependent markets ... ). This is notably the case for goods with a network component, such as electricity, telecoms, railways, airport slot landings or gas, which need dedicated auctions to allocate them efficiently in a market. Most of the time theories fail badly when analyzing these auctions. Even auction theory explains only some data, and may hardly be put to work in practice for these auctions.

Experimental methodology gives economists the opportunity to approach specific aspects of market design, and to go beyond the boundaries of market micro-structure theories. Even if experimental design is simplified as far as possible, this type of experiment remains relatively complex and dedicated to a specific situation and goods as they are close to reality, incorporating a large number of variables that describe the industry and the goods. For this reason results obtained in the laboratory lack generality, but may be used for what they are – empirical regularities obtained in a controlled environment – by the decision maker.

The new electricity markets created to introduce competition among generators are a good illustration of how experimental economics has been used by public authorities to inform deregulation movements in many countries. Pioneering experiments have been carried out by Vernon Smith and his colleagues at the University of Arizona, for the Arizona Corporation Commission in charge of competitive reforms. The key questions addressed by Vernon Smith were: first, to know if decentralization was even feasible; in other words, to question whether decentralized economic coordination, combined with centralized technical coordination, was efficient; and, second, to evaluate how demand-side bidding was affecting market performance. Their study led to many detailed recommendations on the separation of generation and wires, the spot market mechanism, and the allocation of property rights (Rassenti and Smith 1986). Overall, they concluded that experimental markets figuring energy sales and purchases expressed as offers to sell and bids to buy (so that allocation were determined simultaneously given physical properties of the grid) was not only feasible but also efficient. Although the authors experienced negative feedback from Arizona Corporation Commission in response to their final recommendations for a highly decentralized, vertically unbundled, and privatized electricity system,[11] their study triggered a large agenda of research by both theorists and experimentalists.

Notably, they emphasized the fundamental role of demand-side bidding in ensuring real competition, whereas traditionally, the industry had a strong supply-side orientation. Initially, short-term demand response was not considered an issue, probably because electricity demand is considered quasi-inelastic in the short term. Since the seminal contribution of Rassenti and Smith (1986), the impact of demand-side bidding has been tested in the laboratory (Rassenti, Smith, and Wilson 2002). Their significant result is that demand-side bidding completely neutralizes market power and prices spikes in the laboratory. Analyzing further on the conjunction effects of demand-side bidding and market concentration (three versus six generators) in Denton *et al.* (2001), the authors report no differences in market prices and performance related to the market structures, the participation of the demand providing the condition for high market efficiency in both situations. In terms of policy conclusion, they claim that empowering the wholesale buyers is a credible alternative to the control of supply-side market power and the control of price volatility. These conclusions can still hardly be sustained analytically. However, they support what is progressively done in practice.

As said below, one advantage of experimental economics is to be able to deal with complexity under controlled environment notably by using smart market. It is particularly useful in the case of electricity industry. Complications with the operation of an electric grid, including the stochastic nature of load, the associated need to maintain reliability voltage and line limits, the locational variability of transmission losses, and the existence of constraints in the network, may be incorporated in the experience environment. Taking into account transmission constrained networks is a first step that can easily be passed in the laboratory. It permits dealing with important issues regarding local market power and monopoly power of the owner of wires, as well as allocation of ownership rights to use the network. Analytical results are limited to two-node market designs, since in multi-node networks countervailing effects make an analytic analysis difficult.

The efficiency of an electricity auction, which is very complex and often specific to each market, can be assessed in the laboratory. Models are limited in their capture of important features of the electricity auction rule. Indeed, most of them assume that bidders make competitive bids, once only, for unique goods and that they are risk-neutral. Nevertheless, in reality, games are frequently repeated, bids may run over multiple periods, and multiple units are sold simultaneously. Analytically, it is impossible to extend the properties of a simple auction to a complex one, notably those of a single-unit to a multiple-unit auction (Klemperer 2002).

Experimental studies on electricity auctions focus on two key issues. The first is the timing of the auction in the spot market, that is, to know whether sealed-bid auctions (i.e. simultaneous auction) perform better than continuous double auctions (i.e. sequential), or not. The second issue concerns the price outcome in auctions and differentiates between uniform price and discriminatory price auctions. Experimental results on both issues have helped assess some interesting features of these institutions, which usually do not fall in line with theoretical results or practical use. This is the case with experiments dealing with multi-unit uniform and discriminatory auctions. It is often argued that discriminatory pricing may help lower prices and reduce volatility in electricity markets. However, experimental results suggest the contrary. Exploring the issue of market power effects on the two institutions, Rassenti, Smith, and Wilson (2003) show that in discriminatory auction markets, in the absence of market power, market prices converge to higher prices than those obtained in experiments with uniform price auction and market power. Overall, they conclude that the discriminatory institution in a no-market-power environment is as anti-competitive as a uniform-price institution with structural market power. Abbink, Brandts, and McDaniel (2003), investigating the effect of information uncertainty about demand in both the uniform-price and the discriminatory price auction, reveal no major differences in terms of average transaction prices and price volatility exist in the laboratory, between the two institutions, when the information is symmetric and common. But with asymmetric information among sellers, the discriminatory auction is significantly less efficient than uniform price auction, with price spikes more frequent under discriminatory auction.

## 7.5    Conclusion

This chapter suggests how experimental economics may usefully complement the already existing empirical methodologies used by NIE to test its theoretical predictions. We chose to focus on two fields of research: studying individual behaviour and market performances. We revealed how EE may contribute to a deeper characterization of the main behavioural hypothesis of NIE (bounded rationality and opportunism). Analysing learning processes in the laboratory, which are central to understanding bounded rationality and impact of social preferences that may characterize some opportunistic behaviour, and explaining the degree of opportunism might thus be helpful to NIE. In the market analysis, we revealed how EE and NIE both share common interests in the details of the market functioning. Institutional comparison is easily implemented in the laboratory since the experimental design restricts the decision situation in a way similar to that of the *ceteris paribus* clause in normative theory. Applied to NIE issues, it enlarges the spectrum of alternative governance structures that can be compared, with regard to the remediableness criteria (Williamson 1996). It also helps deal empirically with the search of the efficient alignment between governance structures and contractual hazards, but also between institutional environment and institutional arrangement, another important issue in organization theories. Even if EE has a more limited definition of institutions, it has the same approach as NIE in that the performance of an institution largely depends on the circumstances surrounding it. While EE still focuses on formal institutions it could benefit from taking into account more systematically informal institutions, and the link between institutional environment and arrangements, as does NIE. More generally, we claim that EE and NIE have already research points in common and that they could mutually gain from carrying out joint projects.

# 8 Game Theory and Institutions

*Thierry Pénard*

## 8.1 Introduction

Since the seminal book by Von Neumann and Morgenstern (1944), *Theory of Games and Economic Behavior*, game theory has progressively permeated all fields of economics (industrial organization, labor, financial and international economics) and extended its influence on the other social sciences (politics, sociology, and law). It has become an essential tool for studying interpersonal relationships and provides a rigorous and useful methodology for modeling and analyzing strategic decisions. Game theory methodology has also incited profound and far-reaching changes in the way markets, organizations, and institutions are viewed; it has contributed to better understanding the rationale of many private and public institutions, such as contracts, franchising, insurance, certification agencies, and standardization committees.

This chapter is aimed at revealing the contribution of game theory to the analysis of institutions. The goal herein is not to propose an exhaustive course in game theory (for good introductions to game theory, *see* Gibbons 1992 or Osborne and Rubinstein 1995), but rather to focus on the main results and lessons that can be drawn from game theory with respect to institutions.[1]

Institutions may basically be characterized in two ways. They can, first, be defined as the set of fundamental political, social, and legal ground rules that establish the bases for production, exchange, and distribution (Davis and North 1971). From this perspective, institutions appear as the rules of the game imposed on all economic actors. Yet, an institution may also be considered in a more endogenous manner, in being defined as a player who can interact with the game's other strategic players, albeit with a specific status since it can influence or modify the rules of the game and directly affect the outcome, for example by helping players to coordinate their strategies or select an equilibrium. This chapter will adopt the latter approach in order to examine how institutions may be modeled within strategic games and what can be learned about the role of institutions.

For this purpose, it is helpful to define what exactly a strategic game is: a strategic game is characterized by its players (number of players, their features), the set of strategies assigned to each player, players' information set and payoff function (or utility function), and, lastly, by the sequence of moves (and scope of the game). This chapter is intended to show how institutions interact with these various dimensions. Institutions can actually extend or restrict the set of strategies; they can also modify the quality and quantity of information available to players or change the sequence of moves or number of periods during which the game is played. In basic terms, institutions have three main purposes: (1) to facilitate coordination and commitment; (2) to improve information; and (3) to promote cooperation. In all three cases, the rationale behind institutional intervention is often aimed at improving efficiency in interpersonal relationships. From the viewpoint of game theory therefore, institutions appear as multipurpose and multifaceted efficiency-enhancing devices.

The chapter has been organized into four sections. Section 8.2 presents coordination and trust games which emphasize the role of institutions as commitment devices. Section 8.3 will then consider signaling games in the presence of incomplete information and show that institutions may be helpful in improving information. Section 8.4 is devoted to repeated games, within which institutions are used as cooperation-enabling devices. Finally, Section 8.5 illustrates the multiple roles institutions play through two case studies: first, the case of the medieval merchant guilds inspired by the paper from Greif, Milgrom, and Weingast (1994); and, second, the case of eBay, the well-known online auction website that has recently been receiving widespread attention from academics.

## 8.2    Coordination, commitment, and institutions

Here subsection 8.2.1 will examine the role of institutions in a classical coordination game, while subsection 8.2.2 presents a more general framework based on a principal-agent relation in order to introduce the problem of credibility in player announcements. Subsection 8.2.3 illustrates how an institution can become a commitment device.

### 8.2.1    Coordination games

For game theorists, a strategic decision always constitutes a conditional decision, based not only on the intrinsic characteristics and preferences of the decision maker, but also on his beliefs and expectations about the

Table 8.1 *A standardization game*

|  |  | Firm 2 | |
| --- | --- | --- | --- |
|  |  | Standard 1 | Standard 2 |
| Firm 1 | Standard 1 | (4.2) | (1.1) |
|  | Standard 2 | (0.0) | (2.4) |

decisions of other decision makers with whom he interacts. The predictable outcome of a strategic game is displayed as a Nash equilibrium; this corresponds to a stable situation in which no decision maker has an incentive to change strategy given the strategies chosen by the others. A Nash equilibrium thus appears as a self-enforcing or self-organized state; that is, a spontaneous order without any apparent link to institutions and organizations. What game theory does not mention, however, is how decision makers reach this stable state or how they coordinate themselves around this outcome. The first lesson drawn from game theory is essentially that the rationale of many institutions and organizations is to help decision makers coordinate their strategies on an equilibrium – especially when multiple equilibria exist. Institutions can facilitate the convergence of beliefs and expectations toward the same equilibrium. This role of coordination has been well illustrated in the following strategic game.

Consider a market where two firms compete to impose their own standard. Standardization (achieving a common standard) is collectively optimal because it stimulates demand through network externality (as consumers highly appreciate compatibility). Yet each firm has elected to sponsor a different technology: Firm 1 promotes Standard 1, while Firm 2 promotes Standard 2. If Standard 1 were implemented, then Firm 1 would benefit to a greater extent thanks to its technological advantage in this standard and ownership of some patents that could be licensed. Table 8.1 shows the payoff associated with standardization on Standard 1. Firm 1 obtains a profit of 4, whereas Firm 2 obtains just 2. If Standard 2 were adopted then the payoffs would be reversed: Firm 2 would receive more profit than Firm 1. In the absence of standardization (a *standards war*), both firms would obtain less profit than they could obtain with standardization; in particular, they would receive no gain if each firm chose the rival standard (i.e. when Firm 1 adopts Standard 2 and Firm 2 adopts Standard 1) and a profit equal to 1 when each firm opts for its own standard. This strategic game is called a "coordination game."[2]

Such a game has two Nash equilibria in pure strategies:[3] a de facto *standardization* on Standard 1 and a de facto *standardization* on Standard 2. Which of these two Nash equilibria will prevail? In the absence of institutions, it is likely that neither will emerge: the firms may fail to coordinate on a common standard and decide to launch a standards war, which could lead to an inefficient and unstable situation.

This risk of coordination failure explains the emergence of private institutions (in the form of a working group, or a national or international standards body) which help firms discuss and converge on either one of the sponsored standards or a hybrid technology which mixes some elements of the two competing standards. For example, the telecommunications industry is familiar with such standardization committees and forums (European Telecommunications Standards Institute, GSM Forum, and 3G Forum for wireless telecommunications). Similar private institutions exist in other industries (electronics, computer science, aviation, and so on).

Another solution to the coordination problem is a mandated standardization, whereby a public authority (i.e. a public institution) imposes an equilibrium upon all actors. Such was the case for the third generation of wireless telephony in Europe, as the European Commission (with the agreement of every member country) decided to mandate a harmonized standard called W-CDMA; this standard was competing with another standard, CDMA-2000 (*see* Gandal, Salant, and Waverman 2003).

In a strategic game, coordination issues are frequently linked with commitment problems, since players often seek to coordinate themselves by means of announcements, threats, or promises. Another rationale for institutions is to make these commitments credible and efficient.

### 8.2.2 The commitment problem

A decision maker may seek to manipulate a strategic situation by unilaterally changing some rules of the game, in particular the sequence of moves. For example, instead of moving simultaneously, one player may obtain a strategic advantage by moving either before or after the other players (depending on the nature of the game). In the previous coordination game, moving first provides a strategic advantage (it enables one firm to launch its technology ahead of time and to market its product earlier). The other firm will then have no other choice but to adopt the rival standard (de facto *standardization*).

A decision maker may obtain a similar advantage by committing himself to take a specific action in the future (or not to take such action); for example, Firm 1 can commit itself to playing Standard 1 regardless of the decision of Firm 2 (or, on the other hand, commit to never playing Standard 2). Dixit and Nalebuff (1993) defined a commitment as a response rule that prescribes a response to the decisions of the other players. This rule is generally communicated at the beginning of the game. There are two broad categories of response rules, according to Dixit and Nalebuff: threats and promises. A threat is a response rule that punishes others who fail to cooperate: "I will punish you if you don't play the specified action." A promise is an offer to reward someone who cooperates: "I will reward you if you play the specified action." The goal of these announcements is to influence the actions of the others. To return to our standardization game example, Firm 1 can either threaten to trigger a price war if Firm 2 does not choose Standard 1, or promise a reward if Firm 2 adopts Standard 1. Through these commitments, a player can expect coordination on his most preferred equilibrium.

Such a commitment, however, may only influence the other player if the latter is convinced that threats or promises will indeed be carried out. In the standardization game, suppose that Firm 1 announces that it is committing to Standard 1. If Firm 2 considers that this announcement is of no value, then it has no reason to abandon its own technology. It can instead decide to launch its standard in order to force Firm 1 to adopt Standard 2, which implies that a pre-announcement has no strategic effect if it cannot be trusted or if the other players doubt the credibility of such commitments. Game theory has highlighted these issues and incites us to rethink many institutions and organizations as credible commitment devices. Technically speaking, Selten (1975) underscored the fact that some Nash equilibria may be inconsistent or fallacious if they rely on non-credible commitments. He proposed a more restrictive concept of equilibrium: the concept of subgame-perfect equilibrium. A Nash equilibrium satisfies the criterion of subgame–perfection if each strategy yields a best response to the strategies of other players in all of the subgames.[4] Players should not normally reach subgames that are out of equilibrium; but if such a subgame should be reached, each player would implement the prescribed strategy. If a player shows no interest in carrying out the prescribed strategy, then his strategy relies on non-credible commitments (reward or threat), and the other players will not take such a strategy into consideration when deciding on their own strategies.

This idea may be illustrated by the following game: consider two players, where one is the principal who delegates decisions to a second player, called the agent. This describes the classic principal–agent relation. The agent (Player 1) must undertake a project or action that has an impact on the utility or payoff of the principal (Player 2).

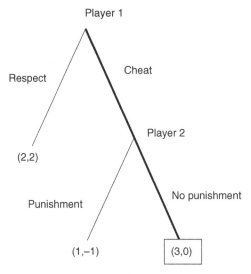

**Figure 8.1** A principal–agent game.

Now assume that the principal and the agent have divergent interests on the optimal actions to be undertaken. The agent should act in the interest of the principal, but he has the opportunity to cheat by choosing actions that yield higher utility for himself. The alternative for Player 1 is thus to behave either honestly (respecting the interest of Player 2) or opportunistically (cheating). Consider the decision tree and payoffs of this game, as displayed in Figure 8.1.

If Player 1 respects the interest of the principal, the game ends and each player will receive a gain of 2. If Player 1 decides to behave opportunistically, then Player 2 can either punish him or play laissez-faire (i.e. tolerate the cheating). Punishing Player 1 is costly and leads to a payoff of -1 for Player 2. But Player 1 also receives a smaller gain in comparison with the situation in which he does not cheat. Lastly, if Player 2 does not punish Player 1, then Player 2 obtains a zero payoff and Player 1 reaps all the benefits (a payoff of 3).

Let us consider the threat by Player 2 to punish Player 1 if the latter betrays his trust. Can this threat deter Player 1 from cheating? Player 1 is apparently better off being honest than being punished. Yet being honest cannot be part of a subgame–perfect equilibrium, since the threat of punishment by Player 2 is not credible. When Player 2 is in a situation to carry out his threat, he would not be inclined to do so. Laissez-faire proves to be a better strategy than punishing Player 1 because punishments are costly to implement. Since the threat of reprisal is not credible, Player 1 will ignore this threat and cheat. The predictable outcome of this strategic game is thus (cheat, no punishment). In anticipating this outcome, the principal is likely to give up playing with the agent. The absence of credible commitment can therefore undermine a valuable relationship, in which the potential value created equals 4 (2 for Player 1 plus 2 for Player 2 when both cooperate).

How then can credibility be restored and the principal be convinced to continue interacting with the agent? Institutions might provide a response to the lack of credibility encountered in many strategic situations, such as the principal–agent relationship.

### 8.2.3   Institutions as commitment devices

One key function of many institutions and organizations is to help decision makers credibly commit themselves. For Dixit and Nalebuff (1993), various ways exist for a decision maker to establish credibility:

- First, he can *burn bridges behind him*: This means that he would eliminate all other options or actions, except those he wishes to exercise. This strategy has long been used in military tactics. "In 1066, William the Conqueror's invading army burned its own ships, thus making an unconditional commitment to fight rather than retreat. Cortes followed the same strategy in his conquest of Mexico. Upon his arrival in Cempoalla, Mexico, he gave orders that led to all but one of his ships being burnt or disabled. Although his soldiers were vastly outnumbered, they had no other choice but to fight and win" (Dixit and Nalebuff 1993, p. 153). A similar strategy consists of *cutting-off communications* with the other players in order to deny oneself any opportunity to back down (i.e. to change the initial move).

- Second, he can *establish and utilize a reputation*: This strategy is only viable if the game is repeated, in which case the initial cost of building a reputation is more than offset by the benefit the player can reap from his strengthened credibility.

- Third, he can *write contracts* to reduce the cost of punishment and amplify the loss incurred by the cheat. A contract represents a means for partners to make their relationship enforceable. If one partner seeks to breach the terms of the contract, then the other party can sue him and force respect of the contract. Signing a contract eliminates the possibility of cheating even though contracting is a costly process (writing and negotiating the terms of a contract).[5]

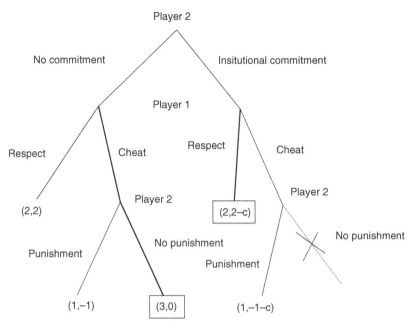

**Figure 8.2** A principal–agent relation with institutional commitment.

Institutions definitely provide the means for a decision maker to *establish a reputation, cut off communications with others, burn bridges,* or *write contracts.* In a principal–agent relation for example, the principal can hire a supervisor in charge of punishing the agent in case of opportunistic behavior. The supervisor would then receive a fixed payment whether he punishes the agent or not. The threat of punishment thus becomes credible; in other words, the creation of hierarchy (i.e. an organization) overcomes the problem of commitment (*the principal cuts off direct communications with his agent*). It is also easier for a principal to build a reputation and then exploit it through setting up a hierarchical organization, thanks to the longevity of an organization.

Insurance companies provide another example of institutions that enable *burning bridges.* When the principal uses the service of an insurance agent, he obtains a payoff guarantee (i.e. a fixed gain). Regardless of the agent's behavior, the principal is certain to earn a payoff of 2-P, where P is the premium paid to the insurance agent. If Player 2 receives less than 2-P from Player 1, then the insurer compensates for the differential and is responsible for punishing Player 1 (obtaining reimbursement for the damages caused by Player 1).

In order to more formally represent the impact of an institutional device in the previous game, let us suppose that the principal can initially use an institutional device (contract, insurance, hierarchy, and so on) at a cost of $c$ (*see* Figure 8.2). This device enables him to credibly commit himself to punish his partner in case of cheating (by eliminating the "no punishment" option), so that Player 1 will behave honestly to avoid reprisals. When institutions are introduced into the principal–agent relation, the subgame–perfect equilibrium becomes (respect, punishment if cheating). Player 2 then obtains a gain of $2-c$ and Player 1 a gain of 2. Finally, Player 2 will invest in the institutional device if the cost $c$ is not excessive: by implementing the institutional solution, Player 2 anticipates a payoff of $2-c$ instead of 0 (without any device). If $c < 2$ then commitment constitutes the best strategy for Player 2.

Let us now consider the second rationale for institutions: the reduction of imperfect information in interpersonal relationships.

## 8.3    Imperfect information and institutions

Game theory has strongly highlighted the importance of information in interpersonal relationships and has largely contributed to the current focus of micro-economics on information issues. Subsection 8.3.1 will consider a principal–agent relation submitted to imperfect information and will underscore the source of inefficiency in this context. Subsection 8.3.2 will show how institutions may overcome imperfect information.

### 8.3.1    A principal–agent game under asymmetric information

Consider the principal–agent game presented in the previous section and assume now that the agent (Player 1) can be highly competent (type H) or incompetent (type L) (Figure 8.3). These two types will influence the payoff of the principal (Player 2) since the principal may expect to obtain a higher gain with a type H agent than with a type L.

Assume that the agent is type H with probability $a$ and type L with probability $1-a$. The true type is, of course, private information held by Player 1 (the choice of the nature is only observed by the agent). Given his type, Player 1 may decide either to cheat or to be honest. Player 2 does not observe the action chosen by Player 1 (respect or cheat) but receives a signal imperfectly correlated with Player 1's behavior. Player 2 can, in fact, receive three kinds of signals: positive, neutral, and negative. When a negative signal is received, Player 2 can perfectly infer opportunistic behavior by an incompetent agent. Likewise, a positive signal

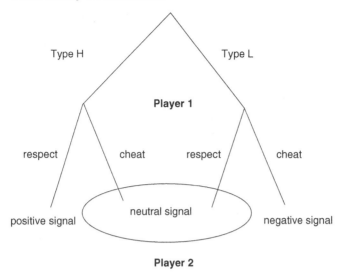

**Figure 8.3** Principal–agent game under imperfect information.

indicates honest behavior by a highly competent agent. However, a neutral signal is compatible with either honest behavior by a type L or opportunistic behavior by a type H agent. In this situation, the deterring of cheating is more complex because even if Player 2 holds credible threats of reprisals, he must apply them cautiously. When observing the neutral signal, Player 2 may make two kinds of errors: punishing an honest agent or playing laissez-faire with an opportunistic agent.

In such a game, we can restrict the set of predictable outcomes to the perfect Bayesian equilibria (PBE). Two potential classes of PBE emerge:

- Pooling equilibria, in which Player 1 sends the same signal regardless of his type (here, a neutral signal). The goal of this strategy is to maintain Player 2's initial beliefs (i.e. to maintain his initial ignorance);

- Separating equilibria, in which Player 1 sends a different signal depending on his type: a positive signal when he is highly competent, and a neutral signal when incompetent. The goal of this strategy is to perfectly inform Player 2.[6]

The first type of equilibrium is observed when Player 2 holds a priori beliefs that lead him to adopt a laissez-faire strategy (beliefs that $a$ is low). Player 2 thus considers that the probability of a neutral signal stemming from an opportunistic agent is low and finds it optimal to react with a laissez-faire attitude. Consequently, it is in the interest of the agent to maintain the principal's a priori beliefs, which would allow a type-H agent to act opportunistically without being punished. In a pooling equilibrium, the rent captured by the agent (called "informational rent") represents a source of inefficiency. If this inefficiency becomes too great, it is then possible that the principal will put an end to the relationship in order to protect himself against opportunistic behavior by the agent.

The second type of equilibria (separating equilibria) appears when Player 2 holds, a priori, belief that $a$ is high. In this case, Player 2 will punish Player 1 in response to a neutral signal. To avoid being systematically punished (in particular when he is of type L and behaves honestly), it is in the interest of Player 1 to reveal his private information. The signal received then enables Player 2 to revise his a priori belief. In a separating equilibrium, however, the credibility of signals proves important: Player 1 must have no incentive to send a neutral signal when his type is H. The source of inefficiency may stem from either the absence of credibility or the cost incurred to make the signal credible.

### 8.3.2    Institutions as information-enhancing devices

The role of institutions is to restore efficiency in relations characterized by imperfect information. Institutions may facilitate the transmission and dissemination of information among players; they may also incite players to reveal their private information or deter them from retaining information. Moreover, they can make signals more credible. The following examples serve to illustrate these various functions.

In the used-car market, buyers do not perfectly observe the quality of cars; they have a positive probability of acquiring a poor-quality car. This problem was highlighted by Akerlof (1970) in his seminal paper entitled "The Market for Lemons: Quality, Uncertainty, and the Market Mechanism" and leads to a phenomenon of adverse selection. Buyers react to imperfect information on quality by lowering their willingness to pay; however, this eliminates all high-quality cars for which sellers have a high reservation price. In the end, all quality cars are withdrawn from the market and only poor-quality cars may be found. Many institutions have been set up to overcome adverse selection problems; for example, the obligation of a technical verification before selling a car is an institutional device that partially handles this problem. The presence of car dealers (intermediaries) in the used-car market can also be explained by the quality guarantee they provide for buyers.

Table 8.2 *The prisoners' dilemma*

|  |  | Player 2 | |
|---|---|---|---|
|  |  | Cooperation | No cooperation |
| Player 1 | Cooperation | $r_c, r_c$ | $r_p, r_d$ |
|  | No cooperation | $r_d, r_p$ | $r_{nc}, r_{nc}$ |

A certification agency is another kind of institution created to reduce information asymmetry. Certification agencies have expanded their activity in recent decades, especially in the food processing industries. On the buyer's side, the role of these institutions is to facilitate screening between good and bad products. On the seller's side, they allow for credible quality signals of the seller's products.

Another institution that tackles the problem of information asymmetry is franchising. A franchise contract is an agreement in which a franchisee obtains the right to operate the business concept of a franchiser by agreeing to pay royalties, which are generally based on revenues. Franchising constitutes an organizational innovation in retailing and has grown tremendously in all developed countries since 1970. Its success may be attributed to its ability to reduce moral hazard in the agency relations that tie the owner of a business concept and the managers in charge of operations. The owner cannot perfectly monitor all his managers; he cannot be present at all times to ensure that they are furnishing the appropriate effort. Franchise contracts which provide the manager with the status of residual claimant deter shirking by the manager because they align the interests of the franchisee with those of the franchiser. A considerable body of literature has focussed on the rationale of franchising as an institution that mitigates moral hazard issues and enhances business performance (Mathewson and Winter 1985; Lafontaine 1993).

The role of institutions is not only to overcome problems of adverse selection or moral hazard, but also to facilitate mutual cooperation in repeated relationships.

## 8.4    Repeated cooperation and institutions

Many relationships in the real world are repeated over a finite time horizon (if people know exactly when the relationship will end) or, more generally, over an infinite horizon (should there be some uncertainty about the ending time). The theory of repeated games provides the simplest approach for considering the effects of long-term interactions. Subsection 8.4.1 presents the general framework of repeated games and subsection 8.4.2 highlights the role of institutions as a facilitating device for enforcing cooperation within a repeated relationship.

### 8.4.1    Prisoners' dilemma and repeated games

The prisoners' dilemma (Table 8.2) is the most famous and certainly the most useful game for analyzing social relationships. Let us consider a symmetric prisoners' dilemma game. Two players have the opportunity to cooperate or cheat. If both cooperate, they will earn more than if both decide to cheat ($r_c > r_{nc}$). If one cooperates and the other cheats, then the cheat earns more than the cheated ($r_d > r_p$). In this game, cheating (no cooperation) is a dominant strategy for both players and constitutes the predictable outcome. However this Nash equilibrium is suboptimal since both players will be better off if they cooperate.

How can trust be restored? In fact, cooperation can emerge from such a relationship if the game is repeated. Cooperation may be a Nash equilibrium of an infinitely repeated game because actions beyond the short-term self-interest of a player may be consistent with his long-term self-interest. Two underlying effects may intervene:

- *reputation effect*: "One cooperates so as to incite the other to cooperate in the future";
- *deterrent effect*: "One does not cheat because of fear of reprisal."

To better understand these two effects, let us assume that the two players agree to follow decision rules that consist of cooperating as long as the other player has chosen cooperation during past periods. In case of cheating, they agree to revert indefinitely to the one-shot Nash equilibrium (no cooperation). The deterrent effect here lies in credibly threatening to punish the other player forever. This strategy is called a "trigger strategy" (Friedman 1971).[7] Under which conditions may a cooperative outcome be enforced by trigger strategies?

The expected value of respecting cooperation, given the other player is behaving honestly, is given by:

$$V^c = \sum_{t=0}^{\infty} \delta^t r_c = \left(\frac{1}{1-\delta}\right) r_c,$$

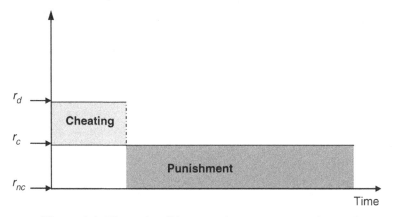

**Figure 8.4** The trade-off between short-term temptation to cheat and long-term costs under trigger strategies.

where $\delta$ is the discount factor, and the expected value of cheating is given by:

$$V^d = r_d + \sum_{t=1}^{\infty} \delta^t r_{nc} = r_d + \left(\frac{\delta}{1-\delta}\right) r_{nc}$$

where the cheat obtains an instantaneous payoff of $r_d$ and then receives $r_{nc}$ indefinitely.

Each player will elect to cooperate if cooperating yields more than cheating over the long term; that is, if:

$$V^c > V^d$$

This incentive condition may be rewritten as follows:

$$r_d - r_c \le \left(\frac{\delta}{1-\delta}\right)(r_c - r_{nc}) \qquad \text{(C1)}$$

The net benefit of cheating (the left-hand term) must be more than offset by the opportunity cost of being punished (the right-hand term). This trade-off is well illustrated in Figure 8.4, where each player must balance the expected gain of betrayal with the cost of reprisal.

This theoretical framework suggests that many institutions may be cooperation-enhancing devices capable of relaxing incentive conditions. Subsection 8.4.2 will examine how institutions can practically facilitate cooperation and will illustrate this role through the example of cartels (price-fixing agreements).

### 8.4.2    *Institutions as cooperation-enhancing institutions*

Let us now consider the incentive condition (C1); it can be reformulated in terms of a threshold discount factor, that is:

$$\delta \geq \frac{(r_d - r_c)}{(r_d - r_{nc})} \tag{C2}$$

The right-hand term corresponds to the minimum value of the discount factor below which players cannot sustain a cooperative outcome. If the discount factor lies above this threshold (which means that players' preference for the future is sufficiently high) then cooperation is likely to emerge as a Nash equilibrium of the repeated game.

The value of the threshold discount factor appears as a measure of the likelihood of a long-term cooperative relationship. The lower the threshold discount factor, the higher the propensity to cooperate. Note that this threshold value increases in both $r_d$ (the cheating payoff) and $r_{nc}$ (the punishment payoff), whereas it decreases in $r_c$ (the cooperation payoff).

From this perspective, an institution is likely to facilitate cooperation if it acts to decrease the threshold discount factor. To be more precise, an institution may facilitate cooperation by increasing the severity of punishments (by reducing the punishment payoff $r_{nc}$) or by reducing the cheating benefits (increasing the cooperative payoff $r_c$ or reducing the cheating payoff $r_d$, or both).

Moreover, if players face imperfect monitoring (e.g. if they do not perfectly observe the past decisions of their partners), then cooperation will be more difficult to sustain, since a cheat is not detected systematically and may escape reprisals. The role of institutions might then be to improve the detection of cheating by facilitating the monitoring of partners' behavior and increasing the speed of reprisals.

In sum, repeated games capture an important aspect of interpersonal relations: most economic relationships are embedded within *relational contracts*, in which cooperation or agreement is enforced by reputation and trust rather than by the courts (Gibbons 2000, 2001). These *relational contracts* are omnipresent in markets and inside firms (in labor relations, supplier relations, pricing agreements, and so forth). They appear as a set of informal rules and codes of conduct backed by formal institutions or formal contracts to enhance performance in long-term relations (Kreps 1990). This notion may be clearly illustrated by cartels and price-fixing agreements.

A cartel is a kind of institution designed to facilitate cooperation between competing firms. An oligopoly faces the same dilemma as players in the prisoners' dilemma: collectively, they should relax price competition, yet individually each firm has an incentive to undercut the rival's prices in order to increase market share and profit.

The role of cartels is to facilitate enforcement of a cooperative outcome. Considerable research has been devoted to understanding how firms organize collusion (Salop 1986; Jacquemin and Slade 1989). Much recent research is aimed at responding to the criticism of Fisher (1989) that too little effort has been dedicated to this issue: "I think game theoretic oligopoly theorists are studying the wrong thing. They are accumulating a wealth of anecdotal material about one-shot oligopoly games when what one wants to know concerns the factors that lead to the collusive equilibrium to be chosen in repeated games" (Fisher 1989).

The facilitating factors (factors leading to the collusive equilibrium) emphasized by Fisher refer in part to institutions and organizations. In all cartels detected and sued in Europe over the recent decades, antitrust authorities actually had obtained evidence of committees, agencies, or associations set up in which firms discussed their intentions (price, capacity, production, and so on) and exchanged information. These facilitating devices not only improve market transparency, but also enable firms to negotiate collusive agreements and decision rules more efficiently (especially the rules of punishment).

As an example, concerning the cement decisions (1994), the European Commission suspected the main European cement firms of having organized a cartel in order to restrain competition in Europe. The objective of the agreement was to regulate capacities and sales, as well as the "non-transshipment to the home markets of the Member States." After several investigations and audits, the Commission found that cement firms had created various institutions to sustain this cooperative agreement; they had set up an export committee and task force in charge of examining and preparing different dissuasive and persuasive measures to stabilize the market (*stick and carrot policy*). The main objective of this policy was to eliminate imports from central Europe and Greece. These measures included the creation of the Joint Trading Company, an institution whose function was:

... to capture the orders of the principal export markets supplied by countries threatening the stability of the Member Countries' markets; to purchase cement and clinker from countries threatening the stability of the Member Countries' markets; to market the quantities purchased through market intervention; to export cement and clinker to countries threatening the stability of the Member Countries; a committee was to designate the markets for purchases, marketing and exports and to set the purchase and selling prices.[8]

All these institutions were intended to enhance the collusive agreement.

Along the same lines, the "UK Agricultural Tractor Registration Exchange" antitrust is most insightful. On January 4, 1988, the UK trade association of manufacturers and importers of agricultural machinery notified the existence of an information exchange agreement; this agreement concerned the registration of new tractors and permitted members to perfectly identify the volume of retail sales and market shares of the eight biggest manufacturers and importers of agricultural tractors in the UK market (sales by model, geographical area, weeks, and so on). The collection and dissemination of sales data were conducted by a specific institution, called the Agricultural Engineers Association Ltd (AEA). Even if firms argued that this information exchange was pro-competitive, the European Commission forbade the agreement because it suspected that this institutional arrangement was designed to relax price competition and promote a self-enforcing cartel: "The high market transparency between suppliers on the United Kingdom tractor market which is created by the Exchange takes the surprise effect out of a competitor's action, thus resulting in a shorter space of time for reactions with the effect that temporary advantages are greatly reduced."[9]

Any temptation to cheat could thus be deterred thanks to this information agreement because each cheat was sure to be detected and punished. The rationale of this institution (AEA) was actually to promote price cooperation between competitors.

Evidence on the self-enforcing role of institutions in collusive agreements has also been provided by Dick (1996), who conducted an empirical study on the determinants of cartel longevity using a database on US exportation cartels. These cartels are legal under the Webb–Pomerene Act, but firms cannot enforce them via the courts. Dick (1996) found that these cartels were more stable when firms had created a common sales agency (an institution) that enabled discussing and monitoring their sales.

The next section illustrates the various roles of institutions (coordination, commitment, information, and cooperation-enhancing devices) through two detailed case studies.

## 8.5 Rethinking institutions: two case studies

The first case study is owed to Greif, Milgrom, and Weingast (1994), who studied in detail the medieval merchant guilds in Europe (see 8.5.1). The second is more recent and concerns eBay, the well-known online auction website (see 8.5.2). These two examples will further our understanding of how institutions improve efficiency in interpersonal relationships and emphasize the multifaceted roles of institutions.

### 8.5.1 Merchant guilds as a contract-enforcing device in medieval trade

In a survey on game theory applied to economic history, Greif (2000) noted that explicit models of repeated games with imperfect information have been used successfully to understand historical institutions.[10] In particular, Greif (1989, 1993) examined the agency relationships in Mediterranean and European long-distance trade between merchants and their overseas agents. Greif analyzed the institutional rules applied by Jewish Maghribi traders, who operated during the eleventh century in the Muslim Mediterranean to overcome moral hazard by agents tempted to act opportunistically and steal a part of the merchants' goods.

Greif, Milgrom, and Weingast (1994) examined the role of merchant guilds in medieval European trade. A guild was "an administrative body that supervised the overseas operations of merchant residents of a specific territorial area and held certain regulatory powers within that territorial area (a town or city)" (Greif, Milgrom, and Weingast 1994). These guilds were organized at the city level (in Italy) or at a regional level (German *Hansa*). According to Greif, Milgrom, and Weingast (1994), these guilds should not be seen as a monopoly that restrained trade, but rather as an institution that secured trade and solved contractual problems. During medieval times, rulers (local authorities) were indeed tempted to abuse the property of alien merchants; such abuse was detrimental to the development of trade. The lack of security was costly and inefficient for both traders and rulers.

Merchant guilds credibly threatened to boycott the city or territory of any cheating ruler. Guilds had the ability to coordinate an embargo and ensure traders' compliance with boycott decisions. They facilitated communications between traders and collected information about conflicts and abuse. Without this institution merchants failed to enforce any embargo. Many merchants were not informed of what happened to other merchants, or had no incentive to respect an embargo; consequently, rulers never committed themselves to securing alien merchants' rights.

To better understand the impact of merchant guilds, let us consider the following model, inspired by Greif, Milgrom, and Weingast (1994), in which $M$ individual merchants have the opportunity to trade with a city. The value of trade is $V(x)$, where $x$ is the number of active merchants. Let $c$ be the variable costs incurred by the ruler of the city for the purpose of securing traders. $V(x)(1-c)$ is the net value of trade. Let $x^*$ be the efficient level of trade ($x^* = \text{argmax } V(x)$). Assume that the ruler finances his service by charging a toll $\tau$ on the volume of transactions.

The ruler faces two possible decisions: to respect his obligation of guaranteeing security or to cheat. An opportunistic behavior for the ruler would thus consist of saving on protection costs. If the ruler upholds his promises, his payoff is $V(x)(\tau - c)$; if he decides to undermine a fraction $e$ of traders, his payoff becomes $V(x)(\tau - (1 - e)c)$. For those traders not cheated, their payoff is $(1 - \tau)V(x)/x$, while cheated traders incur a loss equal to $\tau V(x)/x$.

Now consider the infinitely repeated games, in which at each period the ruler has to choose the level of security provided to the merchants, and the merchants decide whether to continue trading with the city or boycott it. How can merchants force the ruler to play honestly? Each merchant can unilaterally threaten to boycott the city forever if he is cheated (trigger strategy according to *Friedman*). This bilateral reputation mechanism, however, cannot sustain an efficient trade level since the ruler always maintains an incentive to violate the rights of a few traders. To prove this result, consider the incentive constraints of the ruler when the trade level is efficient ($x^*$ merchants). Mistreating $e$ merchants yields: $r_d = [\tau - c(1 - e)]V(x^*)$.

Given the unilateral threat of a boycott, according to condition C2 (*see* 8.4.2), a ruler will be deterred from cheating if for any $e \in [0, x^*]$:

$$\delta \geq \frac{ceV(x^*)}{[\tau - c(1 - e)]V(x^*) - [\tau - c]V(x^*(1 - e))}$$

The right-hand term represents the threshold discount factor, where $r_{nc}$, $r_c$ and $r_d$ in the general expression of the threshold discount factor $\frac{(r_d - r_c)}{(r_d - r_{nc})}$ have been replaced by their specific values. This expression can then be reformulated as follows:

$$\delta \geq \frac{cV(x^*)}{[\tau - c]\left(\frac{V(x^*) - V(x^*(1-e))}{e}\right) + cV(x^*)}$$

As $e$ tends to 0, the threshold discount factor tends to $1$,[11] which means that the ruler still has an incentive to cheat *de minimis* (i.e. to despoil a few merchants) regardless of its preference for the future. The efficient trade level is therefore not sustainable. A bilateral reputation mechanism (based on individual boycotts) is not severe enough to deter the ruler from cheating given that the loss of one merchant is marginal for the city.

What then is the value of a guild? The guild can enhance trading by increasing the severity of reprisals. This institution can in fact impose a complete boycott as soon as one merchant is violated. The credibility of this collective embargo can be ensured by the ability of the guild to sanction those merchants not respecting the embargo. If the ruler wants to cheat, he would know that all merchants would have to be mistreated ($e = 1$) since regardless of the number of cheated merchants, he will be boycotted (no activity and no revenue during the punishment phase). In such a case, the efficient trade level is sustainable if $\delta \geq \frac{c}{\tau}$.[12] Thanks to the guild, trading can be stimulated and reach the efficient volume provided the ruler is sufficiently patient. According to Greif, Milgrom, and Weingast (1994) the existence of merchant guilds lends an explanation for the expansion of medieval trading.[13]

### 8.5.2 *eBay as a reputation-building device for online traders*

The worldwide internet network can create and convey an unlimited number of remote trading relationships. Yet the anonymity of internet users and the ease of internet entry and exit may also incite opportunistic behavior. A seller, for example, may agree to trade with a buyer, promising to deliver goods upon receipt of payment. But once payment has been received, the seller can decide to exit the internet market without delivering the product or after delivering a poor-quality substitute product (not conforming to the original description provided). In such cases, the buyer has no ability to punish the seller since the latter can easily change his identity and return as a new seller without incurring any reprisal (a situation similar to the principal–agent game in which the principal is the buyer and the agent the seller). The ability to avoid punishment (owing to the relative anonymity and distance separating the trading partners) may hinder the development of online commerce, and especially C-to-C (consumer-to-consumer) commerce, since C-to-C is highly subject to fraud and opportunism.

In order to resolve this problem, private institutions have emerged. eBay is the most famous of these institutions. Its role is to provide traders with credible means or tools to retaliate against opportunistic behavior. Its function is not to directly sanction an opportunistic seller or buyer, but, rather, to offer the means to make their trading self-enforceable. For this purpose, eBay has established a reputation mechanism that enables anyone to know whether or not a buyer or seller may be trusted. Following a transaction, each side can evaluate his partner by giving him a positive $(+1)$, neutral $(0)$, or negative $(-1)$ score. Opportunistic behavior can, for example, be sanctioned by a negative evaluation. The evaluations are then summed to generate the agent's overall score: the higher this score, the more trustworthy the agent. Each evaluation can also be accompanied by comments, especially in the case of a negative assessment.

Resnick and Zeckhauser (2002) examined all transactions conducted on eBay between February and June 2001. They noted that 60% of all buyers evaluated their trading partners and that 99% of these evaluations were positive. They described this evaluation system as a public good that helps the community of eBay users in their future transactions.[14] This mechanism serves as a substitute for the classic mechanism of bilateral reputation, which is not adapted to online transactions since repeated transactions between two partners are rare. How does this reputation mechanism actually discipline eBay users?

Since sellers are more likely to behave opportunistically (given that buyers have to send payment before the goods are delivered, their ability to cheat is very limited), we will only consider herein the incentives of the seller. His incentive to be honest stems from the expected long-term benefits of enjoying a good reputation. These benefits are twofold: first, a good reputation can increase the probability of attracting many bidders for his products; moreover, a good reputation can increase the bid amounts that buyers are posting for his products.

If the seller is sufficiently patient and if reputation matters for his future expected auctions, then he should be deterred from acting opportunistically. Even though he can obtain instantaneous benefit by cheating (i.e. keeping the product), he will receive a negative evaluation and buyers will not trust him in subsequent transactions.[15]

Many empirical studies have sought to measure the impact of reputation on future transactions. Houser and Wooders (2005) found that a positive reputation on eBay enables a seller to obtain a better price. Buyers tend to accept paying a premium when the product is sold by a highly reputed seller. This result is based on a data-set of Pentium III chips sold in online auctions during fall 1999 (a total of ninety-five auctions were observed). The authors found that a seller who increases the number of positive evaluations by 10% can expect a price 0.17%

higher for his chips, whereas a 10% increase in the number of neutral or negative evaluations lowers the price by 0.24%.

Resnick and Zeckhauser (2002) found a more ambiguous result. They observed that reputation has no impact on the bids for MP3 players. However, reputation influences the probability that the transaction takes place. For example, a seller with no reputation (score of 0) has a 72% probability of selling his MP3 player, whereas the same seller with a score of 70 has a 96% probability.

Another experimental study conducted by Resnick *et al.* (2006) found results similar to those derived by Houser and Wooders (2005). The authors attempted to determine the willingness-to-pay for old postcards on eBay. They compared the bids for postcards offered by a seller with a good reputation to those for the same postcards offered by a seller without any reputation; the difference in bid prices amounted on average to 8%.[16]

## 8.6    Conclusion

This chapter has highlighted that game theory is highly useful in examining the rationale of institutions. Game theory is a rigorous framework for questioning the nature of interpersonal relationships (Who are the decision makers? What sets of actions do they implement? What information is available?), and for capturing the essential feature of institutions along with their impact.

Integrating game theory and institutions offers a promising and fruitful avenue for the field of new institutional economics (NIE). In return, the body of institutional literature may also enrich game theory by giving insight into how players actually behave during strategic situations (how they choose their decision rules, form their expectations, and select an equilibrium).

*Part III*

# Strategy and Management

# 9 New Institutional Economics, Organization, and Strategy

*Jackson Nickerson and Lyda Bigelow*

## 9.1 Introduction

Although the roots of research into business strategy were seeded in the late 1960s with Igore Ansoff and Richard Brandenburg (1967), the field broke through to the surface and began to grow quickly in the 1970s and early 1980s. In particular, 1980 was a watershed year because of the launching of the field's first major journal, the *Strategic Management Journal*, and Michael Porter's (1980) book , *Competitive Strategy*, which was heralded in the business community. Since then research into business strategy has been a "growth opportunity," attracting scholars from many disciplines and subdisciplines and publishing an increasing number of papers each year in a widening number of journals of both general and special interest. Transaction cost economics (TCE) is one of the subdisciplines that planted seeds in the strategy field and nurtured them with notable success. The good news for those studying TCE is that the field of strategy remains fertile and, in our opinion, TCE remains a useful tool for planting many more seeds as well as for harvesting opportunities.

Research into business strategy is motivated by three questions: (1) Why do some firms earn more rents than other firms, even in the same industry? (2) Why do performance differences persist? And (3) what can managers do to earn higher and enduring rents for their firms? (For a discussion, *see* Rumelt, Schendel, and Teece 1991.) At first glance, these questions may seem distant from TCE. The implied unit of analysis of the first two questions is the firm, not the transaction, which is the traditional unit of analysis of TCE. Performance is another point of difference. Oliver Williamson (1991a) focusses on autonomous and coordinated adaptation as metrics of differentiated performance for transaction cost scholars. In contrast, strategy scholars are specifically interested in economic rents rather than the types of adaptation engendered by alternative governance structures. Another difference is that business strategy either implicitly or explicitly considers the effects of competition, whereas TCE is not easily structured to fold competitors into the analysis. Yet, it is consideration of the third question that reveals the applicability of TCE for strategy scholars and enables responses to the first two questions. If managerial decision making underlies firm performance, then the micro-analytics of many decisions involve not just the firm as the unit of analysis but also the individual decisions managers make, which are at a less aggregate unit of analysis than the firm. If at least some managerial decisions are made with reference to transactions and can be cast in a comparative institutional framework, then TCE may offer a useful lens for understanding why some firms persistently out-perform other firms.

TCE, and, in particular, Williamson's variant of it, is broad and deep, touching many fields and subfields with a multitude of applications. Indeed, this *Guidebook* touches upon many of these areas. Before pro-ceeding, we need to narrow the scope of this chapter to those aspects of TCE that attempt to directly link governance choice to firm perform-ance. For instance, in this review we will not discuss the vast warehouse of theoretical and empirical research which relates the attributes of transactions to governance choices (*see* chapters 1, 2, 10, and 11, *and especially* chapters 12, 14, and 20). Instead, we will explore three areas of TCE research that relate directly to strategy's motivating questions.

The first (Section 9.2) discusses research focussed on the relationship between exchange attributes, organizational choice, and performance. We also discuss the ability of so-called "shift parameters" to differen-tially shift the comparative costs of contracting and how this shift affects exchange performance. A final aspect of this section explores why exchange conditions are chosen in the first place, which links Michael Porter's strategic position approach with Oliver Williamson's TCE. For each of these areas we assess the direction of recent research and suggest opportunities for adding value to the literature.

The second area (Section 9.3) is internal organizational choice and performance. We touch on recent advancements in internal corporate structure, such as the M-form, U-form, and others, and how these choices affect firm performance. Although beyond the scope of this chapter we nonetheless touch on opportunities to test the discriminating alignment hypothesis empirically with respect to other aspects of cor-porate governance, including the choice of capital structure. Finally, we highlight that the comparative contractual perspective has rarely been applied to empirical examination of the shop floor and highlight opportunities for future research.

The third area we explore (Section 9.4) is organizational change and performance, which TCE relates to in three ways. One nascent stream of research evaluates Williamson's weak-form selection hypothesis, which posits that firms that align "significant" transactions according to TCE prescriptions are more likely to survive – another measure of performance – than those that do not align transactions in a transaction cost economizing way. Although largely absent in the economics literature, organizational inertia provides another context in which TCE relates to organizational change and performance. This stream investigates the relationship between the extent to which firms invest in idiosyncratic assets and their adjustment costs in response to environmental shocks. The initial predicted relationship originated in sociological work in population ecology. This logic, which resonates with, and is refined by, TCE, helps to explain the source and effect of organizational inertia on rates of change, profitability, and survival at the firm level. Recent empirical research provides quantitative estimates of these relationships. Finally, research observes that it is not uncommon for at least some firms to vacillate back and forth between or among governance modes in order to enhance performance. TCE provides a theoretical lens that utilizes inertia to explain this phenomenon, although research to empirically explore these predictions has not yet sprung forth from these seeds.

The final area this chapter briefly explores involves a new framework – the problem-solving perspective – that perhaps can best be described as a close relative of TCE. This perspective takes the problem, instead of the transaction, as the unit of analysis. It seeks to explain how different modes of governance affect both the likelihood and cost of arriving at valuable solutions, which therefore informs performance. Although this research is embryonic, it is emerging, and recent theoretical and empirical papers are discussed along with future research possibilities.

Before providing detailed discussions of these three areas of TCE research in the field of business strategy, it is important to highlight several important caveats about this chapter. The goal of the chapter is intendedly narrow. Strategy research with respect to TCE easily could be described more broadly by focussing on organization choice without directly assessing performance benefits. Such topics include diversification, alliances and other inter-firm collaborations, mergers and acquisitions, and so on. Fortunately for the reader, at least some of these topics are discussed in other chapters of this book.

This chapter is not meant to provide a comprehensive review of the extant literature on business strategy. Rather, it is designed as a launching point – to understand key ideas, progress to date, and, more importantly, possible opportunities for dissertation topics and future research.

Finally, the categorization proffered here is based largely on not only our reading of the literature but also our research. Therefore, the reader should be forewarned that the categorization in this chapter derives from our personal biases, which undoubtedly leads us to overemphasize (perhaps excessively) our own research and underemphasize other research. We hope you will read the remainder of the chapter with these caveats in mind.

## 9.2    Exchange attributes, organizational choice, and performance

Williamson's variant of TCE has been in the making for more than thirty-five years. His discriminating alignment hypothesis – the basis for many of his insights – predicts that managers who align organizational structures with exchange attributes will achieve performance benefits. The source of these performance benefits comes from the investment in co-specialized assets *and* the choice of governance. Co-specialization represents investments that lead to value enhancements, such as improved quality or unique product or service features, or lower cost. Thus, co-specialized investments expand the wedge between willingness-to-pay and cost, which is critical for creating and capture value – the central goal of strategy. Oliver Williamson points out that this added value created through specialization may never arise or could be fritted away if managers do not choose governance structures wisely. It is this match between the attributes of the exchange, for which co-specialization is the most important attribute, and governance choice that make up his discriminating alignment hypothesis. Over the long term his hypothesis predicts that firms that align efficiently will enjoy survival advantages. Over the short term his hypothesis presumably implies that alignment translates into economic performance advantages.

These long- and short-term theoretical constructs provide the lynchpin between TCE and the strategy field. Making this connection explicit did not occur until after the foundational TCE empirical work on governance structure occurred in the late 1970s and early 1980s (e.g. Armour and Teece 1978; Monteverde and Teece 1982). Emphasizing and investigating the performance implications of the discriminating alignment hypothesis for strategically relevant outcomes has proved to be a challenging but fruitful area of current research with many more opportunities available.

A common criticism of TCE in the 1990s was that it lacked research on the discriminating alignment hypothesis – the relationship between performance and organizational alignment with exchange attributes (e.g. Winter 1990; Gulati 1999). Indeed, as recently as 2000, Christopher Boerner and Jeffrey Macher concluded that after more than six hundred papers empirically examining TCE predictions, no study directly links alignment between transaction attributes and organizational form to economic profitability at the transaction level. Recent empirical research has begun to respond to this lacuna. Below we summarize three different literatures. In the first, we summarize the most recent research on organizational choice and performance, and discuss opportunities for future research. In the second case we discuss how "shift parameters" affect organizational choice and the resulting impact on performance. We conclude this section with a brief summary of a research stream that integrates the seminal strategic insights of Porter with TCE, emphasizing, yet again, how organizational choice affects firm performance. And we once more highlight future research opportunities.

### 9.2.1   Organizational choice and transaction performance

Henry Armour and David Teece (1978) offered one of the earliest empirical tests of the impact of organizational choice on performance from a transaction-cost perspective. They found that large, complex firms organized as a multi-divisional (M-form) rather than a centralized function (U-form) enjoyed better performance measured as a higher rate of return on equity as predicted by Oliver Williamson (1975). As an early empirical test, this paper launched, albeit with delay, an empirical literature on the discriminating alignment hypothesis and performance.

It was some time before other studies followed. For instance, is was not until 1991 that Gordon Walker and Laura Poppo found that transaction-cost-predicted alignment led to lower comparative negotiation and bargaining difficulties. Mohr and Spekman (1994) found empirical support for the positive effects of partnership attributes of commitment, coordination, and trust; communication quality and participation; and conflict resolution techniques of joint problem solving led to higher partnership performance. Laura Poppo and Todd Zenger (1998) found that increasing asset specificity leads to the diminishing effectiveness of market governance of information services. Using data on semi-conductor devices, Leiblein, Reuer, and Dalsace (2002) found that the alignment of governance choice and contracting hazards ultimately mediates technological performance. In a study of research and development (R&D) alliances Rachelle Sampson (2004) found that the alignment of transactions according to TCE predictions conferred collaborative benefits not found in transactions organized otherwise. Glenn Hoetker (2005) found evidence that organizational performance is enhanced when organizational choice mitigates contracting hazards in a way consistent with TCE. All of these studies report on various aspects of performance. The discriminating alignment hypothesis has begun to mass a body of research that indicates efficient alignment corresponded with various hallmarks of performance. However, none of these studies estimated economic performance. Indeed, estimating the economic profitability of adherence to the discriminating alignment hypothesis at the transaction level greatly retarded the acceptance of TCE as one of the pillars of strategic management.

The first study to provide estimates of economic performance at a transaction level was Scott Masten, James Meehan, and Edward Snyder (1991). Measuring cost savings of the organization of shipbuilding components (pipe fitting), they found that overall organization costs in ship construction were lower when transactions and organizational forms were aligned according to the discriminating alignment hypothesis. In developing their empirical estimates they also utilized econometric methods that statistically remedied the endogeneity problem (*see* Chapter 6) inherent in doing comparative analysis that accounts for selection of discrete organizational forms. Whilst this study offered a breakthrough in empirical transaction cost research by estimating the added costs of misalignment, it still did not achieve the long-sought-after goal of estimating economic profits at the transaction level.

To our knowledge, the first and only study to provide estimates of profitability at a transaction level is Kyle Mayer and Jackson Nickerson (2005). Studying the contracts of an information technology company the authors apply the discriminating alignment hypothesis to predict why firms organize their knowledge workers as employees rather than independent contractors, and predict the performance implications of this choice. Their theory assesses contracting difficulties arising from expropriation concerns, measurement costs, and interdependence rather than from asset co-specialization, and the alignment implications for profitability when governing the transaction through integration or outsourcing for 190 information technology service projects. Using a two-stage switching regression model, their analysis shows that projects aligned according to their version of the discriminating alignment hypothesis are, on average, more profitable than misaligned projects and that firm capability affects organizational choice but not profitability.

Their strongest profitability findings come from estimates of the effects of expropriation and measurement costs. The project's profit margin drops by 20.8% and 200% (negative profit) for the former, and by 99.6% and 28.6% for the latter, depending on whether they predict outsourcing or insourcing, when the project's organization is misaligned with project attributes. These results indicate an asymmetry in the penalty for misalignment – it seems that a lack of measurement difficulty strongly favors independent contractors, whereas the presence of expropriation concerns strongly favors employees. Masten, Meehan, and Snyder (1991) and Rachelle Sampson (2004) also found asymmetry in the cost of misalignment in their studies.

Although 1978 saw the first published empirical study of transaction cost alignment, the number of studies that report economic performance at a transaction level – three decades later – remains remarkably sparse. This body of work suggests several opportunities for future research. The cost of organizational misalignments remains difficult to estimate *ex ante* and across different industrial settings. More studies which assess the impact of organizational alignment on performance would help managers and scholars alike to better understand the costs and benefits of organizational choices. Any research that provides additional estimates of the cost of misalignment would add value to the literature.

The recurring theme of asymmetry in the performance penalty paid by integrating when the theory predicts outsourcing, and outsourcing when the theory predicts integration, represents an important opportunity for additional research not only on the source for the asymmetry but also its implications for strategic management. Toward this end, case studies that document more precisely why these costs are asymmetric could provide particularly useful insights in generating theory to explain the phenomenon. Any research that could provide insight into the micro-mechanisms surrounding this asymmetry would provide value to the literature.

### 9.2.2   *Shift parameters, organizational choice, and transaction performance*

Oliver Williamson (1991b) first articulated his shift-parameter framework in 1991, but empirical work has only recently appeared. A shift parameter is Williamson's terminology for describing variations across institutional environments, like the strength of legal institutions, and the differential effect these institutional factors have on the make-or-buy decision. For instance, the discriminating alignment hypothesis is different for the USA compared to China. Shift parameters may be used to represent these institutional differences and to incorporate them into the discriminating alignment hypothesis to make predictions about governance choice and performance in each environment.

The focus on shift-parameters, as elaborated by Joanne Oxley (1999), Witold Henisz and Oliver Williamson (1999), and Witold Henisz

(2000a) has led to a new stream of research that offers many opportunities to scholars interested in international or multi-national strategy. This line of research incorporates features of the institutional environment in combination with features of the exchange so as to address questions concerning the trade-offs of modes of governance. For instance, countries with weak institutional environments increase the costs of using the market, and writing and enforcing contracts, as well as affect the cost of using hierarchy. How these institutional environments differentially affect the cost of governance alternatives is the focus of inquiries into shift parameters. Alternatively, transactions may differ in terms of other factors like the level of pre-existing trust. Pre-existing trust is an institutional factor that can be recast as a shift parameter. In this case, trust might differentially affect the cost of market, hybrid, and hierarchy. Oliver Williamson considers these institutional features and incorporates them into his discriminating alignment hypothesis in terms of shift parameters.

In a study of technology transfer alliances across countries and industries, Joanne Oxley (1999) provided the first empirical support of Williamson's shift-parameter framework. Joanne Oxley argued that as the intellectual property protection regimen strengthens (the appropriability hazard diminishes) the need for hierarchical control in alliances between US and non-US firms diminishes. Her results show that the features of a transaction do explain much of the variation in choice of alliance governance form, but that the institutional regimen also shifts this decision. The paper demonstrates empirically, then, that both transaction variables and institutional shift parameters must be specified in models estimating governance choice. As the first paper to develop and empirically examine Williamson's shift-parameter logic, it has received much attention.

Another important paper explored the shift-parameter logic in an international context. Using a novel data set on 3,389 international manufacturing operations by 461 firms in 112 countries Witold Henisz (2000b) posits that the effect of political hazards on the choice of market entry mode varies across multi-national firms based on the extent to which they face expropriation hazards (or contracting hazards) from their potential joint-venture partners in the host country. As political hazards increase, the multi-national may mitigate opportunistic expropriation threats by the government by partnering with a host-country firm. Partnering with host-country firms that possess a comparative advantage in interactions with the host-country government may safeguard against this hazard. However, as contractual hazards increase, the potential benefit to the joint-venture partner of manipulating the political system for its own benefit at the expense of the multi-national increases as well, thereby diminishing the hazard-mitigating benefit of forming a joint venture. Results indicate that as political hazards outweigh contracting hazards, firms' entry mode favors partnering with host-country firms but that as this political hazard diminishes relative to the contracting hazards majority-owned plants become the favored market-entry mode.

Whilst these two papers provide support for the logic of shift parameters in understanding organizational decisions, they do not link directly to economic performance. One paper that has used the logic of shift-parameters to link them to performance, albeit measured qualitatively, is Ranjay Gulati and Jackson Nickerson (2005). Instead of focussing on the weakness in the institutional environment, they investigate the extent to which pre-existing inter-organizational trust acts as a shift parameter to differentially shift the cost of markets, hybrids, and hierarchy.

Gulati and Nickerson (2005) argue that trust acts as a shift parameter that lowers governance costs for all modes of governance whenever exchange hazards are present and thus enhances performance regardless of the mode of governance chosen. This lowering of governance cost arises because trust, which is less formal than either contracts or ownership, facilitates adaptation – exchange partners are more likely to avoid disputes or resolve them quickly when trust is present (Gulati, Lawrence, and Puranam 2005). Gulati and Nickerson's (2005) theory also suggests that trust can lead to a substitution of less formal for more formal modes of governance, because governance cost-reducing benefits of trust are greater for market than for hybrid and greater for hybrid than for hierarchy. These differences arise because trust proves a less useful safeguard when formal mechanisms like contracts and ownership are utilized. The result of this differential impact is that the market mode of governance, with the addition of pre-existing trust, may be used over a broader range of exchange hazards than markets can without trust, which in turn offers lower governance costs and enhances exchange performance. Also, a hybrid with pre-existing trust can substitute over some range of exchange hazards for hierarchy, which enhances exchange performance. Drawing on a sample of 222 sourcing arrangements for components from two assemblers in the automobile industry, Gulati and Nickerson (2008) find broad support for both substitutive and complementary effects of inter-organizational trust on qualitative measures of perceived exchange performance.

Beyond these papers, few have focussed on Williamson's shift-parameter logic and its impact on organizational choice and performance. This literature could be advanced in many ways. For instance, with respect to trust and its impact on organizational choice and performance, researchers could assemble panel data on how inter- and intra-firm relationships evolve over time. (*See* Bercovitz *et al.* 2006 for an initial analysis. For a longitudinal case study illustrating one such approach, *see* Argyres and Mayer 2004). We could extend this framework to consider under what conditions and the extent to which relationship networks affect organizational choice and performance. For inter-firm R&D relationships as well as for foreign country entry modes, the shift-parameter framework has yet to be applied to investigate exchange performance. Any advancement in these directions would add value to the literature.

This recent research stream on shift parameters also suggests that there may be other potential candidates for consideration as shift parameters beyond those described above. At the very least, unpacking the determinants of institutional political hazards or trust would be worth additional explorations. Leveraging extant theoretical research on expropriation hazards, reputation effects, or network ties, for example, through combining with the TCE shift-parameter perspective could generate worthwhile new insights. As we discuss in the next section, this sort of theory integration may be usefully employed to demonstrate the power of TCE research in the strategy field.

### 9.2.3    TCE and strategic positioning: organizational choice and firm performance

TCE and Michel Porter's strategic positioning framework (SPF) are two economic theories that have had an immense impact on modern strategic management research (Rumelt, Schendek, and Teece 1991). Although both theories have contributed to our understanding of strategic management and to the choice of strategy and structure, each theory offers managerial prescriptions that are incomplete at best. If followed in isolation, each theory may lead to inferior performance.[1]

George Day and Saul Klein (1987, p. 62), in a discussion of cooperative behavior in vertical markets, argue that the "weaknesses of [Oliver Williamson's] market failure approach are the strengths of [Michel Porter's] strategic perspective and vice versa." George Day and Peter Klein call for research that combines SPF and TCE analyses. "Such a combination," they maintain, "would allow strategically relevant activities to be analyzed with the context of efficient organization, and thereby overcome the deficiencies of each perspective in isolation" (Day and Klein 1987, p. 62). However, both theories have talked past each other, even when a dialogue seems useful.

In response to this call for integration, several researchers have attempted integrations. Jackson Nickerson (1997) and Marinal Ghosh and George John (1999) conceptually suggest an integration of Michel Porter's and Oliver Williamson's theoretical perspectives to account for the role of exchange conditions on organizational choice and performance. Jackson Nickerson, Barton Hamilton, and Tetsuo Wada (2001) develop a more complete theoretical foundation for integration by arguing that the assumptions underlying Porter's SPF and Williamson's TCE are not inconsistent. They utilize the constellation of activities in the vertical chain as a unit of analysis and operationalize the relationships described by Jackson Nickerson (1997) and Marinal Ghosh and George John (1999) by defining the resource profile – the set and type (i.e. the degree of idiosyncrasy) of resources and capabilities employed in the constellation of activities in a vertical chain – as the central measure driving the perspective. Thus, rather than choosing the level of asset specificity for a single transaction they investigate choosing different types of investments (e.g. human, physical, and so on) and the degree of co-specialization across all transactions in the value chain. They also parse the perspective into three relationships that make it easier to develop specific predictions. The main argument works as follows: a target market position is supported by an underlying resource profile, which is paired with an organizational structure to generate product attributes consistent with the target position.

Jackson Nickerson, Barton Hamilton and Tetsuo Wada (2001) used this framework to develop hypothesis for international courier and small package (IC&SP) services in Japan as a good context for their analysis. Their empirical results provide broad support for their industry-specific predictions and hence for their main proposition. A courier's resource profile, which was limited in their empirical context to the level of idiosyncratic information technology resources in each transportation segment, is chosen to support a courier's market position as a package specialist, full-service courier, or document specialist. Different levels of idiosyncratic information technology support each market position, which is consistent with the SPF literature. Idiosyncratic resources in information technology, in conjunction with temporal specificity, generate exchange conditions that influence the choice of organization form in the way predicted by TCE for each activity. Vertical integration is paired with high levels of asset-specificity, and contracting is paired with low levels of asset-specificity. The resulting resource-profile or organization pairing affects delivery time and possibly delivery reliability and transportation cost, although these latter two performance dimensions were not assessed directly except for delivery to financial cities around the world. Differences in delivery time (and presumably in the other performance dimensions not measured directly) influence a shipper's choice of type of courier.

This stream of research opens several paths for future research. First, it provides a theoretical basis for examining through the lens of TCE firm strategies across a constellation of transactions, not just the governance of transactions in isolation. Thus far, only one paper uses this framework to assess the strategies of firms competing against each other. Additional empirical research on firm in different industries is needed to validate the framework. Second, while some have examined firm survival (Silverman, Nickerson, and Freeman 1997; Argyres and Bigelow 2005) and economic performance (Nickerson and Silverman 2003) based on the alignment of a single important transaction, no study examines economic performance or organizational survival for competing organizations based on a constellation of transactions. Doing so would provide a definitive link between transaction-level analysis, firm strategy, and performance.

## 9.3    Internal organizational structure and performance

The make-or-buy decision has dominated TCE research on organizational strategy, but it is not the only domain of strategy and firm performance that TCE informs. TCE offers many predictions through its comparative contracting lens about the internal organization of firms and how these predictions translate to performance. Below we highlight the areas of corporate governance including M-form versus U-form, capital structure, and governing the corporation. We also explore TCE predictions for organizing the shop floor. We provide entry points into these literatures, describe recent research, and highlight opportunities for future research.

### 9.3.1    M-Form versus U-form

Oliver Williamson (1975, 1985) makes clear in his discussion of the M-form, that internal organizational structure matters and that the implications of structure go beyond that which may be explained by incentives alone. M-form stands for a multi-divisional structure. This innovation in organizational structure was made famous by Chandler's path-breaking study "Strategy and Structure," which identified the M-form structure as an organizational form distinct from the U-form, which is a centralized, functionally departmentalized, or unitary structure, and traced the M-form's origins. Chandler also characterized the costs and benefits derived from this new structure.

For many years, David Teece's work (e.g. Armour and Teece 1978; Teece 1980, 1981) on the M-form remained the rare empirical investigation of the effect of hierarchical structure. Recent work by Nicolas Argyres and colleagues revisited and extended the work on hierarchical governance and its effect on firm performance focussing on R&D activities. Comparing GM and IBM, Nicolas Argyres (1995) refined the M-form hypothesis by offering an elaboration of the centralized M-form (CM-form) as an explanation for why performance gains from reduced opportunism have not been consistently detected in the handful of earlier studies. The presence of technological interdependencies require greater coordination, thus the loss of incentive intensity is trumped by the coordination gains for related diversifiers that adopt the CM-form over the M-form. Previous research does not stipulate this distinction.

Nicolas Argyres (1996) continued to elaborate on extensions of the M-form hypothesis by blending concepts from the resource-based view with transaction-cost reasoning to investigate and develop hypotheses about the degree of divisionalization within an M-form organization and about the scope of research activities. His empirical results support the argument that firms with greater divisionalization engage in narrower, more fragmented R&D projects since bargaining and coordination costs increase.

Nicolas Argyres and Brian Silverman (2004) extend this research by measuring the degree of centralization in R&D activities and then measuring the type of innovations that result. Whilst admitting that they do not assume that more impactful or broader innovations are more profitable to the firm, they argue that the form of hierarchical governance has a direct effect on the type of innovations which are generated within the firm. As in Nicolas Argyres (1996) the study uses data on patenting activity as well as a host of industry- and firm-specific variables to show that formal structure matters in terms of influencing the type of R&D activity and what types of innovations are adopted.

These studies suggest that several areas of interest to strategy, transaction cost, and technology scholars remain to be explored. Although Nicolas Argyres (1996) finds that broadening R&D activities is associated with fewer divisional boundaries, he contends that the degree to which this matching of structure with technological strategy better positions the firm vis-à-vis rivals still needs investigation. Further, he suggests that little work investigates the ability of firms to adjust technological strategy and structure, that is, to what extent are firms constrained in their ability to modify divisionalization, coordination, and scope of R&D activities.

In contrast to the robust literature on inter-organizational governance and its impact on the development and diffusion of technological know-how, there is still a paucity of research on how intra-organizational or hierarchical governance affects these technology outcomes. Similarly, just as much recent research has been devoted to understanding hybrid forms of exchange between firms (e.g. Oxley 1997; Sampson 2004; *see also* Chapter 10) there is very little work on hybrid forms of exchange within firms, either within the R&D area or in any other functional area of the firm. In a rare exception, Shelanski (2004) studied intra-firm transfer pricing and found evidence that transaction-specific investment and quality requirements increase the likelihood that headquarters will centrally administer the pricing of transactions between divisions. Nonetheless, applying transaction analysis to intra-firm exchanges could provide new insights into the internal organization of large industrial enterprises.

Finally, questions regarding the link between formal and informal hierarchical governance have yet to be explored. For example, when formal structure adjustments change the nature of informal exchange – for an exception *see* Jackson Nickerson and Todd Zenger (2002), discussed below – as well and, if so, to what extent does this affect a firm's research and technology strategies. These questions are intriguing and provide a gateway to link topics of organizational structure and change from sociology and psychology to issues of hierarchical governance and strategy. Providing such linkages adds value by providing a more comprehensive and integrative science of organizations.

### 9.3.2    Corporate governance

Oliver Williamson's (1985) comparative contracting approach has implications for the overall governance of the corporation. In particular, Oliver Williamson argues that the comparative contracting perspective may inform the composition and functions of the board of directors and management. The literature on corporate governance is large, spans many disciplines, and taking stock of this literature is beyond the scope of this chapter. Nonetheless, it is worth noting that corporate governance is of interest to strategy scholars because of the expectation that the governance of the firm has implications for firm performance. For instance, one specific application of this comparative contracting perspective to corporate governance is Oliver Williamson's (1988) discussion of debt and equity as alternative governance mechanisms. Extending his discriminating alignment hypothesis Oliver Williamson argued that firms that align debt and equity with the underlying profile of assets will receive performance advantages. Unfortunately, few, if any, papers in strategy empirically explore these performance predictions: which suggests a substantial opportunity for scholars. Pursuing a research program to empirically evaluate the performance implications of TCE on corporate governance decisions may provide new opportunities, at least among US-based firms, because of the recent imposition of Sarbannes–Oxley regulations.

### 9.3.3 Team organization

Another area of opportunity for research exists in the area of the organization of labor and utilization of types of teams within organizations, especially on the shop floor. Oliver Williamson (1985, p. 247) presents a framework positing four basic types of internal organization: internal spot market; primitive team; obligation market; and relational team. He maintains that the type of internal organization is discriminatingly aligned to the level of co-specialization and degree of non-separability for the production activity. For instance, he anticipates that an internal spot market offers the efficient organizational choice when the activity involves little asset specificity and that tasks within the activity are separable. A primitive team is efficient when the activity involves little asset specificity but the tasks are not separable. An obligation market is efficient when the activity involves co-specialization and the tasks are separable, and a relationship is efficient when the activity involves co-specialization and the tasks are non-separable. To date, only Barton Hamilton, Jackson Nickerson, and Hideo Owan (2003) empirically explore the economic performance implications of two of these alignments: internal spot market and relational team. Thus, the organization of labor from a discriminating alignment standpoint has received little empirical attention.

## 9.4 Organizational change and performance

In the late 1990s research on performance developed a critical mass as researchers took advantage of advances in methods and adopted creative solutions to theoretical and empirical challenges. Longitudinal, intertemporal studies followed and complemented the emerging cross-sectional research on performance. Such panel-data research designs also allowed for investigation into the role of the selection environment and the firm's ability – or lack thereof – to adapt to changes in the selection environment. We turn to these studies in the next two sections.

*9.4.1    Evaluating Williamson's weak-form selection hypothesis*

As a positive theory, transaction cost theory assumes that efficient discriminating alignments will be observed much more frequently than misalignments, because misalignments "invite their own demise" (Williamson 1996). Essentially it is assumed that weak-form selection pressures exist. There is little discussion of how these pressures may change over time due to either endogenous (e.g. industry evolution) or exogenous (e.g. regulatory change) factors.

In an early test of the impact of alignment in concert with an assessment of an exogenous shift in selection pressures, Brian Silverman, Jackson Nickerson, and John Freeman (1997) find evidence that misalignment of transactions in the trucking industry lowered annual profitability and increased the failure rate. The authors present an analysis of mortality of large motor carriers in the US interstate for-hire trucking industry after deregulation. They examine this phenomenon through a multidisciplinary lens that encompasses organizational ecology, neoclassical economics, and TCE. The paper posits that carrier mortality is a function of both firm- and industry-level attributes, which are drawn from both ecological and economic theories. Although each of these theories separately informs motor carrier mortality, the inclusion of predictions derived from both disciplines in one model significantly increases explanatory power over either theory evaluated alone. The empirical analysis is among the first to show increased mortality when firms do not adhere to operating policies consistent with transaction cost minimization principles.

Selection pressures can also shift owing to the evolution of industry. Yet the presumption in TCE that market forces tend to select firms which economize on transaction costs and achieve efficient alignment is made without further discussion of factors such as the industry life cycle, level of competitive intensity, and degree of technological and product market uncertainty.

Thus, an important question remains regarding the time required before the market forces which promote efficiency have their effects. How long before a truly inefficient policy will be eliminated, either through the exit of the firm promulgating it, or by adjustment of the policy by the firm? Oliver Williamson (1985, p. 23) briefly suggests that efficient transaction cost economizing might occur over five to ten years, though the timescale required to achieve efficient organization is rarely addressed in empirical studies. One exception is Jackson Nickerson and Brian Silverman (2003), who found that institutional constraints on firms in the US trucking industry slowed their efforts to economize on transaction costs after deregulation. We will discuss that paper further below.

Evolutionary theories of economic organization, on the other hand, have paid explicit attention to selection processes and their implications for efficiency. Moreover, because selection occurs at the level of the firm, rather than at the level of the transaction, evolutionary theory suggests that firms may carry inefficiently organized transactions along with them for some time. Winter (1988, p. 191) writes:

> ... it is the interdependent system as a whole that is subject to the most significant informational feedback the market provides to the firm – its overall profitability ... it is quite possible that a very good solution to one part of the system problem can carry, at least for a time, the cost burdens of a number of blunders in other areas."

Evolutionary theories therefore suggest that forces of natural selection may not always operate with the speed and efficacy assumed in the Alchian–Friedman tradition. Industry life cycle theories are of particular interest because they postulate general patterns in the waxing and waning of selection forces that may be, and have been, made subject to empirical confirmation. Thus, integrating theories of industry evolution, competitive intensity, or technological uncertainty with TCE may help address the need for estimating the selection pressures in operation in a given empirical context.

In the first study of this kind, Nicolas Argyres and Lyda Bigelow (2005) integrate industry life cycle theory with TCE to examine the impact of organizational choice and firm survival over time. The authors find that firms that misalign transactions face increased risk of failure. However this risk is mitigated by environmental selection pressures. Research on industry life cycles demonstrates that competitive pressures are more severe during the shake-out stage, which could be associated with the emergence of a dominant design, than at other stages. Transaction cost theory, on the other hand, assumes generally competitive markets and does not address the industry lifecycle. It therefore implies that transaction cost economizing is a superior firm strategy regardless of the stage of the life cycle. This paper seeks to reconcile these two streams of research by investigating whether transaction cost economizing has a differential effect on firm survival in pre-shake-out versus shake-out stages of the industry life cycle. Analyzing data from the early US auto industry they find that while transaction cost economizing did not have a significant impact on firm survival during the pre-shake-out stage it did have a significant positive impact on survival during the shake-out stage. This suggests that applications of transaction cost theory which assume uniformly severe selection pressures across the industry life cycle could be misleading. It also suggests that theories of the industry life cycle could usefully take transaction costs into account along with production costs in their analyses of competition over the life cycle.

In a related paper, Lyda Bigelow (2006) extends this work on the impact of industry conditions and its mitigating effect on the link between organizational choice and performance by adding the role of technology choice to the analysis. Using insights regarding competitive intensity and sub-population density derived from organizational ecology theory this worker tests for evidence of the role of aggregate sub-population organizational choice within a technology class. This study also uses data on the early US auto industry's make-or-buy decisions. The primary preliminary findings suggest that within a population, individual misalignment diminishes survival. However, the aggregate governance structure of firms within a technology sub-population has a greater effect on the survival of a local firm than the governance choice of the individual firm. These findings suggest that governance choices in aggregate within technologically localized sub-populations may influence firm survival in conjunction with overall industry conditions.

### 9.4.2    Organizational inertia and its effects on rates of change, profitability, and firm survival

Since we argue the efficient alignment of organizational form affects firm survival, the question of competing risks arises. Is it riskier to undergo core structural change and adapt governance mode or to remain misaligned? As in the previous section on cross-sectional studies of organizational choice and performance, recent research investigating adaptation to misalignment has relied on integrating organizational theories with TCE to provide additional insight.

Organizational ecology theory, at least in its strong form, argues that much of the change in the organizational landscape comes about through an evolutionary process in which incumbents fail to adapt and are selected out and new entrants flourish due to their improved organizational forms. In other words, though we may observe changes in organizational structure as environmental conditions change, closer inspection often reveals that it is new entrants rather than incumbent firms who display the new, better-aligned structure. As a theory devoted to understanding population vital rates, for example the entry and exit of firms, a central hypothesis of the theory, is that core structural change is positively associated with failure.

This insight became a lightning rod for critics who interpreted this selectionist view as ignoring the empirical reality that, indeed, firms seem to be constantly undergoing change, and that often, the most successful firms in an industry are those firms that pursue wholesale change in the face of competitive shifts. This perspective on the theory is an exaggerated interpretation, based as it is on the strong form of the theory. A better perspective might be that the theory emphasizes that the change process itself, particularly when the process involves changes in core features of the firm, is in and of itself inherently risky – even if the change represents an improvement in the alignment of the firm with its competitive environment.

Michael Hannan and John Freeman's (1984, 1989) structural inertia theory provides the framework for analyzing change within organizational ecology. Their principle argument suggests that the probability of organizational change diminishes over time as a result of both internal and external pressures. To survive, organizations develop co-specialized routines and make co-specialized investments which facilitate interactions within the organization as well as with external agents. As these routines become institutionalized they contribute to an increase in structural inertia. Structural inertia, as its name implies, reduces the firm's ability to change. But it also confers benefits. For example, there are economic efficiencies associated with this institutionalization of organizational routines. The reduction of uncertainty as to how things will be done, as well as the incremental improvements which can be generated once a given procedure is decided upon, help to increase organizational efficiency.

But Michael Hannan and John Freeman also build a case for the sociological notion of constituitive legitimacy. The idea that a routine, structure, or organizational form has become taken for granted implies that resources need no longer be expended on the process of garnering support for that routine or structure. This concept of the continuity of routines being beneficial to the firm and facilitating the leveraging of those resources is entirely consistent with the concept of co-specialized firm-specific investment in assets developed in TCE. Though the link between these two concepts is not made explicit within the original articulation of the theory, Jackson Nickerson and Brian Silverman (2003) exploit this link in their paper examining the cost of adapting misaligned transactions

Of particular importance here, the theory predicts that there are real hazards associated with core change. Core change can disrupt relationships within the organization, for example among employees, strategic groups, and subsidiaries as well as between the organization and other outside entities, such as suppliers, customers, regulatory agencies, and so on. Usurping institutionalized practices makes it more difficult for external and internal agents to predict and understand firm behavior. This in turn makes it more difficult for the firm to attract and retain resources. Based on this, the theory predicts that core change in the boundaries of the firm will be riskier than less extensive or peripheral change undertaken by the firm.

Jackson Nickerson and Brian Silverman (2003) extend the study of organizational choice and performance by considering the efforts of firms to adapt their organizational choices so as to be aligned according to TCE predictions. This paper integrates content-based predictions of TCE with process-based predictions of organizational change to understand adaptation to deregulation in the for-hire trucking industry. They predict, and find, that firms whose governance of a core transaction is poor (according to transaction cost reasoning) will realize lower profits than their better-aligned counterparts and that these firms will attempt to adapt so as to better align their transactions. Results show that several organizational features affect the rate of adaptation: (1) firms with large investments in specialized assets adapt less readily than firms that rely on generic assets; (2) firms with unions adapt less readily than firms without unions; (3) firms that must replace employee drivers with owner-operators adapt less readily than firms that must replace owner-operators with employee drivers; and (4) entrants adapt more quickly than incumbent carriers. There is evidence of institutional isomorphism in that although carriers move systematically to reduce misalignment, they do so less assiduously when this will make their governance of drivers look less like that of nearby, similar carriers. Finally, their results indicate that firms that ultimately exited adapted more quickly than firms that survived.

### 9.4.3    Organizational vacillation

A central proposition in organization theory and TCE is that discrete organizational forms are matched to environmental conditions, market strategies, or exchange conditions. Jackson Nickerson and Todd Zenger (2002) use TCE to develop a contrary theoretical proposition. They argue that efficiency may dictate modulating between discrete governance modes (i.e. structural modulation) in response to a stable set of exchange conditions. If governance choices are discrete, as much of organization theory argues, and firms display inertia in the face of pressures to change, their theory shows that a static environment (or market strategy) often demands a dynamic organizational response. They argue that when no discrete structural organizational mode provides a precise match to exchange attributes, managers can capture efficiency benefits by modulating between organizational modes – what some refer to as vacillating between or among organizational modes such as make or buy, or centralization versus decentralization – in order to approximate the optimal level of functionality, so long as the costs of change are sufficiently low. The pursuit of efficiency leads to dynamic instead of static alignment that implies endogenous organizational change. Perhaps the most intriguing result of the model is the finding that inertia, at least up to a point, may yield efficiency advantages by allowing an organization's actual functionality to temporarily achieve intermediate levels. This improved efficiency occurs because inertia in actual functionality reduces the need or frequency with which an organization must change organizational modes.

They develop an analytical model of structural modulation based on TCE notions of discrete structural alternatives and through simulation examine factors that influence when modulation is efficiency enhancing as well as the optimal rate of modulation. Contrary to theories that highlight the potentially destructive consequences of inertia on organizational survival, they identify important efficiency yielding benefits of inertia. Whilst the authors motivate their research with a case study of Hewlett-Packard, their theory awaits further empirical examination.

## 9.5    The problem-solving perspective

The problem-solving perspective (PSP) is an emerging area of TCE that links strategy, organizational choice, and value creation. This new perspective, articulated in Jackson Nickerson and Todd Zenger (2004), was developed in response to observed inconsistencies and shortcomings in the knowledge- or resource-based view concerning how firms organize to generate knowledge efficiently. Rather than using the transaction as the unit of analysis, the PSP adopts the problem as the unit of analysis.

PSP has three elements. Managers choose problems to solve, knowledge must be assembled in such a way as to increase the likelihood and lower the cost and time of finding viable solutions, and managers must be able to capture a portion of the value that is created by solution. Jackson Nickerson and Todd Zenger (2004) argue that all three questions must be addressed simultaneously and in an ongoing way.

Much of strategy research is focussed on the third issue, capturing value. Jackson Nickerson and Todd Zenger's (2004) paper focusses on the second question: how to organize knowledge sets to solve a problem. Their theory conceptualizes searching for solutions to problems on rugged solution landscapes. The ruggedness of a solution landscape is determined by the complexity of the problem. They rely on Herbert Simon's (1962) archetypes of problem decomposability, near decomposability, and non-decomposability to parameterize the complexity of problems. As the ruggedness of these solution landscapes increase the most efficient way of searching the landscape also changes. Jackson Nickerson and Todd Zenger (2004) argue that different organizational forms have comparative costs and competencies for performing the different types of search necessary to find solutions, that is, high peaks, on the landscapes.

Their theory articulates the knowledge-based advantages and disadvantages of both markets and hierarchy for overcoming knowledge formation hazards in searching solution landscapes. These hazards limit people's willingness to exchange knowledge and may lead to the manipulation of trial and error because of opportunism and bounded rationality. Markets do not overcome these hazards. Hierarchy, of which there are two kinds, may overcome knowledge-formation hazards. One type of hierarchy – they call authority-based hierarchy – overcomes certain knowledge-formation hazards because constraints and conflicts are resolved through fiat by a central administrator. It facilitates searching over nearly decomposable landscapes but does poorly at encouraging the exchange of knowledge and depends critically on the cognitive capacity of the central administrator. The other type of hierarchy is referred to as consensus-based hierarchy, in which constraints and conflicts are resolved through consensus. Consensus-based hierarchy encourages knowledge sharing through socialization of a common goal and common language, but is costly to organize and maintain. Ultimately, their theory predicts that decomposable problems organized across the market interface, merely decomposable problems are organized by authority-based hierarchy, and non-decomposable problems are organized in consensus-based teams. Although correctly aligning governance with problem complexity does not guarantee the rapid discovery of a valuable solution, they nonetheless expect that over a large number of solution searches, efficient alignment yields superior performance by enhancing the probability of discovering a valuable solution.

Whilst the paper proposes a rather static alignment between problem choice and governance choice, the impetus for dynamic changes in the composition of the firm are inherent in PSP. Firms shift their boundaries and organizational structures in response to changes in the problems that they address. Moreover, problems have life cycles. Such strategic and dynamic choices represent a substantial arena for further inquiry.

Jackson Nickerson and Todd Zenger's (2004) theory highlights both the perils and virtues of authority in managing knowledge formation.

Managers must recognize that the domain of problems for which their direction is of value is bounded on two sides. Effective knowledge management requires managers to recognize both limits. On one hand, when problems are quite decomposable, managers must resist the temptation to assume value in their direction by integrating relevant knowledge sets. Instead, the manager must trust the market's intense motivation to specialize and guide directional search when problems are decomposable. Managers must recognize that cognitive constraints limit their capacity to possess the specialized knowledge to guide directional search and integration will simply dull the incentives of those specialists who do possess the required knowledge. On the other, when problems are non-decomposable, managers must also resist the temptation to assume value in their directing the path of search. Again, the manager must recognize that cognitive constraints limit his or her capacity to understand the wide-ranging knowledge interactions required to develop heuristics useful in guiding search. Instead, the manager must trust that a culture of widespread knowledge sharing and consensus decision making is the organizational approach most likely to yield a valuable solution. Therefore, depending on the set of problems pursued by the firm, those gaining from direction (substituting for education) may be quite limited.

Bruce Heiman and Jackson Nickerson (2004) and Jeffrey Macher (2006) provide the first empirical tests of the PSP. Bruce Heiman and Jackson Nickerson (2004) explore how knowledge-based attributes of an inter-firm collaboration – knowledge tacitness and problem-solving complexity – influence the governance choice of the collaboration. They argue that knowledge tacitness and complexity create costly problems with knowledge transfer. These problems are subsequently addressed by deploying knowledge management practices (KMPs), for example high-bandwidth interactions or co-specialization of communication codes, which are generated through equity-based governance as opposed to non-equity-based governance. An initial empirical test using the CATI database provides preliminary support for their hypotheses. Questionnaires filled out by thirty-six collaboration managers and personnel along with interviews of eighteen of the respondents provide further qualitative support for their theory.

Jeffrey Macher's (2006) paper examines how firms in the semi-conductor industry most efficiently organize to solve different types of problems related to technological development. He argues that vertically integrated firms realize performance advantages when problems are ill-structured and complex, while the same is true for specialized firms when problems are well-structured and simple. He collects measures that capture important dimensions of performance and finds empirical support for his propositions. He also finds that performance differences arise from the presence of scale economies and scope economies.

These early empirical findings support the theme addressed in our previous section on hierarchical governance – that there are abundant opportunities to refine and extend our understanding of the link between internal governance structure and firm outcomes, particularly as they relate to the areas of knowledge transfer, R&D, and technological know-how. Again, understanding the links between formal and informal governance mechanisms and how they constrain or facilitate the problem choice and solution search process represents fruitful areas of future research in this area.

## 9.6    Conclusion

This chapter discussed the intersections among NIE, organization, and strategy. Although at first glance the three questions that motivate research in business strategy – (1) Why do some firms earn more rents than other firms, even in the same industry? (2) Why do performance differences persist? (3) What can managers do to earn higher and enduring rents for their firms? – may seem distant from TCE, this chapter highlighted at least some research that informs why and how TCE may address these questions, which makes it one of the core theories for thinking about and understanding business strategy.

The chapter began by providing a long summary of Williamson's discriminating alignment hypothesis. Notably, we drew a connection between the manager's decision about how to organize a transaction and the profitability of the transaction. Williamson's (1991a) model provides the necessary theoretical foundation for much of the research in TCE that addresses organizational choice and performance. We used this model to categorize and discuss research in three broad areas.

The first area focussed on studies that connected exchange attributes with organizational choice and performance. We summarized cross-sectional research that connected organizational choice and performance at the transaction level. While a growing number of papers have been published in this domain, only one thus far has been able to assess the profitability of the transaction with respect to organizational choice. Given the paucity of papers that measure performance at a transaction level, this stream of research offers many potential opportunities for further research. There is also ample room to expand the repertoire of performance outcome measures, utilizing proxies which capture more nuanced details of costs, innovation, growth, and technological performance.

We also reported on recent research that focussed on how shift-parameters affect the choice of organization and thereby impacted performance outcomes. Very little empirical research has used Williamson shift-parameter logic, which suggests a substantial opportunity for future research. This may be of particular importance to those interested in comparative economic or international research.

Another stream of research in this area investigates why particular exchange conditions are chosen in the first place. It links Porter's strategic-positioning logic with Williamson's TCE to identify alternative strategies. A key feature of this research is use of the investment profile across a constellation of transactions instead of just one transaction. Thus far, only one empirical paper, which does support the framework, has been published, which may indicate an opportunity for further research inquiries.

The second research area we explored focussed on organizational change and performance. We discussed the limited research that has investigated Oliver Williamson's weak-form selection hypothesis. We also discussed how this hypothesis may change over the industry life cycle and new research that is investigating these potential changes. We described another stream of research that looks at the interaction of organizational inertia, TCE, and their combined effect on the rates of change, profitability, and firm survival. This research begins to unpack the extent to which firms change or are selected out of environments based on transaction cost notions of misalignment in structural inertia theory. A final stream of research discussed in this area pertains to organizational vacillation. The existence of discrete structural organizational alternatives as proposed by Williamson may lead firms to vacillate between or among organizational modes in order to improve efficiency. Organizational inertia, we argued, provides the key elements to determine the rate of such modulation. As indicated by the small number of research articles described in this area, many opportunities are available to expand research in this domain.

The third and final research area focussed on in this chapter was PSP. This close cousin to TCE provides a new framework to think about the hazards of knowledge formation and the organizational alternatives which may be chosen to mitigate these concerns. This new theory is the first knowledge-based theory to predict when hierarchy supplants markets and when markets supplant hierarchy. It has the added feature of being able to predict the use of alternative hierarchical forms as well as the use of markets in the same model. This theory is in need of further development and enhancement, and many empirical opportunities exist to examine its validity. Given the continuing increase in interest in theories of the firm, this theory is likely to receive increasing attention in the years to come.

The good news for scholars interested in the intersection of institutional economics, organization, and performance is that the field continues to offer many opportunities to plant, grow, and harvest new and value-creating research projects, especially for aspiring scholars.

# 10 Inter-Firm Alliances: A New Institutional Economics Approach

*Joanne E. Oxley and Brian S. Silverman*

## 10.1 Introduction

When examining firm boundary issues, researchers in new institutional economics (NIE), in particular transaction cost economists, have traditionally focussed on the choice between market and hierarchy (Williamson 1975, 1979). However, as acknowledged by Williamson (1985) and expanded by Hennart (1991, 1993), this dichotomy overlooks the fact that the economic landscape is littered with organizational forms which look neither like pure market nor like pure hierarchy. Thus, rather than a market or hierarchy dichotomy, it is more useful to think of transaction governance along a continuum, with market and hierarchy as the end points, and hybrid arrangements such as partnerships and alliances making up the "swollen middle" (Hennart 1993).

Academic interest in alliances as a distinct organizational form began in earnest during the early 1980s, coinciding with a rise in the rate of alliance formation. Early treatments in the management literature sought to understand and classify the variety of organizational forms that may be collected under the alliance rubric (e.g. Contractor and Lorange 1988). Whilst they are useful starting points, these early taxonomies lacked a theoretical underpinning and, although some of the ordering of organizational forms was intuitive, left much room for debate. Thus, the early alliance literature tended to be fragmented and non-cumulative. In the subsequent two decades, however, a voluminous theory-driven literature on alliances has emerged, and significant progress has been made in understanding the motivations, organization, and effects of inter-firm arrangements. This progress has, in large part, been driven by the development and application of transaction cost economics (TCE), often in combination with ideas drawn from the resource-based view (RBV) of the firm.

In this chapter we summarize and survey those strands of alliance research that have most relevance to the NIE agenda, notably those from the TCE or RBV perspective. After providing some additional background information on the motives and challenges of alliance partners, we suggest that there exist seven key questions associated with the study and management of alliances. We then lay out the basic transaction cost theory of alliances, which has been quite successful at addressing many – but not all – of these seven questions. Notably, TCE has been particularly successful at predicting and explaining the existence of alliances as a "hybrid" governance form between markets and hierarchies, as well as the range of governance arrangements within alliances, particularly with respect to discrete comparisons among majority equity, minority equity, and non-equity relationships. In conjunction with RBV, TCE has been successful at predicting alliance partner choice. TCE also provides a systematic way to consider the effect of alliance context (institutional environment, competitive context, and reputation or network effects) on partner choice and governance structure choice.

Following our general survey of the literature, we focus on several areas at the leading edge of alliance research and identify opportunities for future researchers. In particular, we suggest possible avenues for research – often involving integration of NIE with alternate approaches such as social network theory – that will help scholars address the remaining key questions about alliances. This research entails moving beyond governance choice to alliance outcomes; beyond discrete structural alternatives to particular contract terms; and beyond the dyad to network-embedded relationships.

## 10.2    The phenomenon

### 10.2.1    Alliance motives

Although we often think of the inter-firm alliance as a recent phenomenon, firms have long relied on joint ventures and other partnerships or long-term agreements. Joint ventures have frequently been motivated by government restrictions on internationalizing firms: many countries have traditionally restricted foreign firms' access to their markets unless these firms enter via joint ventures with local firms. Consequently, *market-access alliances* have been a common feature of the international business landscape throughout the twentieth century. Industries where entry restrictions (and therefore market-access alliances) are most common include extractive and other natural resource industries and, more recently, those industries that are deemed important to national security or national competitiveness, such as telecommunications and information technology.

The rapid increase in alliance formation in the last twenty-five years reflects a more diverse set of motives, however. As the pace of technological change accelerated and industry boundaries began to blur, many firms found that they did not possess all the necessary resources to sustain competitive advantage in their industry (or to enter an attractive new industry segment); nor were they able to easily acquire the requisite resources in a timely fashion by simply purchasing them in the market or growing them internally. In this context, alliances were seen as useful vehicles for combining alliance partners' resources to increase competitive advantage.

In some instances, partners can effectively combine resources simply by combining the output of their independent activities. In such an alliance, often called a *co-specialization alliance*, operational integration may be quite low, reducing the need for high levels of information exchange. The international alliance that produced the V2500 jet engine, International Aero Engines (IAE), is an example of this type of undertaking. This alliance, managed by Rolls Royce and Pratt & Whitney as the senior participants, was structured to enable each participant to specialize in the development and manufacture of specific portions of the engine, and actually included restrictions on information and technology exchange among partner firms (Mowery 1987). Airbus Industrie, the European producer of large commercial transporters, is another example of such an alliance, in as much as its member firms specialize in the design and manufacture of specific components of the overall aircraft (Mowery, Oxley, and Silverman 2002).

In other instances, partners wish to actually acquire each others' knowledge or capabilities. In such an alliance, often referred to as a *learning alliance*, partners must invest greater effort in activity integration and knowledge-sharing to accomplish their objectives. A classic example of an alliance of this type is the NUMMI joint venture between Toyota and General Motors (GM). This alliance was undertaken by GM to learn Toyota's production system and labor management techniques, while Toyota hoped to access GM's knowledge of the US market and to gain experience working with a unionized US labor force (Womack 1989). To facilitate the desired learning, GM and Toyota jointly operated an automobile plant in Fremont, California, in which the partners employed Japanese processes and a US labor force. GM's learning objective was explicitly recognized within the alliance agreement, which included provisions for site visits by managers from the entire GM network to enable diffusion of the acquired capabilities to other production plants.

In industries where demand-side economies of scale or scope are important drivers of competitive advantage, firms may also form alliances as a means of rapidly increasing scale or filling in gaps, or both, in a product line. The battle between Sony and JVC in the video cassette industry is the iconic example here, as the alliances that JVC formed with other Japanese firms were crucial in rapidly building production capacity and installed base of the VHS tape format, ultimately driving out the superior Beta format. More recent examples of alliances aimed at increasing network scale are airline alliances such as One World and Star Alliance. Because these alliances often bring together current or potential competitors, they are often referred to as *Co-option alliances* (Gomes-Casseres 1996). Co-option alliances may entail virtually no integration of activities across partners – for example, early airline alliances usually entailed little more than code-sharing agreements that allowed passengers to make connections on different member airlines' routes under a single ticket – but over time the level of integration may increase significantly as alliances take on a broader range of tasks, such as common procurement, joint branding, and advertising.

### 10.2.2  Alliance forms

Just as alliances may be established to achieve a wide variety of objectives, they may also assume a wide variety of forms. The "classic" alliance form is the joint venture, which involves the creation of a new venture jointly owned and operated by two or more firms. Equity ownership in the joint venture is divided among the owners, as are the profits generated by the venture. The classic joint venture has its own management team, but ultimately reports to a board of directors comprising members from the parent companies, often in proportion to equity shares. The board provides a direct conduit for communication with senior managers of the parent companies, facilitating negotiation of strategic and operational priorities for the venture, as well as monitoring of partner firms' activities (Kogut 1988).

Although the joint venture is often considered the prototypical alliance, many other alliance forms exist, most of which do not entail the formation of a new stand-alone venture. The alliance rubric also encompasses contractual agreements of various types, including technology, business format, or know-how licenses (both unilateral and bilateral agreements); manufacturing, marketing or research and development (R&D) agreements; and other more esoteric forms such as production buy-back agreements or oil exploration syndicates.

This diversity of organizational and legal forms certainly posed challenges to development of a "unified theory" of alliances, and led to an early proliferation in alliance taxonomies (e.g. Contractor and Lorange 1988; Killing 1988; Lorange and Roos 1992; Gomes-Caseres 1996). However, as we shall see below, the application of TCE has brought significant discipline to this area of study, allowing more cumulative understanding of the nature and role of alliance governance.

The observed diversity of organizational and legal forms of alliances includes arrangements that appear to be quite close relatives of the buyer–supplier relationships and other forms of vertical cooperation that have been the traditional focus of TCE – and the subject of other chapters of this book. Although the conceptual boundary between alliances and buyer–supplier relationships is not sharp (*see* discussion of the market–hierarchy continuum of alliances below), one orienting distinction is the idea that alliances represent collaborations among peers in some sense. Thus, even where an alliance relationship is "vertical," in that output from the alliance is used as an input by one of the partner firms, the existence of an alliance indicates that each firm brings specialized assets and capabilities to the alliance which, for example, brings issues of partner selection more to the fore in alliance research than is commonly the case in the study of buyer–supplier relationships.

Another body of literature that is closely related to NIE research on alliances is the literature on strategic networks. Indeed, academic interest in alliances was in part fueled by observations that firms are often embedded in dense networks of alliances and other inter-organizational relationships. Although in this chapter we primarily concern ourselves with analysis of individual alliances – reflecting the focus of TCE research on the topic to date – we return to the issue of alliance networks and social context toward the end of the chapter. We point to ways that network analysis can inform NIE, and to ways that NIE can do the same for network analysis.

### 10.2.3 Collaboration and competition

Irrespective of the motive for collaboration or the form of the alliance, all alliances embody a basic tension. On one hand, partners need to collaborate and behave cooperatively to create value. On the other, the interests of the firms inevitably diverge when it comes to claiming value generated within the alliance. As a result, partners compete to divide value. This can be exacerbated by the fact that firms which act as partners within an alliance often compete in important areas and markets outside the scope of the alliance. Given this tension, and the implicit motivations that partners have to "defect" as an alliance proceeds, one of the primary concerns in an alliance is that it be structured in a way that satisfactorily protects the interests and investments of the partners.

Depending on the motives and context of the alliance, this tension can take different forms (see Table 10.1). In a market access alliance, one partner – often a multi-national company (MNC) – may possess significant proprietary assets and capabilities and, without government regulation, would prefer to enter the market autonomously to maintain control

Table 10.1 *Alliance motives and cooperative challenges*

| Motive | Goal | Classic business case examples | Key cooperative challenges |
|---|---|---|---|
| Market access | Access geographic market otherwise inaccessible due to government regulations | Fuji-Xerox | Maintaining adequate control while inducing partner's continued cooperation; protecting proprietary assets |
| Co-specialization | Access complementary resources and capabilities possessed by partner | International Aero Engines; Airbus | Managing integration; rent sharing; monitoring changes in capabilities and outside options |
| Learning | Build new competencies by acquiring partner's technological, product or market knowledge | NUMMI | Learning versus leakage; avoiding destructive race to learn |
| Co-option | Build critical mass by partnering with complementors and competitors (current or potential) | VHS video; Airline alliances | Managing incentives to prevent free-riding, rent sharing and destructive rent seeking |

of these assets. In this situation, the key cooperative challenge is to adopt a governance structure that provides an adequate level of control for the foreign partner while inducing the local partner's continued cooperation, particularly where the local partner must make investments specific to the needs of the MNC. Control of proprietary assets is particularly important in order to avoid the situation where the local partner internalizes the MNC's capabilities, exits the alliance, and uses its privileged local status to compete effectively with its erstwhile partner.

In co-specialization and in some co-option alliances managing integration is a key challenge: even though partners remain relatively autonomous and do not cooperate directly on individual tasks, significant knowledge-sharing is nonetheless needed to effectively integrate the products of their individual activities. This again may raise issues related to protection of proprietary assets. Free riding may also be a concern if partners find it difficult to monitor and assess individual contributions, particularly in co-option alliances. In addition, to the extent that a firm customizes its operations to the needs of the alliance, decreasing viable outside options, concerns will arise over rent-sharing within the alliance. Similarly, if circumstances change so that the value of partners' resources and capabilities shift dramatically, this can lead to destructive rent seeking and instability in the alliance. Designing an alliance to align incentives in these circumstances is a significant challenge.

Learning alliances are often viewed as the most challenging, however, as they most clearly embody the tension between value creation and value division in a "learning versus leakage" dilemma (Oxley 2003): effective inter-partner learning requires openness and extensive information sharing, but the very practices that promote learning also seem to facilitate leakage of proprietary assets. This may lead the partners to engage in a "race to learn" (Hamel 1991; Khanna, Gulati, and Nohria 1998) as each partner tries to gain maximum benefit from the alliance and avoid becoming asymmetrically dependent on the other partner. As a result, many see the learning alliance as an unstable or transitory alliance form (Nakamura, Shaver, and Yeung 1996; Dussauge, Garrette, and Mitchell 2000). As we discuss below, however, appropriate governance can play an important role in resolving this and the other collaborative tensions identified here.

### 10.2.4  The seven questions of alliance formation and management

Managers face seven major questions as they consider forming an inter-firm alliance: Why/when do we ally? With whom do we ally? How do we design the alliance? How does the appropriate alliance design depend on the context in which it will operate? How do we manage the alliance over time? How do we extract benefits from the alliance? How do we manage a network of alliances? Figure 10.1 shows connections among these seven questions, which serve to structure our analysis in this chapter. Below we summarize how the NIE approach sheds light on most of these questions, although to date attention by transaction cost economists in particular have predominantly focussed on the first four questions. We then go on to identify opportunities for future research which might shed additional light on the remaining underexplored questions.

## 10.3    The transaction cost theory of alliances

The primary hypothesis of TCE is that organizational actors attempt to economize on transaction costs by assigning transactions (which differ in

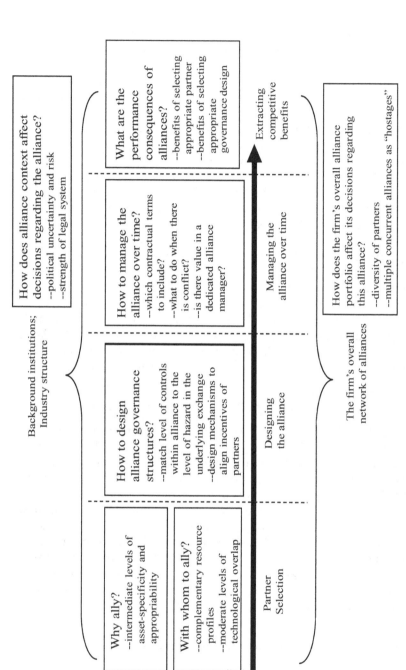

**Figure 10.1** NIE research on the seven questions about alliances.

their attributes) to governance structures (the adaptive capacities and associated costs of which differ) in a discriminating way (Williamson 1985, p. 18). Resting on the behavioral assumptions of bounded rationality and opportunism, TCE asserts that transactions will be governed in ways that accord with their characteristics, chiefly uncertainty, frequency, asset-specificity, and appropriability. Generally, the most important of these is asset specificity, or the degree of specific investment associated with a transaction (Klein, Crawford, and Alchian 1978; Williamson 1979). In the context of knowledge-based transactions, almost equally important is appropriability, or the ability to maintain control over particular elements of knowledge and the income streams that accrue to them (Teece 1986; Oxley 1997).

When exchange hazards are negligible – broadly, when the assets supporting a transaction are generic and the appropriability regime is strong – spot markets offer the least-cost form of governance. Such markets provide strong incentives for effort, and parties incur few if any set-up costs for spot market transactions. At the same time, relying on generic assets means that disputes between transacting parties may be resolved at low cost by exiting the exchange. When exchange hazards are high – when the assets are transaction-specific and appropriability is weak – hierarchy is the least-cost governance solution. Although hierarchy involves muted incentives and high fixed set-up costs, it can support coordination of investments and activities that are difficult to coordinate through markets. Within a hierarchy, authority ultimately can resolve disagreements, which provides tighter control of specific assets and knowledge.

As we discuss below, when a transaction is characterized by intermediate levels of exchange hazards, alliances offer the least-cost method of governance. Further, variations in the level of exchange hazards can be matched with varied levels of hierarchy-style control within an alliance.

### 10.3.1  Why ally? Alliances within the market–hierarchy continuum

Alliances are characterized within TCE as "hybrid" organizations – neither market nor hierarchy, but possessing governance characteristics somewhere between these two polar forms. Williamson (1991a), discussing hybrid organizations in the context of the "market–hierarchy continuum" suggests that the key governance instruments that distinguish governance structures along the continuum are incentive intensity, administrative controls, and contract law. These instruments give rise to differential performance attributes, that is, autonomous adaptability and bilateral adaptability. Hybrid organizations lie between market and hierarchy in all these respects (Table 10.2). Notably, since the parties to

Table 10.2 *Alliances as Hybrid Governance Structures*

|  | Governance structure | | |
| --- | --- | --- | --- |
|  | Market | Hybrid | Hierarchy |
| **Instruments** | | | |
| Incentive Intensity | ++ | + | 0 |
| Administrative Controls | 0 | + | ++ |
| Contract Law | ++ | + | 0 |
| **Performance Attributes** | | | |
| Autonomous Adaptability | ++ | + | 0 |
| Bilateral Adaptability | 0 | + | ++ |

*Note:* ++, strong effect; +, semi-strong effect; 0, weak effect; Adapted from Williamson (1991a)

the exchange maintain independent identities, the bilateral adaptability features associated with hierarchy are partially sacrificed in favor of the autonomous adaptability of the market; at the same time, since the parties establish greater administrative controls and deeper commitments than they would in pure market exchange, some bilateral adaptability is maintained. Williamson (1985, pp 70–72) further suggests that bilateral adaptability in hybrids is also enhanced by reliance on "relational contracting" (Llewellyn 1931), whereby contracts are viewed as frameworks for the agreement rather than as blueprints for specific action or performance. Here, arbitration and other dispute resolution mechanisms largely replace the court ordering associated with market transactions. However, in contrast to organization within a hierarchy (where the law of forbearance prevails and courts will generally decline to hear internal disputes), the court remains available to alliance partners as a forum of ultimate appeal.

Most of the early work on inter-firm alliances (e.g. Geringer and Hebert 1989; Gomes-Casseres 1989; Hennart 1991) focussed on one hybrid archetype, the equity joint venture.[1] In governance terms, the shared equity in such a venture acts as an effective hostage exchange (Williamson 1983): because the value of the joint venture relies critically on continued operation: each firm effectively posts a bond equal to its equity share, the value of which is only partially redeemable should operations cease. Furthermore, the ongoing returns to each partner are based on the profits of the venture as a whole (usually with distributions in proportion to the equity shares), so that the incentives of the parent firms are clearly more closely aligned than is the case in a pure market transaction.

The administrative controls present in an equity joint venture – for example, the parent's control of seats on the venture's board of directors – also serve to facilitate coordinated control over specialized assets. The board provides a direct conduit for communication with senior managers of the parent companies and facilitates monitoring of partner firms' activities (Kogut 1988). Note, however, that in contrast with directives from the senior management or directors of an integrated company, the directives from the joint venture's parents are subject to negotiation and compromise if conflict arises in the goals and aspirations of the firms. Indeed, the right of veto over a venture's strategic decisions is often explicitly incorporated into the joint venture agreement (Geringer and Hebert 1989; Killing 1983).

Evidence of discriminating alignment in the choice between autonomous investment (hierarchy) and establishment of joint venture may be found in empirical studies examining the mode of entry into new international markets. Prominent examples of this large body of research include Hennart's (1991) study of Japanese entry into the US market and studies by Gomes-Casseres (1989), Agarwal and Ramaswamy (1992), and Kim and Hwang (1992) examining US entry into foreign markets. Emblematic of these studies, Hennart (1991) finds that Japanese firms choose joint ventures when they must access complementary inputs for which markets are subject to contractual hazards, and choose autonomous investment when they own all necessary resources.

Interpretation of the results of these studies is often hindered by data limitations, necessitating that only firm- or industry-level measures are employed (rather than the transaction-level characteristics featured in TCE). Nevertheless, the results are generally consistent with TCE's predictions that a firm will rely on a wholly owned subsidiary (hierarchy) when expanding to a new geographic environment that is characterized by significant exchange hazards, but will rely on an alliance (hybrid) in situations that involve "moderate" exchange hazards.

### 10.3.2   With whom to ally? Complementary resources and technological overlap

For a long time, transaction cost economists were silent concerning the question of with whom to ally. This is not surprising given that TCE traditionally does not emphasize firm heterogeneity in productive capability, in order to better focus on governance issues. At the extreme, the identity of an exchange partner often does not matter *ex ante* – it is only *ex post*, after specific investments have been made, that the identity of the exchange partner becomes salient. Hence, the issue of partner selection has not featured heavily in the TCE research agenda.

Scholars in the complementary branch of organizational economics known as RBV have, in contrast, devoted considerable effort to this question. The general consensus of research in this vein is that partner selection is best driven by a search for crucial complementary assets or capabilities (Pisano 1990). For example, in a market access alliance frequently one firm provides technological or manufacturing capabilities in exchange for the other's marketing strengths. Alliances that focus on joint R&D or product development often involve the marriage of partners' distinct technological strengths, as in the previously noted Airbus Industrie example. An important twist in this story, however, is that, in technology-driven alliances, partners should have capabilities that are different but not too different: firms jointly pursuing collaborative development of a technology or product within an alliance are likely to require some level of technological "overlap" to facilitate knowledge exchange and development. Similarly, when an alliance is used by one firm to internalize new technology-based capabilities from a partner, the "student" must have considerable in-house expertise that complements that of its partner in order to properly assess and transfer the desired capabilities (Cohen and Levinthal 1990).

One empirical study that explores this is the work of Mowery, Oxley, and Silverman (1998). Using patent cross- and common-citations to proxy for technological overlap, they contrast the degree of technological overlap between alliance partners with that between a matched-sample of non-partners. They find that partners have a significantly greater degree of technological overlap than do non-partners. Further, their logit estimations indicate that increased technological overlap between two firms increases the likelihood of their forming an alliance up to a point, but then decreases the likelihood of an alliance. This appears to support the RBV prediction that the best partner is one that is different but not too different – a firm needs sufficient overlap with its partner that they can understand each other, but if there is too much overlap this reduces the gain from working together (at the limit, there is no point in partnering with a firm that has the identical capabilities as your own).

### 10.3.3   How to design alliance structures: the continuum of market and hierarchy features within alliances

Just as the prototypical alliance is conceived as a point on the continuum between market and hierarchy, alliances themselves exhibit a range of governance mechanisms that can also be conceived as lying along this continuum. Oxley (1997) extended the basic TCE logic to consider the governance attributes of various alliance types. She argued that, ideally, we would like to rank all alliance types according to the governance instruments shown in Table 10.2 – incentive intensity, administrative controls, and contract law supports – so making the choice of alliance form susceptible to straightforward transaction cost reasoning: alliance forms would be chosen based on the extent of contracting hazards present in the exchange relationship, with more hierarchical alliances being chosen in situations where contracting hazards are higher. Unfortunately, this exercise is far from simple, given the diversity of organizational forms that come under the rubric of alliances; for example, how do we begin to compare the governance features of a marketing service agreement with those of a co-development agreement or oil exploration syndicate?

One approach to this problem would be to catalogue and evaluate individual contract provisions and other safeguards, including formal and informal reporting requirements, assignments of managerial control, third-party arbitration requirements, and effective hostage exchanges built into the agreement. This approach is very demanding in terms of the level of micro-analytic data involved and, furthermore, it is not readily apparent how one would rank alliances in which different combinations of these various governance instruments are present.[2] Added to this is the fact that the universe of alliances covers a wide variety of different activities which embody idiosyncratic governance features such as hostage exchanges that are as much a feature of the activities themselves as of the organizational form *per se*.

Responding to this complexity, Oxley (1997) argued that alliances tend to cluster in discrete forms, within which there is significant variation but between which we can nonetheless identify step function differences in governance attributes. By focussing on these distinctions across clusters, we may develop a simplified ranking of alliance forms, with the caveat that only alliances within broadly comparable activity classes are ranked. Such a ranking for technology-related alliances (going from market towards hierarchy) comprises unilateral contractual agreements (unilateral licenses, long-term supply contracts, R&D contracts); bilateral contractual agreements (technology-sharing or cross-licensing agreement, joint research agreements); and equity-based alliances (joint ventures and research corporations).

Comparing contract-based alliances in the market–hierarchy continuum the key distinguishing feature is greater incentive alignment in a bilateral agreement, based on the ability to effect in-kind hostage exchanges. When an agreement also involves an equity component, this increases the variety of administrative controls and monitoring rights available, as discussed earlier in the context of an equity joint venture; in tandem with the greater incentive alignment achieved via shared equity, this means that equity-based alliances lie closest to the hierarchy end of the market–hierarchy continuum of alliance forms. It is interesting to note that, if we apply this typology beyond the bounds of technology-related alliances, the continuum may encompass various types of complex supply or distribution agreements. This suggests that, although the alliance literature has, by and large, been developed separately, insights from the existing body of research on vertical relationships may usefully be integrated into future research on alliances.

In terms of the empirical evidence regarding the choice of governance structure within alliances, the earliest studies to apply the lens of TCE are those by Pisano and co-authors (Pisano, Russo, and Teece 1988; Pisano 1989), examining the choice between equity-supported agreements and complex contracts in R&D collaboration (in telecommunications equipment and biotechnology). In each case, the authors conclude that equity arrangements are favored when contracting hazards related to small-numbers bargaining and uncertainty are present to a significant degree. More specifically, Pisano (1989) found that collaborators tended to use equity forms when the activities included R&D, when the scope of collaboration extended beyond a single project, and when collaboration took place in industry segments with relatively few active players.

Gulati (1995a) found similar effects in a study of alliances in the bio-pharmaceuticals, new materials, and automotive industries, and further observed that the form of the alliance depended on the collaborative history of the participants: when a pair of firms had collaborated in the recent past, subsequent alliances were less likely to be equity-based. This finding is consistent with the idea that firms learn about the behavioral characteristics of their alliance partners over the course of collaboration and, assuming that repeat collaboration is reserved for "trustworthy" partners, this lowers the need for formal controls in subsequent alliances with repeat partners. To the extent that multiple alliances connect the same partners at a given point in time, overlapping alliances may also create effective hostages, again reducing the need for formal controls.

Oxley (1997) and Garcia-Canal (1996) examine the entire market–hierarchy continuum of alliance forms for technology collaborations and, again, find evidence consistent with transaction cost theory (TCT): in an ordered probit specification examining the choice among unilateral, bilateral, and equity-based technology alliances, Oxley (1997) finds that more hierarchical alliance forms are chosen when the alliance activities are exposed to greater levels of exchange hazards – specifically, when they involve product or process design in addition to manufacturing or marketing, when the scope of activities is broad, and when there are multiple firms involved in the collaboration (so making monitoring more difficult). Adopting a multinomial logit specification on a more varied sample of alliances, Garcia-Canal (1996) also shows a positive relationship between the number of partners and/or the scope of activities in an alliance and the likelihood that an equity joint venture will be formed, relative to contractual arrangements – again, evidence that firms that engage in alliances systematically match governance mechanisms to the exchange hazards that the alliances must deal with.

### 10.3.4 Alliance context and alliance design choices

Transaction cost economists have increasingly paid close attention to the context in which an alliance takes place, suggesting that context matters in determining the appropriate governance structure of an alliance (in addition to transaction and relational characteristics). Applying Williamson's (1991a) "shift parameter framework," Oxley (1999), for example, argues that, all else equal, when background institutions supporting property rights are weak, firms prefer more hierarchical arrangements to facilitate greater control of intellectual property and other knowledge-assets that are otherwise subject to leakage to alliance partners. Her empirical evidence demonstrates that a US firm undertaking an alliance with a partner in, say, China (a nation whose legal system provides relatively weak intellectual property protection) will demand a more "hierarchical" alliance than it would if it were to undertake the same alliance with a partner in Japan.

Henisz and Williamson (1999) and Henisz (2000b) extend this logic and marry it to insights from the international business literature. In market access alliances, joint ventures are often motivated by the need for a "local face" in dealings with government, in particular to reduce expropriation risk: without a local partner, foreign entrants are particularly vulnerable to expropriation during times of political upheaval, since governments focus their attention (and favors) on domestic constituents during these times. As Henisz (2000b) demonstrates in an empirical study of multi-national investment strategies, this "liability of foreignness" leads firms to favor joint ventures over independent entry when political uncertainty is high. However, high political uncertainty also creates opportunities for local joint venture partners to manipulate the political system to expropriate the returns of the joint venture, and this will be particularly problematic when the venture involves complex operations. As a result, the presence of political uncertainty has an additional effect of amplifying the impact of contractual hazards on the choice of governance structure. These findings thus highlight the potentially complex impact that differences in the legal and political context can have on governance choice in general and for alliances in particular.

In addition to the institutional environment, competitive and (to a lesser extent) social context have also been considered as important factors in alliance governance choice. Oxley and Sampson (2004), for example, argue that when alliance partners are direct competitors the hazards of cooperation are increased and, thus, even "protective" governance structures at the hierarchy end of the market–hierarchy continuum of alliances may be inadequate to support cooperation. In their empirical study of R&D alliances in the micro-electronics and telecommunication equipment industries, they show that when a firm allies with a competitor (indicated by involvement in the same primary product or geographic markets) there is a tendancy to reduce the scope of activities in the alliance – limiting activities to "pure" R&D, rather than extending the alliance activities to cover manufacturing and/or marketing – and that this in turn affects the alliance governance structure chosen.

In terms of social context, the early work of Gulati (1995a, 1995b) points to the role of prior social interaction in mitigating contracting hazards in alliances. Others have argued that more indirect ties, such as shared third-party linkages and position within a wider social network, may also facilitate reputation-based disciplining of partner behavior (e.g. Powell, Koput, and Smith-Doerr 1996). Although this is consistent with core ideas in NIE (e.g. Greif 1993), there has until recently been little examination of the impact of social networks on alliance governance. This issue is taken up below, where we explore the leading edge of research in this area and identify opportunities for future researchers.

## 10.4    Current issues: how can the new industrial economics approach make further progress on the seven questions of alliances?

As the above discussion highlights, alliance research in the NIE tradition has made significant headway in addressing many of the seven major alliance management questions: compared with the situation of twenty-five years ago we have a much greater understanding of why and when firms become allies; with whom they generally ally; and the logic underlying alliance design and governance. We have also begun to explore how appropriate alliance design depends on context. In the process of this research we have also begun to develop insights into how firms extract benefits from an alliance, although this and the remaining questions are arguably still underdeveloped within TCE. Below, we describe the current challenges to NIE research, in general, and how they relate to alliance research, in particular. We outline recent research that addresses these challenges, and propose some directions for future research that can push the field further.

### 10.4.1  Extracting benefits from alliances

As described above, NIE studies of alliances have primarily focussed on predicting alliance governance and partner identity, rather than on predicting alliance success. The NIE approach generally presumes that actors who err in selecting partners or governance form will suffer adverse performance consequences.[3] However, until recently this assumption has not been tested.

Studying performance effects of alliances and alliance governance is quite difficult for several reasons.[4] Most obvious, it is often difficult to measure alliance outcomes. Unlike public companies, alliances do not regularly publish financial information. Further, although the dissolution of a firm may be interpreted as a negative performance outcome, alliance dissolution may reflect positive as well as negative outcomes. For example, an alliance may be dissolved because it fails to meet partners' expectations – or because it has successfully accomplished all of the tasks its partners desired. Consequently, scholars are justifiably suspicious of using alliance survival as an outcome measure. In sum, none of the most commonly used measures of firm-level performance is easily applicable to alliance research.

Recent research has addressed this challenge through three avenues: alliance case studies and surveys of alliance participants; event-studies of alliance announcements; and studies on narrower, non-financial measures of performance that are intuitively connected to alliance activities (e.g. changes in a firm's patenting behavior or innovative search patterns).

*10.4.1.1  Survey- and case-based studies*  Case studies and survey research offer the potential benefit of measuring outcomes – or at least the perceived outcomes – specific to an alliance. Although some have questioned the reliability of managerial assessments of alliance performance, recent studies that combine both subjective and objective measures of performance suggest that survey responses may indeed be accurate (Geringer and Hebert 1991; Kale, Dyer, and Singh 2002). Specifically related to the NIE research program, Lane and Lubatkin (1998) survey pharmaceutical firms about their alliances with biotechnology start-ups. They find that their respondents report significantly greater benefits for those alliances which involve partners with whom they have higher levels of overlap in basic technological knowledge. Kale, Dyer, and Singh (2002) find that alliance participants report significantly greater benefits as their prior alliance experience increases and when their firm has a dedicated alliance management function.

One challenge for much of the extant survey research is that it relies on a single respondent to provide information, often both for alliance organization and alliance success. Unless carefully designed, such surveys run the risk of mono-method bias (Podsakoff and Organ 1986). Future research could make better use of surveys by, among other things, surveying managers from all parties to an alliance (for an example that gets part way there, see Luo and Park 2004). In addition to overcoming mono-method bias, such research could enable scholars to address questions that they otherwise could not, such as: What happens when partners to an alliance have dramatically different perceptions of its goals and performance?

*10.4.1.2 Event studies*    Some scholars have applied event-study methods to measure the *anticipated* performance of alliances. In an event study, a researcher identifies the precise date on which each alliance in his or her alliance sample is announced, and then explores whether the alliance partners experienced "abnormal" stock market returns upon the announcement of the alliances. The event-study methodology rests on the assumption that the stock market is efficient – that is, the stock market responds immediately to any new news about a firm so that the firm's stock price reflects all existing information. Given this assumption any abnormal change to the share price of a firm on the day of (or multi-day window around) an alliance announcement may be interpreted as the market's expectation of the performance impact of the announced alliance. Most event studies have found small but significantly positive stock market reactions to the announcement of a new joint venture (e.g. Koh and Venkatraman 1991; Anand and Khanna 2000; but *see also* McGahan and Villalonga 2005 for negative findings). Factors found to significantly increase the magnitude of the imputed value of the venture include greater alliance experience (Anand and Khanna 2000), relatedness of the joint-venture partners and higher overlap between the joint-venture activities and the focal firm's existing product or geographic markets (Koh and Venkatraman 1991), and the presence of a dedicated alliance function within the firm (Kale, Dyer and Singh 2002).

There are no event studies to date that explicitly consider the effect of appropriate governance on stock market reaction. This reflects significant challenges in implementing such a study: beyond the usual problems associated with identifying an appropriate event date and eliminating the effect of potential "confounding events" which may produce a spurious stock market reaction unrelated to the alliance announcement itself, we must deal with the issue of how to measure "appropriate" governance (or lack thereof). This represents a significant challenge in itself (*see* discussion of endogeneity, below) which has, at least to this point, defied implementation in the event study context, but which represents a potential avenue for ambitious future research.

*10.4.1.3 Patents, knowledge flows, and alliance outcomes*   A third method for studying alliance performance has been to focus on a specific, non-financial set of outcomes that are plausibly related to the goals of an alliance. For example, a large proportion of inter-firm alliances are technology-based R&D alliances. Such alliances are most likely to influence a firm in terms of research productivity or, even more specifically, the accessing and acquisition of its partner's technological capabilities. Given this, several scholars have explored the effect of a firm's alliances on the evolution of its technological knowledge base (Mowery, Oxley, and Silverman 1996, 1998, 2002; Sampson 2004, 2006; Oxley and Wada 2007).

Mowery, Oxley, and Silverman (1996) study changes in pre-alliance versus post-alliance technological overlap across a sample of allying firms, as captured by changes in patent citation patterns. They interpret an increase in technological overlap as a measure of successful knowledge transfer. They find that, for learning alliances, increases in technological overlap are positively associated with absorptive capacity between partners, and that the use of equity-based governance is associated with higher levels of knowledge transfer.

Oxley and Wada (2007) push the idea of governance structures shaping the knowledge outcomes of alliances one step further. In a study of patent in-licensing by Japanese firms, they show that – in line with prior research – bilateral agreements lead to greater knowledge transfer to the Japanese firm (as measured by increased patent citation to the licensor's patents). However, when the licensing activity takes place within the context of an equity joint venture linking the licensor and licensee, they show that this increases knowledge transfer in areas closely related to alliance activities (as indicated by citations to patents in the same technology class as the licensed patent) but that knowledge transfers in unrelated areas are actually reduced, relative to that observed in a "bare" license. They suggest that the restricted scope of knowledge flows in the equity joint venture may reflect the enhanced control features of this governance structure and argue that the ability of the licensor to prevent unintended leakage of knowledge unrelated to alliance activities is an important underpinning of the enhanced alliance-relevant knowledge flows in joint ventures observed in prior research.

*10.4.1.4 Alliance decisions, alliance outcomes, and endogeneity*  As noted above, alliance research faces a distinctive challenge in the measurement of performance outcomes. Even when this problem is solved, however, studying the performance effects of alliances and their governance is quite difficult for a more general reason: concern about endogeneity (Masten 1993). Since economic actors are presumed to behave as boundedly rational profit maximizers, it follows that each firm makes optimal governance decisions, conditional on its own idiosyncrasies. Given this presumption, what should a researcher conclude when she sees that: firms whose alliances have similar attributes vary in their alliance governance decisions; firms whose alliance governance choices vary from those prescribed by TCE also have lower performance? Without other information, she must conclude that for those firms whose alliances are "misaligned," being misaligned is optimal owing to some unobserved firm or transaction characteristics (which may also affect performance). Anything else would be hubris.

One way to overcome this is to correct for selection bias in the estimation process, as in the structural modeling approach used by Masten, Meehan, and Snyder (1991) in their study of transaction costs in shipbuilding. Two recent papers provide excellent reviews of the endogeneity problem as well as instructions on how to overcome it (Shaver 1998; Hamilton and Nickerson 2003). The most significant challenge associated with econometric techniques is that to do this properly we need to have at least one "instrument" – a variable that affects the alliance choice but does not affect the performance of the alliance. This variable is included in the selection model (e.g. a model predicting choice of alliance governance form) but not in the performance model. Coming up with an appropriate instrument requires creativity, insight, and – sometimes – a little luck. In short, it is an art.

Most extant research on alliances has not fully addressed this issue. For example, immediately above we described the finding in Mowery, Oxley, and Silverman (1996), that equity governance in an alliance is positively associated with the knowledge transfer in that alliance. Back in 1996, we interpreted that as evidence that the presence of an equity stake facilitated the flow of knowledge across firms. However, when recognizing that the choice to include an equity stake is an endogenous decision of the partners, this interpretation becomes less clear; perhaps the appropriate interpretation is that those alliances that are undertaken with aspirations to transfer a lot of knowledge are those in which firms choose to include an equity stake.

Fortunately, Sampson (2006) provides confirmation of the link between equity governance and enhanced knowledge flows in a study that directly addresses the endogeneity issue. Analyzing a sample of R&D alliances she employs a two-stage method and demonstrates that alliance outcomes vary systematically with governance form even after correcting for governance selection. More specifically, she shows that when the technological diversity of alliance partners is high – a situation that poses the most challenges for effective knowledge-sharing – partners' post-alliance patenting (an indication of innovative output) is significantly higher in equity joint ventures than in non-equity alliances – up to a hundred times higher, depending on the level of technological diversity.

These recent developments notwithstanding, future alliance research would benefit more generally from careful consideration of unobserved heterogeneity. Effort devoted to surmounting these issues is well spent; investigating how firm strategy and alliance organization interact to affect firm performance presents one of the most exciting frontiers of research in NIE today.

### 10.4.2 How to manage the alliance: beyond discrete structural alternatives to contractual terms

Another exciting current area of research is exploration of the role of individual contractual provisions in alliance governance. As the discussion so far suggests, prior alliance research has tended to focus on the choice between two or three discrete governance structures. This in part reflects the underlying logic of TCE, whereby markets, hybrids, and hierarchies are viewed as discrete governance alternatives that are supported by "syndromes" of governance instruments (see Table 10.2). In addition, as suggested by the discussion of Oxley (1997), above, the focus on discrete structural alternatives in TCE research also reflects difficulties in obtaining information on the actual provisions of alliance contracts, as well as a lack of nuanced theory to guide our understanding of the role and consequence of individual contract provisions.[5]

One of the earliest examinations of alliance contract provisions, Parkhe (1993), used a computer-assisted search of the legal literature and identified eight provisions that were commonly (but by no means universally) adopted in alliance contracts. These were: (1) periodic written reports of all relevant transactions; (2) prompt written notice of any departures from the agreement; (3) the right to examine and audit all relevant records through a firm of CPAs; (4) designation of certain information as proprietary and subject to confidentiality provisions of the contract; (5) non-use of proprietary information even after termination of the contract; (6) termination of agreement; (7) arbitration clauses; and (8) lawsuit provisions. Parkhe (1993) used the information gathered on these contract provisions to create measures of contractual complexity for a sample of alliances (based on a count of provisions employed, weighted by the level of stringency). This approach – or variants thereon – has subsequently been adopted in a few studies seeking to understand the relationship between formal and informal ("trust-based") alliance governance (e.g. Kale, Singh, and Perlmutter 2000; Poppo and Zenger 2002).

A more recent survey of alliances in the German telecommunications industry by Reuer, Arino, and Mellewigt (2005) using Parkhe's (1993) classification of contract provisions, highlights both the significant heterogeneity in the use of various provisions across alliance agreements, and a lack of systematic differences between equity and non-equity alliances in the use of specific provisions (with the exception of the right to reports of relevant transactions and auditing rights). Notably, these authors find that factors such as the "strategic importance" of an alliance to a partner affects the complexity of the contract that formalizes the alliance, but does not affect the choice of governance mode for the alliance; in contrast, the asset specificity inherent in the alliance affects governance choice but does not affect contractual complexity. These findings suggest that we have much to learn about how specific contract structures "map" onto the discrete structural alternatives that have been the focus of previous alliance research, and how the use of different contract provisions is shaped by characteristics of the underlying alliance activities, partner resources and capabilities, and relational history.

Although work in this arena is still in its infancy, one early empirical study speaks of the promise of the approach: In a detailed examination of a small sample of forty-two alliance contracts extracted from SEC filings, Ryall and Sampson (2003) again highlight the observed heterogeneity in the level and detail of contract specification and in the specific provisions included. They further show that – at least in this sample of contracts – as firms gain greater alliance experience (whether or not with the current partner) they tend to write more "complete" contracts, particularly in terms of development specifications or time frame, but when alliance partners have other concurrent alliances together, contracts tend to be less complete. This evidence is consistent with research on supply contracts suggesting that firms tend to adopt more complex contracts over time as they learn about new contingencies that may usefully be specified in the agreement (Mayer and Argyres 2004), as well as research on the hostage value of overlapping agreements (Gulati 1995b). The authors of the study nonetheless emphasize that the substantial variation in the contract terms employed (illustrated effectively in detailed case studies of three alliance contracts) make direct cross-case comparisons difficult. This once again highlights the need for additional theory building by both economists and lawyers, to better understand how individual contract provisions coalesce in alliance governance structures.

Another promising approach to this set of issues is to focus on cases where contractual terms are renegotiated. To the extent that renegotiation of specific terms can be tied to changes in the alliance activities or environmental context of the alliance, this approach may shed further light on the factors that lead to the adoption of specific contractual provisions. Reuer and Arino (2002) offer a first step in this direction with their study of renegotiation, at a highly aggregate level, within Spanish firms' collaborative agreements. They find evidence that renegotiation is positively associated with initial "misalignment" in alliance governance, with asset-specificity (if asset specificity is low, partners are likely to exit the agreement rather than spend time renegotiating it), and with changes in partners' strategies. In this study it is not possible to tell whether renegotiation represents a jointly beneficial move toward greater efficiency or whether it represents an opportunistic demand by one of the partners; (in fact, another finding is that renegotiation occurs less frequently when the contract includes specific deterrents to renegotiation, which may suggest that renegotiation represents opportunistic behavior). Future work along this line of inquiry may further inform these questions by explicitly connecting renegotiation to (actual or perceived) performance effects, and to unpacking more disaggregated detail about which types of provisions are renegotiated in the presence of which triggering factors.

### 10.4.3 Managing networks of alliances

Sociology-based network theorists often argue that the emphasis of NIE on dyadic relationships leads NIE scholars to ignore the challenges and benefits associated with engaging in a portfolio, or network, of alliances. This criticism typically comes in two inter-related categories. First, focussing on the dyad obscures the fact that broader social networks provide a potent context in which an alliance takes place. Second, focussing on the dyad ignores the unique challenges and benefits associated with engaging in a portfolio or network of alliances.

*10.4.3.1 The social network as a relevant context for alliances*
Sociology-based organization theorists often criticize NIE for under-emphasizing the impact of social processes on the nature of economic activity. In particular, the atomistic, calculative approach embodied in organizational economics allegedly ignores the fact that transactions are embedded in a rich social context (Granovetter 1985), which leads the theory to underemphasize the contextual effect that an actor's social network may have on governance. Thus, in a study of the social networks in the New York City garment industry, Uzzi (1997) finds evidence that in socially embedded relationships, "an actor's motivation and rationality resist characterization within [the traditional] distinctions" of the NIE framework.

Recent research has begun to demonstrate the benefits of incorporating social structure into an NIE perspective. One example is Jones, Hesterly and Borgatti (1997), which attempts a synthesis between TCE and embeddedness, proposing that in some circumstances embeddedness may safeguard against opportunism by diffusing information about reputations and by facilitating collective sanctions. Of particular interest, these authors also demonstrate how ideas from TCE can inform network theory. Network analysis has traditionally taken network position as given, and has underemphasized the idea that actors will make efforts to gain advantageous network positions. Jones, Hesterly, and Borgatti (1997) point to ways that insights from NIE may help to explain how network positions arise and change. This echoes the pioneering work of Avner Grief who has argued both that social relations and other mechanisms can help to overcome opportunism-related hazards that otherwise would have prevented a wide range of exchanges, and that economic actors will seek to create or influence such mechanisms in the pursuit of their interests (e. g. Greif 1993). Recent network research has begun to incorporate such ideas. For example, Robinson and Stuart (2007) demonstrate convincingly that the prior network of relationships among biotechnology firms serves as a substitute for hierarchical arrangements in newly founded alliances. Specifically, they analyze the network of alliances assembled by all firms in the biotechnology industry, and find that as the centrality of the partners increases and as the partners' proximity within the network increases, equity-based governance decreases even as the dollar-value of the alliance increases – plausible evidence that network embeddedness can go some way toward mitigating the hold-up problem that, according to NIE scholars, is traditionally solved by more hierarchical governance. Looking more closely at the effect of firms' actions to shape their network position, Baum, Shipilov, and Rowley (2003) study the evolution of investment bank networks over time, and find evidence that the "small world" network structure in investment banking arose in large part due to the "insurgent" actions of peripheral firms that established new connections in ways that would destabilize the network and improve their own positions.

*10.4.3.2 Managing a network of alliances*  A related criticism from scholars of "strategic networks" is that the emphasis of NIE on dyadic relationships leads NIE scholars to ignore the challenges and benefits associated with engaging in a portfolio, or network, of alliances (Gomes-Casseres 1994; Powell, Koput, and Smith 1996). Recent research has begun to explore how governance or partner selection in a particular alliance may be affected by a firm's other alliances. For example, as noted above, Ryall and Sampson (2003) find that two partners will tend to rely on less stringent contractual terms when they have multiple alliances running concurrently, presumably because these other alliances serve as a form of hostage for each other.

In a different vein, Baum, Calabrese, and Silverman (2000) find that Canadian biotechnology firms benefit from having a portfolio of alliances with a wider variety of partner types (i.e. pharmaceutical firm, university, and so on) as compared with an equal number of alliances with a narrower range of partner types. This appears to be consistent with some network theorists' predictions that a firm will benefit from tapping into more diverse sources of knowledge and information rather than into redundant sources (Burt 1992). This suggests additional insights on how to manage a portfolio of alliances – at the very least partner selection in one alliance (and governance of that alliance) may usefully be influenced by the identity of a firm's partners in its other alliances. These issues may be particularly salient when one firm's alliance with a key partner pre-empts that partner from allying with other firms (Gomes-Casseres 1994; Silverman and Baum 2002). Future research along these lines can further refine prescriptions for managers regarding the management of an alliance network as well as the governance of the constituent alliances.

## 10.5   Conclusion

In this chapter we have reviewed the burgeoning NIE literature on alliances. We have organized the literature as a set of explorations into seven key questions concerning the establishment and management of alliances. NIE scholars, primarily from the TCE and RBV branches, have made significant progress in pushing the frontiers of knowledge associated with at least four of these questions. Although progress on the other three questions has lagged, we suggest that NIE – often in conjunction with insights from sociology-based organizational theory and in particular "strategic network" theory – is poised to make great strides on these questions in the near future. It is an exciting time to be involved in alliance research, and we hope that the field will benefit both from continued contributions from the "usual suspects" and from new scholars who find these issues compelling.

# 11 Governance Structure and Contractual Design in Retail Chains

*Emmanuel Raynaud*

## 11.1 Introduction

A recent bestseller by Naomi Klein (*No Logo*) argued against the invasion of brand names in our everyday lives. Brands are everywhere, but there are most likely economic reasons for this. Brand names provide consumers with information and reduce information and search costs. As a traveler, I know that McDonald's hamburgers will taste more or less the same in Paris and Los Banos (Philippines). At the same time, in developed countries, firms are increasingly focussing on channeling branded products to consumers, especially in sectors where competitive advantage depends on organizational approaches.

This chapter focuses on the provision of branded products by retailers. More specifically, it studies relations between retailers and producers when several retailers are part of a shared retail chain. When talking about a retail chain we include several types of retail distribution systems where trademarks are prominent. The rest of the paper focusses mainly on franchising, for two reasons. First, most of the empirical literature on contracting in distribution channels concerns franchising. Insights gleaned from studies on franchised chains enable researchers to develop a better understanding of how firms organize their activities much more generally, both in-house and across firms. Second, franchising agreements include several contractual provisions, sometimes called "vertical restraints" (e.g. selective or exclusive distribution), which may be used to analyze the rationale behind contractual design.

This chapter adopts a new institutional economics (NIE) approach to the study of retail chains. It explores the existence and role of franchising as an efficient device. It therefore leaves outside its scope the literature on industrial organization which attempts to explain governance choice as a strategic tool to mitigate actual or potential competition (*see* Rey and Stiglitz 1995; Slade 1998, for examples). The organization of chains is then viewed as a governance device. The NIE approach in this chapter includes both transaction cost economics (TCE), à la Williamson, and

235

also agency theory and recent literature on incomplete contracts (see the contributions of Brousseau, and Garrouste and Saussier, in this book for relevant references). This is an extensive version of what the profession calls "contract theory" (speaking about contract *theories* should be more relevant as alternative frameworks analyze contractual relations). This also implies that several types of coordination problems will be assessed in our framework.

In order to study governance of retail chains, the overall governance design may be broken down into a two-step, sequential decision: first, get the allocation of ownership right (the "make-or-buy" decision); second, get the contractual design right. An extension of step one will focus on understanding an interesting stylized fact: the coexistence of both company-owned and franchised units within the same chain. Whether or not this sequence corresponds to the decision-making process in the real world is not important. It is useful as an expository device.

The chapter is structured as follows: Section 11.2 provides a short overview of the different contractual relations in retail chains and the main contractual terms in franchise agreements; Section 11.3 focusses on vertical integration in chains (get the governance right); Section 11.4 assumes the ownership decision has been taken and studies the structure of franchise contracts (get the contractual design right). Finally, the last section illustrates how the NIE approach may shed light on more normative uses. It focusses on two issues: legal analysis of the franchisor's right to unilaterally terminate the agreement and the treatment of contractual terms in antitrust policy.

## 11.2    Legal definition of franchising and main provisions

What is franchising? From a legal standpoint, a retail contract is a franchise contract in the USA if three main conditions are met: (1) the franchisee operates under the franchisor's brand name and trademarks; (2) the franchisor provides ongoing support and exerts, or can exert, significant control over the franchisee's operations; and (3) the franchisee is required to pay more than US $500 to the franchisor before the end of the first six months in operation. The legal definition of a franchise in the European Union is similar, except that it is more specific about the requirement that the franchisor transfers know-how to the franchisee.[1] Within franchising, the US Department of Commerce further categorizes relationships either as "Product and Trade Name", also called "Traditional" franchises, and "Business Format" franchises (*see* Lafontaine 1992, for more on this). However, from an economic perspective, franchisors involved in business format or traditional franchising, or both, face similar challenges.

Franchising organizes the vertical relationship between an upstream firm (the franchisor) and a network of downstream firms (franchisees). So a franchise chain is the sum of bilateral vertical agreements between the franchisor and each individual outlet (franchisee or company-owned units). Several contractual provisions usually form part of a "typical" franchise contract and fix the transfer of property rights over assets, the monetary transfer from the franchisees to the franchisor, and restrictions on the behavior of each party (*see* Lafontaine 1992; Dnes 1993; OECD 1994, for more on this). To name just a few, exclusive territory, exclusive dealing and tie-ins are typical contractual provisions. Others specify the minimum level of quality for final products or services, the minimum amount for national advertising that the franchisor must spend each year, the minimum level of training for franchisee staff, and so on.

## 11.3   Choosing the right governance structure

One of the most important empirical regularities in franchising is the existence of both franchised and company-owned units in most chains. So it is hardly surprising that much of the relevant literature studies the determinants of vertical integration in chains, that is, the "make-or-buy" problem. However, a recent wave of papers also attempts to understand governance of chains as a way to "make *and* buy."

### 11.3.1   Franchising versus company-ownership as a governance decision

*11.3.1.1 Franchising as a way to speed up chain expansion*   The desire to avoid capital constraint during chain expansion has been historically identified as the key driver behind franchising (Caves and Murphy 1976). If franchisors do not have enough capital to open their own stores, franchisees may reduce this constraint by providing their own capital. The ability of franchising to ease chain expansion is especially important because of significant economies of scale, for example for promotions and marketing.

Despite its popularity among professionals, this approach has been widely criticized. Rubin (1978) convincingly argues that if franchising is a way for the franchisor to alleviate a capital constraint there is a more efficient alternative in terms of risk allocation. If an individual franchisee owns a single outlet this results in a poor diversification of his capital, and, according to finance theory, he should request an additional risk premium. Instead of "selling" the right to run an outlet on a unitary basis, the franchisor should create a portfolio of all the individual outlets and sell a share of this portfolio. If individual profits and risks are not completely correlated, this produces a less risky allocation of capital and more profits for the chain.

At the same time, data fail to back up the main empirical proposition deduced from the capital constraint argument. If chains are successfull, the capital constraint should be reduced over time. So, mature chains should less heavily rely on franchised units.[2] Empirical works using panel data reach a different conclusion: the extent of company-owned units is stable over time (*see* Furquim de Azevedo and Dos Santos Silva 2001; Pénard, Raynaud, and Saussier 2003; Lafontaine and Shaw 2005, for similar studies in different countries). Furthermore, it is not unusual for a franchisor to provide their franchisees with funding, which appears to contradict the capital constraint explanation.

The previous argument may be further extended to another form of capital scarcity, namely managerial human capital scarcity (Norton 1988). Chain expansion may also suffer from "adjustment costs." For instance, potential incumbents must be selected, screened, and trained. Chains, however, have some alternative tools for mitigating these costs. For instance, by providing two kinds of contract (franchised and employment), the chain can sort applicants and select the most talented. Potential applicants with poor skills or little motivation are more reluctant to accept a contract where their wealth depends more on residual income than are more talented applicants.

The empirical propositions derived from this approach are partly similar to the previous one on financial capital constraints. If selection and human resources scarcities decrease with chains' maturity, there should be less reliance on franchising. As pointed out earlier, this is not backed up by empirical results. This suggests that chains probably use other means to mitigate this problem.[3]

*11.3.1.2 Make-or-buy as a way of mitigating contractual hazards*
The study of the governance of chains is an application of the paradigmatical "make-or-buy" problem (Coase 1937). Different theories focus on different aspects of governance, but, in general, they highlight the coordination hazards of opportunistic behavior attributed to incomplete contract and costly enforcement.

A breakthrough paper along these lines is that of Brickley and Dark (1987). The authors focus on agency costs as the main driver of governance decision making. Two agency problems are identified. The first is related to imperfect observability of manager behavior (either an employee or franchisee). Franchising an outlet mitigates this moral hazard problem. By becoming a residual claimant of the outlet's profits (after deducting royalty rates), the manager has a strong incentive to work hard. High-powered incentives replace direct monitoring. However, providing strong incentives to maximize the outlet's profits is not cost free. A franchisee may maximize his sales *and* minimize his costs (e.g. by reducing quality, *see* Lafontaine and Raynaud 2002, for more on this). One way of reducing the incentive to free ride on the goodwill of the chain is to increase the extent of vertical integration in the chain. Because in most cases, salaried managers' compensation is not directly related to the outlet profits they have a lower incentive to free ride. As the incentive to freeload increases with the value of the brand we should observe a higher proportion of company-owned units for valuable brands.

Most of the empirical literature on franchising strongly supports the shirking or monitoring costs theory (Brickley and Dark 1987; Norton 1988; Lafontaine 1992) and shows mixed support for the free riding hypothesis (*see* Lafontaine and Slade 2002, for an overall survey). These results seems robust to changes in the proxies used to measure the theoretical variables.[4] This does not necessarily mean the free riding problem is not a relevant risk. This suggests that franchisors can use other tools to mitigate this problem. For instance, exclusive territories can successfully reduce free riding (Brickley 1999).

Other contractual hazards are also highlighted to explain the extent of vertical integration in franchising. Most of them concern the conse-quences of incomplete contracts and opportunistic behavior. Minkler and Park (1994) argue that the manager of an outlet has an incentive to hold-up part of the value of the brand. This approach is quite similar to the previous free riding story. The more specific the brand name, the higher the level of quasi-rents and the stronger the incentives for fran-chisee to be opportunistic by cheating on quality.[5] One way of solving this problem is for the franchisor to rely on vertical integration, for a reason similar to the one given earlier. Maness (1996) offers an alter-native explanation based on the inability to contract over costs. Because an outlet owner is residual claimant of any cost reductions, he has a strong incentive to minimize costs. Ownership of the unit should be allocated to the party with the greatest ability to control costs. Another paper by Lutz (1995) adopts a similar approach. In a double moral hazard scenario, it also emphasizes the consequences of incomplete contracts on the allocation of unit ownership.

### 11.3.2 Dual distribution as a governance decision – make and buy?

What, if instead of trying to solve the make-*or*-buy problem, chains are willing to make *and* buy at the same time? What is the added value? This phenomenon is called "dual distribution," or sometimes, "plural form." Several explanations have been put forward, and these may be divided into two categories – those which explain dual distribution as a temporary phenomenon and those arguing that dual distribution is an efficient governance structure.

### 11.3.2.1 Dual distribution as transitory

As illustrated earlier, papers dealing with the make-or-buy decision also explain dual distribution. Explanations based on capital constraints, either financial and/or human, predict that as the chains become mature there should be an increase in the extent of company ownership. The opposite is proposed by Gallini and Lutz (1992). Their paper is about the efficiency of dual distribution as a signaling device. They assume the chain knows its value more than potential franchisees. Their main conclusion is that "good" franchisors can signal their type in a credible way by showing their confidence in the value of the chain.[6] One possibility for doing this is to "have a large stake in the business," namely, to own some units directly. Consequently, the proportion of company-owned units should increase with the chain "quality" (Lafontaine 1993).[7] The extent of company-owned units should also decrease with chain maturity.

As pointed out earlier, empirical studies with longitudinal data reveal the stability of dual distribution. As is usual in literature on contracts and organizations, when economists discover an empirical regularity they seek explanations based on efficiency.

### 11.3.2.2 Dual distribution as a tough organization

Most papers on dual distribution explain it in terms of heterogeneous outlets or managers, or both. Such heterogeneity may take many different forms, such as distance to headquarters (Brickley and Dark 1987), percentage of repeated business (Brickley 1999), or risk (Norton 1988). Different economic circumstances require different organizational solutions (Lewin-Solomons 1999). The overall governance of the chain, that is the extent of dual distribution, is simply the aggregation of governance decisions made at the store level. This implies that if all units are similar the chain should be either wholly franchised, or company-owned. However, there are counter-examples (e.g. Minkler 1990). More generally, this raises the question of whether different characteristics are needed for dual distribution to emerge, or whether dual distribution arises for other (maybe complementary) reasons.

Recent papers study dual distribution as an efficient governance structure for homogeneous units. In Gallini and Lutz (1992), all units are identical and dual distribution is an efficient response to asymmetric information on the chain value. Similarly, Bai and Tao (2000) constructed a multi-task model, based on Holmström and Milgrom (1991), to illustrate that even for identical units dual distribution may emerge as an efficient governance structure. The premise of the paper stresses the importance of two types of effort for chain profitability: sales effort and effort to enhance the chain goodwill, for example by providing high-quality products. If the two tasks are substituted in the agent's cost function and measured with more or less the same precision, the power of incentives for both tasks should be "balanced." However, it is difficult to assess individual contribution to the chain goodwill. Sales at store level are a poor proxy because goodwill effort at one store increases not only the sales here, but also sales at other stores. Consequently, the efficient contract must also reduce the incentive intensity for the effort on sales. Another solution is to "specialize" agents in either sales or goodwill improvements, and to provide two different contracts. The chain offers some unit managers a balanced contract to induce goodwill effort and a more high-powered incentive contract on sales for the remainder. Dual distribution emerges as an optimal organization for providing incentive for both tasks. This theory has not yet been proved. The importance of brand name value in influencing the extent of company ownership, implied by Bai and Tao (2000), is however corroborated by Lafontaine and Shaw (2005), who show how brand value has a positive and significant impact on the proportion of company-owned units.

Another related explanation for dual distribution with homogeneous outlets is provided by Scott (1995). He emphasizes the importance of franchisor effort for the profitability of individual outlets. The franchisor must monitor outlets, train managers, and so on. However, the franchisor also needs an incentive to make these efforts. One possibility is to set a high royalty rate, but the more you increase it the weaker the incentives for franchisees. One alternative is for the franchisor to have a stake in the business and own some units. The larger the proportion of company-owned units the greater the franchisor interest in maintaining chain goodwill. This conclusion is similar to ones reached by Lutz (1995) and Lafontaine and Shaw (2005).

More recently, literature on franchising suggests dual distribution should be studied at a more "systemic" or "chain" level. The point here is to assess the governance benefits of "make *and* buy." Braddach (1997) emphasizes the complementarities between the two contractual arrangements in order to maintain quality and homogeneity of the business concept across the units while promoting innovation. Combining both governance modes creates "synergy benefits." What it is important to explore in more detail is the sources of these synergy gains.

For instance, Dutta *et al.* (1995) identified two main benefits of dual distribution. The first relates to asymmetric information; the second concerns credible commitment. Exclusive reliance on market governance to distribute a firm's products can be plagued with information-related problems. Firms may be limited in their ability to evaluate *ex ante*, and monitor *ex post*, the performance of distributors. In-house operations allow firms to mitigate these problems. Basically, by carrying them out itself the chain is better able to assess the costs and difficulties of the task. It may use this information to design a performance evaluation and monitoring system. This is clearly stated by Braddach (1997, p. 287): "the performance of one arrangement was often used to set the standard for the other." The other benefit relates to *ex post* governance issues. Terminating a partnership with an opportunistic distributor is an efficient sanction when assets are non-specific. If the firm had invested in specific assets in its transaction with a distributor, premature termination is a less credible sanction because part of the quasi-rents will be lost by the firm.[8] An in-house operation restores part of the threat of termination as an incentive device. If the firm terminates its relation with the supplier it can use the internal agent as an alternative. Both franchised and company-owned units co-exist side by side because one governance structure supports the other.

In a more dynamic setting, Lewin-Solomons (1999) justified the existence of dual distribution as a commitment device used by a franchisor to give franchisees incentives to innovate. Innovation is fundamental for most chains, as they must find new ways of generating additional profits. In most chains, franchisees pay a royalty rate as a fraction of their revenues (not their profits). With this royalty structure, chains will favor innovations that are good for revenues, sometimes at the expense of franchisees' profits, if innovation increases franchisees' costs at the same time. By owning some units in the chain the franchisor's interest is more aligned with that of its franchisees. Chains may prove that some innovations are worth implementing, by testing them first in their own units and by showing financial results.

Until now, this chapter has focussed on determining factors for vertical integration in chains. However, this is not the only margins chains may use to mitigate contractual hazards. Another key aspect of the relationship is the design of contractual provisions for the part of the units to be franchised.

## 11.4    Choosing the right contractual design: aligning incentives in chains

Franchising basically involves franchisors granting franchisees the right to operate under their trademarks and use their business procedures. But as these intangible assets remain the property of the franchisor, the granting of these rights results in incentive problems and agency costs.[9] Two main types of incentive mechanisms have been highlighted in the literature as ways of reducing these problems: the granting of residual claimancy rights through monetary provisions, as emphasized in principal–agent literature (*see* Mathewson and Winter 1985) and the reliance on self-enforcement (*see*, in particular, Klein and Saft 1985; Klein 1995). Other non-monetary dimensions of franchise contracts have also been recently explored.

### *11.4.1   Franchising as an incentive contract: monetary provisions*

As legally independent businesses, franchisees have a claim on profits generated by their outlet(s) (after deduction of usual sales-based royalties and advertising fees they pay to their franchisors). As these payments normally represent 6–10% of revenues, franchisees obtain the bulk of every additional dollar of sales generated within their outlet(s). Also, since royalty and advertising fee payments are based on revenues, not profits, franchisees reap the full benefit from every additional dollar decrease in operating costs. Most literature on franchise contracts and incentives focus on monetary provisions, namely establishing the "right" royalty rates and initial franchise fees.

When franchisee effort is not observable, and thus cannot be contracted on directly, the best option for the franchisor is to sell the outlet to the franchisee for a fixed price. This outright sale makes the franchisee a full residual claimant, thereby giving him incentives to put forth the optimal level of effort (Mathewson and Winter 1985). Selling the outlet for a fixed price to the franchisee fully resolves franchisee incentive issues. The franchisor can extract all the profits from the outlet operations by setting the initial franchise fee. However, in practice, the typical franchise contract involves sharing. Yet, sharing prevents first-best outcome, since the franchisee has an incentive to reduce his effort. Literature provides two alternative amendments to the model to account for the use, in practice, of sharing arrangements. The first, the most traditional, assumes the franchisee is risk-averse. In this case, the franchisee no longer maximizes expected profits, but, rather, expects utility instead. Sharing in this model then becomes a means of shifting risk from risk-averse franchisees to risk-neutral franchisors. The second amendment to the model relies, instead, on the assumption that the franchisor brings some valuable input to the production process and that his behavior, like that of the franchisee, is difficult to monitor. In this double-sided, moral hazard model, sharing arises from the need to provide incentives to both franchisees and franchisor (*see*, in particular, Rubin 1978; Lal 1990; Bhattacharyya and Lafontaine 1995).

Three main testable implications arise from this principal–agent model. The share parameter will be higher: (1) the lower the importance of franchisee effort; (2) the higher the level of risk involved (assuming the franchisee is more risk-averse than the franchisor); (3) the greater the importance of franchisor effort (assuming this effort is non-observable). Empirical literature on franchising has found support for the first and the last, but not for the second implication.

### 11.4.2  Self-enforcement in contracting

With regard to self-enforcement (Klein and Saft 1985; Klein 1996) in franchise contracting, parties to a contract may be given incentives to put forth effort by making sure that they derive a benefit from the relationship that is at risk if they do not behave as requested. Incentives embedded in a franchise contract in this case do not stem from residual claims, but rather from the combined effect of three elements: (1) an ongoing stream of rents that the franchisee earns within the relationship, but forgoes if he "leaves" the franchised chain; (2) franchisee monitoring by the franchisor; and (3) franchisor ability to terminate the franchise contract. Since the ease or cost of termination is largely determined by the legal system, the franchisor is left with the tasks of choosing the level of ongoing rent to be left with franchisees and selecting the frequency of monitoring so as to minimize the *ex post* costs of enforcing the desired level of effort.[10]

More specifically, let $W_t^1$ represents the (expected) franchisee gain from deviating from the franchisor's requested behaviour; a gain that may be the same from period to period, or vary somewhat across periods. If $W_t^2$ is the present value of the ongoing rent the franchisee can earn through the partnership, a franchise contract is self-enforcing if, and only if, $W_t^2 > W_t^1$ at every $t$. For the contract to be continuously self-enforcing, the franchisee must have a minimum amount of rent to look forward to at each point in time. For that reason, given that the expected rent over the remainder of the contract decreases as the franchise gets closer to expiration, $W_t^2$ must include not only this rent, but also rent associated with future additional outlets, and with the probability of contract renewal.[11]

In this context, specific contract terms play different roles (Klein 1995, 1996), influencing either $W_t^1$ or $W_t^2$. Some specify certain franchisee obligations, for example the mandatory level of input purchases from the franchisor. These contract terms limit $W_t^1$ as they make it easier for the franchisor to detect non-conformance and intervene quickly. They also make it less costly for the franchisor to rely on third parties, or court enforcement, as they provide more objective bases for establishing non-conformance. Other contract terms ensure the stream of ongoing rent, whose potential loss gives incentives to the franchisee. Although Klein does not specify exactly how the stream of rent is created, he suggests that clauses such as exclusive territories limit intra-brand competition, and thus contribute to the franchisee's profitability. As noted earlier, guarantees about future expansion opportunities and the likelihood of contract renewal further affect the levels of expected rent.

The combination of uncertainty and complexity mean all aspects of the desired behavior of franchisees cannot be specified in the contract. Hence $W_t^1$ is never zero. Consequently, the contract must always give rise to positive rent $W_t^2$ if the incentive constraint above is to be continuously satisfied. At the same time, there exists a maximum amount of rent to which the franchisor may credibly commit. If the franchisor prefers franchising to company-managed stores, it is presumably because vertical integration is less profitable. This implies the difference in profits between operating a unit under vertical integration versus franchising is positive. So the franchisor's promise of rent to the franchisee is credible if the present value of the rent, $W_t^2$, is less than the discounted profit difference, at every $t$. If this condition is met continuously, then it is in the best interests of the franchisor to pay the rent. Otherwise, it is more profitable for the franchisor to vertically integrate and appropriate the rent.

Empirically, Kaufmann and Lafontaine (1994) have shown, through a detailed analysis of the economics of McDonald's restaurants in the USA, that there is indeed rent left downstream in that chain. Following a similar methodology, Michael and Moore (1995) confirm the existence of rent in a number of other franchised chains.

### 11.4.3  More on non-monetary contractual provisions

So far, most literature on franchising focusses on monetary terms, namely royalty rates and franchised fees. This is not surprising, given that incentive contracts are the cornerstones of contract theory. Data limitations also play a role. Information on non-monetary terms is extremely limited. Nevertheless, despite their scarcity, studies on non-monetary contractual terms are beginning to appear.

Arruñada, Garicano, and Vázquez (2001) studied the alignment between the allocation of what they call "decision rights" and incentive mechanisms in Spanish automobile distribution. Owing to incompleteness, the contract is unable to specify *ex ante* the relevant decisions to take. However, the contract does specify who, in the future, will have the right to make these decisions. They reveal that the allocation of "decision rights" is rather unbalanced. Franchisors own many more decision rights than franchisees (a point already noted in Hadfield 1990). Arruñada, Garicano, and Vázquez (2001) also find that this degree of asymmetric allocation is explained by the extent of franchisee moral hazard. The more severe the likelihood for franchisee moral hazard, the more the contract allocates decisions and enforcement rights to the franchisor.[12]

In a similar vein, several other papers focus on more narrowly defined contractual provisions. Brickley (1999) links the occurrence of contractual restrictions (such as exclusive territories) to the likelihood of free riding among franchisees. Contractual provisions may mitigate this problem by either increasing investment benefits and/or by committing franchisees to make minimum contractible effort on some specific tasks.[13] Consistent with this proposition, Brickley (1999) shows that the occurrence of contractual restrictions increases with the level of horizontal externalities (proxied here by the extent of repeated customers). What is interesting here is that Brickley also tested the impact of externalities on the extent of vertical integration and found a non-significant result. It seems that the favored margin by which chains adjust to free riding hazards risks is contractual design. Similar works explain contract duration in franchising (*see* Bercovitz 2001; Brickley 2002).

Finally, Bercovitz (2003) studies the use of multi-unit ownership as a way of supporting self-enforcement. By increasing the potential of *ex ante* and *ex post* rents, multi-ownership should mitigate franchisee opportunistic behavior. Instead of trying to measure the level of franchisee opportunism directly, which seems impossible, she looked at the results of active monitoring by chains, that is, levels of termination and litigation. If forced to leave the chain the franchisee will not only lose the current stream of rents attached to his unit, but also the expected value of additional rents attached to others. Empirical results support the idea that litigation and termination rates are negatively related to multi-ownership.

More generally, the issue of multi-ownership is interesting because it shows how chains have greater margins for organizing than what was initially presumed. The chain not only chooses the kind of contract and extent of vertical integration, but also the concentration of ownership among franchisees, the spatial distribution of unit ownership among franchisee, and so on. All of these are relevant issues which may be studied in terms of efficiency. Findings on governing and contracting raise some normative conclusions for the law and economics of contractual relations. The next section will briefly describe two particular areas.

## 11.5 Food for thought for lawyers and policy makers

Here, I will illustrate the relevance of a contractual approach to analyze some debates about the goal and effects of governance structures. The first debate is about the design of regulatory rules on franchising. The second deals with NIE ramifications on antitrust issues, especially the treatment of vertical restraints in antitrust law.

### 11.5.1 Unfairness versus efficiency in contracting

NIE is quite often motivated by real-world contracting problems and should play a role in controversies about real contracting practices. One controversial area in franchising is about the ability of chains to prematurely terminate the contract. Some scholars, mostly lawyers and practitioners, argue that, because of an unbalanced bargaining power (the "small" guy versus the "big" one), termination provision is imposed by franchisor when negotiating the agreement (*see* Brickley, Dark, and Weisbach 1991; Beales and Muris 1995). Chains want the freedom to terminate the contract "at will" because this is mostly a tactic to increase the potential for future rent extraction.[14] Implicit in this approach is the fact that potential franchisees underestimate the risk of hold-up, more generally of franchisor misbehavior. The legal system should correct this assymmetric power by providing franchisees with financial compensations for premature termination or by restricting the franchisor ability to terminate the contract. One example is the "good cause" doctrine, according to which the law should impose on the franchisor a "good cause" limitation on termination and non-renewal.

Others, mostly economists, argued that this provision is an essential part of the enforcement mechanism that is needed to mitigate franchisees' opportunistic behavior (the efficiency hypothesis). They do not deny the fact that the allocation of decision rights is unbalanced in franchised contract. What they argue is that such (unbalanced) contract is a mutually advantageous exchange. A law that reduces the chains' ability to terminate the contract easily increases the costs of monitoring franchisees and make franchising a less desirable option. Franchised contracts are inevitably incomplete because of bounded rationality or verifiability problems. Parties thus have an incentive to complement the legal enforcement mechanisms by self-enforced one. If we go back to the description of how this self-enforcement mechanism à la Klein operates, its effectiveness depends on the expected value of rents (the "carrot") and the threat of losing these rents (the "stick"). Limiting the franchisor's ability to terminate the contract at will reduce the potential threat of losing the expected rents and reduce the franchisee's incentive to behave in accordance with the contractual understanding. In equilibrium, this increases the relative costs of franchising compared to vertical integration. The main empirical prediction is that, *ceteris paribus*, the extent of franchising should be reduced after the implementation of a "good cause" termination law.

What do the data say about this issue? Both anedoctical evidences and statistical results are relevant here. First, the assumption that potential franchisees are naïve and underestimate hold-up potential seems exaggerated. Beales and Muris (1995) showed that many potential franchisees obtain assistance before signing a contract (from lawyers or consultants). Furthermore, most of them had previous experience in the business. Finally, regulation in a lot of countries requires the franchisor to disclose information about termination and non-renewal. Statistical evidence seems also to support the efficiency hypothesis. We should expect litigation and termination rates to be lower when the franchisees are protected with a good cause provision. However, available evidence contradicts this proposition. Termination rate is higher in states where legislation protects franchisees from at-will termination.[15,16] Moreover, Brickley, Dark, and Weisbach (1991) have shown that the proportion of corporate units in franchised chains is higher in US states that restrict the termination of contracts. The stronger effect is found in industries in which the problem of franchisee free riding is the most severe (sectors where the level of non-repeat customers is weak). Finally, Brickley (2002) shows that chains whose headquarters are located in states with restrictive non-renewal or termination rules charge higher fees than their counterparts established in non-restrictive states. These results suggest that the cost of termination indeed affects franchisors' decisions to franchise or vertically integrate outlets or the terms of their contracts, thereby lending support to the idea that franchisors rely on rent and termination in their dealings with their franchisees. It also shows that chains react to the mandatory requirement by modifying the pricing of franchise contracts.

## 11.5.2 *Monopolization versus efficiency in contracts: consequences for antitrust*

Here, we briefly discuss the application of NIE to antitrust legal rules, especially those dealing with vertical restraints. According to Williamson (1985, pp 23–30), there are two different views on the purpose and effects of what he calls "non-standard" contractual forms. The first is based on the view that the main purpose of non-standard contractualization is to reduce actual or potential competition, or both. Any vertical restraint which may be rationalized as a tool to reduce competition should be prohibited *per se*. Williamson (1985) calls this the "monopoly" approach. On the other hand, the main presumption of the "efficiency" approach is that vertical integration and non-standard or restrictive vertical contracts are quite often necessary to mitigate contractual hazards. An efficiency purpose may explain most of the governance structures that are different from "pure" market governance.[17]

This debate is important in itself, but also because, depending on the implicit understanding antitrust authorities have in mind (and the economic framework used to convince them) their decision may have important consequences for business. A "bad" application of competition law can distort the costs and benefits of alternative governance structures, and provides inadequate incentives. If, for instance, the antitrust regulation prohibits as anti-competitive a particular contractual provision, say exclusive territory, and that this provision is vital for mitigating *ex post* opportunistic behavior, the final result of the antitrust decision could be increased incentives for parties to vertically integrate (*see* Ménard 1998 for a similar concern). Does an increase in vertical integration or concentration improve the intensity of competition and consumer welfare?

The fact that we have two distinct frameworks is both good and bad news. On one hand, this means that for most contractual practices, it is often possible to find an efficiency rationale and a more strategic one. Both approaches ("monopoly" and "efficiency" approaches) could provide rational explanations of contractul practices, and this gives a more "balanced" view of the main purpose and potential effects of a particular provision. On the other, the coexistence of alternative frameworks is relevant to policy makers only if they are able to formulate different empirical propositions. Which one will survive the "data test" better? In this respect, NIE seems to be in relatively good shape. As pointed out by Joskow (2002, p. 104):

Post-Chicago antitrust law and economics has not produced much in the way of solid empirical research that demonstrates that these theoretical possibilities are, in fact, observed in real markets, the situation where they are most likely to be observed and, where they are, they lead to significant increase in prices and/or costs and reduction in economic efficiency.

Some scholars in the NIE field have attempted to provide refutable propositions and empirical tests (*see*, for instance, Masten and Snyder 1993; Sass and Saurman 1993).

Finally, the antitrust attitude toward the motivations behind vertical restrictions in distribution contracts has evolved considerably over the years. This is true both in the USA and Europe (see OECD 1994, for more on this). We have shifted from a regime of open hostility to a new one where the benefits of vertical restraints in promoting efficient coordination are more explicitly recognized and accepted. At European Union level, competition policy explicitly takes into account the efficiency benefits of vertical restrictions when creating competition law.[18]

## 11.6    Conclusion

This chapter has highlighted numerous issues for which the contractual perspective appears to be very fruitful. It shows that chains have different margins for efficiently governing their contractual relations with individual outlets. First, the chain decides on the extent of vertical integration. Furthermore, it can also influence the allocation of outlet ownership among existing franchisees, more precisely the extent of multi-unit ownership and its spatial distribution among outlets (*see* Kalnins and Lafontaine 2004). Second, the chain also designs the contractual provisions of franchise agreements. Monetary as well as non-monetary provisions do respond to incentives and coordination issues. More generally, all these margins are largely explained by expected contractual hazards being vertical (between franchisees and franchisor) or horizontal (among franchisees). Issues such as the difficulties of monitoring outlets, the relative importance of outlet and chain effort levels, and free riding, are also involved.

Empirical findings provide a set of stylized facts and generally support most of the efficiency explanation on franchising. We would again like to emphasize the importance of this empirical support. Most of the work in contract theory is based on theoretical models that provide important insights into the determinants of contractual and organizational choice, but for which some empirical validation is missing. Franchising is a strong counter-example where available data exist on a large scale. Furthermore, empirical regularities found in franchising are also relevant for other contractual issues. For example, a typical franchise contract involves sharing the outlet revenues between franchisees and the chain.

Sharing also occurs in sharecropping, licensing, film distribution, and publishing contracts. The same is true when studying other contractual terms. Even if the real world is complex and subtle, the imaginary worlds of theories are potentially infinite. A logical explanation does not necessarily mean an empirically relevant one. It is therefore important to generate testable propositions in order to move out of "nirvana economics," as described by Harold Demsetz.

Lastly, the final point concerns the performance implications of an efficient alignment between governance structure and contractual hazards. This is important both for positive and normative reasons. Most studies on NIE consider that "organization matters" for the efficiency of an economic system. However, is this strictly true? What drives economic agents to adopt efficient governance structures? It is vital to know how much we lose when choosing the "wrong" governance. Preliminary empirical evidences suggest the effects are real and large.[19] The same applies on a normative level, too. For instance, in antitrust economics, some guidelines must be offered to assess the effects of a particular provision. This implies more than simply acknowledging that vertical restraints may indeed affect efficiency.

*Part IV*

# Industrial Organization

# 12 Make-or-Buy Decisions: A New Institutional Economics Approach

## Manuel González-Díaz and Luis Vázquez

### 12.1 The problem: make versus buy

Goods and services are produced through a sequence of activities depicted by the vertical chain of production. For example, at the top of the vertical chain for automobiles are the raw materials, such as plastics, aluminum, steel, rubber, and so on. These inputs are carried to firms which produce the intermediate parts that are used in the final construction of automobiles, such as the chassis, frames, dashboards, cover for seats, and other parts. These intermediate goods are, in turn, assembled into systems. For example, seat systems may incorporate frames, levers, springs, padding, cover, and so on. The intermediate goods are transported to companies which assemble them into cars. Finally, the automobiles are transported to car dealerships, which sell them to customers and provide after-sales services.

When a firm participates in more than one stage in the vertical chain of production it is said to be "vertically integrated." Firms may have different degrees of vertical integration. For example, in the automobile industry, at one theoretical extreme, a fully vertical integrated car manufacturer would own mines from which to obtain raw materials, rubber plantations, tire plants, plastics factories, mills to produce steel and aluminum, spare parts factories, car dealerships, and so on, providing the facilities for operations from digging the raw materials to the final distribution of cars.

At the other theoretical extreme, each stage of the chain of production might be performed by a single firm, which buys inputs for the next firm upstream and sells its outputs to firms that are one step downstream. In this situation, we will say that upstream firms buy or subcontract all inputs and services on the market. In this sense, the term "subcontracting" is frequently used to describe a movement away from integration – moving an activity outside the firm. That term is also used to describe an ongoing arrangement whereby a firm obtains a part or service from an external firm. When the activity was formerly done within the limits of the firm, "outsourcing" is the term usually employed, especially in business literature.[1]

In past decades there has been a move among firms toward subcontracting. For instance, between 1982 and 1995 the size of the workforce employed through some form of external arrangement in the US outsourcing market grew by more than 500%, surpassing the 30% growth rate in the general labor market. By some estimates, as much as a quarter of US employees were working through some form of external arrangement in 1996 (Kosters 1997).

At least three factors have contributed to this trend to subcontract. First, new flexible production technologies allow suppliers to adapt more easily to buyer demands. Thus, in some cases, assets required for production are becoming less firm-specific, which favors subcontracting over vertical integration. Second, there has been an extraordinary increase in world-wide competition. This competition has placed pressure on firms to reduce costs and become more efficient. Third, improvements in information and communication technologies make it easier to identify potential partners and to communicate with them.

In earlier times, outsourcing was focussed on clerical staff and blue-collar labour. However, external labor arrangements now also include an increasing number of highly skilled workers: technical workers (particularly in electronics), accountants, and many other professionals. In fact, today's knowledge- and service-based economy offers innumerable opportunities for companies to increase profits through strategic outsourcing. Increasingly, executives understand that outsourcing for cost cutting yields nearly as much as outsourcing for strategic benefits – obviously, some companies subcontract litigation, tax, advertising, and research and development (R&D) mainly for such benefits rather than for lower costs.

## 12.2    Theoretical background

Since economic agents look for efficient ways of organizing their activities,[2] their main problem is to choose the appropriate structure to govern the transactions. Each transaction yields costs (called "transaction costs") because the parties need to obtain information, negotiate the terms of the exchange, and enforce agreements.[3] Consequently, the contractors' main objective is to organize the transactions in such a way as to economize on transaction costs.

Transaction costs depend on: the dimensions (nature) of the transactions and the effectiveness of devices (mechanisms of governance and safeguards) which parties introduce to attenuate transaction costs attributed to the nature of the transactions. Let us analyze both separately, starting from the nature or dimensions of the transactions.

### 12.2.1 Dimensions of transactions

Transaction costs depend, first, on the features or dimensions of the transaction. We differentiate five dimensions that have been analyzed in the literature as determinants of transaction costs.

*12.2.1.1 Specificity* Specificity is probably the most well-known feature. It refers to the degree to which an investment may be redeployed to alternative uses without reducing its value (Williamson 1996, p. 59). The higher the reduction of its value in alternative uses the greater the specificity. In fact, Klein, Crawford, and Alchian (1978) have suggested measuring the specificity according to the quasi-rents generated in the investment (the difference between the value in their actual use and in its [best] alternative).[4] Consequently, a transaction which requires specific investments creates high transaction costs because contractors anticipate that, once the investment is made, they are "held-up" in the transaction. They can not easily escape from that investment if the present conditions change and they may even be forced to agree to conditions more favorable for the counterpart. Then transaction costs arise because both parties try to anticipate all the relevant contingencies and agree to an efficient response. In other words, the intensity of this problem depends on the incompleteness of the contract.[5] The difficulty in the redeployment of a pipeline or a mold for the hood of a car makes these investments quite specific.

*12.2.1.2 Uncertainty and complexity* Williamson (1975, pp 23–25, 1985, pp 43–63) argues that an increase in the difficulty of foreseeing the evolution of transactional variables – that is, uncertainty – increases the cost of establishing how the participants should act in each possible contingency. Transactional variables may be related to clients (demand uncertainty), technology (including changes in the production process and new products), and suppliers. Likewise, when a transaction deals with a commodity or another kind of standardized product (e.g. steel of predetermined quality, grains, memory chips, and so on), the transaction is quite simple. However, when the product is not so easy to standardize or when it is difficult to anticipate all the relevant variables (e.g. the construction of a turnkey facility) the transaction is much more complex. Thus, transaction costs rise with uncertainty and complexity.

*12.2.1.3 Frequency and duration*    The frequency with which a transaction occurs and the duration of the relationship also affect transaction costs. On one hand, some transactions are unique. This is the case when a firm buys a new building as its headquarters. However, other transactions are repeated frequently, such as the purchase of raw material. Generally speaking, the higher the frequency, the lower the *average* transaction cost of each exchange. This is because the marginal transaction costs are decreasing. The second time a firm buys the same raw materials from the same provider both parties save the same transaction costs, taking advantage of the previous information and checking fewer details than in the first contract. Probably the third time they will invest even fewer resources and so on. On the other hand, "duration" refers to the period of time during which the parties agree *ex ante* to commit themselves to the terms and conditions specified in the agreement (Joskow 1987, p. 169). The longer the period, the higher the transaction costs. This is because parties have many more details to negotiate in the long term than in the short term. For example, a long-term supply contract for a raw material needs to negotiate the incorporation of new technologies. Otherwise, the suppliers may not be interested in changing their production process.

*12.2.1.4 Measurement or search cost*    The difficulty of measuring the output attributes varies from one transaction to another (Barzel 1982, 1989). For example, it is easier to evaluate the output of a painter who is painting your house than the performance of the lawyer who is negotiating your divorce. The argument is simple: the parties do not easily know the output of a transaction, which enhances the risk of opportunism and thus the transaction costs. In our example, the lawyer's chances of opportunism seem greater than the painter's options, since the latter's work is easier to observe and requires less technical knowledge. We can also say that we have measurement problems because there are some aspects of the transaction that are non-contractible.[6] The parties are unable to introduce all future contingencies and agree on the actions they should make. Even when they are able to introduce all relevant actions and payments, some of them may not be verifiable by the counterpart (e.g. when we take out life insurance) or by a third party (e.g. an oral agreement). Under these circumstances, economic agents commonly arrange their transactions to either make measurement easier or to reduce the importance of accurate measurements. However, these arrangements are costly and they are probably more costly the higher the measurement or search costs.

*12.2.1.5 Connectedness* According to Milgrom and Roberts (1992, p. 32), transactions differ in how they are connected to other transactions. Some transactions are quite independent, in the sense that their output or conditions do not affect others. This may be the case, for example, when a secretary buys some flowers to decorate the office or when you decide on your local power provider. However, other transactions should be coordinated. A bank branch cannot decide by itself the software it will use because if it is not perfectly compatible with the software of other branches essential information for the success of the business may be lost. Likewise, in a building project all transactions must be perfectly connected to avoid high coordination costs (e.g. the plumber did not set a drainpipe for the kitchen sink). This kind of interdependent transaction is more costly because more details must be taken into account and the parties should agree on it. It is also the same when we are dealing with strong complementary assets (e.g. the computer software and hardware). Since their coordination is essential, they create high transaction costs.

### 12.2.2 Mechanisms of governance

The above analysis reflects transaction costs generated by the nature of the transaction. In other words, they are the transaction costs depending exclusively on the features or dimensions of the transactions. The parties have not invested at all in reducing the conflicts of the exchange. However, contractors may use many tools to solve the problem of opportunism with different cost and competencies. For example, a contractor may hire the services of a specialist consultant company to select different subcontractors. They use contract law and commerce codes as guides to negotiate all relevant aspects of the contract. They introduce penalties for breaching the contract, termination sanctions, reference prices, incentive systems, a predetermined duration for the relationship, and formalize the contract in a written document. Broadly speaking, these tools are what transaction cost economics (TCE) calls "mechanisms of governance," in the sense that they are devices to reach efficiency in a set of transactions (Williamson 1996). They include all governance structures and safeguards.[7] Consequently, we do not perceive transaction costs directly derived from the nature of the transactions as we described above. On the contrary, we observe transaction costs resulting from the modulation of the mechanisms of governance.

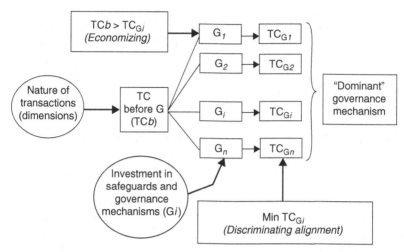

**Figure 12.1** The choice of the governance mechanism.

It is worth noting that each mechanism of governance and safeguard yields costs by itself. In our previous example of the contractor, the formalization of the contract, the introduction of incentive systems, and so on, are not without cost. All these devices generate costs, which are also generally denominated transaction costs. Consequently, the transaction costs we observe in the economy include both transaction costs referred to in the previous section and those costs directly yielded by the chosen mechanism of governance and safeguards (*see* Figure 12.1). Clearly, the savings yielded by the introduction of mechanisms of governance should be greater than the cost generated by them.[8] Otherwise, no mechanism of governance or safeguard will be considered.

*12.2.2.1 Relative performance of governance mechanisms*    Since the costs of each governance mechanism differ, the parties should compare the relative performance of all of them in order to economize. From among the solutions that they will be able to formulate they will choose one that minimizes their joint transaction costs.[9] In fact, Masten (1993, p. 119) argues that what we should focus on is analyzing the *relative merits* of alternative governance arrangements. Thus, the key question in our case is not only ascertaining when the transaction costs of using the market (buy) are greater than those of internal organization (make), but also comparing any alternative governance form, such as a classical subcontracting relationship with the just-in-time (JIT) or lean purchasing style. This means comparing the performance of a transaction (or set of transactions) governed by different mechanisms. To do this, we assess the costs and competences of different mechanisms of governance regarding the dimensions of transactions.

*12.2.2.2 Specificity*   Vertical integration always solves the hold-up problem. Since it gathers all assets under a common property, there is no conflict of interest in expropriating quasi-rents and, hence, the risk of hold-up disappears. However, this is not always the chosen solution. Other governance forms such as formalized long-term contracts, reputation, and hybrid forms may also mitigate the problem (but it does not disappear as in vertical integration) and, depending on the circumstances, they may be optimal. In this sense, Dyer (1997) shows how Japanese automakers incur lower transaction costs than US auto makers, despite the higher specialization of the Japanese suppliers (and their greater reliance on subcontracting). This finding is explained by differences in the mechanisms of governance. Dyer argues that engaging in repeated (long-term) transactions helps to share information and to make credible any promise of the firm. This reduces both production and transaction costs. The former decrease because those features help the firm to invest in specialized and co-specialized assets and the latter decrease because if the promise of no opportunism is credible, the parties do not need to invest in any other safeguards. Although building trust and engaging in repeated trades is not costless, these mechanisms seem to work properly in a long-term relationship in which relation-specific investments are essential. Of course, solving the hold-up problem does not guarantee that other problems can be solved so easily, as, for example, monitoring.

*12.2.2.3 Uncertainty*   The increase in transaction costs derived from uncertainty is present in both market and hierarchies. However, it is frequently considered to be smaller within organizations.[10] The reason is that vertical integration makes it easier to adjust to unforeseen situations. Whereas in most market relationships parties have to agree on detailed plans of action to safeguard themselves from opportunisms, contracts are more "relational" in a hierarchy. This means that *ex ante* agreements only allocate residual decision rights, so that *ex post* decisions are more flexible.[11] This flexibility facilitates self-enforcement because it reduces the risk of transactors taking advantage of the necessarily imperfect terms of explicit and detailed agreements.[12]

Nevertheless, this argument must be qualified. In fact, uncertainty may actually be faced through subcontracting in some situations:

• First, when the demand changes sharply, companies frequently turn to the market (subcontracting) for the need of capacity in the short term.

This effect is usually attenuated in the long term because the firm has the opportunity of adjusting its capacity to the demand. However, this adjustment is not so easy when the demand changes unpredictably, which leads some companies to merely keep the same capacity in the long term as in the short term. They assume the cost of leaving clients unattended during peak periods but do not bear the risk of adjusting their capacity to the changing demand.

- Second, technological uncertainty reduces the use of integrated solutions because of their lack of flexibility to jump to a new technology.[13] However, they protect proprietary knowledge and reduce the leakage of information better than any other market solution.[14] Additionally, new technology might not be available unless it was developed in house because it is extremely difficult to persuade technological suppliers to invest in new technology if the standard is unclear.

- Third, environmental uncertainty (e.g. about the trend of the economic cycle, the evolution of prices, consumption, and so on) may reduce interest in vertical integration because, unlike subcontracting, it is likely to facilitate opportunistic behavior (moral hazard). The reason is that environmental uncertainty makes it very costly to ascertain whether the performance of a transaction comes from the agents' effort or from random components. Thus, this lack of information leads to moral hazard problems, which are usually solved by introducing high-powered incentives.[15] However, integrated solutions (i.e. hierarchy) do not easily offer this type of incentive because fiat and administrative controls are not as effective in the alignment of incentives as market pressure.[16]

- Finally, uncertainty is only relevant for make-or-buy decisions if a certain degree of specificity exists:[17] if a transaction does not require specific investments, contracting costs are small and a new agreement could easily be reached in any new situation.

*12.2.2.4 Frequency*  The market is probably more appropriate for a one-time transaction. The parties may use general-purpose mechanisms (e.g. courts) to solve their contractual hazards, thus avoiding investing in developing specific mechanisms for just a single transaction. However, when the transactions are frequent, the choice is not so easy. It is clear that highly frequent transactions merit investment in developing specific mechanisms. Parties may find it valuable to design and introduce low-cost routines to manage transactions. Small companies do not create, for example, a complaints office because they do not have enough complaints. However, both polar governance mechanisms (market and hierarchy) develop particular safeguards to deal with repeated transactions. Initially, it seems that hierarchy facilitates the design and introduction of this type of device because of the repeated and long-term orientation of all contracts (Williamson 1985). However, equivalent devices appear when we introduce repeated and long-term transactions into market relationships. Thus, reputation, relational contracts, and supervision authorities in stock exchange markets all play the same role as routines throughout the hierarchy. Consequently, it is difficult to ascertain which governance mechanism performs better concerning highly frequent transactions.

Regarding the length of the period over which contractors interact, the longer the period, the less likely it will be to use a pure market relationship. A long-term, arm's-length relation is very costly because parties have to anticipate all relevant variables and contingencies in order to avoid opportunism. However, it is not so important to anticipate all future problems in a relationship within the firm. A firm works as a relational contract in which parties only explicitly allocate well-defined property rights. Other property rights that are not so well defined are not allocated until they are relevant. Parties only agree *ex ante* on the devices they will use to decide the owner of those property rights. This pre-agreement helps to reduce transaction costs. Additionally, it avoids the contractual rigidity that arises when parties are obliged to strictly obey the formalized content of the contract.[18]

*12.2.2.5 Measurement costs*  Theoretically, measurement costs should be the same regardless of the mechanism used to govern a transaction. However, parties may arrange their transactions to either make measurement easier (the best-informed party does the measuring) or to reduce the importance of accurate measurements. The right allocation of property rights is a paradigmatic example of how to reduce the measurement costs.[19] The owner of an asset (e.g. a truck) keeps proper incentives for maximizing the residual value of the asset because he bears the economic consequences of his decisions. Then, if the owner is also the user of an asset (e.g. the driver of the truck) we avoid contracting explicitly on attributes that are difficult to measure (e.g. proper maintenance).[20] This may, for example, explain why some companies subcontract for-hire carriers (owner-operators) instead of using private carriers (the driver is an employee and does not own the truck): They save on transaction costs because the company does not need to negotiate with the drivers the proper maintenance of its trucks. The theoretical question is who should own the asset (the truck): the driver or the company? Barzel (1989) offered an explanation that helps to understand many real-world arrangements: the party that has the greater capacity to affect the value of the asset should be the owner. The driver has greater capacity to affect the value of a truck concerning maintenance, so the best solution is that the driver should own the truck.

However, allocating the ownership to the user is not always applicable. First, it generates a risk allocation that may generate costs. Risk allocation is optimal when the risk is borne by the risk-neutral transactor. In this situation, bearing risk does not generate costs. However, the driver of our example is likely to be risk-averse. Broadly speaking, workers are risk-averse and stakeholders are risk-neutral. Thus, when workers become residual claimants of an asset (owners), they bear a risk and the associated cost. They would not bear this cost if the ownership had been allocated to a risk-neutral part. Second, assets may be used for more than one economic agent and we do not know the individual contributions to the output (negative or positive). In this case, a team production situation, the allocation of the ownership to the users does not solve the problem because it creates an incentive problem of shirking. Alchian and Demsetz (1972) argued that, in this situation, we should have someone specialize in monitoring the team and he or she should be paid for that activity with residual returns of the team. Thus, the solution will be the classical firm, that is, vertical integration.

*12.2.2.6 Connectedness*   The choice of the mechanism of governance depends on the nature of the coordination or connectedness problem. Vertical integration (i.e. an authority) seems more appropriate for solving problems with design attributes (Milgrom and Roberts 1992, p. 33, p. 91). These are problems in which: parties know ex ante how resources should be coordinated to reach the optimal solution (or at least have good knowledge about it); and the most important error is failing to achieve the right coordination. The hierarchy (vertical integration) performs better than the market because design problems (the steel mill production plan) can be solved without taking into account local information (workers prefer not to work during the weekend) since the central authority knows the optimal solution. Hayek (1945) has argued that the market is more efficient using local information than a central authority. Consequently, when this local information is not useful, the central authority performs better because its decisions are faster and more secure than using the market. The authority does not bear the cost of using the price mechanisms (the negotiation of a price) because it just orders (the ex ante known solution) and the workers obey.

There is, however, another kind of coordination problem with innovation attributes, apart from design attributes (Milgrom and Roberts 1992, pp 92–93). These are characterized by the lack of ex ante knowledge about the optimal solution and by the relevance of local information. In this case, the central authority (hierarchy) does not have a clear advantage over the price mechanisms (markets). In fact, the information needed is not usually within a particular firm (e.g. the launching of a new product). Conversely, it is spread throughout the market (clients, suppliers, workers, and so on). Someone should gather and develop the information needed to then implement a solution (the production of the new product). The market sometimes offers better incentives to perform this task than companies. A visionary entrepreneur may see his market opportunity and, since he would earn the whole residual returns of his solution, he is better motivated than a salary-compensated employee.

### 12.2.3  Re-interpreting traditional arguments

Many of the alternative theories that have been offered to explain the degree of vertical integration may be re-interpreted taking into account transaction costs arguments.

*12.2.3.1 Technological factors*  A traditional explanation for make-or-buy relies on technological factors. Some people explain the common ownership of steel milling and steel production by the close technological links between the two processes. This argument is flawed, however. Whilst it is true that there are benefits from having these operations at one location, technology does not dictate ownership. Steel mills could buy hot steel ingots from other companies located in the same building. The reasons why they do not depend on contracting problems rather than technological factors – independent companies do not want to expose themselves to the hold-up problems that arise from this kind of firm-specific investment (Williamson 1985).

*12.2.3.2 Exploiting scale and learning economies*  An advantage of using market contracting instead of vertical integration takes place when there are scale economies – specifically, when the production of an input the company needs involves important up-front set-up costs and its own level of consumption of that input would not allow the firm to achieve the minimum efficient scale. In this context, the firm should rely on independent suppliers for the input. This will often be the case for standard products and services whose production requires the development of know-how and are capital intensive.

The previous argument, however, does not justify why the firm cannot integrate the optimal size of the input production, selling the idle capacity into the market. The reasons may be the complexity of managing that kind of firm and that potential buyers of the input do not trust the integrated firm because they are probably rivals and they do not want to give advantages to the integrated firm. Therefore, the "scale economies" argument really is a transaction cost and strategic argument.

*12.2.3.3 Better coordination between suppliers and buyers* Without good coordination of the flows through the vertical chain, firms cannot effectively achieve the economies of scale that exist in most of the steps of the vertical chain of production. Coordination costs are particularly relevant when downstream companies know how the several inputs and outputs should relate to each other, but the different inputs suppliers may not effectively coordinate with each other, and when failing to achieve the right relationship among inputs may be very costly. In these circumstances, the market mechanism does not work well because it would be slower, as a result of the existence of various transactions and agents.

But the previous explanation is rooted in a transaction cost argument: When the relevant information for the optimal solution is known, the easiest way of reducing the transaction cost is to normalize the process through the creation of routines, which is easier in a hierarchy than in the market because within an integrated company coordination can be achieved through centralized administrative control. Such control is absent when independent firms contract through the market.

Nevertheless, some firms have achieved high levels of coordination through subcontracting. For instance, Toyota relies on outside suppliers not just for its basic inputs like sheet steel and tires, but also for other complex components, such as headlamps, brake systems, and fuel-injection system. Toyota has long-term relationships with a small number of suppliers. These long-term relations facilitated communication and made the suppliers willing to face the risks of investing heavily in both skills and machinery to satisfy Toyota's needs.

*12.2.3.4 Leakage of capabilities and private information* Firms use vertical integration to avoid sharing information about production know-how, customer information, and product or process design with other firms (Besanko, Dranove, and Shanley 1996). For instance, a company might be reluctant to provide an independent supplier with detailed information about such issues because it fears that the supplier will share the information with other companies. This argument assumes that it is easier to control the leakage of critical information when dealing with one's own employees, but it does not consider that these employees could also use the critical information in other companies (for instance, if they are recruited by such companies). In this case, it is necessary to protect the property rights on that information, which depends on the efficacy of judicial institutions. Therefore, this argument may also be interpreted in terms of transaction costs explanations.

### 12.2.4 Dynamic evolution of firm boundaries

A step further in the analysis of firm boundaries is taken when we do not compare transactions at a fixed point but over time. We thus include an additional variable in TCE analysis: the institutional environment. North (1991, p. 97) defines institutions as the "humanly devised constraints that structure political, economic, and social interactions. They consist of both informal constraints [...] and formal rules [...]." Consequently, they are the set of fundamental political, social, and legal rules which define the context in which economic activity takes place (Williamson 1996, p. 378).

Since the institutional environment constrains and affects the transactions, it also probably influences the governance mechanisms that structure those transactions. Thus, Williamson (1991a) proposes to treat the institutional environment as a set of parameters. A variation of one of these parameters shifts the comparative cost of governance, which may change the optimal organizational form for a given set of transactions (*see* Figure 12.2).

#### 12.2.4.1 Changes in the institutional environment   The main candidates among institutional parameters are tax and labor regulations.[21] Changes in labor law and taxation shift the comparative cost of governance forms and move the intercept or the slope of governance cost curves –expressed as a function of transaction dimensions (*see* Figure 12.2). González-Díaz, Arruñada, and Fernández (1998) show, for the case of Spanish construction firms, how more restrictive labor and tax regulations have induced parties to substitute market contracts (subcontracting) for labor contracts (integration); (Figure 12.2 (b) represents this situation). They observe that the fragmentation process is stronger in activities in which the monitoring problem is higher. They explain this contractual swap because a new regulation changes the relative performance of each governance form. Regulation from 1975 to 1995 altered the cost of hiring workers because it restricted the variability of wages and increased the firing cost. Thus the industry lost its capacity to avoid moral hazard, leading to an inefficient situation. Firing the workers and then subcontracting them as self-employed was a way to recover efficiency

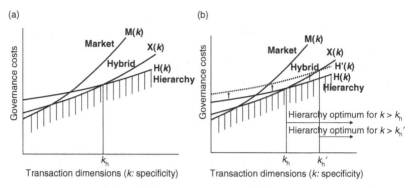

**Figure 12.2**  (a) Governance costs; (b) Governance costs with an institutional change.

because those new (market) contracts were not subject to labor restrictions. A comparison between US and European trucking carriers (Arruñada, González-Díaz, and Fernández 2004) reaches similar conclusions. A substantial difference is observed between both areas. European carriers are much smaller and contract their drivers mainly as owner-operators while US carriers are bigger and rely mostly on employees as drivers. Since technology is ruled out because it is similar in both areas and the similar organizational factors (transactional dimensions) tested for US industry also apply in European trucking, the only explanation for the differences is the institutional environment. Particularly, they show that countries with less flexible labor regulation use owner-operator (subcontracting) more heavily.

*12.2.4.2 Changes in the technological environment*  Until now, we have not considered the influence of technology. All our considerations about the choice of the mechanisms of governance have considered the technology as constant. However, it seems that it is not. The evolution of computers and cell phones are some examples that show the dynamics of certain industries. How does technology affect the organizational form? To answer this question we treat technological change as shift parameters, so it will affect the comparative cost of governance, modifying the optimal organizational form.

Baker and Hubbard (2003) offer an excellent example of the influence of information technology (technological change) on organizational patterns. They explain that trucking faces two main organizational problems. First, there is a coordination problem because shippers rarely have demand for a round trip. So it is necessary to identify complementary hauls for the return trip. The dispatcher's capacity to match trucks to hauls in the very short term is then essential in order to minimize the number of miles driven without the full haul. As we have argued above, this requisite had been reached through integrated companies because of the advantages of this solution regarding market-based solutions. The second problem refers to the driver's motivation because it is not easy to monitor (driving behavior and maintenance tasks). This problem has been traditionally solved by allocating the residual control rights to the driver, who was frequently an owner-operator.

The introduction of trip recorders and electronic vehicle management systems (EVMS) altered both solutions. First, trip recorders, which measure trucks' operation, such as turning the engine on and off, speed, accelerations and decelerations, and various engine performance statistics, solved company-drivers' incentives because they provided verifiable information about how trucks were operated. Since the main limitation of integrated solution (measurement costs) was partially solved, the new technology improved the interest of this governance mechanism. Therefore, for the same set of transactions, company drivers (integration) are now used more frequently than before. Second, EVMS, which are similar to trip recorders but additionally record the truck's geographic location and can transmit information online, improve resource-allocation decisions because their capabilities help dispatchers match trucks to hauls better. Thus, coordination costs are less important, reducing the appeal of integrated solutions.

Finally, the technology may not always be available as we have assumed in our previous trucking example. This can be the case, for example, in the computer industry. Afuah (2001) argues that governance forms that are more suitable for facing a technological change depend on whether you have the new technology or not. If a firm has the new technology vertical integration improves the performance of the company. However, if the firm has the old technology, subcontracting improves its performance. This means that the optimal governance mechanism may evolve as the technology does. To check his argument he analyzed a technological change in the computer industry. In the 1980s, RISC technology overcame CISC and firms had to change to the new technology.[22] Afuah observed that the best performance was obtained for companies that had not been vertically integrated into the old technology but were vertically integrated into the new one. In contrast, the worst output was reached by firms that had been vertically integrated into the old technology but were not vertically integrated into the new one. The explanation is that vertical integration performs worse when it is needed to take advantage of new information that is spread all around the company. Furthermore, the routines that were efficient for using the old technology could prevent the firm from going outside to new suppliers and learning the new technology. In contrast, when the firm is vertically integrated into the new technology there is no need for change and the firm only needs to develop the most efficient routines to take advantage of its technology.

## 12.3    Limitations and future of empirical research

Despite the huge number of studies on the issue analyzed, the empirical literature has several weaknesses. Future empirical research should mitigate these limitations.

First, we observe a large amount of divergence about the operationalization of the core constructs (asset specificity, uncertainty, and transaction costs) used to explain organizational choice. For example, there are numerous measures of asset specificity, which may be grouped according to the five higher-level categorizations defined by Williamson (1991a). As with asset specificity, there is considerable diversity in the measurement of uncertainty. The several measures used to operationalize this construct may be grouped under the larger categories of market conditions, technology, and behavior. There is also significant variety in capturing transaction costs directly, not as a function of transaction characteristics such as asset specificity and uncertainty. Some tests measure the transaction costs associated with monitoring exchanges (Oxley 1999), whereas others measure transaction costs through performance ambiguity (Poppo and Zenger 1998). Given the huge number of measures of key constructs used in the empirical literature, we believe that greater consensus on the operationalization and measurement of core constructs would allow the theory to advance more consistently.

Second, while asset specificity and uncertainty have received considerable analysis in the empirical literature, other important TCE variables, such as frequency and performance, have not. Notably, very little attention was given to TCE propositions regarding the relative performance of governance forms. We found this lack of empirical attention troubling, given the central position that the comparative performance of governance forms occupies within TCE. In this respect, Silverman, Nickerson, and Freeman (1997) attempted to address the discriminating alignment hypothesis. They found that the alignment of governance form with transaction characteristics had no effect on survival rates (the measure of performance used in this study). However, the fact that recent work has begun to examine the performance implications of TCE is encouraging (Leiblein, Reuer, and Dalsace 2002; Nickerson and Silverman 2003). For example, Nickerson and Silverman (2003) found that companies whose governance choices are not aligned with transaction cost predictions obtain lower profits than other firms whose organizational forms are better aligned with those predictions.

Third, important methodological problems should be avoided. Tests on the effects of governance forms on performance are problematic because they are likely to suffer from self-selection issues. That is, unobserved variables may affect both organizational choice and performance, thus potentially biasing estimates (Masten 1993). For example, firms choosing to manufacture in-house may have particular production capabilities (e.g. first-line technology) that make this a highly profitable choice. On the other hand, firms choosing to buy may not have these special production capabilities. As a result, a regression of performance on the make-or-buy choice that does not allow for endogeneity of the organizational choice may not answer the relevant question. Although some studies were explicit about controlling for this problem (i.e. Silverman, Nickerson, and Freeman 1997; Poppo and Zenger 1998; Nickerson and Silverman 2003), others were not. If future research focusses increasingly on the performance implications of organizational choice, then it is important that researchers be aware of such problems and employ methodologies that account for them.

Similarly, most analyses of the relationship between asset specificity and governance form are tests of the largest, surviving firms; that is, they may suffer from survivor bias. One way to overcome this problem is by taking an ecological approach. For example, Bigelow (2003) tested the same transaction over an entire population during multiple periods of observation and she proved that companies that fail to organize according to transaction cost reasoning have a higher risk of mortality than companies that adhere to transaction cost logic.

# 13 Transaction Costs, Property Rights, and the Tools of the New Institutional Economics: Water Rights and Water Markets

*Gary D. Libecap*

## 13.1 Introduction

Throughout the world there are growing problems of a scarcity of fresh water relative to demand.[1] These problems are particularly critical in more arid regions, such as the Middle East, North Africa, Mediterranean Europe, Australia, north-west China, northern Mexico, parts of South America, and the western USA. In the American West there are rapidly growing urban and environmental demands for water, but virtually no new supplies to meet them. Conservation of existing urban water is not a solution, given the magnitude of urban growth relative to supply. The water must come from somewhere else. Similarly, rising per capita incomes have brought greater demands for water to meet environmental and recreational uses. Historically, little water has been directed to those areas so that conservation of existing uses will not release major new amounts of water. And, there are no new dam sites or large, untapped aquifers to quench this thirst. To meet growing urban and environmental demands, water must be reallocated from agricultural uses, where most water is consumed.

For other resources, such as land, shifts in demand and associated reallocation are accommodated routinely with little fanfare through market transactions. When values in new uses exceed those in existing ones, the resource is transferred to new applications. For instance, in areas where there is urban growth, adjacent farmland gradually shifts from crops to housing and commercial activities through the real-estate market. In areas where there is growing recreational and amenity demand, local governments purchase properties for parks or wildlife habitat. There generally is little controversy. Markets perform these services because property rights and contracts are well defined and enforced, providing the basis for exchange among competing users.

This is not the case for water, however. In general, water does not flow easily or routinely through market transactions from one application to another – in the American West from agriculture to urban and environmental uses. This chapter explores why. It also describes how the insights of new institutional economics (NIE), in particular transaction cost and property rights concepts, reveal why markets have not developed as effectively for water as they have for land, and what useful policy responses might be considered to promote smoother, more timely reallocation.

## 13.2  Political or bureaucratic versus market allocation of water

For many, water is viewed as too special or too essential a commodity for private markets. They argue that markets are both irrelevant and impractical for water allocation and management. For these critics, the ownership and provision of water should be left to the state because water is a public resource and low-cost access should be regarded as a fundamental human right.[2] But advocates of state solutions to water supply problems fail to specify the political and bureaucratic models they have in mind for assurance that the state would perform better than would a market alternative. They do not articulate the circumstances under which political and bureaucratic allocation decisions would be more welfare-enhancing than would market exchange.

There are some reasons for skepticism. While the problems of market failure are well known and emphasized by those who favor bureaucratic allocation of water, public choice theory and research also has demonstrated the problems of government failure, whereas political decisions are dominated by interest group politics and short time horizons.[3] Under these circumstances, unless there are competitive interest groups and governments, private interests rather than public concerns are more likely to be advanced by government allocation.[4] Accordingly, caution and clarity are required by both advocates of market or state solutions to water allocation problems.

The provision of non-rivalrous or non-excludable (public) goods is one argument for state allocation of water since markets are likely to underprovide such goods owing to lack of appropriability and freeloading. But these characteristics do not apply to most new water demands. They are largely for private consumption (residential or manufacturing uses) or for a mixture of rivalrous goods (irrigation, urban consumption) and non-rivalrous goods (instream flows for recreation as well as amenities and aquatic habitat). Older uses are dominantly in agriculture for irrigation. Hence, most water reallocation involves moving water from one private (excludable) use to another. Under these circumstances, market distributions are appropriate. If there are important third-party effects, as is possible and described below, then regulatory oversight is warranted for proposed water exchanges.

Where new water demand involves a mixture of rivalrous and non-rivalrous goods, then the relative sizes of the values determine whether or not state allocation is preferable. Although non-rivalrous public goods are notoriously difficult to value, there are techniques in economics, such as contingent valuation, for estimating their values. Where private consumptive water values appear to dominate those for non-rivalrous water uses, then market, rather than state, allocation of water is likely to be most efficient. Where amenity and other non-rivalrous values dominate, then state allocation is required. And where there are important public goods considerations, even if private water uses are more valuable, then regulatory oversight of water exchanges to protect public uses is appropriate.

Some other points are worth considering concerning state versus market allocation of water for rivalrous, private uses. The political supply of private goods is potentially contentious, costly, and slow. Politicians must weigh the relative merits of competing demands. Because politicians and bureaucrats are not residual claimants to the higher resource values brought about by allocation to high-valued uses, they consider other factors, such as political influence. In this case, the total economic contribution or value of water is reduced. Entrenched interest groups have an advantage in this process.

Political, rather than market, allocation occurs without the information about competing uses generated by market trades. Hence, there is no clear mechanism for new demands and values to stimulate reallocation smoothly and flexibly. Further, because current claimants have limited ability to capture the economic gains from political reallocation or to be compensated for any losses should it take place, they resist adjustments, even if they are socially beneficial in the aggregate. Because of their established ties to politicians, current users are well placed politically to block reallocation. Accordingly, current resource allocations are unlikely to respond to the emergence of new social and economic uses, as occurs regularly in markets. With many constituencies having a stake in existing allocations and a potential veto in any reallocation, a paralysis in present uses emerge as a type of anti-commons.[5]

In contrast, where relatively competitive markets exist, those who hold property rights to private goods can quickly respond to new market demand and supply conditions, and they have incentive to do so because they are residual claimants to the gains involved. They also have incentive to invest in the resource (to conserve, augment, or improve it), motivations that are lacking with state ownership and provision.

There is, however, another legitimate cause for concern about the efficacy of market allocation of water. Markets require clearly defined and enforced property rights to provide the basis for exchange. Yet and perhaps surprisingly in the American West, property rights to water are incomplete, vaguely defined, and subject to state appropriation. Weak property rights are an outcome of the physical characteristics of water that raise the costs of measuring, bounding, and enforcing individual claims. There are also legal and organizational factors that raise the costs of exclusion and defining and enforcing rights. Where the costs of measurement and exclusion are very high then it may not be efficient to precisely define property rights and rely on unregulated markets for reallocation. As described below, because surface water flows and therefore is difficult to partition, and is often hydrologically linked to ground water, which is not observable or easily measured, it is more difficult to define property rights to water than to other stationary resources like land. For these reasons efficient reallocation of water requires both the better definition of water rights where possible, and likely a regulatory role for the state in addressing externalities.

This essay uses the tools of the NIE to examine the nature of the transaction costs which inhibit the definition of property rights and trade in water. The policy response to water allocation problems emphasized here is a Coasean one, rather than a call for more direct state provision. Instead we examine the ways that the state might assist in the definition of property rights to water and in lowering the transaction costs of exchange to promote its more effective redistribution.

The works of Coase (1960), Demsetz (1967), Cheung (1970), Williamson (1975, 1985), Dahlman (1979), Barzel (1982, 1989), Libecap (1989), and others provide a critical foundation for understanding property rights and transaction costs. The insights from this literature help in determining what actions might be taken to better define property rights to water, to lower the transaction costs of exchange, and to ascertain when market allocation will be possible when it will not be.

## 13.3    The mis-allocation of water in the American West

In the western USA (the region west of the 98th meridian, running from North Dakota to Texas), rapid population growth, greater environmental and recreational demands, and persistent drought are fueling water demand that exceeds available supplies. Most water, however, is currently used in agriculture, which accounts for approximately 80% of consumptive use. Farmers typically pay only for the pumping or conveyance costs for the water, which often ranges from $15 to $25 per acre foot (326,000 US gallons, where 1 US gallon = 3.8 liters). An acre foot (a.f.) is the amount of water that would cover one acre (0.4 hectares) of land with one foot (0.3 meters) of water. It is a lot of water. As a result, much agricultural water use at the margin is in low-valued crops. In contrast, cities and agencies charged with supplying water for environmental or recreational demands are paying $350 per a.f. and often much more. Accordingly, there are significant allocative gains from moving some water from agricultural to urban and environmental uses.

These price differences have existed for a long time. For example, in a 1992 study in Texas the value of water in agriculture was reported at $300 to $2,300 per a.f., whereas in urban uses, it was $6,500 to $21,000 per a.f. The mean estimated net gains from the transfer of water were $10,000 per a.f.[6] As so much water is often included in a transfer the amount of money involved can be very large. For instance, in 1993, the Metropolitan Water District of Southern California agreed to pay the Imperial Irrigation District, also of Southern California, $233 million for a capitalized price of $1,500 per a.f. for 109,000 acre feet per year for 35 years.[7] Yet, as described below, water transactions generally are extremely difficult to negotiate and to complete. As a result, the price gap between urban or environmental and agricultural uses of water is growing, not declining as would be the case if market arbitrage were widespread. Figure 13.1 shows mean transfer prices for twelve western US states, compiled from 1987 through 2003.[8]

The data in the figure show mean agriculture-to-non-agriculture (urban and environmental) and "other" transaction prices by year. The "other" category is primarily agriculture-to-agriculture trades, but there are also some urban-to-urban, and urban-to-environmental transactions. As the figure shows, water values tend to be lower in those trades that do not involve the reallocation of water from agriculture to urban and environmental uses. And the difference in prices is increasing.

There have been growing water trades, but they have not been sufficient to narrow the price gaps. Indeed, Figure 13.2 shows the amount of water moved annually from agriculture to urban and environmental uses, again for 1987 to 2003.[9] Further, Figure 13.3 shows the number of transfers by category over the same period. In the face of increased demand in other sectors, in general more water is being sent from agriculture, and, since 1996, the number of agriculture-to-urban-and-environmental transactions has exceeded those among farmers and other transactions. Even so, water markets are controversial and water trades are too

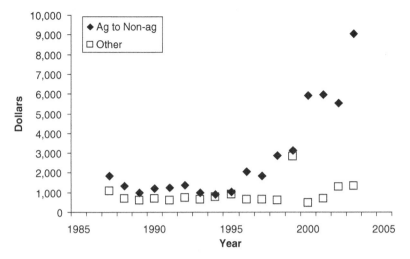

**Figure 13.1** Mean transfer prices for agriculture-to-urban-and-environmental uses and for agriculture-to-agriculture and other transactions for twelve western US states, 1987–2003.
*Source:* Libecap (2007).

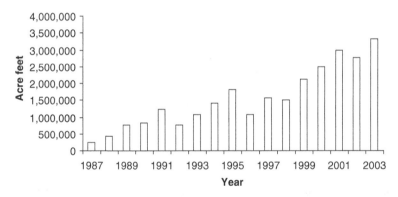

**Figure 13.2** Annual water transfers from agriculture-to-non-agricultural uses for twelve western states, 1987–2003.
*Source:* Libecap (2007).

limited to arbitrage a way those price differences which are not attributed to conveyance costs and variation in water quality.

There are estimates of the transaction costs of water trades across the western states. In 1990 in Colorado and New Mexico, for example, transaction costs ranged from $200 to $380 per a.f. At that time mean price in water sales in New Mexico was $2,167.[10] Estimates of

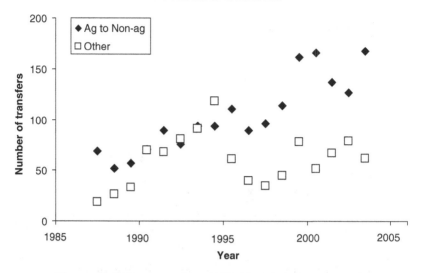

**Figure 13.3** Water transfers, 1987–2003, by category.
*Source:* Libecap (2007).

transaction costs in 1993 in those same two states varied from a few hundred dollars to $50,000, with mean costs of $300 per a.f. on transfers of twenty acre feet or less. With a mean transaction price of $1,500, transaction costs could account for 20% of the purchase price or more.[11] Processing times took from slightly over four months in New Mexico and five months in Utah to twenty-nine months in Colorado.[12]

The question, then, is why are water exchanges more limited than we might expect and what are the sources of high transaction costs? In answering this question, it makes sense to examine the nature of rights to water in the western USA. In doing so, we find that water rights are weaker than are rights to other natural resources.

## 13.4    Legal and organizational reasons for weak water rights

### 13.4.1    Non-vested usufruct rights

Many of the problems of water lie in the complex system of property rights and the difficulty of defining them. In western states, individuals do not own water as they might own land. Water is "owned" by the state in trust for its citizens, and its use is regulated based on public interest or welfare concepts. As stated in Wyoming law, for example: "Because water is so important to the economy of this state, its use is always limited by a concept of public trust; the only uses for which water rights may be established are those which receive 'public recognition' under the law of the state."[13]

Accordingly, individuals generally hold only usufruct rights to the water, subject to the requirement that the use be beneficial and reasonable and to oversight by the state in monitoring transfers to ensure that they are consistent with the public interest. Since individuals have use rights, rather than absolute title, their ownership of water is conditional to actions by the state and regulatory interpretations as to whether particular private actions are "beneficial and reasonable." These requirements are sufficiently vague that they may be interpreted in a variety of ways that can undermine existing ownership patterns.

One major source of uncertainty is regulatory application of the public trust doctrine. The "public trust" is a common law principle creating the legal right of the public to utilize certain lands and waters, such as tidewaters or navigable rivers, and other waters and natural resources with high amenity or public goods values. Under the doctrine, the rights of the public are vested in the state as owner of the resource and trustee of its proper use. In a far-reaching ruling by the California Supreme Court in 1983 in the Mono Lake case (*National Audubon Society* v. *Superior Court* 685 P.2d 709) the court stated that the "core of the public trust doctrine is the state's authority as sovereign to exercise a continuous supervision and control over" the waters of the state.[14] This opinion energized expansion of the public trust doctrine in other court rulings in western states to restrict "excessive" diversions from non-navigable streams to protect aquatic environments. And state legislatures have been involved. For example, a 1988 Oregon statute that allowed water users to sell or lease any water they conserved, included a tax that required about 25% of the saved water be given to the state and held for in-stream flow maintenance.[15]

The public trust doctrine may be applied retrospectively to roll back pre-existing water rights that appear inconsistent with the public trust. Under the doctrine, private water usufruct rights are non-vested and revocable and that any reallocation of water by the state may be done without compensation to existing water claimants.[16] The doctrine also lowers the costs of hold-up strategies by providing legal standing for parties to contest private water diversions or proposed trades as violations of the public trust. These broad regulatory powers, then, potentially add important uncertainty to water ownership, weakening existing property rights and their ability to promote investment, trade, and efficient use of water.

This is not to say that the public trust doctrine is never warranted. Indeed, where there are important non-exclusive values in augmenting stream flows for aquatic habitat, riparian restoration, and other amenity and recreational goods, then state intervention to reallocate water from existing irrigation uses may be called for. But the state should then compensate existing users for their lost water. This accomplishes two objectives. One is that it forces the state to calculate the monetary benefits of greater instream flows because it has to pay for them and equating marginal benefits with marginal costs can then lead to determination of just how much water should be diverted. This information leads to a more efficient redistribution of water. Currently, such decisions are made solely on biologic or hydraulic grounds with little economic consideration. The other gain is that compensation reduces the resistance of current users who will lose their water. Compensation allows the reallocation to be a positive sum game rather than a negative sum where parties are made worse off by the redeployment of water. The resistance of uncompensated parties may raise the costs of providing and defending the provision of the new non-rivalrous public good.

### 13.4.2  Appropriative water rights subject to state regulation

Private claims to surface and ground water in the West are made under the doctrine of prior appropriation: First in time, first in right.[17] In the case of surface water, such as that found in streams, the appropriative doctrine allows rights-holders to withdraw a certain amount of water from its natural course for private beneficial purposes on land remote from the point of diversion. The water may be separated from the land on which it flows and shipped elsewhere via aqueducts, ditches, or other means of conveyance. This approach to water ownership is quite different from that found in the eastern USA where the riparian system dominates. Under the riparian system, water ownership comes with the land that borders flowing streams. Water is not separable from the land that is appurtenant to it. In this case, water is held in common with other property owners.

The appropriative doctrine emerged in the nineteenth century in response to the development of mining and agriculture in the semi-arid West where growing numbers of people and economic activities were concentrated increasingly in areas where there was too little water. There was a need to move the water to where the people were located.

The maintenance of appropriative rights is based on placing claimed water into beneficial use, whereby parties can only divert what they use productively and leave the rest for subsequent claimants. Those with the earliest water claims have the highest priority and those with ensuing claims have lower-priority or junior rights. These junior claims are often to water that has previously been diverted by senior rights-holders, but not consumed. For example, when farmers withdraw water for irrigation, as much as 50% may percolate back through the soil to the original stream or ditch. As a consequence, water claimants within a single draining area are intricately intertwined. This creates potential externalities from water sales. Diverted agricultural water which is sold and shipped to urban or environmental uses will no longer be available for later use by junior parties. Accordingly, water trades that involve changes in nature, timing, or location of use must demonstrate that there is "no harm" to third parties, giving state regulatory agencies a mandate to review proposed water exchanges to minimize or compensate for the negative third-party effects on junior rights-holders.

The resulting regulatory policies differ across the states. California has the strongest pro-transfer laws, but the state's regulatory and property rights environments are less supportive. These include mixed jurisdictions among state and federal agencies, a patchwork of county regulations and restrictions on water export, and a complex system of water rights with differential requirements for agency review. As a result, the administrative process may be lengthy and complex, and the outcome uncertain. These factors reduce the expected gains from trade.

Among other states, New Mexico is also viewed as having a supportive legal and regulatory structure for water trades. Approval of trades can occur within three months.[18] In Colorado there are different regulatory structures within the state. In most of Colorado, water courts handle damage claims for proposed water transactions, and these are often hotly contested. Indeed, more water trades are opposed in Colorado than in New Mexico.[19] Wyoming's legal system has been interpreted as being hostile to water trading. Arizona has had relatively fewer agriculture-to-urban transactions owing to a relatively unfriendly court system and prohibitions against transferring water outside a major water supply organization within the state.[20] Further, all water supply organizations within a drainage area in Arizona must approve proposed transfers before state approval may be given. This authority gives those organizations a potential veto on any proposed transfer without having to prove harm.

Potential third-party effects from water trades are a legitimate basis for regulatory review of proposed transactions, but the procedures for such review should be transparent and tightly defined. The aim is to reduce the transaction costs of exchange and at the same time limit rent-seeking, whereby parties claim a "harm" in order to slow the transfer and extract a portion of the (often very large) rents that are associated with water reallocation.

### 13.4.3  Multiple decision makers with mixed incentives for trade

Weak water rights and an extensive regulatory mandate mean that multiple parties have a say in any proposed water trades. Most are not residual claimants to the allocative gains for transferring water from agriculture to urban and environmental uses and therefore have unclear motives for water transfers.

*13.4.3.1 State regulatory agencies*    State water regulatory agencies are staffed by state employees with technical or legal training who are charged with administering state law regarding water rights, approving certain water transfers, and regulating water use, including application of the public trust doctrine. For water transfer applications, agency officials examine the documents, scrutinize data to ensure compliance with the "no harm" provisions of state law, conduct hearings involving potential protests, and decide on the amount, timing, and nature of any approved trade. As with regulatory agencies in general, agency officials are not benefited directly by any changes in value from approving or denying water trades or from implementing other aspects of state water law. Hence, they are unlikely to be influenced by the economic implications of their decisions. Like all bureaucratic officials, they are motivated by a variety of factors, including professionalism, regulatory mandates, ideology, and political pressure.[21] Their actions may lower or raise the transaction costs of exchange, and the exact impact depends on state legal requirements, the structure of the regulatory body, as well as their personal motivations and qualifications.

*13.4.3.2 Irrigation districts and other water supply organizations*
Almost all agricultural water is supplied to farmers through an irrigation district or other type of water supply organization. These institutions vary widely in terms of governance structure, membership, decision-making authority, and water rights. The majority of districts legally own water rights on behalf of their members, who have contracted amounts of water delivered to them. In other cases, members retain their water rights and have water service contracts with the district. In either case water allocation and use are governed by a district governing board. This organizational complexity increases the transaction costs of defining clear property rights and of transferring water.

The district governing board is elected and voting rules vary, either where only district members have the right to vote or where there is a broader franchise, including citizens in any community surrounding the district. The nature of voting rules for board membership can importantly affect district support for water transfers. Because current marginal urban water values are high relative to similar agricultural values, farmers generally are motivated to sell or lease at least some of their water. They capture most of the returns. If farmers elect the governing board of the district, the board is apt to support those transfers. If board members are elected by a broader electorate with differential incentives to transfer water, then the board may not be as supportive of water exchanges.

District officials often are much less interested in selling or leasing water under their jurisdiction than are their members. There are several reasons why governing board officials oppose water transfers desired by some of the district members. The authority of district managers can be reduced if fallowing is extensive and district agricultural activities decline. Irrigation districts can be harmed financially if reduced water requirements leave them with stranded non-deployable fixed capital investments. There also can be increased administrative costs for the board as it evaluates and monitors the effects of water sales.

Because of a lack of clarity in district charters as to profit and cost sharing, the distribution of the revenues and costs of transfers is not straightforward and discretionary board decisions may be divisive and politically costly for officials. District members, who are not part of the transaction, will not want to shoulder costs involved. They also will be concerned about any spillover effects on their water supplies. These allocation problems are more challenging if the district is heterogeneous with respect to farm size, crop patterns, water use, and farmer support for transfers.[22] Board officials must also manage ground water withdrawal if surface sales lead farmers to turn to ground water for replacement. The board is responsible for the district-wide effects of subsurface water draw-down.

*13.4.3.3 The Federal Bureau of Reclamation*    Much of the water supplied to agricultural water organizations, such as irrigation districts, comes from Bureau of Reclamation Projects. The Bureau is the largest wholesaler of water in the USA. The water is transmitted either through long-term service contracts to those who hold water rights or, in some cases, the Bureau holds the water rights and distributes the water within its reclamation projects. As a federal agency there are mixed incentives for water transfers. It is subject to constituent political pressure in Congress from groups that may or may not support water trades. And as with state regulatory agencies, federal civilian employees do not benefit financially from any water reallocation.

*13.4.3.4 Indian tribes*  The water held by Indian tribes is potentially a major source of water for marketing. Indian tribes have reserved water rights sufficient for the development of agriculture on their reservations. Their water rights date from when the reservation was established by treaty with the federal government, which was usually in the nineteenth century, and therefore generally supersede the priority of non-Indian claimants. Many of these treaty provisions have only been recently enforced and Indian water rights adjudicated through litigation or congressional statute. This water often must come from existing users. Tribes own their resources communally, and their decision-making processes vary. As a result, tribal water litigation may, in the short term at least, increase uncertainty about water rights and transfers. Water may not be exchanged if it is potentially subject to Indian treaty claims.

## 13.5    Physical characteristics of water and weak water rights

Water rights are weak because of legal constraints on ownership, state regulatory intervention, and the existence of multiple decision makers with mixed motives for market trades. The physical characteristics of water also play a very critical role in complicating the assignment of clear property rights and raising the costs of defining them precisely.

### 13.5.1  The high costs of bounding

Owing to its physical mobility, water cannot be bounded easily or partitioned across claimants and uses. Streams move across the ground and seep within it. They cross both multiple private land holdings and political jurisdictions. Water in lakes is less migratory, but particular parcels of water cannot be constrained within property lines at low cost. Ground water also migrates, and it is unobserved. For all of these reasons, it is difficult to define and enforce property boundaries to fresh water.

Accordingly, exclusive control of moving water is difficult to achieve. As a result, numerous parties typically use the same body of water either simultaneously or sequentially. As demand grows relative to a relatively fixed water supply, disputes develop as use by one party conflict with the use of another. Opportunity costs rise, and without clear property rights the parties have little basis for exchange, as occurs, for example, with land, to address conflicting demands. Access to a defined amount and quality of water becomes less certain, making production and consumption of water services less predictable. Resource values decline relative to what might be possible with more secure rights.

Over the long term, the gains from defining more precise property rights may offset bounding costs, and new rights arrangements may emerge. The mobility of water, high measurement costs, distributional disputes, and public good claims, however, will make this process of institutional change more complex than envisioned by Demsetz (1967).

### 13.5.2  The high costs of measurement

Fluidity and lack of observability raise the costs of measuring the amount of water held in a water right. These effects are most critical for ground water. The quantity in any particular location is not precisely known, and it is affected by a variety of forces which deplete or augment it in ways that cannot be easily determined or measured. Extraction by one user drains the water that is available elsewhere for another party. Many aquifers are replenished gradually, both from natural sources and from the recharge of the very ground water which is extracted but not fully consumed. These processes are slow and very complex, affected by intricate hydraulic factors, variable precipitation, evaporation, and the nature of ground water–surface water exchange.

A property right to surface water can be measured more accurately because it is observable. Because water is mobile, the amount claimed is demarcated in terms of diversion. The extent of each diversion, however, varies over time owing to fluctuating precipitation. These seasonal precipitation patterns are predictable and are incorporated into a water claim. This is not the case, however, for annual precipitation variation which leads to uncertainty in water supply. Drought patterns are highly erratic and difficult to forecast with existing models. As a result it is hard to define an exact amount of water that will be available for diversion at any point in time. This supply uncertainty complicates the granting of definite water rights and the writing of contracts for water exchanges because neither buyers nor sellers know exactly how much water may be transacted at any specified period.

Water diversions can be measured more easily than actual consumption, which is affected by the nature of use, and by geologic and hydraulic conditions. Measuring consumption is important because it indicates the amount of diverted water that is released as recharge for subsequent claiming and use by others. Some surface water used for irrigation is consumed by plants, some evaporates, and some seeps into the soil to ground water, streams, or ditches. This released water is available for successive uses in irrigation, urban and industrial consumption, or in aquatic habitat. But because consumptive use is imprecisely known, the size of return flows is difficult to determine and, accordingly, the quantity of water which may be granted subsequently to downstream water rights claimants is not certain.

### 13.5.3  The interconnected private and public goods characteristics of water

Because of the high costs of bounding and measuring water claims, there is a high degree of interaction among claimants and the multiple applications of water, both public and private. Indeed, the simultaneous and sequential provision of private and public goods is an important complicating factor in assigning of property rights to water because it is physically difficult to segment into its various uses. Consider the production of both rivalrous and non-rivalrous goods using water as introduced earlier.

Private goods production from water involves competing, rivalrous uses, but most do not consume all of the water devoted to them. As noted above, an upstream farmer who diverts water for irrigation will use only part of it, with the remainder percolating through the ground back to aquifers, streams, or to ditches for repeated access by other parties. This relationship, however, ties users together because variations in upstream consumption can have important implications for downstream claimants.

There are similar problems of interconnected claims for ground water. Ground water often is in hydrologic communication with surface flows, so that those who consume surface water affect the quantity and quality available to those who extract ground water. In the same way, those who pump ground water reduce surface supplies that otherwise are replenished by springs and other subterranean seepage. Pumping by one user also decreases the amount of ground water available to others by lowering water tables and raising extraction costs. In transfers involving ground water there is significant hydrologic uncertainty in determining how other parties will be affected.

By definition, public goods production using water involves noncompeting or non-rivalrous uses of water. A free-flowing stream is available to all; consumption by one party has negligible impact on consumption by others. For this reason, most public goods are provided by the state either because of the inability to prevent access leads private parties to focus on activities with greater appropriability or because private efforts to limit access reduce production of public goods. But, critically, the decision by the state to provide public goods from water is *rivalrous* because it constrains the provision of private goods. In most cases, historical use of water has been in private agriculture, mining, or hydro-electricity production. The decision to divert some of this water to maintenance of instream flows for aquatic habitat, recreation, or visual amenities then necessarily requires constraints on previous uses. But unless rights have been well defined and recognized, trade and voluntary reallocation of water may not occur. Arbitrary reassignment of water, as occurs under the "public trust" doctrine, as described above, results in wasteful conflict and delay, dissipating both private and public values.

Accordingly, the concurrent or sequential use of water, or both, caused by the high cost of bounding and measurement, may result in numerous interdependent claims. Multiple parties can be affected inadvertently by any change in use to allocation. As noted earlier, because the potential for harm, transfers of surface water rights in western states require that there is "no harm or injury" to downstream rights holders. Compliance with this requirement is difficult to demonstrate if the transfer involves changes in the timing, location, or use of water. As a consequence, water transfers may be restricted to historical consumption, not water diverted. But the former is more difficult to document. Further, the no harm rule makes any trade vulnerable to a variety of constituent claims, some legitimate and some pure hold-up. State agencies enforce these and other regulations, and most water trades that involve new uses must be approved by them. As demonstrated above, the process of application, processing, and evaluation can be lengthy and complicated. This raises the transaction costs of defining clear property rights to water and facilitating its exchange.

The protection of public, non-exclusive goods also raises the transaction costs of water trades. Regulatory interventions in the absence of clear private property rights result in arbitrary and often uncompensated reallocation of water. These actions further weaken property rights, reducing incentives for investment in water and its trade. Reduced investment means foregone improvements in water quality or conservation, and lost trade means not only alternative, valuable uses foregone, but also the loss of useful information about alternative water uses that otherwise would be generated by water market trades.

Avoiding these losses of the common pool requires the definition of clear property rights to water. Defining private property rights must involve the many parties who draw from the same mobile water source and whose uses are intertwined. Determination of the number of parties requires information on the size of the water area and drainage from one use to another. It requires an allocation mechanism that is acceptable, measurable, and enforceable. The mechanism must be responsive to inherent variation in water supplies caused by seasonality and the vagaries of precipitation.

## 13.6     Policy responses

Useful public policy responses to promote property rights definition are to provide: (1) climatic, geologic, and hydraulic information for the definition of water rights; (2) registration and demarcation institutions to record water rights and to accurately measure historical consumption; (3) conflict resolution and enforcement institutions; and (4) overall support for the concept of private water rights and exchange. The latter should include the recognition and purchase of private water rights when it is necessary to provide public goods, rather than arbitrary seizure or taking of water without fair compensation. In the case of ground water, government-mandated unitization (single ownership and management) of ground water, as is done with oil and gas reservoirs, is a solution to excessive access and drawdown. In the case of unitization, a single "unit operator" extracts from and develops the reservoir. All other parties share in the net returns as share holders. This arrangement eliminates competitive withdrawal and directs extraction toward maximization of the economic value of the entire reservoir, rather than of the segments (leases) held by individual parties.[23]

The definition of secure water rights allows for the development of water markets. Legal and political institutions which support clear property rights will lower the transaction costs of trade and facilitate the voluntary, smooth exchange of water from low to higher-value uses. Such institutions are critical as new competing uses for water emerge in the presence of traditional allocations.

All of this sounds formidable, but it has been successfully tackled in other difficult settings. Consider fisheries. Wild ocean fisheries are the classic open-access resource with over-entry, over-fishing, over-capitalization, falling catch per unit of effort, and depleted stocks. These conditions follow from the fugitive nature of offshore species, huge distances involved, overlapping political jurisdictions, and large numbers of heterogeneous, competing fishers.[24] Unfortunately, the implications of open access have been understood for a very long time. Scott Gordon described it in 1954, yet forty-six years later Grafton, Squires, and Fox (2000) could still describe the dramatic wastes of over fishing and regulation in the Pacific Northwest halibut fishery, and a 2003 *Nature* article by Myers and Worm (2003) could report that the world's major predatory fish populations were in a state of serious depletion.

Historically, the initial regulatory response has been to deny access to certain groups based on political influence – non-citizens with expansion of the Exclusive Economic Zones (EEZs), sports versus commercial fishers, inshore versus offshore fishers, large-vessel versus small-vessel fishers, or vice versa, and so on. This action temporarily reduced fishing pressure, but it did not solve the fundamental problem which is that rents exist for those who can find ways around the regulations.

As these failed, new regulations such as fixed seasons, area closures, and gear restrictions were put in place. These arrangements are politically attractive to regulators because they do not upset status quo rankings, minimize existing transaction costs, and call for major regulatory mandates, which are attractive to regulators and politicians. But they have not been successful. They do not align the incentives of fishers with protection of the stock. Further, given heterogeneous fishers and limited and asymmetric information about the stock and the contribution of fishing relative to natural factors, there are disputes about the design and efficacy of these regulations. Finally, there is no basis for fishers to contract among themselves to reduce fishing pressure and thereby to capture the returns from an improved stock. There are no property rights to exchange.

There has been a turn to individual transferable quotas (ITQs) in some fisheries, almost always after continued declines in the stock under centralized regulation. ITQs require restrictions on entry, the setting of an annual total allowable catch, TAC, the allocation of rights or quotas to a share of the TAC, and enforcement. Thus, ITQs are a usufruct right – the right to fish – not a right to the stock and the aquatic habitat. This limited rights arrangement is similar to western US water rights.

The more secure, definite, durable, divisible, and permanent the ITQ, the stronger is the property right. And stronger property rights better link the incentives of fishers with the goal of maximizing the economic value of the fishery. Government regulators still determine the annual catch and then distribute that catch among ITQ holders. With permanent and transferable catch quotas, the quota holders find it to their advantage to preserve and if necessary rebuild the marine resources. The value of the share of the TAC depends on the state of fish stocks and the sustainability of the fishery. Enforcement costs may decline relative to those under other forms of regulation because fishers have a stake in the preservation of the stock as shareholders in the right to fish and self-monitor.

The general consensus is that ITQs have been very successful in restraining fishing pressure and in rebuilding the economic value of the stock. They require the collaboration of fishers and regulators in gathering information to set the annual allowable catch. They also require that fisheries be bounded and protected, and given mobile fish stocks this may be at significant cost. Individual quotas must be defined clearly and exclusively and be enforced. They also must be transferable.

All of these requirements are similar to those encountered in water. The success of ITQs and their gradual spread across countries and fisheries, despite the high costs involved, provides optimism for similar success in defining water rights more completely and in promoting their reallocation.

## 13.7    Concluding remarks

This chapter outlines the complex nature of water rights and the high transaction costs of trading them. It uses the tools of NIE to explain why price disparities between water uses have been so profound and persistent. And it draws on transaction cost economics (TCE) to derive useful state responses to promote markets and the reallocation of water from agriculture to urban and environmental uses. Water trades take place and are growing in frequency and magnitude, but they are not sufficient to cause water prices to equalize on the margin, adjusting for transport costs. Transfers that involve changes in use and the timing and location of use are heavily regulated with options for multiple constituencies to challenge. These transfer regulations vary across the states and, in part, explain the observed differences in the extent of transfers. The basis for strict state regulation lies in the interconnected nature of water uses, some rivalrous and some not, and the public trust doctrine.

As described here, a key problem lies in the fact that individuals do not have clear, complete private property rights to water. The states hold water rights in trust for their citizens and private parties hold usufruct rights. Additionally, even these rights are often held by third parties, irrigation districts, or similar organizations. Profit- and cost-sharing rules within districts are complex so that there may be no clear residual claimants to the returns from any transfer. Moreover, expansion of the public trust doctrine threatens to weaken water rights by stressing their non-vested, revocability without compensation. For all of these reasons water markets will require significant institutional change toward greater precision in the definition of individual water rights, if voluntary market transactions are to be the primary way of reallocating water in the western USA. Similar issues are likely to exist in other semi-arid regions where increased fresh water scarcity will provide pressure for water reallocation.

An advantage of markets is their flexibility in responding to changes in water values. Of course, there is the problem of valuing non-traded, public goods uses of water. But there are increasingly sophisticated mechanisms for quantifying non-market values for guidance in allocation. Another advantage of markets is that they can make reallocation routine, rather than relying on the political process, which, by definition, will be politicized and potentially contentious.

Meeting new and often conflicting demands for scarce water involve reallocation from past uses to new ones. Water markets may be more effective than the political and regulatory process for many reallocations. Even where provision of public goods requires limits on private water use, water rights may be purchased and retired. In that way, more voluntary and less contentious redistributions are possible. Markets, however, require the definition of property rights and the lowering of transaction costs. Useful public policy responses, then, are to provide for the clearer definition and enforcement of property rights to water and to lowering the transaction costs of trading those rights. Given the dramatic differences in observed values, water will be reallocated one way or another. The question is whether this will take place smoothly and routinely in a manner that minimizes waste or whether it will be slow, contentious, and costly. NIE and property rights theory provide the conceptual bases for understanding the challenges at hand and offer useful policy responses for addressing them. Given the critical importance of the water resource and the limited nature of current markets, this is a task worth undertaking.

# 14 Contracting and Organization in Food and Agriculture

*Michael L. Cook, Peter G. Klein, and Constantine Iliopoulos*

## 14.1 Introduction

The food and agriculture sector offers many opportunities to apply concepts from the new institutional economics (NIE). Indeed, some of the earliest modern studies on economic organization focussed on agricultural contracting such as cropsharing (Stiglitz 1974), land tenancy arrangements (Roumasset and Uy 1980; Alston and Higgs 1982; Alston, Datta, and Nugent 1984; Datta, O'Hara, and Nugent 1986), marketing cooperatives (Hendrikse and Bijman 2002), and markets for commodities like honey (Cheung 1973) and fresh fish (Wilson 1980; Acheson 1985). Food and agriculture contracting are particularly interesting because of their unique characteristics. First, agricultural commodities are produced according to biological production functions, meaning that their production schedules are often "fixed" by nature. Combined with the seasonal nature of production, this typically leads to high levels of uncertainty and physical, site, and temporal asset specificity. Second, because agricultural commodities are often highly perishable, monopolistic and monopsonistic market structures are common. Third, agriculture operates in a unique political and regulatory environment, with substantial effect on ownership patterns and economic incentives. Agriculture is often viewed by policy makers as a "special" sector, not only because food is a basic human need but also because the independent farmer – often in a highly romanticized caricature – is usually viewed as an essential element of a nation's character.

Operating in this unique institutional environment, food and agricultural producers have adopted a number of specialized institutional arrangements to increase productivity, improve quality and variety, and protect relationship-specific investments, among other objectives. Hybrid governance structures such as cooperatives and other forms of network organizations are common (Ménard 1996). Unlike virtually every other mature industry, commodity production remains dominated

292

by small, family-owned farms (Allen and Lueck 2002). Informal contracts are common. This chapter describes recent changes to the food and agriculture sector, and shows how concepts from NIE help to shed light on these developments. Until recently, economists approached the food and agriculture sector with the tools of neoclassical industrial organization. Market power in agricultural markets (typically monopsonistic, not monopolistic) was assessed by use of concentration ratios and Herfindahl indices, with the usual remedies proposed to increase competition (in the case of buyer power, this meant increasing, not reducing, commodity prices). Vertical integration was viewed with suspicion because it was typically seen as an attempt by monopsonistic processors to leverage market power. Unfortunately, these approaches left economists unable to explain the variety and richness of contractual arrangements observed in the food chain.

Beginning with a brief review of economic research on the food system, we turn to a discussion of vertical contractual relationships, followed by an examination of network organizations. The organizational forms dominating the governance of exchange in the food system are rapidly changing. Consolidation at every level – from input supply (seeds, plant food, plant protection, animal health products) to food retail – has been caused by technological advances, globalization, domestic and trade policy changes, and tighter vertical coordination across sectors and markets. Throughout the discussion, we show how concepts from NIE, transaction cost economics (TCE) and agency theory, provide valuable insights into the nature and evolution of the main organizational arrangements in agriculture as they adapt to these exogenous forces. Because of the vastness of the topic, we limit our discussion to several specific organizational arrangements.

## 14.2 Research on the economic organization of food: a brief history

Food system organization has been a topic of analytical interest since the seminal work by Bakken and Schaars (1937), but not until the 1950s did it gain its current academic stature.[1] Figure 14.1 describes the evolution of agricultural and organizational economists' thinking about the system. Davis and Goldberg (1957) introduced the concept of inter-firm coordination by referring to the post-Word War II phenomenon of increasing "unified functions" and "interdependency" between the agricultural production sector and the complementary input production and food processing systems. Subsequently, coordination studies evolved

**Get inter-firm coordination right**

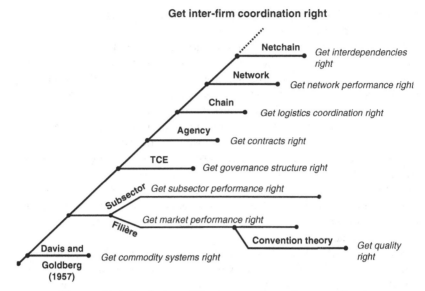

**Figure 14.1** Evolution of food system inter-firm coordination research.

along two loosely parallel levels of analysis: the study of coordination between vertical and horizontal participants within the food chain (inter-firm coordination) and the micro-analytic study of decision making within alternative food chain governance structures (intra-firm coordination).

Starting with an input–output model emphasizing dependence among sectors, Davis and Goldberg (1957) found that value-adding economic activities at the input production and processing levels were increasing while decreasing at the farm production level. Interest immediately arose as to how and why inter-firm coordination arrangements took the form that emerged within individual commodity systems. The first node in Figure 14.1 denotes this "Get commodity systems right" approach which focussed analysis on exchange coordination and harmony, particularly in vertical relationships among firms. Proponents of this approach argued that tightly coordinated systems would lower per-unit costs, increase system and participant profits, increase responsiveness to market demand, and, in many cases, increase output.

Shortly thereafter, a more theoretical yet complementary approach to agrifood system coordination emerged rooted in applied micro-economics and the workings of agricultural marketing researchers. Utilizing the industrial organization model, agricultural economists concentrated their analysis on two major issues: a market structure–performance approach to the agrifood system and analysis of the agricultural indus-trialization process. Evolving simultaneously, the French *"filière"* con-cept and the American "subsector" approach incorporated a more dynamic paradigm than the static, horizontally oriented, structure-conduct–performance approach of traditional industrial organization. "Getting market performance right" was the policy objective of researchers applying the *filière* and subsector approaches. Correcting for vertical market constraints, market failures, and coordination frictions motivated these schools to expand industrial organization models toward more integrative analysis of supply-and-demand conditions, price management relationships, and government–market interfaces. These schools of research emphasized a more dynamic research process and broadened the set of dependent variables to encompass not only efficiency but also social and equity measures (Shaffer 1983). More recent work (albeit efficiency oriented) extends these approaches to diagnostic research methodologies (convention theory) in the study of inter-firm coordination (Sauvée 1998; Boomgard *et al.* 1991).

As exchange in the global food system became more vertically coordinated, new frameworks for understanding vertical contractual relations emerged. Initially, researchers turned their attention to TCE. This "get governance structures right" approach to vertical systems introduced a set of concepts and tools for addressing the increasing importance of relationship-specific investments in inter-firm relations. As the food system became increasingly industrialized and regulated, more transactions were carried out in non-market, non-hierarchical arrangements. Consequently, hybrid governance structures became more important and contracts more complex. With the onset of more complicated contract design, contractual incompleteness became increas-ingly important. And in the absence of credible and enforceable contractual arrangements, the opportunity for a transacting party to extract appropri-able quasi-rents accruing to a relationship-specific investment led to the standard underinvestment problem.

Accompanying TCE, another contractual approach to understanding the inter-firm coordination process emerged. To address the role of contract design in tightly coordinated and owner-manager separated agrifood systems, agricultural economists began turning to principal-agent models. Applied studies of moral hazard and adverse selection represented by Lajili *et al.* (1997), Hayami (1998), and Knoeber (2000) demonstrate the breadth of applicability of this "getting contracts right" approach to the issue of inter-firm coordination.

By the 1990s, supply chain management (SCM) surfaced as an alternative paradigm. First put forth by logistics scientists as a method to improve technical efficiency in procurement and inventory control management processes, SCM soon developed a following among food system economists. Defined as an integrative philosophy to manage the total flow of a distribution channel from supplier to ultimate user, SCM has expanded into a more comprehensive coordination analysis approach. The unit of analysis is the coordinated chain, not the firm. Beers, Beulens, and van Dalen (1998) summarize the origins and conceptual background of the "getting agri-chain performance right" approach. But logistical inter-firm coordination analysis in the form of SCM was not the only academic methodology informing the understanding of the global food system. Exogenous forces such as increased liberalization of market policies, privatization initiatives, and globalization during the 1990s also had important effects on the organization of food production. Simultaneously, the adaptation of information technology and biogenetic technologies affected quality screening, animal safety, traceability, community development, and other sensitive social, environmental, and behavioral objectives (Van Hoek 1999). To analyze these more complex environments and the consequent challenges for coordination, new frameworks such as networking models, system simulation, ecological footprinting, and reverse logistics received increasing attention.

The "netchain" concept exemplifies this more complex modeling approach. The netchain, a set of networks comprising horizontal ties between firms within a particular industry or group, are sequentially arranged based on vertical ties between firms in different layers. Lazzarini, Chaddad, and Cook (2001) model how sources of value and coordination mechanisms correspond to particular and distinct types of interdependencies: pooled, sequential, and reciprocal. The reciprocal interdependency nature and the interdisciplinary origin of these organizational arguments create a natural platform to analyze vertical coordination in the agrifood system. Transaction costs and agency cost minimization play a major part in this approach to inter-firm coordination.

In short, as food production has become increasingly industrialized and globalized, and vertical and horizontal relationships more tightly coordinated, agricultural economists have sought new ways to understand the complex organizational arrangements they observe. As shown in this section, they have turned to various aspects of NIE.

## 14.3    Contracts and vertical integration

As the above discussion makes clear, many of the important changes in the food-system organization involve the relationships between input suppliers, producers, processors, and distributors. Of course, as food product attributes become more measurable and less like the generic commodities caricatured in perfectly competitive general equilibrium models, horizontal relationships among rivals become important as well. To date, however, much of the theoretical and empirical work in the economic organization of food and agriculture emphasizes the vertical dimension.[2]

As briefly explained earlier, the vertical structure of the agricultural production process has changed dramatically in recent decades. One of the most salient features is a rapid increase in contract farming. In the USA, for example, contracts now govern 36% of the value of all agricultural production, up from 12% in 1969 (MacDonald et al. 2004). The adoption of contracting has not proceeded evenly across commodities, however. Between 1991 and 2001 the value of rice production under contract increased from 20% to 39%. For cotton the increase was from 31% to 52%; for hogs, 30% to 61%; and for tobacco, less than 1% to 48%. For livestock commodities such as milk, hogs, and broilers, and for crops such as sugar beets, fruit, and tomatoes, contracts are the primary means of handling production and sales. In France more than 80% of the growers in the poultry industry operated under contracts in 1994, though the contracts varied widely in form (Ménard 1996).

Moreover, data on contracts tell only part of the story. For instance, Grimes, Plain, and Meyer (2004) report that the percent of hogs sold on the US negotiated cash market fell from 62% in 1994 to 12% in 2004, suggesting an increase in vertical integration to accompany the increase in contracting for hogs. Vertical integration is also common in the production of poultry, turkey, and, particularly, eggs. Similar trends are observed in Europe and other parts of the developed world.

### 14.3.1 Why contract?

What explains this increase in vertical coordination? Contracts allow parties to share risks and provide incentives for effort, quality control, and investment. Contracts may also reduce the costs of quality measurement and effort monitoring. And, as emphasized by TCE, contracts can mitigate the hold-up problem associated with relationship-specific investments. These are all important in agriculture, but the precise roles of risk, transaction costs, asset specificity, and other factors in determining the use and structure of contracts is subject to considerable controversy.

*Risk.* Much of the early literature on agricultural contracting, such as the work of Stiglitz (1974) on share cropping, focussed on the trade-off between risk sharing and incentives. Share contracts shift yield and price risks from farmers to commodity buyers, who ameliorate this risk by investing in diversified portfolios. More recent work, in particular a series of papers by Allen and Lueck (summarized in Allen and Lueck 2002), question the role of risk in explaining the particular features of agricultural contracting. They show, for example, that riskier crops are more likely to be associated with fixed-rent contracts, rather than share contracts, contrary to the predictions of standard agency models. Moreover, individuals often act simultaneously as principal in one transaction and agent in another, making it unlikely that contracting arises in response to differences in individuals' tolerances for risk. Allen and Lueck (2002) suggest instead that contracts serve primarily to reduce measurement costs and mitigate moral hazard problems arising from the unique characteristics of land.[3]

*Asset specificity and uncertainty.* Many studies use a TCE framework to explain the time-series and cross-sectional variety of observed contractual arrangements, focussing on the roles of asset specificity and uncertainty (Frank and Henderson 1992; Martinez 1999, 2002; Masten 2001; Ménard and Klein 2004). Egg production is highly vertically integrated while poultry and turkey production rely more on production contracts. All these production and transformation processes are increasingly mechanized and subject to quality standards that require highly specialized equipment. Egg, poultry, and turkey production is characterized by high degrees of physical asset specificity, and, because of perishability, site- and temporal-specificity. Because hogs can be transported greater distances without losing value, and may be slaughtered at different ages, site and temporal specificities are less important in the pork industry where (less tightly coordinated) marketing contracts appear sufficient to mitigate opportunism.

*Quality control.* Tight vertical control can also improve quality control, which is increasingly important as consumers increase their demands for quality, safety, and traceability. In the EU, new regulations making large retailers liable for the quality and identity preservation of the food they sell impose a new set of problems that vertical coordination may alleviate. Similarly, new quality certification and grading systems for protecting consumers that have emerged in Europe over the last ten years require tighter coordination. Recent studies on agricultural contracting in France and in the EU (Mazé 2002; Raynaud, Sauvée, and Valceschini 2002) show that contracts involve an increasing number of detailed clauses concerning quality and the control and monitoring processes which render inputs traceable, all of which require increasingly tight control of the supply chain. On the other hand, the need for flexibility – for instance, matching producers' livestock to the ever-changing quality needs of packers –sometimes leads to an increase in informal, relational contracting, rather than explicit agreements.

### 14.3.2   Small-numbers bargaining

Another reason for the complexity of vertical relationships in food production is the growing consolidation of food production, processing, and distribution. In 1920 the USA had about six and a half million farms with an average of 149 acres per farm. In 1997 there were fewer than two million farms, averaging 487 acres per farm. It is estimated that less than 350,000 farmers generate 80% of the agricultural cash flows in the USA. The European situation is similar. In France, the EU's leading agricultural producer with 21% of total production in 2000, there were 660,000 farms that year compared with over two million in 1958. The average French farm in 2000 had 104 acres compared to half that area forty years earlier. The processing and distribution sectors are also becoming more concentrated. The twenty largest US grocers had a combined market share of 48.2% in 1998; up from 37% in 1992. The thirty largest European grocers held 68.5% of the market in 2001, up from 51.5% in 1992 (French and German companies dominate the top ten with 41% of the market).

At the same time, farming – unlike virtually every other mature industry – has remained largely a family-owned business. In the USA in 1997, "other than family-held," corporate farms owned only 1.3% of total farm acreage and generated only 5.6% of total sales receipts. In France, 75% of farms are family-owned with no employees. Allen and Lueck (2002) argue that this ownership pattern results from agriculture's unique combination of seasonality and random variation, which makes it difficult to design and enforce effective incentive contracts which minimize moral hazard. Instead, sole proprietorships, with the farmer or farm family as residual claimant, outperform joint ownership arrangements such as corporations.

The combination of dispersed family ownership and highly concentrated processing and distribution sectors poses unique challenges for vertical coordination and quality control over the supply chain. Contracts are rarely negotiated among "equals" in size and market influence, but between parties with very different characteristics. In the USA, marketing cooperatives were formed in the early twentieth century for this exact reason – to help small producers negotiate with large processors. Today, in many sectors in both Europe and the USA, formal negotiating bodies and hybrid organizational forms and networks have been established to handle contractual arrangements between diverse producers and an increasingly concentrated processing and distribution sector.

## 14.4    Network organizations

Collaborative or network organizations, such as joint ventures, cooperatives, and other hybrids have always been important in US and European agriculture. As the term "hybrid" implies, network organizations represent a blend, or compromise, between the benefits of centralized coordination and control and the incentive and informational advantages of decentralized decision making. Although network members pool significant resources, they often rely on relational contracts rather than formal written agreements, though they do establish some formal mechanism for coordinating.

Two complementary factors may explain the emergence of network organizations in the food and agriculture sectors. First, agricultural policy in most industrialized agricultural countries over the last half-century was designed to achieve restructuring while retaining family ownership. Coinciding with the major concentration in input distribution and food manufacturing, this dispersed ownership puts the coordination problem at the center of organizational issues. Second, consumers have increased dramatically their demands for quality certification. In Europe the certification movement began in France in the early 1960s, with a small group of poultry producers, and increased dramatically during the late 1970s. For instance, the high-quality segment of the poultry industry (the "red-label" system) represented over 30% of the French poultry market in 1994; up from 2% in the late 1970s (Ménard 1996). This system, made up of tightly coordinated groups of producers who agree to meet certain quality specifications in exchange for the right to display a special label, spread quickly to the pork and beef sectors and diffused to other European countries (in particular Italy and, to a lesser extent, the Netherlands and Spain). This evolution was formally endorsed by the adoption in 1992 of a certification system by the EU (Regulation 2081/92). In other European countries, quality certification has also become more important but is handled by private firms (brand-name certification) or quasi-governmental organizations such as the British "Meat and Livestock Commission."

As was the case with vertical coordination, we observe substantial variety in how these networks are organized. Three stylized types are identifiable. First, some networks are organized around a leading firm. The leader is often a large processor coordinating and monitoring a vast network of suppliers, eventually spread over different countries with different regulations and institutions. To manage these contracts while guaranteeing consistency and quality of supply and maintaining adequate incentives for producers, leading firms tend to rely on a stable network of producers. We see this model both in the USA (Knoeber 1989) and the EU (Sauvée 2000). A second, more "egalitarian," form of network organizes a large number of participants with similar rights and duties. The firms that developed the red-label system in France are a good illustration. To guarantee quality, reduce contractual hazards, and prevent freeloading among legally independent partners, mechanisms must be designed to monitor the partners. Coordinating structures tend to emerge with significant authority on the parties (Ménard 1996), such as Loué in the European poultry industry or Savéol in the market for high-quality tomatoes.

The agricultural organization most analyzed from a new institutional economics approach is the network referred to as a cooperative. Traditionally organized cooperatives, characterized by open membership, redeemable yet non-transferable ownership shares, and a residual claims based on patronage suffer from what Cook and Iliopoulos (2000) call "ill-defined property rights." These ill-defined property rights result in various conflicts of interest among members. Multiple mixes of selective incentives, degrees of decentralization, and coercion have been designed to ameliorate the internal conflicts inherent in these latent formal groups. Given the aforementioned globalization and industrialization forces, a rapid increase in producer heterogeneity follows, and consequently producer-owned and controlled organizations demand a dynamic and flexible design mechanism. Numerous hybrid cooperative organizational forms addressing these incomplete contract and property rights constraints have emerged recently (Cook and Chaddad 2004). One of these hybrids is the "new generation" cooperative whose structure is being adopted in Oceania, North America, and Europe. New generation cooperatives attempt to solve these ill-defined property rights by restricting membership, allowing transferability of equity shares, and making ownership rights unredeemable. Alternatively, rearranging certain ownership rights within the traditional cooperative structure may help to improve members' investment incentives (Hendrikse and Bijman 2002).

Because of their importance in the agricultural sector, cooperatives have been the focus of extensive study, but only recently from an NIE approach. Both TCE incomplete contract theory and agency theory studies attempt to explain the ownership rights, control rights, and incentives of these mutually owned and controlled governance structures.

*Transaction cost economics.* Organization economists have applied TCE concepts to examine two related questions: (1) What type of governance structure is the cooperative firm? (2) Under what conditions is the cooperative the least costly way to govern a transaction? Like all hybrids and networks, cooperatives combine elements of market and hierarchy. Members own the cooperative but remain independent, as the cooperative firm does not control its farmer members. And because of this ownership relation, transactions between the cooperative and its farmer-members are not pure market transactions. The relationship can best be described as contingency contracting since the value of the contract is contingent on the performance of the cooperative. In other words, coordination within a cooperative is similar to market coordination, with the added potential of member patrons influencing the cooperative's behavior and performance by ceasing to use it ("exit," in Hirschmann's [1970] terminology) or influencing its decisions through an elected board of directors (voice).[4]

In the first comprehensive organizational economics summary of cooperative issues, Staatz (1989) uses TCE to examine the conditions under which farmers benefit from forming a cooperative. The combination of small numbers in the product market, increasing asset specificity, and uncertainties associated with rapidly changing consumer demands, production technologies, and regulatory conditions puts farmers at a considerable risk in their dealings with their trading partners. Farmers may attempt to counteract opportunism by forming an association or lobbying the government to enforce particular contractual terms with input suppliers or processors. However, contract enforcement is costly in many situations, and internalizing the transaction by forming a vertically integrated cooperative may be beneficial. "Because farmer cooperatives combine elements of both vertical integration and contingency contracting, they may offer more ways of dealing with uncertainty than either investor-owned firms (IOFs) or bargaining associations," (Staatz 1987, p. 94). This is so because cooperatives' flexibility in pricing renders unnecessary costly contract renegotiation. In addition, the pooling form of payment in marketing cooperatives provides an income insurance function that reduces risk to individual farmers.

More recently Hendrikse and Veeman (2001a) utilize TCE to study the relationships between investment constraints and control constraints within an agricultural marketing cooperative. Employing a TCE framework, these authors develop a logical sequencing for members in deciding on the optimal form of governance structure subject to financial constraints. Analyzing temporal and physical site asset specificity hold-ups, TCE analysis informs the solution to the temporal hold-up and narrows the options to the solution of the second.

*Agency theory.* Agency models view the cooperative firm as a "nexus of contracts" between agents (managers) and principals (members, boards of directors). The key contracts are those that specify the nature of the residual claims and the allocation of decision control among the organization's stakeholders. Cooperative residual claims have unique attributes, not found in IOFs, which distinguish these claims from those found in other types of economic organization. Residual claims in cooperatives are restricted to patrons (i.e. cooperative members) and thus remain in force only in as much as the agents (members) holding them patronise the cooperative. Also, residual claims of traditionally organized cooperatives are not alienable, nor are they separable from any other agent roles in the organization. They are thus not marketable.

Cooperatives are generally complex organizations in which decision management and residual risk-bearing are separated, primarily because the main group in the organization consists of the customers or patrons for the organization's produced goods or services, who do not typically have the decision skills necessary to manage a complex organization. Agency problems arise in cooperatives because management and risk-bearing are separated and performed by specialized agent groups. And because the residual claims of cooperative organizations are not marketable and only incompletely redeemable, members lack the market information that would enable them to exercise more effective decision control.

Another agency problem in cooperatives is that the boards of directors consist, almost exclusively, of members who are not professional managers and who often lack the necessary information to practice decision control effectively. However, cooperative boards often excel at short-term decision making because they have direct knowledge of the near-term impact of management's decisions. This may not be true, nevertheless, with respect to long-term decisions.

Additional mechanisms for aligning cooperative directors' interests with those of member patrons include reputation – directors are often active in their local communities – and the threat of takeover from another cooperative or IOF. Specialized cooperative banks may also be in a position to limit cooperative managers' discretion. These farmer-owned lending institutions specialize in providing capital to cooperatives. Their experts can monitor lending agreements with cooperatives more effectively than can non-cooperative banks which have specialized knowledge of the cooperative form and the unique attributes of the agency relationships within cooperatives.

When analyzing the plethora of network forms in the food sector, an interesting question appears – who is the principal and who is the agent?

Eilers and Hanf (1999) use a principal–agent model combined with detailed fieldwork-generated knowledge to address the opportunistic behavior, conflicts of interest, asymmetric information, and stochastic conditions which emanate from detailed exploration of this issue. This work, heavily influenced by NIE, generates questions seldom raised and never analyzed in the context of agricultural marketing organizations. The approach offers insights and solutions where the manager, acting as principal or agent, offers a contract to a farmer and where the farmer, acting as agent or principal, offers a contract to the cooperative.

## 14.5    Conclusion

The global food system is in the process of radical transformation. This process, often called agro-industrialization, has two major characteristics: (1) production agriculture is becoming more specialized and dependent on outsourcing inputs and services; and (2) food-system participants are using tighter vertical coordination and networking between participants. NIE sheds light on several aspects of this transition, such as the replacement of spot-market exchange for increasingly complex contractual arrangements, and the emergence of new transaction-cost-minimizing structures, replacing spot markets, and exchanges organized by means of transaction-cost-minimizing governance structures. By endogenizing "institutions," organizational economists are beginning to crack open the institutionally rich sector of agriculture.

Several observations may be extracted from the review of agricultural contracts and network literature. The first is the rapid advance in the application of NIE approaches to the understanding of food and agricultural sector inter-firm coordination. Second, since the mid-1980s analytical approaches we recognize an increase in the number of more institutionally friendly theoretical developments, namely TCE, incomplete contracts, and agency approaches. Third, we notice an increasing emphasis on governance structure analysis – particularly emanating from the contract and network literature and analytical insights gained. Fourth, we observe that the analysis of the role of the agent and the role of the principal in inter-firm coordination decision making is increasing. This work is laying the groundwork for more sophisticated risk and influence cost research. The final observation – a plea is emerging from the authors and readers of this literature – in a field so rich in institutional organizational arrangements and complex institutional environments, the need for detailed, painstakingly thorough fieldwork becomes increasingly important in advancing the organizational economist's theoretical and empirical work in agricultural contracts and organization.

*Part V*

# Institutional Design

# 15 Buy, Lobby or Sue: Interest Groups' Participation in Policy Making: A Selective Survey

*Pablo T. Spiller and Sanny Liao*

## 15.1 Introduction

The participation of interest groups in public policy making is unavoidable. No society can be so repressed – nor individual's power so extreme – that decisions are undertaken by a narrow clique of individuals, without consideration of others. Its inevitable nature is only matched by the universal suspicion with which it has been seen by both policy makers and the public. Recently, however, there has been an increase in literature which examines the participation of interest groups in public policy making from a new institutional economics (NIE) perspective. The distinguishing feature of the NIE approach, as it is understood today, is its emphasis on opening up the black box of decision making with reference to, among other things, understanding the rules and the play of the game. Indeed, as Oliver Williamson (2000) says, "NIE has progressed not by advancing an overarching theory but by uncovering and explicating the micro-analytic features [of institutions] to which Arrow refers and by piling block upon block until the cumulative value added cannot be denied."

Thus, in this chapter we do not attempt to describe the vast literature on interest groups' behavior. Instead, we review recent papers that follow Williamson's NIE mantra. That is, these papers attempt to explicate the *micro-analytic* features of the way interest groups actually interact with policy makers, rather than providing an abstract high-level representation.[1]

We start this survey by emphasizing that to understand the role of interest groups in the modern administrative state it is fundamental to recognize that whilst legislatures enact statutes, and often supervise their implementation, it is bureaucracies which, via the administrative process, make and implement the bulk of policies. Consider, for example, telecommunications in the USA. For more than sixty years the main body of telecommunications legislation in the USA was the Federal

Communications Act (FCA) of 1934.[2] This piece of legislation specifically directed the newly created Federal Communications Commission (FCC) to regulate interstate communications so as to provide telecommunications services at "just, fair, and reasonable prices." Nowhere in the Act were there specific instructions about how to obtain that general goal. Furthermore, the Act presumed the existence of a monopoly supplier of long-distance services. The fostering of competition was not one of the stated goals of the Act. Even though the FCA was silent about competition, from the late 1950s until the Telecommunications Act of 1996 the FCC was engaged in a process of partially deregulating the long-distance and customer-provided equipment segments of the industry, which culminated with the passing of the 1996 Telecommunications Act. This process was partially triggered by various interest group actions, which included introduction of multiple pieces of legislation, continuous lobbying of congress and the agency, and, naturally, suing for policy changes in courts.[3]

Indeed, the potentially large distributional effects of legislation provide the affected groups with strong incentives to attempt to control what policies are made and how they are enforced. Thus, much of interest group action in the modern administrative state is geared toward influencing the implementation of, often vague, policies.

In this chapter we first discuss the role of interest groups in the policy-making process, and we then explore how this is affected by the nature of the institutional environments in which interest groups operate.

## 15.2    Buy, lobby, or sue

The literature normally refers to the activities of interest groups generically as "lobbying," whereby this term refers to actions such as transferring resources – normally in the form of campaign contributions, but also in the form of bribes – or information to policy makers. These two, however, are drastically different actions, and in this survey we will not follow the usual definition of lobbying as the quintessential interest group activity. Instead, we look at three main ways by which interest groups may sway policy outcomes their preferred way: *buying* influence; *lobbying* for influence; and *suing* for influence. Buying influence reflects the actions, often legal and sometimes illegal, by which interest groups may attempt to get decision makers (whether politicians or bureaucrats) to listen to their needs, and, they hope, act accordingly. Lobbying for influence consists of the various actions, also often legal, and sometimes illegal, by which interest groups attempt to transfer information to politicians and bureaucrats about issues (such as voters' preferences, impact of particular agency or legislative proposals, and so on) which may affect decision makers' political and bureaucratic calculus. Suing for influence is the art of using the judicial process to change the arena where the game is played, away from the legislative and administrative process, toward the judicial process. Judicial action may be pursued against a particular policy or its implementation depending on the nature of the case and, more importantly, the general environment in which the interest group operates.[4]

### 15.2.1 Direct and indirect influence

Buying, lobbying, and suing may take both direct and indirect forms. Interest groups pursue a *direct* action when the target of their action is intended to act directly on the matter, and pursue an *indirect* action when the target is expected to be persuaded into using its power to influence the actions of another party. For example, interest groups may lobby legislators with the specific intent of changing their votes on particular bills; or may lobby legislators with the intent that the legislators use the information to exert their authority to influence the way a particular agency implements a statute. Likewise, interest groups may make direct monetary contributions to legislators' campaigns so as to obtaining favorable votes on specific pieces of legislation, or to obtain their influence over actions of the bureaucracy. The dichotomy between direct and indirect influence is less apparent for interest groups' suing activities. The purpose of suing is to shift the arena of the game away from the legislative or bureaucratic arena, toward the judicial arena, expecting to obtain – via litigation – what the interest group was unable to obtain by other strategies. In this context, litigation may be used both in a direct or indirect fashion. Direct suing is an attempt to reverse a particular bureaucratic or legislative action, whereas indirect suing attempts to put the government – that is, a regulatory agency – on notice that pursuing particular policies might be extremely expensive.[5]

### 15.2.2 Buying

Legislator buying, the most publicized form of interest-group influence, has attracted the most attention from scholars and pundits alike.[6]

*15.2.2.1 Buying direct influence*   The classical interest-group literature focuses on direct vote-buying. Scholars model this interaction as a game in which interest groups compete with each other to capture legislators by making contributions (to campaigns, or illegally, for profit) in return for politicians' votes.[7] Empirical evidence on the pay-for-vote interaction between interest groups and legislators is, at best, inconclusive. Stratmann (1998) studies time patterns in Political Action Committee (PAC) contributions and finds that changes in PAC contributions are correlated with the voting schedule on relevant policies, independent of the electoral cycle. The extent to which direct vote buying by interest groups actually takes place, however, is unclear. Indeed, more than thirty years ago, Gordon Tullock (1972) asked the fundamental question of why there is so little money going to US policy makers. Ansolabehere, de Figueiredo, and Snyder (2003), investigating the size and make-up of political contributions, and their effect on politicians' behavior, find that, considering the effect of policies on interest groups' welfare, these groups give far less than they should, and, furthermore, that contributions have little effect on politicians' behavior.[8] These findings contradict the classic perception that contributions are made mainly to influence politicians' voting behaviors.

An alternative explanation for campaign contributions is that they are made as a source of ideological consumption. Bronars and Lott (1997) find that politicians in their last term do not alter their voting behavior significantly compared with their preceding term, indicating that interest groups contribute to politicians who are more aligned with their political views, rather than buying votes, a view consistent with campaign contributions being more a consumption than an investment activity.[9] Finally, campaign contributions could be the key to gain access to legislators.[10] Indeed, Ansolabehere, Snyder, and Tripathi (2002) find a strong connection between buying (campaign contributions) and lobbying, suggesting that campaign contributions may indeed be used to gain and maintain access.

*15.2.2.2 Buying indirect influence*    The "Congressional Dominance" and the "Separation of Powers" hypotheses suggest that the power of the legislature is not limited to the immediate effects of their voting outcomes, but extends to its ability to credibly threaten agencies with legislative action (such as a congressional reversal) if administrative outcomes deviate sufficiently from legislative preferences. The wide span of congressional power provides an additional venue for interest groups to control policy outcomes – through buying legislators' influence on bureaucrats and courts. A central element of the Congressional Dominance hypothesis is that formally independent agencies are not truly independent, as they are subject to continual – although not necessarily proactive – congressional oversight.[11] Thus, interest groups may also attempt to control policy outcomes through buying legislators' influence on bureaucrats or courts. Gely and Spiller (1990) show that the discretion of independent administrative agencies in any system of division of powers depends, among other things, on the composition of the legislature and the executive (i.e. on their internal cohesiveness and relative stance on particular issues to determine the threat of congressional reversal).[12] In a system of division of powers, however, full Congressional Dominance is a corner solution and requires a particular type of political composition of the legislature and the executive. Spiller (1990), for example, examines congressional budgetary decisions concerning regulatory agencies and shows that they reflect an internal rather than a corner solution. Thus, in political environments with divided governments, agencies do not always, nor fully, respond to Congressional desires. As a result, buying indirect influence may not always be an efficient or effective strategy for interest groups.

There is some recent evidence of buying indirect influence. De Figueiredo and Edwards (2004) find that telecommunications policy decisions by state regulatory commissions (in particular, interconnection charges) are closely aligned with campaign contributions to key legislators by both incumbents and new entrants. Indirect buying provides, then, a third explanation to the scant evidence concerning the link between campaign contributions and observable policy outcomes.

### 15.2.3  Lobbying

An alternative way for interest groups to exert influence is to provide legislators with valuable information. The purpose of this information is potentially to alter legislators' support for a particular policy.[13] We call the transfer of information "lobbying."[14] Interest groups may transfer information to legislators and other decision makers in various ways. Interest groups may, for example, participate in hearings, may directly provide background documentation, or organize protests. To be of value, these costly actions must transfer relevant information to decision makers, whether legislators, bureaucrats, or judges. The information may concern the value, cost, and distributional implication of a particular policy to the legislators' constituents, the saliency of the issue to the interest group's constituency, or the implication of alternative technologies or policy implementation.[15] The information transfer may be done after formal procedures, such as participating in congressional hearings and directly lobbying agency staff, or via informal means, such as participating in protests or demonstrations. As influence-buying, lobbying for influence may be direct or indirect.

*15.2.3.1 Lobbying for direct influence*    An interest group providing information about the consequences of a particular bill is attempting to get legislators to pay attention to that information when voting on the bill.[16] In recent years scholars have given much attention to the informal and formal rules by which interest groups engage in information lobbying, where the target of influence is usually presumed to be policy outcomes. A key issue in lobbying is the inherent bias in the information transmission process. Interest groups will only provide information when it is in their advantage to do so. Calvert (1985) shows,[17] however, that even biased information may be preferred to no information. From legislators' perspective, because politicians cannot eliminate informational bias if information arises from a single interested group,[18] legislators will benefit from facilitating access to multiple interests, even from those whose desired policy outcomes are not aligned with their own (Austen Smith and Wright 1994; Epstein and O'Halloran 1995; De Figueiredo, Spiller, and Urbiztondo 1999). From the interest groups' perspective, De Figueiredo, Spiller, and Urbiztondo (1999) show that, under some conditions, open participation by multiple interest groups cancels the information advantage each interest group may have vis-à-vis the politicians.

*15.2.3.2 Lobbying for indirect influence*    As it concerns lobbying for indirect influence, the information to be transmitted may be about constituents' interests or about agencies or courts' potential decisions. The interest group transmits the information with the expectation that the agency or court, knowing that such lobbying is taking place and that it will affect legislators' reaction to the proposed decision, will adjust the proposed decision accordingly.

Indeed, apart from the direct monetary advantages that legislators may obtain from interest groups' participation,[19] legislators may value interest groups' participation in the administrative process because of their informational advantage. Since policy outcomes can also affect re-election probabilities, or, more generally, a politician's career advancement, legislators have incentives to provide interest groups with access both to the regulatory process, and to themselves. This is the essence of the "fire alarm" theory of congressional oversight (McCubbins and Schwartz 1984), whereby congressional supervision is triggered by interest groups' detection of bureaucratic "misbehavior."[20] As agency delegation is the natural consequence of increased policy complexity, legislators find it increasingly difficult to supervise the growing bureaucracies. One way to solve the supervision problem is to create intermediary monitors, thereby increasing the bureaucratic hierarchy.[21] However, as De Figueiredo, Spiller, and Urbiztondo (1999) point out, interest groups have an important advantage over supervising bureaucracies in gathering information. Since interest groups' constituents are directly affected by policies, they are naturally motivated to garner policy-relevant information. While supervising bureaucracies require budgets and have to be motivated to undertake the extra effort, interest groups' research and monitoring activities are done for their own purpose, and, in general, do not require congressional funding, releasing congressional budgets for other purposes. This is the essence of the "fire alarm" strategy. Hojnacki and Kimball (1998) find that, all else being equal, interest groups are more likely to lobby friends than undecided or opposing legislators in committee. The results are consistent with the theory that interest groups often lobby not to change the minds of legislators, but to provide friendly legislators with valuable information to be used to influence other legislators or bureaucrats. On the other hand, as mentioned above, interest groups are biased, whereas supervising bureaucracies may be less so. As with direct lobbying, promoting multiple interest-groups' participation, including those in opposition to the politician, makes politicians strictly better off, as competing interest groups provide the greatest amount of information at the lowest cost to the elected official. De Figueiredo, Spiller, and Urbiztondo (1999) use this insight to explain the enactment by the US Congress in 1946 of the Administrative Procedure Act which increased interest group participation in public policy making.[22]

The Administrative Procedure Act (APA),[23] as well as most of the enabling legislation of regulatory agencies, set procedural requirements that provide for increased interest-group participation in the regulatory process. These procedural requirements stipulate that regulatory agencies must provide notice, must inform the public about proposed rule-makings, must make their decisions taking into account the submissions of interested parties, and cannot rush nor make decisions in the dark. In this setting, interest groups serve two important roles: first, they provide information to the regulatory agency about the state of the world; and, second, they provide information to legislators about their constituents' preferences. Both are important for the agency and its political masters. On the one hand, agencies are resource constrained and hence information about the state of the world is always beneficial. On the other, information about interest groups' preferences is important as it allows the agency to forecast potential political problems they may encounter at the legislature. The procedural restrictions on decision making also provide the opportunity for interest groups to attempt to thwart potentially harmful agency actions by lobbying for legislative intervention – McCubbins and Schwartz's (1984) "fire alarm" insight. Interest-group participation allows legislators to supervise the agency without having to be actively involved in the regulatory process, and hence limits the time that legislators have to expend in regulating regulators.[24] However, the information revealed through individual interest groups' lobbying activities, even if truthful, is naturally biased. Interest groups will not reveal information that will bring about a regulatory outcome that makes them worse off. APA's widespread facilitation of interest-group participation ameliorates the bias in information provided by each interest group.

Transferring information about constituents' interests also provides an indirect link between lobbying and policy decisions, whether by agencies or courts. Under the *Separation of Powers* hypothesis, courts, understanding that judicial rulings disfavored by a sufficiently cohesive legislature may be overruled by legislative action,[25] would select policies only among those that are immune to legislative reversal. By changing legislators' perceptions of their constituencies' preferences, lobbying may indirectly change the set of judicial policies that are immune to legislative override. Indeed, Iaryczower, Spiller, and Tommasi (2006) find that interest groups lobby more when the courts are more constrained by the legislature.[26]

In sum, the reason why the literature looking for a connection between lobbying or campaign contributions and policy outcomes has failed to provide a direct connection between lobbying and campaign contributions and policy outcomes is that it may have essentially been looking at the wrong place. As Iaryczower, Spiller, and Tommasi (2006) emphasize, "the empirical work on the impact of lobbying has been looking at the wrong policy dimension." Rather than considering the impact on the nature of legislation, empirical research should focus on the way the administered state operates, that is, via bureaucracies and the courts. In this sense, buying or lobbying for indirect influence ought to imply a stronger correlation between campaign contributions and lobbying to legislators and bureaucratic or judicial outcomes.

### 15.2.4 Suing

When buying and lobbying are inefficient or ineffective, the judicial process may still provide satisfaction. Interest groups may employ litigation as means to obtain what they could not obtain via buying or lobbying alone, such as the reversal of an adverse regulatory decision.

*15.2.4.1 Suing for direct influence* Litigation has been a major form interest groups have of influencing public policy. In the regulatory arena, issues as diverse as nuclear power and telecommunications have been fundamentally affected by litigation.[27] Interest groups' use of the judicial process, however, differs substantially across issues, indicating that interest groups differ in their expected returns from pursuing particular issues in courts, and tailor their participation choices accordingly. For instance, Olson (1990) notices that redistributive issues involving citizen groups constitute a disproportionate number of cases seen by the Federal Court for the district of Minnesota, consistent with theories that politically disadvantaged groups (such as citizen groups) who are weak in the legislative and administrative arena resort to work in the judicial arena more often than their politically powerful peers.[28]

*15.2.4.2 Suing for indirect influence* Because litigation is expensive (both monetarily and politically), complex, and time consuming, interest groups which can credibly commit to suing agencies may also use the threat of litigation to obtain policies advocated through their buying and lobbying processes. Via the threat of litigations, interest groups use litigations as a complement to buying and lobbying. Dal Bó, Dal Bó, and Di Tella (2006) highlight the use of judicial threats to discipline public officials, and show how concurrent uses of threat and buying magnify their policy effectiveness. The degree to which litigation threats may alter bureaucratic behavior, though, depends on the probability that the interest group is likely to win. Thus, the composition of the legislature and that of the courts affects the credibility of litigation threats. De Figueiredo (2005) finds, for example, that interest groups are most likely to challenge a Federal Communications Commission when the courts are more likely to rule against the administration.

## 15.3    Strategic choice of instruments

Given the multiplicity of instruments of influence available to interest groups, we now analyze how interest groups may strategically select their choice. Before a policy is implemented, interest groups face the choice of buying or lobbying, or both, and, if lobbying, to whom to lobby. Buying and lobbying are not equally efficient and effective for all groups. Indeed, Hillman and Hitt (1999) propose that the current stage of an issue's life cycle, the firm's monetary and informational resources, and the corporate environment that the firm operates in co-determines the firm's political strategies. For example, Ansolabehere, Snyder, and Tripathi (2002) find that unions and single-issue groups, whose objectives are more clear and partisan than other interest groups, tend to contribute rather than lobby. Such patterns are consistent with theories of strategic interest group behavior. More specifically, groups with large memberships can gain attention by their sheer number, and hence do not need to spend large amount of money buying legislators; groups with extreme ideologic preferences may not reflect a large spectrum of legislative constituencies' preferences, and may be better off engaging in direct or indirect buying (Ansolabehere, Snyder, and Tripathi 2002). Boehmke, Gialmard, and Patty (2005) take a step back and argue that, in fact, such strategic choices among lobbying venues are desired and designed by Congress. In particular, the ideological and jurisdictional differences between the legislature and the bureaucracy drive interest-group self-selection into lobbying activities, thereby revealing to the legislators the nature of the issue at hand.

Once a policy has been implemented, litigation may be the only strategy left to the losing interest group.[29] The optimality of litigation will depend on the relative ideological position of courts, policy makers and the interest group. Indeed, De Figueiredo and De Figueiredo (2002) show that lobbying falls with the probability that the court will reverse the agency. They also find that interest groups take the FCC more to courts when courts are ideologically far from the administration.

### 15.3.1 A model and empirical implications

To highlight the strategic use of instruments, we present here a simplification of a model of indirect lobbying by Iaryczower, Spiller, and Tommasi (2006).[30] There are three players: an *interest group*; a *court* with known preferences; and a *legislature* composed of legislators whose preferences, distributed on a continuum, depend on the state of the world, such as public support for particular policies. The game starts with nature determining the state of the world, and follows with the interest group determining whether and how much to lobby; the court, making a decision about a particular outcome; and the legislature reviewing the court's decision, and possibly reversing it by imposing an alternative policy. Following the standard *Separation of Powers* approach, the court will decide the case so that, given its information, the decision maximizes its utility subject to the legislature not reversing it.[31] It is assumed that the interest group has an informational advantage over the legislators on the state of the world. Using its informational advantage, the interest group chooses how much to lobby legislators, in an attempt to change their stance on the issue, thus indirectly changing the set of court rulings that cannot be overturned by the legislature. Since the court's optimal decision is in that set, lobbying affects judicial decisions. Thus: indirect lobbying.

*15.3.1.1 The model* There are two individual players: the court and the interest group,[32] and a legislature populated by a continuum of legislators with total size one. The policy space is $X = [0,1]$, and given ideal policy $z_i$, player $i$ has preferences over policies $x \in X$ represented by a utility function $u_i(x, z_i) = -\frac{1}{2}(x - z_i)^2$. Without loss of generality, we assume that the interest group's ideal policy is at the right extreme of the policy space, $z_u = 1$, and refer to policy $x'$ as being pro-interest group with respect to $x''$ whenever $x' > x''$.

Legislators and the court differ in their responsiveness to voters. In particular, we assume that the court is completely unresponsive to the position of voters in the policy space, and denote its preferred policy by $z_c \in X$. We assume, though, that legislators are at least partially responsive to voters' stance on the issue. Assuming for simplicity that the distribution of voters in the policy space can be characterized by a single parameter $\theta \in X$, we let the ideal policy of legislator $j$ be given by $z_{Lj}(\theta;\beta_j) \equiv \beta_j + \theta$, where for all $j$, $\beta_j > 0$ and $\beta_j < 1$. The degree of conflict in the legislature is captured by the distribution of points $\beta_j$ among its members, which we describe by the cumulative distribution $G(\cdot)$; that is, for any point $\beta$, $G(\beta)$ denotes the proportion of legislators for which $\beta_j \leq \beta$.

Given the extent of interest group activity, policy outcomes result from the interaction of the court and the legislature. Although the precise form of this interaction depends on specific institutional details, in most politics the elective body may ultimately impose its will under some sufficiently demanding procedure. We represent this idea by assuming that the court chooses a ruling $x_c \in X$, which the legislature can reverse with the votes of a majority $m \in [1/2,1]$ of legislators. We say that a court's ruling is "stable" in the legislature – and therefore final – if no alternative policy exists that a majority $m$ of legislators would prefer to it in a binary choice, and denote the set of stable rulings given the majority rule $m$ by $S_m$.

Legislators and the court are uninformed about the realization of $\theta$, and have common prior beliefs represented by the cumulative distribution function $F(\cdot)$ with density $f(\cdot)$. In contrast, the interest group is perfectly informed about the realization of $\theta$, and can potentially credibly transmit this information through costly actions – lobbying (participating in legislative or regulatory hearings, writing white papers, and even organizing strikes and public demonstrations). In particular, given a realization $\theta'$, the interest group can organize an observable level $a$ of actions bearing a cost $C(a,\theta')$. For simplicity we assume that $C(a,\theta) = a$ $(k - \theta)$, $k>1$; that is, the marginal cost of lobbying is decreasing in the pro-interest group stance of the population.

The timing of the game may thus be described as follows: (1) $\theta$ is realized and privately observed by the interest group; (2) the interest group decides a publicly observable level of lobbying intensity $a$; and (3) the court chooses a ruling $x_c$ in the set of stable policies in the legislature $S_m$.[33]

An equilibrium is a triplet $\Gamma = \{\gamma(\cdot), x_c(\cdot), F(\cdot\,|\,a)\}$ consisting of: (1) a strategy for the interest group, $\gamma : X \rightarrow R_+$, mapping "types" $\theta$ to levels $a$ of lobbying intensity $a$; (2) a strategy for the court, $x_c: R_+ \rightarrow S_m$, mapping observations of lobbying levels $a$ to stable rulings $x_c \in S_m$; and (3) beliefs $F(\cdot\,|\,a)$ by the court and the legislators so that:

(a)   $\gamma(\theta) \in \underset{a\in R_+}{\arg\max}\, u_u(x_c(a)) - C(a, \theta)\ \forall \theta \in X$;

(b)   $x_c(a) \in \underset{x\in X}{\arg\max}\{u_c(x) : x \in S(m|a)\}\ \forall a \in R_+,$ and ;

(c)   whenever $a \in \gamma(X), F(\cdot\,|\,a)$ is determined from $F(\cdot)$ and $\gamma(\cdot)$ using Bayes' rule.

*15.3.1.2 The Symmetric information benchmark*   We first characterize, as a benchmark, the symmetric information equilibrium. Note that in this case legislators are perfectly informed about the value of $\theta$, and the interest group derives no benefit from lobbying, irrespective of the preferences of the electorate. Hence, there will be no lobbying in equilibrium. The relationship between preferences of the electorate and policy outcomes in the symmetric information environment, however, is the key element determining the amount and effectiveness of lobbying in the incomplete information environment.

We start by characterizing the set of stable policies in the legislature given majority rule $m$. Letting $\beta_L^m \equiv G^{-1}(1 - m)$ and $\beta_H^m \equiv G^{-1}(m)$, it is easy to see that $S_m(\theta) = [z_L(\theta; \beta_L^m), z_L(\theta; \beta_H^m)]$. That is, $\beta_L^m$ is the critical legislator for a pro-interest group coalition, in the sense that any policy $x$ to the left of her preferred policy would be replaced by a more pro-interest group policy. Similarly, $\beta_H^m$ is the critical legislator for an

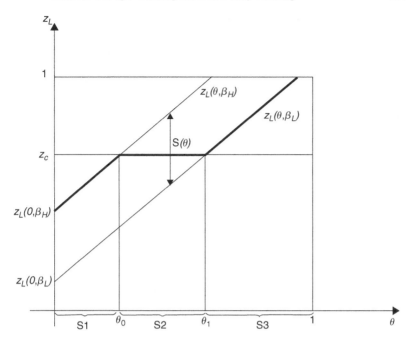

**Figure 15.1** Court's best response to information.

anti-interest group coalition, in that any policy to the right of her preferred policy will be replaced by a more anti-interest group policy. Note
that $\beta_L(m) \leq \beta_H(m)$, and $\beta_L(m) = \beta_H(m)$ only with simple majority rule
$(m=1/2)$, in which case $S_m(\theta)$ collapses to the preferred policy of the
median voter in the legislature, and the court has no policy-making
power. It follows that for $m > 1/2$, the set of possible court's ideal
policies that would be stable given $\theta$ has positive measure.

The court will then select its ideal policy unless it is constrained either
for being "extremely" pro-interest group or anti-interest group in relation to the relevant players in the legislature. In particular, since the
preferred policy of every legislator is strictly increasing in $\theta$, a higher
value of $\theta$ results in a pro-interest group shift of the entire set of stable
policies. A court with a fixed policy preference $z_c$ may then become a
"pro-interest group" court for a legislature observing a low realization $\theta'$
$(z_c > z_L(\theta'; \beta_H))$, or an "anti-interest group" court for a legislature
observing a high realization $\theta''(z_c < z_L(\theta''; \beta_L))$. Figure 15.1 depicts in
bold the resulting court's equilibrium rulings as a function of the state
of nature, $\theta$.

The two parallel lines in the figure represent the preferences of the critical legislators as a function of the state of nature, $z_L(\theta \,;\, \beta_L) = \beta_L + \theta$ and $z_L(\theta \,;\, \beta_H) = \beta_H + \theta$. For each $\theta$, the set of stable policies $S(\theta)$ is the segment between these lines, the interval $[\beta_L + \theta, \beta_H + \theta]$ in the vertical axis. If, for some $\theta$, the court's ideal point $z_c$ is in $S(\theta)$, the court will be able to rule according to its preferred policy, facing no effective legislative constraints. In the example depicted in the figure, this occurs for all states between the (interior) points $\theta_0$ and $\theta_1$. In this region, then, the flat portion of the bold line represents the court's equilibrium ruling. For $\theta < \theta_0$, however, $S(\theta)$ is entirely below $z_c$. Thus, if it were common knowledge among legislators that public sentiment is strongly anti-interest group, the ideal point of the court would not survive the challenge of more anti-interest group legislation. The best choice for the court in such states is, therefore, to enact the most pro-interest group *stable* ruling; that is, $\beta_H + \theta$. For $\theta < \theta_0$, then the bold line representing the court's equilibrium rulings coincides with $\beta_H + \theta$. Similarly, for $\theta > \theta_1$, $S(\theta)$ is entirely above $z_c$. In this sub-set of states the legislature is too pro-interest group compared with the court, and thus the best choice for the court in such states is to enact the most "anti-interest group" stable ruling; that is, $\beta_L + \theta$. Proposition 1 below summarizes the preceding discussion.

The legislature thus effectively constrains the court for some realizations of public opinion when the set $K = \{\theta : \theta \leq \theta_0 \lor \theta \geq \theta_1\}$ is non-empty. In other words, the court will be able to rule its preferred policy completely unaffected by public opinion only if this policy is both: (1) pro-interest group relative to the preferences of the critical legislator for a pro-interest group coalition before a pro-interest group electorate ($z_c > z_L(1; \beta_L) = \beta_L + 1$); and (2) anti-interest group relative to the preferences of the critical legislator for an anti-interest group coalition before an anti-interest group electorate ($z_c < z_L(0 \,;\, \beta_H) = \beta_H$). Note that, as in Gely and Spiller (1990), this condition is more likely to be satisfied when there is significant dissent in the legislature (the critical legislators for a pro- and anti-interest group coalitions are far apart, $\beta_L << \beta_H$).[34]

Moreover, in general, the size of $K$ increases with $\beta_L$ and decreases with $\beta_H$. Thus, the set of realizations of public opinion for which the court is effectively constrained is always smaller the higher dissent in the legislature. Hence, the overall effect of legislators' responsiveness to public opinion on judicial independence depends on the relative position of the court in the policy space.

*15.3.1.3 Informative indirect lobbying*  The previous analysis showed that when the court is constrained for some (publicly known) preferences of the electorate, an increase in $\theta$ induces a more pro-interest group ruling, and thus a more pro-interest group policy outcome in equilibrium. Iaryczower, Spiller, and Tommasi (2006) show that when policy makers are uncertain about the realization of $\theta$, lobbying by the interest group restores the complete information mapping between the preferences of the electorate and policy outcomes. In particular, they show that equilibrium lobbying increases with the realization of $\theta$ when, given $\theta$, the court is constrained by the legislature (i.e. $\theta \in K$), and does not change when the court is unconstrained ($\theta \in [\theta_0, \theta_1]$).[35]

That is, in equilibrium, the level of lobbying will reflect the preferences of the electorate up to the extent that this information may influence a binding constraint for the court (and thus policy outcomes). In other words, lobbying is effectively fully informative. As long as (informed) policy is responsive to the electorate's preferences, interest group types facing different pro-interest group dispositions of the electorate will always choose different levels of lobbying, allowing the reproduction of the complete information link between policies and the preferences of the electorate.

This does not imply, however, that the equilibrium will necessarily involve transmission of information. In fact, lobbying will be completely unresponsive to the preferences of the electorate if (and only if) the court is unconstrained for every possible realization of $\theta$. Conversely, there will be a complete separating equilibrium if (and only if) the court is constrained for every realization of public preferences. That is, only if the court's ideal policy is "extremely anti-interest group" (i.e. $z_c < \beta_L$), or "extremely pro-interest group" (i.e. $z_c > \beta_H + 1$), interest groups will choose different lobbying level for different observed values of $\theta$. This result allows us to develop the response of the expected level of lobbying and pro-interest group rulings to changes in the composition of the legislature. Note that for our purposes changes in the composition of the legislature are relevant only to the extent that they affect the boundaries of the stable set of policies in the legislature, $z_L(\theta;\beta_L) = \beta_L + \theta$ and $z_L(\theta;\beta_H) = \beta_H + \theta$. Moreover, recall from the analysis of the symmetric information benchmark that the set of realizations of public opinion for which the court is effectively constrained decreases with the degree of dissent in the legislature. That is, in general, the size of $K$ increases with $\beta_L$ and decreases with $\beta_H$.

Since the level of interest-group lobbying is decreasing in the constrained court ruling space, it is straightforward to see that a pro-interest group shift in the preferred policy of the critical legislator for a pro-interest group coalition $\beta_L$ (anti-interest group coalition, $\beta_H$) increases the expected pro-interest group tendency of the court's rulings level $E_\theta$ [$x_c$], and increases (reduces) the expected level of lobbying, $E_\theta$ [$\gamma$].[36]

This result has direct implications on the response of equilibrium outcomes to changes in court's preferences. First, the expected level of pro-interest group rulings will increase after a pro-interest group change in the court's preferences unless the court is constrained for every realization of $\theta$ both preceding and following this change. The change in the expected level of lobbying is, however, ambiguous.[37] Likewise, we know from the analysis of the symmetric information benchmark that the effect of legislators' responsiveness to public opinion on judicial decisions depends on the relative position of the court in the policy space. This implies that the relation between lobbying and the responsiveness of legislators to public opinion will also necessarily depend on the relative position of the court in the policy space.

*15.3.1.4 Empirical implications*   This model has direct and empirically refutable implications for understanding interest groups' lobbying strategies, as well as implications concerning the relation between policy outcomes and interest group activity. First, policy outcomes in the form of judicial decisions become more "pro-interest group" the higher the level of the interest group's political activity. In other words, in this model, lobbying influences policies indirectly, via judicial adaptation. Second, the expected level of lobbying decreases the more effective is the separation of powers between the court and the legislature (i.e. the more divided the legislature is on the relevant issues). Specifically, the level of lobbying is decreasing in the magnitude of the set of stable policies in the legislature.[38]

This model also has strategic lobbying implications. Consider Figure 15.1. In the figure, for a given set of preferences $z_c$, $\beta_H$, $\beta_L$, we can partition the set of realizations of the state of the world, $\theta$, in three areas. In regimes S1 and S3 (where the court is constrained either by a pro-interest group or anti-interest group legislature), informative lobbying takes place, whereas it does not in S2. Regimes S1 and S3, however, differ in the individuals over which lobbying effort is being exercised. While in S1[39] the interest group lobbies a *friendly* legislator (i.e. that legislator with a higher pro-interest group tendency), in S2, the interest group is trying to mollify the preferences of the relatively *anti-interest-group* legislator. In other words, lobbying becomes counteractive. In relatively bad states of the world, lobbying is focussed on *friendly* legislators, while in relatively good states of the world, lobbying is focussed on *unfriendly* ones.

Finally, although in regimen S2 lobbying becomes ineffective, suing is effective as legislators cannot agree to move the administration policy in any direction. Thus, we should observe litigation the more divided the legislature is on the interest group's issue, and the stronger the division of powers in the polity, a result consistent with the De Figueiredo (2000) study of telecommunications litigation.

## 15.4    Interest group participation in party-centered systems

The framework presented in the previous sections was based on an institutional environment resembling the separation of powers of the USA. In the USA, members of Congress exhibit remarkable longevity; they also tend to specialize in committees and to play an active role in policy making[40] and in overseeing public bureaucracy.[41] Outside the USA, however, legislatures often do not resemble the US Congress in terms of many or all of these above-mentioned features. This is particularly the case in the party-centered systems (Shugart and Haggard 2001) which dominate the world's democracies,[42] yet are also the least studied.[43] The US Congress is thus a rare outlier in the population of national legislatures, but the most commonly researched one. As a consequence, theoretical models of interest-group participation in the USA, although very helpful in generating general theory, are also limited owing to their status as case studies of an atypical case. In this section we focus our analysis of interest group participation in party-centered systems.[44,45]

Legislatures, and policy making, in general, in these countries differ considerably from their US counterparts. In party-centered systems, legislators may not stay for long in the legislature. As a consequence, they may have little incentives to invest in specialized legislative skills, or to control the bureaucracy. Similarly, in party-centered systems, the focus of policy making tends to be away from the legislature – with the cabinet (as in the case of unified governments) or the government party taking a more fundamental policy-making role. In these instances, interest-group participation in policy making drastically changes its nature. We explore these issues here.

In the previous sections we discussed how legislators benefited from interest-group participation, and thus, how legislators have an incentive to mold the institutional framework in which they participate so as to extract as much information from it as possible. We explore this incentive in alternative institutional environments here.

The key question for comparative work is whether the assumptions which drive the US case are appropriate in understanding how electoral rules shape legislative incentives elsewhere. In principle, non-US politicians are as strategic in their actions as their US counterparts. However, the political institutions which shape legislators' incentives do vary across countries: career structure, electoral laws, and party rules may be very different. The question narrows, therefore, to the incentives these politicians face in different contexts.[46]

For example, if party nomination is inconsequential for electoral success, as is the case for incumbents in the Brazilian Chamber of Deputies (Ames 2001), party renomination will play no substantial role in shaping legislators' behavior. Thus, the US-centered analytical framework may suffice.[47] In contrast, there are situations, as in closed-list PR systems, where nomination at the top of a major party list can virtually guarantee electoral success. In this latter case, legislators' behavior will be constrained by the renomination rules but is essentially unconstrained by the electoral process (Strøm 1997).

In federal countries with a closed-list PR electoral system, the process by which the provincial (district) party lists are formed largely affects which candidates run on each party list, what order they occupy, and, consequently, their chances of winning a seat in Congress. Hence, depending on the role which electoral rules give to local party leaders in the creation of the district-party list, local party leaders may or may not be key determinants of legislators' futures.

In many countries, where local and national party bosses dominate the construction of the local party list, legislators' ability to independently pursue a legislative career is substantially curtailed. Indeed, from legislators' perspectives, in order to pursue their desired career paths, they must maintain a good relationship with their local party bosses, not a good rapport with their constituencies. In some circumstances, such a good rapport may hinder their political progression. Party bosses have a complex political objective. They want to maximize the performance of their party in their province and or nation, but at the same time want to safeguard their position within the provincial or national party structure. The threat of challenge by popular legislators provides local and national party bosses with a strong incentive to reduce the national and provincial visibility of their underlings by rotating them among the various jobs the party can offer.[48] As a result, voters in these PR-based systems tend to vote for the party list, not for the individuals on the list.

Within this institutional context, legislators have little incentive to work hard to improve their visibility in the eyes of the voters, and no incentive to develop legislative policy expertise. A legislator may, at best, be marginally aided in his or her career progression by obtaining public visibility. However, policy expertise is not related to visibility, nor is it relevant for the candidate nomination and general election process. The institutional barriers to re-election, therefore, generate widespread "shirking," providing sub-optimal levels of effort both from an "informational" (Krehbiel 1991) and "institutional" (Fearon 1999; Ferejohn 1999) perspective.

Electoral incentives not only affect a legislature's organization (Weingast and Marshall 1988) but also the design of bureaucratic decision-making processes (Bambaci, Spiller, and Tommasi 2002). In party-centered systems where electoral incentives are centralized on parties, information will follow the same extent of centralization. Baron (2000), for example, shows how interest-group participation is less transparent – but not less active – in Japan than in the USA. Although there are fewer access points, interest groups are able to provide information (lobby) in a systematic, albeit informal and centralized fashion. In party-centered systems, administrative procedures such as the US APA have little purpose because there is no need to inform legislators of the bureaucracy actions. On the one hand, legislators in party-centered systems are not that interested in pursuing bureaucratic supervision. On the other, in party-centered systems with unified governments – such as those in Japan or the UK – the bureaucracy is under substantial control from the Cabinet, with the Cabinet having little incentive for providing the legislature with substantial powers to supervise its own actions. In sum, party-centered systems differ in the incentives faced by legislators and bureaucrats. As a consequence, incentives for lobbying are similarly changed (Bennedsen and Feldmann 2002).

The incentives for campaign contributions also change accordingly. There is little incentive in widely distributing campaign contributions in party-centered systems, as distribution to legislators may have little effect on their re-election, and their post-re-election behavior will be highly affected by the incentives of the political party bosses. Thus, as with lobbying efforts, campaign contributions will be highly centralized in key party decision makers (Bennedsen and Feldmann 2002).

Finally, litigation in party-centered systems may provide less satisfaction than in systems with stronger separation of powers. Because party-centered systems tend to narrow the separation between legislative and executive powers, courts possess a substantially narrower range of discretion. The courts are in a situation where overturning the bureaucracy may imply alienating the cabinet, which may, in turn, trigger retribution. Indeed, evidence from Japan and the UK suggests that progression within the judiciary is dependent on proper behavior vis-à-vis the government of the day.[49] Similarly, Iaryczower, Spiller, and Tommasi (2002) show that in Argentina, strongly unified governments tend to control the judiciary.[50]

## 15.5    Conclusion

In this survey we try to provide a framework to understand interest-group participation in public policy decision making. We show that politics in which legislators have an important policy-making role will tend to develop more transparent and direct interest-group activity. Conversely, politics where policy making is centralized in the Cabinet or the governmental party, though, will tend to reserve interest-group access to key decision-making politicians. The trade-off between campaign contributions, lobbying, and litigation is also affected by the nature of the institutional environment. As a result of the concentration of power in the Cabinet, litigation loses its power in unified systems, limiting successful interest-group activities to direct lobbying and buying. In decentralized politics, the full extent of complementarities between direct and indirect lobbying, buying, and suing become apparent.

These results suggest that interest-group regulatory reform must take the institutional environment into account in order to be successful in delivering the expected effects of increased transparency and improved public policy. It is one thing to implement reforms compatible with the institutional environment, rather than to force inconsistent reforms. A good example is Argentina, which in the middle of its privatization reform in the mid-1990s formally introduced interest-group participation in regulatory proceedings, in an environment in which legislators mostly play the role of a blunt veto player rather than having an active policy-making role.[51] Since then, the response of the executive to attempts by interest groups (mostly consumer and citizen activist groups) to thwart its public utility tariff policies has been the issuing of decrees, thereby sidestepping the formal regulatory process where such interest groups have an advantage, centralizing public policy making, and pushing interest groups to act in the legislative and judicial arena, where the executive has the advantage.[52] Thus, although the reform may have been well intended, its effectiveness has remained limited, thwarted by the intrinsic nature of Argentina's politics.

The late George Stigler admonished survey writers against making grandiose statements about productive future research topics, claiming that "Promising ideas are all that even a rich scholar possesses ... Rather than pursue the economics of scholarly advice, let me simply say that I have always thought that revealed preference is the only reliable guide to what a scholar believes to be fruitful research problems: If he doesn't work on them, he provides no reason for us to do so."[53] We will break apart from Stigler's admonition just a bit, and make the point that this survey has shown that we know quite a bit about how interest groups interact in open societies, such as the USA, and to some extent in Europe, but that there is very little systematic knowledge about their strategic choices in emerging and developing economies. Revealed preference shows our belief that much can be learned from expanding in less-chartered territories. Explore at your peril!

# 16 Regulation and Deregulation in Network Industry

*Jean-Michel Glachant and Yannick Perez*

## 16.1 Introduction

The reform of network industries represents one of the great structural transformations of the economy in the past twenty years. Vast in its scope (covering aviation, telecom, gas, electricity, railways, postal services, and so on), the reform of network industries is also exemplary in its economic content (Newbery 2000).

Previously, the unique characteristics of network industries appeared to set them apart from most other industries, deemed "competitive" (Kahn 1970–1971). The network industries notably feature: significant economies of scale or scope (extending to natural monopolies); far-reaching externalities (positive or negative) in production or consumption; and extensive vertical and horizontal integration (either under a single corporate umbrella or in the form of long-term ad hoc contracts). Within this very specific framework, the successful introduction of competitive mechanisms, substituting for administered regulation or internal corporate management hierarchies, along with the creation of open markets either up- or downstream of the formerly integrated networks, created disruptions and innovations in equal measure (Joskow and Schmalensee 1983; Baumol and Sidak 1994).

New institutional economics (NIE) suggests an analytical framework that differs from, and complements, standard economic theory (Brousseau and Glachant 2002). First, NIE construes market equilibria and prices as the result of an "institutional process for framing transactions" and fashions its analysis from the notions of *transaction costs* and *property rights*. The operation of the price mechanism is neither costless, nor instantaneous, so economic agents cannot benefit from its effects without becoming actively involved in the economic relationships which generate these market prices. Rather than rely on the "wisdom" of the economic calculus of government bureaucracies, the pioneers of NIE proposed creating markets by dismantling the public ownership of network industries (auctioning off property rights for radio bandwidth; Coase 1959) or replacing public agencies overseeing network monopolies with competitive mechanisms for allocating concessions (franchise bidding; Demsetz 1969). However, competitive mechanisms and market institutions are not the only efficient method for framing transactions. Indeed, a whole spectrum of effective alternative arrangements exists, including private agreements and public regulation (Coase 1960, 1988; Williamson 1975, 1985). The efficiency of any conceivable arrangement in network industries should thus not be seen in absolute terms. It remains conditional, and notably depends on the characteristics of the transactions in question.

The competitive reform of network industries has recently experienced a surge of expansion worldwide, with over two hundred new instances of sectoral deregulation between 1990 and 2005 (World Bank 2006). Nonetheless, subsequent to the California electricity crisis (2000–2001) there has been a burgeoning dissatisfaction with regard to the limitations, and in some cases failures,[1] of these new ways of framing network industries (Kessides 2004). We are witnessing a slowdown or, in some cases, a blocking of the reforms, as if the progression of competition policy in network industries had a cyclical component. This brings us to a deeper reflection on the nature of these processes.

The purpose of this chapter is to propose tools for analyzing the process of the competitive transformation of network industries and to shed light on the difficulties encountered. The chapter is divided into six sections. In Section 16.2 we present the first neo-institutional analyses which shed some light on the reform of network industries and emphasized their complementarity to standard micro-economic theory of networks. Whilst standard micro-economic theory delves into the logical underpinnings of rational price setting in networks, NIE focusses on the design of an appropriate institutional framework. In Section 16.3, we extend this basis of institutional analysis by distinguishing several dimensions of competitive network reform policy. In Section 16.4, we demonstrate that the launch of a competitive reform will not result in a credible industrial structure without the creation of a governance structure adapted to the new hybrid nature of the transactions. Although the sequential character of decisions and interaction effects make it difficult, *ex ante*, to define a governance structure that is truly adept at providing prolonged guidance to a lengthy process of competitive reform. Thus, Section 16.5 examines how to build governance structures *ex ante* that will remain adaptable *ex post* to allow imperfections and failures in the competitive reforms to be corrected. Section 16.6 reinserts the long-term evolution of competitive reforms into the framework of structural constraints of an institutional nature. Institutional environments, finally, comprise the ultimate constraints – with varying degrees of rigidity – to the long-term adaptation of the competitive reforms of network industries. It would be very bold to assume ultimate convergence with similar models of competitive functioning, since the reforms are starting from such widely diverging institutional environments.

## 16.2    Two theoretical paths: rational price setting versus adapted institutional framework

Since the middle of the nineteenth century, economic theory has had a particular interest in the problems specific to network industries. However, whilst micro-economics has extended the rationale for, and the foundations of, rational price setting, NIE has revealed the centrality of the design of an adapted institutional framework for managing the competitive functioning of network industries. Here, we present these initial neo-institutional analyses and emphasize their complementarity to the standard micro-economic theory of networks.

### 16.2.1    The theoretical path of rational price setting

For over a century, economic analysis persisted in defining the principal economic feature of network industries as being a "natural monopoly," and devised a rational solution in the form of optimal pricing of network use. The first micro-economic foundations for this theory of rational pricing appeared in France in the nineteenth century in the works of engineers building bridges and railways (Jules Dupuit and Alfred Picard). This work was subsequently taken up at Cambridge in the UK by Alfred Marshall and Arthur Pigou (1920), then in the USA.[2] During the 1930s, a wave of theoretical renewal of this rational price setting was founded on the general equilibrium systems of Leon Walras and Vilfredo Pareto. And, driven by the work of economists like Harold Hotelling (1938), Maurice Allais (1943), and Abba Lerner (1944), these theoretical developments culminated in the famous recommendation that prices be set at marginal cost ($p = mc$). Throughout the 1960s and 1970s, at least two generations of economists learned this from the textbooks of Paul Samuelson (1979). Finally, more recently, a third generation has emerged, notably represented by Jean-Jacques Laffont and Jean Tirole (1993, 2000), who have redefined the economic foundations of rational price-setting on the basis of incentive theory. Concurrently, in the UK Stephen Littlechild (1983) introduced the concept of a price-cap as an innovation applicable to the deregulation of telecommunications. Shortly thereafter he became the first regulator in the world to implement this innovation in the electrical industry.

Thus, for over one hundred years, from the middle of the nineteenth century until the 1970s, a broad theoretical consensus bound rational price setting in infrastructure monopolies to the very core of microeconomic analysis of the functioning of markets. This standard approach to regulating network industries was not subject to significant theoretical challenges.[3] At Cambridge UK – after introducing the notion of externality in 1920 – Arthur Pigou could have pursued the matter of institutional innovation, but neglected to do so. All of the solutions he proposes (taxes, standards, public ownership) derive from the only institutional innovation he retained from the war effort of World War I: the government is an alternative to the market in the "voluntary" administration of economic resources. In practice, externalities may be internalized in the price system by a tax, which later came to be called a "Pigouvian tax." Pigou did not devote any attention to alternative institutional forms, which could provide different solutions to various forms of market failure – of which he deems natural monopoly and externalities to be the most significant. The "Welfare Economics" he founded at the beginning of the twentieth century are thus nothing more than the economics of the "Welfare State."

However, starting in the 1930s and on several occasions over some forty years, a handful of economists (later designated "institutionalists") contested the conclusions and/or premises of the standard reasoning with respect to regulated network industries. To these first "institutionalists," – like Ronald Coase – the rules of the game that intervene, or which should intervene, in the normal functioning of regulated network industries are much more varied than only rational price-setting policy. Also, the economic nature of these rules of the game often differs from the simple promulgation of a price.

### 16.2.2 The theoretical path of the adapted institutional framework

In 1937, today's most famous "institutionalist" economist, Ronald Coase, questioned that prices are freely delivered to economic agents and, instead, advanced the hypothesis that prices are generated from market activity. Thus, these prices themselves had a cost: the cost of producing and disseminating market prices. Moreover, these market prices can only play a limited role in the coordination of behaviour within a firm in which "fiat" authority – an alternative mode of coordination – prevails. Ten years later, when the most distinguished economists in Great Britain recommended nationalizing all monopolies, claiming they could easily manage them with marginal pricing, it is no surprise that Coase (1946) publicly expressed his dissent. In the language that came to be his trademark, we can say that Coase did not believe it possible to use "blackboard economics" to create an optimal pricing system allowing all nationalized firms to be managed efficiently while rendering useless any recourse to real markets for framing real transactions.

Approximately one decade later, Coase (1959) contributed another family of analytical tools to his deconstruction–reconstruction approach to the regulated market. Radio frequencies, he claimed, are not by nature public goods, making it impossible to allocate them by an ordinary market for means of production. It is rather because the existing government regulation did not seek to create the property rights required for the normal functioning of a normal market. Public institutions were intended to regulate this industry in order to correct market failure. In fact, it was these institutional agents which lay at the root of shortcomings in the property rights system required for the good functioning of a market.

In a similar vein, Coase (1960) contested another pillar of the welfare micro-economics of Pigou and Samuelson. Of course the existence of negative externalities in production or consumption gives rise to failure in the market price system. However, according to Coase (1974), this does not necessarily imply that government intervention is preferable to private bargaining for managing externalities. In particular, in the absence of any private bargaining, how would the public authority be able to effectively compare the real economic value of various benefits and damages caused by externalities with the probable economic value of the various alternative remedies[4] proposed?

This contestation of the traditional institutional framework of government regulation reached a zenith toward the end of the 1960s, following in the wake of Coase (1960), with the proposal advanced by Harold Demsetz (1968) to eliminate the agencies regulating network industries and replace them with a competitive mechanism for attributing licences for operating network monopolies. The rationale is striking in its simplicity. The best alternative to competition "*in*" the market is competition "*for*" the market. If the core problem of network markets is truly the monopoly pricing of their services, then why rely on a governmental bureaucracy to tackle this issue in a clumsy and suspect fashion? There exist dynamic competitive auction methods to identify the lowest responsible bidder and provide the service at the best possible price.[5]

Then, the middle of the 1970s saw the arrival of a second wave of institutional analysis (notably Victor Goldberg [1976] and Oliver Williamson [1976]), which both completed and shed some perspective on the first wave of institutional contestation. These two authors underlined that some of the critical dimensions of the services rendered by network industries may go beyond only price setting. Other useful characteristics may be as important as the price, such as the quality of service, the localization of the service, its temporal-seasonal profile, the range and scope of options and potential for individualization, reactions to unforeseen randomness, and so forth.

In these cases, *ex ante* price setting does not eliminate the need for complex contracting *ex ante* and providing for appropriate controls *ex post*. In many other, non-monopoly, industries, the interplay of competition between producers and pressure from consumers provides the context in which transactions occur. However, in network industries, how could a periodic opening to competition, in the form of an *ex ante* competition on prices, substitute *ex post* for competition between producers and pressure from consumers? Outside of the mechanisms of competitive auctions, can consumers really contract *ex ante* with potential producers for non-price characteristics of future services, and then control and enforce compliance with these contractual service commitments *ex post*? We can well believe that some very large consumers may own both the means to contract *ex ante* and the control and reaction structures *ex post*. However, it is more realistic to assume that, for most consumers, this type of bilateral structure governing their transactions with network industries has little chance of spontaneously emerging from the free interplay of market forces. In this case, the rationale of transactions governance suggests a multilateral type of structure, in which large groups of consumers are represented by their "contracting agents." We are led to the conclusion that the construction of a competitive mechanism *ex ante* is no substitute for the usefulness of an *ex post* regulatory structure with complex service contracts and in which the *"right to be served"* implies a real power to sanction *ex post*.

Finally, drawing on assumptions that diverge widely from those of the post-Keynesian world,[6] Douglass North (1991) developed a new branch of institutional analysis to characterize institutional environments. In the "Samuelsonian" post-Keynesian world, the real and precise characteristics of society's general institutions were overlooked in economic analysis. We would, after all, be inclined to believe that open and democratic societies will have developed institutions that are at least reasonably competent, if not nearly perfect, to guarantee the efficient functioning of public economics and markets. In North's universe, we should start from the other corner: institutions are what they are ... nothing more. Also, there are not necessarily any "ready to use" solutions for creating a complete block of perfect institutions starting from the real world as we know it. Nor should we conclude that all existing public institutions have taken a solemn "public choice"-type oath to thwart all manifestations of economic efficiency in all markets. The institutions that actually exist must thus be rationally assessed for the effective capacity to efficiently guide the exact policies we expect.

However, in keeping with the work of North (1990), Aoki (2001), Barzel (2002), and Greif (2006), the characteristics that are truly important in real institutions are not easily renegotiable in the short or medium term. These real characteristics of existing institutions thus appear as true constraints on agents when they need to make decisions, elaborate strategies and interact. Thus, examining relationships between institutional environments such as they are, as we find in Douglass North and in Oliver Williamson's "Economic Institutions" (Williamson 1985) becomes a lynchpin of the analyses of network industry reforms.

## 16.3    Bases for institutional analysis of deregulation policy

Thus, the institutional analysis of the reforms in network industries is complementary to standard analysis. Clearly, institutional analysis recognizes that pricing and markets play or can play a key role in these industries, whatever they may be. Combined with standard analysis, institutional analysis splits the study of network industry reform policy into five segments, which may be separated and then recombined. However, any of these segments requires a robust institutional foundation to be properly implemented.

1. If network industries were solely sources of monopoly rents, then the simplest policy for dismantling a monopoly should be favoured: Directly open the markets wherever possible; set rational prices where that strategy is inadequate. However implementing such a basic policy requires the building of an effective coalition of public and private interests. Any demonopolization has to be made attractive to be able to succeed.
2. If highly protective industrial structures (vertical, horizontal, or spatial) shield these industries and make them unresponsive to governance by the market, it becomes necessary to contemplate industrial surgery, either prior to or after the reforms. The feasibility of such deep property rights reallocation is a "first-order" necessary condition.
3. If these industries have become immune to market forces because of a poor initial configuration of agents' property rights, it becomes vital to create institutional market infrastructures by reconstituting these

rights (definition, allocation, and protection). This is the central argument in the analysis developed by Barzel and North on the role of institutions and inter-individual agreements.[7]

4. If network industries are highly unresponsive to governance by the market owing to the nature of their transactions (as in Williamson: specificity of assets and uncertainty; or, as in Barzel: measurement difficulties), it becomes necessary to construe a governance structure that is adapted and /or a voluntary action for modifying the specificity of these transactions (*see* Glachant 2002).

5. Nonetheless, if governance by the market or governance by a third party is hampered by existing institutional environments, then the surgery of the reforms is confronted with an entirely new, and much more constrained, agenda. Finally, in that case the institutional surgeon needs to operate on himself to stitch up the institutional body differently: Dr Jekyll or Mr Hyde?

*16.3.1   Freeing the sources of monopolistic rents: the issue of the attractiveness of the reforms*

The abusive monopoly is, *a priori*, the simplest case for "blackboard" economic analysis, since it is sufficient to eliminate the monopolization of the rent to provide an incentive to market forces to enter the territory. The main practical problem in conducting this type of public intervention is that it requires the constitution of coalitions that actively support policies to dismantle the monopoly against those interest groups that have traditionally benefited from it (Stigler 1971; Peltzman 1976; World Bank 1995). To the extent that public government intervention is inspired by interest group coalitions that are opposed to other coalitions of interest groups, the future, potentially competitive, market is not necessarily a major force in the political economy of the reforms, a priori. Thus, as a team of researchers from the World Bank (1995, p. 10) observes "The reform can cost a government a support base, because reforms almost invariably involve eliminating jobs and cutting long-established subsidies."

Some of the interest groups benefiting from the status quo may have been traditional targets of government policy for a long time. The best-known of these policies are the European "public service" policies, guaranteeing certain social, territorial, or usage group access to services at a price comprising many transfers and cross-subsidies. Direct challenges to these perks by the government may prove very difficult; sometimes even impossible (Margaret Thatcher was unable to deregulate the British Post Office). Gomez-Ibanez (2003) has shown that, in developing countries, a reform will only be sustainable if it allows for just treatment of the interests of investors and consumers. This practical difficulty is not trivial from an analytical perspective, and institutional analysis characterizes it with the notion of "attractiveness of the reforms" (World Bank 1995). If no robust coalition of interests is built, the reforming pressure may dissipate before materializing or, after it is launched, become bogged down in the tortuous meanders of practical application. If the pro-reform coalition is not sufficiently solid, it could become necessary to exempt a substantial proportion of the vested interests in order to facilitate the launch of the changes. Thus, according to Moravcsik (1993, 1994), it is in the interest of European countries' governments to leave the responsibility of public service reforms in the hands of the European Commission – at the EU level – to the extent that these industries are too entrenched on the various countries' domestic socio-political scene.[8] Some countries' reform policies have thus remained incomplete – in the sense of traditional economic theory – and quite different from one country to the next; or from one industry to the next; or from one period to the next, when they fared poorly on the attractiveness test.

### 16.3.2 Revising industry structures: the feasibility of industrial surgery

Network industries may be unresponsive to governance by the market because they have built protective industrial structures over time. These may take the form of vertical, horizontal, or spatial (over contiguous zones of operation, sometimes smaller than the national territory) concentrations. These cases of industrial structures that are unsuited to market interactions may only be a particular form of monopolization, with the same dimensions in terms of attractiveness of the reforms, coalitions "for" and "against," and compromises making it possible to begin even when the initial conditions are less than ideal. This process is described by Spiller and Tommasi (2003): "Public policies and their features are determined by the functioning of political institutions such as Congress, the bureaucracy, and inter-juridictional relations ... The working of the political system (i.e. the rules of the policy-making game) constitute here the equivalent of the 'institutional environment' in Williamson (1993, 1996) ... Assume that the political game starts with a period in which players can make some agreements. This period captures the notion 'contracting moment,' a time when the parties reach an understanding about how they will restrict their action in the future."

According to these authors, the nature of public intervention will depend on the preliminary distribution of power across the various political and administrative institutions. This *ex ante* distribution of "rights to the reforms" is conceptualized as a game, the rules of which depend on the institutional environment (constitution, electoral rules, the effective functioning of the legislative and executive powers, and so forth). At the beginning, the "contracting moment," political actors fix the limits on their own actions in the subsequent periods.

Therefore, we understand that direct action on industrial structures prior to the reforms poses a quandary for public policy. *A priori*, public authorities (government, legislators, regulators, competition authorities) have access to a much broader slate of tools for modifying legislation and regulation than for overturning the organization of the ownership of industrial and commercial assets. There are few political and legal levers for fundamentally restructuring an incumbent, often very capital-intensive, industry around a competitive paradigm that will disrupt the financial and asset value of its industrial and commercial base. The government itself is rarely able to fully achieve the competitive restructurings of its own asset base. Even England was unable to escape that principle, and privatized British Gas as a monopoly and electricity as a duopoly, and so on. This is because a drastically pro-competition industrial restructuring will dissipate the receipts that governments may expect from their privatization programs.

In practice, therefore, the "industrial restructuring" phase of these reforms is the Achilles' heel of these policies. We saw this in the pioneering countries, the UK and the USA (Sioshansi and Pfaffenberger 2006), but also throughout the European Union (EU).[9] In many cases, during the initial phase of the reforms, implementation of industrial restructuring is intentionally dilute or makeshift to limit domestic opposition. Subsequently, after a market of some kind has begun to operate between the operators in the sector, it may be difficult to resume industrial surgery at the expense of stakeholders. Nonetheless, in practice many reforms strive to spread the magnitude of the desired changes over time and proceed in a progressive, sequential, and "modular" fashion. For example, European telecoms were initially deregulated at the terminals, then in professional services, then in the long-distance and cell-phone service and their new infrastructures, and finally in the old infrastructure of the local loop.

Competitive reform policies may also be implemented over transition periods that may last as long as a decade or two. Thus, the first European Directive on the "internal energy market" was voted in 1996. Its mission was to initiate the opening of the electricity and gas sectors. Seven years later, the second Directive of 2003, "harmonization" of the reforms, was to be implemented stage-wise through July 2007. And, since January 2008, a third Directive, focussed on intensifying the competition at the European level, is under discussion.

The voluntary segmentation of the reforms into successive modules presupposes, at least implicitly, that this will not significantly affect the trajectory of the reforms as a whole. However, this has not been proven, either theoretically or empirically. In network industries in which the infrastructures are not easy to duplicate[10] (railways and aviation, gas and electricity), the most basic form of reform modularity is the institutional separation ("unbundling") of the operation of the network infrastructures from production to final sales (which may be the transportation of merchandise or passengers, or the provision of energy). This separation of the two activity types protects against the spectre of "foreclosure" of infant markets. However, decisions about major investments and technology choice must be coordinated over long periods between infrastructure operators and competitive entrepreneurs.

Finally, the content of the initial industrial restructuring may be objectively difficult to define at the beginning of the reforms, owing to ignorance of the general architecture of critical details which will be revealed as critical only at a further stage. An initial leap into the unknown may subsequently produce all sorts of collisions between the various modules of the industry, or between its sequential components (examples abound from electricity in the UK and California). We have also found surprising offshoots, such as after-the-fact pressure for vertical or horizontal reintegration (Codognet, Glachant, and Plagnet 2003), and even some re-nationalizations of European railways and electricity (*see* Glachant and Lévèque 2007; Barquin *et al.* 2006).

The modular and sequential nature of the competitive reforms of network industries is thus a recurring problem in institutional analysis. Notably, it is a matter of establishing how structures built *ex ante*, at the launch of the reforms, might interact *ex post* with an institutional design that has either never, or only very recently, been in existence.

### 16.3.3    *Recasting industries that are constrained by the initial configuration of their rights*

When it is not a matter of rapidly freeing up a potential market which is already bogged down with the industrial structures and rents that are found with monopoly, another institutional problem arises. It becomes necessary to lay the groundwork for a new market in a milieu that always has been a stranger to all types of market relationships. Here, market failure is first and foremost endogenous – and it is deeply entrenched.

For a market to emerge, first the institutional foundations must be laid. Thus, the reform policy must explicitly address the market design, and not limit itself to "demonopolizing" the traditional industry. For lack of appropriate definitions, allocations, and protections of agents' new property rights, they will be unable to engage in market relationships. This type of reasoning has become common in radio and television, where the attribution of radio waves is performed with the sale at auction of licences. This also obtains for the frequencies of new telephony services, such as UMTS. We know that this was not at all the case in 1959 when Coase discussed the role of the FCC as communications regulator. Today, in the world of telecoms, the internet, and the digital economy, as innovation in processes and services accelerates, the creation of new "appropriate" rights becomes essential for developing all the new markets (Brousseau and Glachant 2002; Brousseau and Curien 2007). Here we may think, for example, of the configuration of the market for downloading music, which remains fragile in the absence of a better definition of the usage rights of the users.

In the field of transportation, the proposal to create real property rights for infrastructure users is still debated for the allotment of slots in airports or railways. However, this procedure has not become commonplace in practice. Even the use of auctions for licences to exploit infrastructure monopolies is not widely implemented. The UK, for example, did not use them in the water, gas, or electricity sectors, probably because this procedure would have driven down the sale or re-sale price of network concessions. However, this competitive allocation procedure has become commonplace for allotting exclusive supply contracts for services such as operating school cafeterias, school bussing services, London transit busses, and sometimes even for operating turnpikes. Likewise, the auctioning of private infrastructure concessions to supply services to large consumers is now a fundamental principle in the development of private urban projects in the UK (supplies of power or water to airports, to corporate manufacturing or shopping areas, and so on).

To internalize the negative externalities of pollution from $CO_2$ emissions, the EU recently introduced a system for allocating pollution rights that has become an international point of reference for the recourse to market mechanisms in a field that has traditionally fallen under the sphere of "pure" government policy (Boemare and Quirion 2002; Buchner, Carraro and Ellerman 2006). Similarly, to manage short-term externalities in the flows on electrical transmission grids, it is now possible to compute the economic value of congestion effects (at each minute) on each of the thousands of nodes on a grid covering a territory much larger than France. These computational techniques may be introduced into the conduct of "ordinary" auctions on a wholesale market for commodities, as is currently the case in the USA in the electrical zones named PJM (Pennsylvania, New Jersey, Maryland) or MidWest ISO, and, soon, Texas. Now market operators can even hedge against random movements in "nodal" electricity prices on a parallel market for financial rights to the revenues from electricity transmission (*Financial Transmission Rights*, as in Joskow and Tirole 2000).

Thus, all of these actual cases of competitive reform of network industries combine principles from NIE with principles from classical micro-economics. When industries have been rendered impervious to market effects by the initial assignment of rights, a market basis[11] may be recreated by reconfiguring these rights (their definition, allocation, and protection). The engineering of competitive mechanisms and the architecture of organized markets are disciplines that have become indispensable to the conduct of these reforms. Consider the design of the auctions for allocating radio frequencies, or the allocation of capacity for transporting gas or electricity, or the design of wholesale markets for power. Following Coase and Demsetz, we have thus been able to reassess the capacity of private arrangements and competitive mechanisms specifically designed to overcome failures in the standard market mechanisms. However, for all that, governance by the market has not become the unique universal mechanism for reforming network industries.[12]

*16.3.4  Adapting governance structures to the nature of the transactions*

Governance by the market is not a universal solution, applicable regardless of the nature of the transactions. The *ex ante* introduction of a competitive mechanism upstream from a transaction does not always yield the expected results when this transaction is performed *ex post*. Network industries may remain relatively impervious to "pure" governance by the market owing to the nature[13] of their transactions. To simplify, the difficulty of adequately framing the markets for certain types of transactions may come from the fact that these transactions require a cooperative governance type. Parties to these exchanges must continue to cooperate to conclude the transactions successfully, be it in the definition and normalization of the expected useful properties; the creation of ad hoc information and measurement structures, linked to the appropriate incentive mechanisms; the design of credible commitments and guarantees; the resolution of litigation; and even the future adaptation of their behaviours and arrangements to unforeseen eventualities of a significant and disruptive nature ("*coordinated adaptation*" in Williamson, or renegotiation).

These provisions for cooperative governance are not part of standard market mechanism, though they are not incompatible with some competitive mechanisms. The range and variety of governance structures adapted to these specialized transactions has not been fully counted. We can, however, identify several forms that are currently in use: bilateral, multilateral, or tri-lateral governance, with a private[14] or public third party (*see* Table 16.1).

To the extent that real markets for final services open up, the respective roles of third parties, whether public or private, may develop considerably. A public third party is not actually designed to provide an adapted, open-ended, and differentiated intermediation service between the consumers and producers of the service over a long period of time. By their very nature, public bodies are not adept at rapid and differentiated adaptation. To the contrary, they must comply with all the formal constraints of neutrality, prudence, impartiality, and due process imposed on the activities of all government institutions. And they must bear in mind that there are independent law courts above them to act as "courts of last resort."

Thus, to a large extent, the outlook for the reform of network industries is an expansion in the authority of private regulation, private governance, and private intermediation. As of a certain level of maturity, third party services in a tri-lateral governance incorporate a market, intermediate or final, on which intermediation services may be sold, either individually or as part of the final service ("rebundling"). At the end of this evolution, third-party services may end up as intermediation services like any other. For centuries, such intermediation services have been at the "transactional" heart of intermediation professions, such as the functions of agent and trader, wholesaler and retailer.[15] An alternative to this commercial normalization of intermediation services is the constitution of private intermediation clubs that operate as "production–consumption cooperatives," though these are likely to be the exclusive enclave of large agents – except in innovative and up-to-date "internet communities".

Can government authorities accelerate this "privatization" of intermediation services by limiting the specificity of assets used by network industries? In fact, the theoretical body of work developed by Williamson between 1985 (*The Economic Institutions of Capitalism*) and 1996 (*The Mechanisms of Governance*) insists on the existence of different forms of asset specificity, and that the treatment afforded to each of these forms cannot be the same. Glachant (2002) extended these initial efforts and applied them to network industries. The most important specificities of network industries are as follows: (1) site specificity; (2) physical

Table 16.1 *The principal forms of governance structures in network industries*

| | Examples | Limits |
|---|---|---|
| **Bilateral governance structures**<br>The "simplest" governance is a bilateral structure in which buyers and sellers collectively manage the definition and execution of their transactions. | The owner of a fleet of cars for transporting specialized merchandise; a micro hydro power plant linked by contract to an integrated electricity monopoly. | This simple form presupposes that the buyer and the seller invest in resources and skills. This is justified by the expected volume of transactions from a good "alignment." |
| **Multilateral governance structures**<br>Many multilateral governance structures are designed and spearheaded by groups of professionals, or professional associations, in the form of "user clubs," "normalization committees," or "panels." The roles of the many participants are symmetric. | The governance structure of the first English electricity wholesale market (Electricity Pool) worked in this way; the operator of the electricity transmission grid in Texas (ERCOT) still does. | In the event of significant disagreement between members, or between a specialized subgroup and the rest, decision making power falls to the general assembly of members having delegated the authority. |
| **Private and asymmetric multilateral governance structures**<br>This is the manner in which airlines group into alliances, operating shared reservation systems and capitalizing on positive externalities and economies of scale and scope in their scheduling slots, their flights, and their hubs, by selling combined packages. Microsoft validates the definition and controls the evolution of operating standards allowing the interconnections and interoperability that continually yield positive externalities between tens of thousands of innovating operators and hundreds of thousands of final consumers. | Private clubs<br><br>Microsoft | |

## Tri-lateral governance structures

The basis of the tri-lateral model is the permanent delegation to a third party the power to evaluate or decide on a defined set of data or events. An expert role is thus superposed on the roles of the participants. However, the expert does not possess asymmetric power vis-à-vis the participants.[i] When the expert also possesses asymmetric authority, it is, in fact, a "regulatory authority."

The most common case of an expert lacking asymmetric authority is that of a panel of experts. It may intervene *ex ante* to define shared rules of operation, and *ex post* to address conflicts between users of the network, or with their clients.[ii] The typical case of an expert with asymmetric authority is the sectorial regulatory agency (telecom, gas, electricity).

There are not always clear borders between multilateral and bilateral governance structures.[iii] The asymmetric authority conferred on sectorial regulators may motivate them to acquire an independent expertise and transform them into specialized judges, but still lacking a unanimously acknowledged level of professional competence.

[i] On the other hand, though the expert effectively participates in maintaining the quasi-rent by contributing to a good "alignment" of transactions, it does not have direct access to the mechanisms for disbursing this quasi-rent and, in particular, it cannot appropriate the quasi-rent to itself.

[ii] The delegation of regulatory powers to experts that are distinct from the sectorial regulator is also practised in Great Britain for handling conflicts between small consumers and the operators of network industries (for example Energy Watch, the independent gas and electricity consumer watchdog).

[iii] A number of multilateral structures frequently or exclusively resort to experts for various types of evaluations or decisions. This is because such recourse can simplify the functioning of multilateral structures and make them more efficient.

specificity (the procedure or product being "customized"); (3) the dedicated asset (production capacity with no other outlet); and (4) temporal specificity (adjusting production to consumption "just-in-time").

Only one of these forms of specificity, site specificity, provides a compelling argument for the integration of activities into a vertically integrated firm. This integrated firm thus constitutes the *ex post* governance structure for the transactions (Williamson 1985, chapters 4, 5, and 10). Site specificity characterizes the greater dependence of a "brick and mortar" network industry on its infrastructures. In contrast, physical specificity may normally be managed with competitive mechanisms if it can be detached from site specificity. Since, in this case, purchasers of the final service can themselves integrate ownership of the specific equipment. These purchasers can then call on several suppliers to compete for the use of their equipment, all the while retaining the ability to switch supplier. Thus, the competitive pressure on suppliers remains credible *ex post*. Furthermore, managing the specificity of dedicated assets can be facilitated by the *ex ante* reciprocal exchange of hostages, or by some other *ex ante* guarantee remaining credible *ex post*, such as "*take-or-pay*" clauses, or the creation of new marketplaces designed to promote the liquidity of exchanges (as "secondary markets" for transmission capacity, interconnection capacity, storage capacity; or coupling transmission capacity with the commodity – which is practiced in Europe under the name "implicit auctioning," and so on). Finally, temporal specificity requires an *ex post* governance structure, but several different governance types remain feasible. Temporal specificity may lead to vertical integration ("unified governance") if the dependence relationship between users and suppliers are very asymmetric. This is because, in this case, "bilateral" governance is not an adequate guarantee, *ex post* (Masten 1993, 1996). However, the management of interdependencies resulting from temporal specificity may occur within a bilateral structure if the commitments of the partners are relatively symmetric (Aoki 1988), or it may be efficiently monitored by a specialized authority in the case of a multilateral relationship (Ménard 1996, 1997; Glachant 1998).

In conclusion, we observe that institutional arrangements adapted to different forms of asset specificity cannot be reduced to universal recourse to government intervention. On the other hand, we must also consider the capacity of some types of targeted public intervention to either modify the nature of the contracting difficulties *ex ante*, or the characteristics of the adopted solutions *ex post*. Notably, there exist government policies to promote the interconnection and interoperability of network equipment and services *ex ante*. Everyone has heard of the success of the GSM standard in European cellular telephony or, conversely, the abysmal incompatibility of the electrical power engines on European railroads. It is less well known that the Treaty of Maastricht, which created the EU, contained an entire chapter dedicated to European policy for "major Trans-European networks" in communications, transportation, and energy.[16] By intentionally reducing the specificity of assets *ex ante*, government policy can expand the normal sphere of action of private governance.

## 16.4    Why building an appropriate governance structure is still problematic?

The idea common to all economic analyses in favor of the competitive reforms is that the creation of markets within network industries presupposes preliminary acts of "industrial surgery." Prior to creating these markets or seeing them appear spontaneously, it is necessary to end the traditional vertical and horizontal integration of the incumbent monopolies. Thus, those links that will permanently be monopolistic must be separated from those with competitive potential with as much precision as possible. This cannot be accomplished overnight – it requires incremental experimentation with new procedures for segregating activities that have been integrated for decades. Thus, there is a transition period during which the new markets are weak and the incumbent monopolies remain quite strong. Consequently, a governance structure supporting the competitive reform throughout this transition period is useful, even indispensable.

The duration of this transition period depends on many conditions, including the characteristics specific to each network industry. As early as 1985, Oliver Williamson foresaw that aviation and roadways would be easier to reform along sustainable competitive lines than railways or electricity. Aviation reorganized itself independently and durably[17] on the *"Hub & Spokes"* model with large airports and "private" interconnections between the flights of a single company or a pool of affiliated companies. At the same time, the design of the competitive electricity market remained heterogeneous and unstable, made up of many distinct industrial and transactional modules, variously disassembled and reassembled, and, sometimes, though not always, associated with competitive mechanisms or true markets. In fact, with regard to electricity reforms, which began in the UK in 1989–1990, the architecture of the competitive market design proved to be an unstable hodgepodge of market and non-market mechanisms. In keeping with the principle of separating monopolistic activities from those that are potentially competitive, the industry splintered into several distinct operational and transactional modules. However, the entire chain of all modules often required a more comprehensive and far-reaching governance structure than that provided for by the initial competitive paradigm.[18]

The electrical industry has proven itself unable to present a robust single competitive market design that garners universal acceptance or, for that matter, that is capable of instantaneously and simultaneously coping with all the new problems having arisen as of the launch of the competitive process. In practice, electrical industry reforms were highly sequential, initially accepting imperfect provisional solutions for this or that module and then staggering successive redesigns of the modules over time. For this reason, the creation of competitive electricity markets is much more frequently the result of the governance structure of the reforms than the direct or indirect offshoot of the legal or political actions (the *blueprint*, the *road map*) that initiated the reforms. The following schema shows this.

The initial market design, introduced by a road map is, in practice, only the first act in the construction of markets. These markets are then built sequentially, module by module, often in a different order, or rank, from one country to the next or (in the USA) from one state to the next. These various modules, which are not defined in the same way, nor implemented in the same order, are articulated around interfaces which may also be defined differently. It follows that the true nature of the interdependencies between modules varies considerably from one reform to the next, but also from the initial phase of the reform to later stages in its competitive evolution (Figure 16.1).

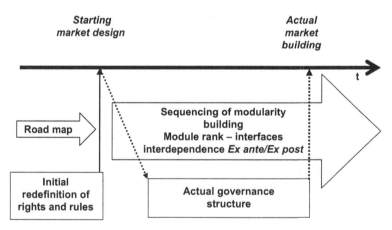

**Figure 16.1** From market design to market building: sequencing the reform modularity.

The true unfolding of reforms frequently appears much more like the *ex post* sequential construction of modules (*ex post* sequential modularity) than like an activity of *ex ante* market design. Here constructing "modules" means allocating tasks and assets among separated sets of tasks and assets names "modules." Thus, the building of competitive markets in network industries can combine up to three dimensions: (1) the overall separation of potentially competitive activities from inherently network activities ("unbundling"); (2) the segregation of all the operations and transactions of the industry into modules organized around various mechanisms for internal coordination ("modularity"); and (3) the implementation of the various modules in the chain to carry the competitive transactions (*"sequentiallity"*).

### 16.4.1   Competition where possible: the unbundling and its boundaries.

As emphasized by Stephen Littlechild (2006a), the first British regulator and inventor of the notion of Price Cap as applied to telecoms, the principle of "Competition where possible" is central to the reform of network industries and their transformation into vehicles for competitive markets. This type of division is expected to free competitive forces, on one side of the new boundary, and to concentrate the regulatory activity in the network monopolies, on the other.

For example, in the electrical industry, the high-tension transmission grid and medium- and low-tension distribution lines will be found on the side of the regulated monopoly, while the generation and sale of electrical power may be devolved to wholesale and retail markets. The regulator and the regulation, in turn, are expected to facilitate market activities and not substitute for the agents performing these activities.

However, the principle of unbundling assumes that there exists a "natural" demarcation, clear and robust – by nature almost technical, or at least technico-economic – between these two universes: the market for services and the infrastructure monopolies. Sometimes this is true. Roads and highways are infrastructures that may easily be differentiated from taxis, buses, and trucks. This remains the case, though a little less unambiguously, in aviation. Flight corridors and airport runways are clearly distinct from the airplanes chartered by airlines. However, it is also necessary to prescribe how these air routes and runways are to be allotted to the various users when the sum of all possible usage slots is less than the airlines' demand, in particular in the case of new entrants, and especially when these new entrants are the then famous "low-cost" airlines. Are the airlines' large hubs private infrastructures with strictly controlled access, or are they provisional private empires built on essential infrastructures freely accessible to all? A similar question arises with reference to telecoms. However, we generally consider that competitors to incumbent telecom operators have no difficulty duplicating their infrastructures and creating their own private grid, at least outside the local terrestrial loop.[19]

The same question is quite prickly in the case of electricity, because the service rendered is not storable[20] and there are no waiting lines. Furthermore, the entire supply–demand equilibrium is a global phenomenon, common to the entire industry and extending beyond the ownership boundaries of dozens of different generators or sellers of electricity.[21] In practice, it is not difficult to see why this issue of global equilibrium in electricity must be ensured by a third party with decision authority over all immediate and very short-term time horizons (from "real time" to one or three hours before real-time). Thus, the transmission grid must directly administer all short-term imbalances between the consumption and generation of power (*balancing*) and between the flows of current and line capacity (*congestion*). We observe here that activities specific to the network monopoly are very strongly enmeshed with, and weakly separable from, all activities that are characteristic of the competitive businesses. The very precise allocation of tasks and decision-making rights between competitive and monopolistic modules, as well as the detailed design of the interface mechanisms connecting these two module types, here continue to be central and decisive questions about the real nature of the competitive reforms. "Where are the activity boundaries and who sets them?"

### 16.4.2    Boundaries are set by "modularity" decisions

Boundaries between monopolistic activities and potentially competitive activities, like the boundaries between the firms themselves, between their respective tasks, and between their real or potential transactions and the corresponding markets, are thus not given once and for all prior to the launch of the competitive reform. Quite the opposite, these boundaries are primarily defined over the course of the long process of creating the reform. They are the result of segregating the industry into new operational modules. The competitive reform is thus a giant "*modularization*" of the network industry, a giant industrial and transactional "Lego set."

According to the most famous analysts of industrial modularity, Baldwin and Clark (2000), "Modularity is a particular design structure, in which parameters and tasks are interdependent within modules and independent across them." This technical definition of modularity is well suited to the new modularity of network industries. It nicely complements the work of Williamson and Joskow on "technological separability" which distinguishes between the hold technological constraints have within non-separable clusters of tasks and a strong institutional constraint on the design of interfaces connecting task clusters that are technologically separable.[22] To Baldwin and Clark: "The ideal of perfect modularity is full 'plug and play' flexibility." They then add, "but in a complex design, there are often many levels of visible and hidden information". Perfect modularity is thus not universal.

In the competitive reforms of network industries, the ideal of "perfect modularity," the hermetic separation of task modules having different natures, is far from universally implemented. The boundaries between modules split up by the competitive reforms remain porous to many leaks. Some modules retain interdependence between each other in their operational functioning, even if, of course, the interdependencies are stronger and more frequent within the modules than between them. Thus, it is useful to bear in mind, as a sort of benchmark, how perfect modularity operating within a perfectly designed competitive reorganization of the chain of tasks within a network industry would look.

Perfect modularity would define "independent task blocks," build "clean impermeable interfaces," and separate "hidden and visible information." Three invaluable characteristics would result for the process of performing these tasks. First, perfect modularity would increase the potential for managing complex chains of operations. Second, perfect modularity would allow the various modules of a complex chain to operate in parallel with a certain degree of autonomy. Third, and finally, perfect modularity would make it easier to react to uncertainty, provided the uncertainty was confined to a single module.

We recognize here the motivation for separating the professions and tasks, as well as the corresponding assets, in the initial implementations of competitive reforms. However, we must acknowledge that market-building often fails to reach that degree of perfect modularity in the competitive reforms. The actual modularity of the competitive reforms of network industries frequently consists of nothing other than a flawed chain of imperfect modules and faulty interfaces. Porous borders and non-exclusive interfaces have been inserted between the monopolistic and competitive module clusters, as well as between the specific modules. At the same time, incomplete rules of operation have been imposed within the various modules. It follows that all of this modularity remains flawed, notably with numerous operational "leaks" across modules. Thus, many direct dependencies persist in the operational functioning of a number of these modules, which are designated, in the jargon of

| **English Transport System Operator (TSO)** |
| --- |
| • Owns the assets and is a "for profit" company<br>• Plans and builds new lines<br>• Manages internal congestion with physical redispatching<br>• Manages connections with other TSOs as boundary<br>• Prices access with regional "postal stamp"<br>• Charges new generator connection with shallow costs |
| **American Independent System Operator (ISO)** |
| • Doesn't own the assets and is a "not for profit" entity<br>• Doesn't plan or build new lines<br>• Manages internal congestion with nodal pricing<br>• Manages connections with other ISOs as new nodes<br>• Prices access by calculating prices at each node<br>• Charges new generator connection with deep costs |

**Figure 16.2** An example of sub-modularity within the module "monopoly transmission network." (After Rious 2005)

economics, as externalities, on the one hand, and incompleteness, on the other.

Let us look at two examples of this issue of "imperfect" or "weak" modularity in network industries. The first is the co-existence of fundamentally divergent alternatives in terms of how to create competitive wholesale markets. In the electricity sector Chao and Peck (1998), Oren (1997), and Wilson (2002) have demonstrated that there are three different solutions to the structure of these markets: compulsory organized multilateral markets (*mandatory pools*), voluntary organized multilateral markets (*voluntary exchanges*), or markets that are uniquely bilateral (*"OTC" markets*).

A second example is the organization of task modules pertaining to monopolistic transmission activities, as Figure 16.2 shows.

The pivotal architecture of electrical networks is the transmission grid, since this transports the energy generated by power plants over long distances and on a huge scale. This component also underlies the spectacular "blackouts" that have shaken up this industry on several occasions since the beginning of the twenty-first century (USA and Canada, Italy, Denmark, Germany and France, and so on). Comparing the typical organization of transmission activity in the competitive reforms of the USA (the *Independent System Operator*; ISO) with its European analog (the *Transmission System Operator*; TSO) immediately reveals the diversity of the transmission modules put into place.[23]

In England, the transmitter is a private firm that is listed on the stock exchange, owns its own transmission facilities, and plans and finances investments in the grid. It manages congestions with the physical method of changing the electrical flows outside the market known as "redispatching." Accordingly, it does not transmit a direct price signal to the users of the grid who are liable to be at the source of this congestion. The cost of congestion is socialized across all grid users during periods of congestion (via a half-hourly "postage stamp" pricing). A direct consequence of this method for managing congestion is the existence of a real border, both physical and price based, that completely surrounds the zone administered by the transmitter. Furthermore, the transmitter charges the costs of transmission (especially the costs of infrastructures) in fees that are socialized across a regional grid, with a dozen or more "postage stamps" for generators and a similar number of other "postage stamps" for consumers. Finally, the cost of new connections to the grid are also largely socialized, since the hook-up fee does not account for the cost of adapting the network upstream from the point of connection. This method of pricing connections is called "shallow cost."

In the USA, most typically in the PJM zone (Pennsylvania, New Jersey, Maryland, and so on), the transmitter is composed of a club of electricity professionals. Thus, it functions as a cooperative, making no profits and distributing no dividends. This club does not own the transmission grid facilities, which remain the property of the incumbent operators. It is, however, their only operator. It is the *System Operator*, and is distinct from the proprietor of the network, the *Transmission Owner* (TO). From the point of view of ownership of the network equipment, this system operator is designed to be independent of the incumbents owning the grid, making it an "*Independent SO*," or ISO. This ISO neither plans nor finances investments on its grid. The users, generators, and distributors, take the initiative of requesting modifications or extensions to the transmission grid, and then pay for them fully. This ISO manages congestion with an economic method known as "nodal pricing," transmitting a direct and individualized price signal to each grid user liable to have an impact on congestion (by creating, exacerbating, or easing it). The cost of congestion is thus only borne by those who directly contribute to it, and only for as long as they to so, being calculated in very short time frames that are recomputed every ten minutes. Each of the thousands of nodes in the grid is handled independently, with a vast technical and economic program of costing congestion for each entry and exit node on the transmission system. That is why this pricing is called "nodal." A direct consequence of this method for managing congestion is that no real border exists, either physical or price-based, around the zone administered by the transmitter. Its zone is nothing other than a collection of computation nodes. To the extent that adjacent transmitters practice the same nodal method of pricing and collaborate in its application, there are no real borders between neighboring transmission zones. This ISO does not charge users the other costs associated with transmission (notably the cost of infrastructures) – they are recovered through fees that are socialized across a local grid and administered by state public utilities commissions (PUCs). Finally, the cost of new connections to the transmission grid is not socialized. The hook-up fee imposes all the costs created by this connection in terms of upstream grid development on the new user (called "*Deep Cost*" pricing).[24]

### 16.4.3  Sequencing matters

The various modules created by the competitive reforms are not perfectly modular: They were neither perfectly designed nor perfectly implemented. They also continue to sequentially interact in the actual functioning of the competitive reforms. When a new module, or a new interface between modules, appears, all of the modules of tasks and assets that are already in place may need to be adapted to the interactions in the new sequence. Thus, the order in which modules appear, or are reconfigured and adapted, is of great practical importance. The sequencing of the decisions in the construction of competitive modular chains is nearly as important as the actual structure of these chains.

This is why David Newbery (2002) emphasizes the importance of a solid reform strategy, which must include all of: the privatization process, the type of unbundling between monopolistic and competitive activities, the initial market design, the powers and functions of the sectoral regulator, and so on. According to Newbery (2002), "the logical sequence of events, some of which can happen simultaneously, is to first create the legislative and regulatory framework and institutions, and to restructure the state-owned ESI. Unbundling and corporatizing the generation companies, national grid, and distribution companies while they are still in public ownership can precede the legislation and setting up the regulatory agencies, but privatisation cannot. Unbundling generation from transmission will require a restructuring of any contractual relationships between the two."

Newbery stresses that the sequencing of the reform is critical, since it structures the behavior of the stakeholders by creating new interests and new rights over the various modules of activity and over the transactions that come into play between these modules. One of the most important consequences of this type of modularity is that certain models of network industry reform, while working well under some circumstances and in some areas, are not easily transferable elsewhere.

This phenomenon has already been examined in the analysis of institutional change developed by Masahiko Aoki (2001). His analysis sheds a good deal of light on the particular nature of this phenomenon. To Aoki, the explicit modification of formal rules is not the entire story in the matter of institutional change. On one hand, since an institution's influence on economic agents fundamentally relies on their "shared beliefs," it can only fully exercise its influence if agents believe in this influence. On the other, any particular institution is always party to a variety of interactions with related and complementary institutions.[25] Any creation of institutions occurs in a world that is already "saturated" – populated with other institutions. Consequently, the compatibility and complementarity between the new institution and other, pre-existing institutions are fundamental objective characteristics that define the new institution.[26] Aoki (2001) specifically notes that the overlap of existing institutions affects the evolution and combination of their activities. The prior existence of given institutions may facilitate, hamper, or sidetrack the desired evolution and the actual consequences of the creation of new institutions.[27] This is why, in theory as much as in fact, the *ex ante* choice of a good competitive reform strategy for entire blocks of industry is more difficult than some optimists had prematurely announced. According to Rufin (2003), "in these industries, the institutional framework plays such a crucial role that it provides an excellent setting for analyzing processes of institutional change."

## 16.5   Is "institution-building" a remedy to governance failure?

Building a complete industrial and commercial chain of modules that are sufficiently competitive thus involves long stretches of time, always exceeding one decade. This is why the governance structure of the reform of a network industry is, in and of itself, as important as the initial design of the very first competitive modules (Levy and Spiller 1994; World Bank 1995; Saleth and Dinar 2004). Why, therefore, at the launch of these reforms, are new governance structures not defined that are more suited to their specific nature? They would be more robust and reactive, and thus more conducive to prolonged adaptation of the industry and its chain of modules, until it finally reaches the stage of sustainable competition. This new way of thinking focusses on guaranteeing the final goal of *ex post* perfect modularity of network industries by the *ex ante* initial design of a perfect governance structure for the reforms. Unfortunately, this notion of perfect governance is plagued by numerous difficulties, not unlike the previous notion of perfect modularity.

### 16.5.1 Is perfect governance possible?

Building a governance structure for reforms that is perfect in the long term essentially consists of defining, allocating, and securing the rights to future implementations of the reforms. This is how the governance structure is able, when the need arises, to define and allocate new rights to be used by this or that industry stakeholders. These new rights, which would obtain in the future and could be useful for steering the course of the reforms after the start-up period, might combine with pre-existing rights – already defined and allocated and protected by assorted institutional guarantees, such as those studied by Pagano (2002).

The institutional hurdle encountered here is that all rights having existed for a long period are anchored in strong guarantees entrenched in their institutional environments. Thus, the notion of creating a perfect governance structure *ex ante* to steer the reforms over a long time horizon seems contradictory. Over the course of the long implementation of these reforms, the various stakeholders, whether private or public, and the new governance structure may, only sequentially, uncover the exact character and relevance of existing rights. Therefore, they can only intervene sequentially in the redefinition and reallocation of these rights in order to sequentially adapt the various modules of the industry and the markets[28] (Prosser 2005). This is because, in North's (1990, 2005) view, we only discover the long-term properties of existing rights and institutional changes by a process of trial and error, and sometimes by blind chance. How could we design *ex ante* a potentially perfect structure that, at some future time during the latter stages of the reform, only allows modification of rights that significantly block adaptations that are truly required? In Williamson's view, private economic agents are unable to create, *ex ante*, a perfect contract to frame their future relationship. And, similarly, according to North, public and private institutional agents are unable to build, *ex ante*, a perfect structure for reconfiguring industry modules and redefining the corresponding rights.

In real institutional change, the long-term governance structure of reforms can only act over the existing endowment of decision-making power and veto power. This endowment is structured by the combination of rights entrenched in the arrangement of the various modules of the reform. Thus, the long-term governance structure of these reforms cannot be immutable throughout the sequential rearrangement of the chain of modules. Any after-the-fact reconfiguration that was not anticipated *ex ante* may yield unexpected configurations of decision-making and veto rights *ex post*. Such undesirable developments may then successfully anchor themselves in strong guarantees that are vigorously protected by the most fundamental elements of the institutional environment (political, executive, and legal). In practice, those who are piloting the competitive reforms cannot do all they would like in the long term to significantly reshuffle rights that have already been acquired, even when major adaptations that were not foreseen at the launch of the competitive reforms become imperative. Institutional environments are inherently rigid, or semi-rigid, provisions that only rarely allow for a redefinition of existing rights.

### 16.5.2    The operationalization of North's analysis

The operational content of the competitive reforms thus acts as a set of rules and rights that constrain the behavior of economic agents and allow conflicts arising from such constraints to be addressed. Levy and Spiller (1994) emphasize that the real operational content of these reforms depends on the functioning of other institutional provisions, such as the legislative, legal, and executive framework specific to each country. Consequently, the institutional endowment of each country constitutes a unique context of guarantees and constraints which must be accounted for in the definition of the nature of the rules and governance structures of the reforms. Differing solutions for the reform may be required in institutional situations that are durably divergent.[29]

There are few comprehensive comparative studies of transformations from old regulatory systems into new, pro-competitive regulatory systems. Guasch and Spiller (1999) make a contribution that is central to network industries by analyzing failures in the legal system and their irrevocability. They present a model that analytically distinguishes between the notions of *"stability"* of the new competitive rules and of *"consistency"* with the nature of the institutional environment that prevailed at the launch of the reforms. In their analysis, the most stable institutional environments are characterized by the presence of numerous veto players, as they embody the principle of checks and balances. These veto powers are bolstered by the existence of administrative procedures which are quite strict and precisely define the procedures for modifying existing rules and rights, while providing for the right to appeal these changes to entirely independent courts of law.[30] The USA typifies that type of institutional environment.[31]

Analytically, we then move on to environments classified as "second-best" in terms of the stability of the competitive commitments. One of these second-best arrangements is found in another type of institutional environment, "centralization." This is the case in the UK. Here, a strong protection of the rights of economic agents is ensured by a special regimen of "professional licenses" safeguarded by private law and regular courts of law. Of course, this second-best cannot provide stability guarantees exactly equal to those in the USA, as it lacks both the credibility of institutional checks and balances, and the stability of the strict US administrative procedures.

Here the introduction of a supreme, "asymmetric" decision maker, endowed with the power to modify existing rights and future rules unilaterally, does not provide any greater long-term guarantee of the longevity of the reform's pro-competitive orientation. Consequently, we have to assume that the initial arrangements are close enough to an *ex ante* perfect configuration that only minor adaptations will be required *ex post*. However, had we begun from the opposite perspective, we would have needed to postulate the long-term necessity of making major *ex post* adaptations in the reforms, with a poor *ex ante* predictability of their future modalities. Thus, an institutional structure guaranteeing a great deal of stability *ex ante* – like in the USA – could ultimately constitute a major obstacle to necessary adaptations to the unexpected, *ex post*.

### 16.5.3    Accounting for the issue of adapting the reforms

As demonstrated by Macintyre (2003) (Figure 16.3), Tsebelis (2002), and Perez (2002), we can look for a more general analytical framework. This framework links "*adaptive governance*" of the reforms to the concentration of decision-making power, as expressed in the number of veto players in the institutional environment. Two issues with governance are thus identified. The first is the inevitably discretionary behavior of individual veto players. As the literature has amply demonstrated, an *ex ante* irrevocable commitment is necessary to guarantee the stability, and thus the credibility, of the competitive nature of the reforms (Levy and Spiller 1994; Weingast, 1995). But the second issue pertains to the paralysis of structures that are too decentralized with multiple veto players. This arises when accounting for all the *ex post* adaptation needs of reforms only appearing over a lengthy period of time (Haggard 2000; Macintyre 2003).

According to Weingast (1995), "government strong enough to protect property rights is also strong enough to confiscate the wealth of citizens." Some institutional systems are sufficiently strong *ex ante* to modify all the

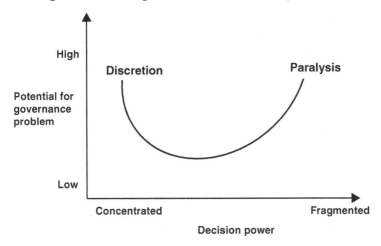

**Figure 16.3** The Macintyre (2003) introduction to veto player problems.

rules impeding the establishment of new competitive regimens in network industries *ex post*. Consequently, these systems are sufficiently powerful to create robust new governance structures capable of administering a drawn out transition to the new competitive order. However, governments with that much power have little political incentive to curtail the exercise of their own power and enforce a neutral long-term policy of establishing a competitive regimen in network industries. Such "strong" governments typically have other political agendas, characterized by another structure of interests in their political systems (for example France, or ... Russia).

At the other extremity of the institutional spectrum, "Fragmentation and dispersal of power stemming from the interplay of constitutional structure and party system leads to policy delay, gridlock, and immobilism" (Tsebelis 1995, 2002) (for example Belgium, Germany, and the USA). "Weak," or "relatively weak," governments are clearly unable to vigorously undertake grandiose reform projects on a vast scale. They prove virtually powerless to correct their course if it later proves that errors were made at inception or if major adaptations to the unforeseen are required *ex post*. This is because veto players can easily block any *ex post* developments to the reforms (as in the quandary facing local and federal authorities during the California electricity crisis of 2000–2001).

Consequently, to understand how the competitive reforms work out over a long period of time, it is necessary to combine the usual notion of an *ex ante* "institutional endowment," which provides the static environmental context for the reforms, with an analytical grid of veto players, as in Tsebelis (2002), to provide *ex post* illumination of the evolution and adaptation. A comparative analysis of government policy and the political economy of reforming network industries must thus make room for an approach in terms of veto points and veto players. A number of domains of government policy may be studied in this framework, and the literature is accumulating rapidly. The most elaborate approach can be found in George Tsebelis (1995, 2002), who, rather than explaining a particular policy, seeks to provide a unified framework for a variety of problems and institutional systems.

Veto players are actors, either individuals or groups, whose agreement is explicitly required for decision making in some fields of public policy. These veto players can be parties, institutions (such as a parliament or senate), independent government authorities (such as a sectorial regulator or a competition watchdog), or a self-regulating structure composed of different sorts of professional groupings[32] (Brousseau and Raynaud 2006). Application of this analysis to typical institutional environments is the subject of a growing literature. For example, Holburn and van den Bergh (2004) demonstrate how to influence the decisions made by focussing lobbying efforts at the swing voter closest to one's particular preferences. We assess the determinants of choices between three alternative instruments for influencing government decisions: disbursing funds (with, or without, corruption); revealing or manipulating information (this is lobbying proper); or litigation (*ex ante* or *ex post*). They show that the choice between these instruments depends upon their institutional effectiveness, and that this effectiveness is bounded by the structural characteristics of decision making in different institutional environments.[33]

The underlying idea – common to all approaches in terms of veto players – is simple. If certain actors, individuals, or groups, have true veto power, and may thus stymie decision making by withholding their consent, they will use this power to advance their own agenda and interests. They will, in fact, block anything counter to their own interests. This is why the institution's receptiveness to competitive reforms which are adaptable in the long term will be a function of three variables: (1) the number of veto players; (2) the objective gap between the ideal preferences of the various veto players; and (3) the internal cohesiveness of each collective veto player.

An analysis in terms of veto players thus sheds new light on the implementation of competitive reforms in network industries. Raising the number of veto players tends to increase the stability of policy conducted in a given system, and cannot reduce it. A high level of policy stability reduces the importance of being able to set the decision making agenda (a power that is typical, for example, of the European Council and the European Commission), since the individual responsible for setting the agenda will have a relatively small set of significantly different policies from which to select. This high degree of policy stability may also contribute to governmental instability in parliamentary systems, since governments will be less able to impose decisive results on the interest groups that support them. High policy stability may also lead some civil servants and bureaucrats to be much more active, or even activist. This is especially true in the case of independent authorities, such as sectorial regulators and judges, as well as for competition watchdogs, who act with the independence of judges. This situation may arise because of the inability of other institutions to coalesce and stake out strong preferences of their own or to block top bureaucrats from directly expressing their own preferences.

## 16.6 Is "institutional endowment" the ultimate (hard or soft?) constraint?

Throughout the world, a large number of very diverse countries have initiated competitive reforms in their network industries. Does the constraint embodied by the initial institutional endowments constitute a strong, or a weak, constraint on the achievement or longevity of these reforms?

### 16.6.1 The example of the English and German electricity reforms

The English competitive reform of electricity in 1990 featured five main structural traits. They were: (1) the vertical and horizontal unbundling of generation and distribution; (2) the vertical unbundling, and horizontal consolidation, of transmission grid infrastructures and the center of operation of the grid; (3) the creation of a mandatory centralized wholesale market (the *Power Pool*) and the prohibition of direct bilateral contracts on physical energy; (4) restrictions on the network monopolies and their services by regulation on the conditions of third-party access to the grid; and, finally, (5) the attribution of regulatory powers to a new independent sectorial authority (The *Office of Electricity Regulation*, or OFFER) (Helm 2004).

It is altogether noteworthy that not one of these points can be found in the German reform of electricity in 1998. Indeed: (1) neither generation nor distribution were vertically unbundled; (2) transmission grids and control centers were not vertically unbundled or horizontally consolidated; (3) there was no mandatory wholesale market; all exchanges being conducted by bilateral contracts on physical energy; (4) there was no detailed regulatory provision for the terms of third-party access to the grid; these third-party access terms were, rather, negotiated on a case-by-case basis between the parties; and, finally, (5) there was no energy-specific regulator (until 2005); the competent independent authority being the competition watchdog (the *Bundeskartellamt*), which essentially intervenes *ex post* in response to complaints received.

These pronounced differences between the German and English modalities of competitive electricity reform did not all appear by chance. Rather, they reflect the differences between their institutional regimens. In England, the government owned all the property rights on every component of the electrical industry; in Germany, the federal government owned none, while local and regional public authorities possessed a very large share. In England, the government fully controls the progression of the legislative process in parliament, and the government–parliament tandem possess full regulatory power over electricity, to the exclusion of all other public bodies (including the competition authority and judges). In Germany, the government is more reliant on accommodation with the Chamber of Deputies (the *Bundestag*). The federal government–Chamber of Deputies tandem must, in turn, share legislative and regulatory powers over electricity with regional bodies (the *Länder*) and their federal legislative representation (the *Bundesrat*) and with local public authorities. Legislation that is passed by a majority of deputies, but that jeopardizes the rightful powers of regional or local authorities, may be challenged before a constitutional judge. This is why, in the absence of cooperation and compromise between the various levels and instances of public authority, the powers specific to the federal government in the matter of electricity reform would not even be adequate for the creation of a German energy regulator endowed with ad hoc powers. It took seven years more and a second European directive to get a weak federal energy regulator.

This comparison of the English and German institutional regimens and their electricity reforms clearly reveals the impossibility of the German institutional regimen reproducing the strong structural modalities of the English electricity reform. Owing to its more demanding modalities, the English model for competitive electricity reform requires more coordination among the various authorities, executive, legislative, and regulatory, as well as more far-reaching powers for reallocating property rights.

### 16.6.2  The issue of convergence

The fact that institutional regimes diverge does not necessarily mean that they are intrinsically incapable of converging toward some competitive reform or other (Glachant and Finon 2000). However, they can only converge to some particular subset among all the possible competitive reform types. Comparing the electrical reforms implemented in England and Germany allows us to explore the potential for institutional convergence. Even though the English and German reforms effectively diverge in important ways, they do not appear to be systematically incompatible. True, the English reform does appear inaccessible to the German institutional regimen, but not the converse. Also, a "German-style" electricity reform has, in fact, been introduced in Scotland, which was under the jurisdiction of the same government and parliament as England at the time of the Electricity Act of 1989.

The institutional path dependency of competitive reforms is greater when veto players are not prepared to willingly negotiate a different orientation for the reform, including bilateral payments between each other, where appropriate. It is characteristic of highly decentralized institutional environments, such as Germany and the USA, that the interplay between veto players may easily stymie an intensification of competition in network industries. This is particularly true in the electricity sector, which is frequently very local in federal systems, with little federal ownership and in which federal power to induce industrial restructuring is limited.

Centralized forms of government appear relatively better suited for conducting this type of reform. The constraint of institutional dependence is weaker here, where central institutions cannot be blocked by other veto players. However, in Europe we observe that France did not succeed in following the English example, despite the fact that the French government owned the incumbent operators. In fact, these incumbent operators assumed the mantel of veto players. The upshot has been a decision-making duopoly, Government of France–incumbent operators, which continues to be the backbone of governance that is strongly bilateral, *ex post*, while the market structure remains highly concentrated with a limited competitive fringe (Glachant and Finon 2006).

## 16.7   Conclusion

Neo-institutional analysis of the competitive reforms of network industries is complementary to the micro-economics of rational pricing, since it accounts for the decisive role of an institutional framework adapted to new transactions. We have seen the importance of the political reform process, which draws on the conditions of attractiveness and feasibility to define an initial reorganization of property rights in these industries.

Once this type of reform has been accepted in principle, the crucial issue is the existence of a governance structure adapted to the transactional characteristics of these industries. We have identified three principal hurdles to the building of this adapted governance structure: where and when to introduce competitive mechanisms; how modularity organizes these various options of segregation and interface between competitive activities and network monopoly; and, finally, the profoundly sequential nature of the implementations of these reforms.

This is why the definition of a perfect governance structure presupposes an improbable perfect coincidence between the definition and allocation of new rights and their correlation with previously existing institutions and rights. The analysis in terms of veto players illuminates the difficulties adapting the initial design of the reforms in an institutional environment that will rarely tolerate several major reorganizations of the rights in effect. Thus, the need to adapt competitive reforms in the long term appears to be central to their analysis. This is revealed by the electricity reforms, for example. In this case, the institutional environment appears as the ultimate constraint on reforms to network industries and on their potential to converge to a sustainable long-term competitive framework.

# 17 Constitutional Political Economy: Analyzing Formal Institutions at the Most Elementary Level

*Stefan Voigt*

## 17.1 Introduction

The economic analysis of constitutions is a fledgling research program also known as "constitutional economics" or "constitutional political economy." It has broadened the standard research program of economics: standard economics is interested in studying choices within rules, thus assuming rules to be exogenously given and fixed. Constitutional economics broadens this research program by analyzing the choice of rules using the standard method of economics, that is, rational choice. Constitutional political economy (CPE) is part of new institutional economics (NIE) because constitutional rules are institutions. They can be considered the most basic layer of formal institutions.

James M. Buchanan, one of the founders of the new research program, defines constitutions as "a set of rules which constrain the activities of persons and agents in the pursuits of their own ends and objectives" (Buchanan 1977, p. 292). Defined as such, quite a few rule systems could be analyzed as constitutions: a firm's partnership agreement as well as the statute of a church. This chapter focusses, however, on the constitution of states.

There are two broad avenues in the economic analysis of constitutions: (1) the normative branch, which is interested in legitimizing the state and actions of its representatives; it is thus interested in identifying conditions in which the outcomes of collective choices can be judged as "fair" or "efficient"; and (2) the positive branch, which is interested in explaining: (a) the (economic) effects of alternative constitutional rules; and (b) the emergence and modification of constitutional rules.

To date, most contributions to the positive branch deal with the economic effects of constitutions, and only a handful deal with the emergence and modification of constitutional rules. In a sense, endogenizing constitutions is the core of the research program. Focussing first on the effects of constitutions seems a logical step, though, as if constitutions did not have any economically significant effects on economic outcomes, trying to explain the emergence of constitutional rules would be pointless. But by now, there is overwhelming evidence that constitutional rules do have important economic effects.

This survey is divided into three main parts: conceptual foundations; the description of recent trends; and speculation on possible future developments.

## 17.2    Conceptual foundations

This section presents the research program of CPE (*see* 17.2.1), describes the various concepts of the constitution used (*see* 17.2.2) as well as the tools used to generate positive knowledge (*see* 17.2.3), and, finally, relates CPE to NIE (*see* 17.2.4).

### 17.2.1    *The research program of constitutional political economy*

Normative constitutional economics could deal with a variety of questions, such as: how societies should proceed to bring about constitutional rules which fulfill some criteria, such as being "just" or "efficient;" the contents of constitutional rules; which issues should be dealt with by the constitution – and which left to subconstitutional choice; and what characteristics should constitutional rules have? Buchanan does not answer any of these questions directly, but tries to offer a conceptual frame to make them answerable. The frame is based on social contract theory as developed most prominently by Tomas Hobbes. According to Buchanan (1987, p. 249), the purpose of this contractarian approach is justificatory in the sense that ". . . it offers a basis for normative evaluation. Could the observed rules that constrain the activity of ordinary politics have emerged from agreement in constitutional contract? To the extent that this question can be affirmatively answered, we have established a legitimating linkage between the individual and the state."

The value judgment that nobody's goals and values should, a priori, be more important than those of anybody else, that is, normative individualism, forms the basis of Buchanan's entire model. One implication of this norm is that societal goals cannot exist. According to this view, every single individual has the right to pursue her or his own ends within the framework of collectively agreed rules. Therefore, a collective evaluation criterion that compared the societal "is" with some "ought" cannot exist, since there is no such thing as a societal "ought." But it is possible to derive a procedural norm from the value

judgment stated. James Buchanan borrowed this idea from Knut
Wicksell (1896): agreements to exchange private goods are judged
advantageous if involved parties agree voluntarily. The agreement
is supposed to be "efficient," "good," or "advantageous" because
involved parties expect to be better off with the agreement than without
it. James Buchanan follows Knut Wicksell, who had demanded the
same evaluation criterion for decisions affecting more than two parties,
or at the extreme, an entire society. Rules that have consequences for
everybody in society may only be judged advantageous if every single
member of that society has voluntarily agreed to them. This is the
Pareto criterion applied to collectivities. Deviations from the unanimity
principle may occur during a decision-making process on the production of collective goods, but this would only be within the realm of
the Buchanan model as long as the constitution itself provided for a
decision rule below unanimity. Deviations from the unanimity rule
would have to be based on a provision that was brought about
unanimously.

Normative constitutional economics thus reinterprets the Pareto criterion in a twofold way: it is not outcomes, but rules or procedures that
lead to outcomes evaluated by use of the criterion. The evaluation is not
carried out by an omniscient scientist or politician but by the concerned
individuals themselves: "In a sense, the political economist is concerned
with 'what people want'" (Buchanan 1959, p. 137). In order to find out
what people want, James Buchanan proposes a consensus test. The
specification of this test will be crucial as to which rules may be considered legitimate. In 1959, James Buchanan had factual unanimity in
mind, and those citizens who expected to be worse off owing to some
rule changes would have to be compensated factually. So the test would
be equivalent to a modified Kaldor–Hicks criterion. In the meantime,
James Buchanan seems to have changed position: hypothetical consent
deduced by an economist is considerd sufficient in order to legitimize
some rules (see Buchanan 1977, 1986). This position may be debated
because a large variety of rules seem to be legitimizable depending on the
assumptions of the scientist carrying out the test. Scientists arguing in
favor of an extensive welfare state will most likely assume risk-averse
individuals, while scientists who argue for cuts in welfare budgets will
assume people to be risk-neutral.

Often, representatives of normative constitutional economics use
social contract theory – not only for *justifying* certain constitutional rules
but also for *explaining* the emergence of the state. Such an endeavor is,
however, highly problematic. Individuals who would like to enter into a
mutually beneficial exchange are not able to do so because there is no

third party to give both of them incentives to stick to the terms of their contract. Since both players anticipate this, it is rational for both of them not to cooperate, but to defect. In other words, the prisoners' dilemma prevails. It is now argued that both could be made better off if there were a third player – the state – to force them to cooperate. Suppose that the players establish a social contract to settle their dilemma. This is an attempt to overcome their inability to comply with a mutually beneficial (private) contract by entering into yet another (now social) contract. Compliance with the social contract, that is, enforcement of the private contract, would make all parties better off. However, it is still dominant not to cooperate. The social contract needs to be enforced in order to enforce the private contract. This would require yet another contract, and so forth, which leads to infinite regress.

But suppose, for the sake of the argument, that the parties who failed to solve the prisoners' dilemma enter into a social contract and found the state with the intention of establishing an impartial arbitrator and an enforcement agency. They disarm themselves and endow a third party with the monopoly of using force. But what are the incentives for the third party to stick to its role of impartial arbitrator, instead of expropriating the two – now disarmed – parties? Here, the social contract needs some external enforcement.

If constitutional rules are assumed to be the most basic layer of rules, they need to be self-enforcing. Kirstein and Voigt (2006), for example, attempt to identify parameter settings ensuring that an autocrat with a comparative advantage in violence remains within the realm of a social contract. Another way to escape this problem is not conceptualizing constitutional rules as the most basic rule set. If constitutional rules are to constrain the governing, they might try to renege upon them in order to make themselves better off. If the governed are able to coordinate their behavior against such attempts at transgressing the constitution, the expected value of reneging might not be positive. Here, formal constitutional contracts need to be backed by informal conventions (*see* Voigt 1999 for more details). Both approaches thus stress the limited leeway that constitution makers have in passing documents if they are to become effective. Supporters of social contract theory sometimes neglect some of these constraints, and then commit what Hayek termed "constructivistic rationalism" or "rationalistic constructivism" (*see* Hayek 1973).

This section has dealt with the research program of CPE, and has described and assessed the approach of normative constitutional economics. Let us now describe the various meanings of the term "constitution" as used in this new research program.

## 17.2.2 Concepts of the constitution

### 17.2.2.1 The constitution as social contract

James Buchanan has not reinvented social philosophy, but has made extensive use of Thomas Hobbes and others. The situation from which the social contract emerges is the "equilibrium of anarchy," where marginal costs and returns for producing, stealing, and protecting goods are equally high. Individuals realize that they could all be better off if they agree on a disarmament contract allowing them to reduce the resources used for protecting – and stealing – goods. Since individuals find themselves in a prisoners' dilemma situation, they all have an incentive to sign a disarmament contract and to break it subsequently. As they all foresee this, they are nevertheless able to create a protective state to protect their private spheres. Additionally, they create the productive state to provide the society with those (collective) goods whose private production would not be profitable.

The idea that individuals create a state by way of contract is not meant to be a historically correct description, but simply a heuristic means. Buchanan (1975b, p. 50) considers it helpful not only for explaining existing institutions, but also hopes to be able to derive some criteria from it for evaluating them. The notion of social contract has often been criticized as being based on logical inconsistency: why should individuals be able to cooperate in the Prisoners' Dilemma (PD) of founding a state if the desire to found a state is driven by their incapacity to cooperate in daily exchange situations? The notion of social contract retains its important status, nevertheless, because it is the first heuristic means of assessing whether a proposed constitutional change may be argued to be a Pareto-improvement or not.

### 17.2.2.2 The constitution as incomplete contract

Supporters of NIE have convincingly shown that all contracts are – because of our constitutional ignorance – incomplete. This concept has been developed with business contracts in mind. But if we are interested in contracts used to bind entire societies the systematic incapacity to foresee all contingencies becomes even more obvious. The incomplete contract view is interested in setting up certain procedures to be applied if certain classes of contingencies arise. For example, an attempt to set up a constitutional rule that helps society choose the equilibrium (among a number of equilibria) which maximizes welfare or similar. Aghion and Bolton (2003) show that with a complete constitutional contract unanimity is an optimal *ex post* decision rule, whereas in situations where unforeseen contingencies may arise, societies might be better off to draw on less than unanimity *ex post* decision rules. They explicitly deal with the resulting trade-off between minority protection (which is maximized under the unanimity rule) and flexibility (which is increased by decision rules below unanimity). Other scholars who have lent support to the incomplete social contract approach include Jean-Jaques Laffont (2000) and Hans Gersbach (2004), among others.

### 17.2.2.3 The constitutional contract as principal-agent relationship

The principal–agent theory emerged from the observation that contracting partners often possess different information. A principal entrusts an agent with a number of tasks, but cannot observe the actions of the agent costlessly. In addition, the agent might have to act in situations too complex for a clear-cut assessment of the respective aim. So the agent has a certain degree of liberty to act, which he will use to optimize his own – and not the principal's – utility function. The main focus of the principal–agent theory therefore is on the design of the optimal contract under the assumption of asymmetrically distributed information.

Conceptualizing members of society as the principals, and the government as the agent, almost suggests itself. The problem is to draw up a contract – in this case the constitution – in such a way that agents will maximize the expected utility of the principals, while simultaneously maximizing their own. It is therefore normative theory. Merville and Osborne (1990) show that under a number of fairly restrictive assumptions, politicians only have a chance of being re-elected if they break the principal–agent contract, implying that elections do not function quasi-automatically as monitoring or enforcement mechanisms for the original contract.

### 17.2.2.4 The constitutional contract as pre-commitment device

The ability to credibly commit to our own promises can be a valuable asset and potentially benefit all parties concerned; for example if wealth-enhancing contracts are only entered into given a device that all partners can use in order to credibly commit to their promises. The most famous example of such a use of pre-commitment dates back to antiquity: Ulysses had himself bound against the mast to resist the singing of the Sirens. In economic speak, the problem of *akrasia* is often discussed in terms of time-inconsistent preferences. Whereas the principal–agent theory modifies traditional theory by taking asymmetrical information into account, the pre-commitment-approach contains a modification with regard to the imputed rationality of players.

If both individuals and entire groups may be subject to time-inconsistent preferences, are societies capable of protecting themselves from these inconsistencies using pre-commitment devices? This would presuppose that: (1) members of the respective society know their own weaknesses; (2) they possess adequate technology for pre-commiting themselves; and (3) a vast majority of the society's members, including its politicians, are willing to restrain themselves with such mechanisms. Weingast (1995) works within the commitment frame.

*17.2.2.5 The constitution as bundle of conventions*   Some scientists argue that the constitution cannot meaningfully be conceptualized as a contract, but that it is more comparable to social norms which emerge unintentionally, and which are accepted by most members of society in a general and unconscious way (Hardin 1989; Ordeshook 1992; Voigt 1999). Constitution making may then be considered an attempt to hasten the emergence of conventions and guide it in a certain direction. Hardin (1989, p. 119) writes: "Establishing a constitution is a massive act of coordination that creates a convention that depends for its maintenance on its self-generating incentives and expectations." Since the concept arises from dissatisfaction with, and in explicit distance from, the constitution as contract-notion, here are four differences between the two concepts: (1) a contract serves to solve a prisoners' dilemma; whereas a constitution serves to solve a coordination game that can, however, include a considerable degree of conflict; (2) in order for a contract to be valid, the explicit consent of the contracting parties is needed; whereas a constitution may be viable without the explicit consent of a majority, as long as there is no serious opposition; (3) enforcement of a contract is usually ensured by the availability of external sanctions; whereas a constitution is secured by the immense difficulty of establishing an alternative constitution; (4) contracting parties frequently try to take as many contingencies as possible into consideration, which often makes contracts static, whereas constitutions are more easily amenable to evolution.

This section reveals the many different ways of conceptualizing constitutions, which do not only lead to differences in the specific research questions dealt with, but also in possible policy implications. The next section presents some of the research tools used by CPE.

*17.2.3   Tools of constitutional political economy*

*17.2.3.1 Econometric tests*   Quantifying specific constitutional rules opens the door to applying conventional econometric tools. Ten years ago, very few adequate data sets allowing for such tests were available. This situation has changed dramatically and a vast number of studies based on econometric tests have been published in the meantime. Recently, however, many of these studies have been criticized as relying on inadequate – or even patently false – indicators (Glaeser *et al.* 2004). We will return to this criticism in Section 17.4.

*17.2.3.2 Comparative institutional analysis*    Comparative institutional analysis (CIA) is the attempt to identify the consequences of alternative institutional arrangements on various variables of interest to the economist, and to compare them. Supporters of NIE claim Ronald Coase (1964) was the first to use CIA in economics. CIA is a departure from another kind of comparison often observed in traditional theorizing, where an empirical result is compared with theoretically derived optima. In such comparisons, reality generally appears suboptimal and state interventions are often justified on these grounds. In CIA, however, we compare only realized with realized institutions and so avoid what has been termed the "Nirvana approach" (Demsetz 1969). Since the number of theoretically possible cause–effect relationships will often be high, concrete analysis will be confined to testing a rather small number of theoretically derived relationships. CIA is thus based on deductive reasoning; an evaluation not shared by all proponents of this approach.[1]

*17.2.3.3 Laboratory experiments*    *Homo economicus* is an extremely simple model that allows for accurate predictions. It is therefore tempting to test predictions in the laboratory, where conditions may be controlled. Over the last couple of years, it has been shown not only that many predictions are consistently falsified, but that subjects behave within certain boundaries and that their actions may thus be predicted on the basis of such experiments (Kagel and Roth 1995 provide an overview of this mushrooming field). Although a number of experiments have recently endogenized institutional choice, much more appears possible with regard to this tool.

*17.2.4    Constitutional political economy as part of new institutional economics*

After having looked at the various concepts of the term "constitution" used by different researchers, and having described a number of research tools, we now present this research program as a genuine part of NIE. Supporters of NIE ask very similar, yet broader questions: they analyze the (economic) effects of alternative institutions and the determinants for institutional change (*see* North 1981, 1990). Institutions may be defined as commonly known rules used to structure recurrent interaction situations that are endowed with a sanctioning mechanism which can be used in case a rule has been reneged upon. Constitutional rules may be subsumed under this definition of institutions. This means that CPE may be interpreted as part of NIE. This argument can be re-enforced by considering the tools used by representatives of both CPE and NIE: their toolkit is largely identical.

As long as constitutional rules are viewed as a specific kind of institution, NIE may be interpreted as the more inclusive research program. Surveys or textbooks of NIE might thus include the economics of constitutions. But they usually do not. Neither the book-length survey by Eggertsson (1990), nor the work by Furubotn and Richter (1997) pay special attention to constitutional rules (both surveys do, however, include a chapter on the theory of the state, in which the emergence of states is conceptualized using the economic approach). In short, representatives of both research programs seem to treat each other with benign neglect.

CPE could greatly profit from positioning itself within the broader NIE by explicitly taking two important issues dealt with in NIE into account: (1) the restrictions internal or informal institutions can constitute when trying to establish new constitutional rules by design; and (2) the very special commitment problems that loom large when trying to establish new constitutional rules.

## 17.3 Positive constitutional economics

### 17.3.1 Introductory remarks

Since the main focus of this chapter is on positive constitutional economics, we now turn to the questions dealt with by the positive branch of the research program. In broad terms, the positive constitutional economist is interested in two questions: namely, the (economic) effects of alternative constitutional rules, on the one hand, and how constitutional rules are brought about and changed, on the other. This section presents research on various constitutional rules. This includes electoral rules (*see* 17.3.2), horizontal as well as vertical separation of powers (*see* 17.3.3 and 17.3.4), and direct versus representative democracy (*see* 17.3.5). More topics would have been possible; some of them will at least be mentioned in the summary of this section (*see* 17.3.6).

Every topic is structured in a similar way: first, the effects of the constitutional rule in question are presented. Only in a second step are specific constitutional rules dealt with as endogenous. When constitutional rules are assumed to be exogenously given, they serve to explain different (economic) variables. Traditionally, economists look at effects on income and growth first. Other variables of interest include (*see* Persson and Tabellini 2003 for a similar list): (1) fiscal policy, in particular, the size of the government, the composition of government spending, and the size of the budget deficit; (2) rent extraction by the government, in particular, the perceived corruption of government and the effectiveness with which government provides public goods and services; and (3) composite measures of growth-promoting policies, such as the protection of private property rights that should then be reflected in labor, as well as total factor productivity. At the end of the day, all these measures should be reflected in per capita income and its – long-term – growth rate.

### 17.3.2  Electoral rules

The insight that electoral rules may have a crucial effect on the number of parties has been recognized for a long time. Maurice Duverger's (1954) observation that constitutions providing for first-past-the-post or majority rule often induce two party systems, whereas systems which provide for proportional representation often induce the existence of more parties, has even been coined "Duverger's law," in order to express its general validity. Although this has been known for a long time, occupation with the economic consequences of electoral systems has only just begun. It has been argued (Austen-Smith 2000) that since the number of parties presented in parliament is higher under proportional representation, tax rates will not be determined by one single party, but will be the result of legislative bargaining between various parties with different constituents. This would explain why tax rates are, on average, higher under proportional representation than under majority rule. Lizzeri and Persico (2001) compare the structure of government spending under alternative electoral rules. They distinguish between providing a genuine public good, on one hand, and of pork-barrel projects which serve to redistribute, on the other, and ask whether incentives to provide these goods differ systematically between systems with majority rule (called "winner-take-all systems" by them) and proportional representation. In majority-rule systems, politicians have incentives to cater to the preferences of those who can help them obtain plurality of the vote. They will do so by promising pork-barrel projects. In proportional representation systems, targeting makes less sense because every vote counts, which is why politicians will provide more public goods.

In their study on the economic effects of electoral systems, Persson and Tabellini (2003) deal with two additional aspects, namely district size and ballot structure. "District size" refers to the number of legislators in a voting district. Suppose single-member districts are combined with the plurality rule. A party only needs some 25% of the national vote to win the elections (50% of half of the districts; Buchanan and Tullock 1962). Contrast this with a single, national district combined with proportional representation. Here, a party needs some 50% of the national vote to win. Persson and Tabellini (2000) argue that this gives parties under proportional representation strong incentives to offer general public goods, whereas parties under plurality rule have an incentive to focus on the swing states and promise policies specifically targeted to meet the the preferences of constituents.

It is the ballot structure that determines whether voters can vote for individual candidates, or for party lists. Often, majority rule systems rely on individual candidates, whereas proportional systems rely on party lists. Party lists may be interpreted as a common pool, meaning that individual candidates may be expected to invest less in their campaigns under proportional representation than under majority rule. Persson and Tabellini (2000) argue that corruption and political rents should be higher, the lower the ratio between individually elected legislators to legislators delegated by their parties.

What do the data say? Persson and Tabellini (2003) find that the electoral system has (economically and statistically) significant effects on a number of economic variables: (1) in majoritarian systems, central government expenditure is some 3% of gross domestic product (GDP) lower than in proportional representation systems; (2) expenditure for social services ("the welfare state") are some 2–3% lower in majoritarian systems; (3) the budget deficit in majoritarian systems is some 1–2% below that of systems with proportional representation; (4) a higher proportion of individually elected candidates does indeed result in lower levels of (perceived) corruption; (5) countries with smaller electoral districts tend to have more corruption; (6) a higher proportion of individually elected candidates leads to higher output per worker; and (7) likewise, countries with smaller electoral districts tend to have lower output per worker.

Boix (1999) is interested in endogenizing electoral institutions, and asks under what circumstances incumbent parties will change electoral systems. As a starting point, he assumes that incumbents are interested in maximizing their parliamentary representation (as well as government positions). The emergence of new parties is modeled as an exogenous shock which can, for example, be caused by a move toward universal suffrage. If the newly emerging parties (usually leftist ones) are perceived as weak, the electoral system remains unchanged; if they are perceived as strong, electoral systems change from majoritarian to proportional rule. Boix (1999) tests this hypothesis for the electoral systems of twenty-two countries between 1875 and 1990 and finds it is broadly confirmed. Furthermore, he shows that internal fragmentation (measured by ethnic as well as religious fragmentation) has different consequences, depending on the size of the country: in small countries, high levels of fragmentation are one factor leading to proportional representation. Large countries may be highly fragmented at the national level, yet quite homogenous at the local or regional ones. If this is the case, federalism serves as a substitute for proportional representation.

Boix (1999) showed that changes in electoral systems may be explained as the consequences of giving the right to vote to a larger number of citizens, that is, franchise extensions. But changes in the franchise are also chosen, so the question is: Why do the elite extend the franchise to larger parts of the population? Voigt (1999) suggests thinking of constitutional change as the outcome of a bargaining game in which a variable number of interest groups participate. Only powerful groups will be bargaining over a constitutional contract, interpreted as a real contract, between identifiable parties.[2] The bargaining power of a group is determined by its ability and willingness to inflict costs on others, and thereby reduce the net social product and resulting rents. Owing to, say, technological changes, the relative bargaining power of the various groups may change over time. This means that the number and identity of the parties bargaining over a constitutional contract may change over time. It further means that those groups whose relative bargaining powers have increased will demand constitutional renegotiation. Acemoglu and Robinson (2000) also deal with the issue of franchise extension. According to these scholars, the franchise is extended if the hitherto disenfranchised were able credibly to threaten a revolution if not granted the franchise. Extending the franchise is interpreted as a commitment to future redistribution that prevents social unrest.

Iversen and Soskice (2006) note that three out of four governments under majoritarian systems have been center-right between 1945 and 1998, whereas three out of four governments have been center-left under proportional representation. But if this is the case, a closer look at the transmission mechanism that leads from electoral systems to government expenditures is necessary because it is unclear if the difference may be attributed to the constitutional rule or the different government ideologies – and citizens at large. It may, hence, not be excluded that more conservative populations tend to choose majority rule, and more leftist ones proportional representation. To sum up: if electoral rules are assumed to be given exogenously, their economic effects appear stunning. Their endogenization leads to a number of puzzles, such as whether the connection between electoral rules and economic outcomes is causal, or primarily a – very strong – correlation. It appears plausible that strong players can influence both electoral institutions and policy choices. More research on precise transmission channels is thus needed.

### 17.3.3    Horizontal separation of powers

*17.3.3.1 Introductory remarks*    The concept of the separation of powers may be classified into horizontal separation (legislature, executive, and judiciary) and vertical separation (federalism). But the horizontal separation of powers still remains an extremely broad term. This is why we deal with it in small portions: first, with the most general consequences of having two or three branches – and not just one (*see* 17.3.3.2). We then study the different forms of government, more specifically, whether there are systematic differences between presidential and parliamentary systems. This may be interpreted as an aspect of the separation of powers because presidential systems have a higher degree of separation than parliamentary ones (*see* 17.3.3.3). The economic consequences of the judiciary – and the reasons for the very different ways in which judiciaries are organized across countries – have been entirely neglected by economists for a long time. This has recently changed, and Section 17.3.3.4 gives an overview of such recently gained insights.

*17.3.3.2 Horizontal separation in general*    Brennan and Hamlin (1994) offer a "revisionist view" of the separation of powers. To make their point, they draw on standard monopoly models used in economics, and distinguish between horizontal and a vertical separation of powers. Starting out with a monopoly, the introduction of horizontal separation amounts to two (or more) suppliers competing for demand, and thus involves the introduction of duopoly (or oligopoly). The equilibrium price will then be below the monopoly price and consumer rent will subsequently increase. Vertical separation of powers also results in a division of the original monopoly, albeit in a different way: now, single functions of the process are divided; there is, for example, one monopolistic firm which produces goods and a second monopolistic firm that distributes them; Brennan and Hamlin (1994) also call this functional separation of powers. The (individually) maximizing strategies of vertically separated firms will, at best, result in the monopoly price, but usually the price will be even higher and the accruing consumer rent will thus be lower than in the original monopoly. Brennan and Hamlin (1994) argue that the separation of powers doctrine, as conventionally understood, is equivalent to the functional separation of powers and will therefore not protect citizens from being exploited by governing bodies. They further argue that the horizontal separation of powers could, on the other hand, have beneficial results. In order to unfold, it must include an "exit" option for citizens, plus there must be an absence of strong externalities between competing states.

Persson, Roland, and Tabellini (1997) argue that politicians have two possibilities for enriching themselves to the detriment of citizens: the first based on the misuse of power; the second on exploiting information advantages. These authors reveal that both possibilities may be reduced by implementing checks and balances between the legislature and the executive. This was one of the first models dealing with the (horizontal) separation of powers. Yet, it falls short of the traditional notion going back to Montesquieu, as it is based on two government branches and does not take a third branch (the judiciary) into account.

*17.3.3.3 Forms of government: presidential versus parliamentary regimens*    The degree of separation of powers is higher in presidential than in parliamentary systems, as the survival of the president does not depend on the confidence of parliament. Persson, Roland, and Tabellini (1997, 2000) argue that it is easier for legislatures to collude in parliamentary systems, which is why they expect higher corruption levels and higher taxes than in presidential systems. They further argue that the majority (of both voters and legislators) in parliamentary systems may pass spending programs aimed at their own benefit, implying that they can make themselves better off to the detriment of the minority. This is why Persson, Roland, and Tabellini (2000) predict that both taxes and government expenditures will be higher in parliamentary, rather than in presidential, systems.

In order to test their hypotheses, Persson and Tabellini (2003) needed to code presidential as opposed to parliamentary systems. If there was no vote of no-confidence, they coded the country as "presidential." The results are quite impressive: (1) government spending is some 6% of GDP lower in presidential compared to parliamentary systems;[3] (2) the size of the welfare state is some 2–3% of GDP lower in presidential systems; (3) the influence of government form on the budget deficit is rather marginal, the binary variable explains only a small proportion in the variation of budget deficits; (4) presidential systems seem to have lower levels of corruption; (5) there are no significant differences in the level of government efficiency between the two forms of government; (6) presidential systems seem to be a hindrance to increased productivity but this result is significant on the 10% level only. These results are impressive and intriguing: presidential systems seem to do better than parliamentary systems, according to a bunch of different criteria. Yet, when it comes to income and growth (i.e. productivity development), parliamentary systems seem to have an advantage over presidential systems, if only on a low level of significance. More detailed research on the transmission channels is therefore needed.

This result is backed by Persson (2005), who asks whether changes in the form of government matter for the likelihood of governments implementing structural policies aimed at economic growth. He finds that reforms to parliamentary arrangements have an important growth-promoting effect. Introducing parliamentary democracy in a non-democracy, or in a presidential democracy, would improve structural policy so that long-term productivity growth would increase by an impressive 50%.

Economic literature on the horizontal separation of powers is still in its infancy. Therefore, many potentially relevant aspects have not yet been dealt with. If interested in the ability of constitutional rules to constrain politicians, we could, for example, question whether governments display systematic differences in complying with constitutional rules depending on the form of government. It could be argued that presidential systems should have a higher likelihood of politicians breaking the rules of the game, *although* the formal degree of separation is higher here. Presidents often claim they are the only ones who represent the people as a whole, which might make them more daring than, say, prime ministers, in reneging upon constitutional constraints. Political parties are regularly weaker in presidential than in parliamentary systems.[4] This might further increase the incentives of presidents not to take constitutional rules too seriously: if parties are weak, the possibility of producing opposition to a president who reneges on the constitution might be less than in systems with strong political parties. A reduced likelihood of opposition does, of course, make reneging on constitutional rules more beneficial. There might yet be another transmission mechanism for political parties. Brennan and Kliemt (1994) show that organizations like political parties often develop longer time horizons than individual politicians: whereas presidents will be out after one or two terms (as in Mexico or the USA), political parties might opt for staying in power indefinitely (like in Japan). If the discount rate of presidents is indeed higher than that of, say, prime ministers or party leaders, this also means offenses against formal constitutional rules may appear more beneficial to presidents than to prime ministers. Persson and Tabellini (2003) call their book *The Economic Effects of Constitutions* and they do not try to explain the emergence of different forms of government in any detail, yet they note that differences seem to be strongly linked to geographical variables: presidential systems are more likely to be found in Latin America and closer to the equator. Acemoglu *et al.* (2001) argue that settlers brought (good) European institutions where their mortality was low. Persson (2005) endogenizes the choice of parliamentary as opposed to presidential regimens by using this variable, as well as different periods of constitution making (1921–1950 versus 1951–1980), as exogenous variables, and finds that settler mortality is correlated in a negative and significant way with parliamentary regimens. Constitutional birth between 1951 and 1980 is positively correlated with parliamentary democracy, and constitution making between 1920 and 1950 negatively (but insignificantly) so. Aghion, Alesina, and Trebbi (2004) point out that ethnically and linguistically fragmented societies are more likely to have a presidential form of government. These can, however, only represent the very first steps in endogenizing forms of government.

*17.3.3.4 A forgotten branch: the judiciary*  The independence of the judiciary vis-à-vis the other two government branches may be crucial to the notion of separation of powers. One way of conceptualizing judicial independence is to think of it as the implementation of judicial decisions by representatives of other government branches, even if they are not in their (short-term) interests. An independent judiciary may be one way to solve the dilemma of the strong state: on the one hand, a state strong enough to protect private property rights is needed; on the other, a state that is sufficiently powerful to protect private property rights is also sufficiently powerful to attenuate or totally ignore private property rights. This is to the detriment of all players involved: citizens who anticipate that their property rights may not be completely respected have fewer incentives to create wealth. The state, in turn, will receive a lower tax income and will have to pay higher interest rates as a debtor. An independent judiciary may be an institutional arrangement to solve the dilemma of the strong state because it enables the state to enforce private property rights but prevents it from giving in to the temptation of attenuating property rights. The independent judiciary is, in other words, a pre-commitment device that can turn promises of those governing to respect private property rights into credible commitments.

Is this theory supported by data? One huge problem is to measure the degree of independence the judiciary enjoys in various countries. In their attempt to measure it, Feld and Voigt (2003, 2004) explicitly distinguish between law in the books (*de jure* judicial independence [JI]) and its factual implementation (de facto JI). Feld and Voigt (2004) find that whilst *de jure* JI does not have an impact on economic growth, de facto JI positively influences real GDP per capita growth in a sample of seventy-three countries. The impact of de facto JI on economic growth is robust to outliers, to the inclusion of several additional economic, legal, and political control variables and to the construction of the index. The authors thus conclude that JI matters for economic growth.

Voigt (2008) points out that: not only is JI a necessary condition for ensuring the impartiality of judges, it may also endanger it; judges who are independent could have incentives to remain uninformed, become lazy, or even corrupt. It is therefore often argued that JI and judicial accountability (JA) are competing with each other. Voigt (2008) suggests, however, that they are not necessarily competing, but may complement each other in that judges are *independent from* the other government branches and, at the same time, *accountable to* the law. The first tests on the economic effects of JA were carried out based on the absence of corruption within the judiciary, as well as on data collected by the US State Department as proxies. On the basis of seventy-five countries, these proxies are highly significant for explaining differences in per capita income.

After having dealt with some economic effects of JI, we now turn to theories dealing with the determinants of JI. Conventional wisdom has it that an independent judiciary constrains the other two branches of government. The other two branches would therefore be interested in a judiciary without teeth. It was Landes and Posner (1975) who first questioned conventional wisdom from an economic point of view. According to them the legislature is not controlled by the judiciary, but legislators have an interest in an "independent" judiciary because its existence makes it more valuable to be a legislator, as it can prolong the life span of the legislative deals legislators strike with representatives of interest groups. The paper by Landes and Posner (1975) may also be interpreted as a theory concerning the choice of JI. Later papers have partially challenged and complemented this view. For Ramseyer (1994), the independence of courts depends on the expectations of politicians: if they expect their own party to remain in power, they have less incentive to create an independent judiciary than if they expect to lose power to a competing party. Ginsburg (2002) expands on

Ramseyer's approach: for him, politicians are likely to choose a higher degree of judicial review (as one important aspect of JI); the higher the degree of political uncertainty at the time of constitution making.

Hanssen (2004) tested two predictions first generated by Ramseyer (1994), namely, that JI will be higher if politicians fear losing power and the further apart are the ideal points of the rival parties. Using judicial retention procedures as the proxy for JI, Hanssen (2004) finds empirical support for these hypotheses in his analysis of panel data covering US states between 1950 and 1990. Besley and Payne (2003) have used a similar approach to explain differences in judicial behavior: they find that judges make decisions favoring important sections of the electorate as this might increase their chances of re-election. These empirical studies deal with the USA; cross-country studies are clearly a desideratum.

Hayo and Voigt (2007) is a first attempt to explain variation of de facto JI across countries. They find that high levels of *de jure* JI, the extent of democratization, and higher degrees of press freedom, are good predictors for high levels of de facto JI. The question of which particular design of constitutional rules enhances the judges' incentives so as to take the intentions of the constitution makers into consideration has not been dealt with extensively until now. More work is needed which inquires into the utility functions as well as the (perceived) constraints of judges in their professional activities. It is interesting that Mueller (1996) does not think that formal institutions could be sufficient to ensure a judiciary which is not only independent but also accountable. For incentives to make judges decide impartially (Mueller 1996, p. 284), "one has to rely on 'the culture of the judiciary' and the great status (and possibly financial rewards) that surround it." This view entails at least two implications: first, an independent and accountable judiciary might simply be unattainable if the respective culture does not support it. Second, informal institutions might be an important factor determining the factually realized level of JI. Hayo and Voigt (2006) test for a number of potentially relevant informal factors, such as the capacity to overcome the problem of collective action, religious affiliation, ethno-linguistic fractionalization, and the level of trust found among members of society, and find that none of them survives the rigorous model-reduction process employed by them.

This completes our overview of the traditional horizontal separation of powers. Over the last couple of decades, a number of additional players, such as independent central banks, competition offices, regulatory agencies, and so on, have been created and have the potential to substantially modify the traditional separation of powers. An in-depth, economic study of this "new separation of powers" (Ackerman 2000) is needed.

### 17.3.4  Vertical separation of powers: federalism

We now turn to federalism, that is, the vertical separation of powers. It has entered into mainstream economics as "fiscal federalism." Besides incorporating a second – and possibly third – layer of government into their studies, supporters of this approach based their theories on the traditional economic model; that is, assuming government to be efficiency-maximizing. Representatives of fiscal federalism, then, ask at what governmental level public goods are (optimally) provided, taking externalities explicitly into account. This approach thus need not concern us here (Inman and Rubinfeld 1997; Oates 1999 are surveys).

Federalism may be described as having two closely inter-related effects: lower government levels compete for tax-paying citizens, and this gives them incentives to cater to the preferences of their citizens. In terms of its economic effects, federalism will thus lead to fiscal policies more in line with the preferences of the median voter on a local or state level. Whether this automatically translates into lower taxes, lower budgets, and lower deficits is a different matter, because this argument implicitly assumes that the median voter will always want taxes, budgets, and deficits to be low. Further, the effects of federalism on other variables of interest, such as corruption, are a priori uncertain: on the one hand, iterated games between local politicians and local interest groups could make it easier for them to establish long-lasting relationships conducive to corruption. On the other, the higher degree of transparency associated with the local provision of public goods could have an opposite effect. Likewise, the effect of federalism on productivity levels is unclear from a theoretical point of view: it could be that public goods are provided in suboptimal quantities, and that those providing them are insufficiently specialized (Tanzi 2000). Yet, if factors are mobile and they settle where the provided infrastructure best fits their needs, competition might force lower level governments to provide goods that help increase productivity. Estimating the effects of federalism presupposes the possibility of ascertaining it. Depending on the specific research question, different dimensions might be desirable. *The Database of Political Institutions* (Beck *et al.* 2000) alone contains five different indicators, asking: (1) whether autonomous regions exist; (2) whether municipal governments are locally elected; (3) whether state governments are locally elected; (4) whether sub-national governments have extensive taxing, spending, or regulatory authority; and (5) whether the constituencies of upper house members are states in the federation. Adserà, Boix, and Payne (2001), as well as Elazar (1995), have provided alternative indicators. The Elazar variable is based on Riker's (1964) definition of federalism. A potential problem with this variable is that for a country to be classified as federal the mere promise of some autonomy at each government level, as specified in the constitution, might be sufficient. It is, in other words, an indicator of *de jure*, rather than de facto, federalism.

Based on OECD revenue statistics, Stegarescu (2004) proposes a new indicator not based on the expenditure shares of central- and state-level, but, instead, on the revenue side, arguing that autonomy in determining tax levels, or even in introducing entirely new taxes, is the single most important criterion. He shows that countries such as Austria and Germany score a lot worse with regard to decentralization in his indicator than in previous ones. More generally, Stegarescu (2004) reveals that measurement errors can lead to erroneous conclusions, in particular with regard to the effects of fiscal decentralization.

What do the data say? For a long time, evidence on the effects of federalism on overall government spending was mixed. Over recent years, this seems to have changed, though; Rodden (2003) shows, in a cross-country study covering the period from 1980 to 1993, that countries where local and state governments have the competence for setting the tax base, total government expenditure is lower. Feld, Kirchgässner, and Schaltegger (2003) find that more intense tax competition leads to lower public revenue.

Treisman (2000) finds that federal states have higher corruption levels than unitary states, based on the Elazar variable. Fisman and Gatti (2002), on the other hand, find that fiscal decentralization is strongly and significantly associated with lower corruption levels. Their result is based on a specific aspect of federalism, namely decentralization, which they proxy for by the share of sub-national spending over total government spending. We have just presented arguments claiming that this is a bad measure for federalism. In addition, we could argue that it does not even measure institutions, but, rather, policies (based on institutions; *see* Section 17.4). On the other hand, we might argue that this is a good way to proxy for de facto federalism. It could, for example, be the case that the formal institutions of a country assign far-reaching autonomy in tax issues to the states, but that, in fact, autonomy is restricted at the federal level, by cartels among the states, and so on. Stegarescu (2004) even claims that his indicator contradicts the common claim that federal countries are more decentralized than unitary ones. Persson and Tabellini (2003, p. 61) find that federalism is not a significant variable in explaining rent extraction (which they use as a proxy for corruption). Thus the evidence is unclear and more fine-grained research is needed.

With regard to productivity, Persson and Tabellini (2003, p. 71) find that the federalism variable is highly significant for explaining differences in both labor and total factor productivity, with federations having higher levels. Existing evidence on the effects of federalism (or decentralization) on economic growth reflects the ambiguity of theoretical conjectures. There are only half a dozen studies with cross-country evidence. Often, these studies are limited to OECD member states. Based on a cross-section of ninety-one countries, Enikopolov and Zhuravskaya (2003) are an exception. They find that higher decentralization of revenue reduces growth of real GDP per capita in developing countries. Davoodi and Zou (1998) also report similar results, based on decentralization of spending in forty-six countries. Thiessen (2003) finds the opposite for a cross-section of twenty-one developed countries and a panel of twenty-six countries. Feld, Zimmerman, and Doring (2004) surveyed the literature in more detail, including empirical results for individual countries. The results of these studies are just as ambiguous as those mentioned here.

Measuring federalism with a dummy variable allows for comparisons between federal and unitary constitutions. But, important institutional aspects within the group of federal states might simply be overlooked. It would thus be interesting to generate a more fine-grained indicator that takes possibly relevant aspects into account. One problem that such a research strategy would immediately encounter would be the low number of observations, as the entire group of federal states is rather small (fewer than twenty countries). One possible escape route consists of drawing on case studies instead of econometric estimates. This is exactly what Blankart (2000) has done by comparing the development of two federally organized states over time, namely Switzerland and Germany. It is often presumed that there are inherent centralizing tendencies, even in federal states. Blankart (2000) now asks whether the so-called "law of the attracting power of the highest budget" (also called "Popitz's law") is a natural sciences type of law – or whether it is rather a consequence of constitutional choices. He conjectures that centralization is a function of cartelization tendencies between federal and state government levels, which, in turn, would be a function of constitutional rules. He then shows that the competence of the federal level to appropriate tax competence from the state level is crucial for explaining differences in the centralizing tendencies of different federations.

Vaubel (1996) has analyzed the process of centralization in federal states empirically. His first result is that federal states are indeed less prone to centralization than states with a non-federal constitution. Centralization is measured as the share of central government expenditure in total government spending. If we replace the binary dummy variable for federalism by quantitative constitutional variables, the most powerful single explanatory variable is the age of the constitutional court (for the entire sample) or the independence of the constitutional court from the organs of central government (for the industrialized states). If we take into account the degree of control that the lower level governments have over changing the federal constitution and whether tax increases require popular referendum, the explanatory power may be raised further. It thus seems that some constitutional provisions may make a difference in constraining centralization.

Our knowledge of the conditions under which constitutional assemblies choose federal, rather than unitary, structures leaves much to be desired. Figueiredo and Weingast (2005) have recently dealt with the issue of how the institutions of federalism may be sustained. They introduce a two-stage game: in the first stage, the institutions of federalism are determined ("institutional game"); in the second, a repeated game is played in which the participants can either act in accordance with the institutions established in the first stage or renege upon them. Figueiredo and Weingast (2005) stress the need of federal institutions to be self-enforcing; they show that constitutional rules can serve as a coordination device which permits the members of a federation to act collectively in case the center tries to exploit rents from one or more members. Figueiredo and Weingast (2005) demonstrate that sustained federalism may be equilibrium of the game. Although they look at some countries in order to demonstrate some of the implications of their model, their emphasis is clearly on the theoretical issues.

What is still lacking, then, are empirical insights dealing with the conditions under which constitutional assemblies choose federal structures. It almost seems to suggest itself that countries with a rather high degree of internal diversity which appears along geographical lines (e.g. ethnic, religious, or linguistic) which simultaneously need to stay together because of external threats, the small size of the states that would result if they tried to go it alone, and so on, have a higher tendency to choose federal structures than do countries which do not have these attributes. The identity of the former colonial power could also be relevant, as quite a few former British colonies have a federal structure today (Australia, Canada, India, Malaysia, Nigeria, South Africa) but hardly any French ones do. It is also worth noting that – with the exception of Russia – none of the newly passed constitutions of Central and Eastern Europe have a federal structure, which means it makes sense to analyze the age of constitutions. But these are nothing more than some ad hoc observations and the issue surely deserves thorough analysis.

### 17.3.5 Representative versus direct democracy

If we choose a broad notion of separation of powers, this also includes direct democratic institutions: here, it is the citizens who may act as an additional veto player. It has been hypothesized that direct democratic institutions make politicians more accountable – and that this would lead to policy choices that are closer to the preferences of the citizens. In real-world societies beyond a certain size, representative and direct democracy are not an alternative. Rather, a different degree of direct democratic institutions is combined with representative institutions, as no sizeable society can decide on all issues directly.

Matsusaka (1995, 2004) has estimated the effects of the right to an initiative on fiscal policy among all US states except Alaska. He finds that states that have that institution have lower expenditure and lower revenues than states which do not. With regard to Switzerland, Feld and Kirchgässner (2001) have dealt with the effects of a mandatory fiscal referendum on the same variables. They find that both expend-iture and revenues in cantons with the mandatory referendum are lower by about 7% and 11% compared to cantons without mandatory referenda.

The next question we are interested in is whether direct democratic institutions have any effects on rent extraction, that is, the perceived level of government corruption, as well as the efficiency with which public goods are provided. With regard to US states, Alt and Lassen (2003) find that states in which a referendum may be initiated by a certain number of citizens demanding it (a so-called "right of initiative") have significantly lower levels of perceived corruption than states with-out the initiative institution. Blomberg, Hess, and Weerapana (2004) ask whether there is any significant difference in the effective provision of public capital between initiative and non-initiative states, among the forty-eight continental US states between 1969 and 1986. They find that non-initiative states are some 20% less effective in providing public capital than initiative states.

Finally, do direct democratic institutions have any discernible effects on productivity, and thus on per capita income? Feld and Savioz (1997) find that per capita GDP in cantons with extended democracy rights is some 5% higher than in cantons without such rights. Voigt and Blume (2006) present the first cross-country study on the economic effects of direct democratic institutions; they find most (but not all) of the results obtained by the within-country studies confirmed. Frey and his various co-authors argue that we should not only look at the outcomes that direct democratic institutions produce, but also at the political process they induce (*see* Frey and Stutzer 2006). Kirchgässner and Frey (1990) speculate that the readiness of voters to incur information costs would, *ceteris paribus*, be higher in democracies with direct-democratic institutions because they participate more directly in decision making (Kirchgässner and Frey [1990, p. 63]). Benz and Stutzer (2004) have provided evidence in favor of the conjecture that citizens in states with direct-democratic institutions are better-informed than citizens in purely representative states. Some European states used referenda to pass the Maastricht treaty, whereas others did not. Relying on Eurobarometer data, Benz and Stutzer (2004) find that citizens in countries with a referendum were indeed better informed both objectively (i.e. concerning their knowledge of the European Union [EU]) as well as subjectively (i.e. their feelings about how well they were informed).

There are seemingly no systematic attempts to explain the emergence of direct democratic institutions. It has been noted (Matsusaka 2005) that current knowledge is poor: "A difficulty in developing instruments is that we do not yet understand why certain states adopted the process and others did not." So there is still much work to be done, in particular with regard to endogenizing direct democratic institutions.

### 17.3.6 Summary

We now complete our *tour d'horizon* on the consequences and causes of various constitutional rules. Owing to limited space, other institutional devices, such as bi-cameralism, the delegation of competences to independent agencies, the economic effects of individual rights, and procedural rules (such as constitutional amendment rules or rules for exiting as a group from an existing constitution), cannot be included here (Voigt 2006 offers a longer survey in which these topics are taken up). To sum up, quite a few constitutional rules seem to have important economic consequences. These results clearly indicate that endogenizing these institutions is desirable. Yet, it has been argued (Acemoglu 2005) that these might merely be strong correlations rather than causal effects. It may well be that (omitted) third variables determine both institutions and policies. But even if this argument is entirely correct, the conditions responsible for creating different institutions still need to be studied, as this will also clarify whether they have a direct impact on policies.

## 17.4  Possibilities and desiderata for future development

Throughout Section 17.3, we implicitly assume that measuring institutions, or more particularly, specific constitutional arrangements, is not a fundamental problem. We now move on to make this implicit assumption explicit – and to discuss some possible problems that might occur when ascertaining institutions.

Institutions may be defined as generally known rules used to structure recurrent interaction situations which are endowed with a sanctioning mechanism. In order to serve their function of reducing uncertainty, they need to be rather stable. Prima facie, ascertaining formal institutions, that is, those institutions based on written law, should not be a problem: the rule component, as well as the possible sanction we might have to face in case we breaks the rule, are both codified. Yet, in many cases, a glance at legal texts offers little information on the factual functioning of the institutions. The probability of being sanctioned after breaking some rule might vary widely between states, although their institutions are formally identical.

Glaeser *et al.* (2004) attack the NIE by claiming that much of the empirical work pretending to measure the economic effects of institutions has, indeed, not been measuring institutions, but rather policies. Drawing on a standard definition of institutions, they stress two qualities, namely that they constrain behavior and that they are permanent or stable. Some of the frequently used measures would neither measure policy constraints nor would they be stable. They would rather measure outcomes, that is, policy choices. In addition, the subjectivity of these measures would make it highly likely that they "increase" when income increases. But if their ascertainment is influenced by income levels, they are not an adequate measure for explaining changes in income levels.

The criticism of the measurement problems of institutions by Glaeser *et al.* (2004) is well taken. But, how do we measure institutions properly? Glaeser *et al.* (2004) offer some general observations – but no concrete proposals. If (formal) institutions may only be expected to have beneficial economic effects if implemented factually, then some kind of de facto measures must be used. It is hard to see how these could entirely abstain from taking certain outcomes into account. Of course, this promises to be messy because, when there is congruence between *de jure* and de facto, we wants to know whether the institution was complied with because of its constraining powers – or because the relevant player simply chose to do so.

Section 17.3 largely attempts to isolate the causes and consequences of single constitutional rules. This has been coined the business of "unbundling" (Acemoglu, Daron, and Johnson 2005). It is important in order to avoid wrongly attributing some consequences to a specific institution, although it is the general quality of institutions which drives the result. It is also important because it should enable us to identify those components crucial for achieving a high average quality of institutions – and those which have only marginal effects. On the other hand, introducing a specific constitutional rule without a number of other rules which might also be necessary might not induce the desired effects. The study of interdependencies – or interaction effects – seems, therefore, just as important as "unbundling." It might even be coined the business of "bundling."

A key presumption shared by both the normative and positive branches of CPE is that constitutional rules matter because they constrain human behavior and can therefore explain it. Yet, not all constitutions seem capable of constraining and enabling politicians effectively. It has been argued that it is not only the structure of formal constitutional rules, such as the separation of powers, which determines whether constitutions are effectively enforced, but informal rules or institutions may also have an important influence here (*see* North 1990; Kiwit and Voigt 1998). Our knowledge about transmission mechanisms leaves much to be desired.

# 18 New Institutional Economics and Its Application on Transition and Developing Economies

*Sonja Opper*

## 18.1 Introduction

In departures from centrally planned economies the threat of financial crisis, breakdown of political order, and re-evaluation of social values cause what Williamson (2000a) has termed "defining moments." Transition economies share broad similarities with other developing economies with respect to the importance of building institutions that can enable, motivate, and guide economic actors to create private and social wealth. Dismantling centrally planned economies to construct the institutional foundations of a market economy entails far-reaching and rapid institutional transformations. Whilst developing countries seek to optimize economic growth within the context of a relatively stable institutional framework, transition economies face the immense task of replacing socialist planning apparatus with a new economic system (Nee and Opper 2007). The standard economic toolkit does not include guidelines to deal with the intractability of informal constraints in the effort to build new economic institutions. Hence, transition economies offer rare windows of opportunity for economists to examine under conditions of punctuated equilibrium the dynamics of institutional change wherein informal and formal institutional elements collide, interact, and recombine to shape the institutional foundations of an emergent market economy.

This chapter reviews the transition economy literature with an emphasis on the two levels – institutional environment and governance – in Williamson's (1994) multi-level model of economic systems. A broader approach, incorporating two or more levels of analysis of Williamson's multi-level model, is needed to cover appropriately the complex inter-actions between formal and informal institutional elements driving insti-tutional change and economic performance in transition economies. Analysis of transition countries opens up the opportunity to tackle new questions exploring the interdependence between embeddedness and institutional environment (linking levels 1 and 2 analysis) and between the institutional environment and the emergence of particular institutional arrangements (linking levels 2 and 3 analysis) of Williamson's multi-level model (Figure 18.1).

The focus throughout this chapter will be on examples of new institutional economics (NIE) research, which illustrate the fruitful application of Williamson's multi-level perspective. Two major research directions, particularly relevant to understand institutional change in transition economies, are explored in detail: First, well-specified and secure property rights and mechanisms to safeguard economic transactions are generally regarded as crucial preconditions for economic development. Recent experiences of transition and developing economies, however, testify that there are no simple recipes on the *right* structure of property rights. In contrast, the effectiveness of property arrangements seems to depend partly on the embeddedness of the market infrastructure in social institutions. How else could we explain the breathtaking economic development in China in comparison to Russia? Both countries were equally characterized by weak property rights and the lack of an independent judiciary able to guarantee effective and unbiased litigation at low cost. Hence, from the point of view of standard institutional thought, both countries were deemed to fail economically. Nonetheless, China emerged as the world's most dynamic market economy, while Russia's transition led to a steep decrease in growth and economic wellbeing.

Second, contractual choice is a classical application of transaction cost economics at the micro-level. With respect to its application to transition and developing economies, a recurrent theme is once again the fact that the institutional environment can affect contract choices. According to Williamson, shift parameters of the institutional environment affect the economizing of the optimal institutional arrangement. The application of contract theory therefore demands a careful incorporation of the institutional environment if contractual choices are to be properly understood. For instance, identical asset specificity and frequency of transaction are likely to yield a different contractual choice in Vietnam than in mature market economies such as the USA. Contractual choices in transition economies are embedded in a distinct institutional environment that clearly diverges from steady-state economies. This means also that policy recommendations regarding particular contract types may prove ill if enforceability constraints are not taken into account.

The following applications of NIE emphasize the analysis of transition economies. Sections 18.2 and 18.3, deal with property rights arrangements and contractual choices as central institutional requirements of

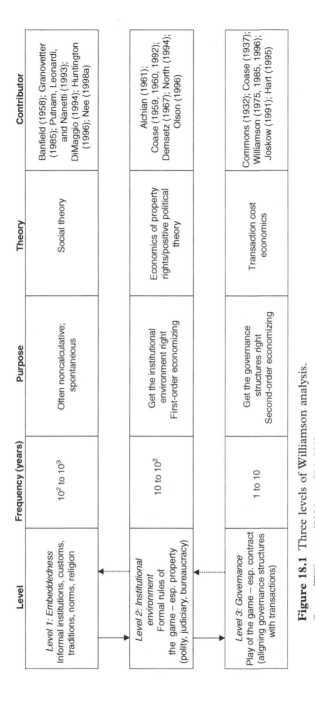

| Level | Frequency (years) | Purpose | Theory | Contributor |
| --- | --- | --- | --- | --- |
| *Level 1: Embeddedness* Informal institutions, customs, traditions, norms, religion | $10^2$ to $10^3$ | Often noncalculative; spontaneous | Social theory | Banfield (1958); Granovetter (1985); Putnam, Leonardi, and Nanetti (1993); DiMaggio (1994); Huntington (1996); Nee (1998a) |
| *Level 2: Institutional environment* Formal rules of the game – esp. property (polity, judiciary, bureaucracy) | 10 to $10^2$ | Get the institutional environment right First-order economizing | Economics of property rights/positive political theory | Alchian (1961); Coase (1959, 1960, 1992); Demsetz (1967); North (1994); Olson (1996) |
| *Level 3: Governance* Play of the game – esp. contract (aligning governance structures with transactions) | 1 to 10 | Get the governance structures right Second-order economizing | Transaction cost economics | Commons (1932); Coase (1937); Williamson (1975, 1985, 1996); Joskow (1991); Hart (1995) |

**Figure 18.1** Three levels of Williamson analysis.
*Source:* Williamson (2000, pp 596–600).

economic development and market transitions. In Section 18.4 the focus shifts to issues related to the complex task of instituting and managing institutional change in transition economies. Section 18.5 summarizes the practical impact of NIE on the problem of economic development and transition, and suggests promising fields for future research.

## 18.2    Privatization and organizational hybrids: in search of the "right" property rights

Privatization was assigned top-priority within most reform packages for developing and transition economies. Privatization encompassed not only the redistribution of property rights from the state to private investors, but also the creation of institutional arrangements to manage trading and provide property protection of land, intangibles, and securities. For illustrative purposes we derive some crucial lessons from one of the most intensively debated fields of privatization, the redistribution of state corporate assets to private investors.

It is generally assumed that the quality of property rights, as reflected by the rule of law and security of property rights, affects national growth through four major causal mechanisms. First, secure property rights reduce insecurity and thereby increase national investment activities and foreign direct investment. Second, property rights influence investment in technology and human capital. If property rights of the investment and expected revenue streams are perceived to be sufficiently secure, the relative attractiveness of long-term, high value-added investment in capital or technology-intensive investments increases in comparison to short-term, often labor-intensive endeavors (Keefer and Knack 1997). Third, secure property rights reduce transaction costs, as private ordering becomes obsolete within a secure institutional framework. Finally, insecure property rights may cause resource misallocation if personal ties with the ruling elite are developed as substitutes for impartial formal rules. Economic success is often affected by personal ties, relative bargaining power and corruption within politicized networks while economic efficiency may play a minor role.

The surprising outcome of the recent privatization wave, however, was that privatization effects clearly varied across countries and were obviously responsive to the privatization method. Although sole reliance on inferences from the Coasian theorem had led to the expectation that privatization methods should not affect resource allocation as property rights would eventually be efficiently allocated, early reform experience suggested that the choice of privatization models in Central and Eastern European (CEE) countries critically determined the emerging ownership structure and thereby locked in firms on distinct development paths. Ownership structures established through privatization turned out to be relatively invariant due to illiquid markets impeding the retrading of shares, which had a lasting impact on firm restructuring and performance. Phenomena such as the widespread emergence of insider control and the concentration of extremely large proportions of shares in the hands of only a few investment funds indicated that the specific method of privatization is not a trivial choice. Moreover, the costs and benefits of distinct types of ownership distribution were clearly determined by the embedded institutional environment.[1] Djankov and Murrell (2002) were the first to draw some general lessons based on a meta-analysis of twenty-four studies in twenty countries. They found that investment funds and foreigners had the strongest positive effect on firm performance; banks and blockholders reached almost comparable effects, while employee ownership is detrimental and diffuse individual ownership has no effect.

The majority of the empirical studies on privatization effects seem to confirm that increasing exclusivity of property rights is connected with growing economic efficiency. Fast privatizers, such as Estonia (Jones and Mygind 2000), as well as those that opted for slow privatization, such as Poland (Grosfeld and Nivet 1999), both presented favorable privatization effects; even countries under persisting communist leadership, which chose only partial privatization of their state-owned firms, realized positive privatization effects through the introduction of non-state shareholders (Wong, Opper, and Hu 2004). On the other hand, clear counter-examples without positive privatization effects, such as Russia (Brown and Earle 2000) and Mongolia (Anderson, Lee, and Murrell 2000) undermined the widespread euphoria that considered privatization a universal remedy. This inconclusive casual account was confirmed by Djankov and Murrell (2002), who conducted a meta-analysis investigating more than a hundred empirical studies on the economic performance of privatized firms in order to provide more systematic evidence. Overall, they found convincing evidence that privatization is strongly associated with more enterprise restructuring. Quite in conflict with inferences from property rights theory, however, statistically significant positive privatization effects were not confirmed for the countries of the Commonwealth of Independent States (CIS).

Causal explanations for the regional disparity of restructuring results were diverse, but there is a broad consensus that the simple establishment of *de jure* property rights, that is, the formal transfer of property titles from the state to private economic actors, underestimated the complexity of the transition task. In particular, the substandard quality of complementary institutions impeded inefficient enforcement of contractual rights. Most transition economies have dysfunctional legal systems characterized by either missing laws and regulations or the inadequate enforcement of existing laws (Anderson, Lee, and Murrell 2000; Johnson, McMillan, and Woodruff 2000). Although the property rights approach does not usually include analysis of the institutional environment, it implicitly presupposes the existence of an institutional environment characterized by mature markets, and independent and impartial legal systems guaranteeing the de facto implementation of *de jure* rights for individual actors (North 1991). None of these assumptions are usually valid for emerging markets and transition economies, however. Instead, transition economies are typically characterized by underdeveloped product and capital markets, the absence of a market culture, and dysfunctional legal systems. Briefly, the institutional environment is quite different from the model world, which Coase (1960), Alchian (1961) and Demsetz (1967) as the founders of the property rights school had conceptualized.[2] Further supporting mechanisms providing crucial incentives for efficient firm management and restructuring such as bankruptcy laws, private banks with market-oriented lending policies, and a widely accepted code of conduct for corporate governance are also simply assumed as given and to be operating efficiently. Overall, the prognostic power of arguments derived from property-rights theory was necessarily limited.

Not just the lack of positive privatization effects in the CIS challenged common thinking on property rights. A narrow interpretation of property rights theory was also unable to account for the exceptional economic performance of China and Vietnam since the beginning of economic reforms in 1978 and 1986, respectively. In particular, the outstanding performance of China's so-called township–village–enterprises (TVEs), an organizational hybrid characterized by formally "collective" property arrangements and intense involvement by local government, party, and bureaucracy, undermined the idea of a universally applicable "right structure of property rights."

Williamson's transaction cost economics offer a more comprehensive approach to analyzing property rights. With "transaction costs as the basic unit of analysis" and governance as "the means by which to infuse order, and thereby to relieve conflict and realize mutual gains," Williamson (2002a, p. 439) offers an alternative to the normative postulate of exclusive formal property rights and shifts attention from *de jure* to de facto property rights. The focus on de facto property rights implies that the security of individual rights does not rely solely on court ordering and formal rules of the game. Instead, individuals try to secure their interests by means of private ordering if they detect security hazards resulting from weak formal institutions that will not provide adequate protection from expropriation. Hence these theoretical directions take diametrically opposed views on the role of state. Although the property rights approach assigns a dominant role to governments and polity, the transaction-cost view shifts attention to the way individuals and social groups actually "play-the-game" (Greif 1993). Self-help complements the formal rules of the game and may thereby improve the quality of trading relations. Thus, "getting the governance structures right" replaces "getting the property rights straight" as the core objective of firms in developing or transition economies facing large-scale institutional reforms (Williamson 2002a, p. 438).

The extended perspective on de facto rights is indeed better equipped to explain the emergence of hybrid organizational forms characterized by non-private property rights, and helps to disclose when and why privatization efforts succeed or fail (Williamson 1998). Through the lens of governance, the above mentioned TVEs are an organizational form which is intentionally chosen to economize on transaction costs accruing from an intermediate economy regulated by socialist-style redistributive institutions and market mechanisms (Nee 1992). Linking levels 2 and 3 analysis, Peng (2001) studied firm-level data from TVEs, and found empirical evidence that informal or ambiguous property rights may be the most efficient property arrangement under a given set of partial institutional reforms. Owing to the active involvement of township and village governments they receive higher political protection, enjoy reduced insecurity, and benefit from preferential treatment on the immature capital market and markets for scarce resources (Nee 1992). Network ties provide the social basis of informal property rights that enable and facilitate private sector entrepreneurship in a transition economy (Nee and Su 1996). Che and Qian (1998) focus on the ability of local governments to limit state predation and thereby mitigate excessive revenue hiding compared to "private ownership forms." The emergence of organizational hybrids, such as China's TVE clearly reflects the organizational result of transaction cost economizing within a specific (non-market) institutional environment. Their persistence is inevitably only temporary. Parallel to a maturing institutional market environment, transaction cost economizing gradually forces their conversion to more private ownership forms as has been observed since the mid-1990s.

## 18.3   Contracts

Another focal point in the application of NIE on transition economies is contract theory, including the analysis of contractual choices, and contract enforcement. One major lesson to be learned was that the distinct institutional quality of transition economies, characterized by high levels of uncertainty critically affects the profitability of contractual choices. In comparison to established market economies, transition economies provide high-risk environments with an above-average level of uncertainty resulting from frequent policy changes, inadequate transparency, low predictability, and bureaucratic red tape. In addition, markets, particularly credit markets and markets for scarce material, are underdeveloped, which adds to overall uncertainty. Uncertainty resulting from weak political and economic institutions is further aggravated, since most of the transition economies have dysfunctional legal systems. These legal systems are so poor either because laws do not exist or because law enforcement is inadequate, owing to insufficient financial resources, human capital, or simply due to a lack of legal independence on the part of the judiciary (McMillan and Woodruff 2000). Whilst higher uncertainty resulting from immature institutions is likely to affect the contract choice, dysfunctional public order will invariably affect the relative importance of public enforcement and diverse types of self-help mechanisms. Subsequently, transition economies, with their distinct institutional settings, provide an informative place to observe the interaction between contract choice and institutional environment, and the interaction between public and private ordering.

One of the early examples shedding light on the interplay between contractual choice and institutional environment was provided by Stiglitz (1974) with his principal–agent model on sharecropping. Under consideration of risk taking, share tenancy may evolve as an effective instrument to distribute risk and incentives between sharecropper and land owner. Based on the tenant's risk aversion, sharecropping contracts were interpreted as convenient contractual choices within high-risk environments typical for developing economies. Although operators have stronger incentives to work more efficiently than on a wage contract, they have to shoulder a smaller share of the financial risk than on a rental contract. In economies where landlords have weak monitoring facilities over paid labor, and peasants behaviour is highly risk-averse because of poverty, this intermediate contract-type may be particularly appealing to both landowner and peasant. Similarly, Laffont and Matoussi (1995) develop a theory of sharecropping which emphasizes the role of weak credit markets as a critical financial constraint in explaining which type of contract is selected. Incentive contracts such as rental contracts are often impossible because of the tenant's financial constraints, while sharecropping contracts offer a better opportunity of risk sharing. These workers support their theory with empirical evidence from Tunisia, showing that financial variables play a significant role in explaining the type of contract chosen. The sharecropping example suggests that contractual choices depend crucially on the institutional environment (e.g. existence of competitive markets) owing to its impact on the individual risks for contract partners. Similarly, transaction cost reasoning lends itself to the analysis of a broad range of contractual choices, such as tax collection, manufacturing, mining, education, and so on.

Mechanisms to secure contracts vary significantly in transition economies. In general there are two methods to secure the transaction: by means of law enforcement and through private safeguard mechanisms, such as reliance on relational contracting and choice of specific contract types. The relative importance of both methods obviously depends crucially on the adequacy of the legal system. In developing and transition economies, where judiciaries are not independent, access to the court is restricted, and lawsuits easily entail substantial costs that may surpass the amount in dispute, business partners are often left to their own devices.

A common self-help mechanism to secure contracts is to rely on repeated transactions and relational contracting. Bilateral cooperation between two trading partners is likely to emerge if they find themselves in a situation of limited alternatives that (temporarily) lock contractors together. Underdeveloped market institutions, weak competition (either few buyers or sellers), poor market information when looking for alternative contractors, or high transportation costs for non-local transactions, for instance, may easily lock in contract partners with each other (Kranton 1996). Without lock-ins between contractors, and if trading relations are rather infrequent, only multilateral relational contracting may provide an effective self-help mechanism. In this case, private ordering relies on membership to close-knit social groups that can make a credible threat to punish contract breach through multilateral retaliation, which may lead to a complete loss of business (McMillan and Woodruff 2000). Social sanctions can further support economic sanctions and seem to be of particular importance within close ethnic networks. As illustrated by recent East Asian development, ethnic groups still play a crucial role in facilitating contracting and trading in the absence of market institutions. A broad literature studies network-based trading relations in China. "*Guanxi*" (Chinese for personal relations) with business partners (horizontal networking) as well as party and bureaucracy (vertical networking) were confirmed to be significant determinants of economic success of private entrepreneurs and rural collective firms giving rise to a specific type of "network capitalism"

(Boisot and Child 1996). Xin and Pearce (1996) show that, in particular, private businesses critically depend on connections linking entrepreneurs with the local bureaucracy and political elite in order to mitigate business risks resulting from their weak legal status. As to business-to-business relations, *guanxi* become crucial, wherever market institutions are not fully developed and information flows are deficient. Whyte (1995), for instance, asserts that family and kinship ties facilitate subcontracting by allowing entrepreneurs to adjust flexibly to changing market conditions. In this setting *guanxi* provide opportunities to secure information and to access scarce resources, thereby critically shaping resource flows within the economy. This suggests that the need to invest in personal relations is by no means identical for all firm types. To the contrary, there is evidence that *guanxi* utilization is heterogenous across firms. Organizational, institutional, and strategic settings of distinct firms determine the need to complement weak market institutions with personnel networks (Park and Luo 2001). Likewise, labor contracts are determined by social networks. There is evidence that both the probability of securing a non-farm job in China, as well as the type of job, are determined by the different types of *guanxi* (Zhang and Li 2003).

The emergence of self-help mechanisms in the absence of functional public order is not to be taken for granted, however. Relational contracting within social and business networks varies greatly across the developing and transition economies. The crucial question is, therefore, under which circumstances individual actors rely on network trading in order to bridge the gap left by dysfunctional public order. Under which circumstance does multilateral relational contracting develop, and under which circumstances is private entrepreneurship impeded? Customs, traditions, and norms are assumed to influence the individuals' ability and willingness to organize self-help within social groups. Greif (1993) introduced the idea that differing cultural beliefs significantly shape the emergence and persistence of distinct organizational forms. His comparative analysis of the Maghribi traders and the Genoese suggests that members of collectivist societies, such as the medieval Maghribi traders, are more prone to transactions with members of specific religious, ethnic, or familial groups in which contract enforcement is achieved through informal institutions. Individualist societies, such as the Genoese, are associated with integrated social structures, allowing frequent shifts of individuals between specific groups, which demand more formal mechanisms to secure contract enforcement. Culturally differing levels of interpersonal trust and kinship ties therefore emerge as a central determinant of the need to develop formal institutions (Knack and Keefer 1997).

But the existence and prominence of multilateral relational contracting does not simply depend on cultural beliefs. Polities affect business environments in ways that either induce or impede the emergence of relational contracting to substitute formal institutions. Given the assumption that business partners' incentive not to breach relational contracts depends on their expectation of future profits resulting from their business relations, predictability of the future is a central precondition of effective self-help. Corruption, overtaxing, high inflation rates, weak public security, and any circumstances that reduce future profits or impede calculations on the expected pay off from continuing business relationships may easily impede the development of relational contracting.[3]

It would be a clear misconception, however, to regard relational contracting as a universal remedy for countries with weak public order. First of all, it has a downside risk, as trading within social networks may preclude specialization advantages and collusion between network members may reduce efficiency. Furthermore, multilateral relational contracting does not always offer satisfactory solutions. While multilateral relational contracting usually works well for small firms and start-ups, large-scale firms with highly diversified product portfolios and complex production processes will find it difficult to secure their contracts within locally limited social networks. From a dynamic perspective, sole reliance on multilateral relational contracting impedes growth beyond a certain firm size. Significant national and especially global market shares demand anonymous contracting based on reliable formal institutions and effective public order. Finally, economies of scale are hard to achieve if transactions are based on personalized mutual exchange, as significant long-term investments pose a severe risk for the manufacturer. Once the manufacturer faces a critical amount of investment in fixed assets, these sunk costs become hostage to the buyer who may now threaten to severe the contract unless prices are renegotiated (McMillan and Woodruff 2002).

Other contract types re-emerged, which aim to allow impersonal trade in spite of weak legal enforcement mechanisms. Marin and Schnitzer (2002) explore the re-emergence of barter as an optimal contractual choice for firms acting in business environments characterized by weak financial systems, high inflation rates, and immature legal systems. They show that barter allows trading partners to mitigate risks stemming from a deficient institutional environment. In international trade, barter may mitigate the credit worthiness problem of highly indebted countries. As barter also provides collateralization of a trade credit, it may even provide a superior enforcement mechanism compared to reputation building (Marin and Schnitzer 2003). Barter trade, however, also has its limitations, as the matching of trading partners and traded goods imposes additional transaction costs compared to impersonal market trading backed by reliable and fair legal institutions.

All these observations support the idea that transaction cost reasoning serves as a core mechanism to dictate the choice between relational contracting and coercive enforcement mechanisms (Milgrom, North, and Weingast 1990). With growing trade, the costs of relational contracting (e.g. information costs, control costs) and specific contract types such as barter will grow and eventually exceed the costs of operating a coercive enforcement mechanism backed by the state. Subsequently, incentives arise to replace one enforcement mechanism with another. The importance of the current cost structure for the choice of the appropriate enforcement mechanisms therefore suggests one central lesson for transition and developing economies: whereas the creation of effective legal systems is an essential element of any reform agenda, recent experience suggests that under a certain set of preconditions, entrepreneurs may find alternative solutions to deal with the problem of contract enforcement in a Hobbesian world.

## 18.4    Managing institutional change

Although some crucial elements of ideal transition strategies, such as private property rights, market liberalization, and rule of law, seemed indisputable from the outset of economic reforms, the design and implementation of the respective institutional reform packages replacing the existing economic system, posed an even greater challenge to reformers, and advisors. Unexpectedly steep economic declines of the economies, high inflation rates, and persistently high unemployment rates signaled that the replacement of one economic system by another was not an easy undertaking. It became evident, that the state's ability to manage effectively country-specific institutional reforms, in particular, turned out to be a crucial determinant of the overall reform success. Whilst some countries could return to positive growth rates after a short economic downturn, others, such as Russia, struggled for more than fifteen years just to regain the economic strength of the pre-reform period. Russia's per capita gross domestic product (GDP) (PPP in US $2,000) was, in 2004 (US $9,128), still lower than in 1989 (US $10,417) (world development indicators). Management of institutional change may be broadly divided into two core competencies of the state: crafting an appropriate reform agenda, and the political and bureaucratic ability to effectively implement and enforce institutional change on a national scale.

First of all, governments need to identify appropriate institutions to support economic growth and development. Here, governments can build on a broad basis of empirical findings on essential institutions supporting economic development (Aron 2000; Rodrik 2006). It is generally accepted that politically open societies, which respect the rule of law and private property rights, have growth advantages over societies where these rights are restrained (Scully 1988). Keefer and Knack (1997) studied rule of law, pervasiveness of corruption, and risk of expropriation and contract repudiation as typical institutional outputs of insecure property rights. Their estimates suggest that per capita growth in the period 1960–1989 was actually significantly and negatively affected by weak protection of property rights. Henisz (2000a) applies an even stronger focus on the role of politics and developed an index to measure political institutions. He provides convincing evidence that political constraints have a statistically significant influence on national growth rates in 157 countries in the period between 1964 and 1994.

In addition, two major determinants are likely to affect the short-term prospects of institutional reform. The successful reform of a country's institutions will critically depend on the government's incentives to implement institutional reforms, and the technical capacity to implement and enforce institutional reforms.

First of all, politicians' and bureaucrats' rent-seeking behavior may constrain the incentives to implement growth-promoting institutional reforms. States do not, in general, act as welfare maximizers in a Benthamite sense, as politicians tend to maximize their own benefits, which need not be consistent with long-term national development goals. A core problem with institutional reforms, therefore, is that "Institutions are not necessarily or even usually created to be socially efficient; rather they, or at least the formal rules, are created to serve the interests of those with the bargaining power to create new rules" (North 1994, p. 360). In addition, the newly emerging young CEE democracies and developing countries often lack the necessary insulation of political decision makers and bureaucracies to avoid state capture. Under these preconditions, powerful interest groups and firms are well-positioned either to defend their vested interests or to influence institutional reforms in order to secure private advantages over competitors (Hellman, Jones, and Kaufmann 2003). Opper (2004) provides sector-independent, cross-country evidence for the explanatory power of political economy arguments. Her panel analysis of fourteen CEE transition economies between 1994 and 2000 supports the idea that divergent experiences in large-scale privatization may be explained to a large extent with political interests and national constellations of interest groups. Similarly, less democratic governments tend to employ market regulation for their rent-seeking activities (Djankov *et al.* 2002). Examples abound which show how state actors may have a strong motivation to defend socially inefficient institutions. Transparent bureaucratic rules and independent monitoring by the judicial system and media may provide remedies against politician's rent-seeking behavior and state capture.

But even if optimal political and bureaucratic reforms were guaranteed, institutional reforms still pose an immense technical challenge. As specified above, good institutions cannot simply be transplanted into developing and transition economies. Institutional reforms require a "goodness of fit" between the specific innovation and the country's broader institutional environment, including its norms and beliefs (Levy and Spiller 1994). As a crucial lesson from the partly dismal experience of transition and developing economies it turned out that capitalism by design ignored "the persistence of routines and practices, organizational forms and social ties that can become assets, resources, and the basis for credible commitments and coordinated actions in the post-socialist period" (Stark 1996, p. 995).

State-directed institutional reforms are inevitably limited to changes in the formal rules. Informal rules, on the other hand, are beyond the reach of the state, hard to change, and usually exert "a pervasive influence upon the long-term character of economies" (North 1991, p. 111). Although North (1990) argues that economic performance is shaped by both formal and informal norms, economists so far have paid particularly little attention to the embeddedness of institutions. Research and theorizing on the mechanics of informal norms were left to other social sciences, in particular to sociologists, who have a comparative advantage when it comes to questions that focus on the social mechanisms that channel economic interests and shape economic behavior (Nee and Swedberg 2005; Smelser and Swedberg 2005). Granovetter's (1985) concept of embeddedness has been the most influential approach so far, though it still awaits greater theoretical specification.

Closely connected with the search for an explication as to when and how informal norms emerge and persist, is the highly relevant question, of how informal norms and formal norms combine to shape economic performance. Economic sociology may provide useful insights into the way informal norms within close-knit social groups may interact, de-couple, and combine with formal rules. The structure of transaction costs are embedded in the interaction of informal and formal institutional elements (Nee and Ingram 1998). For reform and transition economies it would be particularly important to identify the circumstances under which a de-coupling of formal and informal norms may actually cause the emergence of opposition norms. The economic effect of new banking laws in China, for instance, crucially depends on the implementation and behavioral changes of bank employees and customers. As long as both parties stick to a century-old Chinese tradition that loans are best secured by personal connections and long-established business relations instead of expected profitability and business plans, the ratio of policy loans and default loans is unlikely to decrease. If sanctions for malfeasance are weak, informal norms may even develop into opposition norms (a direct resistance against formal norms), which could eventually cause organizational conflict and factionalism. Russia's mafia-like business networks clearly worked in an effort to obstruct and undermine ongoing economic reforms. Nee's (2005) study of organizational dynamics in China's institutional reforms suggests that oppositional networks and norms explain the organizational inertia of state-owned enterprise and why this organizational form is structurally unable to adapt to the market environment. Instead, new organizational forms, including private enterprise and hybrids, adapt readily to the new institutional environment because they are not encumbered by powerful inertia forces within the firm. As long as interaction effects between formal and informal institutional elements of organizations as they respond to change in relative prices are not studied carefully, a theory of institutional change as envisioned by North will inevitably suffer from severe indeterminacy.

## 18.5   Conclusion

The diverse strands of NIE certainly touch on important issues relevant to both development and transition economies. Yet, to be honest, NIE has neither the golden formula to escape underdevelopment nor the recipe for how to build a market economy. The lack of clear-cut policy advice and reliance on rather broad suggestions has been rightly criticized (Smyth 1998). Nonetheless, to blame NIE for not having solved the pressing problems of underdevelopment, poverty, and institutional change after less than two decades of serious application, would be obtuse.

A fair and honest account should focus on the question of what NIE application actually has achieved and whether concepts and solutions outperformed the mainstream neoclassical view. Such a comparative view will certainly be in favor of NIE. There is little doubt that a more consequent and assiduous application of institutional knowledge on reform economies would have significantly reduced the costs of transition (Roland 2000). In this sense, Williamson (2000) states that "NIE is informative and should be included as part of the reform calculus."

Not surprisingly, an increasing diffusion of institutional thought into the fields of development and transition economics may be observed. The observed shift toward institutional approaches in developing and transition economies may therefore clearly be interpreted as a search for alternatives more appropriate for the explanation and understanding of real-world phenomena, which were insufficiently covered by neo-classical models. The shift is most apparent in academic publishing, where the proportion of NIE-oriented analysis in development economics and transition economics increased rapidly. A changing perception and a stronger recognition of institutions as critical factors determining development is also testified by the rapidly growing provision of databases such as the International Country Risk Guide, BERI, and Heritage Foundation Index of Economic Freedom (for a comprehensive overview, *see* Aron 2000) providing indicators aimed at the measurement of a country's institutional quality.

Despite broad achievements, we nonetheless have to agree with the critical assessment that "NIE is much less successful as a grand theory of the development process in its entirety" (Toye 1995) than for limited micro-applications. It is, however, exactly the application of NIE to transition and developing economies and the intrinsic need for a broader analytical approach not confined to one level of institutional analysis which seems to further the limits of NIE, thereby giving justice to North's (1991, p. 108) conjecture that in order to understand institutional change "we need to dig deeper into ... the relationship between the basic institutional framework, the consequent organizational structure, and institutional change."

Recent findings and related questions are opening up promising directions for future research. Two major directions are emphasized here, which both demand the consequent application of NIE's interdisciplinary approach. First of all, the relation between formal and informal norms is one of the critically under-researched topics that came to light during the last decade. Which norms – formal or informal – actually matter? Which institutions matter most? What are the determinants of their relative importance? When do opposition norms emerge? Answers to these crucial questions will be indispensable elements of a grand theory of institutional change, but surely need joint efforts from within the social sciences. Mutual benefits between economics and sociology, for instance, have been pronounced, and should inspire further coordinated efforts to solve the mystery of institutional performance and change. Likewise, a stronger association of behavioral scientists and anthropologists appears most promising.

A second important issue is the prominent role of the state in defining and implementing formal institutions. This issue calls for stronger interdisciplinary research efforts if institutional change is to be understood. As we still know too little about "the interplay between economic and political markets" (North 1995, p. 20), a systematic incorporation of the new political economy might provide new insight. So far, research in the new political economy has been largely focussed on the USA and other selected developed countries. Research on different political systems is needed if NIE is eventually to be integrated into a political economy.

The puzzle of institutional change surely has many more missing pieces and we are far away from seeing the full picture in the near future, but the empirical application of NIE to the highly dynamic developing and transition economies undoubtedly provides fertile ground for the advancement of the discipline.

*Part VI*

# Challenges to Institutional Analysis

# 19    Law and Economics in Retrospect

*Antonio Nicita and Ugo Pagano*

## 19.1    The case for law and economics: beyond disciplinary nirvanas?

In recent years, as Mercuro and Medema (1997, pp ix–x)[1] point out, "Law and Economics has developed from a small and rather esoteric branch within economics and law, to a substantial movement that has helped to both redefine the study of law and expose economics to the important implications of the legal environment." Although the standard law and economics approach typically refers to legal rules (Friedman 1998), recent developments have focussed more on "institutional" rules, including informal and customary ones, and the wide range of institutions performing private orderings and enforcement.

Traditional "law and economics" is mainly identified with the Chicagoan tradition, starting in the 1950s, and covers a number of long-investigated topics (such as economic analysis of contract law, property law and torts, criminal law, competition law, and corporate governance). However, according to many researchers in the field, law and economics would now include also the theory of the firm, the analysis of institutions and regulations, and the evolution of norms and behaviour. The complexity surrounding current methods and approaches to law and economics involves the need to go beyond the Chicagoan tradition, and even beyond the important contribution of new institutional economics (NIE), in order to assess the full range of interdependencies among legal rules, economic behaviour, motivation, and institutional change.

Before "law and economics," traditional approaches to the disciplines of law and economics were generally embedded in two separate "nirvanas": states of ultimate perfection characterized by ideal conditions hardly encountered in real-life societies. The *pure economics* advocated by Walras, and developed in neoclassical economics, turns out to be an economic nirvana characterized by internal consistency (equilibrium) and efficiency of all decentralized, perfectly rational decisions. However, if we look at some of the conditions surrounding this "economic nirvana," we find that the independence of its supposed purity is doubtful because it depends on the existence of a "legal nirvana": it assumes the existence of well-defined and complete rights for every contractible use of each resource.

A "legal nirvana" was also assumed in "pure theory of law": according to Kelsen's (1992) *Pure Theory of Law*, the law, or legal order, is a completely coherent *system of legal norms* and its typical questions relate to what constitutes unity in diversity of legal norms, and why a particular legal norm belongs to a particular (but always perfectly consistent) legal order.

In Kelsen's view, a multiplicity of norms constitutes a unity, a system, or an order when validity may be traced back to its original source. Thus, *pure law* concentrates on the validity of laws or the internal consistency of legal systems which may ultimately be traced to a founding norm (*grundnorm*). Pure law assumes that legal ordering can be completed and made consistent by public authorities implicitly assumed to be unlimited by bounded rationality, cognitive ability, failure of collective action, and all the other forms of economic scarcity. In other words, in this case, the relation between the nirvanas was reversed: the legal nirvana was implicitly based on an economic one.

These interdependencies explain why the escape routes of Coase (1937, 1960) and Fuller (1969) from their respective nirvana fallacies did not only mean a new relationship between law and economics but the reshaping of both, and the creation of a large intersection between the new fields, which eventually became the innovative field of law and economics (Pagano 2000).

In Fuller's (1969) work, law is defined as "the enterprise subjecting human behaviour to rules." Since this activity is a real-life human activity, it is characterized by opportunity costs attributed to competing uses arising in other spheres, and within the law-making process itself. Thus, economic opportunity costs imply that no legal nirvana may ever be achieved. Completeness, unity, and consistency may be the aim of a legal ordering, but they cannot be taken for granted in real-life societies. Moreover, the enterprise of "subjecting human behavior to rules" is too costly to be carried out solely by a centralized ordering system. The costs of law may be, and are, decreased by decentralizing many pieces of its enterprise to different orderings. Trade unions, churches, universities, firms, and many private orderings all contribute to the economically costly activity of law making.

In particular, according to Fuller (1969), within the firm, the entrepreneur or manager is actively engaged in setting up a private ordering whose rule can guide the behaviour of its members, and top management is actively involved in adjudicating the disputes between members of firms. Thus, some of the typical activities generally attributed to public legal ordering are decentralized to a firm's internal governance.

A striking consequence of the interdependence of pre-existing legal and economic nirvanas is Coase's departure from the zero transaction costs of "pure economics," which results in the same conclusion: only outside this world do activities by institutions such as firms make sense.

In a world of zero transaction costs, we would live in what would later become the world of the "Coase theorem." Despite numerous unjustified misunderstandings, this world is the opposite of Coase's world: it is a world which, according to Coase, economists should leave if their discipline is to gain any relevance. In Coase's world, all institutions are costly: a complex mix of institutions is required to eliminate externalities and, given that even the most efficient institution is not a "free lunch," it would be economically unsound to eliminate all externalities. By contrast, in the nirvana world of the Coase theorem, all possible externalities, including those related to economies and diseconomies of scale would be internalized by market transactions. Firms, state regulations, and other arrangements may only appear in a world where no alternative institution is available at zero costs.

The Coase (1960) article also has striking implications for the activities of courts. In the Coase-theorem world with zero transaction costs, attributing rights to a particular individual has no "economic" consequences. In any case, rights will flow to the individual who values them most. We are in a legal and economic nirvana where judges can ignore the economic consequences of their decisions. By contrast, in a world with positive transactions, the decisions of judges have economic consequences because rights will not necessarily flow efficiently to the individuals who value them most. Far from being in a world separate from economic activities, judges' decisions have important implications for the allocation of resources and their efficiency. This conclusion had a huge impact on Chicago law and economics.

According to Posner (*see* Section 19.2), judges should, and do, in fact, allocate rights according to criteria of economic efficiency to the individuals who value them most. On this view, judges are aware of the Coasean implications of their decisions in a world of positive transaction costs, and perform the role that markets cannot play when transaction cost are positive. It is up to judges to allocate resources efficiently.

Although inspired by Coase, Posner's approach had a non-Coasean flavor. The nirvana hypothesis was not removed, but simply shifted from markets to judges, and this contradicted the Coasean insight that all institutions are costly and no institutional nirvana exists.

In the subsequent sections, we briefly outline the evolution of law and economics paradigms, and compare them with the evolution of NIE approaches to studying transactions. We suggest that the way ahead for trespassing on economic and legal nirvanas relies on redefining transactions through the lens of old institutional economics, which linked private and legal orderings in a complex relationship. On our view, an *institutional law and economics* approach should resort to the notion of institutional complementarity as a powerful tool for analyzing the dynamics and structuring of transactions.

## 19.2    From Chicago with law: the evolution of law and economics paradigms

### 19.2.1    The first wave in Chicago

Posner (1975) distinguished two main schools of thought in Chicago. The "first wave" refers to the works of Aaron Director, Ronald Coase, and Guido Calabresi (even if Calabresi is considered the founder of the so-called New Haven School[2] in law and economics thought), and some others, as further refinements of an early tradition in legal theory that evolved from continental Europe to the USA (Mattei 1994). This approach emerged in the 1960s as an application of methodological individualism and mainstream economics (Rutherford 2003), with the aim of applying "economics to core legal doctrines and subjects, such as contract, property, tort and criminal law" (Duxbury 1995, p. 340; Mackaay 1999). The impulse toward revisiting the meaning and extent of antitrust law was the key that opened the way to the law and economics movement. Studies on the economics of competition became thus the privileged field of investigation and application of new ideas. The main argument developed is that in many antitrust cases, by applying simple micro-economic tools (such as analysing the well-known "double mark-up problem"; Hovenkamp 1994), it is possible to show how several strategies enacted by dominant firms are not the result of a monopolization attempt, but, rather, are aimed at pursuing efficiency in terms of transaction cost minimization. In this respect, Coase's work on the efficiency of vertical integration within the firm, and on the efficiency of property rights allocation in the presence of transaction costs, was retained as a distinct framework for developing a new theory on the efficiency of vertical restraints together with a renewed inclination towards "big dimensions" in firms. According to the new wave, antitrust statutes, as well as any form of state regulation, should be considered, in order to absorb externalities, only when the level of transaction costs is so high that it inhibits any Pareto relevant market exchange of well-defined property rights.

This approach is clearly shaped in the Coase Theorem. Moving beyond Pigouvian theory, Coase (1960) observed that externalities are reciprocal in nature, and that, in principle injurers as well as victims may eliminate harm. Coase undermined Pigou's analysis by conjecturing a frictionless state where transacting is costless. In such a world, he revealed how entitlements would eventually end up in the hands of whoever valued them most through private bargaining and regardless of to whom the entitlements were initially assigned, provided that clearly defined property rights were in place (*see* Nicita and Rizzolli 2004). However, as we have seen in Section 19.1, the main message of the 1960s article was that economists should focus their analysis on the real world where both market arrangements and state intervention are costly.

### 19.2.2 Chicago and New Haven

The "property rights approach" rapidly grew in the New Haven School with Calabresi's (1965, 1968, 1970) theory of liability and his distinction among property, liability and inalienability rules (Calabresi and Melamed 1972). In his theory on the costs of accidents, Calabresi pointed out that it would be prohibitive to define and bargain *ex ante* property rights on uses in a context exposed to a high risk of *ex post* third-party interference. To face these problems – so Calabresi's argument goes – legal systems have developed liability rules, and mainly tort law, as an efficient response to the problem of *ex post* absorption of externalities. Later on, Calabresi and Melamed (1972) organized the vast array of tools for externality absorption into a coherent, tripartite family made up of property rules, liability rules, and inalienability rules. Property rules confer to the holder of the entitlement the exclusive power of excluding others from using it, along with the power of alienating it at the price fixed exclusively by him. Thus, all non-consensual transfers would meet with an injunction by the courts. Conversely, liability rules grant non-holders the power to take the entitlement, even without the consent of the holder, and pay a price accordingly determined by the courts or the legislator. The holder, in this case, retains the right to seek damages, but no longer exclusively controls the entitlement. Finally, the inalienability rule applies when transactions are incompatible with fundamental rights and ethical principles, and it typically involves the application of criminal law. The work of Calabresi and Melamed suggests that in contexts where transaction costs are high, the courts should opt for liability rules, whereas when transaction costs are low, the opposite holds true. Calabresi and Melamed (1972) argued that entitlements should be assigned according to criteria based on *economic efficiency*, as well as on other considerations such as society's *distributional preferences* and other *justice reasons*, and went beyond the limits of the efficiency-driven Chicago School approach.

### 19.2.3   The second wave in Chicago

According to Richard Posner, unanimously viewed as the most important contributor to the second wave (starting from 1973) of Chicago law and economics, the legal system aims (or at least should aim) to produce and enforce efficient rules, that is, to maximize the *Kaldor–Hicks* criterion of efficiency. Common law, as a judge-made law, "is best understood not merely as a pricing mechanism, but as a pricing system designed to bring about an efficient allocation of resources in the Kaldor–Hicks sense" (Posner 1987). According to Posner, judges, aware of the economic consequences of their actions, should behave like quasi-markets, attributing rights to individuals who, in a world of zero transaction costs, would have acquired them. They apply the Kaldor criterion, according to which an allocation is efficient if the gainers could compensate the losers. Posner claims this criterion is in line with an intuitive view of justice. If avoiding some damages is extremely costly for some agents and not costly for the others, the latter are responsible for the damages. Consequently, "development of common law could be explained if its goal was to maximize allocative efficiency" (Mercuro and Medema 1997). In this respect, any human behavior subject to a legal rule, and not exclusively economic decisions (as Becker's studies on divorce, family, and religion have shown), could be regulated by a legal norm performing an efficiency purpose.

In Posner's work, the economic nirvana of neoclassical economics somehow shifts from markets to law making, and applies to the emergence and enforcement of legal rules. In Posner's approach, individuals are always informed rational maximizers, and their behavior is easily formalized and predicted. Economic agents respond to price incentives, and the simple tools of micro-economics always work well. This approach has been successfully extended to non-market decision making (theory of the state, voting rules, bureaucratic choice, regulations, corruption, and so on) and to studies on *rent-seeking* (Tullock 1965; Peltzman 1976). However, from 1983 onwards, "the confidence with which Chicago research agenda for law and economics was taken for granted as the only game in town appears shaken. The debate allows viewpoints dissonant from strict neoclassical economics to come out of the shadows" (Mackaay 1999).

## 19.3    Does new institutional economics meet law and economics?

One of the main criticisms of the Posnerian approach to law and economics has been made, in recent years, by those whose works were heavily cited by Posner as the best examples of the economic analysis of law and economic institutions: Ronald Coase and Oliver Williamson. In a special issue of the 1993 *Journal of Institutional and Theoretical Economics*,[3] Posner had the misfortune of being attacked both by Coase and Williamson on the nature of the economic nirvana of his studies. Posner's starting point was that "NIE, save in Coase's version, is just economics . . . and the L&E movement is economics too." Posner's attitude toward the use of mainstream economics was clear: "We should be pragmatic about theory. It is a tool, rather than a glimpse of ultimate truth, and the criterion of a tool is its utility." However, since economics is, in Posner's view, an ideal example of mainstream neoclassical economics, Coase's reaction was rather strong: "after having read Posner's paper, I felt I could not remain silent . . . [on] Posner's highly inaccurate account of my views . . . The trouble with Posner . . . is not what he doesn't know, but what he knows 'ain't so'."

Looking at the original Coasean approach, we can easily see the void between Coase and Posner. In his 1937 paper on the nature of firms, Coase derived the notion of transaction costs first from the limits of rationality and knowledge embedded in human action, in a context of uncertainty – either when searching for the best market options or when governing a growing organization. As Coase (1937) comments, "the question of uncertainty is often considered extremely relevant to studies on the equilibrium of the firm. It seems improbable that a firm would emerge without the existence of uncertainty." Looking at Frank Knight's influential theory of uncertainty, we suggest that in Coase, the "second-best" world produced by the existence of transaction costs generates first in the human mind and, in particular, in the agents' inability to immediately adopt, without costs, first best choices. In Posner's view, a court surprisingly has all the virtues (in terms of knowledge, rationality, and certainty) that conflicting parties lack when trying to settle their disputes autonomously. In setting efficient rules, courts and the legal system use superior rationality unavailable to parties involved in a dispute. In Posner's approach, whereas economic agents do not have the ability to run their relations autonomously in an efficient way, the legal system is able to provide, at zero cost, efficient solutions to market failure. Unsurprisingly, this contradiction could hardly be conciliated within the Coasean framework. In this framework, institutions are not the source of efficient solutions to the emergence of externalities. They are second-best devices which internalize externalities possibly at the lowest level of transaction costs. Thus, we ask in Coasean terms, if courts and the legal system perform efficiently, how can we explain the emergence and the persistence of institutional structures as firms? If courts always perform well, why should firms often act as private courts? According to the Posnerian study, we should expect a lower level of private orderings in common law countries, whereas the realm of modern societies suggests quite the opposite.[4]

The tone of the debate between Posner and Williamson is similar. The key feature of Williamson's (1985, 1996) *new institutional economics* is the idea that the unit of analysis is represented by a transaction, and, as its paradigmatic problem, the minimization of transaction costs. The distinguishing features of a transaction are bounded rationality, incompleteness of contracts, opportunism, and asset specificity. And economic agents generate economic institutions (private orderings) to deal with their costs. The economic institutions that survive over time are those that best perform agents' behaviour in terms of minimizing transaction costs. Posner (1993) disregarded the distinguishing feature of NIE or transaction cost economics (TCE) and pointed out that "in the process of moderating Coase, Williamson collapsed the NIE back into mainstream economics – which is fine with me . . . The L&E movement differs from new institutional economics in that it has shows no desire, or at least very little, to change economic theory or economists' empirical methodology." In Posner's view, "bounded rationality" simply states that "economic players have, and must (rationally) act on, less than full information" and as for the idea that "mind is a scarce resource," according to Posner, this idea simply implies that "the mind has limited information-processing capabilities." The same is true, in Posner's analysis, for the notion of opportunism to which a large part of Williamsonian work is devoted: "as used by Williamson and other economists, it means taking advantage . . . it is self-interest in setting in which private incentives cannot be relied on to promote social welfare." Thus Posner's conclusions on Williamson's work are simple: "they are merely new words for old themes in economics," whereas "the novelty of Williamson's works . . . lies in attracting the attention of economists to a host of unexplored problems."

Also in this case, the answer given by Williamson is rather harsh: "Posner has not understood the Coasean message (or does not like what he hears); he misconstrues game theory; he has a truncated understanding of bounded rationality, the economics of information and maximizing; he mischaracterizes empirical research in transaction cost economics."

From the above debate we conclude that NIE did not meet Posnerian law and economics. However, as Mercuro and Medema (1997) observe, the NIE/TCE approach is fully integrated into the law and economics approach, and has also been applied to comparative studies of legal systems and of misalignment incentives in courts in common law countries (Glaeser and Shleifer 2003).

Coase and Williamson are clearly dissatisfied with Posner's transfer of the economic nirvana hypothesis to the behaviour of courts. However, they share his over-optimistic view of the legal process: when property rights do exist, in Coase and Williamson's studies, they are always well-defined, complete, clear, and fully enforced at zero cost. In other words, Coase and Williamson fail to apply the same paradigm for the governance of costly market transactions to the process of creation, emergence, and enforcement of property rights. It seems as if, in the NIE world, a pre-existent ideal world has produced property rights and continues to maintain an efficient enforcement system over them, without incurring any of the failures generally attributed to market transactions (Pagano 2000). This implies, in our view, that the economic notion of transaction generated by the NIE/TCE approach, although aimed at removing the economic nirvana, still includes a legal nirvana, taking as given the legal process of creation and enforcement of well-defined property rights. In the next section, the comparative study of the notion of transaction in NIE and in old institutional economics will help to investigate the complexity of transactions at the intersection of law and economics.

## 19.4    Meaning of transaction costs: new versus old institutional economics

Section 19.3 illustrated the main differences between NIE and Posnerian law and economics. However, if we investigate the surrounding notion of transactions, which seems to emerge from scholarly works by both schools of thought, we find that Coase, Posner, and Williamson share similar views. This section compares a stylized NIE notion of transaction with a complex notion of transactions as outlined by the so-called old institutional economics (OIE). Whilst the NIE concept of transactions (mainly in Williamson's view) tends to focus exclusively on the role of private orderings, taking public legal orderings for granted, the OIE concept of transactions tries to illustrate the endogenous interdependence between legal orderings (defined as *authorized transactions*) and private orderings (defined as *authoritative transactions*).

NIE approaches neglect relevant aspects such as the emergence and change of legal rights and preferences,[5] the organisational diversity of firms and their persistence over time, the impact of ex-post potential competition over contracts and between firms, the endogenous and reciprocal shaping of legal and private orderings.

There is no common vision of the meaning and evolution of property rights among authors like Coase (1988), Barzel (1989), Williamson (1985), and North (1990). However, the resulting NIE approaches to the governance of transactions are all characterized, to different degrees, by a pervasive incoherence: on one hand, institutions such as firms are always an efficient adaptation to market failure generated by high transaction costs in carrying out a given transaction in the open market; on the other, the market for property rights and control must work efficiently if firms are to adapt efficiently to problems of market failure.[6] Thus, while some property rights do not exist, others must be efficiently enforced by a costless public ordering. This dichotic view of public ordering reaches a rather extreme level in the new property right approach by Hart (1995), where some rights (those on human capital investment) cannot be defined, exchanged, and enforced, and other rights (those on machines) may be defined, enforced, and exchanged at zero cost – an assumption entailing a complete transformation of the uneven and lumpy Coasian buttermilk-like markets into a smooth Swiss cheese where empty holes of unenforceable claims exist in a flat surface of perfectly defined property rights (Pagano 2000).

Obviously, as Fuller (1969) emphasized, the existence of a legal system and its capacity to define and enforce rights is rather more often a matter of uneven degrees than of absolute capacities and incapacities to do so.

Barzel (1989) has emphasized that property rights are a bundle of rights, and that different transaction cost structures imply different de facto rights.[7] In Barzel's view, there is potential for enlarging the framework to assess the full range of interdependency among legal rules, economic behaviour, and institutional change. In this respect, Barzel's contribution is strictly related to the notion of transaction as outlined by OIE and, in particular, Commons (1924), where the issue of defining and enforcing property rights plays a central role and greatly increases the complexity of transactions.

### 19.4.1   Defining complex transactions: the old institutional economics approach

In Commons's (1924) view, in order to properly assess the nature and extent of transaction costs, the notion of transactions must be investigated in further detail. A transaction is thus a complex interaction involving relations of rights, power, competition, and enforcement.

Table 19.1 *First-order jural relations*
*(authorised transaction)*

| Right of $i$ | Duty of $j$ |
|---|---|
| Exposure of $i$ | Liberty of $j$ |

Consider transactions between two agents $i$ and $j$. According to Commons, who built on Hohfeld's (1919) contribution, "first-order" jural relations define some necessary relations between the two agents $i$ and $j$. For instance, $i$ may (may not) claim that $j$ saves him when his ship is in trouble (Action A), and $j$ may be deprived of the corresponding liberty to leave without assisting.

In other words:

(1)   Claim (right) of $i$ ⇔ Duty of $j$;

or, in other words, agent $i$ has legal claim on agent $j$ that $j$ performs action A if, and only if, $j$ has a duty to perform A with respect to $i$:

(2)   No right (exposure) of $i$ ⇔ Liberty of $j$;

or, in other words, agent $j$ has the legal liberty toward agent $i$ to perform A if, and only if, $i$ has no right over $j$ to prevent $j$ from performing A and is, therefore, exposed to the liberty of $j$. Of course, similar relations hold true for the claims of $j$ and liberties of $i$.

In this simple two-individual relationship, the set of actions, for which $i$ has rights, do not only define the duties of $j$. They also define the remaining actions for which $j$ has the liberty to act (i.e. the set of actions for which $i$ has no right to interfere and is exposed to the liberties of $j$). In other words, in this simple framework, jural relations must ensure that the boundary between the rights and exposures of $i$ should coincide with the boundary between the duties and liberties of $j$ and vice versa, as is made clear in Table 19.1 on first-order jural relations.

Besides the above relationships, we have "second-order" jural relations in terms of powers and immunities that involve changing first-order relations. Thus second-order jural relations are characterized by the following relations, which are analogous to those described above:

(1')   Power of $i$ ⇔ Liability of $j$;

or, in other words, $i$ has legal power over agent $j$ to bring about a particular legal consequence C for $j$ if, and only if, some voluntary actions by $i$ are legally recognized to have such a consequence for $j$.

(2')   Disability of $i$ ⇔ Immunity of $j$;

Table 19.2 *Second-order legal relations (authoritative transaction)*

| Power of $i$ | Liability of $j$ |
|---|---|
| Disability of $i$ | Immunity of $j$ |

or, in other words, agent $j$ has legal immunity with respect to agent $i$ from a specific legal consequence C if, and only if, $i$ does not have the legal power to take any action which, according to law, would have consequence C for $j$. (Again, similar relations hold for the powers of $i$ and immunities of $j$).

Second-order jural relations also entail similar correlations between the positions of the two agents. In this case, too, the boundary between the powers and disabilities of $i$ should coincide with the boundary between the liabilities and immunities of $j$, and vice versa. Again, focussing our attention on relations (1') and (2'), we obtain the following (Table 19.2) on second-order legal relations.

The working rules for transactions include a definition of the rights, duties, liberties, and exposures of agents or, in other words, their entitlements. However, there is no guarantee that these rules satisfy the relations considered above. Much "legal dis-equilibrium" may exist in real-life societies. If we focus on the two agents $i$ and $j$ involved in the transactions, the two agents may well hold different views on their entitlements. For instance, the rights of agent $i$ may not match the duties of $j$, and the liberties of $j$ may not match the exposures to these liberties of $i$. In other words, the boundary between the rights and exposures of $i$ may not coincide with the border between the duties and liberties of $j$.

Both first- and second-order jural relations play a prominent role in Commons's analysis of transactions and, in particular, in his distinction between authorised and authoritative transactions. Whilst *authorized transactions* depend directly on the "hierarchy" of a judge or third party with respect to well-defined rights, *authoritative transactions* depend on relationships of power.

*19.4.1.1 Authorized transaction*    An "authorized transaction" is defined as a transaction governed by "the will of a superior party or parties to impose limits on their transactions, by imposing or interpreting a rule of conduct applicable to dispute" (Commons 1924, p. 87). Thus, it occurs when, because of the activity of a fifth agent (public authorities), the border between the rights and exposures of each agent coincide with that between the duties and liberties of the other agent. "Legal dis-equilibrium" is eliminated by the superior party. However, "authorized transactions" cannot be taken for granted unless we imagine a world of complete law, or of complete rights (and related duties) for every possible action or use potentially exposed to an externality.[8] As long as we live in a world of incomplete rights, most potential relationships among economic agents are governed by "authoritative transactions" or second-order jural relations, which means that they are governed by rules of power and liability.

*19.4.1.2 Authoritative transactions* An "authoritative transaction" is a transaction governed by a power relationship where "the subject person is not permitted to choose any alternative once the superior person has decided" (Commons 1924, p. 107). This power depends on the completeness of the legal system and the dimension and actual configuration of the market in which the transaction occurs. The "legal dis-equilibrium" is here partially eliminated by the private sphere of the economy.

Thus we can see how at any time, in a given legal system, there is reciprocal shaping between authorized and authoritative transactions. This relationship between "authorized transactions" and "authoritative transactions" strictly depends, in a given legal system, on the degree of completeness of property rights: the more complete and defined the property rights, the greater the predominance of "authorized transactions" over "authoritative transactions," and the weaker the impact of market discipline on contractual or vertical relationships. On the other hand, when rights are poorly defined, authoritative transactions act as a surrogate for the legal system, and actual contractual parties are exposed to relations of economic power. The above conclusions stress that the OIE notion of transactions has been recouped by the works of Demsetz (1967), Barzel (1989), and North (1990), in their studies of the emergence and evolution of property rights, norms, and institutions resulting from inter-individual exchanges between institutional environments based on trust, bilateral retaliation, and power to anonymous market exchange. But the next section illustrates how interactions between authorized and authoritative transactions do not necessarily and automatically give rise to a unique pattern of evolution, being influenced by the structuring of reciprocal complementarities among distinct institutional domains.

## 19.5    Setting the research agenda: complex transactions and institutional complementarities

As the above analysis reveals, Commons developed a complex concept of transactions which included all the possible social interactions that actually affect it. As a consequence, Commons's transactions generate a rich governance structure that relates to the relative dimension of "authorized transactions" and "authoritative transactions." The relative weight of the two depends on many variables, and mainly on the way in which legal positions structure themselves as institutional complementarities (Pagano 2007). This final section illustrates how the concept of institutional complementarities may be used to investigate the dynamics of complex transactions and the endogenous structuring of authorized and authoritative transactions, according to initial institutional conditions.

As Aoki (2001) has recently pointed out, the notion of institutional complementarity (Milgrom and Roberts 1990; Pagano and Rossi 2004) is a useful tool for studying how equilibria are selected in a complex transaction characterized by multiple equilibria. The concept of institutional complementarity is based on the idea that, in a given institutional framework characterized by complex transactions, economic agents face different domains and do not strategically coordinate their choices across domain games. Consequently, institutional choices in one domain act as exogenous parameters in others, and constitute the "institutional environment" where choices are made. In this setting, "one type of institution rather than another becomes viable in one domain, when a fitting institution is present in another domain, and vice versa" (Aoki 2001).

The emergence of institutional complementarities between legal and economic domains in transactions results in the possibility of equally (in)efficient multiple equilibria that tend to persist over time. Studies of institutional complementarities in the context of complex transactions result in the following: (1) interdependence between legal and economic domains may generate multiple institutional arrangements; (2) according to initial conditions affecting the available choices in one domain, some Pareto-inferior institutional arrangements may emerge; (3) since institutional arrangements are self-enforcing in nature, they are destined to perpetuate over time (because of path dependency and cumulative causation) unless some exogenous change affects one domain or the other so as to shift the choice to another institutional arrangement.

These outcomes completely reverse the Posnerian view of the process of legal change as a continuous and progressive tendency toward a systemic efficiency, rather than the emergence of diversity and fragmentation in legal systems. Moreover, since interdependence between legal and economic domains may strictly depend on the degree of discretionary power on the definition and allocation of rights, the co-evolution of economic and legal domains may well be shaped by reasons other than the maximization of aggregate wealth. This is in line with recent studies showing that, even in common law countries, the rise of the regulatory state has been an institutional response to the belief that private litigation is the sole appropriate response to social wrongs. As Glaeser and Shleifer (2003) point out, since private litigation is subject to "subversion" (the power exerted by authoritative transactions), the regulatory state has grown as an institutional response to (the excesses of) discretionary power in private litigation. This has another consequence contrary to the claimed "efficiency of property rights." Not only the allocation of well-defined property rights, but also the process of defining rights is subject to discretionary powers, and in a theoretical framework, nothing guarantees that property rights are defined in principle to perform efficient transactions.

This is one of the main conclusions of the approach known as *critical legal studies*, for which law is a social institution. The Posnerian idea of a world of (wealth-maximizing) efficient norms may mask a policy to preserve the existing social order, where the evolution of law and rights depends on the allocation of power.[9] When property rights are poorly defined or incomplete, their allocation may affect the actual shape of these rights and is not in itself a prerequisite for efficiency (Usher 1998). The ultimate effect of property rights on the efficient governance of a given transaction depends on how property rights are defined, enforced and exerted.

Setting a future research agenda, post-Chicago developments are heterogeneous in their objectives, but they share a common feature in challenging traditional assumptions (bounded rationality but predictable maximizing behaviour; explicit consideration of agents' hidden purposes). Norms result from complex, institutional complementarity relations among several domains of choice (Cafaggi, Nicita, and Pagano 2007), which may easily bring about multiple (and often inefficient) equilibria. The enforcement of legal rules is the complex result of complementary devices (such as the state, the market, and firms), and the impact of legal change needs to be assessed and predicted within a wide and enlarged framework according to the actual behavior of real-life agents. Self-enforcing, path-dependent equilibria in the governance of transactions between economic and legal domains can easily emerge. This explains the variety of legal systems, and the structuring of alternative governance systems for transactions, according to historical local conditions.

When legal relations are inconsistent, this means not only that there is a better alternative but also that the consequent mismatch in the expectations of agents will create some costly conflict in the economic system. Both public and private orderings are costly and imperfect systems for aligning expectations *ex ante* and avoiding costly conflicts *ex post*.

The institutional comparative advantages of the public and private orderings depend on their relations of complementarity with other institutional domains where individuals exercise their choices and which are, in turn, affected by the relative efficiency of the different types of legal orderings.

None of the institutional domains outlined may be considered an independent nirvana capable of supporting an a-historical efficiency of its own domain and of the other domains. And, indeed, in our opinion, it is this definitive removal of all the nirvana assumptions that should characterize an *institutional law and economics* approach which, building on the early insights of Commons and Coase, aims at fruitful exploration of the complex relations among the arrangements existing in the different domains and, eventually, at less naïve policies grounded in the historical specificity of each system.

# 20 The Theory of the Firm and Its Critics: A Stocktaking and Assessment

*Nicolai J. Foss and Peter G. Klein*

## 20.1 Introduction

Since it emerged in the early 1970s new institutional economics (NIE) has been the subject of intense debate. As an important part of NIE, the modern theory of the firm – mainly transaction cost economics (TCE) and property rights theory, but also agency theory and team theory – is no exception.[1] Much of the debate on the theory of the firm has been "internal," in the sense that it has been conducted between scholars who are generally sympathetic to the new institutional approach (e.g. Hart 1995; Kreps 1996; Maskin and Tirole 1999; Brousseau and Fares 2000; Foss and Foss 2001; Furubotn 2002; MacLeod 2002).

However, there also exists a substantial, though somewhat amorphous, set of "external" critiques, arising from sociologists, heterodox economists ("old" institutionalist, Austrian, and evolutionary), and management scholars, mainly in the organization and strategy fields. Williamson's TCE has been a favorite *Prügelknabe* for about three decades (e.g. Richardson 1972; Hodgson 1989; Perrow 2002), but agency theory has also drawn a fair amount of fire (Donaldson 1996). For instance, early critics argued that TCE ignored the role of differential capabilities in structuring economic organizations (Richardson 1972); neglected power relations (Perrow 1986), trust, and other forms of social embeddedness (Granovetter 1985); and overlooked evolutionary considerations, including Knightian uncertainty and market processes (Langlois 1984). Such critiques have been echoed and refined in numerous contributions, and criticizing NIE remains a thriving industry. The incumbents are mainly sociologists (Freeland 2002; Buskens, Raub, and Snijders 2003; Lindenberg 2003) and non-mainstream economists (Hodgson 1998; Loasby 1999; Witt 1999; Dosi and Marengo 2000), but new entrants are increasingly recruited from the ranks of management scholars (Pfeffer 1994), in particular from the strategic management field (Kogut and Zander 1992; Conner and Prahalad 1996; Ghoshal and Moran 1996; Madhok 1996).

This chapter offers an idiosyncratic review and assessment of this critical literature.[2] Our assessment aims to be constructive, in that we ask if the critiques can advance the modern economic theory of the firm by identifying weak points, suggesting improvements, and the like. We do not claim to be comprehensive; unavoidably many authors, papers, and insights must be left out. However, we aim to capture what we see as the fundamental critiques.

We begin with a brief summary of core ideas in the modern economic theory of the firm, highlighting the key assumptions at which the critics have concentrated their fire. We turn next to the substance of these critiques, focussing on cognitive and behavioral issues, firm heterogeneity and production costs, and market characteristics such as path dependence, the survivor principle, and other evolutionary issues. As we consider each challenge, we discuss its implications for theoretical and applied research on the firm. In other words, we ask what, if anything, each critique suggests about how to address the three key *explananda* of the theory of the firm: existence, boundaries, and internal organization.

## 20.2    The Coasian theory of the firm

### 20.2.1    Coase and later work on the theory of the firm

The basic features of the emergence of the theory of the firm are well known. As the story is normally told, the theory of the firm traces its existence back to Coase's (1937) landmark article, "The Nature of the Firm," with its key conjecture that the main *explananda* of the theory of the firm (existence, boundaries, and internal organization) may be explained by incorporating the "costs of using the price mechanism" into standard economic analysis. For various reasons, Coase's seminal analysis was neglected for more than three decades; the analysis was known, but not used, as Coase (1972, p. 68) himself has noted. However, about the same time as Coase's lamentation, serious work on the theory of firm began to emerge, with four seminal contributions defining the central streams of research in the theory of the firm, namely TCE (Williamson 1971), the property rights or nexus-of-contracts approach (Alchian and Demsetz 1972), agency theory (Ross 1973), and team theory (Marschak and Radner 1972).

Of these four approaches, only the transaction costs approach and the property rights approach are conventionally considered theories of the firm in the strict sense. Neither team theory nor principal–agent theory explains the boundaries of the firm, defined in terms of asset ownership

(Hart 1995). Such an explanation must presuppose that contracts are incomplete, otherwise everything can be stipulated contractually and there is no need for ownership, the "residual right" to make decisions under conditions not specified by contract. TCE and property rights theory, by contrast, assume that contracts are incomplete, meaning that some contingencies or outcomes are not specified in the contract. Accordingly, our main emphasis will be on the latter two approaches.[3]

### 20.2.2  A simple representation

The basic incomplete contracting argument is illustrated by the strategic-form games shown in Figure 20.1. We choose this representation not for its own sake, but, rather, because it brings out many of the crucial underlying assumptions in the modern theory of the firm.

Following Hurwicz (1972), we can imagine economic agents choosing game forms, and the resulting equilibria, for regulating their trade. Efficiency requires that agents choose the game form and equilibrium that maximizes the gains from trade. The two players begin by confronting Game 1. The problem here, of course, is that the Pareto criterion is too weak to select a unique equilibrium since both {up, left} and {down, right} are Pareto-efficient. However, the {down, right} equilibrium has a higher joint surplus than the {up, left} equilibrium, so that it will be in A's interest to bribe B to play {right}. Given complete contracting, as in agency theory, $u$, the side payment, may be chosen ($1 < u < 2$) to implement the equilibrium in which A plays {down} and B plays {right}. But under incomplete contracting, side payments may not be sustainable in equilibrium.[4]

The inefficiency may be remedied by contract; for example, A may agree to pay a penalty to B if he does not pay $u$, or B may agree to pay a

| Game 1 | | | | Game 2 | | |
|---|---|---|---|---|---|---|
| | B | | | | B | |
| | left | right | | | left | right |
| up | 2,2 | 0,0 | | up | 2,2 | 0,0 |
| | A | | | | A | |
| down | 0,0 | 4,1 | | down | 0,0 | 4-u,1+u |

**Figure 20.1**  Conflict in organizations.

penalty to A if he does not play {right} after receiving $u$. However, such contracts may not always be feasible. Contracts cannot completely safeguard against the reduction of surplus or loss of welfare stemming from incentive conflicts (given risk preferences). The analytical enterprise is therefore one of comparing alternative contracting arrangements, all of them imperfect. For example, we may compare Nash equilibria that result from different distributions of bargaining power (e.g. as given by ownership patterns) (Hart 1995).

### 20.2.3 Basic characteristics of the modern theory of the firm

The above strategic-form representation helps illustrate several crucial underlying assumptions of the modern theory of the firm:

*Cognition.* Particularly in its formal versions, the theory of the firm follows neoclassical economics in making strong assumptions about the cognitive powers of agents. This reflects the dependence of the modern theory of the firm on mainstream information economics and game theory. Although bounded rationality is invoked by some writers (in particular Williamson 1985, 1996), virtually all the contracting problems studied in the modern theory of the firm may be modeled using the more tractable notion of asymmetric information (Hart 1990). Moreover, the Bayesian notion of uncertainty underlying game-theoretic models of contracting leaves no room for "Knightian," "deep," or "radical" uncertainty. In the above representation, players can thus never experience genuine surprise.

*Everything is given.* Because of strong assumptions about agents' cognitive powers, modern theories of the firm portray decision situations as always unambiguous and "given." The choice of efficient economic organization is portrayed as a standard maximization problem, as in contract design, or as a choice among given "discrete, structural alternatives" (Williamson 1996), as in the choice of governance structure. There is no learning, no need for entrepreneurial creation or discovery, and explicit room for the emergence of new contractual or organizational forms. In the representation above, the strategy spaces are fully specified *ex ante*.

*Motivation.* In the modern theory of the firm motivation is assumed to be wholly extrinsic (Frey 1997). Stronger monetary incentives always call forth more effort (in at least a particular dimension). Low-powered incentives play a role only in multi-task agency problems (Holmström and Milgrom 1991).

*Explaining economic organization.* Problems of economic organization may be represented as games where the Nash equilibrium is not Pareto optimal. Whilst this includes some coordination games, such as the stag-hunt game (Camerer and Knez 1996), the modern theory of the firm generally disregards coordination problems. The focus is on aligning incentives, rather than coordinating actions. The function of contracts, hierarchies, reputation, and the like is to give agents incentives to choose the strategies that result in a Pareto-superior equilibrium. Transaction costs, and not production costs, are seen as the main obstacles to achieving first–best outcomes.

*Methodological individualism.* Aggregates play no independent role in explaining economic organization. The aim is to explain contractual and organizational form in terms of individual actions. Thus, aggregate constructs such as trust, embeddedness, organizational cognition, and capabilities are not considered part of the *explanans* of the modern theory of the firm; moreover, they are only seldom treated as *explanandum* phenomena (an exception is Kreps 1990, on corporate culture).

*Mode of explanation.* As a first approximation, efficient economic organization is supposed to be consciously chosen by well-informed, rational agents. If pressed on the issue economists of organization may also invoke evolutionary processes that are assumed to perform a sorting between organizational forms in favor of the efficient ones (Williamson 1985). Thus, explanation is either fully "intentional" or "functional-evolutionary" (Elster 1983; Dow 1987).

### 20.2.4   What are the critics criticizing?

Most of the above characteristics are not particular to the economic theory of the firm; they also describe any part of game-theoretic micro-economics. Critics of the theory of the firm may thus appear simply to be criticizing modern micro-economics more generally. However, while this may indeed be the case for some critics, a different interpretation is possible: the critics are protesting the application of concepts designed for analysis of *market exchange* to the study of firm organization. While some economists maintain that there is no real difference between firms and markets (Alchian and Demsetz 1972; Cheung 1983), and most econo-mists would agree that the same analytical tools are applicable to firms as well as to markets, the critics seem to argue that firms are essentially different from markets; many of the critics (in particular sociologists) argue that firms need to be studied using different tools (Freeland 2002).

Thus, while some critics may balk at methodological individualism and assumptions of full, instrumental rationality in general, they are likely to find such assumptions *particularly* objectionable when they are applied to the theory of the firm. In the literature that criticizes the modern theory of the firm firms are often portrayed in rosy terms as "mini-societies" (Freeland 2002) which provide "identity" (Kogut and Zander 1996), "higher-order organizing principles" (Kogut and Zander 1992), trust relations (Ghoshal and Moran 1996), and collective learning (Hodgson 1998) that, purportedly, "atomistic" markets cannot provide. Firms exist because and to the extent that they can supply "identity," "collective learning," and so on.

Although we are skeptical of such arguments, we acknowledge that they may point to unresolved issues and weak spots in the modern theory of the firm. For example, we may reject methodological holism and still hold that there are firm-specific cultures and capabilities, the understanding of which is inadequate in the modern theory of the firm (in spite of the efforts of, for example, Kreps 1990). Or one can argue that there is too little room for bounded rationality in this body of theory. In the following sections, we discuss and assess a number of such critiques of the modern theory of the firm in greater detail.

## 20.3    Cognitive and motivational issues

### 20.3.1  Bounded rationality

Formal, mainstream economics typically assumes that agents hold the same, correct model of the world and that this model does not change. The theory of the firm is no exception. More precisely, these assumptions are built into formal contract theory through the assumption that payoffs, strategies, and the like are common knowledge. These assumptions are clearly at variance with the notion of bounded rationality (Simon 1955). Indeed, the game-theoretic models used in most theoretical research on the theory of the firm ignore bounded rationality altogether, although it may play a role in the "rhetorical" motivation of such research (*see* Foss 2003).

In contrast, bounded rationality is often invoked in Oliver Williamson's (1985, 1996) less formal work. "But for bounded rationality," he argues (1996, p. 36), "all issues of organization collapse in favor of comprehensive contracting of either Arrow–Debreu or mechanism design kinds." What Williamson calls "comprehensive contracting" does not allow for "governance structures" in the sense of mechanisms which handle the coordination and incentive problems produced by unanticipated change (Williamson 1996). However, the role of bounded rationality in Williamson's work is mainly to provide a reason why contracts are incomplete.[5] It is a sort of background assumption that, while necessary, never really assumes a central role. Indeed, many critics have observed that to the extent that bounded rationality enters the theory of the firm, it is in rather "thin" forms (e.g. MacLeod 2000; Foss 2003). The reason is presumably that the theory is taken up with comparative institutional exercises, focusing on transaction cost economizing, and hence has no room for the process aspects introduced by more substantive notions of bounded rationality (e.g. Furubotn 2002).

Still, even the rather limited use of bounded rationality in the theory of the firm has been criticized. Hart (1990) argues that bounded rationality may not be necessary at all, because asymmetric information (in the form of imperfect verifiability) can do the job that bounded rationality is supposed to do, and may do so more elegantly and more consistently with mainstream modeling (*see also* Posner 1993). From a different position, Dow (1987) argues that it is inconsistent to invoke bounded rationality as a necessary assumption in the analysis of contracts and governance structures, and then assume that substantively rational choices can be made with respect to the contracts and governance structures (that are imperfect because of bounded rationality). This point is echoed in Kreps's (1996) critique of contract theory. Contract theory assumes that although the parties to a contract cannot describe the benefits from an exchange relationship, they can perfectly anticipate the benefits produced by the different contractual arrangements that can structure such a relationship. Of course, this assumption is made to rationalize the *ex ante* choice of ownership or incentive structures. While it may make formal sense (*see* Maskin and Tirole 1999), "not everything that is logically consistent is credulous," as Kreps (1996, p. 565) laconically observes in a comment on Maskin and Tirole. He argues that the Maskin and Tirole argument (and virtually all of contract theory) simply takes rationality too far, and that more attention should be paid to bounded rationality.[6]

In contrast, bounded rationality has long been a central assumption in organization theory (e.g. March and Simon 1958; Cyert and March 1963). In fact, recent critics of the theory of the firm have drawn explicitly on these older sources to develop alternative, evolutionary views emphasizing the role of bounded rationality in problem solving, and the role of firms as cognitive structures around such problem-solving efforts (e.g. Dosi and Marengo 1994). Other critics, also echoing behaviorist organization theory, argue that a key characteristic of firms is that they tend to shape employee cognition (Kogut and Zander 1996; Hodgson 1998; Witt 1999). For example, starting with social learning theory, Witt (1999) argues that individual cognitive frames are socially shaped and that firms can accomplish such shaping. In particular, entrepreneurs form business conceptions that underlie their "cognitive leadership," making employees internalize and collectively share the cognitive categories embodied in the business conception.

## 20.3.2 Motivation

Whilst the role of bounded rationality in the theory of the firm has given rise to a fair amount of debate, it is nothing compared to the enormous amount of critical writings on the motivational assumptions. Opportunism, in particular, seems to be the favorite bête noire. The critique of opportunism takes various forms. Empirically, the relevance of opportunism is dismissed by pointing to difficulty in observing it, for instance in industrial networks or in long-term associations between firms and their suppliers (see Håkansson and Snehota 1990). The obvious problem with such arguments is that they misunderstand the counterfactual nature of reasoning in the theory of the firm: opportunistic behavior is seldom observed because governance structures are chosen to mitigate opportunism. Another claim is that opportunism is not a necessary assumption in the theory of the firm (e.g. Kogut and Zander 1992), but this line of reasoning fails to provide convincing alternative accounts.

According to a more recent and more sophisticated set of arguments, the primary problem with the treatment of motivation in the theory of the firm is not opportunism *per se*, but rather that modern economic approaches assume that all motivation is of the "extrinsic" type (Ghoshal and Moran 1996; Osterloh and Frey 2000). In other words, all behavior is understood in terms of encouragement from an external force, such as the expectance of a monetary reward. (In contrast, when "intrinsically" motivated, individuals wish to undertake a task for its own sake.) These arguments do not necessarily deny the reality of opportunism, moral hazard, and so on; they assert instead that there are other, better ways of handling these problems besides providing monetary incentives, sanctions, and monitoring. The arguments are often based on social psychology (notably Deci and Ryan 1985) and on experimental economics (e.g. Fehr and Gächter 2000).

In one version of the argument, Pfeffer (1994) and Ghoshal and Moran (1996) argue that the theory of the firm misconstrues the causal relation between motivation (e.g. the tendency to shirk) and the surrounding environment (the type of governance structure in place). For example, Ghoshal and Moran (1996, p. 21) claim that individuals within an organization perform not according to the incentives and opportunities offered, but to their "feelings for the entity." "Hierarchical" controls, they state, reduce organizational loyalty and thus increase shirking. Reliance on internal governance in the presence of relationship-specific investments, they hold, causes the very problems it is designed to alleviate: Williamson's approach becomes a "self-fulfilling prophecy," and is therefore "bad for practice."[7] In another version of the argument Osterloh and Frey (2000) ask which organizational forms are conducive to knowledge creation and transfer. They note that elements of market control (e.g. high-powered incentives) are often introduced in firms to accomplish this. However, Osterloh and Frey argue that this only works to the extent that there is no "motivation crowding-out effect," in which extrinsic motivation does not crowd out intrinsic motivation. They draw on Deci and Ryan (1985) and other contributions to social psychology to argue that motivation may be harmed when agents perceive that their actions are subject to external control (as with a performance-pay system). Osterloh and Frey argue that forms of internal organization that foster intrinsic motivation can more successfully create and transfer tacit knowledge because such activities cannot be compelled – only enabled.

### 20.3.3   Challenges to the theory of the firm?

Few economists of organization have reacted to the above critiques. We suspect this is partly because taking these critiques seriously means questioning fundamental tenets of mainstream economic modeling. For example, taking bounded rationality seriously opens up a Pandora's box because bounded rationality challenges the game-theoretic foundations underlying the formal literature on the theory of the firm (subjective expected utility theory, the independence of payoff utilities, the irrelevance of labeling, and common prior beliefs [Camerer 1998]). Organizational economists may also question what bounded rationality adds to the theory (Hart 1990). Williamson (1999c, p. 12) notes that "organization can and should be regarded as an instrument for utilizing varying cognitive and behavioral propensities to best advantage," and that the many ramifications of bounded rationality should be explored to help identify those regularities in decision making that differ from the classical von Neumann–Morgenstern–Savage model. The implications of these regularities for efficient organization can then be developed and incorporated into the theory of the firm (Williamson 1999c, p. 18). However, Williamson (1999c) mainly emphasizes that the findings of cognitive psychology are consistent with "[t]he transaction cost economics triple for describing human actors – bounded rationality, far-sighted contracting, and opportunism." Moreover, many bounds on rationality are substantially mitigated by organization, because organization has recourse to specialization, which allows for economizing with cognitive effort. Such arguments cast doubt on the belief that taking bounded rationality more seriously will yield theoretical advances.

However, a handful of contributions, mainly to contract theory, do try to model agents that are boundedly rational in a more substantive sense. For example, Mookerjee (1998) shows how ambiguity may lead to incomplete contracting; Carmichael and MacLeod (2003) show that if boundedly rational agents care about sunk costs, the hold-up problem may be solved. There are various problems with such approaches. Notably, there may be too many "degrees of freedom," in the sense that virtually any cognitive bias may be thrown into a standard contracting model, thus producing a non-standard result. Moreover, how does the theorist decide which manifestation of bounded rationality to model? The danger is that we end up with a string of unconnected and extreme partial models with no apparent connection to empirical reality.

In our opinion, working with alternative motivational assumptions may be a more fruitful way forward. It is easier to doctor utility functions than cognitive assumptions. There is established social psychology work, the insights of which may be fed relatively directly into modeling efforts (*see* Benabou and Tirole 2003). Moreover, the implications for economic organization may also seem more immediate (*see* Lazear 1991; Fehr and Gächter 2000 for concrete examples).

## 20.4    Firm heterogeneity, capabilities, and production costs

### 20.4.1    *The knowledge-based view*

A growing number of writers within heterodox economics (in particular evolutionary economics) and strategic management now embrace "capabilities," "dynamic capabilities," or "competence" approaches (e.g. Winter 1988; Langlois 1992; Kogut and Zander 1992; Foss 1993; Dosi and Marengo 1994; Teece and Pisano 1994; Langlois and Robertson 1995; Loasby 1999). We lump all these together here under the heading "knowledge-based view of the firm." Contributions to the knowledge-based view are usually launched on a background of critique of NIE, in particular Williamson's version of TCE. The critique concerns the reliance on opportunism and the neglect of differential capabilities (i.e. firm heterogeneity) and dynamics (e.g. Winter 1988; Langlois 1992; Kogut and Zander 1992).

In contrast, contributors to the knowledge-based view typically begin from the empirical generalization that firm-specific knowledge is sticky and tacit, and develops through path-dependent processes. This implies that organizations are necessarily limited in what they know how to do well.[8] Differential capabilities imply differences in terms of the efficiency with which resources are deployed. Superior capabilities, if hard to imitate, can generate long-lived rents (Lippman and Rumelt 1982; Wernerfelt 1984; Barney 1991; Peteraf 1993). Beginning perhaps with Kogut and Zander (1992) and Langlois (1992), adherents of the knowledge-based view have also argued that the characteristics of capabilities that make them relevant to the study of competitive advantage are also crucial for the study of the main issues in economic organization. Thus, knowledge-based writers argue that a theory of the firm should be based on considerations of knowledge, rather than incentives, opportunism, and transaction costs.

### 20.4.2 The knowledge-based view as a theory of economic organization

The idea that knowledge matters for economic organization is hardly new. George B. Richardson (1972) suggested that we begin, not from the Coasian idea of transaction costs, but from the idea that production may be broken down into activities underpinned by firm-specific capabilities. Some activities are similar, in that they draw on the same general capabilities; activities may be complementary, in that they are connected in the chain of production; and similarity and complementarity may obtain to varying degrees. The main point in Richardson (1972) is that the boundaries of the firm are strongly influenced by these dimensions of activities.[9] However, it is unclear in Richardson's paper how exactly capabilities are supposed to influence economic organization.

Some papers (e.g. Kogut and Zander 1992; Langlois 1992) argue that differential capabilities give rise to different production costs, and that such cost differentials may crucially influence the make-or-buy decision. Thus, firms may internalize activities because they can carry out these activities in a more production (not transaction) cost-efficient way than other firms are capable of. The factors that make capabilities distinctive and costly to imitate (e.g. complexity and tacitness) also make such differences in production costs long-lived. Thus, one firm's agents may literally fail to understand what another firm wants (e.g. in supplier contracts) or is offering (e.g. in license contracts). The costs of making contacts with potential partners, of educating potential licensees and franchisees, of teaching suppliers what it is we need from them, and so on – what Langlois (1992) christens "dynamic transaction costs," to distinguish them from the transaction costs usually considered in the theory of the firm – may influence where the boundaries of the firm are placed.

Knowledge-based writers also claim that the existence of the firm may be explained in knowledge terms and without invoking opportunism

(Hodgson 2004a). Demsetz (1988) argues that firms exist for reasons of economizing on expenditures on communicating and coordinating knowledge. Thus, the employment contract, and hierarchy more generally, may exist because it is efficient to have the less knowledgeable being directed by the more knowledgeable. A very different argument is forwarded by Kogut and Zander (1992), who argue that firms exist because they can create certain assets – such as learning capabilities or a "shared context" – that markets purportedly cannot create: "organizations are social communities in which individual and social expertise is transformed into economically useful products and services by the application of a set of higher-order organizing principles. Firms exist because they provide a social community of voluntaristic action structured by organizing principles that are not reducible to individuals" (Kogut and Zander 1992, p. 384). This view, they claim, "differs radically from that of the firm as a bundle of contracts that serves to allocate efficiently property rights." Firms' advantages over markets derive from their being able to supply "organizing principles that are not reducible to individuals" (Kogut and Zander 1992, p. 384).

The problem with this argument is that it does not apply exclusively to *firms*: markets may also cultivate learning capabilities and shared context (as in industrial districts, for instance). Moreover, embeddedness of the kind that Kogut and Zander talk about does not require firm organization: in a moral utopia, characterized by the absence of opportunistic proclivities, the gains from embeddedness could be realized over *the market.* Agents could simply meet under the same factory roof, own their own pieces of physical capital equipment or rent it to each other, and develop value-enhancing "organizing principles" (to use Kogut and Zander's term) among themselves, or in other ways integrate their specialized knowledge (as a team). Firms would not be necessary.[10]

### 20.4.3  Challenges to the theory of the firm?

Whilst we are skeptical of the specific knowledge-based explanations for economic organization, we acknowledge that the knowledge-based view does point to some weak points in the theory of the firm.[11] For example, differential capabilities probably do play a role in determining the boundaries of the firm (Walker and Weber 1984; Monteverde 1995; Argyes 1996). However, there are two major problems in this area that may hinder progress. The first is that the nature of the central construct (i.e. capabilities) is highly unclear. It is not clear how capabilities are conceptualized, dimensionalized, and measured, and it is not clear how capabilities emerge and are changed by individual action (Felin and

Foss 2004). The second problem partly follows from the first: the mechanisms between capabilities and economic organization are unclear (Heiman and Nickerson 2002; Foss 2005).

One of the few attempts to provide such a mechanism is Langlois (1992), who gives a key role to dynamic transaction costs. In other words, economizing with costs of communication (i.e. dynamic transaction costs) is a possible determinant of the boundaries of the firm (*see* Monteverde 1995 for this). More generally, the genuine challenges that the knowledge-based view represents has more probably more to do with the non-standard transaction problems relating to the exchange of knowledge than with the fuzzy notion of "firm capability." In other words, exchanging knowledge may lead to contractual frictions and hazards that do not involve opportunism and it may involve transaction costs that have nothing to do with misaligned incentives and everything to do with costly communication.

## 20.5    Entrepreneurship

A major problem with modern economic theories of the firm is that they ignore the entrepreneur (Furubotn 2002; Foss and Klein 2005). Thus, Furubotn (2002, pp 72–73) points out that "profit is always in the background of TCE analysis because it is impossible to say whether a particular action (and contractual arrangement) undertaken by the firm is desirable or not purely on the basis of the costs of transacting . . . There is reason, then, to give greater consideration to the question of how profits are generated." And this leads to the theory of entrepreneurship. However, in the modern theory of the firm reference to entrepreneurship is passing at best. These approaches are largely static and "closed," meaning that they focus on solutions to given optimization problems.[12]

### 20.5.1    Concepts of entrepreneurship

Probably the best-known concept of entrepreneurship in economics is Schumpeter's (1934) idea of the entrepreneur as innovator, who introduces "new combinations" – new products, production methods, markets, sources of supply, or industrial combinations – shaking the economy out of its previous equilibrium. Entrepreneurship can also be conceived as "alertness" to profit opportunities. Although present in older notions of entrepreneurship, this concept has been elaborated most fully by Kirzner (1973). Kirzner's formulation emphasizes the nature of competition as a discovery process: the source of entrepreneurial profit is superior foresight – the discovery of something (new products, cost-saving technology) unknown to other market participants. Success, in this view, comes not from following a well-specified maximization problem, but from having some knowledge or insight that no one else has. None of these accounts, however, links entrepreneurship closely to the theory of the firm. Small-business management is only one manifestation of entrepreneurship. Creativity, innovation, and alertness are undoubtedly important, but neither activity must take place within a firm. Charismatic leaders work with teams, but need not own physical assets, around which the boundaries of the firm are drawn.

### 20.5.2 Putting entrepreneurship into the theory of the firm

Various attempts to put entrepreneurship into the theory of the firm exist (e.g. Langlois and Robertson 1995; Casson 1997). An attempt that stays relatively close to the new institutional theory of the firm is Foss and Klein (2005). They outline an alternative account of entrepreneurship as judgmental decision making under conditions of uncertainty. Judgment refers primarily to business decision making when the range of possible future outcomes, let alone the likelihood of individual outcomes, is generally unknown (what Knight [1921] terms uncertainty, rather than mere probabilistic risk). The concept of entrepreneurship as judgment has a direct and natural link to the theory of the firm. Because markets for judgment are closed, the exercise of judgment requires starting a firm; moreover, judgment implies asset ownership. In this approach, resource uses are not data, but are created as entrepreneurs envision new ways of using assets to produce goods. The entrepreneur's decision problem is aggravated by the fact that capital assets are heterogeneous, and it is not immediately obvious how they should be combined. Asset ownership facilitates experimenting entrepreneurship: acquiring a bundle of property rights is a low-cost means of carrying out commercial experimentation. Moreover, important features of internal organization such as delegation and contractual incompleteness may be understood in terms of employers' attempts to facilitate "productive" entrepreneurship while discouraging non-productive forms of decision making. In short, firm boundaries and internal organization may be understood as responses to entrepreneurial processes of experimentation.

### 20.5.3 Challenges to the theory of the firm?

Will these insights be incorporated into the economic theory of the firm? Because these concepts lie fundamentally outside the standard constrained optimization framework, they are inherently difficult to model mathematically. Modern economists have difficulty appreciating ideas that are not expressed in this familiar language. Indeed, most recent theoretical advances in the economic theory of the firm have been developed within the more formal framework associated with Grossman, Hart, and Moore (Grossman and Hart 1986; Hart and Moore 1990), not the more "open" framework associated with Williamson.[13] Relaxing this constraint may lead to considerable advances in economists' understanding of the firm.

## 20.6    Process issues

### 20.6.1    Path dependence

The claim that the theory of the firm, because of its emphasis on efficiency at a point in time and on cross-sectional variation, is a-historical and neglects process has often been made by economists and management scholars within both the knowledge-based and the evolutionary perspective. Thus, according to Winter (1988, p. 178), "in the evolutionary view – perhaps in contrast to the transaction cost view – the size of a large firm at a particular time is not to be understood as the solution to some organizational problem. General Motors does not sit atop the Fortune 500 . . . because some set of contemporary cost minimization imperatives (technological or organizational) require a certain chunk of the US economy to be organized in this manner. Its position at the top reflects the cumulative effect of a long string of happenings stretching back into the past."

One way to interpret this critique is that the theory of the firm seeks to explain the governance of individual transactions (Williamson 1996), or clusters of attributes (Holmström and Milgrom 1994), without identifying how the governance of a particular transaction may depend on how *previous* transactions were governed. Argyres and Liebeskind (1999) term this historical dependency "governance inseparability." Where governance inseparability is present, firms may rely on governance structures that appear inefficient at a particular time, but which make sense as part of a longer-term process. Changes in governance structure affect not only the transaction in question, but the entire temporal sequence of transactions. This may make organizational form appear more "sticky" than it really is.

This criticism will sound familiar to Austrian and evolutionary economists, who have long argued for a "process" view of economic activity that takes time seriously (Hayek 1948; Kirzner 1973; Dosi 2000). Hayek (1948) distinguished between the neoclassical economics notion of "competition," identified as a set of equilibrium conditions (number of market participants, characteristics of the product, and so on), and the older notion of competition as a rivalrous process. Practices that appear inefficient or even anti-competitive at a given moment are better understood as part a process of competition through time; it is the process that should be evaluated in welfare terms, not the conditions that obtain at a particular moment in the process.

Williamson (1996), recognizing the need to incorporate history into TCE, has introduced the notion of remediableness as a welfare criterion. The outcome of a path-dependent process is suboptimal, he argues, only if it is remediable; that is, an alternative outcome can be implemented with net gains. Merely pointing to a hypothetical superior outcome, if it is not attainable, does not establish suboptimality. Thus, a governance structure or contractual arrangement "for which no superior *feasible* alternative can be described and *implemented* with expected net gains is *presumed* to be efficient" (Williamson 1996, p. 7) (for a critique, *see* Furubotn 2002, pp 89–90).

### 20.6.2    Selection and survival: are all organizations "efficient"?

The explanation of economic organization in terms of efficiency has been one of the most frequently criticized characteristics of the theory of the firm: Assuming that agents can figure out the efficient organizational arrangements seems to collide with the assumption of bounded rationality (Dow 1987; Furubotn 2002). Presumably in response to this problem, early work in the theory of the firm often explicitly assumed that market forces work to cause an "efficient sort" between transactions and governance structures, an assumption that is not in general tenable.

While appealing to market selection, Williamson (1988, p. 174) also clearly recognizes that the process of transaction cost economizing is not automatic. Still, he maintains that the efficiency presumption is reasonable, offering the argument that inefficient governance arrangements will *tend* to be discovered and undone.[14] Clearly, this assumption is not an innocuous one. It is in fact a key underlying assumption in virtually all empirical work in the theory of the firm. A general problem with the empirical literature on organizational form is that we usually observe only the business arrangements actually chosen. However, *if* these arrangements are presumed to be efficient, *then* we can draw inferences about the appropriate alignment between transactional characteristics and organizational form simply by observing what firms do. The problem is that the efficiency assumption has always been taken as an essential, but untested, background assumption.

In one of the few attempts to grapple empirically with the efficiency assumption, Lien and Klein (2004) examine the assumption that decisions or behaviors that occur frequently in a population of competitive firms are on average more efficient than those that occur rarely. They conduct the test in the context of corporate diversification. If the survivor principle holds, those pairs of industries most frequently combined within firms ("related" businesses) should tend to represent more efficient combinations than those pairs that are rarely combined. As firms strive to improve their performance, they tend to exit "unrelated" industries, that is, industries that are poor matches for their other businesses. Using detailed data on firms' business portfolios from the AGSM/Trinet database for the early 1980s, Lien and Klein (2004) show that the survivor-based measure of relatedness is a strong predictor of exit, even when controlling for other firm and industry characteristics which might affect the decision to withdraw from a particular industry. During that period, then, the competitive selection process did tend to filter out inappropriate business combinations.[15]

Another approach is to see if "appropriately" organized firms, that is, firms organized along the lines recommended by the theory of the firm, out perform the feasible alternatives. Several papers in the empirical TCE literature use a two-step procedure in which organizational form (in particular, the relationship between transactional characteristics and governance structure) is endogenously chosen in the first stage, and then used to explain performance in the second stage. By endogenizing both organizational form and performance this approach also mitigates the selection bias associated with OLS regressions of performance on firm characteristics.[16]

These evolutionary approaches shed considerable light on the processes by which organizations adapt and change, along with the costs of misalignment or maladaptation. However, reliance on evolutionary models introduces additional problems. In many cases, survival may not be the best measure of performance, compared with profitability or market value. Poorly performing firms may survive due to inefficient competitors, regulatory protection, or legal barriers to exit such as anti-takeover amendments or an overprotective bankruptcy code. In short, efficient alignment between transactions and governance should be expected only if the selection environment is strong. Moreover, when market conditions change rapidly and unexpectedly, *ex post* survival may not be a good measure of *ex ante* efficiency; a particular organizational form may be right for the times, but the times change. Indeed, the optimal organizational forms may be those that adapt most readily to new circumstances (Boger, Hobbs, and Kerr 2001).

## 20.7    Conclusion

Almost two decades ago Milgrom and Roberts (1988, p. 450) argued that the "incentive-based transaction costs theory has been made to carry too much of the weight of explanation in the theory of organizations," and predicted that "competing and complementary theories" would emerge, "theories that are founded on economizing on bounded rationality and that pay more attention to changing technology and to evolutionary considerations." However, despite the importance in the management literature of knowledge-based or capabilities theories of the firm, this body of thought cannot yet be considered a serious competitor to the "incentive-based transaction costs theory." No other serious competitors have emerged.

There are many reasons for this. One possible reason is that the conventional theory of the firm is sufficiently successful, theoretically and empirically, that competitors have a hard time gaining a foothold. Still, as we have stressed throughout this chapter, many of the critiques do, in fact, point to weaknesses in the theory of the firm that should ideally be remedied. A further reason is that the critics tend to focus on phenomena that are difficult to model, phenomena that are not readily "tractable" in the sense familiar to mainstream economists. Innovation, entrepreneurship, bounded rationality, learning, evolutionary processes, and differential capabilities are examples of such phenomena. We should not expect to see these phenomena integrated into the mainstream economic theory of the firm until the formal tools that can handle them have been developed. Moreover, the empirical literature supporting the challenges outlined above tends to be idiosyncratic, based on experimental or qualitative work rather than the standard econometric analysis familiar to economists. Finally, the various critiques are not separate but overlapping or complementary. For example, the claim that the theory of the firm neglects bounded rationality is very close to the claim that it ignores differential capabilities, learning, and path dependence. In turn, the complaint that the theory of the firm neglects the latter phenomena is closely related to concerns that it assumes, uncritically, that selection forces operate to produce efficiency. In other words, the critiques come in a package, so that embracing one critique may be taken as embracing the rest – which would mean abandoning the theory of the firm as we know it.

### Acknowledgements

Thanks to Harvey James, Martin Krause, and an anonymous reviewer for helpful comments.

# 21 The Causes of Institutional Inefficiency: A Development Perspective

*Jean-Philippe Platteau*

## 21.1 Introduction

The purpose of this chapter is to probe into the issue of inefficient institutions. Toward that end, I intend to look at the different strands that form the so-called new institutional economics (NIE), and raise the question for each of them as to whether institutions can be inefficient and, if yes, for what reasons. Four economic approaches are reviewed, and these regard and depict institutions as the outcome of individual interactions. These are: the transaction-cost approach; the principal-agent approach; the equilibrium-of-the-game approach; and the evolutionary approach. The discussion will proceed in four successive sections, from Section 21.2 to Section 21.5. In each of these sections, the main features of the approach concerned – how institutions are defined and analyzed – will be summarized before addressing the issue of institutional efficiency proper. Section 21.6 will briefly conclude.

## 21.2 The transaction-cost approach

The transaction-cost (TC) approach is not only well known, but is frequently considered to be the core approach of NIE. A major reason for such a special treatment is historical: pioneers and advocates of this approach (Coase 1960; Williamson 1985; Barzel 1989) have actually established and popularized the name of NIE, helping to convey the message that economists have again begun to be interested in institutions after an eclipse of almost one century (Platteau 2000).

The central concept in the TC approach, as the name indicates, is that of transaction costs. These are the costs that arise whenever agents want to make a deal; this does not need to take the form of a market exchange. In contrast to production costs, which are costs arising from relations between individuals and things, transaction costs originate in relations between the individuals themselves (Matthews 1986). Indeed, economic transactions would not be feasible if agents were unable to enter into

443

contact with each other and to find ways to reach agreement. In short, transaction costs are "the costs of running the system: the costs of coordinating and of motivating" (Milgrom and Roberts 1992, p. 29).[1] What Milgrom and Roberts call "motivation costs" may be of two kinds: first, they may arise from informational incompleteness and asymmetries, such as happens when the parties miss information needed to determine whether the terms of an agreement are mutually acceptable and whether these terms are actually being met. They thus follow from various kinds of incentive problems. Second, there are the costs resulting from imperfect commitment, characterized by "the inability of parties to bind themselves to follow through on threats and promises that they would like to make but which, having made, they would later like to renounce" (Milgrom and Roberts 1992, p. 30).

In the TC perspective, the aim of institutions is to reduce transaction costs so as to allow agents to seize on economic opportunities, and an efficient institution is simply an arrangement that minimizes such costs, or one which maximizes the joint wealth of all the parties concerned net of transaction costs (*see* Allen and Lueck 2002, p. 4). Institutional arrangements aimed at reducing transaction costs are often called "governance structures." For example, a capitalist firm is a governance structure which is characterized by hierarchical relationships between capital owners or their representatives and the workers or employees (Williamson 1985). Indeed, a system of vertical relationships is often considered preferable to the alternative of relying on market relationships because dealing with suppliers and subcontractors entails too many risks and incentive problems, such as moral hazard and adverse selection. Employees may accept being subordinate to the authority of the capital owners or their representatives if, in return, they receive the guarantee of a stable employment. On the other hand, the latter are willing to grant such job stability to their workers because their position of authority enables them the flexibility to adjust the tasks to be accomplished to the current needs dictated by evolving market opportunities (Aoki 1984).

Or, to take another example, ownership regimens may be analyzed as governance structures exhibiting different TC characteristics that themselves depend on things such as the characteristics of the resource or asset considered, those of the social group concerned, the state of the technology, the degree of riskiness of the environment, and so on (for a detailed analysis of property of natural resources, *see* Platteau 2000). Note that there is a clear distinction between the institutional environment, composed of risk and informational characteristics, and governance structures. The efficient governance structure (the optimal institution) depends on the characteristics of the specific institutional environment in which it has to operate.

As emphasized by Milgrom and Roberts (1992, pp 33–35), there are two main problems with the TC approach. For one thing, it implicitly assumes that production costs and transaction costs are independent or separable, the former depending only on the technology and the inputs used, and the latter depending on the manner in which transactions are organized. Two conceptually distinct operations are involved: the production costs are minimized through the choice of an appropriate technique and input mix, and the transaction costs are minimized through the choice of an appropriate institutional arrangement. In reality, it is often the case that production and transaction costs depend both on the organization and the technology. When that is the case, the total costs of an economic activity cannot be minimized as though they were just the sum of production costs and transaction costs.

An immediate consequence of the above is that an institutional choice may be the outcome of a trade-off between technological and transaction cost considerations. To illustrate, consider the problem of the choice between a U-shaped and a star-shaped irrigation system, as depicted in Figure 21.1 (where the U-shaped system is represented by solid lines and the star-shaped system by dotted lines).

If we take the viewpoint of technology alone, the U-shaped system appears as the best option since it economizes on infrastructure-building costs (assuming that such costs are proportional to the length of the canal to build) compared with the star-shaped system. In our example, the total canal length under the former system is measured by $(Xa + ab + bc + Xd + de + ef)$, whereas under the latter it is equal to $(XY + Ya + Yb + Yc + Yd + Ye + Yf)$, which is obviously larger. If, instead, the viewpoint of TC is adopted, the star-shaped system appears as the most cost-effective solution. This is because the field of each farmer is directly connected to a canal, unlike the situation obtaining under the U-shaped system, in which only the head-end farmers, with fields a and d, have a direct access to water. Farmers with fields b, c, e, and f depend on the goodwill of neighbors who precede them along the canal branch.

To mitigate the risk of opportunistic behavior on the part of strategically located farmers, and thereby ensure equitable and reliable distribution of water, costs must be incurred which are not needed when access to water is secured on an individual basis. (Think of the costs required to organize, monitor, and enforce a rotation system of access to water.) Which system, the U-shaped or the star-shaped, is more

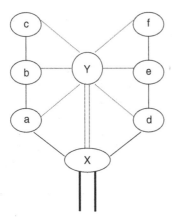

**Figure 21.1** Illustrating interdependence between production and transaction costs: the U-shaped versus the star-shaped irrigation systems.

cost-effective overall? In actuality, it is impossible to determine a priori which system minimizes the sum of production and transaction costs. Choice will ultimately depend on the social capital of the rural community as a greater amount of social cohesion within a group of water users reduces the transaction costs of collective action and, therefore, tilts the balance of (total) costs in favor of the technologically more cost-effective U-shaped system.

The central lesson of this example, thus, is that, contrary to what the TC approach contends, there is no unique cost-effective institutional solution to a problem. Two implications follow. First, the most efficient solution in a given social environment may not be the most efficient in another environment. Second, when an environment is more favorable in the sense that less attention may be paid to transaction cost considerations, total costs generated by an economic activity will be lower. That there is no unique efficient institutional solution to a problem involving transaction costs is also at the heart of the second critique against the TC approach.

Even assuming that transaction costs are independent of production costs, the notion that efficient institutions minimize transaction costs is highly problematic. This is because many different institutional arrangements might be compatible with the efficiency criterion and, as a result, such a criterion considered alone is unlikely to be satisfactory (Milgrom and Roberts 1992, p. 34). It is only under a set of restrictive assumptions – essentially, the possibility of transfer payments, zero negotiating costs, ability to implement and enforce decisions reached in the bargaining process and the absence of wealth effects – that the efficiency criterion may predict a well-defined institutional outcome. Indeed, with such assumptions, the Coase theorem and the efficiency principle[2] mean that institutional forms are determined to maximize the total value of the parties, taking into account transaction costs understood as the costs of managing the transactions (including the costs of writing and enforcing contracts, supervising workers, and resolving disputes). Or, put another way, these forms are determined to minimize transaction costs for any given production plan (implying that resource uses and the aggregate production costs are given).

In such a framework, since parties are assumed to be able to make unlimited transfer payments, the issue of distribution of value is completely separable from the issue of how value is created. Confronted with an institutional choice problem, the agents' only concern is to establish the (uniquely efficient) institution that maximizes the total wealth available for sharing between themselves. In other words, the choice of the efficient institution does not depend on the a priori distribution of power between the parties involved. The latter will only affect the distribution of costs and benefits (Milgrom and Roberts 1992, pp 35–39).

The hypotheses underlying the TC approach are easily violated. Wealth effects are likely to be insignificant only when the sizes of the cash transfers are small relative to the agents' financial resources. Compensatory cash payments may be illegitimate according to cultural prescriptions or social norms. Negotiating costs are important if the number of agents is large and they have heterogeneous characteristics. Decisions reached through decentralized bargaining may be hard to implement and enforce. Finally, as Shapley and Shubik (1969) have shown, when there are more than two agents, a bargaining solution may not exist. More precisely, an efficient solution may exist in a game, but the parties will not be able to reach it through decentralized bargaining (the core being empty). Moreover, whether a bargaining solution is attainable or not may ultimately depend on the initial assignment of rights to the parties, that is, on the initial distribution of bargaining powers (Baland and Platteau 1996, pp 51–52).

In the following, I discuss a number of situations where, for one or several of the reasons mentioned above, the Coasian framework is not a good approximation to reality. As a result, the efficiency and distributive issues are not separable, and no unique efficient institutional solution may be said to exist. Institutional choices can therefore be made that do not maximize the total value available to the parties concerned.

Consider an institutional change (e.g. a land reform) that is liable to increase the total value available to the agents, but from which a sub-group (big landowners) is going to lose. If these agents belong to a powerful elite which has benefited excessively from the existing arrangement in the past, the potential winners (landless or small farmers) might well view any compensation to the losers as unfair or unjustified. In such circumstances, the preferences of the potential winners are not compatible with the requirement of the Pareto criterion since they would imply that the wellbeing of the potential losers will decrease with the institutional change. Note also that, when the potential losers succeed in strategically strengthening their position so as to be able to ask for larger compensatory transfers from the potential winners, the latter are still more likely to resist the former's demand for compensation. If the existing elite are strong enough to block the change, the status quo, which does not maximize the total value, will continue to prevail. In the opposite case, a revolutionary situation will develop with all the costs that it necessarily entails. It needs to be emphasized that, in the above instances, pre-emption of efficient institutional change arises from the irrational behaviour of the potential beneficiaries of such change. If they were rational, indeed, they would not oppose the payment of compensatory transfers which would eventually make them better off. But ideological considerations and value systems (e.g. a notion of fairness) may outweigh rational calculus and drive agents to behave against their own material interests.

The potential losers may not trust the potential winners' promise to compensate them once the institutional change would have occurred. Realizing the transfers before the advent of the change is of no help: the inverse problem will arise since the potential winners may now fear that the incumbents will opportunistically collect the payment and then oppose the agreed change.

The agents may not be able to reach an agreement because their assessment of the costs and benefits of institutional change do not match. Potential losers may, in good faith, exaggerate the costs that they will have to bear, and potential winners will refuse to compensate them on that basis. It might be contended that the former might also try to manipulate information and claim losses larger than in reality, whereas the latter might manipulate information in the opposite direction. However, if agents are rational and have a perfect knowledge of the costs and benefits of the institutional change, such manipulation should only aim at influencing the distribution of these benefits and costs (through bluffing the other party), but can not have the effect of hindering the occurrence of an efficient change available.

In situations where the interests of a large number of individuals are involved, it is likely that only a subgroup of them will effectively communicate with one another and participate in the bargaining process. In these conditions, the agreements reached will not reflect the interests of the people who were excluded from the discussions. Bargaining may then lead to an efficiency-enhancing change, but only relative to the small, effective group that was able to take part in the decision about what institution (or policy) to choose.

By positing zero negotiating costs, the Coasian framework gets rid of the leadership problem that may prevent a group of people from asserting their viewpoint and, perhaps, promoting an efficiency-enhancing institutional change. Acting as a leader involves non-negligible costs, and no member of a group may be willing to bear them. This happens if the payoff matrix of the leadership game has the same structure as the prisoner's dilemma: everyone would prefer someone else to bear the costs of leadership and, as a result, everybody chooses to abstain from taking the initiative. In other words, leadership is a public good and the classic freeloader problem is observed. If, however, the structure of the game is that of a "chicken game," a leader will emerge because, in this case, the individual benefit of collective action exceeds the cost of leadership even when it is borne by a single individual.

In conclusion, when the hypotheses underlying the Coasian framework are not valid, we can no more be certain that an institution that increases allocative efficiency constitutes a Pareto improvement. It is then incorrect to say that only efficiency considerations govern institutional choices, and that distributive choices are only secondary consequences of efficiency choices. In many instances, institutions are the product of distributive conflicts and, depending on whether the preferences of the most powerful coincide with allocatively efficient institutions, the latter will emerge and persist or not (Knight 1992).

In Spain during the early modern period (1500–1700), for example, the powerful shepherds' guild (the *Mesta*) successfully opposed the farmers' demand for secure and exclusive property rights in arable lands at a time when these lands became increasingly scarce and investments were socially profitable. As a matter of fact, shepherds did not want any curtailment of their customary rights to drive their flocks of migrating sheep across Spanish territory. If they came to acquire a strong bargaining position vis-à-vis the farmers, it is ultimately because their privileges were protected by the Crown, which relied heavily on export taxes on wool for meeting its expenditures (North and Thomas 1973, pp 128–129).

## 21.3    The principal–agent approach

For the principal–agent approach, an institution is a contract, that is, an *ex ante* mechanism designed in such a way as to induce an agent to behave spontaneously in accordance with the interests of a principal (for a detailed exposition, *see* Furubotn and Richter [2000]). Whether explicit or implicit, the contractual arrangement is self-enforcing. Being unable to directly observe the agent's actions, the principal sets the terms of the contract by taking the former's optimizing response into account and by ensuring that he will accept the contractual offer. Given the presence of informational asymmetries and the associated market imperfections, the institutions or contracts correspond to second-best optima. In fact, the efficiency losses which they entail are the equivalent of transaction costs under the TC approach. Note that the two approaches address essentially the same problem but from a different angle. Whilst the TC approach considers the costs explicitly incurred to overcome coordination and motivation problems which arise in economic transactions (plus any lost gains from trade that result from the fact that incentive problems are imperfectly surmounted), the principal–agent approach looks at self-enforcing mechanisms devised by principals to discipline agents when the latter's actions cannot be directly monitored. In other words, contracts are viewed as mechanisms giving rise to incentives that substitute for direct monitoring.

Like in the Coasian framework underlying the TC approach, the optimal contract or institutional form predicted by the principal–agent approach is unique. Yet, as aptly pointed out by Aoki (2001, p. 18), the solution arrived at in the TC approach "is usually responsive not only to the technological environment but also to the 'institutional environments' hidden in parameters specifying the objective functions of the principal and agent, and the participation constraints describing the outside options of the agent." The results obtained under this approach may therefore be valid only relative to an implicitly assumed institutional environment of the domain considered, and "may not be exclusively technology-dominated, second-best solutions applicable anywhere."

Contracts in the above perspective often appear as the result of a deliberate will of the parties concerned. Users of the principal–agent approach tend, therefore, to believe that people spontaneously choose optimal contracts, thus obeying to the prescriptions of theory. Note that the concept of constrained efficiency obtaining in the principal–agent approach fundamentally differs from that chosen by strict adherents of the TC approach. For the latter, indeed, an optimal arrangement has the property of maximizing the expected value of the joint wealth of all the parties concerned, net of transaction costs (*see above*). This is because they believe that competition among all parties (e.g. competition among farmers for land, competition among landowners for renters, and competition between on- and off-farm opportunities generally) is strong enough that only the most valuable contract or arrangement is chosen in the sense of being "naturally selected." In the words of two proponents of this orthodox TC approach: "it seems only reasonable to assume that contracts and organization are fundamentally driven to maximize wealth" (Allen and Lueck 2002, p. 6).

If there exists a discrepancy between a theoretical prediction (optimal contracts should be chosen) and a set of empirical observations, the blame is typically put by proponents of the principal–agent approach on policy failures and undue government interferences with the free will of the actors and the free play of market forces. For example, the low incidence of land-rental relative to land-sales contracts is ascribed to uncertain property rights and the fear of losing ownership control of the land by renting it out. Likewise, the low frequency or the absence of sharecropping contracts in risky tropical environments is usually traced back to harmful government prohibitions (Hayami and Kikuchi 1981, 2000; Bliss and Stern 1982; De Janvry *et al.* 2001).

It must be borne in mind that, even assuming the absence of any undue interference with the will of the parties involved, contracts can only be constrained or second-best optima (*see above*). What needs to be emphasized now is that the optimum can be quite severely constrained if several incentive problems plague a particular type of transaction and severely conflict with each other. Indeed, it may well happen that no contractual arrangement is available to solve the existing incentive problems in a satisfactory manner. Just assume that an absentee owner wants to rent out an asset to a renter. If there exist severe problems of risk (that no insurance market can guarantee against) or capital availability (that no credit market may address) combined with serious incentive problems such as labor-shirking, asset mismanagement, output under-reporting, and input overreporting, no type of rental contract will allow the owner to overcome these problems in a satisfactory manner. As a consequence, he will be compelled to manage the asset himself or to leave it unused. The argument may be easily summarized as follows: if the costs of measuring and dividing the output and the inputs are prohibitively high, only a fixed-rent contract may enable an owner to control the associated risks of opportunistic behavior. Yet, on the other hand, such a contractual form is ill-suited in a context of severe insurance and credit market imperfections, and is also the worst arrangement to counter the risk of asset mismanagement.

A striking illustration of such a possibility is provided by the situation prevailing in artisanal or small-scale fisheries all over the world (Platteau and Nugent 1992). In this sector, serious informational asymmetries prevent equipment owners from controlling risks of opportunistic behavior on the part of boat captains and their crews. This explains why the owner himself, or one of his sons or close acquaintances, has to be on board to supervise all the fishing operations, thus removing all information gaps. It is thus not surprising that family undertakings remain an essential characteristic of the artisanal fishing landscape. In an unpublished study conducted along the Senegalese coastline, I found that in as many as 80% of the fishing units the captain was either the owner or one of his close relatives (usually, a son or a son-in-law). In almost all the remaining instances, the captain was a close friend whom the owner considered as entirely trustworthy.

Finally, contract theory does not seem to easily account for the existence of rather uniform terms of contracts even while relevant personal characteristics of the agents (the endowments of the concerned parties, the opportunity costs they face for different inputs, their respective bargaining powers, their degree of risk aversion, and so on) differ. For instance, in a study of a village in Uttar Pradesh (India), it has been observed that landlord and tenant choose between a limited number of standardized sharecropping contracts, each entailing pre-specified input and output shares (Lanjouw and Stern 1998, p. 468). Limited rationality considerations or social norms suggest themselves as plausible reasons for uniform contractual terms (see Stiglitz 1989, pp 22–23). Uniform contractual terms such as the fifty-fifty division rule are often interpreted as useful coordination devices that correspond to prominent focal points. An alternative argument is that a particular rule is uniformly chosen because it is perceived by many people to be fair, and people derive utility from treating others fairly; or, rigid contracts reduce the costs of bargaining (Young 1998, pp 129–130; Young and Burke 2001).

The explanation based on focal length – contracts are rigid around a few focal shares – has been recently called into question by Allen and Lueck (2002, pp 88–92) on the basis of their own US data (from Nebraska and South Dakota) and a revisitation of the data (from Illinois) used by Young and Burke in their aforementioned article. Their point is that input-sharing terms are crucial in understanding the structure of sharecropping contracts. If they are overlooked, differences in output shares may be mistakenly attributed to regional custom based on soil quality (large differences in land quality lead to variations in focal shares across different regions), while they actually reflect differences in input-sharing which may themselves be predicted with the help of contract theory. On the other hand, discrete sharing rules that mimic simple fractions, as they are observed within a particular region, may be viewed "as rules that economize on measurement costs when measurement technology is imprecise" (Young and Burke 2001, p. 91). As a matter of fact, although it is theoretically possible to have finer divisions in sharecropping contracts than those actually observed (e.g. a fifty-two–forty-eight division rule besides a fifty-fifty rule), it makes no sense to use them if the landowner is unable to know the exact relative contributions without incurring enormous monitoring costs.

## 21.4   The equilibrium-of-the-game approach

According to the equilibrium-of-the-game (EG) approach, the major role of institutions is, by establishing a stable structure to human interactions, to reduce the uncertainties arising from incomplete information with respect to the behavior of other individuals (North 1990, p. 6, p. 25). Institutions are rules or humanly devised constraints which structure inter-individual relationships by allowing agents to form expectations about the behavior of others and by thus facilitating coordination among them. If institutions constrain the choices of agents, the question naturally arises as to how consistency can be induced in the players' beliefs regarding the emerging situation and in the actual situation created by their choices based on these beliefs (Aoki 2001, p. 9). In other words, how are convergent beliefs and coordinated actions generated? The question is legitimate since, when choosing an appropriate equilibrium strategy, an actor ignores the equilibrium and is therefore not yet constrained by it.

Clearly, to resolve the above issue, a new definition of institutions is required. It is provided by Aoki: an institution is "*a self-sustaining system of shared beliefs*" about a salient way in which a game is repeatedly played. This way of playing may be viewed as the rules of the game that are "endogenously created through the strategic interactions of agents, held in the minds of agents, and thus self-sustaining" (Aoki 2001, p. 10). A complex feedback mechanism is therefore at work, since all the agents form their own action-choice rules in response to their subjective perceptions (beliefs) of others' action-choice rules, and it is only when these perceptions become stabilized and reproduced that their own action-choice rules also become stabilized and may thus serve as useful guides for playing the game. From there, it is rather straightforward that agents' beliefs and their strategic formation of action-choice rules may be regarded as being in Nash equilibrium. Indeed, as long as beliefs about others' actions are sustained, agents have no incentive to deviate from their own action-choice rules. As for the salient feature of an equilib-rium; it may be tacitly recognized by the agents, or have corresponding representations outside their minds (Aoki 2001, pp 10–11).

To sum up, an institution conceived as an equilibrium of a game is "a socially constructed reality" that helps coordinate the beliefs and actions (understood as strategic choices) of agents. This equilibrium state is being reproduced if actions are made on the basis of beliefs that stand confirmed once the actions of others become observable. As a result of this conception, institutions are seen as emerging endogenously from human interactions to constrain people's behaviour in a self-enforcing manner in a particular domain. In this way they have the effect of linking up actions through time, with the past and the present serving as focal points for the future (Greif 1997, 1998).

A direct implication of the EG approach is that the history and the culture (understood as a set of views and expectations about others' behaviour) of a society are embedded in its institutions. The fact that cultural beliefs are shared binds its members together. As a conse-quence, it is incorrect to say that explanations based on individual rational choice ignore the influence of community and history (Knight 1992, pp 80–82).

Another implication is that the EG approach accounts for informal institutions, such as social norms and conventions. This follows from the definition of a social convention: a behavioral regularity that is self-perpetuating because individual expectations and behaviors are in equilibrium when a convention is well-established (Young 1996). Informal practices therefore qualify as institutions "as long as the agents believe in them as relevant representations." On the other hand, a formal rule, such as a statutory law or a regulation, is not a true institution if the agents do not mutually believe in it (Aoki 2001, p. 13).

A last important implication is that, since institutions correspond to Nash equilibria which are multiple in repeated plays (and in one-stage coordination games), there are typically many possible institutional solu-tions. Emphasis is thus put on the non-arbitrary ("humanly devised") character of institutions rather than on their features that are techno-logically, ecologically, or culturally determined (Aoki 2001, p. 16). Cul-tural specificity often takes on the form of social or cultural norms that embody equity principles which themselves serve as focal points in a given community. Myerson (1991, p. 113) defines cultural norms as "the rules that a society uses to determine focal equilibria in game situations," bearing in mind that "there may be some situations where people of a given culture might look to equity principles to determine a focal equilibrium" (*see also* Young 1994, p. 81).

We are now in a position to discuss the problem of efficiency. From the Nash equilibrium concept and from the existence of multiple equilibria, it is evident that inefficient institutions may well come to be established and sustained over time. Just consider a simple two-agent coordination game in which there are two Nash equilibria in pure strategies, with one equilibrium Pareto dominating the other. For example, two measurement systems are available but one is superior to the other, say, because it is easier to use. For each agent, to coordinate on the same system is always preferable than to have a mismatch of strategies. Whether the convention established favors the socially efficient or the inefficient system will depend on the content of the shared beliefs of the agents and on which equilibrium is a focal point in their minds. The inefficient measurement system may therefore predominate if agents believe that others are going to use it. Moreover, once the inefficient convention is established, the very concept of Nash equilibrium that underlies it implies that it may persist for a long time.

Although under the TC approach status quo situations are explained by the difficulty of making the necessary compensations to the potential losers, under the EG approach cultural inertia appears as a privileged explanation (*see* Basu, Jones, and Schlicht 1987). In the words of Joseph Stiglitz (1989, p. 26), "individuals know more about the institutions and conventions with which they have lived in the recent past than they know of others by which they might live." The preservation of institutions that are inefficient, or have become so following some change in the environment, is caused by self-perpetuating beliefs which receive continuous confirmation from the choice-actions of the other agents.

In the above example, we have used a simple one-stage coordination game to illustrate the possibility of inefficient institutions. An infinitely repeated game based on a principal–agent stage game provides another convenient illustration. We refer to the work of Avner Greif (1989, 1994, 1998), who distinguishes between two sorts of mechanisms to tame opportunistic behavior in pairwise merchant–agent relationships. The first mechanism, known as the "bilateral reputation mechanism," is based on a strategy whereby a merchant hires an agent and keeps him as long as he behaves honestly. If the merchant finds that the agent has cheated him, he fires him and will never re-hire him in the future. Yet, he is ready to employ any unemployed agent indiscriminately. Under the second mechanism, known as the "multilateral reputation mechanism," a merchant adopts the strategy of not employing an agent who once cheated some other merchant belonging to his community. Once he hires an agent who has an honest reputation, he keeps on employing him so long as the agent is honest with him. A dense information network is assumed to exist among merchants so that cheats may easily be identified and punished.

The two strategies described above are equilibrium strategies. Believing that all other agents follow a strategy of bilateral (multilateral) punishment, an individual has an incentive to adopt the same strategy and, at equilibrium, no agent cheats. Expectations are self-enforcing. Greif calls "collectivist" or "segregated" a society, such as that of the *Maghribi* (Jewish) traders who operated in the Muslim Mediterranean during the eleventh century, in which everyone expects everyone else to respond to any act of dishonesty committed in any pairwise encounter within the community space. In contrast, "individualist" societies, such as those of the Italian city states, are those in which anyone only reacts when his own interest has been hurt.

The multilateral reputation system practiced by the *Maghribi* is more efficient than the bilateral reputation system used by the Italian traders. Compared to Italian merchants, the *Maghribi* could afford to pay lower fees to their trading agents because they could rely on the credible threat of a more severe punishment. As a result, thanks to their having a more favorable cultural heritage, they were in a position to earn larger profits and to accumulate more capital. In a more dynamic perspective, however, the advantage may well have turned in favor of the Italian merchants. The case may indeed be made that the limitations of the disciplining mechanism available to them has served to encourage Italian merchants to seek institutional innovations more rapidly than the *Maghribi*. The invention of the family firm (during the thirteenth century) and the establishment of legal and political enforcement organizations (including a legal code to coordinate expectations and to enhance the deterrence effect of these organizations) may be seen as responses induced by the existence of a wide gap between opportunities and existing institutions (Greif 1994).

Finally, it bears emphasis that, even from a static standpoint, the multilateral reputation mechanism cannot be considered as completely efficient. This is because, among the *Maghribi*, the volume of trade was limited by the size of their community which had itself been determined by historical circumstances and could not grow as trade opportunities expanded. In Italy, where the situation was even less efficient, trade magnitude was politically determined under the political coalition system while under the patron system, agency relations could be governed only at a high cost until new organizations were found, as we have just mentioned (Greif 1992). The EG approach thus explicitly allows for inefficient institutions. It can also provide an explanation for those paradoxical situations in which individuals choose to support rules that they do not like or even find oppressive (such as the caste system in India). As shown by Akerlof (1976) and Kuran (1995), it may thus be rational for an individual to comply with unpleasant rules or to obey a totalitarian regime if there exist an effective network of mutually reinforcing social sanctions against disobedience and a system of converging expectations which sustain the existing arrangement. The key intuition is that a bad institution or a harmful rule persists because of mutual suspicion between people: because each person is worried about what the others will do to him, he chooses to cooperate.

The immediate implication of the existence of a web of self-reinforcing sanctions (think of the ostracization of individuals who have violated caste-based rules) is that everyone is both a victim and a supporter of a system in which there need not even be a ruler. For this sort of effective sanctions to prevail, meta-punishment must be applied; that is, a person is considered disloyal to a regime or a rule if either he does not cooperate or he maintains relations with someone who is disloyal. Note carefully that such an explanatory framework sheds light on how the sanctions have been self-reproducing, not on how they arose (Kuran 1995, pp 118–136; Basu 2000, pp 136–147).

## 21.5 The evolutionary approach

All the above economic approaches to institutions are essentially a-historical. They do not explain how a previous equilibrium state affects the set of new equilibria and there is no way to analyze how games are linked with one another through time. The last approach precisely aims at remedying such a lacuna by looking into the problem of the origin of institutions (i.e. the way they are selected), and not only that of their persistence. In the evolutionary (EV) approach, the emergence, diffusion, and demise of particular rules or institutional arrangements appears as the outcome of an organic process of Darwinian natural selection which epitomizes the competitive pressures of the market and the invisible hand. In this perspective, institutions emerge not as a result of rational, purposeful design by any individual or organization of individuals, but as the result of spontaneous evolution, say, because the people learn from experience that following a given constraint or custom can actually serve their own individual interests (Aoki 2001, p. 40). In the orthodox version of the evolutionary account, institutions that are inefficient are expected to have a low evolutionary fitness and, therefore, to be displaced in the long term by more efficient institutions (*see* Schotter 1981; Sugden 1986, 1989).

The evolutionary game theory used in the EV approach has distinct features. Whilst under the EG approach, which uses the classical game theory, the actors' expectations about each other have to be consistent with the experience that is generated by the resulting actions, EV game theory is based on the idea that agents follow trial-and-error behavior: what works well for a player is more likely to be used again, whereas what turns out poorly is more likely to be discarded. Agents look around them, gather information, and ground their decisions on the basis of fragmentary information. They have only an incomplete idea of the way the world in which they operate works, do not fully understand the strategic implications of their choices, and may not be especially forward looking (Young 1998, pp 5–6). Thanks to imitation, trials and errors, and takeovers, however, effective strategies are more likely to be retained than ineffective ones (Axelrod 1997, pp 47–48).

The notion of equilibrium is another feature that fundamentally distinguishes the EV approach from the other approaches. Evolutionary economists believe that equilibrium may be understood only within a dynamic framework that explains how it comes about, if it does (Young 1998, p. 4). After having specified the initial proportions of various types of agents in the whole population, the probabilities of their interactions, and the payoffs associated with every possible pairwise interaction, the evolutionary modeler needs to specify the dynamics (specified as a replicator mechanism) by which the proportions of the agents with higher payoffs (in biologic terminology, individuals with better fitness or reproductive ability) increase in the population. Equilibrium is attained when the proportions of different types of agents able to survive have become stable. It immediately follows that the concept of evolutionary efficiency, based on the idea of maximizing average fitness, differs markedly from the standard economic concepts in either the Pareto or the technical-efficiency sense.

Interestingly, a remarkable result obtained in EV game theory is that evolutionary equilibria have the properties of strategic equilibria. More precisely, for a large class of evolutionary games, if the dynamics converge, they converge toward a steady state in which the limiting distributions are in equilibrium in the same sense as in classical game theory. In other words, even though behavior of the players is not rational, the population seems to learn the rational equilibrium as its distribution evolves (Montet and Serra, 2003, pp 8–9). A nice example is the parable of a proto-institution of property rights developed by Aoki (2001, pp 36–39) and inspired by an ingenious evolutionary bargaining model of Young (1998).

Another central lesson from evolutionary models is still more paradoxical. Bear in mind that, in many of those models, institutions appear simply as the unintended and undesigned outcomes arising gradually from the pursuit of individual interests as agents repeatedly face the same types of social problems or situations: this is the idea of a spontaneous order grounded in the analogy between the invisible hand and the natural-selection arguments. (By contrast, economists using classical game theory to understand institutions, whether they refer to the principal–agent or the EG approaches, are not always clear about whether rules and institutions are the result of conscious design by legislators, political entrepreneurs, or mechanism design economists, or the unintended outcome of long-term dynamics). Yet, it appears that there is absolutely no certainty that optimal rules or institutions will emerge from evolutionary processes. Several reasons can account for this, which deserve to be mentioned (*see* Bowles 2004, pp 90–91).

First, analogues to both external economies (spillovers) and increasing returns may be found in the world of institutions. Thus, "some institutions may be complementary, each enhancing the functioning of the other, while some institutions may reduce the effectiveness of other institutions." As a consequence, there may be multiple stable configurations of institutions, and some of these configurations "may be very inefficient and yet persist over long periods." Second, the analysis of evolutionary processes that select among group-level institutions, which involves a *co-evolution* of preferences and institutions (each exerting an influence on the development of the other), may not support the emergence of efficient solutions. For example, success in inter-group conflict may be caused by a group's military strength rather than by its efficient performance on any other account. Third, "the rates of change induced by real world selection processes may be slow relative to the pace of changes induced by other sources, such as chance events, or exogenous changes in knowledge . . ." (Bowles 2004, pp 90–91).

Finally, the repertoire of institutions and behaviors among which selection operates may be highly restricted. As emphasized by biologists, natural selection works on existing genetic material, which need not include the optimal genetic "program," and, if it does not, optimal adaptation is hampered. Moreover, the fact that gene mutations are blind (their occurrence is assumed to be independent of the needs of organisms) and may represent only gradual variations of existing genotypes precludes them from introducing optimal types in the population (Vromen 1995, pp 95–96). The same conclusion applies, *mutatis mutandis*, to institutions. On one hand, being absent from the available repertoire, many institutions remain unknown or untried. And, on the other, "the creation of novel institutions is akin to the emergence of new species: it requires the confluence of a large number of improbable variations in the status quo" (Bowles 2004, p. 91). It needs to be emphasized that an immediate implication of the above point is that inefficiency may be impossible to measure owing to the lack of a counterfactual. As a matter of fact, it is difficult to compare the efficiency of a selected institution against another because this last one has not been selected.

In a related vein, Ken Binmore has aptly pointed out that in many evolutionary models attention has been artificially restricted to a few strategies, often arbitrarily chosen. No clue is given as to why particular strategies are there while innumerable other conceivable strategies are ignored (Binmore 1992, p. 434). Such an approach may enable the evolutionary modeler to derive efficient institutions but without really explaining their emergence in so far as the appearance of the nice strategies is itself unaccounted for. A vivid illustration of this possibility is provided by the evolutionary account of the emergence of private property rights on the basis of the famous Hawk–Dove game studied by Smith (1982). In the (evolutionarily stable) equilibrium,[3] the agent first arrived at a resource is considered as the legitimate owner and no fight occurs. Unfortunately, the theory does not say anything about how the sophisticated strategy that will eventually lead to that result (the so-called Bourgeois strategy: "if owner fight, if intruder refrain from fighting") has actually come about. Note that, if the Bourgeois strategy is not available the equilibrium of the Hawk–Dove game is inefficient. There may be a positive proportion of aggressive agents (the Hawks) in equilibrium, and average fitness is not maximized in the population.

Even when evolutionary models are made more complex by bringing multi-level selection into the picture and by introducing players who intentionally pursue conflicting interests through collective action (*see* Bowles 2004), the conclusion continues to hold that inefficient (and unequal) institutions may persist over very long periods of time.

Another illuminating lesson to draw from the EV approach is the path-dependent nature of institutional evolution: small initial differences may cause distinct societal histories to emerge. In the words of Bowles (2004, pp 403–404), "This view stresses not institutional convergence but the long-term coexistence of distinct evolutionarily stable institutions." Because the evolutionary process follows paths which have different long-term characteristics, depending on where they start and on the order in which players happen to meet, the paths end up in different equilibrium configurations (Young 1998; *see also* North 1990, pp 92–104). Nothing can be said a priori about the comparative levels of efficiency (or inefficiency) reached by these varied configurations.

Large set-up or fixed costs, learning effects, coordination effects ("which confer advantages to cooperation with other economic agents taking similar action"), and adaptive expectations (where increased prevalence enhances beliefs of further prevalence) all contribute to creating path dependence (North 1990, pp 93–94). Ideology may also play a major role in sustaining a particular path, even though it is inefficient. This will happen if agents construct rationalisations with the aim of vindicating their society's rules and structures, and thereby account for their poor performance.

## 21.6 Conclusion

Two economic approaches to institutions, the EG approach and the EV approach, lead to the conclusion that institutions may very well be inefficient over long periods of time. Whilst such a conclusion is almost embedded in the EG approach, which pays a lot of attention to the role of expectations and beliefs, it may come as a surprise as far as the EV approach is concerned. Indeed, at least in the minds of its pioneers, the latter purported to show that efficient rules and institutions may evolve without conscious human design, gradually arising from the uncoordinated actions of numerous actors over a long period. On the other hand, the idea that economic agents tend to select (second-best) optimal institutional arrangements is inherent in the other two approaches: the TC approach and the princpal–agent approach. However, the assumptions required in the TC approach to generate that result are quite restrictive, and it is therefore not difficult to imagine situations in which inefficient rules or institutions will be established and persist. As for the principal–agent approach, it is an inspiring approach that takes explicitly account of the strategic behavior of agents. To the extent that reality differs from its predictions, the discrepancy may be ascribed to policy failures or to the existence of social norms such as are postulated in the EG approach.

Taken as a whole, NIE thus appears to be rather agnostic about the issue of institutional efficiency. Cultural inertia, vested interests, institutional complementarities, and myopic behavior may explain why inefficient institutions persist. Furthermore, it is possible that institutional arrangements that have been efficient some time in the past do not adapt when circumstances change. For example, the rule of celibacy in the Catholic church was probably efficient when it was set up in medieval times in order to break the formation of priestly dynasties. Yet, it has clearly become dysfunctional now that the supply of catholic priests falls short of demand while priesthood is discouraged by the celibacy rule. One plausible reason why the rule is not rescinded is that the decision makers in Rome, who are all old people, refuse to support a change from which they will not be able to benefit. In terms of the TC approach, they oppose a change because they cannot be properly compensated. If this view is correct, only a shift of power in favor of young priests or willing priests is likely to modify the situation.

# Notes

## FOREWORD

1 See "Reflections on the New Institutional Economics" (Williamson 1985b) and "The New Institutional Economics: Taking Stock, Looking Ahead" (Williamson 2000).

2 My experience as an adviser to Mayor Lindsay's cable television task force in the late 1960s is illustrative. There being little theory that dealt with the issues, I attempted to bring the best theory that was available to bear: Harold Demsetz's (1968) model of franchise bidding for natural monopoly. Non-economist members of the cable television task force were not persuaded, however, and their intuitions prevailed. But the story continues in that shortly thereafter I began to reformulate the vertical integration problem in transaction cost terms (Williamson 1971). And this time the ramifications seemed to be borne out by discussions with practitioners who had experience with make-or-buy decisions (economists, lawyers, and purchasing agents in large corporations). As work of this kind progressed, moreover, it became natural to examine whether the contractual logic of make-or-buy carried over to regulation, in general, and cable television, in particular. As reported elsewhere (Williamson 1976), the theory served to clarify where franchise bidding worked well and where poorly, for which a focussed case study of cable television was broadly corroborative. I interpret these and later developments as being in the spirit of Alan Newell's remark that "theories cumulate. They are refined and reformulated, corrected and expanded ... Theories are things to be nurtured and changed and built up" (Newell 1990, p. 14) – possibly along the lines of the natural progression to which I referred earlier – ideally with value added at each step in the process. Recall, moreover, that good but failed theories help to clear the ground.

3 Implementing discriminating alignment requires that the critical attributes of transactions be named and their ramifications for the comparative efficacy of alternative modes of governance (which are described as syndromes of discrete structural attributes to which distinctive strengths and weaknesses accrue), be worked out.

## A ROAD MAP FOR THE GUIDEBOOK

1 This, together with a new generation of young scholars – such as Daron Acemoglu, Robert Gibbons, or Andrei Shleifer to quote but a few – seems to meet the expectations of Ronald Coase, who predicted in 1998 that with

institutions being the main performance factors of an economy all of economics is going to become what we now call *"New Institutional Economics"* (Coase 1998).

2 Of course, important bodies of literature, which strongly contributed to the field, were initiated before. Law and economics, economic history, and public choice, in particular, were initiated in the 1960s; not to mention the various "institutional" schools of thought that developed in different countries – in particular France, Germany, and the USA – in the late-nineteenth and early twentieth centuries.

3 This remains a differentiating factor across countries. Consequently, nation states remain relevant political arenas despite globalization of the economy and the collapse of barriers to trade and to trans-border financial flows.

## INTRODUCTION

* This section draws heavily on Joskow (2004).

## 1 THE THEORIES OF THE FIRM

1 It should be noted here that TCE mainly looked at transaction costs on the market making the assumption that "substantially the same factors that are ultimately responsible for market failures also explain failures of internal organization" (Williamson 1973, p. 316; Williamson 1996).

2 Only one recent work (Hart and Moore 2005) tries to use an incomplete contract framework and to endogenize the incompleteness level of contracts. Nevertheless, such a framework is based on more (questionable) assumptions concerning the ability of contracting parties to commit (and not to renegotiate) and concerning the way they use contracts (contracts that rule out but do not rule in).

3 For a presentation of the relationships between cognitive psychology and economics on this issue, *see* Festré and Garrouste (2006).

4 In what follows, we believe that what we write also applies to other theoretical frameworks such as evolutionary economics or the competence-based view of the firm. We do not go into details when distinguishing those approaches and focus on what is common to all of them.

5 See Goshal and Moran (1996) and Plunket-Saussier (2004) on these issues.

## 2 CONTRACTS: FROM BILATERAL SETS OF INCENTIVES TO THE MULTI-LEVEL GOVERNANCE OF RELATIONS

1 This second approach either contrasts contract with alternative coordination principles, in particular the market – which in that case is pure price coordination on the basis of public calls and auctions – and the hierarchy – which is charactacterized by coordination based on fiat and authority, or considers that contracts are "everywhere" since explicit mutual promises are

at the root of any bilateral relationship because most actual markets rely on contracts signed among the parties, and because the signature of contracts founds hierarchical relationships.

2 Although as pointed out by Hansmann and Kraakman (2002) on the line of Barzel (1989), contracting may be considered as a way to overcome the limits of an institutional framework. Indeed, within the latter, rights of decision over uses and access of economic resources are bundled in with property rights because it would be too costly to unbundle them. In such a context, contractual agreements allow unbundling property rights and therefore a fine redistribution of rights "to decide" or "to benefit" among agents.

3 MacLeod (2002) nevertheless explores the idea: even very small decisions costs can lead to incomplete contracting. In fact, as in Anderlini and Felli (1994, 2004), the idea is to introduce bounded rationality thanks to complexity.

4 It is important to point out that this makes NIE logically consistent since the same assumptions apply to contracting parties and to those who design and run institutions. Moreover, there is a logical link between cost borne *ex ante* (search, negotiation, "writing") and costs borne *ex post* (due to insufficiencies from the contract: maladaptation, renegotiation, conflict) because they are all linked to the cost of decision, since *ex post* costs are directly related to the savings on decision costs made *ex ante* and/or on the savings made on the design or implementation of perfect institutions.

5 In sociology, the idea of framing states that several "rationalities" or "logics of behavior" are possible and that agents choose one of these logics to interact among each other. Then they can adjust within the frame of one of these logics. See, for instance, Lindenberg (1992).

6 The "efficiency" of market selection remains as discussed, as pointed out in particular by the economics of technology and the analysis of evolutionary processes (especially Arthur 1989; David 1985; Liebowitz and Margolis 1995).

7 As argued by Brousseau and Fares (2000, 2002), the difference between results obtained by Hart and Moore (1988), and by Aghion, Dewagtripont, and Rey (1994), may be attributed to a difference in the enforcement framework. In the Aghion, Dewatripont and Rey (1994) model the judge is able to implement specific performance (of the default option) and to prevent any renegotiation which allows both parties to implement an incentives system that will incite them to behave optimally *ex ante* and *ex post*. In Hart and Moore (1988) the judge either authorizes or does not prevent renegotiation of the default provision, preventing the parties from building an incentive framework guaranteeing efficiency. This may also be interpreted as a contrast between a framework in which perfect judicial enforcement is available and a framework in which it is not the case. In the latter, the contracts are "harm length" and should be drawn to be self-enforceable, which inevitably binds the contracting capabilities of agents.

8 Note that Posner (2005) proposes another typology more in line with actual practices, but conclusions do not differ much. He contrasts four principles: (1) Try to determine what the parties really meant; that is, assume they resolved the interpretive issue in their negotiations but just didn't express

their resolution clearly; (2) Pick the economically efficient solution, on the assumption that it is probably what the parties intended, or would have intended had they thought about the issue; (3) Treat the case as a toss-up, and apply some rule for breaking ties; for example ambiguities are resolved against the party trying to enforce the contract or against the party that drafted the contract; (4) Combine (1) and (3) by pretending a written contract always represents full agreement by the parties and that no other evidence of the contract's meaning, besides the text itself, is to be considered. This is the literalist method of interpretation.

9 Moreover, Posner (2005) insists that optimal contractual regulation also depends on the decision process of the enforcement mechanism. He points out that in different kinds of judicial systems the "interpretive medium" (i.e. jurors, arbitrators, and judges) who have different levels of skills and possibly contrasted incentives, may or may not successfully apply the same principles. We return to the argument by Hadfield (2005), who insists on the influence of the characteristics of the institutional system on the behavior of those in charge of implementing contractual agreements (*see* 3.3.1.2). We will go back to this in Section 2.5.1.

10 Of course this contradicts the idea that parties cannot establish complete incentive contracts because of the observation and decision costs of the judge (which leads to the differences in verifiability and observability and to the idea that certain variables are non-contractible).

11 In general, the judiciary is considered because it is observable and "organizable;" and it makes sense from a legal point of view. But alternatives to the judiciary – from the illegal mafia to private conflict-settlement bodies, and encompassing communitarian oversight – should also be considered. (*See* 2.5.2 below; *see also* Dixit 2004).

## 3  INSTITUTIONS AND THE INSTITUTIONAL ENVIRONMENT

1 For a more in-depth definition, *see* North (1990).

2 For an excellent discussion of the post-war policy consensus and its subsequent failures *see* Easterly (2001).

3 The standard neoclassical growth model simplifies by treating only capital, labor, and natural resources as the inputs to production with technology treated as an exogenous parameter. Theorists understand that this set of three inputs merely stands in place of a variety of possible inputs which could include organizational or institutional quality. But in practice, applied work, in particular that based on official government statistics, tends to treat capital and labor as the primary inputs of interest. Transactions costs are assumed to be of secondary importance and there is no place for them in the official statistics, or in the standard treatments of macro-economic theory.

4 This trend in the mainstream economics literature has only intensified as recent research points to institutions as being more determinative of long run economic performance than labor, capital, natural resources, and sometimes even openness to trade itself (see Rodrik 2003).

## 4 HUMAN NATURE AND INSTITUTIONAL ANALYSIS

1 The idea that individuals (and organizations) decide by using heuristics which work relatively well in a given environment, be it natural or social, was proposed by Simon (1956). Reference to "ecological rationality" is found in Tooby and Cosmides (1992). See also Gigerenzer and Todd (1999), who stressed how the mind makes efficient use of the structure of information available in the environment, and Smith (2003) for a view from experimental economics.

2 See Gigerenzer (2000), whose work has been criticized, however, both in terms of its results (e.g. Kleither *et al.* 1997) and for distorting the position of the "biases and fallacies" paradigm (Markoczy and Goldberg 1998, pp 400–402).

3 For some it is clear that no part of the brain decides, as mental "supervisors" fail systematically and suffer self-deception. Self-control is therefore claimed to be merely a sort of "spin doctor," an illusion (Pinker 2002, pp 42–43). For a more nuanced view, see Ramachandran (2004).

4 In fact, the brain's response to short-term opportunities is mostly emotional, taking place in the limbic system, whereas long-term rewards are governed by reason and calculation, triggering brain activity in the prefrontal cortex (McClure *et al.* 2004).

5 These ideas of "kin selection" or "inclusive fitness" were developed by Williams and Williams (1957), Hamilton (1963, 1964), and Maynard Smith (1964). Brown (1991) pointed out the universal presence of nepotism.

6 The main ideas on what is often labeled "reciprocal altruism" were developed by Williams (1966), Trivers (1971, 1985), and Alexander (1987). Reciprocity has been shown to be a human universal, with similar results being obtained in experiments run in different cultures, and greater cooperation found in societies in which people rely more on market exchanges in their daily lives (Henrich *et al.* 2001, 2005).

7 Tit-for-tat consists of cooperating in the initial round and replicating in other rounds the conduct of the other player in the preceding round.

8 See Maynard Smith and Price (1973) and Frank (1987), and, for a recent empirical test, Kurzban and House (2005).

9 The card with a *D* is informative because if there was not a 3 the rule would be falsified. The card with a 7 is also informative because if there was a *D* the rule would be falsified. The card with an *F* is not informative because whatever the number on the other side it would comply with the rule. The card with a 3 is not informative either because the rule does not forbid having a 3 and any other letter.

10 This argument provides a common and more solid ground to the pioneering and rival arguments by Polanyi (1944) on the limits of market-type relations and the resistance of societies to the dominance of such relations; and Hayek (1944) on the opposing rules of the "extended order of cooperation through markets" and the more intimate and personal order. The danger that the primitive collectivistic leanings of human beings pose to the market has also been stressed by Smith (2003) from the perspective of experimental economics.

11 Excessive attention therefore may be paid now to identifiable individuals, to the detriment of anonymous parties by both the political process (Rubin 2002, pp 153–181) and judges (Arruñada and Andonova, forthcoming).

12 Sometimes institutions also help the individual to enforce the code, as happens in Catholic oral confession (Arruñada 2007).

13 It is therefore Lamarckian. Jean-Baptiste Lamarck argued at the beginning of the nineteenth century that traits acquired by an organism are passed on to its progeny. For example, the long neck of the giraffe would result from generations of animals stretching to reach the highest leaves.

14 Analyzing how institutions are designed would exceed the proper scope of this work as it would make necessary going into the many theories of cultural evolution. *See*, for instance, Dawkins (1976, 1982), Boyd and Richerson (1985) and Sperber (1996).

## 5 THE "CASE" FOR CASE STUDIES IN NEW INSTITUTIONAL ECONOMICS

1 For an earlier discussion of empirical work in the new institutional economics which touches on the use of case studies see the essay by Alston in Alston, Eggertsson, and North (1996).

2 *Analytic Narratives* is the title of a book of case studies compiled by Bates *et al.* (1998).

3 By "historical" I mean an approach that relies on qualitative evidence, which has been one of the hallmarks of historical research. Qualitative evidence may come from any time period.

4 Anthropologists as well as scholars in business schools have relied on surveys for a long time.

5 Paul Joskow was one of the scholars who first worked on the issue of long-term contracting and vertical integration.

6 The work of Oliver Williamson, along with Ronald Coase, may have had the greatest impact on theorists working on contract theory.

7 Douglass C. North was the pioneer in taking "micro" concepts and using them to build an analysis of changes over time. It is important to note that North has been careful not to refer to his work as theory. Indeed, North, like Coase, maintains that economists are far too hasty in modeling an issue before they fully understand it (*see*, in particular, North 2005).

8 For possible explanations for "institutional lock-in" *see* Alston and Mueller (2004).

9 The work of Acemoglu, Johnson, and Robinson (2001) falls into this category.

10 *See* Levy and Spiller (1994) for an analysis of the impact of political determinants on regulatory outcomes for telecommunications.

11 Franchising is a good example of an economic outcome for a micro case study.

12 For one of the best theoretical discussions of the role of property rights in economics *see* Barzel (1989). For good analyses of property rights dealing with the interface of law and economics *see* Anderson and McChesney (2003) and Barzel (2002).

13 Space constraints prohibit equal exposition across the case studies discussed in this chapter. I chose to spend the most space on this case because in it we analyzed the role and determinants of property rights, a concept familiar to most economists. This section draws heavily on Alston and Mueller (2004), Alston, Libecap, and Mueller (1999a, 1999b, 2000); and Alston, Libecap, and Schneider (1996). See Libecap (1989) for an early discussion of property rights which relies on case studies from which he draws generalizations.

14 In our work we produced the figure as an illustrative device and then estimated various hypotheses associated with property rights, which we can visualize on the figure. For example, the vertical distance between Line A–D and Line B–D represents the demand for secure property rights.

15 We could further segment line D–E into the return from a commons versus open access arrangement. The losses from an open access arrangement would increase as we move toward greater scarcity.

16 Cattlemen's associations in the nineteenth century US West are a good example of informal institutions (Dennen 1976). See Umbeck (1981), Eggertsson (1990), Ostrom (1990), and Anderson and Hill (2002) for accounts of local groups allocating resources under "common" arrangements. See Smith (2000) for an analysis of "semi-commons" arrangements.

17 For the households that we surveyed formal property rights always had a positive value, that is no households resided at a distance to the market to the right of F on the figure.

18 The framework accommodates any force that either increases (or decreases) demand or supply.

19 Designing the survey ourselves not only allowed us to construct the proxies for testing the determinants and impact of property rights but it gave us a thorough understanding of the issue prior to modeling and testing.

20 Certainly, those we interviewed stressed the role of title for accessing capital for investments. For example, thirty-one smallholders near the town of Tucumã were asked, in May 1993, what effect having title would have, and the dominant response (by eight of those interviewed) was that title would provide collateral to obtain credit. These responses are representative of those from the other survey sites.

21 Field notes by Ricardo Tarifa, May 18, 1993, for Tucumã indicate that between 40% and 50% of the colonists had sold land, even without title, between visits in 1991 and 1993. The sales appear to be to other colonists in the community. Similarly, in the community of Nova Aliança, Tarifa noted active land exchanges among small holders, none of whom had title. Active land markets exist in all of the survey sites.

22 We estimated a three-equation model with dependent variables as title (0.1), land value per hectare, and land investment (percentage of hectares that received site-specific investments in either permanent crops or pasture requiring costly fencing).

23 Extrapolating to the rest of the world is analytically dangerous unless one is cognizant of the local formal and informal institutions.

24 This section draws primarily from Alston and Gallo (2008).

25  Though independent, the Justices did come from the higher socio-economic class. But this is true in most countries.

26  We performed an econometric counterfactual using county level allegations of fraud as an explanatory variable for the vote for Conservatives. The results indicate that in the absence of fraud the Conservatives would have lost in the Province of Buenos Aires and most likely lost control of the Presidency. Results supplied upon request.

27  In Alston and Gallo (2008) we perform an econometric estimation for the determinants of voting for Juan Peron. One of the explanatory variables is fraud in the 1930s. Our results indicate that those provinces where fraud was the greatest voted most heavily for Peron. Indeed, without fraud our results indicate that Peron would not have been elected. Additional circumstantial evidence comes from the Province of Cordoba located in the rich agricultural Pampas. In Cordoba the Conservatives refrained from fraud in the 1930s and lost the elections, but Cordoba continued to vote for the Radical Party and received more votes than Peron in the Presidential election of 1945.

28  Report from the Deputies Chamber to the Senate accusing the Supreme Court members; Sessions Diary of the Honorable National Senate Constituted in Tribunal. Tomo VI, 1947, p. 29.

29  The USA confronted a similar turning point in its institutional history but the electorate in 1896 came down on the side of maintaining the independence of the Supreme Court. In the election of 1896, the Supreme Court was under assault and one of its Republican defenders presaged the future of Argentina: "There are two places in this country where all men are absolutely equal: One is the ballot-box and the other is the Supreme Court. Bryan (the Populist candidate) proposes to abolish the Supreme Court and make it the creature of the party caucus whenever a new Congress comes in . . . " (Westin 1953, p. 37)

30  See Gallo (2003) for the econometric tests that determined the break point for Argentine GDP per capita with respect to Australia.

31  Examples of the institutional volatility are abundant: in 1955 the military government removed all the Justices of the Supreme Court and nullified the Peronist constitutional reform of 1949 by a simple decree. In 1958 the new Democratic President replaced most of the Justices of the Court and introduced two new Justices. Successive governments frequently either forced judges to resign or impeached them. On the economic side, stop and go policies characterized the post-Peron years. See Spiller and Tomassi (2003) for elaboration on policy volatility.

32  A recent (January 2005) default by Argentina on its debt obligations illustrates this point.

33  This works draws on Alston and Ferrie (1993, 1999).

34  In 1960 Southern farmers still harvested 50% of the cotton crop by hand. We took technological change as exogenous in our analysis.

35  The USA negotiated a "temporary" guest worker program in 1942, during World War II, which recruited workers from Mexico. The program (with a hiatus from 1948 to 1950) remained in existence until 1963. The chairs of the House and Senate agricultural committees, both Southerners, negotiated

the original agreement with Mexico and, after the War, Southerners disproportionately voted in favor of legislation to sustain the guest worker program because it prevented outmigration of Southerners to areas which recruited Mexicans.

36 The Food Stamp program gave "stamps" to poor individuals and households, which could be redeemed for groceries.

37 The significance of encouraging capital to flow to the South is that new factories would compete for Southern agricultural labor.

38 Previously, Southern agricultural interests resisted expenditure on education because educated rural workers tended to migrate away from agricultural jobs.

# 6 NEW INSTITUTIONAL ECONOMETRICS: THE CASE OF RESEARCH ON CONTRACTING AND ORGANIZATION

1 The more realistic assumptions and empirical focus of NIE are also contributing factors in the broad-spread application of the NIE theories in disciplines such as law, political science, sociology, anthropology, accounting, finance, and management.

2 For reviews of the competing theories and their implications, see Brousseau and Fares (2000), Whinston (2001), Saussier (2000b), and Masten and Saussier (2002). Klein (2005) provides a current review of the make-or-buy literature, while Boerner and Macher (2001) provide an extensive summary of empirical work in transaction cost economics (TCE).

3 Throughout the paper I refer to the use of hierarchical managerial coordination as "internalization" rather than as (vertical) integration. While the reader may perceive the two as synonymous, the reason for the distinction is discussed at length in Section 6.4.

4 This simple dichotomy may be deceptive since firms often choose to make and buy. This complication is addressed in Section 6.3.

5 Discussion of econometric models and their statistical properties draw heavily from Chapter 21 in Greene (2003). Any good econometric text (or statistical software manual) should provide a more complete discussion of these models and their applications.

6 G. S. Madalla (1983, p. 23) discusses several formulations for directly comparing coefficient estimates from the two models under the assumption that the probit error terms are distributed $N(0, \sigma^2)$.

7 A most-favored-nations clause, sometimes referred to as a most-favored-customer clause, guarantees the favored trading party (typically a purchaser) will receive the best price offered by the supplier to any of its customers during the duration of the contract regardless of the price stipulated in the original contract terms.

8 For problems with more than three ordinal responses, such as bond ratings, survey responses, and so forth, the model generalizes with additional threshold values, $\mu_i$'s for all $i \leq$ N-1, where N is the highest value of the discrete dependent variable.

9  This ambiguity applies to any interior values of the distribution if the number of discrete values is more than two. The probability $y = 0$ goes down, the probability $y = N$ goes up, and everything in between is ambiguous.

10  The Contracting and Organizations Research Institute (CORI) contracts collection may be accessed through a full-text search engine over the internet at www.cori.missouri.edu. CORI provides specialized access to large subsets of its data collection for academic users upon request.

11  For examples of some attempts to measure the quasi-rent itself, see Abowd and Allain (1996).

## 7  EXPERIMENTAL METHODOLOGY TO INFORM NEW INSTITUTIONAL ECONOMICS ISSUES

1  For a presentation of the early history of experimental economics, see Roth (1993).

2  The seminal research program on experimental economics (EE) applied to market experiments was run to challenge the standard price theory (Chamberlin 1948; Smith 1962). The development of game theory gave particular impetus to this use of experimental economics in the 1950s, just as auction literature did in the 1980s.

3  For discussion on the testability of a theory, see Vernon L. Smith 2002.

4  This difficulty is not limited to NIE. It may also prove difficult to collect field data for standard theories. For example, a supply or demand function is not observable in reality because the postulated limit prices are inherently private and not publicly observable. The "Induced Value Theory" proposed by Smith (1976) aims to induce preferences by a special application of derived demand theory inducing known (to the experimenter) supply or demand on individual subjects thereby ensuring the control.

5  For a complete description of the nature of social preferences, see Fehr and Fischbacher (2002).

6  Foss (2002) defines the "rhetorical use" as "dressing up a theory with arguments that are essentially empty in an explanatory sense, but nevertheless made because they help to persuade."

7  Complexity occurs because there may be many decision alternatives, with many features, so that a situation may be too complex to establish a maximizable utility function.

8  For a survey of the evolutionary models and the related experiments see Ostrom (2000).

9  Experience-weighted attraction models and learning direction theory may be considered hybrid models for reinforcement and belief learning. Rule learning models are, to a certain extent, a reinforcement model whereby agents learn which rules rather than which strategy to use.

10  For a survey on market experiment results, see Plott (1989), Davis and Holt (1993), and Sunder (1995).

11  As suggested by the authors, reticence was mostly due to political factors.

## 8   GAME THEORY AND INSTITUTIONS

1  This chapter will just consider non-cooperative games and leave aside cooperative games and evolutionary games; the latter will be developed in Chapter 15 of this book.

2  A well-known version of such a game is the "battle of sexes," in which a man and a woman are trying to decide on evening entertainment. They prefer spending the evening together, but each has an entertainment preference he or she would like to impose on the other.

3  An equilibrium in mixed strategies also exists, where Firm 1 chooses Standard 1 with a probability of 4/5 and Firm 2 adopts Standard 2 with a probability of 4/5.

4  A strategic game contains as many subgames as decision nodes. For each node, the subgame corresponds to the sequence of all actions or decisions that follow this node.

5  However, one important issue is to prevent renegotiations. The possibility of renegotiating the contract could weaken the credibility of commitment. To avoid this risk, some additional devices may be required, such as employing a neutral party with independent interests or building a strong reputation of no-renegotiation.

6  Hybrid or semi-separating equilibria may also exist, whereby the type-H agent randomizes between the two strategies – respect and cheat.

7  Players can also adopt other strategies in order to sustain cooperation. For example, Abreu (1986) showed that *stick and carrot* strategies, where punishments consist of an extremely severe one-period sanction (stick) followed by an indefinite reversion to the cooperative outcome (carrot), are at least as efficient in sustaining cooperation as any more complex strategy.

8  Decision issued on November 30, 1994, *Ciment*, No. L343, December 30, 1994.

9  Decision issued on February 17, 1992, *UK Agricultural Tractor Registration Exchange*, No. L68, March 13, 1992.

10  "Apart from indicating the empirical relevance of repeated games (with and without imperfect monitoring), these studies demonstrate the extent to which game theoretical analysis can highlight diverse aspects of a society, such as the interrelations between economic institutions and social structures," Greif (2000).

11  Because $lim_{e \to 0}\left(\frac{V(x^\star) - V(x^\star(1-e))}{e}\right) = V'(x^\star) = 0$ since $x^\star$ maximizes the net value of trade.

12  Since $r_d = \tau V(x^\star)$, $r_c = [\tau - c]V(x^\star)$ and $r_{nc} = 0$.

13  A similar example of institutional device is provided in Milgrom, North, and Weingast (1990). They showed that the *Law Merchant* institution in Champagne Fairs (during medieval times) enhanced the multilateral reputation mechanism, which by itself was unable to enforce contracts between merchants.

14  Dellarocas, Ming, and Wood (2004) observed rare coin auctions on eBay and found that 77% of the sellers and 67% of the buyers left feedback.

15 Or he can change his identity, but in this case he would lose his entire reputation and would reappear as a no-reputation seller.

16 *See also* the study by Lucking-Reiley *et al.* (2007) on coin auctions. For a survey of empirical studies on eBay, see Resnick *et al.* (2006).

## 9 NEW INSTITUTIONAL ECONOMICS, ORGANIZATION, AND STRATEGY

1 In his most recent discussion of strategy (Porter 1996), Porter's main claim is that fitting together a firm's activities creates sustainable competitive advantage. Unfortunately, Porter's framework lacks a method for making trade-offs among competing activity systems and resources; for operationalizing fit, which limits its predictive content; and for assessing the choice of organizational form. Williamson's TCE predicts a discriminating alignment between transaction exchange attributes (asset-specificity) and organizational mode (Williamson 1985, 1996). TCE offers almost no prescription for deciding which type of exchange attributes are desirable, which implies it has little to say about which strategy a firm should adopt.

## 10 INTER-FIRM ALLIANCES: A NEW INSTITUTIONAL ECONOMICS APPROACH

1 This section draws heavily on Oxley (1997).

2 Comparison of specific contract terms within particular classes of alliances is nonetheless a very fruitful avenue of research, as discussed later.

3 In general, NIE presumes that actors whose transactions are misaligned are more likely to display poor performance and to fail (or adapt) than those whose transactions are properly aligned, although this is rarely tested (exceptions include Nickerson and Silverman 2003; Argyres and Bigelow 2005). *See* Platteau (Chapter 21) for evidence on the persistence of inefficient institutions.

4 This section and Section 10.3 draw heavily on Silverman (2002).

5 As the discussion in other chapters of this book suggest, much greater attention has been paid to the role and influence of specific contract provisions in other contexts, for example in franchising (e.g. Lafontaine 1992) and supply contracts (e.g. Crocker and Reynolds 1993 and, more recently, the work of Mayer and co-authors [Kalnins and Mayer 2004; Mayer and Argyres 2004; Mayer 2005]. Some provisions, such as territorial restrictions, have also been examined quite extensively in a variety of contexts, such as technology licensing (Mueller and Geithman 1991) and industrial distribution (Fein and Anderson 1997).

## 11 GOVERNANCE STRUCTURE AND CONTRACTUAL DESIGN IN RETAIL CHAINS

1 See FTC, "Disclosure Requirements and Prohibitions Concerning Franchising and Business Opportunity Ventures" (16 CFR § 436.1 et seq.), and European Union rule 4087/88.

2 Franchisors should mostly open company-owned units and/or buy back existing franchised units.

3 For instance, Braddach (1997) shows that new franchisees are quite often previous employees of company-owned units. This reduces the asymmetric information problem concerning their talent and motivation, and decreases the time they need to run the outlet efficiently.

4 Geographical distance between an individual outlet and the chain head-quarter is the most widely used proxy for monitoring costs (Rubin 1978). The value of the brand is proxied by variables such as the age of the chain, or the monetary value of investments in advertising (*see* Minkler and Park 1994; Lafontaine and Shaw 2005).

5 According to Williamson (1991), "brand name capital" is a form of specific asset.

6 The credibility of the signal may be seen because a "good" chain will offer a contract that a "bad" chain has no incentive to offer. Technically speaking, a separating equilibrium exists in the signaling game.

7 Another implication is that if the franchisee participation constraint is bidding, the two monetary terms of the franchise contract, namely the royalty rate and the franchise fee, should be negatively correlated.

8 As pointed out by Williamson (1985), continuity of the relation is important in small bargaining situations.

9 This section draws heavily from Lafontaine and Raynaud (2002).

10 For self-enforcement to work the franchisor must be able to evaluate, *ex post*, whether or not the franchisee's performance is satisfactory, even if the desired effort is too complex to specify in the contract.

11 Indeed, only high-performance franchisees may expect renewal and additional outlets within the same chain. These decisions therefore involve rent that gives further incentives to franchisees.

12 According to them, the potential for franchisors to display opportunistic behaviour is limited by his reputation vis-à-vis actual and potential franchisees.

13 If part of the returns of local marketing investments accrues to other units, an individual franchisee will underinvest. By granting him an exclusive territory, or by requiring a mandatory (and verifiable) minimum level of expenditure on local promotions, the incentive to invest is restored.

14 For example, if one unit is particularly profitable the franchisor could threaten termination to purchase it at a discounted price (regarding its "real" value) and run it directly or re-sell it for a higher price to a new franchisee.

15 Regulating a franchise contract is a state decision in the USA. Some states restrict the ability of franchisors to terminate the contract easily; others do not (*see* Brickley 2002, for more on this).

16 Beales and Muris (1995) explain this contradictory result by arguing that in states with "at-will" termination chains are more tolerant with franchisees whose performance is poor, because they know that if performance is not improving, ultimately they have the possibility of terminating the agreement.

17 NIE partly shares this view with the "Chicago school" of law and economics on antitrust issues (see, for instance, an earlier contribution by Sam Peltzman, R. Posner or R. Bork).
18 Regulation No. 4087/88 of the European Union, and the more recent regulation No. 2790/1999, and the guideline on vertical restraints set by the EU for implementing the regulation.
19 See, for instance, Sampson 2004.


## 12 MAKE-OR-BUY DECISIONS: A NEW INSTITUTIONAL ECONOMICS APPROACH

1 It should be noted that we are referring to vertical integration and subcontracting as alternative organizational forms, confronting both concepts in a way similar to hierarchy versus market or insourcing versus outsourcing. Consequently, for the purpose of this chapter, market relationship, subcontracting, and outsourcing will be treated as equivalent.
2 We have ruled out the technological problem for simplicity. We will introduce this factor in the analysis in Section 12.2.4.2.
3 This concept was introduced by Coase (1937) and developed later by many other authors. Williamson (1975, 1985, 1996) is probably one of the authors who has contributed most.
4 Similarly, a quasi-rent is a return in excess of the minimum needed to keep a resource in its current use (Milgrom and Roberts 1992, p. 602).
5 Principal–agent literature has highlighted this idea. See Hart and Holmström (1987) and Hart and Moore (1988) as pioneering works.
6 This is the typical perspective of the principal–agent theory. See, as an overview, Hart and Moore (1999).
7 Although Williamson (1996, pp 378–379) differentiates governance structures, private ordering, and safeguards, we only differentiate safeguards from governance structures. The latter refers to the general mechanism used to govern a set of transactions (markets, hybrids, and hierarchy) and the former are devices with a more particular purpose used in a contract to deal with problems and contingencies.
8 This is an underlying requirement in Williamson's (1991a and 1991b) concept of economizing (i.e. the elimination of waste).
9 We refer to joint transaction costs because it is the optimal solution (instead of individual transaction costs). Applying Coase's Theorem, the parties will be able to negotiate and agree crossed compensations (if needed) for reaching that (joint) optimal solution.
10 See, for instance, Williamson (1975, p. 25, 1985, pp 79–80), Anderson and Schmittlein (1984, pp 387–388), Masten (1984, pp 405–406), Masten, Meehan, and Snyder (1991, pp 7–8) and Ricketts (1994, pp 185–191).
11 See, for example, MacNeil (1978) and Williamson (1991a).
12 See Barzel (1989) and Klein and Murphy (1997).
13 See, for example, Harrigan (1985) and Balakrishnan and Wernerfelt (1986).
14 See Poppo and Zenger (1998) and Afuah (2001) for a deeper discussion.

15  See Milgrom and Roberts (1992, especially chapters 6 and 7) for a summary of the incentive theory and moral hazard problem.
16  Williamson (1985, p. 76, 1991a).
17  Williamson (1985, pp 59–60) and Shelanski and Klein (1995, p. 339).
18  *See* Klein (1988, 1996), Crocker and Masten (1991), and Al Najjar (1995).
19  *See* Grossman and Hart (1986) and Barzel (1982, 1989) as pioneer works.
20  This kind of maintenance is quite difficult to measure in the short term and consequently it is costly to evaluate.
21  The influence of the institutional environment on organizational form has been studied recently, among other works, in González-Díaz, Arruñada, and Fernández (1998), Nickerson and Silverman (2003), and Lafontaine and Oxley (2002). Additionally, many other works have analyzed the effect of labor regulation on unemployment, wages, hiring and firing patterns, unionization and so on.
22  "RISC is an innovation in the instruction set architecture of a central processing unit that increases its speed" (Afuah 2001, p. 1217). CISC was the slow technology.

## 13 TRANSACTION COSTS, PROPERTY RIGHTS, AND THE TOOLS OF THE NEW INSTITUTIONAL ECONOMICS: WATER RIGHTS AND WATER MARKETS

1  This essay is developed from Libecap (2007).
2  *See* Blumm and Schwartz (1995), for example.
3  *See* the classic by Buchanan and Tullock (1962) on political incentives and Posner (2003, pp 346–349) on agency capture.
4  *See* the role of interest group politics in the ethanol subsidy as described by Johnson and Libecap (2001).
5  Heller (1998).
6  Griffin and Boadu (1992, pp 274–275).
7  Smith (1994), Thompson (1993, p. 729, p. 757).
8  The data in the figures are drawn from a data set compiled by Robert Glennon, Alan Ker, and Gary Libecap as part of a NSF-funded project on western water markets. The data are available upon request.
9  These transactions show annual flows of water, the first year of the contract. Hence, 1,000 acre feet of water leased for one year and 1,000 acre feet of water sold or leased for multiple years will reflect the same amount. This is a standard method of reporting water transactions. Alternatively, the water committed by the contract could be shown. Parts of the data set are reported in Libecap (2007, Chapter 1) and are drawn from a research project with joint principal investigators Robert Glennon and Alan Ker.
10  MacDonnell, (1990, Vol. I, 53, p. 68).
11  Thompson (1993, pp 704–705) claimed that the high costs of procedural requirements deters transfers.
12  Colby (1990, p. 1184).
13  *See* the Wyoming Constitution Art 8, p. 1.

14 *National Audubon Society* v. *Superior Court*, 685 P.2d. 712.
15 Sax (1990, p. 277).
16 Blumm and Schwartz (1995, pp 709–711).
17 For discussion of first-possession rules, *see* Lueck (1998).
18 MacDonnell (1990, Vol I, 27).
19 Howe, Boggs, and Butler (1990, pp. 404–5).
20 MacDonnell (1990, Vol. I, 11–13).
21 For discussion of bureaucratic incentives, *see* the summary in Johnson and Libecap (1994, pp 1–11, pp 154–188).
22 These distributional issues are major ones in the formation of oil field units and in fishery regulation. *See* Johnson and Libecap (1982), Libecap and Wiggins (1985), and Wiggins and Libecap (1985).
23 *See* Wiggins and Libecap (1985), Libecap and Smith (1999).
24 *See* Libecap and Johnson (1982) and Leal (2005) for discussion.

## 14 CONTRACTING AND ORGANIZATION IN FOOD AND AGRICULTURE

1 *See* Cook and Chaddad (2004) for an introduction and more detailed narrative about the evolution of inter-firm coordination research in the food and agriculture sector.
2 This section draws on Ménard and Klein (2004).
3 A potential problem with the empirical literature on contractual choice, however, is the need to control for unobserved heterogeneity within groups of contracting parties. Ackerberg and Botticini (2002) argue that studies of risk and transaction costs in agriculture do not adequately control for endogenous matching between principals and agents with unobserved idiosyncratic characteristics.
4 According to Hirschmann (1970), the members of an organization, when dissatisfied with their organization's policies, have one of the following options: Voice, Exit, or Loyalty. Voice in this context is a means of dynamically demonstrating their dissatisfaction, in order to achieve a change in the organization's policies.

## 15 BUY, LOBBY OR SUE: INTEREST GROUPS' PARTICIPATION IN POLICY MAKING: A SELECTIVE SURVEY

1 An earlier wave of new institutional analysis of interest groups was led by Mancur Olson's (1971) path-breaking *The Logic of Collective Action*. His analysis of the organization of, and individual incentives to, join groups led to a large literature on the formation and organization of interest groups. *See*, for example, Moe (1980) and references therein.
2 47 USC 151 (1934).
3 For a more detailed analysis of the role played by interest groups in the opening of the telecommunications market in the USA, *see* Spiller (1996a).

4 Some countries do not provide for a blanket declaration of lack of constitutionality of a statute, requiring instead its prior application (i.e. an agency decision) to a particular case.

5 The strategies of telecommunication entrants, such as MCI and others, to fight the FCC to open the telecommunications market may be understood in this setting. Indeed, Temin and Galambos (1987) point to MCI's multiple law suits against the FCC as the triggering factor that increased the hostility of the Justice Department against AT&T, and helped motivate it to pursue AT&T's eventual break-up.

6 Even US President Theodore Roosevelt saw the need, in 1906, to coin the term "muckrakers" to refer to those journalists who questioned the influence of business in policy making. See *The Columbia Encyclopedia*, sixth edition, 2001–2005. (Available at www.bartleby.com/65/mu/muckrake.html).

7 Among the classical buying legislators' papers, Denzau and Munger (1986), Snyder (1990, 1991), and Baron (1994) model the effects of tailored contribution schedules to individual legislators on voting outcomes. Dal Bó (2006a) extends the analysis by investigating the effect of general contribution offers to ideologically uniform voters on voting outcomes.

8 We could argue that legislators (and the president) buy each others' votes via pork-barrel legislation. Although the practice is well studied (for a recent application to Brazil, *see* Alston and Mueller 2006), we do not deal with pork-barrel issues here.

9 We could always spin a reciprocity theory whereby interest groups may compensate legislators with post-legislative employment, increasing thus the potential for interest alignment even on legislators' last terms. For a recent survey of theories of capture by interest groups, *see* Dal Bó (2006b).

10 Since the probability that a small contribution will impact on the probability of the legislator's re-election is small, the net gains from the contribution could well be negative.

11 Weingast and Moran (1983), McCubbins and Schwartz (1984), Barker and Ricker (1982), and Fiorina (1982), among others, deal with various forms of oversight employed by the Congress. We focus here on the incentives for buying legislators so as to achieve such influence.

12 The organization and budget of the judiciary (determining the threat of judicial reversal) is also of relevance (Spiller 1992). *See* Spiller and Gely (1992) for a discussion of the econometric implications of separations of powers models, and empirical evidence.

13 Support may depend on the legislator's perception of his or her constituency's preferences over the policy, or of his or her own beliefs about the public good.

14 In principle, conditional campaign or in general monetary contributions may also change legislators' perspectives about particular policies. We focus here, though, on information concerning states of the world, rather than on interest-group actions.

15 The March 2006 students' demonstrations in France represent one excellent example of transferring information to politicians about voters' preferences concerning flexible labor policies.

16 De Figueiredo and Silverman (2002) show large returns to universities from (direct) lobbying with a senator in the Senate Appropriations Committee (SAC), while the returns from lobbying to universities without a senator in the SAC is nil.

17 *See also* Lupia and McCubbins (1994).

18 *See* Calvert (1985), De Figueiredo, Spiller, and Urbiztondo (1999).

19 It may be argued that by allowing interest-group participation in the administrative process, legislators may have increased their usefulness to interest groups, thus, increasing the amount interest groups will pay for access. *See* also Spiller (1990) for a revolving-door theory of interest group influence where politicians benefit from interest group influence on bureaucratic decision making.

20 McCubbins, Noll, and Weingast (1987) view administrative procedures in that fashion. In their view, administrative procedures guide bureaucracies to make decisions consistent with the preferences of the enacting coalition.

21 The creation of a specific organ of the legislature whose purpose is to supervise the actions of the bureaucracy (such as the US General Accounting Office) is one such strategy. The problem remains, though, of who monitors the monitor. For a discussion of hierarchy as an organizational response to information problems, *see* Garicano (2000).

22 McCubbins, Noll and Weingast (1987) present a slightly different view. They see the organization of administrative procedures, in general and as applied to particular agencies, as ways to hard wire and protect the interests of the enacting coalitions, while DeFigueiredo, Spiller and Urbiztondo (1999) focus more on the generic informational benefit to incumbent legislators.

23 5 USC §§ 551–59, 701–06, 1305, 3105, 3344, 5372, 7521.

24 McCubbins, Noll, and Weingast (1989) apply the same "autopilot" explanation to the function of the APA as a safeguard for the enacting coalitions' interest. By including interest group participation in agencies' procedure and structure, agencies will change automatically in response to changes in the enfranchised interest groups' preferences, freeing the legislators from the need to intervene.

25 For evidence on congressional override, *see* Eskridge (1991).

26 Boehmke, Gailmard, and Patty (2006) find a related result that interest groups' lobbying of legislators and bureaucrats is highly correlated. *See also* De Figueiredo and Edwards (2004).

27 For a discussion of the role of new entrants in opening the market for long distance telecommunications, *see* Spiller (1996b). For environmentalist interest groups in limiting the development of nuclear power, *see* Weingast (1981).

28 *See* Epstein (1985) and Olson (1990) for a summary of works on the political disadvantage theory of interest group participation in the judical arena.

29 Interest groups may intensify their lobby and buying activities with the purpose of reversing the policy by direct legislative override. For this strategy to be "optimal," though, the policy implementation must have reflected the erroneous strategic choice by the interest group.

30 De Figueiredo and De Figueiredo (2002) develop a similar vote buying rather than indirect lobbying model. However, in their model there is no uncertainty, a fundamental issue to trigger informative lobbying.

31 *See*, for example, Gely and Spiller (1990).

32 This model may also be applied to a game between the administration and the legislature. Throughout this section, the word "court" may be replaced by the word "agency" to generate a model of indirect lobbying of the bureaucracy.

33 For completeness, there is a fourth stage in which the legislature reviews the court's decision, but given that courts would only make policy choices that are stable, we can, without any loss, discard this last stage.

34 *See* Proposition 1 in Iaryczower, Spiller, and Tommasi (2006).

35 *See* Proposition 2 and Lemma 1 in Iaryczower, Spiller, and Tommasi (2006).

36 See Proposition 3 in Iaryczower, Spiller, and Tommasi (2006).

37 This should come as no surprise, however, since for this purpose, increasing $x_c$ with $\beta_L$ and $\beta_H$ given is qualitatively similar to simultaneously reducing both $\beta_L$ and $\beta_H$ taking $x_c$ as given, and from the prior discussion we know that $\beta_L$ and $\beta_H$ have opposite effects on the expected level of lobbying.

38 This model also has standard separation of powers empirical implications. As in most separation of powers models, the equilibrium level of "pro-interest group" judicial decisions depends on the political composition of the legislature. In equilibrium, a more "pro-interest group" legislature will trigger more "pro-interest group" decisions provided that the court is effectively constrained by the legislature.

39 Recall S1 reflects cases when the state of the world is relatively *anti*-interest group, as $\theta$ is relatively low, given the preferences of the polity.

40 On the longevity of US congressional careers see Polsby (1968) and Ornstein, Mann and Malbin (1998). On committee specialization and the US Congress' policymaking role, see Shepsle (1978), Weingast and Moran (1983), Weingast and Marshall (1988), Krehbiel (1991) and Londregan and Snyder (1994).

41 *See* Weingast and Moran (1983) and McCubbins, Noll, and Weingast (1989). For a differing view on US Presidential powers *see* Moe and Howell (1999), whilst for a critical assessment of the "Congressional Dominance" theory *see* Moe (1987).

42 By party centered we refer to those electoral systems that force the voters' choices among parties rather than across candidates. *See* Carey and Shugart (1995).

43 To the extent that studies of legislatures in other presidential democracies have been conducted, they tend to focus almost exclusively on the least party-centered systems; especially Brazil.

44 This section draws from Jones *et al.* (2002).

45 The establishment of the European Union (EU) presents a unique case of an evolving institutional structure, from party centered to one better characterized as separation of powers. For a discussion of how firms

are adapting their political strategies to the emergence of powerful cross-national regulatory agencies, *see* Coen (1998).

46 For a study of the impact of a country's institutional features on legislators' behavior, *see* Crisp *et al.* (2004).

47 On the interaction between legislators and the President in Brazil, *see* Alston and Mueller (2006). *See also* Samuels (2002) for an alternative explanation of the link between legislators and the executive in Brazil.

48 On the role of party bosses in Argentina, *see* Spiller and Tommasi (2003).

49 *See* Ramseyer and Rasmusen (1997) for evidence on Japan; *see also* Salzberger and Fenn (1999) for evidence on the UK.

50 For a discussion of judicial adaptation to political control, *see* Spiller (1996a).

51 *See* Jones *et al.* (2002).

52 Spiller and Tommasi (2003).

53 Stigler (1981, p. 76).


## 16 REGULATION AND DEREGULATION IN NETWORK INDUSTRY

1 Such as financial crisis, corporate scandals (like ENRON), stock market collapses, California electricity crisis, numerous electricity blackouts around the world, and severe alerts coming from antitrust authorities (including one from the European Union).

2 Thus, as of 1904 John Bates Clark maintained that owners of infrastructures regulated by the public authority de facto forfeit the exclusivity component of their property rights and are obligated to act as employees of their clients!

3 That is, aside from those brought during two phases of internal renewal of the micro-economic theory of markets: first by the Walras–Pareto general equilibrium, which was more far-reaching than the Cambridge partial equilibrium of Marshall and Pigou, then by the "new micro-economics" of market imperfections that successfully laid siege to Arrow–Debreu general equilibrium.

4 Indemnification, buy-back, unilateral protection, technological innovation, and so on.

5 Several years later judge Posner would find a universal method for deregulating all network industries.

6 For example, that of Paul Samuelson.

7 Which was subsequently developed by various scholars (*see* Greif 2005; Hadfield 2005, for surveys).

8 The author demonstrates that this transfer of authority to the European Commission makes it possible to conceal the responsibilities of national bureaucracies by introducing an outside actor into domestic negotiations.

9 Where regulation or deregulation policy is more or less defined collectively in the framework of shared laws (called "Directives" or "Community Regulations"). The politics of industrial restructuring remains exclusively domestic, however (Glachant and Finon 2003; Glachant and Lévêque 2007; Haas *et al.* 2007).

10 On the contrary, when infrastructures may be duplicated by new operators they often remain integrated with the other activities of the incumbent operators (notably in telecoms, but also in postal services, and, sometimes in aviation, in the notion of hubs).

11 In his Nobel Prize acceptance speech, Coase called these market bases the "institutional structures of production."

12 For a survey of different empirical uses of "franchise bidding" we direct the reader to the work by Guash (2004) and Huet (2006).

13 As we have seen, a nature "à la Williamson" means specificity of the assets and uncertainty; a nature "à la Barzel" means measurement difficulties.

14 Another case, also exceptional, is that of gas and electricity in Germany. Between 1998 and 2004, the government conferred on a national consortium of stakeholders (i.e. a multilateral structure) *ex ante* powers to define the rules of network industries, in parallel with the *ex post* intervention of the competition watchdog (by reference or on own initiative) and the absence of a sectorial regulator.

15 This is already the case in the intermediation of telecoms and the internet (access or service provider), as well as in gas (shipper) and electricity (wholesale supplier = balancing authority = aggregator and retail supplier).

16 It is true that this European policy was stillborn, since it was subordinated to two veto rights of the member countries: a general veto for the global budget of this new European policy, plus a specific veto to each country over any project having a direct impact on it.

17 Until the appearance of low-cost airlines.

18 We here recall the operational difficulties encountered by California's electricity markets between the summer of 2000 and the spring of 2001. We also think of the comprehensive redesign of the English system in 2002, leading to the closing of the Electricity Pool of England and Wales, which was mandatory for all generators and resellers as of the beginning of the reform on April 1, 1990.

19 Except for the local landline grid for which it must provide free access to competitors.

20 As in aviation.

21 It is as if all airlines operating in the same control space were obligated to continually equate the number of seats on all their aircraft to the exact number of passengers having boarded them!

22 In other words, transactions arose in specific locations because designers created technologically separable interfaces that made transactions cost effective at those points (Lenfle and Baldwin 2007).

23 Littlechild (2006b) brings two aspects to the debate: he shows that, in Australia, merchant transmission companies have been allowed to compete with incumbent transmission monopolies for the building of new lines; while in Argentina transmission line expansion decisions have to be proposed, approved and paid for by market participants and not by the regulator or the regulated transmission company.

24 For a discussion of the economic consequences of the various methods of recovering connection costs in the electrical industry, *see* Hiroux (2004).

25  For a detailed presentation of institutional change *see* Aoki (2001, chapters 9 and 10). For an overview, *see* Aoki (2004).

26  Aoki's central notion is that each institution generates incentives and manages information autonomously, which may make it difficult for economic agents to utilize and understand the enmeshing of complex institutions.

27  Working from a different analytical framework, Laffont (2005) arrives at the same conclusions regarding the difficulties in transferring regulatory institutions and policies from the developed countries to the developing world.

28  Prosser (2005) argues that the early legal structures adopted for UK utility regulation did have elements of a regulatory contract. However, with the growth of competition and social regulation, a different model, that of a network of stakeholders, has largely replaced it.

29  Levy and Spiller (1994) on telecommunications reform; Guasch and Spiller (1999) on reforms in various network industries in Latin America; Savedoff and Spiller (1999) on reforms in water distribution sectors; Spiller and Martorell (1996); Holburn and Spiller (2002) on electricity reform.

30  *See* McCubbins, Noll, and Weingast (1987, 1989).

31  A growing literature is starting to reconsider the assumptions used – like Rufin (2003), who identifies a "Presidential Bias" in the Levy and Spiller framework.

32  Self-regulation may, therefore, be an appropriate solution where bargaining, at a low cost, can occur between risk creators and those affected; occupational health and safety provides a familiar example (Rees 1988; Greif 1989; Milgrom, North, and Weingast 1990; Ogus 1995; Glachant, Dubois, and Perez 2007).

33  For example, Congress (House of Representatives and Senate) is the key decision maker in the federal system of the USA, as is the President in France and the Prime Minister in England.

## 17 CONSTITUTIONAL POLITICAL ECONOMY: ANALYZING FORMAL INSTITUTIONS AT THE MOST ELEMENTARY LEVEL

1  Greif (1998), for example, describes historical comparative institutional analysis (HCIA) as an inductive tool.

2  This notion of contract is thus closer to private law contracts than to the notion of a social contract.

3  If a country with a proportional and parliamentary system is compared to a country with a plurality and presidential system, government expenditure of the latter is predicted to be some 10% of GDP lower than the former.

4  "Strong" and "weak" here refers to the organizational structure of parties; they are called "strong" if they have many paying members who are active in both political office and closely follow political events. Owing to the organizational structure, strong political parties may mobilize many people within a short period of time. This might enable them to produce focal points different from those the executive would like to create. Executives in an

environment with strong parties are expected to be more likely to play by the constitutional rules than executives in an environment with weak parties.

## 18 NEW INSTITUTIONAL ECONOMICS AND ITS APPLICATION ON TRANSITION AND DEVELOPING ECONOMIES

1 Aoki (1995), for instance, ascribes negative performance effects of insider control in Russian firms to the fact that the Western paradigm of diffuse ownership was applied blindly. Whilst potential principal–agent problems arising from small ownership concentration and widespread shareholdings are mitigated by efficient capital markets, the market for corporate governance, and the market for managers in Western market economies, such corporate governance mechanisms do not yet exist in the transition economies. The malfeasance of agents in transitory firms is therefore shielded by an institutional vacuum, which allows the emergence of opportunistic behavior and insider control.

2 Their assumption "that the legal system will eliminate chaos upon defining and enforcing property rights assumes, that the definition and enforcement of such rights is easy (costless)" (Williamson 2000, p. 599).

3 Johnson, McMillan, and Woodruff (2002) report on a survey of Russian and Polish managers whose concerns about corruption are clearly negatively correlated with firm investment. In the same survey managers were asked whether they would invest $100 today if they expected to receive $200 in two years; 99% of the Russian managers said they would not invest, while only 22% of the Polish managers refused.

## 19 LAW AND ECONOMICS IN RETROSPECT

1 *See also* Backhaus (1999) and Shavell (2003).

2 *See* Mercuro and Medema (1997).

3 *See* Coase (1993a, 1993b); Posner (1993); Williamson (1993).

4 *See* Dixit (2004) for an explanation of the complementary existence of private orderings and the efficiency of common law courts.

5 This is one of the key results of the approach described as behavioral law and economics (Jolls, Sunstein, and Thaler 1998), which investigates how law affects human behavior and the likely response of individuals to changes in the rules. The idea that rationality and institutions should themselves be explained was also central issue to the old institutional approach. From this point of view, neoclassical economics is a special case of institutional economics (Hodgson 2004a, p. 449).

6 In this regard, a brief comment on Williamson's remarks on this chapter expressed in the Foreword to this volume is in order. Indeed, we acknowledge that Professor Williamson explicitly recognizes in a 2000 article the relevance of the transaction costs associated to the functioning of legal orderings. However, this issue was absent from his 1985 book and our

reflections in this regard are meant to provide retrospective insights on the law and economics perspective as it has developed through time.

7 Barzel (1989) observes that, in spite of legally well-defined absolute rights on the slave, slaves were able to buy freedom from their master – a circumstance that may only be explained by the fact that transaction costs involved in extracting effort from the slave gave him some limited form of self-ownership.

8 *See* Nicita (2001); Nicita and Rizzolli (2004).

9 *See also* Bowles and Gintis (1999).

## 20 THE THEORY OF THE FIRM AND ITS CRITICS: A STOCKTAKING AND ASSESSMENT

1 We ignore here the claim that agency theory and property rights theory should not properly be included in NIE (Brousseau and Fares 2000).

2 Some of these criticisms echo even older critiques of the neoclassical theory of the firm by Papandreou, Lester, Cyert, March, Simon, and others. *See* Foss (2000) for brief discussions of these.

3 For expository reasons, we generally suppress the differences between the Williamson's and Hart's versions of the incomplete contracting story. Brousseau and Fares (2000) analyze the differences in detail.

4 For example, if A gives B the bribe before the game begins B will not play {right}, which means that A will decide not to give B any bribe. Or, A may promise B to pay the bribe after game, but B will realize that this will not be in A's interest, and will still play {left}.

5 Therefore, Williamson's treatment of bounded rationality seldom goes beyond quoting Simon's dictum that man is "intendedly rational, but limitedly so." He notes that "[e]conomizing on bounded rationality takes two forms. One concerns decision processes and the other involves governance structures. The use of heuristic problem-solving . . . is a decision process response." (Williamson 1985, p. 46). The latter "form" is not central, however, in TCE, which "is principally concerned . . . with the economizing consequences of assigning transactions to governance structures in a discriminating way."

6 A perhaps deeper problem stems from trying to combine substantive rationality with respect to some variables with rationality about other variables that is very bounded indeed. This is problematic, because in reality knowledge of the former variables (the expected surplus from the relation) is likely to be dependent upon knowledge of the latter variables (the sources of the surplus).

7 However, while Ghoshal and Moran (1996) question the substantial empirical literature supporting Williamson's theory, they offer little systematic evidence for their own view. They simply assert that the strong empirical relationship between specific assets and vertical integration exists because these assets reduce the cost of internal organization, independent of their effects on the hazards of market governance. They cite Masten, Meehan, and Snyder (1991), who have shown that this is a possibility with respect to specific human capital. However, there is no evidence that specific physical assets do reduce the costs of internal organization, nor do Ghoshal and Moran supply a coherent theory for such an effect.

8 Large parts of the knowledge-based view implicitly and sometimes explicitly subscribe to methodological collectivism (e.g. Kogut and Zander 1992; Hodgson 1998).

9 For example, closely complementary and similar activities are best undertaken under unified governance, whereas closely complementary but dissimilar activities are normally best undertaken under some sort of hybrid arrangement (to use Williamson's [1996] terminology).

10 Moreover, even in an opportunism-prone world, there may be much embeddedness "outside" firms, as it were, for example, in single industries, in firm networks, industrial districts, and so on, depending on the presence of various control and enforcement mechanisms.

11 In a recent paper, two leading theorists of the firm, Bengt Holmström and John Roberts (1998, p. 90) observed that "information and knowledge are at the heart of organizational design, because they result in contractual and incentive problems that challenge both markets and firms... In light of this, it is surprising that leading economic theories... have paid almost no attention to the role of organizational knowledge." Similarly, Coase (1988, p. 47) has lamented that in his 1937 paper, he "did not investigate the factors that would make the costs of organizing lower for some firms than for others."

12 Agency theory, for example, has generated important insights on the effects of incentives on effort and the relationship between incentive pay and risk. In explaining how a principal gets an agent to do something, however, the theory overlooks the more fundamental question of what the principal should want the agent to do, or indeed, how the principal got to be a principal in the first place.

13 Bajari and Tadelis (2001) is a prominent exception.

14 Concerning vertical integration, for example, Williamson (1985, pp 119–120) writes that "backward integration that lacks a transaction cost rationale or serves no strategic purposes will presumably be recognized and will be undone," adding that mistakes will be corrected more quickly "if the firm is confronted with an active rivalry."

15 However, the early 1980s was a period of corporate re-focus and de-conglomeration (Bhide 1990; Shleifer and Vishny 1991) and exit decisions during this period may reflect fashion and herd behavior, not efficiency. Moreover, though the findings support using the efficiency assumption in research on diversification, it may not hold for other decisions, such as the choice between market and hierarchical governance.

16 Some representative papers using a two-stage approach (such as Heckman's selection model) in this fashion are Masten, Meehan and Snyder (1991) and Saussier (2000).


21 THE CAUSES OF INSTITUTIONAL INEFFICIENCY: A DEVELOPMENT PERSPECTIVE

1 For property rights theorists, transaction costs correspond only to "the costs of enforcing and maintaining property rights, regardless of whether a market exchange takes place or not" (Allen and Lueck 2002, p. 4; *see also* Barzel 1989).

2 The efficiency principle simply states that if people are able to bargain together effectively and can effectively implement and enforce any agreements they reach, they should be able to realize the gains resulting from a shift from an inefficient situation to an alternative that everyone would prefer (Milgrom and Roberts 1992, p. 24).

3 The basic idea is that of immunity to invasion: a population of players all following an evolutionarily stable strategy will be able to repel an invasion of individuals playing some other strategy.

# References

Abbink, K., Brandts, J., Tanga McDaniel, T. 2003. "Asymmetric Demand Information in Uniform and Discriminatory Call Auctions: An Experimental Analysis Motivated by Electricity Markets," *J. Regul. Econy.*, 23, 2, pp 125–144.

Abowd, J.M. and Allain, L. 1996. "Compensation Structure and Product Market Competition," *Ann. Econ. Statist.*, 41:42, pp 207–218.

Abreu, D. 1986. "Extremal Equilibria of Oligopolistic Supergames," *J. Econ. Theory*, 39, pp 191–225.

Acemoglu, D. 2003. "Root Causes: A Historical Approach to Assessing the Role of Institutions in Economic Development," *Finance Devel.*, 40, 2, pp 27–30.
——— 2005. "Constitutions, Politics and Economics: A Review Essay on Persson and Tabellini's The Economic Effects of Constitutions," *J. Econ. Lit.*, 43, 4, pp 1025–1048.

Acemoglu, D. and Johnson, D. 2005. "Unbundling Institutions". *Journal of Political Economy*, 113, 949–995.

Acemoglu, D. and Robinson, J.A. 2000. "Why Did the West Extend the Franchise?" *Quart. J. Econ.*, 115, pp 1167–1199.

Acemoglu, D., Johnson, S., and Robinson, J.A. 2001. "The Colonial Origins of Comparative Development: An Empirical Investigation," *Amer. Econ. Rev.*, 91, pp 1369–1401.

Acheson, J.M. 1985. "The Main Lobster Market: Between Market and Hierarchy," *J. Law, Econ., Organ.*, 1, 2, pp 385–398.

Ackerberg, D.A. and Botticini, M. 2002. "Endogenous Matching and the Empirical Determinants of Contract Form," *J. Polit. Economy.*, 110, 3, pp 564–591.

Ackerman, B. 2000. "The New Separation of Powers," *Harvard Law Rev.*, 113, 3, pp 633–639.

Adserà, A., Boix, C., and Payne, M.E. 2001. "Are You Being Served? Political Accountability and Quality of Government," *J. Law, Econ., Organ.*, 19, 2, pp 445–490.

Afuah, A. 2001. "Dynamic Boundaries of the Firm: Are Firms Better off Being Vertically Integrated in the Face of a Technological Change?" *Acad. Manage. J.*, 44, 6, pp 1211–1228.

Agarwal, S. and Ramaswarmy, S.N. 1992. "Choice of Foreign Market Entry Mode: Impact of Ownership, Location and Internalization Factors," *J. Int. Bus. Stud.*, 23, pp 1–27.

Aghion, P. and Bolton, P. 2003. "Incomplete Social Contracts," *J. Europ. Econ. Assoc.*, 1, 1, pp 38–67.

Aghion, P., Alesina, A. F., and Trebbi, F. 2004. "Endogenous Political Institutions," *Quart. J. Econ.*, 119, 2, pp 565–611.

Aghion, P., Dewatripont, M., and Rey, P. 1994. "Renegotiation Design with Unverifiable Information," *Econometrica*, 62, 2, pp 257–282.

Akerlof, G. A. 1970. "The Market for 'Lemons' Quality, Uncertainty and the Market Mechanism," *Quart. J. Econ.*, 84, 3, pp 488–500.

1976. "The Economics of Caste and of the Rat Race and Other Woeful Tales," *Quart. J. Econ.*, 90, 4, pp 599–617.

Alchian, A. A. 1961. *Some Economics of Property*. Santa Monica, CA: Rand Corporation.

Alchian, A. A. and Demsetz, H. 1972. "Production, Information Costs, and Economic Organization," *Amer. Econ. Rev.*, 62, pp 772–795.

Alexander, R. 1987. *The Biology of Moral Systems*. Aldine de Gruyter: Hawthorne.

Allais, M. 1943. *A la Recherche d'Une Discipline Economique*. Atelier Industria.

Allen, D. W. and Lueck, D. 1998. "The Nature of the Farm," *J. Law Econ.*, 41, 2, pp 343–387.

1992. "Contract Choice in Modern Agriculture: Cash Rent versus Cropshare," *J. Law Econ.*, 35, 2, pp 397–426.

2002. *The Nature of the Farm – Contracts, Risk, and Organization in Agriculture*. Cambridge, MA, and London: MIT Press.

Al-Najjar, N. I. 1995. "Incomplete Contracts and the Governance of Complex Contractual Relationships," *Amer. Econ. Rev.*, 85, 2, pp 433–436.

Alston, L. J. and Ferrie, J. P. 1993. "Paternalism in Agricultural Labor Contracts in the U.S. South: Implications for the Growth of the Welfare State," *Amer. Econ. Rev.*, 83, 4, pp 852–875.

1999. *Paternalism and the American Welfare State: Economics, Politics, and Institutions in the U.S. South, 1865–1965*. Cambridge University Press.

Alston, L. J. and Gallo, A. 2008. "Electoral fraud, the rise of Peron, and the demise of checks and balances in Argentina," IBS work. Paper PEC2008:0001, University of Colorado. (Available at: www.colorado.edu/ibs/eb/alston)

Alston, L. J. and Higgs, R. 1982. "Contractual Mix in Southern Agriculture since the Civil War: Facts, Hypotheses, and Tests," *J. Econ. Hist.*, 42, pp 327–353.

Alston, L. J. and Mueller, B. 2004. "Property Rights and the State," in Ménard, C. and Shirley, M. M., eds, *Handbook for New Institutional Economics*. Norwell, MA: Kluwer Academic Publishers, pp 573–590.

2006. "Pork for Policy: Executive and Legislative Exchange in Brazil," *J. Law Econ. Organ.*, 22, 1, pp 12–36.

Alston, L. J., Datta, S. K., and Nugent, J. B. 1984. "Tenancy Choice in a Competitive Framework with Transaction Costs," *J. Polit. Economy*, 92, pp 1121–1133.

Alston, L. J., Eggertsson, T., and North, D. 1996. *Empirical Studies in Institutional Change*. Cambridge University Press.

Alston, L. J., Libecap, G. D., and Mueller, B. 1999a. "A Model of Rural Conflict: Violence and Land Reform Policy in Brazil," *Environ. Devel. Econ.*, 4, 2, pp 135–160.

1999b. *Titles, Conflict, and Land Use: The Development of Property Rights and Land Reform on the Brazilian Amazon Frontier*. Ann Arbor, MI: University of Michigan Press.

2000. "Land Reform Policies: The Sources of Violent Conflict, and Implications for Deforestation in the Brazilian Amazon," *J. Environ. Econ. Manage.*, 39, 2, pp 162–188.

Alston, L. J., Libecap, G. D., and Schneider, R. 1996. "The Determinants and Impact of Property Rights: Land Titles on the Brazilian Frontier," *J. Law, Econ. Organ.*, 12, pp. 25–61.

Alt, J. E. and Lassen, D. D. 2003. "The Political Economy of Institutions and Corruption in American States," *J. Theo. Polit.*, 5, 3, pp 341–365.

Ames, B. 2001. *The Deadlock of Democracy in Brazil*. Ann Arbor, MI: University of Michigan Press.

Anand, B. N. and Khanna T. 2000. "Do Companies Learn to Create Value?" *Strategic. Manage. J.*, 21, 3, pp 295–316.

Anderlini, L. and Felli, L. 1999. "Incomplete Contracts and Complexity Costs," *Theory Dec.*, 46, pp 23–50.

2004. "Bounded Rationality and Incomplete Contracts," *Res. Econ.*, 58, pp 3–30.

Anderson, E. and Schmittlein, D. C. 1984. "Integration of the Sales Force: An Empirical Examination," *RAND J. Econ.*, 15, 3, pp 385–395.

Anderson, J. and Young, L. 2002. "Imperfect Contract Enforcement," NBER work. paper, 8847, pp 1–50.

Anderson, J. H., Lee, Y., and Murrell, P. 2000. "Competition and Privatization Amidst Weak Institutions: Evidence from Mongolia," *Econ. Inquiry*, 38, 4, pp 527–549.

Anderson, T. L. and Hill, P. J. 2002. "Cowboys and Contracts," *J. Legal Stud.*, 31, 2, pp 489–514.

Anderson, T. L. and McChesney, F. 2003. *Property Rights: Cooperation, Conflict and Law*. Princeton, NJ: Princeton University Press.

Ansoff, I. H. and Brandenburg, R. C. 1967. "A Program of Research in Business Planning," *Manage. Sci.*, 13, 6, pp 219–241.

Ansolabehere, S., de Figueiredo, J. M., and Snyder, J. M. 2003. "Why Is There So Little Money in US Politics?" *J. Econ. Perspect.*, 17, 1, pp 105–130.

Ansolabehere, S., Snyder, J. M., and Tripathi, M. 2002. "Are PAC Contributions and Lobbying Linked? New Evidence from the 1995 Lobby Disclosure Act," *Bus. Polit.*, 4, 2, pp 131–155.

Aoki, M. 1984. *The Co-operative Game Theory of the Firm*. Oxford: Clarendon Press.

1988. *Information, Incentives and Bargaining in the Japanese Economy*. Cambridge University Press.

1995. "Controlling Insider Control: Issues of Corporate Governance in Transition Economies," in Aoki, M. and Hyung-Ki, K., eds, *Corporate Governance in Transitional Economies: Insider Control and the Role of Banks*. Washington, DC: World Bank, pp 3–30.

2001. *Towards a Comparative Institutional Analysis*. Cambridge, MA: MIT Press.

2004. "An Organizational Architecture of T-Form: Silicon Valley Clustering and Its Institutional Coherence," *Ind. Corp. Change*, 13, 6, pp 473–487.

Argyres, N. S. 1995. "Technology Strategy, Governance Structure and Interdivisional Coordination," *J. Econ. Behav. Organ.*, 28, pp 337–358.

1996a. "Capabilities, Technological Diversification and Divisionalization," *Strategic. Manage. J.*, 17, 5, pp 395–410.

1996b. "Evidence on the Role of Firm Capabilities in Vertical Integration Decisions," *Strategic Manage. J.*, 17, pp 129–150.

Argyres, N. S. and Bigelow, L. 2005. "Do transaction costs matter for survival at all stages of the industry life cycle?" Work paper, Boston University, presented at the 2004 ISNIE meetings in Tucson, AZ. (Available at: http://smgnet.bu.edu/mgmt_new/profiles/ArgyresNicholas.html).

Argyres, N. S. and Liebeskind, J. P. 1999. "Contractual Commitments, Bargaining Power, and Governance Inseparability: Incorporating History into Transaction Cost Theory," *Acad. Manage. Rev.*, 24, 1, pp 49–63.

Argyres, N. S. and Mayer, K. J. 2004. "Learning to Contract: Evidence from the Personal Computer Industry," *Organization Sci.*, 15, 4, pp 394–410.

Argyres, N. S. and Silverman, B. S. 2004. "R&D, Organizational Structure, and the Development of Corportae Technological Knowledge," *Strategic Manage. J.*, 25, pp 929–958.

Armour, H. O. and Teece, D. J. 1978. "Organizational Structure and Economic Performance: A Test of the Multidivisional Hypothesis," *Bell J. Econ.*, 9, 1, pp 106–122.

Aron, J. 2000. "Growth and Institutions: A Review of the Evidence," *World Bank Res. Observer*, 15, 1, pp 99–135.

Arrow, K. 1971. *Essays in the Theory of Risk*. Amsterdam, North Holland Publishing.

1987. "Reflections on the Essays," in Feiwel, G., ed. *Arrow and the Foundations of the Theory of Economic Policy*. New York University Press, pp 727–734.

Arruñada, B. 2001. "The Role of Institutions in the Contractual Process," in Deffains, B. and Kirat, T., eds, *Law and Economics in Civil Law Countries*. Amsterdam: Elsevier Science, pp 177–196.

2003. "Third Party Moral Enforcement: The Rise and Decline of Christian Confession," Universitat Pompeu Fabra, Economics and Business. Work paper 653. (Available at: www.econ.upf.es/cgi-bin/onepaper?653).

2004. "The Economic Effects of Christian Moralities," Universitat Pompeu Fabra, Economics and Business. Work paper 743. (Available at: www.econ.upf.es/cgi-bin/onepaper?743).

Arruñada, B and Andonova, V., forthcoming. "Judges' Cognition, and Market Order," *Review of Law and Economics*.

2005. "Market Institutions and Judicial Rulemaking," in Ménard, C. and Shirley, M., eds, *Handbook of New Institutional Economics*," Norwelll, MA: Kluwer Academic Publishers, pp 229–50.

Arruñada, B. and Garoupa, N. 2005. "The Choice of Titling System in Land," *J. Law Econ.*, 48, 2, pp 709–727.

Arruñada, B., Gonzále Díaz, M., Fernández, A. 2004. "Determinants of Organizational Form: Transaction Costs and Institutions in the European Trucking Industry," *Ind. Corp. Change*, 13, 6, pp 687–692.

Arruñada, B., Garicano, L., and Vázquez, L. 2001. "Contractual Allocation of Decision Rights and Incentives: The Case of Automobile Distribution," *J. Law Econ. Organ.*, 17, 1, pp 257–284.

Arthur, B. W. 1989. "Competing Technologies, Increasing Returns, and Lock-in by Historical Events," *Econ. J.*, 99, 394, pp 116–131.

Austen-Smith, D. 2000. "Redistributing Income under Proportional Representation," *J. Pol. Econ.*, 108, 6, pp 1235–1269.

Austen-Smith, D. and Wright, J. R. 1994. "Counteractive Lobbying," *Amer. J. Polit. Sci.*, 38, 1, pp 25–44.

Axelrod, R. 1997. *The Complexity of Cooperation – Agent-Based Models of Competition and Collaboration*. Princeton University Press.

Backhaus, J. 1999. "Introduction," in *The Elgar Companion to Law and Economics*. Cheltenham: Edward Elgar, pp 1–4.

Bai, C.-E. and Zhijian, T. 2000. "Contract Mixing in Franchising as a Mechanism for Public-Goods Provision," *J. Econ. Manage. Strategic.*, 9, 1, pp 85–113.

Bailey, M. J. 1992. "Approximate Optimality of Aboriginal Property Rights," *J. Law Econ.*, 35, pp 183–198.

Bajari, P. and Tadelis, S. 2001. "Incentives versus Transactions Costs: A Theory of Procurement Contracts," *RAND J. Econ.*, 32, 3, pp 387–407.

Baker G. P. and Hubbard, T. N. 2001. "Empirical Strategies in Contract Economics: Information and the Boundary of the Firm," *Amer. Econ. Rev.*, 91, 2, pp 189–194.

2003. "Make or Buy in Trucking: Assets Ownership, Job Design and Information," *Amer. Econ. Rev.*, 93, 3, pp 551–572.

2004. "Contractibility and Asset Ownership: On-Board Computers and Governance in US Trucking," *Quart. J. Econ.*, 119, 4, pp 1443–1479.

Baker, G. P., Gibbons, R., and Murphy, K. 2004. "Strategic Alliances: Bridges Between 'Islands of Conscious Power'," Work paper: Harvard Business School, Massachusetts Institute of Technology, University of Southern California.

Baker, M. 2001. *The Atoms of Language*. New York, NY: Basic Books.

Bakken, H. and Schaars, M. 1937. *The Economics of Cooperative Marketing*. New York, NY: McGraw-Hill.

Bakos, Y. and Dellarocas, C. 2003. "Cooperation Without Enforcement? A Comparative Analysis of Litigation and Online Reputation as Quality Assurance Mechanisms," MIT Sloan Work paper 4295-03, pp 1–33.

Balakrishnan, S. and Wernerfelt, B. 1986. "Technical Change, Competition and Vertical Integration," *Strategic. Manage. J.*, 7, 4, pp 347–359.

Baland, J.-M. and Platteau, J.-P. 1996. *Halting Degradation of Natural Resources – Is There a Role for Rural Communities?* Oxford: Clarendon Press.

Baldwin, C. and Clark K. 2000. *Design Rules: The Power of Modularity*. Boston, MA: MIT Press.

Bambaci, J., Spiller, P. T. and Tommasi, M. 2001. "Bureaucracy and Public Policy in Argentina," *American Political Science Association Meetings*.

Banerjee, A. V. and Duflo, E. 2000. "Reputation Effects and the Limits of Contracting: A Study of the Indian Software Industry," *Quart. J. Econ.*, 15, 3, pp 989–1017.

Banerjee, A. V. and Iyer, L. 2004. "History, Institutions, and Economic Performance: The Legacy of Colonial Land Tenure Systems in India," Mimeo, MIT. (Available at: http://econ-www.mit.edu/faculty/download_pdf.php?id=517).

Banerjee, A. V. and Munshi, K. D. 2004. "How Efficiently is Capital Allocated? Evidence from the Knitted Garment Industry in Tirupur," *Rev. Econ. Stud.*, 71, 1, pp 19–42.

Banfield, E. 1958. *The Moral Basis of a Backward Society.* New York, NY: Free Press.

Barker, R. P., and Ricker, W. H., 1982. "A Political Theory of Regulation with some Observations on Railway Abandonments," *Public Choice*, 39, pp 73–106.

Barnard, Chester. 1938. *The Functions of the Executive.* Cambridge: Harvard University Press.

Barney, J. B. 1991. "Firm Resources and Sustained Competitive Advantage," *J. Manage.*, 17, 1, pp 99–120.

Baron, D. P. 1994. "Electoral Competition with Informed and Uninformed Voters," *Amer. Polit. Sci. Rev.*, 88, 1, pp 33–47.

2000. *Business and Its Environment*, third edition. Englewood Cliffs, NJ: Prentice Hall.

Barquin, J., Bergman, L., Crampes, C., Green, R., Glachant, J.-M., Hirchhausen, C., *et al.* 2006. "The Acquisition of Endesa by Gas Natural: Why the Antitrust Authorities Are Right to Be Cautious," *Electricity J.*, 19, 2, pp 62–68.

Barzel, Y. 1982. "Measurement Cost and Organization of Markets," *J. Law Econ.* 25, pp 27–48.

1989. *Economic Analysis of Property Rights.* New York, NY: Cambridge University Press.

2002. *A Theory of the State: Economic Rights, Legal Rights, and the Scope of the State.* New York, NY: Cambridge University Press.

Basu, K. 2000. *Prelude to Political Economy – A Study of the Social and Political Foundations of Economics.* Oxford: Oxford University Press.

Basu, K., Jones, E., and Schlicht, E. 1987. "The Growth and Decay of Custom: The Role of the New Institutional Economics in Economic History," *Explorations Econ. Hist.* 24, 1, pp 1–21.

Bates, R., Greif, A., Levi, M., Rosenthal, J.-L., and Weingast, B. 1998. *Analytic Narratives.* Princeton University Press.

Baum, J. A. C., Calabrese, T., and Silverman, B. S. 2000. "Don't Go It Alone: Alliance Networks and Startup Performance in Canadian Biotechnology," *Strategic. Manage. J.* 21, 3, pp 267–294.

Baum, J. A. C., Shipilov, A. V., and Rowley, T. J. 2003. "Where Do Small Worlds Come From?" *Industrial Corpor. Change.*, 12, 4, pp 697–725.

Baumol, W. and Sidak, G. 1994. *Toward Competition in Local Telephony*, Boston, MA: MIT Press.

Beales, H. J. and Muris, T. J. 1995. "The Foundation of Franchise Regulation: Issues and Evidence," *J. Corp. Finan.*, 2, pp 157–197.

Beck, T., Clarke, G., Groff, A., Keefer, P., and Walsh, P. 2000. "New Tools and New Tests," in *Comparative Political Economy: The Database of Political Institutions*, Washington, DC: World Bank.

Beers, G., Beulens, A., and van Dalen, J. 1998. "Chain Science as an Emerging Discipline," in Ziggers, G. W., Trienekens, J. H., and Zuurbier, P. J. P, eds, *Proceedings of the Third International Conference on Chain Management in Agribusiness and the Food Industry.* Wageningen University, Management Studies Group, pp 295–330.

Benabou, R. and Tirole, J. 2003. "Intrinsic and Extrinsic Motivation," *Rev. Econ. Stud.*, 70, 3, pp 489–520.

Bennedsen, M. and Feldmann, S. E. 2002. "Lobbying Legislatures," *J. Polit. Econ.*, 110, 4, pp 919–948.

Benz, M. and Stutzer, A. 2004. "Are Voters Better Informed when They Have a Larger Say in Politics? Evidence for the European Union and Switzerland," *Public Choice*, 119, 1–2, pp 31–59.

Bercovitz, J. 2001. *An Analysis of Contract Provisions in Business-Format Franchise Agreement*. Mimeo, Duke University, Fuqua School of Business.

2003. *The Option to Expand: The Use of Multi-Unit Opportunities to Support Self-Enforcing Agreements in Franchise Relationships*. Mimeo, Duke University, Fuqua School of Business.

Bercovitz, J., Jap, S. and Nickerson, J. A. 2006. "The Antecedents and Performance Implications of Cooperative Exchange Norms," *Organization Science*, 17, 6, pp 724–740.

Bergara, M., Richman, B. D., and Spiller, P. T. 2003. "Modeling Supreme Court Strategic Decision Making: the Congressional Constraint," *Legisl. Stud. Quart.*, 28, pp 247–80.

Bernstein, L. 1992. "Opting out of the Legal System: Extralegal Contractual Relations in the Diamond Industry," *J. Legal Stud.*, 21, 1, pp 115–157.

2001. "Private Commercial Law in the Cotton Industry: Creating Cooperation through Norms, Rules, and Institutions," *Mich. Law Rev.*, 99, pp 1724–1788.

Besanko, D., Dranove, D., and Shanley, M. 1996. *Economics of Strategy*. New York, NY: John Wiley & Sons.

Besley, T. and Payne, A. 2003. "Judicial Accountability and Economic Policy Outcomes: Evidence from Employment Discrimination Charges." Mimeo, June.

Bhattacharyya, S. and Lafontaine, F. 1995. "Double-Sided Moral Hazard and the Nature of Share Contracts," *RAND J. Econ.*, 26, 4, pp 761–781.

Bhide, A. 1990. "Reversing Corporate Diversification," *J. Appl. Corp. Fin.*, 3, 2, pp 70–81.

Bigelow, L. 2003. "Transaction Alignment and Survival: Performance Implications of Transaction Cost Alignment," Work paper, Olin School of Business, Washington University.

2006. "Technology Choice, Transaction Alignment and Survival: The Impact of Sub-Population Organizational Structure," *Advan. Strategic. Manage.*, 23, pp 301–334.

Binmore, K. 1992. *Funs and Games: A Text on Game Theory*. Cambridge, MA: DC Heath & Co.

Blankart, C. B. 2000. "The Process of Government Centralization: A Constitutional View," *Constit. Polit. Econ.*, 11, 1, pp 27–39.

Bliss, C. and Stern, N. 1982. *Palanpur*. Oxford University Press.

Blomberg, B. S., Hess, G. D., and Weerapana, A. 2004. "The Impact of Voter Initiatives on Economic Activity," *Europ. J. of Polit. Econ.*, 20, 1, pp 207–226.

Blumm, M. C. and Schwartz, T. 1995. "Mono Lake and the Evolving Public Trust in Western Water," *Arizona Law Rev.*, 37, pp 701–738.

Boehmke, F. J., Gailmard, S., and Patty, J. W. 2005. "Whose Ear to Bend? Information Sources and Venue Choice in Policy Making," *Quart. J. of Polit. Sci.*, 1, pp 139–169.

2005. "Patterns of Interest Group Lobbying Across Venues and Policies," paper presented at the 2005 Annual Meetings of the Midwest Political Science Association.

Boemare, C. and Quirion, P. 2002. "Implementing Greenhouse Gas Trading in Europe – Lessons from Economic Theory and International Experiences," *Ecolog. Econ.*, 43, 2–3, pp 213–230.

Boerner, C. and Macher, J. 2001. "Transaction Cost Economics: An Assessment of Empirical Research in the Social Science," Georgetown University, work paper. (Available at: www.msb.edu/faculty/jtm4/Macher.CV.htm).

Boger, S., Hobbs, J. E., and Kerr, W. A. 2001. "Supply Chain Relationships in the Polish Pork Sector," *Suppl. Chai. Manage.*, 6, 2, pp 74–83.

Boisot, M. and Child, J. 1996. "From Fiefs to Clans and Network Capitalism: Explaining China's Emerging Economic Order," *Admin. Sci. Quart.*, 41, 4, pp 600–628.

Boix, C. 1999. "Setting the Rules of the Game: The Choice of Electoral Systems in Advanced Democracies," *Amer. Polit. Sci. Rev.*, 93, 3, pp 609–724.

Bolton, G. E. 1991. "A Comparative Model of Bargaining: Theory and Evidence," *Amer. Econ. Rev.*, 81, 5, pp 1097–1136.

Boomgard, J. J., Davies, S. P., Haggblade, S. J., and Mead, D. C. 1991. "A Subsector Approach to Small Enterprise Promotion and Research," *Worl. Devel.* 19, pp 199–212.

Bowles, S. 2004. *Microeconomics – Behavior, Institutions, and Evolution.* New York, NY: Russell Sage Foundation and Princeton, NJ: Princeton University Press.

Bowles, S. and Gintis, H. 1999. "Power in Competitive Exchange," in Bowles, S., Franzini, M., and Pagano, U., eds, *The Politics and the Economics of Power.* London: Routledge, pp 13–31.

Boyd, R. and Richerson, P. 1985. *Culture and the Evolutionary Process.* Chicago University Press.

Braddach, J. L. 1997. "Using the Plural Form in the Management of Restaurant Chains," *Admin. Sci. Quart.*, 42, 2, pp 276–303.

Brennan, G. and Hamlin, A. 1994. "A Revisionist View of the Separation of Powers," *J. Theo. Polit.*, 6, 3, pp 345–368.

Brennan, G. and Kliemt, H. 1994. "Finite Lives and Social Institutions," *Kyklos*, 47, 4, pp 551–571.

Brickley, J. A. 1999. "Incentives Conflicts and Contractual Restraints: Evidence from Franchising," *J. Law Econ.*, 42, 2, pp 745–774.

2002. "Royalty Rates and Upfront Fees in Share Contracts: Evidence from Franchising," *J. Law Econ. Org.*, 18, 2, pp 511–535.

Brickley, J. A. and Dark, F. H. 1987. "The Choice of Organizational Form: the Case of Franchising," *J. Finan. Econ.*, 18, pp 401–420.

Brickley, J. A., Dark, F. H., and Weisbach, W. S. 1991. "The Economic Effects of Franchise Termination Laws," *J. Law Econ.*, 34, 1, pp 101–132.

Bronars, S. G. and Lott, J. R., Jr. 1997. "Do Campaign Donations Alter How A Politician Votes? Or, Do Donors Support Candidates Who Value the Same Things That They Do?" *J. Law Econ.*, 40, 2, pp 317–350.

Brousseau, E. 2000a. "Confiance ou Contrat, Confiance et Contrat," in Aubert, F. and Sylvestre, J.-P., eds, *Confiance et Rationalité*. INRA: Les Colloques, 97, pp 65–80.

2000b. "Processus Evolutionnaires et Institutions: Quelles alternatives à la rationalité parfaite ?" *Revue Economique*, Special Issue, 51, 5, pp 1185–1213.

2000c. "What Institutions to Organize Electronic Commerce: Private Institutions and the Organization of Markets," *Econ. Innovation New Tech.*, 9, 3, pp 245–273.

2004. "Property Rights in the Digital Space," in Colombatto, ed., *Companion to Economics of Property Rights*. Cheltenham, UK, and Northampton, MA: Edward Elgar, pp 438–472.

Brousseau, E. and Bessy, C. 2006. "Public and Private Institutions in the Governance of Intellectual Property Rights," in Andersen, B., ed, *Intellectual Property Rights: Innovation, Governance and the Institutional Environment*. Cheltenham, UK and Northampton, MA, USA: Edward Elgar Publishers, pp 243–277.

Broussea, E. and Curien, N., eds. 2007. *Internet and Digital Economics: Principles Methods and Applications*. Cambridge University Press.

Brousseau, E. and Fares, M. 2000. "Incomplete Contracts and Governance Structures: Are Incomplete Contract Theory and Transaction Cost Economics Substitutes or Complements?" in Ménard, C., ed., *Institutions, Contracts and Organizations: Perspectives from the New Institutional Economics*. Cheltenham: Edward Elgar, pp 399–421.

2002. "Règle de Droit et Exécution des Contrats : Réflexion d'Économistes sur le Droit comparé des Contrats," *Revue Econ. Politique*, N° Spécial "L'Economie du Droit", sld Deffains, B., 112, 6, pp 823–844.

Brousseau, E. and Glachant, J. M. 2002. *The Economics of Contracts: Theories and Applications*. Cambridge: Cambridge University Press.

Brousseau, E. and Raynaud, E. 2006. "The Economics of Private Institutions: An Introduction to the Dynamics of Institutional Frameworks and to the Analysis of Multilevel Multi-Type Governance," Mimeo, EconomiX, University of Paris X.

2007. "The Economics of Multilevel Governance," Mimeo, EconomiX, University of Paris X.

Brown, D. 1991. *Human Universals*. New York, NY: McGraw-Hill.

Brown, D. and Earle, J. 2000. "Privatization and Enterprise Restructuring in Russia: New Evidence from Panel Data on Industrial Enterprises." Work paper 1, RECEP, Moscow.

Brown, M., Falk, A., and Fehr, E. 2003. "Relational Contracts and the Nature of Market Interactions," IZA Discussion Paper, 897.

*Brown* Versus *Board of Education of Topeka, Kansas*, 347 U.S. 483, 47 S. Ct. 686, 98 L. eds. 873.

Buchanan, J. 1977. *Freedom in Constitutional Contract – Perspectives of a Political Economist*. London: College Station and Texas, TX: A&M University Press.

1984. "Sources of Opposition to Constitutional Reform," in *Constitutional Economics – Containing the Economic Powers of Government*. McKenzie, R. B., ed. Lexington: Lexington Books. pp 21–34.

1986. "Political Economy and Social Philosophy," in Buchanan, J., ed., *Liberty, Market and State – Political Economy in the 1980s.* New York, pp 261–274.

1987. "Constitutional Economics," in *The New Palgrave.* Basingstoke: Macmillan, pp 588–595.

Buchanan, J. M. 1959. "Positive Economics, Welfare Economics, and Political Economy," *J. Law Econ.,* 2, pp 124–138.

1975a. "A Contractarian Paradigm for Applying Economic Theory: Conflict and Contract," *Amer. Econ. Rev.,* 65, 2, pp 225–230. (Papers and Proceedings of the Eighty-Seventh Annual Meeting of the American Economic Association.)

1975b. *The Limits of Liberty – Between Anarchy and Leviathan.* Chicago University Press.

Buchanan, J. and Tullock, G. 1962. *The Calculus of Consent: Logical Foundations of Constitutional Democracy.* Ann Arbor, MI: Michigan University Press.

Buchner, B., Carraro, C., and Ellerman, D. 2006. "The Allocation of European Union Allowances: Lessons, Unifying Themes and General Principles," FEEM work paper, 116, Milan.

Bueno de Mesquita, E. and Stephenson, M. 2006. "Legal Institutions and the Structure of Informal Networks," *J. Theoret. Pol.,* 18, 1, pp 40–67.

Bull, J. and Watson, J. 2001. "Evidence Disclosure and Verifiability," *J. Econ. Theory,* 118, 1, pp 1–31.

Burt, R. 1992. *Structural Holes: The Social Structure of Competition.* Cambridge, MA: Harvard University Press.

Buskens, V., Raub, W., and Snijders, C. 2003. *The Governance of Relations in Markets and Organizations.* Amsterdam: JAI Press.

Cafaggi, F., Nicita, A. and Pagano, U. 2007. "Law, economics and institutional complexity: An introduction," in *Legal Orderings and Economics Institutions.* in Cafaggi, F., Nicita, A. and Pagano, U., eds. London, Routledge.

Calabresi, G. 1965. "The Decision for Accidents: An Approach to Non-Fault Allocation for Costs," *Harvard Law Rev.,* 78, 4, pp 713–745.

1968. "Transaction Costs, Resource Allocation and Liability Rules: A Comment," *J. Law Econ.,* 11, 1, pp 67–73.

1970. *The Costs of Accidents: A Legal and Economic Analysis.* New Haven, CT: Yale University Press.

Calabresi, G. and Melamed, D. A. 1972. "Property Rules, Liability Rules, and Inalienability: One View of the Cathedral," *Harvard Law Rev.,* 85, 6, pp 1089–1128.

Calvert, R. L. 1985. "Robustness of the Multidimensional Voting Model: Candidate Motivations, Uncertainty, and Convergence," *Amer. J. Polit. Sci.,* 29, 1, pp 69–95.

Camara de Senadores de la Nacion. 1947. *Diario de Sesiones del Honorable Senado de la Nacion. Constituido en Tribunal.* 4, Buenos Aires.

Camerer, C. F. 1998. "Behavioral Economics and Nonrational Organizational Decision Making," in Halpern, J. J. and Stern, R. N., eds, *Debating Rationality.* Ithaca, NY: Cornell University Press, pp 53–77.

1999. "Behavioral Economics: Reunifying Psychology and Economics," *Proceed. National Acad. Sci.,* 9, 19, pp 10575–77.

2003. *Behavioral Game Theory: Experiments in Strategic Interaction.* New York, NY: Princeton University Press and Russell Sage Foundation.

Camerer, C. F. and Ho, T.-H. 1999. "Experienced-Weighted Attraction Learning in Normal Form Games," *Econometrica,* 67, 4, pp 827–874.

Camerer, C. F. and Thaler, R. H. 1995. "Anomalies: Ultimatums, Dictators and Manners," *J. Econ. Perspect.,* 9, 2, pp 209–219.

Camerer, C. F. and Knez, M. 1996. "Coordination, Organizational Boundaries and Fads in Business Practice," *Industrial Corp. Change,* 5, 1, pp 89–112.

Carey, J. M. and Shugart, M. S. 1995. "Incentives to Cultivate a Personal Vote: A Rank Ordering of Electoral Formulas," *Elect. Stud.,* 14, 4, pp 417–439.

Carmichael, L. H. and MacLeod, B. W. 2003. "Caring About Sunk Costs: A Behavioral Solution to the Hold-up Problem," *J. Law Econ. Organ.,* 19, pp 106–118.

Cashdan, E. A. 1980. "Egalitarianism Among Hunters and Gatherers," *Amer. Anthropol.,* 82, 1, pp 116–120.

Casson, M. 1997. *Information and Organization.* Oxford University Press.

Castalia Strategic Advisor. 2005. *Explanatory Notes on Key Topics in the Regulation of Water and Sanitation Services,* World Bank edition.

Caves, R. E. and Murphy, W. F. 1976. "Franchising: Firms, Markets and Intangible Assets," *Southern Econ. J.,* 42, 4, pp 572–586.

Chakravarty, S. and MacLeod, B. 2004. "On the Efficiency of Standard Form Contracts: The Case of Construction," USC CLEO Research paper series, C04-17.

Chamberlin, E. H. 1948. "An Experimental Imperfect Market," *J. Polit. Econ.,* 56, 2, pp 95–108.

Chao, H.-P., and Peck, S., 1998. "Reliability management in competitive electricity markets," *Journal of Regulatory Economics,* 14, pp 189–200.

Chao, H.-P. and Huntington, H. 1998. *Designing Competitive Electricity Markets.* Kluwer Academic Press.

Che, J. and Qian, Y. 1998. "Insecure Property Rights and Government Ownership of Firms," *Quart. J. Econ.,* 113, 2, pp 467–496.

Che, Y.-K. and Hausch, D. B. 1999. "Cooperative Investments and the Value of Contracting," *Amer. Econ. Rev.,* 89, 1, pp 125–148.

Cheung, S. N. S. 1970. "The Structure of a Contract and the Theory of a Non-Exclusive Resource," *J. Law Econ.,* 13, 1, pp 49–70.

1973. "The Fable of the Bees: An Economic Investigation," *J. Law Econ.,* 16, 1, pp 11–33.

1983. "The Contractual Nature of the Firm," *J. Law Econ.,* 26, 1, pp 1–21.

Coase, R. H. 1937. "The Nature of the Firm," *Economica,* pp 386–405. Reprinted in Coase, R. H. 1988. *The Firm, the Market and the Law.* Chicago Univerrsity Press, pp 55–57.

1946. "The Marginal Cost Controversy," in Coase, R. H., 1988.

1959. "The Federal Communications Commission," *J. Law Econ.,* 2, 2, pp 1–40.

1960. "The Problem of Social Cost," *J. Law Econ.,* 3, 1, pp 1–44.

1964. "The Regulated Industries – Discussion," *American Economic Review,* 54, 3, pp 194–197.

1972. "Industrial Organization: A Proposal for Research," in Coase, R. H. 1988, pp 57–74.

1974. "The Lighthouse in Economics," in Coase, R. H., 1988, Chapter 7.

1976. "Adam Smith View of Man," *J. Law Econ.*, 19, 3, pp 529–546.

1988. *The Firm, the Market, and the Law.* Chicago University Press.

1988. "The Nature of the Firm: Origin, Meaning, Influence," *J. Law Econ. Org.*, 4, pp 3–59.

1992. "The Institutional Structure of Production," *Amer. Econ. Rev.*, 82, 4, pp 713–719.

1993a. "Coase on Posner on Coase and Concluding Comment," *J. Inst. Theoretical Econ.*, 149, 1, pp 73–87.

1993b. "Law and Economics at Chicago," *J. Law Econ.*, 36, pp 239–254.

1998. "The New Institutional Economics," *Amer. Econ. Rev.*, 88, 2, pp 72–74

2000. "The Acquisition of Fisher Body by General Motors," *J. Law Econ.*, 43, 1, pp 15–31.

Codognet, M. K., Glachant, J. M., Lévêque, F., and Plagnet, M. A. 2003. "Mergers and Acquisitions in the European Electricity Sector." GRJM and CERNA, École Nationale Supérieure des Mines de Paris.

Coen, D. 1998. "The European Business Interest and the Nation State: Large Firm Lobbying in the European Union and Member States," *J. of Public Polit.*, 118, 1, pp 75–100.

Coeurderoy R. and Quélin, B. 1997. "Transaction Cost Theory: A Survey of Empirical Studies on Vertical Integration," *Rev. Econ. Polit.*, 107, 2, pp 145–181.

Cohen, M. D., Burkhart, R., Dosi, G., Egidi, M., Marengo, L., Warglien, M., and Winter, S. G. 1996. "Routines and Other Recurring Action Patterns of Organizations," *Contemp. Res. Issues*, Industrial and Corporate Change, 5, 3, pp 653–698.

Cohen, W. M. and Levinthal, D. A. 1990. "Absorptive Capacity: A New Perspective on Learning and Innovation," *Administ. Scien. Quart.*, 35, 1, pp 128–152.

Colby, B. G. 1990. "Transaction Costs and Efficiency in Western Water Allocation," *Amer. J. Agr. Econ.*, 72, 5, pp 1184–1192.

Collis, D. and Montgomery, C. 1995. "Competing on Resources: Strategy in the 1990s," *Harvard Bus. Rev.*, 73, 4, pp 118–128.

Commons, J. R. 1924. *Legal Foundations of Capitalism.* Clifton: Augustus M. Kelley, reprinted: Transaction Publishers, 1995.

1932–1933. "The Problems of Correlating Law, Economics and Ethics," *Wisconsin Law Rev.* 8, 1, pp 3–26.

Conner, K. R. and Prahalad, C. K. 1996. "A Resource-based Theory of the Firm: Knowledge versus Opportunism," *Organ. Sci.*, 7, 5, pp 477–502.

Contractor, F. J. and Lorange, P. 1988. "Why Should Firms Cooperate? The Strategy and Economics Basis for Cooperative Ventures," in Contractor, F. J. and Lorange, P., eds., *Cooperative Strategies in International Business.* Lexington, MA: Lexington Books.

Cook, M. L. 1995. "The Future of U.S. Agricultural Cooperatives: A Neo-Institutional Approach," *Amer. J. Agr. Econ.*, 77, 5, pp 1153–59.

Cook, M. and Iliopoulos, C. 2000. "Ill-defined Property Rights in Collective Action: The Case of US Agricultural Cooperatives," in Ménard, C., ed., *Institutions, Contracts and Organizations*. Cheltenham: Edward Elgar, pp 335–348.

Cook, M. L. and Chaddad, F. R. 2004. "Redesigning Cooperative Boundaries: The Emergence of New Models," *Amer. J. Agr.Econ.* 86, 5, pp 1249–1253.

Cooter, R. D. and Janet, L. T. 1984. "Personal versus Impersonal Trade: The Size of Trading Groups and Contract Law," *Int. Rev. Law Econ*, 4, 1, pp 15–22.

Cooter, R. D. and Rubinfeld L. D. 1989. "Economic Analysis of Legal Dispute and Their Resolution," *J. Econ. Lit.*, 27, 3, pp 1067–1097.

Corts, K. S. and Singh, J. 2004. "The Effect of Repeated Interaction on Contract Choice: Evidence from Offshore Drilling," *J. Law, Econ. Organ.*, 20, 1, pp 230–260.

Cosmides, L. 1985. "Deduction or Darwinian Algorithms? An Explanation of the Elusive Content Effect of the Wason Selection Task." PhD dissertation, Department of Psychology, Harvard University.

1989. "The Logic of Social Exchange: Has Natural Selection Shaped How Humans Reason? Studies with the Wason Selection Task," *Cognition*, 31, 3, pp 187–196.

Cosmides, L. and Tooby, J. 1992. "Cognitive Adaptations for Social Exchange," in Barkow, J. H., Cosmides, L., and Tooby, J., eds, *The Adapted Mind*. New York, NY: Oxford University Press, pp 163–228.

1994. "Better than Rational: Evolutionary Psychology and the Invisible Hand," *Amer. Econ. Rev.*, 84, 2, pp 327–332.

Craswell, R. 2001. "Two Economic Theories of Enforcing Promises," in Benson, P., ed., *Readings in the Theory of Contract Law*. Cambridge University Press.

Crawford, V. P. and Broseta, B. 1998. "What Price Coordination? The Efficiency-Enhancing Effect of Auctioning the Right to Play," *Amer. Econ. Rev.*, 88, 1, pp 198–225.

Crisp, B. F., Escobar-Lemmon, M. C., Jones, B. S., Jones, M. P., and Taylor-Robinson, M. M. 2004. "Vote-Seeking Incentives and Legislative Representation in Six Presidential Democracies," *J. Polit.*, 166, 3, pp 823–846.

Crocker, K. J. and Masten, S. E. 1988. "Mitigating Contractual Hazards: Unilateral Options and Contract Length," *RAND J. Econ.*, 19, 3, pp 327–343.

1991. "Pretia ex Machina?: Prices and Process in Long Term Contracts," *J. of Law and Econ.*, 34, pp 64–99.

1996. "Regulation and Administered Contracts Revisited: Lessons From Transaction-Cost Economics for Public Utility Regulation," *J. Regul. Econ.*, 9, pp 5–40.

Crocker, K. J. and Reynolds J. K. 1993. "The Efficiency of Incomplete Contracts: An Empirical Analysis of Air Force Engine Procurement," *RAND J. Econ.*, 24, 1, pp 126–146.

Cyert, R. and March, J. 1963. *A Behavioral Theory of the Firm*. Englewood Cliffs, NJ: Prentice Hall.

Dahlman, C. J. 1979. "The Problem of Externality," *J. Law Econ.*, 22, 1, pp 141–162.

Dal Bó, E. 2006a. *Bribing Voters*. Mimeo: Haas School of Business, University of California, Berkeley.

2006b. *Regulatory Capture: A Review*. Mimeo: Haas School of Business, University of California, Berkeley.

Dal Bó, E., Dal Bó, P., and Di Tella, R. 2006. "Plato O Plomo? Bribe and Punishment in a Theory of Political Influence," *Amer. Polit. Sci. Rev.*, 100, 1, pp 41–53.

Damasio, A. 1994. *Descartes' Error: Emotion, Reason and the Human Brain*. New York, NY: Grosset/Putnam.

Datta, S. K., O'Hara, D. J., and Nugent, J. B. 1986. "Choice of Agricultural Tenancy in the Presence of Transaction Costs," *Land Econ.*, 62, 2, pp 145–158.

David, P. A. 1985. "Clio and the Economics of QWERTY," *Amer. Econ. Rev.* 75, 2, pp 332–337.

Davis, D. and Holt, C. 1993. *Experimental Economics*. Princeton University Press.

Davis, J. and Goldberg, R. 1957. *A Concept of Agribusiness*. Boston, MA: Division of Research, Harvard Business School.

Davis, L. and North, D. 1971. *Institutional Change and American Economic Growth*. New York, NY: Cambridge University Press.

Davoodi, H. and Heng-fu Z. 1998. "Fiscal Decentralization and Economic Growth: A Cross-Country Study," *J. Urban Econ.*, 43, 2, pp 244–257.

Dawkins, R. 1976. *The Selfish Gene*. Oxford University Press.

1982. *The Extended Phenotype*. Oxford University Press.

Day, G. S. and Klein, S. 1987. "Cooperative Behavior in Vertical Markets: The Influence of Transaction Costs and Competitive Strategies," *Rev. Marketing*, pp 39–66.

De Figueiredo, J. M. 1998. "Litigating Regulation: Corporate Strategy in Telecommunication," unpublished manuscript.

2005. "Strategic Plaintiffs and Ideological Judges in Telecommunications Litigation," *J. Law, Econ., Organ.*, 21, 2, pp 501–523.

De Figueiredo, J. M. and De Figueiredo, R. J. P, Jr. 2002. "The Allocation of Resources by Interest Groups: Lobbying, Litigation, and Administrative Regulation," *Bus. Politics*, 14, 2, pp 161–181.

De Figueiredo, J. P. R, Jr. and Edwards, G. 2004. "Why Do Regulatory Outcomes Vary So Much? Economic, Political and Institutional Determinants of Regulated Prices in the US Telecommunications Industry." Work paper, Haas School of Business, University of California, Berkeley.

De Figueiredo, J. M. and Silverman, B. S. 2002. "Academic Earmarks and the Returns to Lobbying," *J. Law, Econ., Organ.*, 49, pp 597–625.

De Figueiredo, J. P. R, Jr., Spiller, P. T., and Urbiztondo, S. 1999. "An Informational Perspective on Administrative Procedures," *J. Law, Econ., Organ.*, 15, 1, pp 283–305.

De Janvry, A., Gordillo, G., Platteau, J.-P., and Sadoulet, E. 2001. *Access to Land, Rural Poverty, and Public Action*. Oxford University Press.

Deakin, S. and Michie, J. 1997a. "Contracts, Co operation, and Competition," in *Studies in Economics, Management, and Law*. Oxford University Press.

1997b. "Contracts and Competition," *Cambridge Journal of Economics*, 21, 2, pp 121–25.

Deci, E. and Ryan, R. 1985. *Intrinsic Motivation and Self-Determination in Human behavior.* New York, NY: Plenum.

Deffains, B. and Kirat, T. 2001, in Mercuro, N., ed., *Law and Economics in Civil Law Countries, the Economics of Legal Relationship.* Amsterdam: JAI Press, Elsevier Science BV.

Dellarocas, C., Fan, M., and Wood, C. 2004. "Self-Interest, Reciprocity, and Participation in Online Reputation Systems," MIT Sloan work paper 4500–04 (Available at: http://ssrn.com/abstract=585402).

Demsetz, H. 1967. "Toward a Theory of Property Rights," *Amer. Econ. Rev.*, 57, 2, pp 347–359.

1968. "Why Regulate Utilities?" *J. Law Econ*, 11, 1, pp 55–65.

1969. "Information and Efficiency: Another Viewpoint," *J. Law Econ.*, 12, 1, pp 1–22.

1988. "Profit as a Functional Return: Reconsidering Knight's Views," in Demsetz, H., ed., *Ownership, Control and the Firm. The Organization of Economic Activity.* Oxford and New York, NY: Blackwell, pp 236–247.

Dennen, T. R. 1976. "Cattlemen's Associations and Property Rights in Land in the American West," *Explorations Econ. Hist.*, 13, 4, pp 423–436.

Denton, M. J., Rassenti, S. J., Smith, V. L., and Backerman, S. R. 2001. "Market Power in a Deregulated Electrical Industry," *Decision Support Systems*, 30, 3, pp 357–381.

Denzau, A. T. and Munger, M. C. 1986. "Legislators and Interest Groups: How Unorganized Interests get Represented," *Amer. Polit. Sci. Rev.*, 80, 1, pp 89–106.

Dick, A. R. 1996. "When are Cartels Stable Contracts?" *J. Law Econ.*, 39, 1, pp 241–283.

DiMaggio, P. 1994. "Culture and Economy," in Smelser, N. and Swedberg, R., eds, *The Handbook of Economic Sociology.* Princeton University Press, pp 27–57.

Dixit, A. 1996. *The Making of Economic Policy: A Transaction Cost Politics Perspective.* Cambridge, MA: MIT Press.

2004. *Lawlessness and Economics. Alternative Modes of Governance.* Princeton University Press.

Dixit, A. and Nalebuff, B. 1993. *Thinking Strategically: The Competitive Edge in Business, Politics, and Every Day Life.* New York, NY: W.W. Norton & Co.

Djankov, S. and Murrell, P. 2002. "Enterprise Restructuring in Transition: A Quantitative Survey," *J. Econ. Lit.*, 40, 3, pp 793–837.

Djankov, S., Glaeser, E., La Porta, R., Lopez de Silanes, F., and Shleifer, A. 2003. "The New Comparative Economics," *J. Compar. Econ.*, 31, 4, pp 595–619.

Djankov, S., La Porta, R., Lopez de Silanes, F., and Shleifer, A. 2002. "The Regulation of Entry," *Quart. J. Econ.*, 117, 1, pp 1–37.

Dnes, A. W. 1993. "A Case-Study Analysis of Franchise Contracts," *J. Legal Stud.*, 22, 2, pp 367–393.

Donaldson, L. 1996. *For Positivist Organization Theory: Proving the Hard Core.* London: Sage.

Dosi, G. 2000. *Innovation, Organization, and Economic Dynamics: Selected Essays.* Cheltenham: Edward Elgar.

Dosi, G. and Marengo, L. 1994. "Some Elements of an Evolutionary Theory of Organizational Competences," in Englander, R. W., ed., *Evolutionary Concepts in Contemporary Economics.* Ann Arbor, MI: Michigan University Press, pp 157–178.

2000. "On the Tangled Discourse between Transaction Cost Economics and Competence-based Views of the Firm: Some Comments," in Foss, N. J. and Mahnke, V., eds, *Competence, Governance, and Entrepreneurship.* Oxford University Press, pp 80–92.

Dow, G. K. 1987. "The Function of Authority in Transaction Cost Economics," *J. Econ. Behav. Organ.*, 8, 1, pp 13–38.

Dubois, W. E. B. 1965. *Three Negro Classics: Up from Slavery. The Souls of Black Folks. The Autobiography of an Ex-Colored Man.* New York, NY: Avon Books.

Dufwenberg, M. and Kirchsteiger, G. 2004. "A Theory of Sequential Reciprocity," *Games Econ. Behav.*, 47, 2, pp 268–298.

Dussauge, P., Garrette, B., and Will, M. 2000. "Learning from Competing Partners: Outcomes and Durations of Scale and Link Alliances in Europe, North America and Asia," *Strategic Manag. J.*, 21, 2, pp 99–126.

Dutta, S., Bergen, M., Heide, J. B., and John, G. 1995. "Understanding Dual Distribution: The Case of Rep and House Accounts," *J. Law, Econ., Organ.*, 11, 1, pp 189–204.

Duverger, M. 1954. *Political Parties: Their Organization and Activity in the Modern State.* New York, NY: Wiley.

Duxbury, N. 1995. *Patterns of American Jurisprudence.* Oxford: Clarendon Press.

Dyer, J. H. 1997. "Effective Interfirm Collaboration: How Firms Minimize Transaction Costs and Maximize Transaction Value," *Strategic Manage. J.*, 18, 7, pp 535–356.

Easterly, W. 2001. *The Elusive Quest for Growth: Economists' Adventures and Misadventures in the Tropics.* Cambridge, MA: MIT Press.

Edlin, A. S. 1998. "Breach Remedies," in *The New Palgrave Dictionary of Economics and the Law.* London: Macmillan, pp 174–179.

Edlin, A. S. and Reichelstein, S. J. 1996. "Holdups, Standard Breach Remedies, and Optimal Investment," *Amer. Econ. Rev.*, 86, 3, pp 478–01.

EDRD (European Bank for Reconstrucion and Development). 2004. Transition Report : Infrastructure, London.

Eggertsson, T. 1990. *Economic Behaviour and Institutions.* Cambridge University Press.

Eilers, C. and Campbell Hanf, C. 1999. "Contracts between Farmers and Farmers Processing Cooperatives: A Principal Agent Approach for the Potato Starch Industry," in Galizzi, G. and Venturini, L., eds, *Vertical Relationships and Coordination in the Food System.* Hiedelberg: Physica, pp 267–284.

Elazar, D. J. 1995. "From Statism to Federalism: A Paradigm Shift," *Publius*, 25, 2, pp 5–18.

Elfenbein, D.W. and Lerner, J. 2003. "Ownership and Control Rights in Internet Portal Alliances, 1995–1999," *RAND J Econ.*, 34, 2, pp 356–369.

Elster, J. 1983. *Explaining Technical Change. A Case Study in the Philosophy of Science.* Cambridge: Cambidge University Press.

1994. "Arguing and Bargaining in Two Constituent Assemblies," unpublished manuscript, remarks given at the University of California, Berkeley.

Enikolopov, R. and Zhuravskaya, E. 2003. "Decentralization and Political Institutions," CEPR Discussion paper 3857.

Ensminger, J. 1992. *Making a Market: The Institutional Transformation of an African Society.* Cambridge University Press.

Epstein, D. and O'Halloran, S. 1995. "A Theory of Strategic Oversight: Congress, Lobbyist and the Bureaucracy," *J. Law, Econ. Organ.*, 11, 2, pp 227–255.

Epstein, L. 1985. *Conservatives in Court.* Knoxville, TN: Tennessee University Press.

Eskridge J.R., William N. 1991. "Overriding Supreme Court Statutory Interpretation Decisions," *Yale Law J.*, 101, 2, pp 331–355.

Fafchamps, M. 1996. "The Enforcement of Commercial Contracts in Ghana," *World Devel.*, 24, 3, pp 427–448.

Fan, J.P.H. 2000. "Price Uncertainty and Vertical Integration: An Examination of Petrochemical Firms," *J. Corp. Finan: Contracting, Governance, and Organ.*, 6, 4, pp 345–376.

Fan, J.P.H. and Lang, L.H.P. 2000. "The Measurement of Relatedness: An Application to Corporate Diversification," *J. Bus.*, 73, 4, pp 629–660.

Fares, M. and Saussier, S. 2002. "Contrats Incomplets et Couts de Transaction," *Rev. Fr. Econ.*, pp 193–230.

Fearon, J. 1999. "Electoral Accountability and the Control of Politicians: Selecting Good Types versus Sanctioning Poor Performance," in Manin, B., Przeworski, A., and Stokes, S., eds, *Democracy, Accountability, and Representation.* Cambridge, MA: Cambridge University Press,

Fehr, E. and Fischbacher, U. 2002. "Why Social Preferences Matter. The Impact of Non Selfish Motives on Competition, Cooperation and Incentives," *Econ. J.*, 112, 478, pp C1–C33.

Fehr, E. and Gachter, S. 2000. "Fairness and Retaliation: The Economics of Reciprocity," *J. Econ. Perspect.*, 14, pp. 159–181.

2002. "Do Incentive Contracts Crowd-out Voluntary Cooperation?" Work paper W34. (Available at: www.iew.unizh.ch/wp/iewwp034.pdf).

Fehr, E. and Gächter, S. 2006. "Reciprocity and Contract Enforcement," *Handbook of Experimental Economics*, in press.

Fehr, E. and Schmidt, K.M. 1999. "A Theory of Fairness, Competition, and Cooperation," *Quart. J. Econ.*, 114, pp 769–816.

Fehr, E., Klein, A., and Schmidt, K. 2001. "Fairness, Incentives and Contractual Incompleteness," CESifo work paper W445, Zurich IEER work paper W72. (Available at: http://ssrn.com/abstract=262015).

Fein, A.J. and Anderson, E. 1997. "Patterns of Credible Commitments: Territory and Brand Selectivity in Industrial Distribution Channels," *J. Marketing*, 61, 2, pp 19–34.

Feld, L. P. and Kirchgässner, G. 2001. "The Political Economy of Direct Legislation: Direct Democracy and Local Decision-Making," *Econ. Pol. Rev.*, 33, pp 329–367.

Feld, L. P. and Savioz, M. R. 1997. "Direct Democracy Matters for Economic Performance: An Empirical Investigation," *Kyklos*, 50, 4, pp 507–538.

Feld, L. P. and Voigt, S. 2003. "Economic Growth and Judicial Independence: Cross-Country Evidence Using a New Set of Indicators," *Europ. J. Polit. Economy*, 19, 3, pp 497–527.

2004. "Making Judges Independent – Some Proposals Regarding the Judiciary," CESifo work paper W1260.

Feld, L., Kirchgässner, G., and Schaltegger, C. 2003. "Decentralized Taxation and the Size of Government: Evidence from Swiss State and Local Governments," CESifo Work paper W1087.

Feld, L., Zimmermann, H., and Doring, T. 2004. "Federalism, Decentralization and Economic Growth," Discussion Paper Series Work papers 200430, Philipps-Universität Marburg, Faculty of Business Administration and Economics, Department of Economics (Volkswirtschaftliche Abteilung).

Felin, T. and Foss, N. 2004. "Methodological Individualism and the Organizational Capabilities Approach," Work paper W2004-5, Center for Knowledge Governance, Copenhagen Business School. (Available at www.cbs.dk/ckg).

Ferejohn, J. 1999. "Accountability and Authority: Toward a Theory of Political Accountability," in Manin, B., Przeworski, A., and Stokes, S., eds, *Democracy, Accountability, and Representation*. Cambridge, MA: Cambridge University Press.

Ferejohn, J. and Shipan Charles, C. 1990. "Congressional Influence on Bureaucracy," *J. Law, Econ., Organ.*, 6, pp 1–20.

Festré, A. and Garrouste P. 2006. "Incentives and Motivations: To What Extent Can Economics Benefit from Psychology?" Mimeo, ATOM, University of Paris 1.

Figueiredo, R. J. and Weingast, B. R. 2005. "Self-Enforcing Federalism," *J. Law, Econ., Organ.*, 21, 1, pp 103–135.

Fiorina, M. P. 1982. "Legislative Choice of Regulatory Forms: Legal Process or Administrative Process?" *Public Choice*, 39, 1, pp 33–66.

Fisher, F. M. 1989. "Games Economists Play: A Non-Cooperative View," *RAND J. Econ.*, 20, 1, pp 113–124.

Fisman, R. J. and Gatti, R. 2002. "Decentralization and Corruption: Evidence Across Countries," *J. Public Econ.*, 83, pp 325–345.

Foss, K. and Foss, N. J. 2001. "Assets, Attributes and Ownership," *Int. J. Econ. Bus.*, 8, pp 19–37.

Foss, N. J. 1993. "Theories of the Firm: Contractual and Competence Perspectives," *J. Evolutionary Econ.*, 3, 2, pp 127–144.

2000. *The Theory of the Firm*. London: Routledge.

2002. "The Rhetorical Dimensions of Bounded Rationality: Herbert A. Simon and Organizational Economics," in Rizzelo S., ed., *Cognitive Paradigms in Economics*. London: Routledge, pp 158–176.

2003. "Herbert Simon's Grand Theme in the Economics of Organization: Much Cited and Little Used," *J. Econ. Psych.*, 24, pp 245–264.

2005. *Strategy and Economic Organization in the Knowledge Economy.* Oxford: Oxford University Press.

Foss, N. J. and Klein, P. 2005. "Entrepreneuship and the Theory of the Firm: Any Gains From Trade?" in Agarwal, R., Alvarez, S. A., and Sorenson, O., eds, *Handbook of Entrepreneurship: Disciplinary Perspectives.* New York, NY: Kluwer.

Frank, R. H. 1987. "If Homo Economicus Could Choose His Own Utility Function, Would He Want One with a Conscience?" *Amer. Econ. R.*, 79, 3, pp 594–596.

Frank, S. D. and Henderson, D. R. 1992. "Transaction Costs as Determinants of Vertical Coordination in the US Food Industries," *Amer. J. Agr. Econ.*, 74, 4, pp 941–950.

Freeland, R. F. 2002. "The Firm as a Minisociety," draft manuscript.

Frey, B. S. 1997. *Not Just for the Money: An Economic Theory of Personal Motivation.* Aldershot: Edward Elgar.

Frey, B. S. and Oberholzer-Gee, F. 1997. "The Cost of Price Incentives: An Empirical Analysis of Motivation Crowding-Out," *Amer. Econ. Rev.*, 87, 4, pp 746–755.

Frey, B. S. and Stutzer, A. 2006. "Direct Democracy: Designing a Living Constitution," in Congleton, R., ed., *Democratic Constitutional Design and Public Policy – Analysis and Evidence*, Cambridge, MA: MIT Press.

Friedman, D. 1998. "Law and Economics," in *The New Palgrave. A Dictionary in Economics.* London: Macmillan, pp 144–147.

Friedman, J. W. 1971. "A Non-Cooperative Equilibrium for Supergames," *Rev. Econ. Stud.*, 28, pp 1–12.

Friedman, M. 1997. "Modern Macroeconomics and its Evolution from a Monetarist Perspective," *Rev. Econ. Stud*, 24, 4, pp 192–222.

Fuller, L. 1969. *The Morality of Law.* New Haven, CT and London: Yale University Press.

Furquim de Azevedo, P. and Dos Santos Silva, V. L. 2001. "Contractual Mix Analysis in the Brazilian Franchising," Work paper, University of Sao Paulo.

Furubotn, E. 2002. "Entrepreneurship, Transaction-Cost Economics, and the Design of Contracts," in Brousseau, E. and Glachant, J.-M., eds, *The Economics of Contracts.* Cambridge University Press, pp 72–97.

Furubotn, E. and Richter, R. 1997. *Institutions and Economic Theory: An Introduction to and Assessment of the New Institutional Economics.* Ann Arbor, MI: University of Michigan Press.

2000. *Institutions and Economics Theory: The Contributions of the New Institutional Economics.* Ann Arbor, MI: University of Michigan Press.

Gagne, M. and Deci, E. L. 2005. "Self-Determination Theory and Work Motivation," *J. Organ. Behavior*, 26, pp 331–362.

Gallini, N. T. and Lutz, N. A. 1992. "Dual Distribution and Royalty Fees in Franchising," *J Law, Econ. Organ.* 8, 3, pp 471–501.

Gallo, A. 2003. *The Political Economy of Argentine Development.* PhD dissertation, University of Illinois at Urbana-Champaign.

Gambetta, D. 1988. *Trust, Making and Breaking Cooperative Relations.* Oxford: Basil Blackwell.

Gandal, N., Salant, D., and Waverman, L. 2003. "Standards in Wireless Telephone Networks," *Telecommunications Pol.* 27, pp 325–332.

Garcia-Canal, E. 1996. "Contractual Form in Domestic and International Strategic Alliances," *Organization Studies*, 17, 5, pp 773–794.

Garicano, L. 2000. "Hierarchies and the Organization of Knowledge in Production," *J. Polit. Economy*, 108, 5, pp 874–904.

Garrouste, P. 2004. "The New Property Rights Theory of the Firm," in Colombatto, E., ed., *The Edward Elgar Companion to the Economics of Property Rights*, E. Cheltenham: Edward Elgar, pp 370–382.

Garrouste, P. and Saussier, S. 2005. "Looking for a Theory of the Firm," *J. Econ. Behav. Organ.*, 58, 2, pp 178–199.

Geddes, R. R. 1997. "Ownership, Regulation, and Managerial Monitoring in the Electric Utility Industry," *J. Law Econ.*, 40, 1, pp 261–288.

Gely, R. and Spiller, P. T. 1990. "A Rational Choice Theory of Supreme Court Statutory Decisions with Applications to the State Farm and Grove City Cases," *J. Law, Econ., Organ.*, 6, 2, pp 263–300.

1992a. "The Political Economy of Supreme Court Constitutional Decisions: The Case of Roosevelt's Court-Packing Plan," *Int. Rev. Law Econ.*, 12, 1, pp 45–67.

Georgescu-Roegen, N. 1971. *The Entropy Law and Economic Process*. Cambridge, MA: Harvard University Press.

Geringer, M. J. and Hebert, L. 1989. "The Importance of Control in International Joint Ventures," *J. Int. Bus. Stud.*, 20, pp 235–254.

1991. "Measuring Performance of International Joint Ventures," *J. Int. Bus. Stud.*, 22, 2, pp 249–264.

Gersbach, H. 2004. "Fiscal Constitutions," *Constit. Polit. Economy*, 15, 1, pp 3–25.

Ghosh, M. and John, G. 1999. "Governance Value Analysis and Marketing Strategy," *J. Marketing*, 63, pp 131–145.

Ghoshal, S. and Moran, P. 1996. "Bad for Practice: A Critique of the Transaction Cost Theory," *Acad. Man. Rev.*, 21, 1, pp 13–47.

Gibbons, R. S. 1992. *Game Theory for Applied Economists*. Princeton University Press.

2000. "Why Organizations Are Such a Mess (and What an Economist Might Do About It)?" MIT Sloan work paper. (Available at: http://web.mit.edu/rgibbons/www/Org_mess.pdf).

2001. "Trust in Social Structures: Hobbes and Coase Meet Repeated Games," in Cook, K., ed., *Trust in Society*. New York, NY: Russell Sage Foundation, pp 332–353.

2005. "Four Formalizeable Theories of the Firm," *J. Econ. Behav. Organ.*, 58, 2, pp 200–245.

Gigerenzer, G. 2000. *Adaptive Thinking: Rationality in the Real World*. New York, NY: Oxford University Press.

Gigerenzer, G. and Todd, P. 1999. "Fast and Frugal Heuristics: The Adaptive Toolbox," in Gigerenzer G., Todd, P. M., and the ABC Research Group, eds, *Simple Heuristics That Make Us Smart*. G. New York, NY: Oxford University Press, pp 3–34.

Ginsburg, T. 2002. "Economic Analysis and the Design of Constitutional Courts," *Theoretical Inquiries in Law*, 3, 1, pp 49–85.

Glachant, J.-M. 1998. "England Wholesale Electricity Market," *Utilities Policy*, 7, pp 63–74.

2002. "Why Regulate Deregulated Network Industries?" *J. Network Industries*, 3, pp 297–311.

Glachant, J.-M. and Finon, D. 2000. "Why do the European Union's electricity industries continue to differ? A new institutional analysis," in Claude Ménard, eds., *Institutions, Contracts and Organizations*. Edward Elgar, pp. 313–34.

2003. *Competition in European Electricity Markets: A Cross Country Comparison*. Cheltenham: Edward Elgar.

2006. "France Electricity Reform: A Competitive Fringe in the Shadow of a State Owned Incumbent," in *Energy Journal*, 26.

Glachant, J.-M. and Lévêque, F. 2007. *European Union Electricity Internal Market: Towards an Achievement?* Cheltenham: Edward Elgar.

Glachant, J.-M., Dubois, U., Perez, Y. 2007. "Deregulating with No Regulator: Is the German Electricity Transmission Regime Institutionally Correct? *Energy Policy*, 36, pp 1600–1610.

Glaeser, E. L. and Shleifer, A. 2003. "The Rise of the Regulatory State," *J. Econ. Lit.*, 41, 2, pp 401–425.

Glaeser, E. L., La Porta, R., Lopez-de-Silanes, F., and Shleifer, A. 2004. "Do Institutions Cause Growth?" *J. Econ. Growth*, 9, 3, pp 271–303.

Gneezy, U. and Rustichini, A. 2000. "Pay Enough or Don't Pay at All," *Quart. J. Econ.*, 115, 3, pp 791–810.

Goldberg, V. P. 1976. "Regulation and Administered Contracts" *Bell J. Econ.*, 7, 2, pp 426–452.

Gomes-Casseres, B. 1989. "Ownership Structures of Foreign Subsidiaries: Theory and Evidence," *J. Econ. Behav. Organ.*, 11, 1, pp 1–25.

1994. "Group vs. Group: How Alliance Networks Compete," *Harvard Bus. Rev.*, 72, 4, pp 62–74.

1996. *The Alliance Revolution*. Boston, MA: Harvard University Press.

Gomez-Ibanez, J. 2003. *Regulating Infrastructure: Monopoly, Contracts and Discretion*. Boston, MA: Harvard University Press.

Gompers, P. A. and Lerner, J. 1996. "The Use of Covenants: An Empirical Analysis of Venture Partnership Agreements," *J. Law Econ.*, 39, 2, pp 405–434.

González-Díaz, M., Arruñada, B., and Fernández, A. 1998. "Regulation as Cause of Firm Fragmentation: The Case of Spanish Construction Industry," *Int. Rev. Law Econ.*, 18, 4, pp 433–450.

Gordon, Scott H. 1954. "The Economic Theory of A Common-property Resource: The Fishery," *J. Polit. Economy*, 62, 2, pp 124–42.

Goshal, S. and Moran, P. 1996. "Bad Practice: A Critique of Transaction Cost Theory," *Academy of Management Review*, 21, 1, pp 13–47.

Grafton, Q. R., Squires, D., and Fox, K. J. 2000. "Private Property and Economic Efficiency: A Study of a Common-Pool Resource," *J. Law Econ.*, 43, pp 679–713.

Granovetter, M. 1985. "Economic Action and Social Structure: The Problem of Embeddedness," *Amer. J. Sociology*, 91, 3, pp 481–510.

Greene, W. 2003. *Econometric Analysis*. Upper Saddle River, NJ: Prentice Hall.

Green, R., Lorenzoni, A., Perez, Y. and Pollitt, M. 2006. "Benchmarking in the European Union," work paper, University of Cambridge.

Greif, A. 1989. "Reputation and Coalitions in Medieval Trade: Evidence on the Maghribi Traders," *J. Econ. Hist.*, 49, 4, pp 857–882.

1992. "Institutions and International Trade: Lessons from the Commercial Revolution," *Amer. Econ. Rev.*, 82, 2, pp 128–33.

1993. "Contract Enforceability and Economic Institutions in Early Trade: The Magrhibi Traders Coalition," *Amer. Econ. Rev.*, 83, 3, pp 525–548.

1994. "Cultural Beliefs and the Organization of Society: A Historical and Theoretical Reflection on Collectivist and Individualist Societies," *J. Pol. Econ.*, 102, 5, pp 912–950.

1997. "Microtheory and Recent Developments in the Study of Economic Institutions Through Economic History," in Kreps, D. and Wallis, K., eds, *Advances in Economic Theory.* Cambridge University Press, pp 79–113.

1998. "Historical and Comparative Institutional Analysis," *Amer. Econ. Rev.*, 88, 2, pp 80–89.

2000. "Economic History and Game Theory: A Survey," in Aumann, R. and Hart, S., eds, *Handbook of Game Theory.* Amsterdam: North Holland.

2004. *Institutions: Theory and History.* Cambridge University Press.

2005. "Commitment, Coercion and Markets: The Nature and Dynamics of Institutions Supporting Exchange," in Ménard, C. and Shirley, M. M., eds, *Handbook of New Institutional Economics*, New York, NY: Kluwer Academic Press, pp 727–786.

2006. *Institutions and the Path to the Modern Economy: Lessons from Medieval Trade.* Cambridge University Press.

Greif, A., Milgrom, P., and Weingast, B. R. 1994. "Coordination, Commitment and Enforcement: The Case of the Merchant Guild," *J. Polit. Economy*, 102, 4, pp 745–776.

Griffin, R. C. and Boadu, F. O. 1992. "Water Marketing in Texas: Opportunities for Reform," *Natural Res. J.*, 32, pp 265–288.

Grimes, G., Plain, R., and Meyer, S. 2004. "US Hog Marketing Contract Study," University of Missouri, Work paper AEWP 2004–07.

Grosfeld, I. and Nivet, J.-F. 1999. "Insider Power and Wage Setting in Transition: Evidence from a Panel of Large Polish Firms," *Europ. Econ. Rev.*, 43, 4, pp 1137–1147.

Grossman, S. J. and Hart, O. D. 1986. "The Costs and Benefits of Ownership: A Theory of Vertical and Lateral Integration," *J. Polit. Economy*, 94, 4, pp 691–719.

Guash, J. L. 2004. *Granting and Renegotiating Infrastructure Concessions: Doing It Right.* Washington, DC: World Bank Institute.

Guash, J. L. and Spiller, P. 1999. *Managing the Regulatory Process: Design, Concepts, Issues, and the Latin America and Caribbean Story*, Washington, DC: International Bank for Reconstruction and Development, Chapter 6.

Gulati, R. 1995a. "Does Familiarity Breed Trust? The Implications of Repeated Ties for Contractual Choice in Alliances," *Academy of Manage. J.*, 38, 1, pp 85–112.

1995b. "Social Structure and Alliance Formation Patterns: A Longitudinal Analysis," *Administrative Science Quarterly*, 40, 4, pp 619–650.

1999. "Network Location and Learning: The Influence of Network Resources and Firm Capabilities on Alliance Formation," *Strategic Manage. J.*, 20, 5, pp 397–420.

Gulati, R. and Nickerson, J. 2005. *Interorganizational-Trust: The Choice of Make, Buy, or Ally; and the Performance of Interorganizational Relationships in the U.S. Auto Industry.* Manuscript, Olin School of Business.

Gulati, R. and Nickerson J. A., forthcoming. "Inter–organizational Trust: the Choice of Make, Buy, or Ally; and the Performance of Interorganizational Relationships in the US. Auto Industry", *Organization Science*.

Gulati, R., Lawrence, P. R., and Puranam, P. 2005. "Adaptation in Vertical Relationships: Beyond Incentive Conflict," *Strategic Manage. J.*, 26, 5, pp 415–40.

Güth, W., Schmittberger, R., Bernd Schwarz, B. 1982. "An Experimental Analysis of Ultimatum Bargaining," *J. Econ. Behav. Organ.*, 3, pp 367–388.

Haas, R., Glachant, J.-M., Perez, Y., Auer, H., and Keseric, N. 2007. "The Liberalisation of the Continental European Electricity Market," *Energy Stud. Rev.*, 14, 2, pp 1–29.

Hadfield, G. K. 1990. "Problematic Relations: Franchising and the Law of Incomplete Contracts," *Stanford Law Rev.*, 42, pp 927–992.

2000. "Privatizing Commercial Law: Lessons from the Middle and the Digital Ages," Work paper 195, John M. Olin program in Law and Economics, Standford Law School.

2005. "The Many Legal Institutions that Support Contractual Commitments," in Ménard, C. and Shirley, M. M., eds, *Handbook of New Institutional Economics*. New York, NY: Kluwer Academic Publishers, pp 175–204.

Haggard, S. 2000. "Interest, Institutions and Policy Reform," in Krueger, A. O., ed., *Economic Policy Reform: The Second Stage*. Chicago University Press, pp 21–61.

Håkansson, H. and Snehota, I. 1990. "No Business is an Island: The Network Concept of Business Strategy," *Scand. J. Man.*, 5, pp 187–200.

Hamel, G. 1991. "Competition for Competence and Inter-Partner Learning within International Strategic Alliances," *Strategic Manage. J.*, 12, pp 82–103.

Hamilton, B. H. and Nickerson, J. A. 2003. "Correcting for Endogeneity in Strategic Management Research," *Strategic Organ*, 1, 1, pp. 53–80.

Hamilton, B. H., Nickerson, J. A., and Owan, H. (2003) "Team Incentives and Worker Heterogeneity: An Empirical Analysis of the Impact of Teams on Productivity and Participation," *Journal of Political Economy*, 111, 3, pp 465–497.

Hamilton, W. D. 1963. "The Evolution of Altruistic Behavior," *Amer. Naturalist*, 97, pp 354–356.

1964. "The Genetical Evolution of Social Behaviour I and II," *J. Theoretical Biology*, 7, pp 1–52.

Hannan, M. T. and Freeman, J. 1984. "Structural Inertia and Organizational Change," *Amer. Sociological Rev.*, 49, pp 149–164.

1989. *Organizational Ecology*. Cambridge, MA: Harvard University Press.

Hansmann, H. and Kraakman, R. 2002. "Property, Contract, and Verification: The Numerus Clausus Problem and the Divisibility of Rights," Harvard Law School Public Law Research paper 37.

Hanssen, A. F. 2004. "Is There a Politically Optimal Level of Judicial Independence?" *Amer. Econ. Rev.*, 94, 3, pp 712–729.

Hardin, R. 1989. "Why a Constitution?" in Grofman, B. and Wittman, D., eds, *The Federalist Papers and the New Institutionalism*. New York, NY: Agathon Press, pp 100–120.

Harrigan, K. R. 1985. "Vertical Integration and Corporate Strategy," *Acad. Manage. J.*, 28, 2, pp 397–425.

Hart, O. D. 1988. "Incomplete Contracts and the Theory of the Firm," *J. Law, Econ., Organ.*, 4, pp 119–141. Reprinted in Williamson O. E. and Winter S. G., eds, 1991, *The Nature of the Firm*. Oxford University Press, pp 138–159.

———. 1990. "Is 'Bounded Rationality' an Important Element of a Theory of Institutions?" *J. Inst. Theoretical Econ.*, 146, pp 696–702.

———. 1995. *Firms, Contracts and Financial Structure*. Oxford University Press.

Hart, O. D. and Holmström, B. 1987. "The Theory of the Contracts," in Bewley, T., ed., *Advances in Economic Theory, Fifth World Congress*. Cambridge University Press, pp 71–85.

———. 2002. "A Theory of Firm Scope," Mimeo. (Available at: http://econ-www.mit. edu/faculty/download_pdf.php?id=514).

Hart, O. D. and Moore, J. 1988. "Incomplete Contracts and Renegotiation," *Econometrica*, 56, 4, pp 755–785.

———. 1990. "Property Rights and the Nature of the Firm," *J. Polit. Economy*, 98, pp 1119–1158.

———. 1999. "Foundations of Incomplete Contracts," *Rev. Econ. Stud.*, 66, 1, pp 115–138.

———. 2004. "Agreeing Now to Agree Later: Contracts that Rule Out but do not Rule In," Harvard Law and Economics Discussion Paper, 465.

———. 2005. "On the Design of Hierarchies: Coordination Versus Specialization with John Moore," *J Political Econ.*, 113, 4, pp 675–702.

Harvey, J. S. Jr. 2005. "Why Did You Do That? An Economic Examination of the Effect of Extrinsic Compensation on Intrinsic Motivation and Performance," *J. Econ. Psych.*, 26, 4, 549–566.

Hatzis, A. 2000. "The Anti-Theoretic Nature of Civil Law Contract Scholarship and the Need for an Economic Theory," Mimeo, Chicago Law School, and University of Thessalonica.

———. 2006. "Civil Contract Law and Economic Reasoning: An Unlikely Pair?" in Grundmann, S. and Schauer, M., eds, *The Architecture of European Codes and Contract Law*. Kluwer Law International, Private Law in European Context Series, 8, pp 159–191.

Hayami, Y. 1998. "Introduction," in *Toward the Rural-Based Development of Commerce and Industry: Selected Experiences from East Asia*, Washington, DC: World Bank.

Hayami, Y. and Kikuchi, M. 1981. *Asian Village Economy at the Crossroads: An Economic Approach to Institutional Change*. Tokyo University Press, Baltimore, MD, and London: Johns Hopkins University Press.

———. 2000. *A Rice Village Saga – Three Decades of Green Revolution in the Philippines, Lanham*. Boulder, CO, and New York, NY: Barnes & Noble.

Hayek, F. A. 1944. *The Road to Serfdom*. Chicago University Press.
1945. "The Use of Knowledge in Society," *Amer. Econ. Rev.*, 35, pp 519–530.
1948. *Individualism and Economic Order*. Chicago University Press.
1973. *Law, Legislation and Liberty, Vol. 1: Rules and Order*. Chicago University Press.

Hayo, B. and Voigt, S. 2007. "Explaining De Facto Judicial Independence," *Int. Rev. Law Econ.*, 27, 3, 269–290.

Heiman, B. A. and Nickerson, J. A. 2002. "Towards Reconciling Transaction Cost Economics and the Knowledge-based View of the Firm: The Context of Interfirm Collaborations," *Int. J. Econ. Bus.*, 9, pp 97–116.
2004. "Empirical Evidence Regarding the Tension between Knowledge Sharing and Knowledge Expropriation in Collaborations," *Managerial Dec. Econ.*, 25, pp 401–420.

Helland, E. and Sykuta, M. 2004. "Regulation and the Evolution of Corporate Boards: Monitoring, Advising, or Window Dressing?" *J. Law Econ.*, 47, 1, pp 167–194.

Heller, M. A. 1998. "The Tragedy of the Anticommons: Property in the Transition from Marx to Markets," *Harvard Law Rev.*, 111, 3, pp 621–688.

Hellman, J. S., Jones, G., and Kaufmann, D. 2003. "Seize the State, Seize the Day: State Capture and Influence in Transition Economies," *J. Comp. Econ.*, 31, 4, pp 751–773.

Helm, D. 2004. *Energy, the State and the Market: British Energy Policy Since 1979*. Oxford University Press.

Hendrikse, G. W. J. and Bijman, J. 2002. "Ownership Structure in Agrifood Chains: The Marketing Cooperative," *Amer. J. Agr. Econ.*, 84, pp 104–119.

Hendrikse, G. W. J. and Veerman, C. P. 2001a. "Marketing Cooperatives and Financial Structure: A Transaction Cost Economics Analysis," *J. Agr. Econ.*, 26, pp 205–216.
2001b. "Marketing Cooperatives: An Incomplete Contracting Perspective," *J. Agr. Econ.*, 52, pp. 53–64.

Henisz, W. J. 2000a. "The Institutional Environment for Economic Growth," *Econ. Politics*, 12, 1, pp 1–31.
2000b. "The Institutional Environment for Multinational Investment," *J. Law, Econ., Organ.*, 16, 2, pp 334–364.

Henisz, W. J. and Williamson, O. E. 1999. "Comparative Economic Organization – Within and Between Countries," *Bus. Polit*, 1, 3, pp 261–276.

Hennart, J.-F. 1991. "The Transaction Cost Theory of Joint Ventures: An Empirical Study of Japanese Subsidiaries in the US," *Manage. Sci.*, pp 483–497.
1993. "Explaining the Swollen Middle: Why Most Transactions Are a Mix of Market and Hierarchy," *Organization Sci.*, 4, 4, pp 529–547.

Henrich, J., Boyd, R., Bowles, S., Camerer, C., Fehr, E., Gintis, H., and McElreath, R. 2001. "Cooperation, Reciprocity and Punishment in Fifteen Small-Scale Societies," *Amer. Econ. Rev.*, 91, pp 73–78.

Henrich, J., Boyd, R., Bowles, S., Camerer, C., Fehr, E., Gintis, H., *et al.* 2005. "'Economic Man' in Cross-Cultural Perspective: Behavioral Experiments in fifteen Small-Scale Societies," *Behavioral and Brain Science*, 28, pp 795–815.

Herbert, S. A. 1962. "The Architecture of Complexity," *Proceedings of the American Philosophical Society*, 106, pp 467–482.

Hill, C. A. 2001. "Why Contracts are Written in Legalese," *Chicago Kent Law Rev.*, 77, 1, pp 59–85.

Hillman, A. J. and Hitt, M. A. 1999. "Corporate Political Strategy Formulation: A Model of Approach, Participation, and Strategy Decisions," *Academy Manage. Rev.*, 24, 4, pp 825–842.

Hiroux, C. 2004. "Shallow Cost and Deep Cost, An Assessment," Work paper GRJM, Université Paris-Sud 11.

Hirschmann, A. 1970. *Exit, Voice and Loyalty: Responses to Decline in Firms, Organizations and States*. Cambridge, MA: Harvard University Press.

Ho, T.-H. and Weigelt, K. 1996. "Task Complexity, Equilibrium Selection, and Learning: An Experimental Study," *Manage. Sci.*, 42, pp 659–679.

Hodgson, G. M. 1989. *Economics and Institutions: A Manifesto for a Modern Institutional Economics*. Oxford: Polity Press.

1998. "Competence and Contract in the Theory of the Firm," *J. Econ. Behav. Organ.*, 35, pp 179–201.

2004a. *The Evolution of Institutional Economics: Agency, Structure and Darwinism in American Institutionalism*. London and New York, NY: Routledge.

2004b. "Veblen and Darwinism," *International R. Sociology*, 14, pp 343–361.

Hoetker, G. 2005. "How Much You Know versus How Will I Know You: Supplier Selection for Innovative Components," *Strategic Manage. J.*, 26, 1, pp 75–96.

Hohfeld, W. N. 1919. *Fundamental Legal Conceptions*. New Haven, CT and London: Yale University Press.

Hojnacky, M. and Kimball, D. C. 1998. "Organized Interests and the Decision of Whom to Lobby in Congress," *Amer. Polit. Sci. Rev.*, 92, 4, pp 775–790.

Holburn, G. and Spiller, P. 2002. "Institutional or Structural: Lessons from International Electricity Sector Reforms," in Brousseau, E. and Glachant, J.-M., eds, *The Economics of Contracts: Theories and Applications*. Cambridge University Press, pp 463–502.

Holburn, G., and van den Burgh, R. 2004. "Influencing Agencies through Pivotal Political Institutions," *Journal of Law, Economics and Organization*, 20, 2, pp 458–483.

Holmström, B. 1999. "The Firm as a Subeconomy," *J. Law, Econ. Organ.*, 1, pp 74–102.

Holmström, B. and Milgrom, P. 1991. "Multitask Principal–Agent Analysis: Incentive Contracts, Asset Ownership and Job Design," *J. Law, Econ., Organ.*, 7, pp 24–54.

1994. "The Firm as an Incentive System," *Amer. Econ. Rev.*, 84, pp 972–991.

Holmstrom, B. and Roberts, J. 1998. "The Boundaries of the Firm Revisited," *J. Econ. Perspect.*, 12, pp 73–94.

Hotelling, H. 1938. "The General Welfare in Relation to Problems of Taxation and of Railway and Utility Rates," *Econometrica*, 6, 3, pp 242–269.

Houser, D. and Wooders, J. 2005. "Reputation in Auctions: Theory and Evidence from eBay," *J. Econ. Manage. Strategy*, 15, 2, pp 353–369.

Hovenkamp, H. 1994. *Federal Antitrust Policy: The Law of Competition and its Practice*. St. Paul, MN: West Publishing Co.

Howe, C. W., Boggs, C. S., and Butler, P. 1990. "Transaction Costs as Determinants of Water Transfers," *University of Colorado Law R.*, 61, pp 393–405.

Hubbard, G. R. and Weiner, R. J. 1991. "Efficient Contracting and Market Power: Evidence from the U.S. Natural Gas Industry," *J. Law Econ.*, 34, 1, pp 25–68.

Hubbard, T. N. 2001. "Contractual Form and Market Thickness in Trucking," *RAND J. Econ.*, 32, 2, pp 369–386.

Huet, F. 2006. "Partenariats Publics–Privés et Concurrence pour le Marché: Quelles Avancées depuis Demsetz (1968)?" Work paper ATOM, Université Paris 1.

Huntington, S. 1996. *The Clash of Civilizations and the Remaking of World Order.* New York, NY: Simon & Schuster.

Hurwicz, L. 1972. "On Informationally Decentralized Systems," in McGuire, C. B. and Radner, R., eds, *Decision and Organization.* Amsterdam: North-Holland, pp 297–336.

Iaryczower, M., Spiller, P. T., and Tommasi, M. 2002. "Judicial Independence in an Unstable Environment, Argentina 1935–1998," *Amer. J. Politic. Sci.*, 46, 4, pp 699–716.

2006. "Judicial Lobbying: The Politics of Labor Law Constitutional Interpretation," *Amer. J. Politic. Sci.*, 100, 1, pp 85–97.

IEA (International Energy Agency). 2001. *Regulatory Institutions in Liberalised Electricity Markets.* AIE OCDE.

Inman, R. P. and Rubinfeld, D. L. 1997. "Rethinking Federalism," *J. Econ. Perspect.*, 11, 4, pp 43–64.

Iverson, T. and Soskice, D. 2006. "Electoral Institutions and the Politics of Coalitions: Why Some Democracies Redistribute more Than Others," *American Political Science Review*, 100, pp 165–181.

Jacquemin, A. and Slade, M. 1989 "Cartels, Collusion, and Horizontal Merger," in Schmalensee, R. and Willigm R. D., eds, *Handbook of Industrial Organization.* Amsterdam: North-Holland, pp 415–473.

James, H. S. Jr. and Sykuta, M. E. 2004. "Generalized and Particularized Trust in Organizations," University of Missouri, work paper, presented at the 2004 ISNIE meetings in Tucson, AZ. (Available at: http://cori.missouri. edu/jamesh/).

2005. "Organizational Antecedents of Trust in Producer-Owned Firms," *Ann. Public Coop. Econ.*, 76, 4.

2006. "Farmer Trust in Producer- and Investor-Owned Firms: Evidence from Missouri Corn and Soybean Producers," *Agribusiness: An International Journal*, 22, 1, pp 135–153.

Johnson, R. N. and Libecap, G. D. 1982. "Contracting Problems and Regulation: The Case of the Fishery," *Amer. Econ. Rev.*, 72, 5, pp 1005–1022.

1994. *The Federal Civil Service System and the Problem of Bureaucracy: The Economics and Politics of Institutional Change.* Chicago University Press.

2001. "Information Distortion and Competitive Remedies in Government Transfer Programs: The Case of Ethanol," *Econ. Governance*, 2, 2, pp 1001–1034.

Johnson, S., McMillan, J., and Woodruff, C. 2000. "Entrepreneurs and the Ordering of Institutional Reform," *Econ. Transition*, 8, 1, pp 1–36.

2002a. "Courts and Relational Contract," *J. Law, Econ., Organ.*, 18, 1, pp 221–277.

2002b. "Property Rights and Finance," *Amer. Econ. Rev.*, 92, 5, pp 1335–1356.

Jolls, C., Sunstein, C. R., and Thaler, R. 1998. "A Behavioral Approach to Law and Economics," *Stanford Law Rev.*, 50, pp 683–668.

Jones, C., Hesterly, W. S. and Borgatti, S. P. 1997. "A General Theory of Network Governance: Exchange Conditions and Social Mechanisms," *Academy of Management Review*, 22, 4, pp 911–945.

Jones, D. C. and Mygind, N. 2000. "The Effects of Privatization upon Productive Efficiency: Evidence from the Baltic Republics," *Ann. Public Coop. Econ.*, 71, 3, pp 415–439.

Jones, M. P., Saiegh, S., Spiller, P. T., and Tommasi, M. 2002. "Amateur Legislators – Professional Politicians: The Consequences of Party-Centered Electoral Rules in a Federal System," *Amer. J. Politic. Sci.*, 46, 3, pp 656–669.

Joskow, P. L. 1985. "Vertical Integration and Long Term Contracts: The Case of Coal Burning Electric Generating Plants," *J. Law, Econ. Organ.*, 1, 1, pp 33–80.

1987. "Contract Duration and Relationship-Specific Investment: Empirical Evidence from Coal Markets," *Amer. Econ. Rev.*, 77, 1, pp 168–185.

1988. "Asset Specificity and the Structure of Vertical Relationships: Empirical Evidence," *J. Law, Econ., Organ.*, 4, 95–117.

1991. "The Role of Transaction Cost Economics in Antitrust and Public Utility Regulation," *J. Law Econ. Organ.*, 7, pp 53–83.

1996. "Introducing Competition into Regulated Network Industries: From Hierarchies to Markets in Electricity," *Ind. Corp. Change*, 5, 2, pp 341–383.

2002. "Transaction Costs Economics, Antitrust Rules and Remedies," *J. Law, Econ. Organ.*, 18, 1, pp 95–16.

2003. "New Institutional Economics: A Report Card," *ISNIE Presidential Address*: Budapest, Hungary.

2004. "Vertical Integration," in Ménard, C. and Shirley, M. M., eds, *Handbook of New Institutional Economics*. Norwell, MA: Kluwer Academic Publishers, pp 319–348.

Joskow, P. L. and Schmalensee, R. 1983. *Markets for Power*, Cambridge, MA: MIT Press.

Joskow, P. L. and Tirole, J. 2000. "Transmission Rights and Market Power on Electric Power Network I: Financial Rights," *RAND J. Econ.*, 31, 3, pp 450–487.

Kagel, J. and Roth, A. 1995. *The Handbook of Experimental Economics*. Princeton University Press.

Kahn, A. 1970–1971. *The Economics of Regulation: Principles and Institutions*. Chichester: Wiley.

Kahneman, D. and Tversky, A. 1979. "Prospect Theory: An Analysis of Decisions Under Risk," *Econometrica*, 47, pp 263–291.

Kale, P., Singh, H., and Perlmutter, H. 2000. "Learning and Protection of Proprietary Assets in Strategic Alliances: Building Relational Capital," *Strategic. Manage. J.*, 21, pp 217–237.

Kale, P., Dyer, J. H., and Singh H. 2002. "Alliance Capability, Stock Market Response, and Long-Term Alliance Success: The Role of the Alliance Function," *Strategic. Manage. J.*, 23, pp 747–767.

Kalnins, A. and Lafontaine, F. 2004. "Multi-Unit Ownership in Franchising: Evidence from the Texan Fast-Food Industry," *RAND J. Econ.*, 35, 4, pp 747–761.

Kalnins, A. and Mayer J. K. 2004. "Relationships and Hybrid Contracts: An Analysis of Contract Choice in Information Technology," *J. Law Econ. Organ.*, 20, 1, pp 207–229.

Kaplan, H. and Hill, K. 1985. "Food Sharing among Ache Foragers: Test of Explanatory Hypotheses," *Current Anthropology*, 26, pp 223–239.

Kaufmann, P. J. and Lafontaine, F. 1994. "Costs of Control: The Source of Economic Rents for McDonald's Franchisees," *J Law Econ.*, 37, pp 417–454.

Keefer, P. and Knack, S. 1997. "Why Don't Poor Countries Catch Up? A Cross-National Test of an Institutional Environment," *Econ. Inquiry*, 35, pp 590–602.

Keeley, L. 1996. *War Before Civilization: The Myth of the Peaceful Savage.* New York, NY: Oxford University Press.

Kelsen, H. 1992. *Introduction to the Problems of Legal Theory.* A translation of the first edition of the *Reine Rechtlehere*. Oxford: Clarendon Press.

Kessides, L. 2004. "*Reforming Infrastructure: Privatization, Regulation, and Competition,*" World Bank Policy Research Report. Washington, DC: World Bank and Oxford: Oxford University Press.

Khanna, T., Gulati, R., and Nitin N. 1998. "The Dynamics of Learning Alliances: Competition, Cooperation and Relative Scope," *Strategic. Manage. J.*, 19, 3, pp 193–210.

Killing, P. 1983. *Strategies for Joint Venture Success.* London: Croom Helm.
   1988. "Understanding Alliances: The Role of Task and Organizational Complexity," in Contractor, F. and Lorange, P., eds, *Cooperative Strategies in International Business.* Lexington, MA: Lexington Books.

Kim, C. W. and Hwang, P. 1992. "Global Strategy and Multinationals' Entry Mode Choice," *J. Int. Bus. Stud.*, 23, 1, pp 29–53.

Kirchgässner, G. and Frey, B. 1990. "Volksabstimmung und direkte Demokratie: Ein Beitrag zur Verfassungsdiskussion," in Klingmann, H. D. and Kaase, M., eds, *Wahlen und Wähler – Analysen aus Anlaß der Bundestagswahl.* Westdeutscher Verlag: Opladen, pp 42–69.

Kirstein, R. and Voigt, S. 2006. "The Violent and the Weak: When Dictators Care About Social Contracts," *Amer. J. Econ. Sociology*, 65, 4, pp 863–889.

Kirzner, I. 1973. *Competition and Entrepreneurship.* Chicago University Press.

Kiwit, D. and Voigt, S. 1998. "The Role and Evolution of Beliefs, Habits, Moral Norms, and Institutions," in Giersch, H., ed., *Merits and Limits of Markets.* Berlin: Springer, pp 83–108.

Klein, B. 1980. "Transaction Cost Determinants of Unfair Contractual Arrangements," *Amer. Econ. Rev.*, 70, pp 356–362.
   1988. "Vertical Integration as Organizational Ownership: The Fisher Body–General Motors Relationship Revisited," *J. Law, Econ., Organ.*, 4, 1, pp 199–213.

1995. "The Economics of Franchise Contracts," *J. Corp. Finan.*, 2, 1/2, pp 9–37.

1996. "Why Hold-Ups Occur? The Self Enforcing Range of Contractual Relationships," *Econ. Inquiry*, 34, pp 444–463.

Klein, B. and Leffler, K. B. 1981. "The Role of Market Forces in Assuring Contractual Performance," *J. Polit. Economy*, 89, 41, pp 615–41.

and Murphy, K. 1997. "Vertical Integration as a Self-Enforcing Contractual Arrangement," *Amer. Econ. Rev.*, 87, 2, pp 415–420.

Klein, B. and Saft, L. F. 1985. "The Law and Economics of Franchise Tying Contracts," *J. Law Econ.*, 27, pp 345–361.

Klein, B., Crawford, R. G., and Alchian, A. A. 1978. "Vertical Integration, Appropriable Rents, and the Competitive Contracting Process," *J. Law Econ.*, 21, 2, pp 297–326.

Klein, P. G. 2005. "The Make-or-Buy Decision: Lessons from Empirical Studies," in Ménard, C. and Shirley, M. M., eds, *Handbook on New Institutional Economics*. New York, NY: Springer, pp 435–464.

Kleither, G. D., Krebs, M., Doherty, M. E., Garavan, H., Chadwick, R., and Brake, G. 1997. "Do Subjects Understand Base Rates," *Orga. Behav. Human Dec. Process.*, 72, pp 25–61.

Klemperer, P. 2002. "What Really Matters in Auction Design," *J. Econ. Perspect.*, 16, 1, pp 169–190.

Knack, S. and Keefer, P. 1997. "Does Social Capital Have an Economic Payoff? A Cross-Country Investigation," *Quart. J. Econ.*, 112, 4, pp 1251–1288.

Knight, F. 1921. *Risk, Uncertainty, and Profit.* 1964 reprint. New York, NY: Augustus M. Kelley.

Knight, Jack. 1992. *Institutions and Social Conflict.* Cambridge University Press.

Knoeber, C. R. 1989. "A Real Game of Chicken: Contracts, Tournaments, and the Production of Broilers," *J. Law Econ. Organ.*, 5, pp 271–292.

2000. "Land and Livestock Contracting in Agriculture: A Principal–Agent Perspective," in Bouckaert, B. and De Geest, G., eds, *Encyclopedia of Law and Economics*. Aldershot, Edward Elgar, pp 1133–1153.

Kogut, B. 1988. "Joint Ventures: Theoretical and Empirical Perspectives," *Strategic. Manage. J.*, 9, pp 319–332.

Kogut, B. and Zander, U. 1992. "Knowledge of the Firm, Combinative Capabilities, and the Replication of Technology," *Organ. Sci.*, 3, pp 383–397.

1996. "What Firms Do? Coordination, Identity, and Learning," *Organ. Sci.*, 7, pp 502–518.

Koh, J. and Venkatraman N. 1991. "Joint Venture Formations and Stock Market Reactions: An Assessment in the Information Technology Sector," *Academy Manag. J.*, 34, pp 869–892.

Korobkin, R. 2003. "Bounded Rationality and Unconscionability: A Behavioral Theory of Policing Form Contracts," law and economics research paper. University of California, School of Law.

Kosters, M. H. 1997. "New Employment Relationships and the Labor Market," *J. Lab. Res.*, 18, pp 551–559.

Kranton, R. E. 1996. "Reciprocal Exchange: A Self-Sustaining System," *Amer. Econ. Rev.*, 86, 4, pp 830–851.

Krehbiel, K. 1991. *Information and Legislative Organization*, Ann Arbour, MI: University of Michigan Press.

Kremer, M. 1993. "Population Growth and Technological Change: One Million BC to 1990," *Quart. J. Econ.*, 108, pp 681–716.

Kreps, D. M. 1990. "Corporate Culture and Economic Theory," in Alt, J. and Shepsle, K., eds, *Perspectives on Positive Political Economy*. New York, NY: Cambridge University Press.

1996. "Markets and Hierarchies and (Mathematical) Economic Theory," *Ind. Corp. Change*, 5, pp 561–595.

Kreps, D. M., Milgrom, P., Roberts, J., and Wilson, R. B. 1982. "Rational Cooperation in the Finitely Repeated Prisoner's Dilemma," *J. Econ. Theory*, 27, pp 245–252.

Kuran, Timur. 1995. *Private Truths, Public Lies – The Social Consequences of Preference Falsification*. Cambridge, MA & London: Harvard University Press.

Kurzban, R. and Houser, D. 2005. "Experiments Investigating Cooperative Types in Humans: A Complement to Evolutionary Theory and Simulations," *Proceedings of the National Acad. Sci.*, 102, pp 1803–1807.

La Porta, R., Lopez-de-Silanes, F., Schleifer, A., and Vishny, R. 1999. "The Quality of Government," *J. Law Econ. Organ.*, 15, 1, pp 222–282.

Laffont, J.-J. 2000. *Incentives and Political Economy*. Oxford University Press.

2005. *Regulation and Development*. Cambridge University Press.

Laffont, J.-J. and Maskin, E. 1982. "The Theory of Incentives: An Overview," in Hildenbrand, W. (with Laffont, J.-J.), eds, *Advances in Economic Theory* (invited lectures from the 4th World Congress of the Econometric Society.) Cambridge University Press, pp 31–94.

Laffont, J.-J. and Matoussi, M.-S. 1995. "Moral Hazard, Financial Constraints and Sharecropping in El Oulja," *Rev. Econ. Stud.*, 62, pp 381–399.

Laffont, J.-J. and Tirole, J. 1993. *A Theory of Incentives in Procurement and Regulation*. Cambridge, MA: MIT Press.

2000. *Competition in Telecommunications*. Cambridge, MA: MIT Press.

Lafontaine, F. 1992. "Agency Theory and Franchising: Some Empirical Results," *RAND J. Econ.*, 23, 2, pp 263–283.

1993. "Contractual Arrangement as Signaling Devices: Evidence from Franchising," *J. Law Econ. Organ.*, 9, pp 256–289.

Lafontaine, F. and Oxley, J. E. 2002. "International Franchising Practices in Mexico: Do Franchisors Customize Their Contracts," *J. Econ. Manage. Strategy*, 13, 1, pp 95–123.

Lafontaine, F. and Raynaud, E. 2002. "The Role of Residual Claims and Self-Enforcement in Franchise Contracting," in Brousseau, E. and Glachant, J.-M., eds, *The Economics of Contract in Prospect and Retrospect*. Cambridge University Press, pp 315–336.

Lafontaine, F. and Shaw, K. L. 2005. "Targeting Managerial Control: Evidence from Franchising," *RAND J. Econ.*, 36, 1, pp 131–150.

Lafontaine, F. and Slade, M. 2002. "Incentive Contracts and the Franchising Decision," in Chatterjee, K. and Samuelson, W., eds, *Game Theory and Business Applications*. New York, NY: Kluwer Academic Press, pp 133–188.

Lajili, K., Barry, P., Sonka, S., and Mahoney, J. T. 1997. "Farmers Preferences for Crop Contracts," *J. Agr. Resource Econ.*, 22, pp 264–280.

Lal, R. 1990. "Improving Channel Coordination through Franchising," *Manage. Sci.*, 9, pp 299–318.

Lamoreaux, N. R. and Rosenthal, J.-L. 2004. "Legal Regime and Business's Organizational Choice: A Comparison of France and the United States During the Mid-Nineteenth Century," NBER Work paper 10288, pp 1–47.

Landes, W. M. and Posner, R. A. 1975. "The Independent Judiciary in an Interest-Group Perspective," *J. Law Econ.*, 18, 3, pp 875–911.

Lane, P. J. and Lubatkin M. 1998. "Relative Absorptive Capacity and Inter-organizational Learning," *Strategic. Manage. J.*, 19, 5, pp 461–477.

Langlois, R. 1984. "Internal Organization in a Dynamic Context: Some Theoretical Considerations," in Jussawalla, M. and Ebenfield, H., eds, *Communication and Information Economics: New Perspectives*. Amsterdam, North-Holland, pp 23–49.

1992. "Transaction Cost Economics in Real Time," *Ind. Corp. Change*, 1, pp 99–127.

Langlois, R. and Robertson, P. 1995. *Firms, Markets, and Economic Change: A Dynamic Theory of Business Institutions*. London: Routledge.

Lanjouw, P. and Stern, N. 1998. *Economic Development in Palanpur Over Five Decades*. Oxford: Clarendon Press.

Lazear, E. P. 1991. "Labor Economics and the Psychology of Organizations," *J. Econ. Perspect.*, 5, pp 89–110.

Lazzarini, S. G., Chaddad, F. R., and Cook, M. L. 2001. "Integrating Supply Chain and Network Analyses: The Study of Netchains," *J. Chain Network Sci.*, 1, pp 7–22.

Lazzarini, S. G., Miller, G. J., and Zenger, T. 2004. "Order with Some Law: Complementarity vs. Substitution of Formal and Informal Arrangements." *J. Law Econ. Org.*, 20, 2, pp 261–298.

Leal, D. 2005. *Evolving Property Rights in Marine Fisheries*, Lanham, MD: Rowman & Littlefield.

Leiblein, M. J., Reuer, J. J., and Dalsace, F. 2002. "Do Make or Buy Decisions Matter? The Influence of Organizational Governance on Technological Performance," *Strategic Manage. J.*, 23, pp 817–833.

Lenfle, S. and Baldwin, C. Y. 2007. "From Manufacturing to Design: An Essay on the Work of Kim B. Clark," Work paper CRG, Paris.

Lerner, A. 1944. *The Economics of Control*. London: Macmillan.

Lévêque, François. 2006a. "La mise en uvre du droit de la concurrence dans les industries électriques et gazières – problèmes et solutions," *Concurrence*.

2006b. *Competitive Electricity Markets and Sustainability*. London: Edward Elgar Publishers.

Levy, B. and Spiller, P. T. 1994. *Regulations, Institutions, and Commitment: Comparative Studies of Telecommunications Regulations, Institutions, and Commitment*. Cambridge University Press.

1994. "The Institutional Foundations of Regulatory Commitment," *J. Law, Econ., Organ.*, 10, 2, pp 201–246.

Lewin-Solomons, S. 1999. "The Plural Form in Franchising: A Synergism of Market and Hierachy," Mimeo, Dept. of Applied Economics, University of Cambridge.

Libecap, G. D. 1989. *Contracting for Property Rights*, New York, NY: Cambridge University Press.

— 2002. "A transaction costs approach to the analysis of property rights," in Brousseau É. and Glachant J.-M. eds, The Economics of Contracts: *Theories and Applications*, Cambridge University Press, Chapter 9.

— 2006. *Chinatown: A Re-examination of the Owens Valley Water Transfer to Los Angeles and What It Means for Western Water Today*. Stanford University Press, in press.

— 2007. *Owens Valley Revisited: a Reassessment of the West's First Great Water Transfer*. Stanford: Stanford University Press.

Libecap, G. D. and Smith, J. L. 1999. "The Self-Enforcing Provisions of Oil and Gas Unit Operating Agreements: Theory and Evidence," *J. Law Econ., Organ.*,15, 2, pp 526–548.

— 2000. "The Economic Evolution of Petroleum Property Rights in the United States," *J. Legal Stud.*, 31, 2, pp 558–608.

Libecap, G. D. and Wiggins, S. N. 1985. "The Influence of Private Contractual Failure on Regulation: The Case of Oil Field Unitization," *J. Polit. Economy*, 93, 4, pp 690–714.

Liebowitz, S. J. and Margolis, S. E. 1995. "Path Dependence, Lock-in and History," *J. Law, Econ., Organ.*, 11, 1, pp 205–226.

Lien, L. B. and Klein, P. G. 2004. "Can the Survivor Principle Survive Diversification?" Norwegian School of Economics and Business Administration work paper. (Available at: http://euro.nhh.no/sol/tceworkshop/).

Lindenberg, S. M. 1992. "An Extended Theory of Institutions and Contractual Discipline," *J. Inst. Theoretical Econ.*, 148, 2, pp 125–154.

— 2003. "The Cognitive Side of Governance," *Research in the Sociology of Organizations*, 20, pp 47–76.

Lippman, S. A. and Rumelt, R. P. 1982. "Uncertain Imitability: An Analysis of Interfirm Differences in Efficiency under Competition," *Bell J. Econ.*, 13, pp 418–438.

Littlechild, S. 1983. *Regulation of British Telecom Profitability*. London: HMSO.

— 2006a. "Beyond Regulation," ESNIE lecture, Cargèse, May.

— 2006b. "Foreword," in Sioshani, F. P. and Pfaffenberger, W., eds, *Electricity Markets around the World*. Amsterdam: Elsevier.

Lizzeri, A. and Persico, N. 2001. "The Provision of Public Goods Under Alternative Electoral Incentives," *Amer. Econ. R.*, 91, 1, pp 225–239.

Llewellyn, K. N. 1931. "What Price Contract? An Essay in Perspective," *Yale Law J.*, 40, pp 701–751.

Loasby, B. 1999. *Knowledge, Institutions, and Evolution in Economics*. London: Routledge.

Londregan, J. and Snyder, J. M. Jr. 1994. "Comparing Committee and Floor Preferences," *Legislative Studies Quarterly*, 19, 2, pp 233–66.

Lorange, P. and Roos, J. 1992. *Strategic Alliances: Formation, Implementation and Evolution*. Cambridge, MA: Blackwell.

Lucking-Reiley, D., Bryan, D., Prasad, N., and Reeves, D. 2007. "Pennies from Ebay: The Determinants of Price in Online Auctions," *J. Ind. Econ.*, 55, 2, pp 223–233.

Lueck, D. 1998. "First Possession," in Newman, P., ed., *The New Palgrave Dictionary of Economics and the Law*. London: Macmillan, pp 132–144.

Luo, Y. and Park, S. H. 2004. "Multiparty Cooperation and Performance in International Equity Joint Ventures," *J. Int. Bus. Stud.*, 35, pp 142–160.

Lupia, A. and McCubbins, M. D. 1994. "Learning from Oversight: Fire Alarms and Police Patrols Reconstructed," *J. Law, Econ., Organ.*, 10, 1, pp 96–125.

Lutz, N. A. 1995. "Ownership Rights and Incentives in Franchising," *J. Corp. Finan.*, 2, pp 56–74.

Macaulay, S. 1963. "Non Contractual Relations in Business: A Preliminary Study," *Amer. Sociological Rev.*, 45, pp 151–175.

MacDonald, J., Perry, J., Ahearn, M., Banker, D., Chambers, W., Dimitri, C., et al. 2004. *Contracts, Markets, and Prices: Organizing the Production and Use of Agricultural Commodities*, Agricultural Economic Report No. 837, US Department of Agriculture, Economic Research Service.

MacDonnell, L. 1990. *The Water Transfer Process as a Management Option for Meeting Changing Water Demands*. Washington, DC: USGS.

Macher, J. 2006. "Technological Development and the Boundaries of the Firm: A Knowledge-Based Examination in Semiconductor Manufacturing," *Manage. Sci.*, 52, 6, pp 826–843.

Macintyre, A. 2001. "Institutions and Investors: The Politics of the Economic Crisis in Southeast Asia," *Int. Organ.*, 55, 1, pp 81–22.

2003. *The Power of Institutions, Political Architecture and Governance*. New York, NY: Cornell University Press.

Mackaay, E. 1999. "History of Law and Economics," in Bouckaert, B. and De Geest, G., eds, *Encyclopedia of Law and Economics*, pp 65–117. (Available at: http://allserve/rug.ac.be/-gdegeest).

MacLeod, B. W. 2002. "Complexity and Contract," in Brousseau, E. and Glachant, J.-M., eds, *The Economics of Contracts*. Cambridge University Press, pp 213–240.

MacNeil, I. R. 1974. "The Many Future of Contracts," *Southern California Law Review*, 47, pp 691–716.

1978. "Contracts: Adjustment of Long-Term Economic Relations under Classical, Neoclassical and Relational Contract Law," *Northwest. U. Law Rev.*, 72, pp 854–906.

Maddala, G. S. 1983. *Limited-Dependent and Qualitative Variables in Econometrics*. Cambridge University Press.

Maddison, A. 1995. *Monitoring the World Economy, 1820–1992*. Paris: OECD.

Madhok, A. 1996. "The Organization of Economic Activity: Transaction Costs, Firm Capabilities, and the Nature of Governance," *Organ. Sci*, 7, pp 577–590.

Maness, R. 1996. "Incomplete Contracts and the Choice between Vertical Integration and Franchising," *J. Econ. Behav. Organ.*, 31, pp 101–115.

March, J. and Simon, H. 1958. *Organizations*. New York, NY: Wiley.

Marin, D. and Schnitzer, M. 2002. *Contracts in Trade and Transition. The Resurgence of Barter*. Cambridge, MA: MIT Press.

2003. "Creating Creditworthiness through Reciprocal Trade," *Rev. Int. Econ.*, 11, 1, pp 159–174.

Marion, Bruce. 1976. "Vertical Coordination and Exchange Arrangements: Concepts and Hypotheses," in B. W. Marion eds, *Coordination and Exchange in Agricultural Subsectors*, North Central Regional Research Publication 228, 2, Madison, Wisconsin, USA, pp 179–95.

Markoczy, L. and Goldberg, J. 1998. "Management, Organization and Human Nature: An Introduction," *Managerial Dec. Econ.*, 19, pp 387–409.

Marschak, J. and Radner, R. 1972. *Economic Theory of Teams*. New Haven, CT: Cowles Foundation and Yale University Press.

Marshall, A. and Pigou, A. 1920. *Principles of Economics*, 8th edn. London: Macmillan.

Martinez, S. 1999. *Vertical Coordination in the Pork and Broiler Industries: Implications for Pork and Chicken Products*, Agricultural Economic Report No. 777, US Department of Agriculture, Economic Research Service.

2002. "A Comparison of Vertical Coordination in the US Poultry, Egg, and Pork Industries," *Current Issues in Economics of Food Markets, Agriculture Information Bulletin* 747, 05, US Department of Agriculture, Economic Research Service.

Martinez, S. and Reed, L. 1996. *From Farmers to Consumers: Vertical Coordination in the Food Industry*. Washington, D. C.: U.S. Department of Agriculture, Economic Research Service.

Maskin, E. 1985. "The Theory of Implementation in Nash Equilibrium: A Survey," in Hurwicz, L., Schmeidler, D., and Sonnenschein, H., eds, *Social Goals and Social Organization: Volume in Memory of Elisha Pazner*. Cambridge University Press, pp 173–204.

Maskin, E. and Tirole, J. 1999. "Unforeseen Contingencies and Incomplete Contracts," *Rev. Econ. Stud.*, 66, 1, pp 139–149.

Masten, S. E. 1984. "The Organization of Production: Evidence from the Aerospace Industry," *J. Law Econ.*, 23, 2, pp 403–417.

1993. "Transaction Costs, Mistakes, and Performance: Assessing the Importance of Governance," *Managerial Dec. Econ.*, 14, pp 119–129.

1996. *Case Studies in Contracting and Organization*. Oxford: Oxford University Press.

1999. "Contractual Choice," in Boukaert, B. and De Geest, G., eds, *Encyclopedia of Law and Economics*. Cheltenham: Edward Elgar and the University of Ghent.

2001. "Transaction-Cost Economics and the Organization of Agricultural Transactions," *Ind. Organ. Rev.*, 9, pp 173–195.

2002. "Modern Evidence on the Firm," *Amer. Econ. Rev.*, 92, 2, pp 428–432.

Masten, S. E. and Saussier, S. 2002. "Econometrics of Contracts: An Assessment of Developments in the Empirical Literature of Contracting," in Brousseau, E. and Glachant, J.-M., eds, *Economics of Contracts: Theories and Applications*. Cambridge University Press, pp 273–293.

Masten, S. E. and Snyder, E. A. 1993. "*United States* v. *Shoe Machinery Corporation*: On the Merits," *J. Law Econ.* 36, pp 33–70.

Masten, S. E., Meehan, J. W., and Snyder, E. A. 1991. "The Costs of Organization," *J. Law Econ. Organ.*, 7, 1, pp 1–25.

Mathewson, F. G. and Winter, R. A. 1985. "The Economics of Franchise Contracts," *J. Law Econ.*, 28, pp 503–526.

Matsusaka, J. G. 1995. "Fiscal Effects of the Voter Initiative: Evidence From the Last 30 Years," *J. Polit. Economy*, 102, 2, pp 587–623.

2004. *For the Many or the Few. The Initiative, Public Policy, and American Democracy*, Chicago University Press.

2005. "Discrete Democracy Works," *Journal of Economic Perspectives*, 19, 2, 185–206.

Mattei, U. 1994. "Why the Wind changed: Intellectual Leadership in Western Law," *Amer. J. Comp. Law*, 42, pp 195–218.

Matthews, R. C. O. 1986. "The Economics of Institutions and the Sources of Economic Growth," *Econ. J.*, 96, pp 903–918.

Mayer, K. 2005. *The Role of Prior Relationships on Contract Design: An Analysis of Early Termination Provisions*. University of Southern California, unpublished manuscript.

Mayer, K. J. and Argyres, N. S. 2004. "Learning to Contract: Evidence from the Personal Computer Industry," *Organization Sci.*, 15, 4, pp 394–410.

Mayer, K. J. and Nickerson, J. 2005. "Antecedents and Performance Implications of Contracting for Knowledge Workers: Evidence from Information Technology Services," *Organization Sci.*, 1, 3, pp 225–242.

Maynard Smith, J. 1964. "Group Selection and Kin Selection," *Nature*, 201, pp 1145–1147.

1982. *Evolution and the Theory of Games*, Cambridge University Press.

Maynard Smith, J. and Price, G. R. 1973. "The Logic of Animal Conflicts," *Nature*, 246, pp 15–18.

Maze, Armelle. 2002. "Retailer's Branding Strategy: Contract Design, Organizational Change, and Learning," *J. Chain Network Sci.* 2, pp 33–45.

McCabe, K. and Smith V. 1998. *Strategic Analysis by Players in Games*, unpublished manuscript.

McCabe, K., Smith, V. and Le Pore, M. (2000) "Internationality Detection and 'Mind Reading': Why Does Game Form Matter?", *Proceedings of the National Academy of Sciences*, 97(8), pp 4404–9.

McClure, S. M., Laibson, D. I., Loewenstein, G., and Cohen, J. D. 2004. "Separate Neural Systems Value Immediate and Delayed Monetary Rewards," *Science*, 306, pp 503–507.

McCubbins, M. D. and Schwartz, T. 1984. "Congressional Oversight Overlooked: Police Patrol vs. Fire Alarms," *Amer. J. Politic. Sci.*, 24, 1, pp 165–179.

McCubbins, M. D., Noll, R. G. 1987. "Administrative Procedures as Instruments of Political Control," *J. Law Econ.Organ.*, 3, pp 243–277.

1989. "Structure and Process, Politics and Policy: Administrative Arrangements and the Political Control of Agencies," *Virginia Law Rev.*, 75, 2, pp 431–482.

McGahan, A. M. and Belen, V. 2005. "The Choice among Acquisitions, Alliances and Divestitures," *Strategic Manag. J.*, 26, pp 1183–1208.

McMillan, J. and Woodruff, C. 1999. "Dispute Prevention without Courts in Vietnam," *J. Law, Econ., Organ.*, 15, 13, pp 637–58.

2000. "Private Order under Dysfunctional Public Order," *Mich. Law Rev.*, 98, pp 2421–2458.

2002. "The Central Role of Entrepreneurs in Transition Economies," *J. Econ. Perspect.*, 16, 3, pp 153–170.

Meidinger, C., Robin, S., and Ruffieux, B. 1999. "Confiance, Réciprocité et Cheap Talk," *Revue Econ.*, 50, 1, pp 5–44.

Ménard, C. 1996. "On Clusters, Hybrids and other Strange Forms: The Case of the French Poultry Industry," *J. Inst. Theoretical Econ.*, 152, pp 154–183.

1997. "Le pilotage des formes organisationelles hybrides," *Revue Économique*, 42, 3, pp 741–750.

1998. "Maladaptation of Regulation to Hybrid Organizational Forms," *Int. Rev. Law Econ.*, 18, pp 403–417.

2001. "Methodological Issues in New Institutional Economics," *J. Econ. Methodology*, 8, 1, pp 85–92.

2004a. *The Foundations of New Institutional Economics, the International Library of New Institutional Economics*, Cheltenham: Edwards Elgar.

2004b. "The Economics of Hybrid Organizations," *J. Inst. Theoretical Econ.*, 160, 3, pp 1–32.

Ménard, C. and Klein 2004. "Organisational Issues in the Agrifood Sector: Toward a Competitive Approach," *American Journal of Agricultural Economics*, 86, pp 750–755.

Ménard, C. and Saussier, S. 2000. "Contractual Choice and Performance: The Case of Water Supply in France," *Revue Econ. Ind.*, 92, pp 285–304.

Mercuro, N. and Medema, S. 1997. *Economics and the Law: From Posner to Post-Modernism*, Princeton University Press.

Merville, L. J. and Osborne, D. K. 1990. "Constitutional Democracy and the Theory of Agency," *Constit. Polit. Economy*, 1, pp 21–47.

Michael, S. C. and Moore, H. J. 1995. "Return to Franchising," *J. Corp. Finan.*, 2, 1/2, pp 133–155.

Milgrom, P. 2004. *Putting Auction Theory to Work*. Cambridge University Press.

Milgrom, P. and Roberts, J. D. 1988. "Economic Theories of the Firm: Past, Present, and Future," *Can. J. Econ.*, 21, pp 444–458.

1990. "Rationalizability, Learning and Equilibrium Games with Strategic Complementarities," *Econometrica*, 59, pp 511–528.

1992. *Economics, Organization and Management*. Englewood Cliffs, NJ: Prentice-Hall International.

Milgrom, P., North, D. C., and Weingast, B. R. 1990. "The Role of Institutions in the Revival of Trade: The Law Merchant, Private Judges, and the Champagne Fairs," *Econ. Politics*, 2, 1, pp 1–23.

Minkler, A. P. 1990. "An Empirical Analysis of a Firm Decision to Franchise," *Econ. Letters*, 34, pp 77–82.

Minkler, A. P. and Park, T. A. 1994. "Asset Specificity and Vertical Integration in Franchising," *Rev. Ind. Organ.*, 9, pp 409–423.

Moe, T. M. 1980. *The Organization of Interests: Incentives and the Internal Dynamics of Political Interest Groups*, Chicago, IL: University of Chicago Press.

1987. "An Assessment of the Positive Theory of Congressional Dominance," *Legislative Studies Quarterly*, 12, 4, pp 475–520.

Moe, T. M. and Howell, W. G. 1999. "The Presidential Power of Unilateral Action," *J. Law Econ. Organ.*, 15, 1, pp 132–179.

Mohr, J. J. and Spekman, R. E. 1994. "Characteristics of Partnership Success: Partnership Attributes, Communication Behavior, and Conflict Resolution Techniques," *Strategic Manage. J.*, 15, pp 135–152.

Mokyr, J. 1977. "Demand vs Supply in the Industrial Revolution," *J. Econ. Hist.*, 37, 4, pp 981–1008.

Montet, C. and Serra, D. 2003. *Game Theory and Economics*. London: Palgrave Macmillan.

Monteverde, K. 1995. "Technical Dialog as an Incentive for Vertical Integration," *Manage. Sci.*, 641, pp 1624–1638.

Monteverde, K. and Teece, D. J. 1982. "Supplier Switching Costs and Vertical Integration in the Automobile Industry," *Bell J. Econ.*, 13, 1, pp 206–213.

Mookerjee, S. 1998. "Ambiguity Aversion and Incompleteness of Contractual Form," *Amer. Econ. Rev.*, 88, pp 1207–1231.

Mookherjee, D. and Sopher, B. 1997. "Learning and Decision Costs in Experimental Constant Sum Games," *Games Econ. Behav.*, 19, 1, pp 97–132.

Moran, P. and Ghoshal, S. 1996. "Theories of Economic Organization: The Case for Realism and Balance," *Acad. Manage. Rev.*, 21, pp 58–72.

Moravcsik, A. 1993. "Preferences and Power in the European Community. A Liberal Intergovernemantalist Approach," *J. Common Market Stud.*, 31, pp 473–523.

1994. *Why the European Community Strengthens the State. Domestic Politics and International Cooperation*. Cambridge, MA: Harvard University Press.

Mowery, D. C. 1987. *Alliance Politics and Economics: Multinational Joint Ventures in the Commercial Aircraft Industry*. New York, NY: Ballinger Publishing Company.

Mowery, D. C., Oxley, J. E., and Silverman, B. S. 1996. "Strategic Alliances and Inter-Firm Knowledge Transfer," *Strategic Manage. J.*, 17, pp 77–91.

1998. "Technological Overlap and Interfirm Cooperation: Implications for the Resource-Based View of the Firm," *Res. Pol.*, 27, pp 507–523.

2002. "The Two Faces of Partner-Specific Absorptive Capacity: Learning and Co-specialization in Strategic Alliances," in Contractor, F. and Lorange, P., eds, *Cooperative Strategies and Alliances*. London: Elsevier.

Mueller, D. 1996. *Constitutional Democracy*. Oxford University Press.

Mueller, W. F. and Geithman, F. E. 1991. "An Empirical Test of the Free-Rider and Market Power Hypotheses," *Rev. Econ. Statist.*, pp 301–308.

Murdock, K. 2002. "Intrinsic motivation and optimal incentive contracts," *RAND J. Econ.*, 33, 4, pp 650–71.

Myers, R. A. and Worm, B. 2003. "Rapid Worldwide Depletion of Predatory Fish Communities," *Nature*, 423, pp 280–283.

Myerson, R. 1991. *Game Theory – Analysis of Conflict*. Boston, MA, and London: Harvard University Press.

Nakamura, M., Shaver, J. M., and Yeung, B. 1996. "An Empirical Investigation of Joint Venture Dynamics: Evidence from US–Japan Joint Ventures," *Int. J. Ind. Organ.*, 14, pp 521–541.

Nee, V. 1992. "Organizational Dynamics of Market Transition: Hybrid Forms, Property Rights, and Mixed Economy in China," *Administrative Sci. Quarterly*, 37, pp 1–27.

1998. "Sources of the New Institutionalism," in Brinton, M. and Nee, V., eds, *The New Institutionalism in Sociology*. New York: Russel Sage, pp 1–16.

2005. "Organizational Dynamics of Institutional Change; China's Market Economy," in Nee, V. and Swedberg, R., eds, *The Economic Sociology of Capitalism*. Princeton University Press, pp 53–74.

Nee, V. and Ingram, P. 1998. "Embeddedness and Beyond: Institutions, Exchange, and Social Structure," in Brinton, M. and Nee, V., eds, *The New Institutionalism in Sociology*. New York, NY: Russell Sage Foundation, pp 19–45.

Nee, V. and Opper, S. 2007. "On Politicized Capitalism," in Nee, V. and Swedberg, R., eds, *On Capitalism*. Stanford University Press.

Nee, V. and Su, S. 1996. "Institutions, Social Ties, and Credible Commitment: Local Corporatism in China," in McMillan, J. and Naughton, B., eds, *Reforming Asian Economies: The Growth of Market Institutions*. Ann Arbor, MI: University of Michigan Press, pp 111–134.

Nee, V. and Swedberg, R. 2005. "Economic Sociology and New Institutional Economics," in Ménard, C. and Shirley, M. M., eds, *Handbook of New Institutional Economics*. New York, NY: Springer, pp 789–818.

Nelson, R. and Winter S. 1982. *An Evolutionary Theory of Economic Change*. Cambridge University Press.

Newbery, D. M. 2000. *Privatization, Restructuring, and Regulation of Network Utilities*. Cambridge, MA: MIT Press.

2002. "Issues and options for restructuring electricity supply industries," DAE work paper WP 0210, University of Cambridge.

Newell, A. 1990. *United Theories of Cognition*. Cambridge, MA: Harvard University Press.

Nicita, A. 2001. "The Firm as an Evolutionary Enforcement Device," in Nicita, A. and Pagano, U., eds, *The Evolution of Economic Diversity*. London: Routledge, pp 240–270.

Nicita, A. and Rizzolli, M. 2004. "Much Ado about the Cathedral: Property Rules and Liability Rules when Rights are Incomplete," University of Siena, Simple: Siena memos and papers in law and economics, 22:04. (Available at: www.unisi.it/lawandeconomics/simple/022_Nicita_Rizzolli.pdf).

Nickerson, J. A. 1997. *Toward an Economizing Theory of Strategy*. Dissertation. US Berkeley Haas School of Business.

Nickerson, J. A. and Silverman, B. S. 2003. "Why Firms Want to Organize Efficiently and What Keeps Them From Doing So: Inappropriate Governance, Performance, and Adaptation in a Deregulated Industry," *Administrative Sci. Quarterly*, 48, 3, pp 433–465.

Nickerson, J. A. and Zenger, T. R. 2002. "Being Efficiently Fickle: A Dynamic Theory of Organizational Choice," *Organization. Sci.*, 13, pp 547–567.

2004. "A Knowledge-Based Theory of Governance Choice," *Organization. Sci.*, 15, 6, pp 617–632.

Nickerson, J. A., Hamilton, B. H., and Wada, T. 2001. "Market Position, Resource Profile, and Governance: Linking Porter and Williamson in the

Context of International Courier and Small Package Services in Japan,"
*Strategic Manage. J.*, 22, 3, pp 251–273.

Noll, Juergen. 2004. *Some Findings on Contractual Penalties*. Mimeo, University
of Vienna, Department of Business Studies.

North, D. C. 1981. *Structure and Change in Economic History*. New York, NY:
Norton.

1990. *Institutions, Institutional Change and Economic Performance*. Cambridge
University Press.

1991. "Institutions," *J. Econ. Perspect.*, 5, 1, pp 97–112.

1994. "Economic Performance Through Time," *Amer. Econ. Rev.*, 84, 3,
pp 359–368.

1995. "The New Institutional Economics and Third World Development,"
in Harriss, J., Hunter, J., and Lewis, C. M., eds, *The New Institutional
Economics and Third World Development*. London: Routledge, pp 17–26.

2005. *Understanding the Process of Institutional Change*. Princeton University
Press.

North, D. C. and Thomas, R. 1973. *The Rise of the Western World: A New
Economic History*. Cambridge University Press.

North, D. C. and Weingast, B. R. 1989. "Constitutions and Commitment: The
Evolution of Institutional Governing Public Choice in Seventeenth-Century
England," *J. Econ. Hist.*, 49, 4, pp 803–832.

Norton, S. W. 1988. "An Empirical Look at Franchising as an Organizational
Form," *J. Bus.*, 61, 2, pp 197–217.

Oates, W. E. 1999. "An Essay on Fiscal Federalism," *J. Econ. Lit.*, 37,
pp 1120–1149.

Ocana, Carlos. 2002. "Trends in Management of Regulation: A Comparison of
Energy Regulators in Member Countries of the OECD," *Int. J. Reg.
Governance*, 3, 1, pp 13–32.

OECD. 1994. *Competition Policy and Vertical Restraints: Franchising Agreements*,
Paris: Publication de l'OECD.

Ogus, A. 1995. "Rethinking Self-Regulation," *Oxford J. Legal Studies*, 15,
pp 97–108.

Olson, M., Jr. 1965. *The Logic of Collective Action: Public Goods and the Theory of
Groups*. Cambridge, MA: Harvard University Press.

1971. *The Logic of Collective Action*. New York, NY: Schocken.

1990. "Interest-Group Litigation in Federal District Court: Beyond the
Political Disadvantage Theory," *J. Politics*, 52, 3, pp 854–882.

Opper, S. 2004. "The Political Economy of Privatization: Empirical Evidence
from Transition Economies," *Kyklos*, 57, 4, pp 567–594.

Ordeshook, P. C. 1992. "Constitutional Stability," *Constit. Polit. Economy*, 3, 2,
pp 137–175.

Oren, Shmuel. 1997. "Economic Inefficiency of Passive Transmission Rights in
Congested Electricity Systems with Competitive Generation," *Energy J.*, 1,
18, pp 63–83.

Ornstein, N., Mann, T., and Malbin, M. 1998. *Vital Statistics on Congress*.
American Enterprise Institute, Washington D. C.

Osborne, M. and Rubinstein, A. 1995. *A Course in Game Theory*. Cambridge,
MA: MIT Press.

Osterloh, M. and Frey, B. 2000. "Motivation, Knowledge Transfer and Organizational Form," *Organ. Sci.*, 11, pp 538–550.

Ostrom, E. 1990. *Governing the Commons: The Evolution of Institutions for Collective Action.* New York, NY: Cambridge University Press.

2000. "Collective Action and the Evolution of Social Norms," *J. Econ. Perspect.*, 14, 3, pp 137–158.

Oxley, J. E. 1997. "Appropriability Hazards and Governance in Strategic Alliances: A Transaction Cost Approach," *J. Law Econ. Organ.*, 13, 2, pp 387–409.

1999. "Institutional Environment and the Mechanisms of Governance: The Impact of Intellectual Property Protection on the Structure of Inter-firm Alliances," *J. Econ. Behav. Organ.*, 38, 3, pp 283–309.

2003. "Learning versus Protection in Interfirm Alliances: A False Dichotomy", in Pedersen, T. and Mahnke, V., eds., *Knowledge, Governance and the MNC.* Basingstoke: Palgrave Macmillan.

Oxley J. E. and Sampson, R. C. 2004. "The Scope and Governance of International R&D Alliances," *Strategic Manage. J.*, 25, pp 8–9.

Oxley, J. E. and Tetsuo, W. 2007. "Alliance Structure and the Scope of Knowledge Transfer: Evidence from US-Japan Agreements," paper presented at the DRUID Summer Conference on Appropriability, Proximity, Routines and Innovation.

Pagano, U. 2000. "Public Markets, Private Orderings and Corporate Governance," *Int. Rev. Law Econ.*, 20, 4, pp 453–477.

2002. "Legal Position and Institutional Complementarities." Unpublished manuscript, University of Siena (Italy).

2005. "Legal Positions and Institutional Complementarities," in *Legal Orderings and Economics Institutions.* Cafaggi, F., Nicita, A., and Pagano, U., eds. London, Routledge.

2007. "Legal Positions and Institutional Complementarities" in Fabrizio, C., Nicita, A., and Pagano, U., eds, *Legal Orderings and Economics Institutions.* London: Routledge.

Pagano, U. and Rossi, M. A. 2004. "Incomplete Contracts, Intellectual Property and Institutional Complementarities," *Europ. J. Law Econ.*, 18, 1, pp 55–76.

Park, S.-H. and Luo, Y. 2001. "Guanxi and Organizational Dynamics: Organizational Networking in Chinese firms," *Strategic Manage. J.*, 22, pp 455–477.

Parkhe, A. 1993. "Strategic Alliance Structuring: A Game Theoretic and Transaction Costs Examination of Interfirm Cooperation," *Academy Manage. J.*, 36, pp 794–829.

Peltzman, S. 1976. "Toward a More General Theory of Regulation," *J. Law Econ.*, 68, pp 211–240.

Pénard, T., Raynaud, E., and Saussier, S. 2003. "Dual Distribution and Royalty Rates in Franchised Chains: An Empirical Exploration using French Data," *J. Marketing Channel*, 10, 3/4, pp 5–29.

Peng, Y. 2001. "Chinese Villages and Townships as Industrial Corporations: Ownership, Governance and Market Discipline," *Amer. J. Sociology*, 106, 5, pp 1338–1370.

Perez, Y. 2002. "L'Analyse Néo-Institutionnelle des Réformes Electriques Européennes." Thèse de doctorat, Université de Paris I Panthéon-Sorbonne.

Perrow, C. 1986. *Complex Organizations: A Critical Essay*, third edition. New York, NY: McGraw-Hill.

2002. "Economic Theories of Organization," *Central Currents in Organization Theory*, 4, pp 244–271.

Persson, T. 2005. "Forms of Democracy, Policy and Economic Development." Mimeo, January.

Persson, T. and Tabellini, G. 2000. *Political Economics – Explaining Economic Policy*. Cambridge, MA: MIT Press.

2003. *The Economic Effects of Constitutions*. Cambridge, MA: MIT Press.

Persson, T., Roland, G., and Tabellini, G. 1997. "Separation of Powers and Political Accountability," *Quart. J. Econ.*, 112, pp 310–327.

Peteraf, M. A. 1993. "The Cornerstones of Competitive Advantage: A Resource-Based View," *Strategy. Manage. J.*, 14, pp 179–191.

Pfeffer, J. 1994. *Competitive Advantage through People: Unleashing the Power of the Work Force*. Boston, MA: Harvard Business Press.

Pigou, A. 1920. *Economics of Welfare*. London: Macmillan.

Pinker, S. 1994. *The Language Instinct: How the Mind Creates Language*. New York, NY: Morrow.

2002. *The Blank Slate: The Modern Denial of Human Nature*. New York, NY: Viking.

Pirrong, S. C. 1993. "Contracting Practices in Bulk Shipping Markets: A Transactions Cost Explanation," *J. Law Econ.*, 36, 2, pp 937–976.

Pisano, G. P. 1989. "Using Equity Participation to Support Exchange: Evidence from the Biotechnology Industry," *J. Law Econ. Organ.*, 5, 1, pp 109–126.

1990. "The R&D Boundaries of the Firm: An Empirical Analysis," *Administrative Sci. Quart.*, 35, pp 153–176.

Pisano, G. P., Russo, M., and Teece, D. 1988. "Joint Ventures and Collaborative Arrangements in the Telecommunications Equipment Industry," in Mowery, D., ed., *International Collaborative Ventures in U.S. Manufacturing*. Cambridge, MA: Balinger.

Platteau, J.-P. 2000. *Institutions, Social Norms and Economic Development*, London: Harwood Academic Publishers.

Platteau, J.-P. and Nugent, J. 1992. "Share Contracts and their Rationale: Lessons from Marine Fishing," *J. of Dev. Stud.*, 28, 3, pp 386–422.

Plott, C. R. 1989. "An Updated Review of Industrial Organization: Applications of Experimental Methods," in Schmalensee, R. and Willig, R, eds, *Handbook of Industrial Organization*. Amsterdam: North-Holland, pp 1109–1176.

1997. "Laboratory Experimental Testbeds: Application to the PCS Auction," *J. Econ. Manage. Strategy*, 6, pp 605–638.

Plunket, A. and Saussier, S. 2004. "Theories of the Firm: How to Rule Out Competing Views?" *Economie et Institutions*, 3, pp 103–130.

Podsakoff, P. M. and Organ, D. W. 1986. "Self-Reports in Organizational Research: Problems and Prospects," *J. Manage.*, 12, pp 531–544.

Polanyi, K. 1944. *The Great Transformation*, Boston, MA: Bacon Press.

Polsby, Nelson W. 1968. "The Institutionalization of the U.S. House of Representatives," *Amer. Polit. Sci. Rev.*, 62, 1, pp 144–68.

Pommerehne, W. W. 1978. "Institutional Approaches to Public Expenditure," *J. Public Econ.*, 9, pp 255–280.

Poppo, L. and Zenger, T. 1998. "Testing Alternative Theories of the Firm: Transaction Cost, Knowledge-Based, and Measurement Explanations for Make-or-Buy Decisions in Information Services," *Strategic Manage. J.*, 19, pp 853–877.

2002. "Do Formal Contracts and Relational Governance Function as Substitutes or Complements?" *Strategic Manage. J.*, 23, 8, pp 707–725.

Porter, M. 1980. *Competitive Strategy*, New York, NY: Free Press.

1996. "What Is Strategy?" *Harvard Bus. Rev.*, vol pp 61–78.

Posner, E. A. 2003. "Economic Analysis of Contract law after three Decades: Success or Failure?" *Yale Law J.* 112, 4, pp 829–80.

Posner, R. A. 1975. "The Economic Approach to Law," *Texas Law Review*, 53, pp 757–782.

1987. "The Law and Economics Movement," *Amer. Econ. Rev.*, 77, pp 1–13.

1993. "The New Institutional Economics Meets Law and Economics," *J. Inst. Theoretical Econ.*, 149, 1, pp 73–87.

2003. *Economic Analysis of Law*, 6th ed., New York, NY: Aspen Publishers.

2005. "The Law and Economics of Contract Interpretation," hosted by the *Berkeley Electronic Press, American Law & Economics Association Annual Meetings*. American Law & Economics Association 15th Annual Meeting, 56, pp 1–49.

Powell, W. W., Koput, K. W., and Smith, L. D. 1996. "Interorganizational Collaboration and the Locus of Innovation: Networks of Learning in Biotechnology," *Administrative Sci. Quart.*, 41, 1, pp 116–145.

Prosser, T. 2005. "Regulatory Contracts and Stakeholder Regulation," *Ann. Public Coop. Econ.*, 76 1, pp 35–57.

Putnam, R., Leonardi, R., and Nanetti, R. 1993. *Making Democracy Work: Civic Traditions in Modern Italy*. Princeton University Press.

Rabin, M. 1993. "Incorporating Fairness into Game Theory and Economics," *Amer. Econ. Rev.*, 83, pp 1281–1302.

Rabin, M. and Thaler, R. 2001. "Risk Aversion," *J. Econ. Perspect.*, 15, 1, pp 219–232.

Ramachandran, V. 2004. *A Brief Tour of Human Consciousness. From Impostor Poodles to Purple Numbers*, New York, NY: PI Press.

Ramseyer, M. J. 1994. "The Puzzling (In)dependence of Courts: A Comparative Approach," *J. Legal Stud.*, 23, 2, pp 721–747.

Ramseyer, M. J. and Rasmusen, E. B. 1997. "Judicial Independence in a Civil Law Regime: The Evidence from Japan," *J. Law Econ. Organ.*, 13, 2, pp 259–286.

Rasmusen, E. B. 2001. "A Model of Negotiation not Bargaining: Explaining Incomplete Contracts," Harvard Law and Economics Discussion paper, 324.

Rassenti, S. J. and Smith, V. L. 1986. "Electric Utility Deregulation," *Pricing Electric, Gas and Telecommunication Services*. Institute for the Study of Regulation.

Rassenti, S. J., Smith, V. L., and Wilson, B. J. 2002. "Using Experiments to Inform the Privatization/Deregulation Movement in Electricity," *The Cato J.*, 21, 3, pp 515–544.

2003. "Controlling Market Power and Price Spikes in Electricity Networks: Demand-Side Bidding," *PNAS*, 100, 5, pp 2989–3003.

Raynaud, E., Sauvée, L., and Valceschini, E. 2002. "Quality Strategies and Producers Organization in the European Agro-Food Sector: Competition Policy and Consumer Information," INRA Work paper.

Reder, M. 1999. *Economics: The Culture of a Controversial Science.* Chicago University Press.

Rees, J. 1988. "Reforming the Workplace: A Study of Self-Regulation in Occupational Safety," University of Pennsylvania Press.

Resnick, P. and Zeckhauser, R. 2002. "Trust Among Strangers in Internet Transactions: Empirical Analysis of eBay's Reputation System," in Baye, M., ed., *Advances in Applied Microeconomics*, vol 11. Amsterdam: Elsevier Science, pp 127–157.

Resnick, P., Zeckhauser, R., Swanson, J., and Lockwood, K. 2006. "The Value of Reputation on eBay: A Controlled Experiment," *Exper. Econ.*, 9, 2, pp 79–101.

Reuer, J. J. and Arino, A. 2002. "Contractual Renegotiations in Strategic Alliances," *J. Manage.*, 28, 1, pp 51–74.

Reuer, J. J., Arino, A., and Mellewigt, T. 2005. "Entrepreneurial Alliances as Contractual Forms," *J. Bus. Venturing*, 21, 3, pp 306–325.

Rey, P. and Stiglitz, J. E. 1995. "The Role of Exclusive Territories in Producers Competition," *RAND J. Econ.*, 26, 3, pp 431–451.

Richardson, G. B. 1972. "The Organization of Industry," *Econ. J.*, 82, pp 883–996.

Richman, B. 2002. *Community Enforcement of Informal Contracts: Jewish Diamond Merchants in New York*, John M. Olin Center for Law Economics and Business Discussion paper 384.

Ricketts, M. 1994. *The Economics of Business Enterprise: An Introduction to Economic Organisation and the Theory of the Firm.* New York, NY: Harvester Wheatsheaf.

Riker, W. 1964. *Federalism: Origins, Operation, Significance.* Boston, MA: Little Brown.

Ring, P. S. and Van De Ven, A. H. 1992. "Structuring Cooperative Relationships Between Organizations," *Strategic Management Journal*, 13, pp 483–498.

Rious, V. 2005. "Comparaison de Deux Gestionnaires de Réseau de Transport Electrique: PJM et NGC," Work paper GRJM.

Robinson, D. and Stuart, T. 2007. "Network Effects in the Governance of Biotech Strategic Alliances," *J. Law, Econ., Organ.*, 23, 1, pp 242–273.

Rodden, J. A. 2003. "Reviving Leviathan: Fiscal Federalism and the Growth of Government," *Int. Organ.*, 57, pp 695–729.

Rodrik, D. 2003. *In Search of Prosperity: Analytic Narratives on Economic Growth.* Princeton University Press.

——— 2006. "Institutions for High-Quality Growth: What They are and How to Acquire Them," in Boy, P. C. and Siredas, J., eds, *Institutions, Globalization and Empowerment*. Business and Economics, pp 19–55.

Roland, G. 2000. *Transition and Economics. Politics, Markets, and Firms.* Cambridge, MA: MIT Press.

——— 2004. "Understanding Institutional Change: Fast-Moving and Slow-Moving Institutions," *Studies in Comparative Industrial Development*, 28, 4, pp 109–131.

Ross, S. A. 1973. "The Economic Theory of Agency: The Principal's Problem," *Amer. Econ. Rev.*, 63, pp 134–139.

Roth, A. E. 1993. "On the Early History of Experimental Economics," *J. Hist. Econ. Thought*, 15, pp 184–209.

1995. "Introduction to Experimental Economics," in Kagel, J. H. and Roth, A. E., eds, *The Handbook of Experimental Economics*. Princeton University Press, pp 3–109.

Roth, A. E. and Erev, I. 1995. "Learning in Extensive-Form Games: Experimental Data and Simple Dynamic Models in the Intermediate Term," *Games Econ. Behav.*, 8, pp 164–212.

Roumasset, J. A. and Uy, M. 1980. "Piece Rates, Time Rates, and Teams: Explaining Patterns in the Employment Relation," *J. Econ. Behav. Organ.*, 1, pp 343–360.

Royer, James and Rogers, R. 1998. *The Industrialization of Agriculture: Vertical Coordination in the U.S. Food System*. Aldershot, U. K.: Ashgate Publishers.

Rubin, P. H. 1978. "The Theory of the Firm and the Structure of Franchise Contract," *J. Law Econ.*, 21, 1, pp 223–232.

2002. *Darwinian Politics: The Evolutionary Origin of Freedom*. New Brunswick: Rutgers University Press.

Rufin, C. 2003. *The Political Economy of Institutional Change in the Electricity Supply Industry*. Cheltenham: Edward Elgar.

Rumelt, R. P., Schendel, D., and Teece, D. J. 1991. "Strategic Management and Economics," *Strategic Manage. J.*, 12, pp 5–29.

Rutherford, M. 2003. "Chicago Economics and Institutionalism," Mimeo, University of Victoria.

Ryall, M. and Sampson, R. 2003. *Do Prior Alliances Influence Contract Structure? Evidence from Technology Alliance Contracts*. Manuscript, University of Maryland.

Saleth, Maria and Dinar, A. 2004. *Institutional Economics of Water: A Cross-Country Analysis of Institutions and Performance*. World Bank Publications.

Salop, S. 1986. "Practices That (Credibly) Facilitate Oligopoly Co-ordination," in Stiglitz, J. and Mathewson, G. F., eds, *New Developments in the Analysis of Market Structure*. Cambridge, MA: MIT Press, pp 265–290.

Salzberger, E. and Fenn, P. 1999. "Judicial Independence: Some Evidence from the English Court of Appeal," *J. Law Econ.*, 42, 2, pp 831–847.

Sampson, R. C. 2004. "The Costs of Misaligned Governance in R&D Alliances," *J. Law Econ. Organ.*, 20, 2, pp 484–526.

2006. "R&D Alliances and Firm Performance: The Impact of Technological Diversity and Alliance Organization on Innovation," *Academy of Management Journal*, 50, pp 364–386.

Samuels, D. J. 2002. "Pork Barreling is Not Credit-Claiming or Advertising: Campaign Finance and the Sources of Personal Vote in Brazil," *J. Politics*, 64, 3, pp 845–863.

Samuelson, P. 1979. *Economics: An Introductory Analysis*. New York, NY: McGraw-Hill.

Sass, T. R. and Saurman, D. S. 1993. "Mandate Exclusive Territories and Economic Efficiency: An Empirical Analysis of the Malt-Beverage Industry," *J. Law Econ.*, 36, pp 153–177.

Saussier, S. 2000a. "Transaction Costs and Contractual Completeness," *J. Econ. Behav. Organ.*, 42, pp 189–206.

2000b. "When Incomplete Contract Theory Meets Transaction Cost Economics: A Test," in Ménard, C., ed., *Institutions, Contracts and Organizations: Perspectives from the New Institutional Economics*. Cheltenham: Edward, pp 376–398.

Sauvée, L. 1998. "Toward an Institutional Analysis of Vertical Coordination in Agribusiness," in Royer, R. and Rogers, R., eds, *The Industrialization of Agriculture*, Aldershot: Ashgate Publishing Co, pp 27–72.

2000. "Effectiveness, Efficiency, and the Design of Network Governance," in Trienekens, J. H. and Zuurbier, P. J. P., eds, *Proceedings of the Fifth International Conference on Chain Management in Agribusiness and the Food Industry*, Wageningen University Press.

Savage, L. 1954. *The Foundation of Statistics*. New York, NY: Wiley.

Savedorff, W. and Spiller, P. 1999. *Spilled Water: Institutional Commitment in the Provision of Water Services*. Inter-American Development Bank editor.

Sax, J. L. 1990. "The Constitution, Property Rights and the Future of Water Law," *U. Colorado Law Rev.*, 61, pp 257–282.

Schotter, A. 1981. *The Economic Theory of Social Institutions*, New York: Cambridge University Press.

Schumpeter, J. 1934. *The Theory of Economic Development: An Inquiry into Profits, Capital, Credit, Interest and the Business Cycle*. Cambridge, MA: Harvard University Press.

Schwartz, A. and Scott, R. E. 2003. "Contract Theory and the Limits of Contract Law," *Yale Law J.*, 113, pp 1–84.

Schwartz, A. and Watson, J. 2004. "The Law and Economics of Costly Contracting," *J. Law, Econ., Organ.*, 20, 1, pp 2–31.

Scott, F. A. 1995. "Franchising vs. Company Ownership as a Decision Variable for the Firm," *Rev. Ind. Organ.*, 10, pp 69–81.

Scott, R. E. 2003. "A Theory of Self-Enforcing Indefinite Agreements," *Columbia Law Rev.* 102, 302, pp 1–70.

Scully, G. W. 1988. "The Institutional Framework and Economic Development," *J. Polit. Economy*, 96, 1, pp 652–662.

Segal, J. A. 2000. "Correction to Separation-of-Powers Games in the Positive Theory of Congress and Courts," *Amer. Polit. Sci. Rev.*, 92, 4, pp 923–26.

Selten, R. 1975. "Reexamination of the Perfectness Concept for Equilibrium Points in Extensive Games," *Int. J. Game Theory*, 4, pp 25–55.

Shaffer, J. D. 1983. "Preference Articulation and Food System Performance," in Farris, P., ed, *Future Frontiers in Agricultural Marketing Research*. Ames, Iowa: Iowa State University Press.

Shapley, L. S. and Shubik, M. 1969. "On the Core of an Economic System with Externalities," *Amer. Econ. Rev.*, 59, 4, pp 678–84.

Shavell, S. 1995. "The Design of Contracts and Remedies for Breach," *Quart. J. Econ.*, 99, 1, pp 121–48.

2003a. "Economic Analysis of Contract Law," NBER work paper 9696, pp 1–74.

2003b. *Foundations of Economic Analysis of Law*. Boston, MA: Harvard University Press.

2005. "Contracts, Holdup and Legal Intervention," NBER work paper 11284, pp 1–34.

2006. "On the Writing and the Interpretation of Contracts," *J. Law, Econ., Organ.*, 22, 2, pp 289–314.

Shaver, M. J. 1998. "Accounting for Endogeneity when Assessing Strategy Performance: Does Entry Mode Choice Affect FDI Survival?" *Manage. Sci.*, 44, pp 571–585.

Shelanski, H. A. 2004. "'Transaction-Level Determinants of Transfer-Pricing Policy: Evidence from the High-Technology Sector," *Ind. Corp. Change*, 13, pp 953–966.

Shelanski, H. A. and Klein, P. G. 1995. "Empirical Research in Transaction Cost Economics: A Review and Assessment," *J. Law, Econ., Organ.*, 11, 2, pp 335–361.

Shepsle, K. 1978. *The Giant Jigsaw Puzzle: Democratic Committee Assignments in the Modern House*. University of Chicago Press.

Shleifer, A. and Vishny, R. 1991. "Takeovers in the '60s and '80s: Evidence and Implications," *Strat. Man. J.*, 12, pp 51–59.

Shugart, M. and Haggard, S. 2001. "Institutions and Public Policy in Presidential Systems," in Haggard, S. and McCubbins, M. D., eds, *Presidents, Parliaments, and Policy*. New York, NY: Cambridge University Press.

Silverman, B. 2002. "Organizational Economics," in Baum, J. A. C., ed, *Companion to Organizations*. London: Blackwell Publishing.

Silverman, B. S. and Baum, J. A. C. 2002. "Alliance-Based Competitive Dynamics,"*Academy Manage. J.*, 45, 4, pp 791–806.

Silverman, B. S., Nickerson, J. A., and Freeman, J. 1997. "Profitability, Transactional Alignment, and Organizational Mortality in the US Trucking Industry," *Strategic Manage. J.*, (Special Issue) 18, pp 31–52.

Simon, H. A. 1947. *Administrative Behavior*. New York, NY: MacMillan.

1951. "A Formal Theory of the Employment Relationship," *Econometrica*, 19, pp 293–305.

1955. "A Behavioral Model of Rational Choice," *Quart. J. Econ.*, 69, pp 99–118.

1956. "Rational Choice and the Structure of Environments," *Psychological Rev.*, 63, pp 129–138.

1957. *Models of Man*. New York: John Wiley.

1962. "The Architecture of Complexity," *Proceedings of the American Philosophical Society*, 106, pp 467–82.

1976. "From Substantive to Procedural Rationality," in Latsis, S., ed, *Methods and Appraisals in Economics*, Cambridge University Press, pp 129–148.

1992. *Economics, Bounded Rationality, and the Cognitive Revolution*. Brookfield, CT: Edward Elgar.

1997. *An Empirically Based Microeconomics*. New York, NY: Cambridge University Press.

Sioshansi, F. and Pfaffenberger, W. 2006. *Electricity Markets around the World*. Amsterdam: Elsevier.

Slade, M. B. 1998. "Strategic Motives for Vertical Separation: Evidence from Retail Gasoline Market," *J. Law Econ., Organ.*, 14, 1, pp 84–113.

Smeers, Y. 2004. "TSO, electricity markets and market power," presentation in *European Regulatory TSO benchmarking*. Den Haag.

Smelser, N. and Swedberg, R. 2005. *The Handbook of Economic Sociology*, second edition. Princeton, NJ and New York, NY: Princeton University Press and the Russell Sage Foundation.

Smith, A. 1759. *The Theory of Moral Sentiments*.

Smith, Henry E. 2000. "Semicommon Property Rights and Scattering in the Open Fields," *J. Legal Stud.*, 29, 1, pp 131–70.

Smith, R. 1994. "Sinking or Swimming in Water Policy?" *Regulation*, 17, 3, pp 35–43.

Smith, V. L. 1962. "An Experimental Study of Competitive Market Behavior," *J. Polit. Economy*, 70, pp 111–137.

1976. "Experimental Economics: Induced Value Theory," *Amer. Econ. Rev.*, 66, 2, pp 274–279.

1981. "An Empirical Study of Decentralize Institutions of Monopoly Restraints," in Horwick, G. and Quirk, J. P., eds, *Essays in Contemporary Fields of Economics in Honor of Emanuel T. Weiler (1914–1979)*. West Lafayette, IN: Purdue University Press.

2002. "Method in Experiment: Rhetoric and Reality," *Exper. Econ.*, 5, 2, pp 91–110.

2003. "Constructivist and Ecological Rationality in Economics," *Amer. Econ. Rev.*, 93, pp 465–508.

Smyth, R. 1998. "New Institutional Economics in the Post-Socialist Transformation Debate," *J. Econ. Surveys*, 12, 4, pp 361–398.

Snyder, J. M. 1990. "Campaign Contributions as Investments: The US House of Representatives, 1980–1986," *J. Polit. Economy*, 98, 6, pp 1195–1227.

1991. "On Buying Legislatures," *Econ. Politics*, 3, pp 93–109.

Solow, R. 2001. "A Native Informant Speaks," *J. Econ. Methodology*, 8, pp 111–112.

Sperber, D. 1996. *Explaining Culture: A Naturalistic Approach*, London: Blackwell.

Spier, K. E. and Whinston, M. D. 1995. "On the Efficiency of Privately Stipulated Damages for Breach of Contract: Entry Barriers, Reliance and Renegotiation," *RAND J. Econ.*, 26, 2, pp 180–202.

Spiller, P. T. 1990. "Politicians, Interest Groups, and Regulators: A Multiple-Principals Agency Theory of Regulation, or Let Them Be Bribed," *J. Law Econ.*, 33, 1, pp 65–101.

1992. "Agency Discretion Under Judicial Review," in *Formal Theory of Politics II*, a special issue of *Mathematical and Computer Modelling*, 16, pp 185–200.

1996a. "Institutions and Commitment," *Ind. Corp. Change*, 5, 2, pp 421–452.

1996b. "A Positive Political Theory of Regulatory Instruments: Contracts, Administrative Law or Regulatory Specificity?" *USC Law Rev.*, 69, 2, pp 477–515.

Spiller, P. T. and Gely, R. 1992. "Congressional Control or Judicial Independence: The Determinants of US Supreme Court Labor-Relations Decisions, 1949–1988," *RAND J. Econ.*, 23, 4, pp 463–492.

Spiller, P. T. and Martorell, L. V. 1996. "How Should It Be Done? Electricity Regulation in Argentina, Brazil, Uruguay, and Chile," in Gilbert, R. J.

and Kahn, E. P., eds, *International Comparisons of Electricity Regulation*. Cambridge University Press, pp 82–125.

Spiller, P. T. and Tommasi, M. 2003. "The Institutional Foundations of Public Policy: A Transactions Approach with Application to Argentina," *J. Law Econ., Organ.*, 19, 2, pp 281–306.

Staatz, J. 1987. "The Structural Characteristics of Farmer Cooperatives and Their Behavioral Consequences," in Royer, J., ed., *Cooperative Theory: New Approaches*. Washington, DC: US Department of Agriculture. ACS Service Report 18, pp 33–60.

1989. "Farmer Cooperative Theory: Recent Developments," ACS Research Report 84. Washington, DC: US Department of Agriculture, Agricultural Cooperative Service.

Stahl, D. O. 1996. "Boundedly Rational Rule Learning in a Guessing Game," *Games Econ. Behav.*, 16, 2, pp 303–330.

Stark, D. 1996. "Recombinant Property in East European Capitalism," *Amer. J. Sociology*, 101, 4, pp 993–1027.

Stegarescu, D. 2004. "Public Sector Decentralization: Measurement Concepts and Recent International Trends," ZEW discussion paper 04–74.

Stigler, G. J. 1971. "The Theory of Economic Regulation," *Bell J. Econ. Manage Sci.*, 2, pp 3–21.

1981. "Comments," in Joskow, P., Noll, R., and Fromm, G., eds, *Studies in Public Regulation: Regulation in Theory and Practice*. Boston, MA: MIT Press.

1983. "Comments," in Kitch, E. W., ed., "The Fire of Truth: A Remembrance of Law and Economics at Chicago, 1932–1970," *J. Law Econ.*, 26, pp 163–234.

Stiglitz, J. E. 1974. "Incentives and Risk Sharing in Sharecropping," *Rev. Econ. Stud.*, 41, 2, pp 219–255.

1977. "Monopoly Nonlinear Pricing and Imperfect Information: The Insurance Market," *Rev. Econ. Stud.*, 44, pp 407–430.

1989. "Rational Peasants, Efficient Institutions, and a Theory of Rural Organization: Methodological Remarks for Development Economics," in Bardham, P., ed., *The Economic Theory of Agrarian Institutions*. Oxford: Clarendon Press, pp 18–29.

Stratmann, T. 1998. "The Market for Congressional Vote: Is Timing of Contributions Everything?" *J. Law Econ.*, 41, 1, pp 85–113.

Strøm, K. 1997. "Rules, Reasons and Routines: Legislative Roles in Parliamentary Democracies," *Journal of Legislative Studies*, 3, 1, pp 155–174.

Sugden, R. 1986. *The Economics of Rights, Co-operation and Welfare*, Oxford: Basil Blackwell.

1989. "Spontaneous Order," *J. Econ. Persp.*, 3, 4, pp 85–97.

Sunder, S. 1995. "Experimental Asset Markets: A survey," in Kagel, J. H. and Roth, A. E., eds, *The Handbook of Experimental Economics*, Princeton University Press, pp 445–500.

Sykuta, M. E. and Cook, M. L. 2001. "A New Institutional Economics Approach to Contracts and Cooperatives," *Amer. J. Agr. Econ.*, 83, 5, pp 1273–1279.

Sykuta, M. E. and James, H. S. Jr. 2004. "Organizational Economic Research in the U.S. Agricultural Sector and the Role of the Contracting and Organizations Research Institute," *Amer. J. Agr. Econ.*, this issue.

Sykuta, M. E. and Parcell, J. L. 2003. "Contract Structure and Design in Identity Preserved Soybean Production," *Rev. Agr. Econ.*, 25, 2, pp 332–350.

Tanzi, V. 2000. "Some Politically Incorrect Remarks on Decentralization and Public Finance," in Dethier, J.-J., ed., *Governance, Decentralization and Reform in China, India and Russia*. Boston, MA: Kluwer, pp 47–63.

Teece, D. J. 1980. "Economies of Scope and the Scope of the Enterprise," *J. Econ. Behav. Organ.*, 1, pp 223–247.

———. 1981. "Internal Organization and Economic Performance: An Empirical Analysis of the Profitability of Principal Firms," *J. Ind. Econ.*, 30, pp 173–199.

———. 1986. "Profiting from Technological Innovation: Implications for Integration, Collaboration, Licensing and Public Policy," *Res. Pol.*, 15, pp 285–305.

Teece, D. J. and Pisano, G. 1994. "The Dynamic Capabilities of Firms: An Introduction," *Ind. Corp. Change*, 3, pp 537–556.

Teece D. J., Rumelt, R., Dosi, G., and Winter G. S. 1994. "Understanding Corporate Coherence: Theory and Évidence," *J. Econ. Behav. Organ.*, 23, pp 1–30.

Temin, P. and Galambos, L. 1987. *The Fall of the Bell System: A Study in Prices and Politics*. New York, NY: Cambridge University Press.

Thaler, R. 1992. *The Winner's Curse*, Princeton University Press.

———. 2003b. Fiscal Federalism in Western European and Selected Other Countries: Centralization or Decentralization? What is Better for Economic Growth. DIW Berlin.

Thiessen, U. 2003. "Fiscal Decentralization and Economic Growth in High Income OECD Countries," *Fisc. Stud.*, 24, 3, pp 237–274.

Thompson, B. H. 1993. "Institutional Perspectives on Water Policy and Markets," *California Law Rev.*, 81, p. 673.

Tietz, R. 1990. "On Bounded Rationality: Experimental Work at the University of Frankfurt/Main," *J. Inst. Theoretical Econ.*, 146, 4, pp 659–672.

Tirole, J. 1999. "Incomplete Contracts: Where Do We Stand?" *Econometrica*, 67, 4, pp 741–781.

Tooby, J. and Cosmides, L. 1992. "The Psychological Foundations of Culture," in Barkow, J. H., Cosimedes, L., and Tooby, J., eds, *The Adapted Mind: Evolutionary Psychology and the Generation of Culture*. New York, NY: Oxford University Press, pp 19–36.

Tooby, J. and DeVore, I. 1987. "The Reconstruction of Hominid Behavioral Evolution Through Strategic Modeling," in Kinzey, W. G., ed., *Primate Models of Hominid Behavior*. Albany, NY: SUNY Press, pp 183–237.

Toye, J. 1995. "The New Institutional Economics and Its Implications for Development Theory," in Harriss, J., Hunter, J., and Lewis, C. M., eds, *The New Institutional Economics and Third World Development*. London: Routledge, pp 49–68.

Treisman, D. S. 2000. "The Causes of Corruption: A Cross-National Study," *J. Public Econ.*, 76, pp 399–457.

Triantis, G. 2002 "The Efficiency of Vague Contract Terms," University of Virginia, School of Law: Law & Economincs Research Paper Series, 02–7.

Trivers, R. 1985. *Social Evolution*. Menlo Park, CA: Benjamin Cummings.

Trivers, R. L. 1971. "The Evolution of Reciprocal Altruism," *Quart. Rev. Biology*, 46, pp 35–57.

Tsebelis, G. 1995. "Decision-Making in Political Systems: Veto Players in Presidentialism, Parliamentarism, Multicameralism and Multipartism," *Br. J. Political Sci.*, 25, 3, pp 289–325.

2002. *Veto Players. How Political Institutions Work*. Princeton University Press.

Tullock, G. 1965. *The Politics of Bureaucracy*. Washington, DC: Public Affairs Press.

1972. "The Purchase of Politicians," *Western Econ. J.*, 10, pp 354–355.

Umbeck, J. 1981. *A Theory of Property Rights: With Application to the California Gold Rush*. Ames, IO: Iowa State University Press.

Usher, D. 1998. "The Coase Theorem is Tautological, Incoherent or Wrong," *Econ. Letters*, 61, 1, pp 3–11.

Usman, Murat. 2002. "Verifiability and Contract Enforcement: A Model with Judicial Moral Hazard," *J. Law, Econ., Organ.*, 18, 1, pp 67–94.

Uzzi, B. 1997. "Social Structure and Competition in Interfirm Networks: The Paradox of Embeddedness," *Administrative Sci. Quart.*, 42, pp 35–67.

Valley, K. L., Thompson, L. L., Gibbons, R. S., and Bazerman, M. H. 2002. "How Communication Improves Efficiency in Bargaining Games," *Games Econ. Behav.*, 38, pp 127–155.

Van Hoek, R. I. 1999. "From Reversed Logistics to Green Supply Chains," *Supply Chain Manag.*, 4, pp 129–134.

Vannoni, D. 2002. "Empirical Studies of Vertical Integration: The Transaction Cost Orthodoxy," *Int. Rev. Econ. Bus.*, 49, pp 113–141.

Vaubel, R. 1996. "Constitutional Safeguards Against Centralization in Federal States: An Independent Cross-Section Analysis," *Constit. Polit. Economy*, 7, 2, pp 79–102.

Voigt, S. 1999. *Explaining Constitutional Change – A Positive Economics Approach*. Cheltenham: Edward Elgar.

2005. "The Economic Effects of Judicial Accountability – Some Preliminary Insights." Mimeo, University of Kassel.

2006. "Constitutional Political Economy – Conceptual Foundations, Recent Trends, Possible Developments" Mimeo, University of Kassel.

2008. "The Economic Effects of Judicial Accountability," *European Journal of Law and Economics*, 25, pp 95–123.

Voigt, S. and Blume, L. 2006. "The Economic Effects of Direct Democracy – A Cross-Country Assessment," University of Kassel, discussion paper.

Von Neumann, J. and Morgenstern, O. 1944. *Theory of Games and Economic Behavior*. Princeton University Press.

Vromen, J. 1995. *Economic Evolution – An Enquiry into the Foundations of New Institutional Economics*. London & New York: Routledge.

Walker, G. and Poppo, L. 1991. "Profit Centers, Single-Source Suppliers, and Transaction Costs," *Admin. Sci. Quart.*, 36, pp 66–87.

Walker, G. and Weber, D. 1984. "A Transaction Cost Approach to Make-or-Buy Decisions," *Admin. Sci. Q.*, 29, pp 373–391.

Weingast, B. R. 1981. "Regulation, Reregulation and Deregulation: The Political Foundations of Agency Clientele Relationships," *Law Contemp. Prob.*, 44, 1, pp 147–177.

1995. "The Economic Role of Political Institutions: Market-Preserving Federalism and Economic Development," *J. Law Econ., Organ.*, 11, 1, pp 269–296.

2007. *Self-Enforcing Institutions.* Cambridge University Press.

Weingast, B. R. and Marshall, W. J. 1988. "The Industrial Organization of Congress; or Why Legislatures, Like Firms, are Not Organized as Markets," *J. Polit. Economy*, 96, 1, pp 132–163.

Weingast, B. R. and Moran, M. J. 1983. "Bureaucratic Discretion or Congressional Control? Regulatory Policy-making by the Federal Trade Commission," *J. Polit. Economy*, 91, 5, pp 765–800.

Wernerfelt, B. 1984. "A Resource-Based View of the Firm," *Strat. Man. J.*, 5, pp 272–280.

Westin, A. F. 1953. "The Supreme Court, the Populist Movement and the Campaign of 1896," *J. Politics*, 15, 1, pp 3–41.

Whinston, M. D. 2001. "Assessing the Property Rights and Transaction-Cost Theories of Firm Scope," *Amer. Econ. Rev.*, 91, 2, pp 184–188.

2003. "On the Transaction Cost Determinants of Vertical Integration," *J. Law Econ., Organ.*, 19, pp 1–23.

Whyte, M. K. 1995. "The Social Roots of China's Economic Development," *China Quart.*, 144, pp 999–1019.

Wicksell, K. 1896. *Finanztheoretische Untersuchungen.* Jena: Fischer.

Wiggins, S. N. and Libecap, G. D. 1985. "Oil Field Unitization: Contractual Failure in the Presence of Imperfect Information," *Amer. Econ. Rev.*, 75, 3, pp 368–385.

Williams, G. C. 1966. *Adaptation and Natural Selection: A Critique of Some Current Evolutionary Thought.* Princeton University Press.

Williams, G. C. and Williams, D. C. 1957. "Natural Selection of Individually Harmful Social Adaptations among Sibs with Special Reference to Social Insects," *Evolution*, 11, pp 32–39.

Williamson, O. E. 1971. "The Vertical Integration of Production: Market Failure Considerations," *Amer. Econ. Rev.*, 61, pp 112–123.

1973. "Organizational Forms and Internal Efficiency. Markets and Hierarchies: Some Elementary Considerations," *Amer. Econ. Rev.*, 3, pp 316–325.

1975. *Markets and Hierarchies: Analysis and Antitrust Implications. A Study in the Economics of Internal Organization.* New York, NY: Free Press.

1976. "Franchise Bidding for Natural Monopolies – In General and With Respect to CATV," *Bell J. Econ.*, 7, pp 73–104.

1979. "Transaction Cost Economics: The Governance of Contractual Relations," *J. Law Econ.*, 22, pp 233–261.

1981. "The Modern Corporation: Origins, Evolution, Attributes," *J. Econ. Lit.*, 19, pp 1537–68.

1993. "Credible Commitments: Using Hostages to Support Exchange," *The American Economic Review*, 734, 519–540.

1985a. *The Economic Institutions of Capitalism: Firms, Markets and Relational Contracting.* New York, NY: Free Press.

1985b. "Reflections on the New Institutional Economics," *J. Institutional and Theoretical Econ.*, 141, pp 187–95.

1988. "Economics and Sociology," in Farkas, G. and England, P., eds, *Industries, Firms, and Jobs.* New York, NY: Plenum Press, pp 159–186.

1991a. "Comparative Economic Organization: The Analysis of Discrete Structural Alternatives," *Admin. Sci. Quart.*, 36, pp 269–296.

1991b. "Strategizing, Economizing, and Economic Organization," *Strategic Manage. J.*, 12 (special issue), pp 75–94.

1993. "Calculativeness, Trust, and Economic Organization," *J. Law Econ.*, 36.

1994. "Transaction Cost Economics and Organizational Theory," in Smelser, N. and Swedberg, R., eds, *The Handbook of Economic Sociology.* Princeton University Press, pp 77–107.

1996. *The Mechanisms of Governance.* New York, NY: Oxford University Press.

1998. "The Institutions of Governance," *Amer. Econ. Rev.*, 88, 2, pp 75–79.

1999a. "Public and Private Bureaucracies: A Transaction Cost Economics Perspective," *J. Law Econ., Organ.*, 15, pp 306–342.

1999b. "Strategy Research: Governance and Competence Perspectives," *Strategic Manage. J.*, 20, 12, pp 1087–1208.

1999c. "Human Actors and Economic Organization," Business and Public Policy Work paper BPP-72, University of California: Berkeley.

2000. "The New Institutional Economics: Taking Stock, Looking Ahead," *J. Econ. Lit.*, 38, pp 595–613.

2002a. "The Lens of Contract: Private Ordering," *Amer. Econ. Rev.*, 92, 2, pp 438–443.

2002b. "The Theory of the Firm as Governance Structure: From Choice to Contract," *J. Econ. Perspect.*, 16, pp 171–195.

2003. "Transaction Cost Economics and Agriculture: An Excursion," *European Agriculture Economics Meeting*, an Invited Address, Antwerp, Belgium.

2005. "The Economics of Governance," *Amer. Econ. Rev.*, 95, pp 1–18.

Willinger, M. and Keser, C. 2000. "La Théorie des Contrats dans un Contexte Expérimental: Un Survol des Expériences sur la Relations Principal–Agent," *Revue d'Economie Industrielle*, 92, pp 237–253.

Wilson, J. A. 1980. "Adaptation to Uncertainty and Small Numbers Exchange: The New England Fresh Fish Market," *Bell J. Econ.*, 4, pp 491–504.

Wilson, R. B. 2002. "Architecture of Power Markets," *Econometrica*, 70, 4, pp 1299–1240.

Winter, S. G. 1988. "On Coase, Competence, and the Corporation," *J. Law Econ., Organ.*, 4, 1, pp 63–80.

1990. "Survival, Selection, and Inheritance in Evolutionary Theories of Organization," in Singh, J. V., ed., *Organizational Evolution: New Directions.* Newbury Park, CA: Sage Publications.

Witt, U. 1999. "Do Entrepreneurs Need Firms? A Contribution to a Missing Chapter in Austrian Economics," *Rev. Austrian Econ.*, 11, pp 99–110.

Womack, J. 1989. *The Machine that Changed the World.* New York, NY: Rawson Associates.

Wong, S. M. L., Opper, S., and Hu, R. 2004. "Shareholding Structure, De-Politicization and Enterprise Performance: Lessons from China's Listed Companies," *Econ. Transition*, 12, 1, pp 29–66.

World Bank. 1995. *Bureaucrats in Business: The Economics and Politics of Government Ownership*. Oxford: Oxford University Press.

2006. *Handbook for Evaluating Infrastructure Regulatory Systems*. Washington, DC: World Bank.

Xin, K. R. and Pearce, J. L. 1996. "Guanxi: Connections as Substitutes for Formal Institutional Support," *Academy Manage. J.*, 39, 6, pp 1641–1658.

Yeon-Koo, C. and Hausch, D. B. 1999. "Cooperative Investments and the Value of Contracting," *Amer. Econ. Rrev.*, 89, 1, pp 125–48.

Young, A. and Levy, D. 2005. "Explicit Evidence on an Implicit Contract," Emory Law and Economics Research paper, 4–05.

Young, P. H. 1994. *Equity – In Theory and Practice*. Princeton University Press.

1996. "The Economics of Convention," *J. Econ. Persp.*, 10, 2, pp 105–122.

1998. *Individual Strategy and Social Structure An Evolutionary Theory of Institutions*, Princeton University Press.

Young, P. H. and Burke, M. A. 2001. "Competition and Custom in Economic Contracts: A Case Study of Illinois Agriculture," *Amer. Econ. Rev.*, 91, 3, pp 559–573.

Yvrande-Billon, A. 2004. "Franchising Public Services: An Analysis of the Duration of Passenger Rail Franchises in Great Britain," in *Economics and Management of Franchising Networks*. Hendrikse, G., Windsperger, J., Cliquet, G., and Tuunanen, M., eds, Heidelberg: Physica/Springer, pp 174–87.

Zhang, X. and Li, G. 2003. "Does *Guanxi* Matter to Nonfarm Employment?" *J. Compar. Econ.*, 21, pp 315–331.

# Index

Note: Page numbers in **bold** refer to Tables; those in *italics* refer to Figures

Printed in the United States
by Baker & Taylor Publisher Services